Agent and Web Service Technologies in Virtual Enterprises

Nicolaos Protogeros
University of Macedonia, Greece

INFORMATION SCIENCE REFERENCE

Hershey · New York

Acquisitions Editor:	Kristin Klinger
Development Editor:	Kristin Roth
Senior Managing Editor:	Jennifer Neidig
Managing Editor:	Sara Reed
Copy Editor:	Erin Meyer
Typesetter:	Jeff Ash
Cover Design:	Lisa Tosheff
Printed at:	Yurchak Printing Inc.

Published in the United States of America by
Information Science Reference (an imprint of IGI Global)
701 E. Chocolate Avenue, Suite 200
Hershey PA 17033
Tel: 717-533-8845
Fax: 717-533-8661
E-mail: cust@igi-pub.com
Web site: http://www.igi-pub.com/reference

and in the United Kingdom by
Information Science Reference (an imprint of IGI Global)
3 Henrietta Street
Covent Garden
London WC2E 8LU
Tel: 44 20 7240 0856
Fax: 44 20 7379 0609
Web site: http://www.eurospanonline.com

Library of Congress Cataloging-in-Publication Data

Agent and web service technologies in virtual enterprises / Nicolaos Protogeros, editor.

p. cm.

Summary: "This book provides a comprehensive review of the most recent advances in agent and Web service technologies. It provides an integrated view of the most recent contributions which support formation, integration, collaboration, and operation in virtual enterprise. Readers will gain insight from examples of applications of these technologies throughout various aspects of the virtual enterprise life cycle"--Provided by publisher.

Includes bibliographical references and index.

ISBN 978-1-59904-648-8 (hardcover) -- ISBN 978-1-59904-650-1 (ebook)

1. Virtual reality in management--Technological innovations. 2. Business enterprises--Computer networks. 3. Software agents (Computer software) 4. Web services. I. Protogeros, Nicolaos.

HD30.2122.A44 2007

006.3'3--dc22

2007007293

British Cataloguing in Publication Data
A Cataloguing in Publication record for this book is available from the British Library.

Table of Contents

Foreword xiii

Preface xiv

Acknowledgment xxii

Section I
Agents and Web Services Overview

Chapter I
Software Agent Technology: An Overview / *Chrysanthi E. Georgakarakou and*
Anastasios A. Economides 1

Chapter II
Web Services Technology: An Overview / *Fani A. Tzima and Pericles A. Mitkas* 25

Section II
Virtual Enterprise Formation

Chapter III
Virtual Enterprise Formation Supported by Agents and Web Services /
Sobah Abbas Petersen, Jinghai Rao, and Mihhail Matskin... 46

Section III
Virtual Enterprise Integration

Chapter IV
Adaptive Service Choreography Support in Virtual Enterprises / *Adomas Svirskas,*
Bob Roberts, and Ioannis Ignatiadis 66

Chapter V
Technologies to Support the Market of Resources as an Infrastructure for
Agile/Virtual Enterprise Integration / *Maria Manuela Cunha, Goran D. Putnik,*
Joaquim Pereira da Silva, and José Paulo Oliveira Santos 76

Chapter VI
The Utilization of Semantic Web for Integrating Enterprise Systems /
Dimitrios Tektonidis and Albert Bokma 97

Chapter VII
A Recommender Agent to Support Knowledge Sharing in Virtual Enterprises /
Renata S. S. Guizzardi, Pablo Gomes Ludermir, and Diego Sona 115

Chapter VIII
Framework of Agent-Based Intelligent System for Distributed Virtual
Enterprise Project Control / *Yee Ming Chen and Shih-Chang Wang* 135

Chapter IX
Sharing Views, Information, and Cross-Enterprise Culture in the Corporate
Situation Room / *Bob Roberts and Adamantios Koumpis* 160

Chapter X
Multi-Agent Systems Integration in Enterprise Environments Using Web Services /
Eduardo H. Ramírez and Ramón F. Brena 174

Chapter XI
Web Service Discovery and Composition for Virtual Enterprises /
Jürgen Dorn, Peter Hrastnik, and Albert Rainer 190

Chapter XII
Achieving Agile Enterprise Through Integrated Process Management:
From Planning to Work Execution / *Ali Bahrami* 208

Section IV
Virtual Enterprise Operation

Chapter XIII
Agents and Multi-Agent Systems in Supply Chain Management: An Overview /
Pericles A. Mitkas and Paraskevi Nikolaidou 223

Chapter XIV
A Conceptual Framework for Business Process Modeling in Virtual Organizations /
Dimitris Folinas, Tania Pavlou, Bill Karakostas, and Vicky Manthou 244

Chapter XV
Towards a Virtual Enterprise Architecture for the Environmental Sector /
Ioannis N. Athanasiadis 256

Chapter XVI
Using VO Concept for Managing Dynamic Security Associations / *Yuri Demchenko* 267

Chapter XVII
Interoperability Middleware for Federated Business Services in Web-Pilacros /
Lea Kutvonen, Toni Ruokolainen, and Janne Metso 288

Chapter XVIII
Web-Based Template-Driven Communication Support Systems: Using Shadow
netWorkspace to Support Trust Development in Virtual Teams / *Herbert Remidez, Jr.,*
Antonie Stam, and James M. Laffey 310

Chapter IXX
Web Service Design Concepts and Structures for Support of Highly Interconnected
E-Health Infrastructures: A Bottom-Up Approach / *Adamantios Koumpis* 327

Compilation of References 341

About the Contributors 370

Index 379

Detailed Table of Contents

Foreword xiii

Preface xiv

Acknowledgment xxii

Section I
Agents and Web Services Overview

Chapter I

Software Agent Technology: An Overview / *Chrysanthi E. Georgakarakou and Anastasios A. Economides* 1

This chapter provides an overview of the rapidly evolving area of software agents and presents the basic aspects of applying the agent technology to virtual enterprises (VE). As the field of software agents can appear chaotic, this chapter briefly introduces the key issues rather than present an in-depth analysis and critique of the field. In addition to, this chapter investigates the application of agent technology to virtual enterprises and presents current research activity that focuses on this field serving as an introductory step. Furthermore, this chapter makes a list of the most important themes concerning software agents and the application of agent technology to virtual enterprises apposing some order and consistency and serve as a reference point to a large body of literature.

Chapter II

Web Services Technology: An Overview / *Fani A. Tzima and Pericles A. Mitkas* 25

This chapter examines the concept of service-oriented architecture (SOA) in conjunction with the Web services technology as an implementation of the former's design principles. Following a brief introduction of SOA and its advantages, a high-level overview of the structure and composition of the Web services platform is provided. This overview covers the core Web services specifications as well as features of the extended architecture stack, which together form a powerful and robust foundation for building distributed systems. The chapter concludes with a discussion of the scope of applicability of SOA and Web services. The overall goal of this chapter is to portray the key assets of the presented technologies and evaluate them as tools for handling adaptability, portability and interoperability issues that arise in modern business environments.

Section II
Virtual Enterprise Formation

Chapter III

Virtual Enterprise Formation Supported by Agents and Web Services /

Sobah Abbas Petersen, Jinghai Rao, and Mihhail Matskin... 46

This chapter describes the use of software agents and Web services to support the formation of virtual enterprises. The partners of a virtual enterprise are represented as software agents. The AGORA multi-agent architecture is used. The focus of this chapter is on the description of the services provided by each partner and the partner selection process. The concept of agent interaction protocols is used to manage the interactions during the formation of the virtual enterprise. An implementation of the ideas and examples from industrial case studies are used for the validation of the approach and discussions. The use of semantic Web technology and Web services with multi-agent systems is discussed as the future directions for this work.

Section III
Virtual Enterprise Integration

Chapter IV

Adaptive Service Choreography Support in Virtual Enterprises / *Adomas Svirskas,*

Bob Roberts, and Ioannis Ignatiadis 66

Service oriented architecture (SOA) approach in general and the Web services technology in particular enable creation of business applications from independently developed, deployed and owned components called services. A service captures a distinct business function offering some value independently of its usage context. However, it is not enough to have the business functionality of the partners packaged as (Web) services; there is also a need for business-aligned order of interaction between these services also known as business protocols, which can also be reused. The contribution of the chapter is two-fold: it explores reusability of the applicable business protocols in different business scenarios and it also suggests possible ways to adapt the implementations of the partners' services (end-points) to the changes in the business protocols.

Chapter V

Technologies to Support the Market of Resources as an Infrastructure for
Agile/Virtual Enterprise Integration / *Maria Manuela Cunha, Goran D. Putnik,*

Joaquim Pereira da Silva, and José Paulo Oliveira Santos 76

The agile/virtual enterprise (A/V E) model is considered a highly dynamic version of the virtual enterprise (VE) model, and its implementation presents several requirements in order to keep the VE partnership aligned with the market, that is, with business. Such requirements include (1) the reduction of reconfiguration costs and effort, and (2) the capability to preserve the firms' private knowledge on products or processes. These must be assured by a specific environment, or, in other words, by organizational infrastructures as a meta-organizational structure for VE design (or integration) and operation, such as the market of resources—an environment developed by the authors to cope with the highlighted requirements, and assuring a better performance than the traditional environments such as the Internet search engines or the electronic marketplaces. The chapter describes the functionalities of the market of resources and explains how does it supports A/V E integration, and addresses some technologies that could support A/V E integration within the market of resources, namely XML/ebXML and Webservices. The chapter proposes an architecture to support the operation of the market of resources, representing a fusion of the peer-to-peer (P2P) architecture with the client-server architecture, as a variant of P2P architecture. Also, a laboratory implementation of the web services for manufacturing is presented too.

Chapter VI

The Utilization of Semantic Web for Integrating Enterprise Systems /
Dimitrios Tektonidis and Albert Bokma... 97

Integrating enterprise system has become an issue of sharing information rather than transforming information due to the increasing complexity and the heterogeneity of the applications. The transition from application centric to integration centric enterprise application integration (EAI) requires methods and technologies that will enable and facilitate the definition of shared information. The use of ontologies semantic Web and technologies can improve the existing EAI methods by providing a framework capable to define shared information. Ontologies-based enterprise application integration (ONAR) framework utilizes semantic Web technologies to define shared information among heterogeneous systems. The present chapter presents the utilization of ontologies for the formation of ONAR framework and its application for service oriented application integration (SOAI).

Chapter VII

A Recommender Agent to Support Knowledge Sharing in Virtual Enterprises /
Renata S. S. Guizzardi, Pablo Gomes Ludermir, and Diego Sona 115

To remain competitive, virtual enterprises depend on effective knowledge management (KM). On the other hand, KM is deeply affected by the virtualization of modern organizations. As a result, KM systems need to be reshaped to adapt to these new conditions. This chapter presents KARe, a multi-agent recommender system that supports users sharing knowledge in a peer-to-peer environment. In this way, KARe reflects the intrinsically distributed nature of virtual enterprises. Supporting social interaction, the system allows users to share knowledge through questions and answers. This chapter focuses on KARe's recommendation algorithm, presenting its description and evaluation.

Chapter VIII

Framework of Agent-Based Intelligent System for Distributed Virtual
Enterprise Project Control / *Yee Ming Chen and Shih-Chang Wang*.. 135

Virtual enterprise-oriented projects need the support of a distributed project management system, which concerns the collaboration of different departments and enterprises. In this chapter, we propose a multi-agent system with negotiation strategies for project schedule control—a collaborative system framework wherein a distributed project can be scheduled dynamically by agents in the virtual enterprise environment. A prototype of the multi-agent systems with the negotiation strategies is implemented by Java, JADE, FIPA-ACL, and the negotiation strategies are experimentally validated. It successfully demonstrates on the online coordination and resolution of scheduling dynamically while encountering unexpected events to meet each project participant's requirements.

Chapter IX
Sharing Views, Information, and Cross-Enterprise Culture in the Corporate
Situation Room / *Bob Roberts and Adamantios Koumpis* 160

A major challenge for virtual organizations is the integration of their various corporate organizational and information assets, as well as their communication infrastructures and personnel. There also remains a need for greater understanding of how such virtual enterprises will operate in a "shared data / information / knowledge environment", through distributed working approaches and based on the paradigm of using the situation room metaphor as the core paradigm for carrying out joint operations. In this chapter, we present a methodology for modelling corporate interactions using the concept of the situation room (SR) as a supporting paradigm. Such an approach enables a way to model interactions of a virtual enterprise nature by means of a information and knowledge auction market that is concerned with the communications and interactions within a virtual enterprise (VE). This forms part of a wider research in defining a methodological framework for situation room analysis (SRA), and its deployment for complex corporate intelligence systems study.

Chapter X
Multi-Agent Systems Integration in Enterprise Environments Using Web Services /
Eduardo H. Ramírez and Ramón F. Brena 174

In this chapter we present a decoupled architectural approach that allows software agents to interoperate with enterprise systems using Web services. The solution leverages existing technologies and standards in order to reduce the time-to-market and increase the adoption of agent-based applications. We present case studies of applications that have been enhanced by our proposal.

Chapter XI
Web Service Discovery and Composition for Virtual Enterprises /
Jürgen Dorn, Peter Hrastnik, and Albert Rainer 190

One main characteristic of virtual enterprises are short-term collaborations between business partners to provide efficient and individualized services to customers. The MOVE project targets at a methodology and a software framework to support such flexible collaborations based on process oriented design and communication by Web services. MOVE's framework supports the graphical design and verification of business processes, the execution and supervision of processes in transaction-oriented environment, and the dynamic composition and optimization of processes. A business process may be composed from a set of Web services, deployed itself as Web service and executed in the framework. The composition of processes from Web services is implemented with methods from AI-planning. We apply answer set programming (ASP) and map Web service descriptions and customer requests into the input language of the ASP software DLV. Composition goals and constraints guide a composition challenge. We show the performance of our program and give some implementation details. Finally we conclude with some insights.

Chapter XII

Achieving Agile Enterprise Through Integrated Process Management:
From Planning to Work Execution / *Ali Bahrami* 208

Project management tools are used to manage projects from time as well as from resource leveling perspectives. Workflow management systems guide users through processes by driving the processes based on formal process definitions also called workflow types. This paper describes integrated process management system that will integrate project management, business process modeling, simulation and workflow technologies in order to support scheduled workflow execution. The target will be achieved by utilizing a tool for modeling work processes which can semi automatically generate workflow processes based on scheduling tool and then exported it to workflow engine via web services using XML process definition language (XPDL). Addition of simulation capability allows testing workflows before deployment.

Section IV
Virtual Enterprise Operation

Chapter XIII

Agents and Multi-Agent Systems in Supply Chain Management: An Overview /
Pericles A. Mitkas and Paraskevi Nikolaidou 223

This chapter discusses the current state-of-the-art of agents and multi-agent systems (MAS) in supply chain management (SCM). Following a general description of SCM and the challenges it is currently faced with, we present MAS as a possible solution to these challenges. We argue that an application involving multiple autonomous actors, such as SCM, can best be served by a software paradigm that relies on multiple independent software entities, like agents. The most significant current trends in this area and focusing on potential areas of further research. Furthermore, the authors believe that a clearer view on the current state-of-the-art and future extension will help researchers improve existing standards and solve remaining issues, eventually helping MAS-based SCM systems to replace legacy ERP software, but also give a boost on both areas of research separately.

Chapter XIV

A Conceptual Framework for Business Process Modeling in Virtual Organizations /
Dimitris Folinas, Tania Pavlou, Bill Karakostas, and Vicky Manthou 244

Among different approaches in business processes modeling procedure are those in virtual and dynamic organizational environments. In this chapter, a conceptual framework for modeling business processes in virtual organizations is suggested, by introducing Web services technology. Web services can be the business enabler for the new organizational form, which is particularly well suited to meet the demands arising from today's turbulent changes in the firms' environment. The proposed framework consists of several steps in a bottom-up approach, aiming to support the modeling and coordination of the complex and shared business processes in the examined environment.

Chapter XV
Towards a Virtual Enterprise Architecture for the Environmental Sector /
Ioannis N. Athanasiadis 256

This chapter introduces a virtual enterprise architecture for environmental information management, integration and dissemination. On a daily basis, our knowledge related to ecological phenomena, the degradation of the natural environment and the sustainability of human activity impact, is growing as a consequence raises the need for effective environmental knowledge exchange and reuse. In this work, a solution among collaborating peers forming a virtual enterprise is investigated. Following an analysis of the main stakeholders, a service-oriented architecture is proposed. Technical implementation options, using Web services or software agents, are considered and issues related to environmental information management, ownership and standardization are discussed.

Chapter XVI
Using VO Concept for Managing Dynamic Security Associations / *Yuri Demchenko* 267

This chapter discusses how the virtual organisation (VO) concept can be used for managing dynamic security associations in collaborative applications and for complex resource provisioning as possible components of the agent-based virtual enterprises. The chapter provides an overview of the current practice in VO management at the organizational level and its support at the security middleware level. It identifies open issues and basic requirements to the VO security functionality and services and suggests possible directions of further research and development, in particular, VO management concept, VO security services operation, and basic VO operational models. The author hopes that understanding the VO concept and current practice in Grid of using VO for managing security associations will help developers effectively use Gird technologies and middleware for building distributed security infrastructure for virtual enterprises.

Chapter XVII
Interoperability Middleware for Ferderated Business Services in Web-Pilacros /
Lea Kutvonen, Toni Ruokolainen, and Janne Metso 288

Participation in electronic business networks has become necessary for the success of enterprises. The strategic business needs for participating multiple networks simultaneously and for managing changes in these networks are reflected as new requirements for the supporting computing facilities. The web-Pilarcos architecture addresses the needs of managed collaboration and interoperability of autonomous business services in an inter-organisational context. The web-Pilarcos B2B middleware is designed for lowering the cost of collaboration establishment and to facilitate management and maintenance of electronic business networks. The approach is a federated one: All business services are developed independently, and the B2B middleware services are used to ensure that technical, semantic, and pragmatic interoperability is maintained in the business network. In the architecture and middleware functionality design, attention has been given to the dynamic aspects and evolution of the network. This paper discusses the concepts provided for application and business network creators, and the supporting middleware-level knowledge repositories for interoperability support.

Chapter XVIII
Web-Based Template-Driven Communication Support Systems: Using Shadow
netWorkspace to Support Trust Development in Virtual Teams / *Herbert Remidez, Jr.,*
Antonie Stam, and James M. Laffey 310

Teams whose interactions might be mediated entirely via Internet-based communication, virtual teams, are emerging as commonplace in business settings. Researchers have identified trust as a key ingredient for virtual teams to work effectively (Aubrey & Kelsey, 2003; Beranek, 2000; David & McDaniel, 2004; Iacono & Weisband, 1997; Jarvenpaa, Knoll, & Leidner, 1998). However, researchers have not identified scalable methods that consistently promote trust within virtual teams. Improved interface design for communication support systems used by virtual teams may contribute to solving this problem. Interface cannot solve the problem of members trusting each other, but it can support the type of activities that do. This chapter describes the development and some initial experiences with a web-based, template-driven, asynchronous communication support tool and how this system can be used to support trust development in virtual teams and performance goals of virtual teams. This chapter presents the capabilities and features of the communication support system. More detailed findings from an experimental study of this system's use can be found in another publication (Remidez, 2003).

Chapter IXX
Web Service Design Concepts and Structures for Support of Highly Interconnected
E-Health Infrastructures: A Bottom-Up Approach / *Adamantios Koumpis* 327

In this chapter we present organizational aspects that appear when considering the case of interconnecting and integrating different compartments of a modern hospital. While the information and communication technologies provide advanced and powerful means for the creation of coherent information supply services, such as the Web service and ontology technologies, there is a lack of appropriate organizational metaphors that will enable the successful assimilation of these technologies, helping to aid in the improvement of critical cost parameters that concentrate a large part of the hospital's management resources, while also helping to improve the knowledge capital and the intangible and immaterial assets of any particular hospital, which are considered as the most essential and scarce resource. In this paper we presents a technology-based approach for solving interoperability problems at the service level, and we deliberately adopt a problem-solving approach that has successfully been adopted by the European IST Project ARTEMIS.

Compilation of References 341

About the Contributors 370

Index 379

Foreword

Use of Internet technologies for the interest of individuals and organizations is becoming more context-related and the center of gravity is correctly placed to the utility and the value that all involved parties are getting from a business transaction, a business venture or a collaborative service.

Therefore, both aspects that are covered in this book are important: software agents and Web services are not treated as enabling technologies for the addressed field of virtual enterprises, but also as paradigms that can govern the organizational or/and social aspects of such constellations. It is expected that this to become a dominating pattern in the next years: the role of technology shall not limit in the realization of our ideas, but will more and more support us in shaping new ones.

Many of the chapters of this book report on first-hand experiences of the authors. The role of the lessons learned is extremely important when considering the combination of new and to great extent immature technologies on the one hand, and still-novel concepts like this of virtual organizations on the other.

Looking back in all the progress that was made in the last 10 years, I am confident that future technologists will integrate an understanding of the concept of virtual enterprises. Much of the work and the research undergone in this area are not related with technologies *per se*, but with several managerial and social aspects. This book therefore presents a valuable collection of articles worth reading that shed light on many different and complimentary issues in the field.

Prof. Georgios I. Doukidis
ELTRUN, Athens University of Economics and Business
Athens, May 2007

Georgios I. Doukidis *has a bachelor's degree in mathematics from the University of Thessaloniki (1980), a master's degree in operational research from the London School of Economics (1981), and a PhD in simulation/artificial intelligence from the London School of Economics (1985). From 1981-1991, he worked at LSE as a teaching assistant in operational research, a lecturer in computing, and an academic visitor in information systems. Currently he is a professor in the Department of Management Science and Technology at the Athens University of Economics and Business (AUEB) and a visiting professor in the Department of Information Systems and Computing at Brunel University, UK. He teaches and researches in the areas of management and strategy of information systems, electronic commerce, and decision support systems. He is chairman of the Department of Management Science and Technology and scientific coordinator of the e-business specialization of the graduate program in decision sciences. He has an extensive 22 years experience with R&D in information systems and e-business. He is initiator and director of ELTRUN (ELectronic Trading Research UNit) and has collaborated with more than 30 research groups worldwide in R&D projects. He has successfully managed more than 35 R&D projects financed by the European Commission, the Greek government, and private organizations. He has participated in various R&D committees and acted as evaluator for the Greek General Secretariat of Research & Technology and DGIII of the European Commission (program ESPRIT). He has published or edited 14 books. He is a member of the editorial board in more than nine international scientific journals and he has presented various scientific papers in more than 120 international and national conferences in 21 different countries.*

Preface

INTRODUCTION

The shift from the industrial economy to the information economy that has happened over the years has led to an enormous increase in competitiveness among companies. This in turn has led to the development of information technology to highly advanced levels. It is now able to support modern enterprise operation in extremely intricate environments where the changing needs of the business community forces firms to be more agile and responsive. The development of technologies that can efficiently handle complex information such as software agents, combined with the development of Internet technologies for business process integration and automation such as Web services, is causing considerable impact on the way economic actors and their roles are implemented in the worldwide market place. This technological evolution has lead to the development of a new value-creating economic paradigm, where the concepts of extended enterprise, the agile enterprise, the smart organization, and the virtual enterprise are starting to hold an important position.

The network based information economy and the virtual-yet-real enterprises are a promising reality. Research on new technologies for the virtual enterprise has released new roads to the design principles and operation approaches, done in order to maximize benefits and overcome any limitations encountered so far, in the real life of the virtual enterprise. New theories and technologies such as agent and Web service supported formation and operation, collaboration requirement planning, active middleware for virtual enterprise operation support and operational parallelism—some of them covered by chapters in this book—present a concrete design framework for virtual enterprise successful operation. At the same time, serious challenges to the future effectiveness of virtual enterprises are also sensed and discussed throughout this book.

In a virtual enterprise, sets of economic actors combine their strengths to provide a specific service traditionally provided by a single enterprise. Such possibilities can greatly influence the economy and enterprise development strategies, and in the long term this will help small and medium enterprises capitalize on the information economy. Historically speaking, small and medium enterprises (SMEs) have founded their competitiveness on static established co-operations, which were based on personal relationships and on the proximity of the involved companies' locations. Groups of SMEs have demonstrated in several regions of Europe and the USA, the ability to successfully exploit a business opportunity that none of its members had the financial and technological ability to realize individually. This approach, although effective in the past, is showing its limitations regarding its capability to face the requirements of the global market, where the search for competitiveness cannot be limited by geographical and personal constraints.

Yet, if we could find a way to exploit the tremendous advancement of ICT and the promises of the border-less electronic market, in order to harvest the cultural attitude toward cooperation of SMEs, and transpose it from its local environment to the worldwide market, we would unleash a tremendous competitive potential in the world global market. Moreover, within both the overall Industrial Policy and the Enterprise Policy, there is a clear imperative to support initiatives that will facilitate and enhance the current operation of SMEs "daily" and "routine" working activities. Particularly, the European Commission White Paper on Growth, Competitiveness and Employment proposed a synergetic strategy to ensure the mobilization of economic operators to support the development of 17 million European SMEs (the number of European SMEs equalizes the number of the unemployed).

Virtual enterprises allow businesses to concentrate on their best skills and be flexible within their environments. Their strategic guideline is the electronic commerce model and more specifically the cooperative business or B2B scenario, where the virtual enterprise offered a new and major step. It defied the conventional organization operation scenario by accomplishing tasks traditionally meant for an organization much bigger with lots of financial, human and technical resources. This is made possible due to there being a collaborative effort. A company having the right know-how, another with the technical capability, the other with the right human skill set, can come together across the Internet to aggregate it all. The Information Economy gifts a virtual enterprise composition for entrepreneurs who want to achieve their dreams (Wikipedia).

Virtual enterprises are a major trend in cooperative business. Specialization and flexibility are some of the key aspects of an every day more dynamic and global market. The concept of virtual enterprise has been applied to many forms of cooperative business relations, like supply chains, construction industry, outsourcing or temporary consortiums.

As with all types of enterprises, virtual enterprises present both benefits and challenges. Organizations can benefit from virtual enterprises through more business opportunities, lower cost connections with suppliers, more chances to create revenue, more efficient operations, and a reduction in administrative costs. The challenges facing virtual enterprises are integration difficulties, security, expense control, inexperienced users and the level of incorporation required to create a successful virtual enterprise (Sun Microsystems, Inc., 2004).

One of the ideas driving virtual enterprise creation is that of processes dynamically constructed out of available Internet-based services, as needed at runtime. In the late 1980's, Marty Tenenbaum talked about a "sea of services" on the Internet that would facilitate virtual enterprise formation. Now that we have Web Services, this idea of finding services at runtime has great potential. Agent technology can help to locate and apply Web Services in virtual enterprises, and also to dynamically construct and operate them.

The most ambitious technologies however, intend to automate the process of formation and operation of virtual enterprises, mainly through multi-agent technology approaches, where each partner enterprises of the virtual enterprise can be represented by an agent. Research on multi-agent technology addresses issues that fit the virtual enterprise scenario. Agents are autonomous, interact with other agents, and enable approaching inherently distributed problems with negotiation and coordination capabilities (Cardoso & Oliveira, 2005).

A lot of academic work has been done so far in applying software agents to virtual enterprises. Due to this work many interesting results have been achieved concerning the virtual enterprise life cycle. However, some of these results mean more confusion rather than clarification. Recent research, for example, proposes abandoning specific implementations of software agents, in favor of building on emerging Web service standards—called service agents—while others propose that we just use MAS technology.

"Agent and Web Service Technologies in Virtual Enterprises" addresses the different dimensions of the above mentioned technologies when applied to virtual enterprises. The book intends to provide an integrated view of the most recent contributions to the agent and Web service technologies in virtual enterprises. Several dimensions can be identified in this mission:

- **The Web service dimension:** This technology is very popular for virtual enterprise integration and operation where the academic approach has not solved the fundamental problems of service discovery as yet. How do interested parties find the capability they're looking for? How do they advertise? How can software do this on behalf (but without the intervention) of a person? Many proposals along these lines exist, ranging from content-based routing in the early 1990's to the use of DAML-S for agents in recent years but none of them has led to deployed, practical systems so far.
- **The software agent dimension:** This includes multi-agent systems (MAS) technology, mobile agents, intelligent agents and other combinations of traditional agent technologies.

The mission of the proposed book is to discuss the main issues, trends and opportunities related to the application of agent and Web service technologies to virtual enterprises, from the above-mentioned dimensions. The book will take a comprehensive approach, and disseminate practical solutions to promote virtual enterprise and interorganizational integration. The overall objectives are:

- To introduce and discuss the business integration requirements in the virtual enterprise and other emerging interorganizational models
- To discuss Web service and software agent technologies and applications
- To discuss Web service and software agent technologies in virtual enterprise formation, integration and operation
- To introduce relevant and recent developments and solutions (academic and industrial) addressing the several dimensions and issues of the book

This book is both for an academic audience (teachers, researchers and students, mainly of post-graduate studies) and professional audience (managers, organizational and system developers and IT specialists) in terms of explaining the requirements and frameworks for IT solutions.

This book is expected to act as a guide for technology solution developers from academia, research institutions and industry, providing them with a broader perspective of Agent and Web Services.

This book contains 14 excellent chapters authored by a group of internationally renowned and experienced professionals and researchers in the field of IT and virtual enterprise (VE) science. Contributors also include younger authors, creating a value-added constellation of dynamic authors. Concerning the environments from which the contributions are presented, the chapters came from academia, research institutions and industry.

ORGANIZATION OF THE BOOK

The 19 chapters in this book are organized into four sections. These sections address the state of the art software agents and Web services areas along with the main phases of the virtual enterprise life cycle, being in a simplified view formation, integration and operation.

The book's organization scheme, in respect to the previously mentioned three phases of the virtual enterprise's life cycle and the technology addressed, is given in Table 1.

- **Section I,** "Agents and Web Services Overview," consists of two chapters that give an overview of the current advances in the software agent and Web service technologies.
- Chapter I, "Software Agent Technology: An Overview," surveys some key research issues in the software agents' area. It annotates several researchers' opinions on many areas concerning software

Table 1. Book organization

Virtual Enterprise phase	Technology	Sections	Chapters
	Overview	1	1, 2
Formation		2	3
Operation	Integration	3	4-9
	Collaboration		
	Applications	4	10-14

agents aiming to give a more documentary point of view on each argued subject. Its main goal is to provide an overview of the rapidly evolving area of software agents, serving as a reference point to a large body of literature and outlining the key aspects of software agent technology.

- Chapter II, "Web Services Technology: An Overview," examines the concept of service-oriented architecture (SOA) in conjunction with Web services technology, as an implementation of the former's design principles. Following a brief introduction of SOA and its advantages, a high-level overview of the structure and composition of the Web services platform is provided. This overview covers the core Web services specifications as well as features of the extended architecture stack, which together forms a powerful and robust foundation for building distributed systems.

- **Section II**, "Virtual Enterprise Formation," consists of one chapter that discusses the application of software agents and Web service technologies in the formation of virtual enterprises.

- Chapter III, "Virtual Enterprise Formation Supported by Agents and Web Services," describes the use of software agents and Web services to support the formation of virtual enterprises. The partners of a virtual enterprise are represented as software agents. The AGORA multi-agent architecture is used. The focus of this chapter is on the description of the services provided by each partner and the partner selection process. The concept of agent interaction protocols is used to manage the interactions during the formation of the virtual enterprise. An implementation of the ideas and examples from industrial case studies are used for the validation of the approach and discussions. The use of Semantic Web technology and Web services with multi-agent systems is discussed as the future direction for this work.

- **Section III**, "Virtual Enterprise Integration," consists of nine chapters that discuss the problems of virtual enterprise integration. Agents and Web services are examined through various aspects of the integration problem such as information and knowledge sharing, distributed project scheduling and views and cross-enterprise culture sharing.

- Chapter IV, "Adaptive Service Choreography Support in Virtual Enterprises," discusses Web service choreography application in virtual enterprises. The contribution of the paper is two-fold: it explores reusability of the applicable business protocols in different business scenarios and suggests ways to adapt the implementations of the partners' services (end-points) to the changes in the business protocols.

- Chapter V, "Technologies to Support the Market of Resources as an Infrastructure for Agile/Virtual Enterprise Integration," describes the functionalities of the market of resources and explains how it supports A/V E integration. It also addresses some technologies that could support A/V E integration based on the market of resources, namely XML/ebXML and Web services, in the integration and automation of processes and services. The chapter proposes an architecture to support the operation of the market of resources, representing a fusion of the peer-to-peer (P2P) architecture with the client-server architecture, as a variant of P2P architecture.

- Chapter VI, "The Utilization of Semantic Web for Integrating Enterprise Systems" presents the utilization of ontologies for the formation of an ONAR framework and its application for service oriented application integration (SOAI). Ontologies based enterprise application integration (ONAR) framework utilizes Semantic Web technologies to define shared information among heterogeneous systems.

- Chapter VII, "A Recommender Agent to Support Knowledge Sharing in Virtual Enterprises," presents KARe, a multi-agent recommender system that supports users sharing knowledge in a peer-to-peer environment. In this way, KARe reflects the intrinsically distributed nature of virtual enterprises. Supporting social interaction, the system allows users to share knowledge through questions and answers. This chapter focuses on KARe's recommendation algorithm, presenting its description and evaluation

- Chapter VIII, "Framework of Agent-Based Intelligent System for Distributed Virtual Enterprise Project Control," the authors propose the multiagent systems with negotiation strategies for project schedule control—a collaborative system framework wherein a distributed project can be scheduled dynamically by agents in the virtual enterprise environment. A prototype of the multiagent systems, with the negotiation strategies, is implemented in Java, JADE, FIPA-ACL, and the negotiation strategies are experimentally validated. The prototype successfully demonstrates the online coordination and resolution in dynamic scheduling, while handling unexpected events to meet each project participant's requirements.

- Chapter IX, "Sharing Views, Information, and Cross-Enterprise Culture in the Corporate Situation Room," presents a methodology for modeling corporate interactions using the concept of the situation room (SR) as a supporting paradigm. Such an approach facilitates a way to model interactions of a virtual enterprise nature, by means of an information and knowledge auction market that is concerned with the communications and interactions within a virtual enterprise.

- Chapter X, "Multi-Agent Systems Integration in Enterprise Environments Using Web Services," presents a decoupled architectural approach that allows software agents to interoperate with enterprise systems using Web services. The solution leverages existing technologies and standards in order to reduce the time-to-market and increase the adoption of agent-based applications. The chapter also presents case studies of applications that have been enhanced by this architecture.

- Chapter XI, "Web Service Discovery and Composition for Virtual Enterprises," presents a methodology and a software framework to support short-term collaborations between business partners within a virtual enterprise, based on process-oriented design and communication by Web services. Their framework developed in the frame of the Austrian project MOVE, supports the graphical design and verification of business processes, the execution and supervision of processes in transaction-oriented environment, and the dynamic composition and optimization of processes.

- Chapter XII, "Achieving Agile Enterprise Through Integrated Process Management: From Planning to Work Execution," describes an integrated process management system that will integrate project management, business process modelling, simulation, and workflow technologies to support scheduled workflow execution. The target will be achieved by utilizing a tool for modelling work processes that can semi-automatically generate workflow processes based on a scheduling tool and then export it to a workflow engine via Web services using XML process definition language (XPDL). In addition, the simulation capability allows testing workflows before deployment.

- **Section IV**, "Virtual Enterprise Operation," consists of six chapters that discuss virtual enterprise operation. Agents and Web Services are examined through various aspects of the virtual enterprise operation such as supply chain management, business process modelling and applications of virtual enterprises in various sectors such as environmental and health care.

- Chapter XIII, "Agents and Multi-Agent Systems in Supply Chain Management: An Overview," discusses the current state-of-the-art agents and multi-agent systems (MAS) in supply chain management (SCM). Following a general description of SCM and the challenges it is currently faced with, we present MAS as a possible solution. The authors argue that an application involving multiple autonomous actors, such as SCM, can best be served by a software paradigm that relies on multiple independent software entities, like agents. The most significant current trends in this area are discussed and potential areas for further research are outlined.

- Chapter XIV, "A Conceptual Framework for Business Process Modeling in Virtual Organizations," suggests a conceptual framework for modelling business processes in virtual Organizations, by introducing Web services technology. Web services can be the business enabler for the new organizational form, which is particularly well suited to meeting the demands arising from today's turbulent changes in the firms' environment. The proposed framework consists of several steps in a bottom-up approach, aiming to support the modelling and coordination of the complex and shared business processes in the examined environments.

- Chapter XV, "Towards a Virtual Enterprise Architecture for the Environmental Sector," explores the potential of formulating virtual enterprises for the environmental sector. In particular, Section II lays the foundations by introducing concepts related to environmental management information systems (EMIS) and the major challenges for environmental information processing and dissemination. In Section III, a virtual enterprise architecture for environmental information management is introduced and Section IV specifies the operational fashion of such a virtual enterprise. Section V summarizes latest developments in the field, and discusses the potential for wide-range adoption of virtual enterprises in the environmental sector.

- Chapter XVI, "Using VO Concept for Managing Dynamic Security Associations," discusses how the virtual organization concept can be used for managing dynamic security associations in collaborative applications and for complex resource provisioning as possible components of the Agent based virtual enterprises. This chapter provides an overview of the current practice in virtual organization management at the organizational level and its support at the security middleware level. It identifies open issues and basic requirements of the virtual organization security functionality and services and suggests possible directions for further research and development. The research presented here is based on experience gained from the major grid-based and grid-oriented projects in collaborative applications and complex resource provisioning.

- Chapter XVII, "Interoperability Middleware for Federated Business Services in Web-Pilarcos," presents the Web-Pilarcos architecture that addresses the needs of managed collaboration and interoperability of autonomous business services in an inter-organisational context. The Web-Pilarcos B2B middleware is designed for lowering the cost of collaboration establishment and to facilitate management and maintenance of electronic business networks. The approach is a federated one: all business services are developed independently and the B2B middleware services are used to ensure that technical, semantic and pragmatic interoperability is maintained in the business network.

- Chapter XVIII, "Web-Based Template-Driven Communication Support Systems: Using Shadow netWorkspace to Support Trust Development in Virtual Teams," describes the development and some initial experiences with a Web-based, template driven, asynchronous communication support tool and how this system can be used to support trust development in virtual teams and performance goals of virtual teams. This chapter presents the capabilities and features of the communication support system.

- Chapter IXX, "Web Service Design Concepts and Structures for Support of Highly Interconnected E-Health Infrastructures: A Bottom-Up Approach," the authors present organizational issues that are revealed when considering the case of interconnecting and integrating different compartments of a modern hospital. They present a technology-based approach for solving interoperability problems at the service level, and they deliberately adopt a problem-solving approach that is successfully adopted in the European IST Project ARTEMIS.

EXPECTATIONS

This book is expected to be read by academics (i.e., teachers, researchers and students), technology solutions developers and enterprise managers (including top level managers). It is expected to be a guide for technology solution developers, from academia, research institutions and industry, providing them with a broader perspective of virtual enterprise technologies. It aims to increase their awareness on how agent and Web stechnologies can best serve the needs of an ever expanding and increasingly competitive organizational model. This book also widens horizons for researchers interested in this emerging field and presents the background and state-of-the-art developments.

As a book it is expected to raise the awareness of the potential of the virtual enterprises model so that managers, who should employ proactive behavior towards new approaches to business, are able to exploit it. In other words, the book provides guidance and helps raise awareness, pro-activeness and agility of enterprise managers. This should include top level and IT managers, for strategic and dynamic alignment with business opportunities, on the problems of virtual enterprise development, implementations and operation as well as on the evolution of their actual enterprises towards virtual enterprise.

This work will support teachers of several graduate and postgraduate courses, from an information technology perspective. In particular, it will support the emerging courses on virtual enterprise technologies and provide a basis for understanding content, and an area for further study, research and solutions development.

The editor is also expecting that the book will contribute to the diffusion of the virtual enterprises technological concept in other parts of the world, not only in the most developed countries.

Finally, the editor is grateful to the readers for any constructive criticism and indication of errors—conceptual, omissions or in typing.

The Editor,
Nicolaos Protogeros

REFERENCES

Wikipedia. Virtual Enterprise definition. Retrieved January 31, 2007, from http://en.wikipedia.org/wiki/Virtual_enterprise

Sun Microsystems, Inc. (2004). *Identity Management: Technology Cornerstone of the Virtual Enterprise.* Retrieved January 31, 2007, from http://www.sun.com/software/products/identity/wp_virtual_enterprise.pdf

Cardoso, H. L., & Oliveira, E. (2005). *Virtual Enterprise Normative Framework within Electronic Institutions.* Retrieved January 31, 2007, from http://paginas.fe.up.pt/~eol/PUBLICATIONS/2005/esaw_post.PDF

Acknowledgment

This book could not have been edited without great help and support from many sources. I would like to acknowledge the help of all involved in the collation, review process and production of the book, without whose support the project could not have been satisfactorily completed.

Deep appreciation and gratitude is due to Dr. Adamantios Koumpis, manager of the Research Programmes Division, ALTEC S.A. and Professor Pericles A. Mitkas of Aristotle University of Thessaloniki for their continuous support during this project.

Most of the authors of the chapters included in this book also served as referees for articles written by other authors. Thanks go to all those who provided constructive and comprehensive reviews. However, some of the reviewers must be mentioned as their reviews set the benchmark. Reviewers who provided the most comprehensive, critical and constructive comments include: Dr. Adamantios Koumpis of ALTEC S.A., Dr. Yuri Demchenko of the University of Amsterdam and Dr. Renata S. S. Guizzardi from ITC-IRST Povo, Trento, Italy. Support from the Department of Accounting and Finance at Macedonia University is also acknowledged for their hosting and e-mail service during the review process.

Special thanks also go to all the staff at IGI Global, whose contributions throughout the entire process from inception of the initial idea to final publication have been invaluable. In particular to Jan Travers, who continuously offered encouragement via e-mail to keep the project on schedule, and to Mehdi Khosrow-Pour whose enthusiasm motivated me to initially accept his invitation to take on this project.

Special thanks to my colleagues at the University of Macedonia for their moral support and help in reading various drafts and manuscripts and provided helpful suggestions for enhancing its content. Last but not least, to my wife Maria for her unfailing support and encouragement during the months it took to give birth to this book and to my children Katerina and George for their love.

In closing, I wish to thank all of the authors for their insights and excellent contributions to this book.

Nicolaos Protogeros
Editor, PhD
Thessaloniki, Greece

Section I
Agents and
Web Services Overview

Chapter I
Software Agent Technology:
An Overview

Chrysanthi E. Georgakarakou
University of Macedonia, Greece

Anastasios A. Economides
University of Macedonia, Greece

ABSTRACT

This chapter provides an overview of the rapidly evolving area of software agents and presents the basic aspects of applying the agent technology to virtual enterprises (VE). As the field of software agents can appear chaotic, this chapter briefly introduces the key issues rather than present an in-depth analysis and critique of the field. In addition to, this chapter investigates the application of agent technology to virtual enterprises and presents current research activity that focuses on this field serving as an introductory step. Furthermore, this chapter makes a list of the most important themes concerning software agents and the application of agent technology to virtual enterprises apposing some order and consistency and serve as a reference point to a large body of literature.

INTRODUCTION

The aim of this chapter is to survey some key research issues in the software agents' area. It annotates several researchers' opinions on many areas concerning software agents trying to give a more documentary point of view of each argued subject. Its main goal is to provide an overview of the rapidly evolving area of software agents serving as a reference point to a large body of literature and outlining the key aspects of software agent technology. While this chapter does not act as an introduction to all the issues in the software agents' field, it intends to point the reader at the primary areas of interest. In addition to, this chapter investigates the application of agent technology to virtual enterprises. It presents basic aspects of applying agent technology to virtual enterprises serving as an introductory step.

First of all, this overview chapter attempts to answer the question of what a software agent is. Secondly, it analyzes the three technologies that distributed artificial intelligence (DAI) has evolved: (1) multi-agent system (MAS), (2) distributed problem solving (DPS), and (3) parallel AI (PAI). Thereinafter, it makes the distinction between single agent and multi-agent systems analyzing their dimensions. In addition to, it goes through the broad spectrum of agent properties. Furthermore, it discusses the most acknowledged classification schemes or taxonomies (typologies) of software agents proposed in the agent research community. Moreover, it presents the most well known agent architecture classification schemes arguing about each distinct architecture. Besides, it explores the two most important agent communication approaches: (1) communication protocols, and (2) evolving languages. It also discusses about a number of languages for coordination and communication that have been proposed. It argues about possible implementations of agent transportation mechanisms as well. Further, it annotates prominent ontology specification languages and editors for ontology creation and maintenance. Then, it lists and argues standard languages and several prototype languages for implementing agent-based systems that have been proposed for constructing agent-based systems. Afterwards, it presents a number of tools and platforms that are available and support activities or phases of the process of agent-oriented software development. Next, it examines several agent oriented software engineering (AOSE) methodologies that have been proposed to assist engineers to create agent-based systems. At the end, it investigates the application of the agent technology to virtual enterprises, answering the question of why to use agents in virtual enterprises and presenting the current research activity that focuses on the agent technology applied to virtual enterprises.

BACKGROUND

As software agents comprise a prominent scientific area of research activity, a plethora of researchers have investigated them and stated their own point of view. Nwana and Ndumu (1996) mention that software agent technology is a rapidly developing area of research. According to Wooldridge and Jennings (1995), the concept of an agent has become important in both artificial intelligence (AI) and mainstream computer science. Oliveira, Fischer, and Stepankova (1999) observe that for some time now agent-based and multi-agent systems (MASs) have attracted the interest of researchers far beyond traditional computer science and artificial intelligence (AI).

Although software agent technology demonstrates expeditious advancement, there is a truly heterogeneous body of work being carried out under the "agents" banner (Nwana & Ndumu, 1996). Nwana and Ndumu (1996) introduce software agent technology by overviewing the various agent types currently under investigation by researchers. Nwana (1996) largely reviews software agents, and makes some strong statements that are not necessarily widely accepted by the agent community. Nwana (1996) presents a typology of agents, next places agents in context, defines them and overviews critically the rationales, hypotheses, goals, challenges, and state-of-the-art demonstrators of the various agent types of the proposed typology. Besides, Nwana (1996) attempts to make explicit much of what is usually implicit in the agents' literature and proceeds to overview some other general issues which pertain to all the types of agents in the typology.

Agent-based and multi-agent systems (MASs) have attracted the researchers' interest to great extents. Oliveira et al. (1999) try to identify focal points of interest for researchers working in the area of distributed AI (DAI) and MAS as well as application oriented researchers coming from related disciplines, for example, electrical and mechanical engineering. They do this by presenting key research topics in DAI and MAS research and by identifying application domains in which the DAI and MAS technologies are most suitable.

Sycara (1998) presents some of the critical notions in MASs and the research work that has addressed them and organizes these notions around the concept of problem-solving coherence. Sycara (1998) believes that problem-solving coherence is one of the most critical overall characteristics that an MAS should exhibit.

Jennings et al. (1998) provide an overview of research and development activities in the field of autonomous agents and multi-agent systems. They aim to identify key concepts and applications, and to indicate how they relate to one another. Some historical context to the field of agent-based computing is given, and contemporary research directions are presented. Finally, a range of open issues and future challenges are highlighted.

Wooldridge and Jennings (1995) aim to point the reader at what they perceive to be the most important theoretical and practical issues associated with the design and construction of intelligent agents. For convenience, they divide these issues into three areas (agent theory, agent architectures, and agent languages). Their paper is not intended to serve as a tutorial introduction to all the issues mentioned and includes a short review of current and potential applications of agent technology.

Wooldridge (1998) provides an introductory survey of agent-based computing. The article begins with an overview of micro-level issues in agent-based systems: issues related to the design and construction of individual intelligent agents. The article then goes on to discuss some macrolevel issues; issues related to the design and construction of agent societies. Finally, the key application areas for agent technology are surveyed.

An article that should not be omitted at this point is Weiß's (2002) paper. Weiß (2002) offers a guide to the broad body of literature of agent-

oriented software engineering (AOSE). The guide, which is intended to be of value to both researchers and practitioners, is structured according to key issues and key topics that arise when dealing with AOSE: methods and frameworks for requirements engineering, analysis, design, and implementation; languages for programming, communication and coordination, and ontology specification; and development tools and platforms.

On the other hand, considering the agent technology application to virtual enterprises, Jennings, Norman and Faratin (1998) exhibit considerable concepts. They argue the case of the agent-based approach showing how agent technology can improve efficiency by ensuring that business activities are better scheduled, executed, monitored, and coordinated.

According to Camarinha-Matos (2002), multi-agent systems represent a promising approach to both model and implement the complex supporting infrastructures required for virtual enterprises and related emerging organizations. The current status of application of this approach to industrial virtual enterprises, virtual communities, and remote supervision in the context of networked collaborative organizations is presented (Camarinha-Matos, 2002). Examples of relevant projects are provided and major challenges and open issues identified as well (Camarinha-Matos, 2002).

Petersen, Divitini, and Matskin (2001) describe how virtual enterprises can be modeled using the AGORA multi-agent architecture, designed for modelling and supporting cooperative work among distributed entities. They underline that the distributed and goal-oriented nature of the virtual enterprise provides a strong motivation for the use of agents to model virtual enterprises. They also mention the main advantages of their approach.

This chapter provides an overview of research activity regarding the scientific domain of software agents. As the field of software agents can appear chaotic, this chapter briefly introduces the key issues rather than present an in-depth analysis and critique of the field. References to more detailed treatments are provided. The purpose of this chapter is to make a list of the most important themes concerning software agents, apposing some order and consistency and serve as a reference point to a large body of literature. In addition to, this chapter makes an introduction of applying agent technology to virtual enterprises and describes current research activity that addresses the above-mentioned issue.

A BRIEF OVERVIEW OF SOFTWARE AGENT TECHNOLOGY

What is a Software Agent?

Software agent technology is a rapidly developing area of research and probably the fastest growing area of information technology (IT) (Jennings & Wooldridge, 1996; Nwana & Ndumu, 1996). Application domains in which agent solutions are being applied or researched into include workflow management, telecommunications network management, air-traffic control, business process reengineering, data mining, information retrieval/management, electronic commerce, education, personal digital assistants (PDAs), e-mail filtering, digital libraries, command and control, smart databases, and scheduling/diary management (Nwana & Ndumu, 1996).

Over the last years, many researchers in the area of agents have proposed a large variety of definitions for the "agent" term. It is stated that it is difficult to give a full definition for the note of agency. Nwana (1996) predicates there are at least two reasons why it is so difficult to define precisely what agents are. Firstly, agent researchers do not "own" this term in the same way as fuzzy logicians/AI researchers, for example, own the term "fuzzy logic"—it is one that is used widely in everyday parlance as in travel agents, estate agents, and so forth. Secondly, even within the software fraternity, the word agent is really an um-

brella term for a heterogeneous body of research and development (Nwana, 1996). Concerning the agent definition, Nwana (1996) states:

When we really have to, we define an agent as referring to a component of software and/or hardware which is capable of acting exactingly in order to accomplish tasks on behalf of its user. Given a choice, we would rather say it is an umbrella term, meta-term or class, which covers a range of other more specific agent types, and then go on to list and define what these other agent types are. This way, we reduce the chances of getting into the usual prolonged philosophical and sterile arguments which usually proceed the former definition, when any old software is conceivably recastable as agent-based software. (p. 6)

Bradshow (1997) identifies two approaches to the definition of an agent as follows: (1) agent as an ascription—this approach is based on the concept that "agency cannot ultimately be characterized by listing a collection of attributes but rather consists fundamentally as an attribution on the part of some person," and (2) agent as a description: agents are defined by describing the attributes they should exhibit.

Jennings and Wooldridge (1996) offer a relatively loose notion of an agent as a self-contained program capable of controlling its own decision-making and acting, based on its perception of its environment, in pursuit of one or more objectives will be used here.

Wooldridge (1998) defines an intelligent agent as a system that enjoys the following four properties: autonomy (agents operate without the direct intervention of humans or others, and have control over their actions and internal state), social ability (agents are able to cooperate with humans or other agents in order to achieve their tasks), reactivity (agents perceive their environment, and respond in a timely fashion to changes that occur in it), and pro-activeness (agents do not simply act in response to their environment, they are able to exhibit goal-directed behavior by taking the initiative).

According to Hayes (1999), an agent is an entity (either computer or human) that is capable of carrying out goals, and is part of a larger community of agents that have mutual influence on each other. Agents may co-exist on a single processor, or they may be constructed from physically, but intercommunicating processors (such as a community of robots) (Hayes, 1999). The key concepts in this definition are that agents can act autonomously to some degree, and they are part of a community in which mutual influence occurs (Hayes, 1999).

Distributed Artificial Intelligence (DAI) Technologies

Distributed artificial intelligence (DAI) is a subfield of artificial intelligence (AI) which is concerned with a society of problem solvers or agents interacting in order to solve a common problem: computers and persons, sensors, aircraft, robots, and so forth (Green, Hurst, Nangle, Cunningham, Somers, & Evans, 1997). Such a society is termed a multi-agent system, namely, a network of problem solvers that work together to solve problems that are beyond their individual capabilities (Green et al., 1997). Software agents have evolved from multi-agent systems (MAS), which in turn form one of three broad areas which fall under DAI, the other two being distributed problem solving (DPS) and parallel AI (PAI) (Nwana, 1996). Therefore, agents inherit potential benefits from both DAI, for example modularity, speed, reliability and AI (e.g., operation at knowledge level, easier maintenance, reusability, platform independence) (Nwana, 1996).

Agent Systems

Jennings et al. (1998) state that an agent-based system is a system in which the key abstraction used is that of an agent. In principle, an agent-based system might be conceptualized in terms of agents, but implemented without any software structures corresponding to agents at all (Jennings et al., 1998). A parallel with object-oriented software can be drawn, where it is entirely possible to design a system in terms of objects, but to implement it without the use of an object-oriented software environment (Jennings et al., 1998). But this would at best be unusual, and at worst, counter-productive (Jennings et al., 1998). According to Jennings et al. (1998), a similar situation exists with agent technology and they therefore expect an agent-based system to be both designed and implemented in terms of agents.

An agent-based system may contain one or more agents (Jennings et al., 1998). There are cases in which a single agent solution is appropriate (Jennings et al., 1998). However, the multi-agent case—where the system is designed and implemented as several interacting agents—is arguably more general and more interesting from a software engineering standpoint (Jennings et al., 1998). Multi-agent systems are ideally suited to representing problems that have multiple problem solving methods, multiple perspectives and/or multiple problem solving entities (Jennings et al., 1998). Such systems have the traditional advantages of distributed and concurrent problem solving, but have the additional advantage of sophisticated patterns of interactions (Jennings et al., 1998). Examples of common types of interactions include: cooperation (working together towards a common aim), coordination (organizing problem solving activity so that harmful interactions are avoided or beneficial interactions are exploited), and negotiation (coming to an agreement which is acceptable to all the parties involved) (Jennings et al., 1998).

As the technology matures and endeavors to attack more complex, realistic, and large-scale problems, the need for systems that consist of multiple agents that communicate in a peer-to-peer fashion is becoming apparent (Sycara, 1998). The most powerful tools for handling complexity are modularity and abstraction (Sycara, 1998). Multi-agent systems (MASs) offer modularity (Sycara, 1998). If a problem domain is particularly a complex, large, or unpredictable, then the only way it can reasonably be addressed is to develop a number of functionally specific and (nearly) modular components (agents) that are specialized at solving a particular problem aspect (Sycara, 1998). In MASs, applications are designed and developed in terms of autonomous software entities (agents) that can flexibly achieve their objectives by interacting with one another in terms of high-level protocols and languages (Zambonelli, Jennings, & Wooldridge, 2003). An MAS can be defined as a collection of, possibly heterogeneous, computational entities, having their own problem solving capabilities and which are able to interact among them in order to reach an overall goal (Oliveira et al., 1999).

Agent Properties

A software agent is a computer system situated in an environment that acts on behalf of its user and is characterised by a number of properties (Chira, 2003). Most researchers agree that autonomy is a crucial property of an agent. Alonso (2002) states about agents that it is precisely their autonomy that defines them. Furthermore, cooperation among different software agents may be very useful in achieving the objectives an agent has (Chira, 2003). According to the weak notion of agency given by Wooldridge and Jennings (1995) the most general way in which the term agent is used is to denote hardware or (more usually) software-based computer system that enjoys the following properties: autonomy, social ability, reactivity and pro-activeness (Wooldridge & Jennings, 1995). Jennings et al. (1998) identify three key concepts in their definition that they adapt from (Wooldridge & Jennings, 1995): situatedness, autonomy, and flexibility (by the term flexible they mean that the system is responsive, pro-active and social). For Wooldridge (1998), an

intelligent agent is a system that enjoys autonomy, social ability, reactivity, and pro-activeness. He also refers to the fact that other researchers argue that different properties, such as mobility, veracity, benevolence, rationality and learning, should receive greater emphasis.

An agent may possess many properties in various combinations. In continuance, we enumerate and define all the properties that we adopt for the purposes of this research:

1. **Autonomy:** It means that the agent can act without direct intervention by humans or other agents and that it has control over its own actions and internal state (Sycara, 1998).

2. **Reactivity or situatedness or sensing and acting:** It means that the agent receives some form of sensory input from its environment, and it performs some action that changes its environment in some way (Chira, 2003; Sycara, 1998).

3. **Proactiveness or goal directed behavior:** It means that the agent does not simply act in response to its environment; it is able to exhibit goal-directed behavior by taking the initiative (Chira, 2003; Odell, 2000; Wooldridge & Jennings, 1995).

4. **Social ability:** It means that the agent interacts and friendliness or pleasant social relations mark this interaction; that is, the agent is affable, companionable or friendly (Odell, 2000).

5. **Coordination:** It means that the agent is able to perform some activity in a shared environment with other agents (Odell, 2000). Activities are often coordinated via plans, workflows or some other process management mechanism (Odell, 2000).

6. **Cooperation or collaboration:** It means that the agent is able to coordinate with other agents to achieve a common purpose; non-antagonistic agents that succeed or fail together (Odell, 2000).

7. **Flexibility:** It means that the system is responsive (the agents should perceive their environment and respond in a timely fashion to changes that occur in it), pro-active and social (Jennings et al., 1998).

8. **Learning or adaptivity:** It means that an agent is capable of (1) reacting flexibly to changes in its environment; (2) taking goal-directed initiative, when appropriate; and (3) learning from its own experience, its environment, and interactions with others (Chira, 2003; Sycara, 1998).

9. **Mobility:** It means that the agent is able to transport itself from one machine to another and across different system architectures and platforms (Etzioni & Weld, 1995).

10. **Temporal continuity:** It means that the agent is a continuously running process, not a "one-shot" computation that maps a single input to a single output, then terminates (Etzioni & Weld, 1995).

11. **Personality or character:** An agent has a well-defined, believable personality and emotional state (Etzioni & Weld, 1995).

12. **Reusability:** Processes or subsequent instances can require keeping instances of the class agent for an information handover or to check and to analyze them according to their results (Horn, Kupries, & Reinke, 1999).

13. **Resource limitation:** An agent can only act as long as it has resources at its disposal (Horn et al., 1999). These resources are changed by its acting and possibly also by delegating (Horn et al., 1999).

14. **Veracity:** It is the assumption that an agent will not knowingly communicate false information (Wooldridge, 1998; Wooldridge & Jennings, 1995).

15. **Benevolence:** It is the assumption that agents do not have conflicting goals and that every agent will therefore always try to do what is asked of it (Wooldridge, 1998; Wooldridge & Jennings, 1995).

16. **Rationality:** It is the assumption that an agent will act in order to achieve its goals, and will not act in such a way as to prevent its goals being achieved—at least insofar as its beliefs permit (Wooldridge, 1998; Wooldridge & Jennings, 1995).

17. **Inferential capability:** An agent can act on abstract task specification using prior knowledge of general goals and preferred methods to achieve flexibility; goes beyond the information given, and may have explicit models of self, user, situation and/or other agents (Bradshow, 1997).

18. **"Knowledge-level" communication ability:** The ability to communicate with persons and other agents with language more resembling humanlike "speech acts" than typical symbol-level program-to-program protocols (Bradshow, 1997).

19. **Prediction ability:** An agent is predictive if its model of how the world works is sufficiently accurate to allow it to correctly predict how it can achieve the task (Goodwin, 1993).

20. **Interpretation ability:** An agent is interpretive if it can correctly interpret its sensor readings (Goodwin, 1993).

21. **Sound:** An agent is sound if it is predictive, interpretive and rational (Goodwin, 1993).

22. **Proxy ability:** An agent can act on behalf of someone or something that is, acting in the interest of, as a representative of, or for the benefit of, some entity (Odell, 2000).

23. **Intelligence:** The agent's state is formalized by knowledge and interacts with other agents using symbolic language (Odell, 2000).

24. **Unpredictability:** An agent is able to act in ways that are not fully predictable, even if all the initial conditions are known (Odell, 2000). It is capable of nondeterministic behavior (Odell, 2000).

25. **Credibility:** An agent has a believable personality and emotional state (Odell, 2000).

26. **Transparency and accountability:** An agent must be transparent when required, but must provide a log of its activities upon demand (Odell, 2000).

27. **Competitiveness:** An agent is able to co-ordinate with other agents except that the success of one agent implies the failure of others (Odell, 2000).

28. **Ruggedization:** An agent is able to deal with errors and incomplete data robustly (Odell, 2000).

29. **Trustworthiness:** An agent adheres to laws of robotics and is truthful (Odell, 2000).

Agent Typology

Agents may be usefully classified according to the subset of these properties that they enjoy (Franklin & Graesser, 1996). There are, of course, other possible classifying schemes (Franklin & Graesser, 1996). For example, software agents might be classified according to the tasks they perform, for example, information gathering agents or email filtering agents (Franklin & Graesser, 1996). Or, they might be classified according to their control architecture (Franklin & Graesser, 1996). Agents may also be classified by the range and sensitivity of their senses, or by the range and effectiveness of their actions, or by how much internal state they possess (Franklin & Graesser, 1996).

There are several classification schemes or taxonomies proposed in the agent research community from which the following three are well acknowledged (Chira, 2003): (1) Gilbert's scope of intelligent agents (Bradshow, 1997), (2) Nwana's (1996) primary attributes dimension typology, and (3) Franklin's and Graesser's (1996) agent taxonomy.

A typology refers to the study of types of entities and there are several dimensions to classify existing software agents (Nwana, 1996). Agents may be classified according to (Bradshow, 1997): (1) mobility, as static or mobile, (2) presence of a symbolic reasoning model, as deliberative or reactive, (3) exhibition of ideal and primary attributes, such as autonomy, cooperation and learning, (4) roles, as information or Internet, (5) hybrid philosophies, which combine two or more approaches in a single agent, and (6) secondary attributes, such as versatility, benevolence, veracity, trustworthiness, temporal continuity, ability to fail gracefully and mentalistic and emotional qualities (Nwana, 1996).

Nwana (1996) identifies seven types of agents (Chira, 2003). Next, we enumerate and describe each agent type:

1. **Collaborative agents:** They are "able to act rationally and autonomously in open and time-constrained multi-agent environments" (Chira, 2003; Nwana, 1996). Key characteristics: autonomy, social ability, responsiveness, and pro-activeness (Chira, 2003; Nwana, 1996).

2. **Interface agents:** They support and assist the user when interacting with one or more computer applications by learning during the collaboration process with the user and with other software agents (Chira, 2003; Nwana, 1996). Key characteristics: autonomy, learning (mainly from the user but also from other agents), and cooperation with the user and/or other agents (Chira, 2003; Nwana, 1996).

3. **Mobile agents:** They are autonomous software programs capable of roaming wide area networks (such as WWW) and cooperation while performing duties (e.g., flight reservation, managing a telecommunications' network) on behalf of its user (Chira, 2003; Nwana, 1996). Key characteristics: mobility, autonomy, and cooperation (with other agents—e.g., to exchange data or information) (Chira, 2003; Nwana, 1996).

4. **Information/internet agents:** They are designed to manage, manipulate or collate the vast amount of information available from many distributed sources (information explosion) (Chira, 2003; Nwana, 1996). These

agents "have varying characteristics: they may be static or mobile; they may be non-cooperative or social; and they may or may not learn" (Chira, 2003; Nwana, 1996).

5. **Reactive agents:** They act/respond to the current state of their environment based on a stimulus-response scheme (Chira, 2003; Nwana, 1996). These agents are relatively simple and interact with other agents in basic ways but they have the potential to form more robust and fault tolerant agent-based systems (Chira, 2003; Nwana, 1996). Key characteristics: autonomy and reactivity (Chira, 2003; Nwana, 1996).

6. **Hybrid agents:** They combine two or more agent philosophies into a single agent in order to maximize the strengths and mini-mize the deficiencies of the most relevant techniques (for a particular purpose) (Chira, 2003; Nwana, 1996).

7. **Smart agents:** They are equally character-ised by autonomy, cooperation, and learning (Chira, 2003; Nwana, 1996).

According to Nwana (1996), there are some applications that combine agents from two or more of the above types. Nwana (1996) refers to these as heterogeneous agent systems. This category of agent systems is generally referred to (by most researchers) as multi-agent systems (Chira, 2003).

Agent Architectures

Researchers working in the area of agents' ar-chitectures are concerned with the design and construction of agents that enjoy the properties of autonomy, reactivity, pro-activeness, and social ability (Wooldridge, 1998). Wooldridge (1999) states that agent architecture is essentially a map of the internals of an agent—its data structures, the operations that may be performed on these data structures, and the control flow between these data structures. Three classes of agent architectures can

be identified (Wooldridge & Jennings, 1995): (1) deliberative or symbolic architectures are those designed along the lines proposed by traditional, symbolic AI, (2) reactive architectures are those that eschew central symbolic representations of the agent's environment, and do not rely on symbolic reasoning, and (3) hybrid architectures are those that try to marry the deliberative and reactive approaches (Wooldridge, 1998). Wooldridge and Jennings (1995) indicate that agent architectures can be viewed as software engineering models of agents and identify the above-mentioned classes of agent architectures.

Wooldridge (1999) considers four classes of agents. In our opinion most agents follow one of these four architectural classes. To continue, we enumerate and give a short description of each class:

1. **Logic based agents:** In which decision-making is realized through logical deduction (Wooldridge, 1999).

2. **Reactive agents:** In which decision-making is implemented in some form of direct map-ping from situation to action (Wooldridge, 1999).

3. **Belief-desire-intention (BDI) agents:** In which decision-making depends upon the manipulation of data structures represent-ing the beliefs, desires, and intentions of the agent (Wooldridge, 1999).

4. **Layered architectures:** In which decision making is realized via various software lay-ers, each of which is more-or-less explicitly reasoning about the environment at different levels of abstraction (Wooldridge, 1999).

Agent Communication Approaches

One of the most important features of an agent is interaction. In other words, agents recurrently interact to share information and to perform tasks to achieve their goals (Kostakos & Taraschi, 2001). Without communication, different agents cannot know from each other who is doing what and how they can cooperate (Bussink, 2004). Therefore communication is a must if we want to set up a useful multi-agent system (Bussink, 2004).

There are several approaches to how this communication can take shape (Bussink, 2004). The two most important approaches are communication using communication protocols, and communication using an evolving language (Bussink, 2004). Both techniques have their advantages and disadvantages (Bussink, 2004). In industrial applications communication protocols will be the best practice, but in systems where homogeneous agents can work together language evolution is a good option (Bussink, 2004). The basis for language evolution is in human communication (Bussink, 2004). The agent languages consist of grammars and vocabularies, just like any human language (Bussink, 2004). Some researchers even do research in the area of language evolution using agents in order to get more understanding of how human communication has evolved (Bussink, 2004). For a long time, the only way agents communicated was using communication protocols (Bussink, 2004). Therefore research often focussed on this area and a lot of specifications have been written (Bussink, 2004). Because of the formal nature of protocols, there are a quite a few widely known and used standards (Bussink, 2004).

Agent Communication Languages (ACLs)

The difficulty to precisely handle coordination and communication increases with the size of the agent-based software to be developed. A number of languages for coordination and communication have been proposed. Weiβ (2002) enumerates a list of such languages. Next, we enumerate and describe the most prominent examples of agent communication languages (ACLs) according to Weiβ (2002):

1. **Knowledge query and manipulation language (KQML):** It is perhaps the most widely used agent communication language (Weiβ, 2002).
2. **ARCOL ("ARTIMIS communication language"):** It is the communication language used in the ARTIMIS system (Weiβ, 2002). ARCOL has a smaller set of communication primitives than KQML, but these can be composed (Weiβ, 2002).
3. **FIPA agent communication language (FIPA-ACL):** It is an agent communication language that is largely inuenced by ARCOL (Weiβ, 2002). Together FIPA-ACL, ARCOL, and KQML establish a quasi standard for agent communication languages (Weiβ, 2002).
4. **Knowledge interchange format (KIF):** It is a logic-based language that has been designed to express any kind of knowledge and metaknowledge (Weiβ, 2002). KIF is a language for content communication, whereas languages like KQML, ARCOL, and FIPA-ACL are for intention communication (Weiβ, 2002).
5. **Domain independent COOrdination language (COOL):** It aims at explicitly representing and applying coordination knowledge for multi-agent systems and focuses on rule-based conversation management (Weiβ, 2002). Languages like COOL can be thought of as supporting a coordination/communication (or "protocol-sensitive") layer above intention communication (Weiβ, 2002).

Apart from these most prominent languages, several others showing unique properties have been proposed (Weiβ, 2002). Some of the above-mentioned languages follow:

1. Interagent communication language (ICL) (Weiβ, 2002)
2. AgentTalk (Weiβ, 2002)

3. Communication and coordination language (CoLa) (Weiβ, 2002)

4. Tuple centres spread over networks (TuC-SoN) (Weiβ, 2002)

5. LuCe (Weiβ, 2002)

6. Simple thread language ++ (STL++) (Weiβ, 2002)

7. Strictly declarative modelling language (SDML) (Weiβ, 2002)

Agent Transportation Mechanisms

In agent environments, messages should be schedulable, as well as event driven (OMG Agent Working Group, 2000). They can be sent in synchronous or asynchronous modes (OMG Agent Working Group, 2000). The transportation mechanism should support unique addressing as well as role-based addresses (OMG Agent Working Group, 2000). Lastly, the transportation mechanism must support unicast, multicast, and broadcast modes and such services as broadcast behavior, nonrepudiation of messages, and logging (OMG Agent Working Group, 2000). Next, we enumerate and describe possible implementations of the agent transportation mechanism:

1. **Common object request broker architecture (COBRA):** It is the acronym for common object request broker architecture, OMG's open, vendor-independent architecture and infrastructure that computer applications use to work together over networks (The Object Management Group). Using the standard protocol IIOP, a CORBA-based program from any vendor, on almost any computer, operating system, programming language, and network, can interoperate with a CORBA-based program from the same or another vendor, on almost any other computer, operating system, programming language, and network (The Object Management Group).

2. **Object management group (OMG) messaging services:** OMG is an international trade association incorporated as a nonprofit in the United States (The Object Management Group). The OMG is currently specifying a new messaging service (The CORBA Object Group Service).

3. **JAVA messaging service:** It is the standard API for sending and receiving messages (Creative Science Systems).

4. **Remote method invocation (RMI):** It defines and supports a distributed object model for the Java language hiding the ORB from the programmer and providing an API for the development of distributed applications (Bracho, Matteo, & Metzner, 1999). Java remote method invocation (Java RMI) enables the programmer to create distributed Java technology-based to Java technology-based applications, in which the methods of remote Java objects can be invoked from other Java virtual machines, possibly on different hosts (Java.sun.com).

5. **Distributed component object model (DCOM):** Microsoft® Distributed COM (DCOM) extends the component object model (COM) to support communication among objects on different computers—on a LAN, a WAN, or even the Internet (DCOM Technical Overview). With DCOM, your application can be distributed at locations that make the most sense to your customer and to the application (DCOM technical overview).

6. **Enterprise Java Beans events:** The newest Java component model is Enterprise Java Beans (Tuukka Vartiainen, Java Beans, and Enterprise Java Beans). Besides its name, the Java language and the idea of component based software re-use; it has little or no similarities with the Java Beans standard (Tuukka Vartiainen, Java Beans, and Enterprise Java Beans). Enterprise Java Beans are located on the server and they support a

distributed programming model that could be described as a flexible, two-way, object-oriented version of traditional client-server programming (Tuukka Vartiainen, Java Beans, and Enterprise Java Beans).

Ontology Languages and Editors

Besides an ACL, a common understanding of the concepts used among agents is necessary for a meaningful agent communication. A common ontology is required for representing the knowledge from various domains of discourse (OMG Agent Working Group, 2000). The ACL remains just syntax without a shared common ontology containing the terms used in agent communication and the knowledge associated with them (Nwana & Wooldridge, 1996). Next, we enumerate and describe the most elaborated examples of such languages according to Weiß (2002):

1. **Ontolingua and frame logic:** They are frame-based languages (Weiß, 2002). Both of them extend first-order predicate logics (Weiß, 2002). The key modeling primitive of these languages are frames as known from artificial intelligence (Weiß, 2002).
2. **CLASSIC and LOOM:** They are description logics that allow an intentional definition of concepts (Weiß, 2002).
3. **CycL:** It extends first-order predicate logic and was developed to enable the specification of large common-sense ontologies (Weiß, 2002).

In addition, we enumerate and describe the most prominent ontology specification languages that are conform to syntactic and semantic Web standards according to Weiß (2002):

1. **Simple HTML ontology extension (SHOE):** It is a language that slightly extends HTML and enables a hierarchical classification of HTML documents and the specification of relationships among them (Weiß, 2002).
2. **Ontology exchange language (XOL):** It is an XML- and frame-based language for the exchange of ontologies (Weiß, 2002).
3. **Ontology inference layer (OIL):** It aims at unifying formal semantics as offered by description logics, rich modelling primitives as offered by frame-based languages, and the XML and RDF Web standards (Weiß, 2002). OIL can be seen as an extension of XOL offering both an XML-based and an RDF-based syntax (Weiß, 2002).
4. **DAML-ONT and DAML-OIL:** They are the DAML (DARPA Agent Markup Language) languages (Weiß, 2002). DAML-OIL, which replaces DAML-ONT and represents the state of the art in the field, has well-defined model-theoretic and axiomatic semantics (Weiß, 2002).

Furthermore, we enumerate and describe three good examples of editors for ontology creation and maintenance according to Weiß (2002):

1. **Protégé:** It supports single-user ontology acquisition (Weiß, 2002).
2. **Webonto:** It supports multiple-user ontology acquisition over the Web (Weiß, 2002).
3. **OntoEdit:** It supports multilingual development of ontologies and multiple inheritances (Weiß, 2002).

Languages for Constructing Agent-Based Systems

Most agent systems are probably written in Java and C/C++ (Weiß, 2002). Apart from these standard languages, several prototype languages for implementing agent-based systems have been proposed that all aim at enabling a programmer to better realize agent-specific conceptions (Weiß, 2002). Three paradigms for implementing agent systems have been proposed: agent-oriented programming, market-oriented programming and interaction-oriented programming (Weiß, 2002). Weiß (2002) lists some of most prominent and best understood prototype languages following the agent-oriented paradigm (references to these languages are provided in Weiß, 2002). Next, we enumerate and describe the above mentioned prototype languages:

1. **AGENT-0, PLACA and AGENT-K:** AGENT-0 realizes the basic ideas of the agent-oriented programming paradigm as formulated by Shoham (Weiß, 2002). A language that extends AGENT-0 toward planning is PLACA, and a language that aims at integrating AGENT-0 and KQML is AGENT-K (Weiß, 2002).

2. **Concurrent MetateM:** It allows specifying the intended behavior of an agent based on temporal logics (Weiß, 2002).

3. **AgentSpeak (L):** It is a rule-based language that has a formal operational semantics and that assumes agents to consist of intentions, beliefs, recorded events, and plan rules (Weiß, 2002). AgentSpeak (L) is based on an abstraction of the PRS architecture (Weiß, 2002).

4. **3APL:** It incorporates features from imperative and logic programming (Weiß, 2002). 3APL has well defined operational semantics and supports monitoring and revising of agent goals (Weiß, 2002).

5. **ConGolog:** It is a concurrent logic-based language initially designed for high-level robot programming (Weiß, 2002).

6. **Agent process interaction language (APRIL), multiagent interaction and implementation language (MAIL/MAI2L), and VIVA:** Other examples of languages following the agent-oriented programming paradigm (Weiß, 2002).

Nwana and Wooldridge (1996) classify constructing agent application languages according to a typology. Next, we present the above-mentioned classification (Nwana & Wooldridge, 1996):

1. **Collaborative agents:** The actor language actors and the agent-oriented programming languages Agent-0 and Placa.

2. **Interface, information and mobile agents:** The scripting languages TCL/Tk, Safe-TCL, Safe-Tk, Java, Telescript, Active Web tools, Python, Obliq, April and Scheme-48.

3. **Reactive agents:** The reactive language RTA/ABLE.

However traditional languages are still used to construct agent applications (Nwana & Wooldridge, 1996). It is possible to implement agent-based systems in languages like Pascal, C, Lisp, or Prolog (Nwana & Wooldridge, 1996). But as a rule, one would not choose to do so because such languages are not particularly well suited to the job (Nwana & Wooldridge, 1996). Typically, object-oriented languages such as Smalltalk, Java, or C++ lend themselves more easily for the construction of agent systems (Nwana & Wooldridge, 1996). This is because the concept of an "agent" is not too distant from that of an "object": Agents share some properties with objects such as encapsulation, and frequently, inheritance and message passing (Nwana & Wooldridge, 1996). However, agents differ distinctly from objects vis-à-vis polymorphism (Nwana & Wooldridge, 1996).

Tools and Platforms

A number of tools and platforms are available that support activities or phases of the process of agent-oriented software development (Weiß, 2002). Most of them are built on top of and integrated with Java (Weiß, 2002). While almost all available tools and platforms have their focus on implementation support, some of them do also support analysis, design, and test/debugging activities (Weiß, 2002).

Weiβ (2002) makes a list of such tools and platforms separating them into often-sited academic and research prototypes and into commercial products for development support. References to the following tools and a brief description as well can be found in (Weiβ, 2002). Next, we present the above-mentioned classification:

1. **Academic and research activity:** ZEUS, Java Agent DEvelopment framework (JADE), Lightweight extensible agent platform (LEAP), agenTool, RETSINA, Java agent template, lite (JATLite), FIPA-OS, MADKIT, SIM_AGENT, Java-based agent framework for multi-agent systems (JAF-MAS), agent building shell (ABS), open agent architecture (OAA), and Agentis
2. **Commercial activity:** AgentBuilder, JACK, intelligent agent factory and grasshopper

Serenko and Detlor (2002) state about the term agent toolkit that each vendor uses its own explanation of the term and for the needs of their report define an agent toolkit as any software package, application or development environment that provides agent builders with a sufficient level of abstraction to allow them to implement intelligent agents with desired attributes, features and rules. Some toolkits may offer only a platform for agent development, whereas others may provide features for visual programming (Serenko & Detlor, 2002). Serenko and Detlor (2002) categorize the available agent toolkits on the market into four major categories. Next, we present the four categories and the representative toolkits of each category:

1. **Mobile agent toolkits:** Concordia, Gossip, FarGo, and IBM Aglets
2. **Multi-agent toolkits:** MadKit, ZEUS, JADE, JATLite, and MAST
3. **General purpose toolkits:** FIPA-OS and Ascape
4. **Internet agent toolkits:** Microsoft Agent, Voyager, and NetStepper

Agent-Oriented Software Engineering (AOSE) Methodologies

Agent researchers have produced methodologies to assist engineers to create agent-based systems (Agent-Oriented Software Engineering). Some researchers have taken agent theory as their starting point and have produced methodologies that are rooted in that theory (Agent-Oriented Software Engineering). Other researchers have taken object techniques as their point of departure and have enriched them to be suitable for agents (Agent-Oriented Software Engineering). Others have taken knowledge engineering concepts and have extended them (Agent-Oriented Software Engineering). Researchers also have tried to assemble methodologies by combining features from different methodologies (Agent-Oriented Software Engineering). Yet other researchers have produced methodologies based on both agent and object technologies (Agent-Oriented Software Engineering).

Methodologies having as background the agent and multi-agent technology are characterized by a clear focus on capturing social-level abstractions such as agent, group, or organization, that is, on abstractions that are above the conventional object level (Weiβ, 2002). Methodologies having as background the object orientation are characterized by the attempt to appropriately extend existing object-oriented techniques such that they also capture the notion of agency (Weiβ, 2002). Methodologies having engineering background knowledge are characterized by an emphasis on the identification, acquisition and modeling of knowledge to be used by the agent components of a software system (Weiβ, 2002).

The most popular approaches based on agent and multi-agent technology are the following:

1. **Generic architecture for information availability (GAIA):** This is a method that distinguishes between analysis and design and associates different models with these two phases (Weiβ, 2002). Gaia focuses on organizational aspects in terms of concepts such as roles, interactions and acquaintances (Weiβ, 2002).

2. **Societies in open and distributed agent spaces (SODA):** This is another good example of an analysis and design method that concentrates on the social (interagent) aspects of agent systems and that employs the concept of coordination models (Weiβ, 2002).

3. **Cassiopeia:** This is a design method that distinguishes three levels of behavior—elementary, relational, and organizational—and aims at capturing both structural and dynamic aspects of the target system (Weiβ, 2002).

4. **Aalaadin:** This is a general analysis and design framework that has its focus on the organizational level of multi-agent systems and is built on the three core concepts of agents, groups, and roles (Weiβ, 2002).

The most popular approaches based on object-oriented technology are the following:

1. **KGR:** This is a design and specification method for a particular class of agents, namely, BDI agents (Weiβ, 2002).

2. **Multiagent systems engineering (MaSE):** This method covers design and initial implementation through two languages called agent modeling language (AgML) and agent definition language (AgDL) and builds upon OMT and UML (Weiβ, 2002).

3. **Multiagent systems iterative view engineering (MASSIVE):** This method covers analysis, design and code generation, and combines standard software engineering techniques such as multi-view modeling,

round-trip engineering, and iterative enhancement (Weiβ, 2002).

4. **Agent-oriented analysis and design (AOAD):** This analysis and design method proposes the use of extended class responsibility cards (CRCs) and the use of both the object modelling technique (OMT) and the responsibility driven design (RDD) method known from object-oriented development (Weiβ, 2002).

5. **Multi-agent scenario-based (MASB):** MASB is an analysis and design method that covers issues of both objects and agents via behavior diagrams, data models, transition diagrams, and object life cycles (Weiβ, 2002).

The most popular approaches based on knowledge engineering technology are the following:

1. **Conceptual modelling of multi-agent systems (CoMoMAS):** This is an elaborated extension of the CommonKADS methodology, supporting analysis, design, and automated code generation (Weiβ, 2002).

2. **Multi-agent system commonKADS (MAS-CommonKADS):** This is another extension of CommonKADS that supports analysis and design of agent-oriented systems (Weiβ, 2002).

Other agent-oriented software engineering methodologies (AOSE) are tropos, agent-oriented analysis and design, agent modelling technique for systems of BDI agents, agent oriented methodology for enterprise modelling, a process for agent societies specification and implementation (PASSI), prometheus, AOR, ROADMAP, OPM /MAS, ingenias, DESIRE, AAII methodology, cooperative information agents design, adept, AUML, ADELFE, MESSAGE /UML, the styx agent methology, SABPO, expectation-oriented analysis and design (EXPAND) and ODAC (Cernuzzi, Cossentino, & Zambonelli, 2004; Iglesias,

Garijo, & Gonzalez, 1999; Agent-Oriented Software Engineering; Faculty Science Unitn; Weiβ, 2002; Wooldridge & Ciancarini, 2000).

AGENTS IN VIRTUAL ENTERPRISES (VES)

What is a Virtual Enterprise?

The term, and the concept, "virtual enterprise" (VE) emerged already in the beginning of the 1990s and could be seen as the further optimization and perfection of the basic ideas about dynamic networking (Putnik, 2004). Although the virtual enterprise research represents a growing and multidisciplinary area it still lacks a precise definition of the concepts and an agreement on the used terminology (Camarinha-Matos, 2002). So far, there is no unified definition for this paradigm and a number of terms are even competing in the literature while referring to different aspects and scopes of virtual enterprises (Camarinha-Matos, 2002). Akin concepts are supported by Gijsen, Szirbik, and Wagner (2002); Freitas Mundim, Rossi, and Stocchetti (2000); Putnik (2004) and Petersen et al. (2001).

The definitions range from the virtual enterprise as a simple subcontracting network to the virtual enterprise as a dynamic network, in which the partners share that share resources, risks and even markets, and which operates in a virtual environment or with virtual agents (Putnik, 2004). According to Do, Halatchev, and Neumann (2000) a virtual enterprise is a form of cooperation of independent market players (enterprises, freelancers authorities, etc.) which combine their core competencies in order to manufacture a product or to provide a service. Marík and McFarlane (2005) conclude that a virtual enterprise represents a cluster of organizations collaborating to achieve one or more goals. Katz and Schuh (1999) define that the virtual enterprise is based on the ability to create temporary co-operations and to realize

the value of a short business opportunity that the partners cannot (or can, but only to lesser extent) capture on their own. Other attempts at defining virtual enterprises are listed in (Petersen et al., 2001).

In our opinion, an interesting definition that we adopt is the following:

A goal-oriented constellation of (semi)autonomous distributed entities. Each entity, which can be an organization and/or an individual, attempts to maximize its own profits as well as contribute to defining and achieving the overall goals of the virtual enterprise. Virtual enterprises are not rigid organizational structures within rigid frameworks, but rather (heterogeneous) ensembles, continuously evolving over time. (Petersen et al., 2001, p. 2)

Why to Use Agents in Virtual Enterprises?

Marík and McFarlane (2005) state that a virtual enterprise might address problems ranging from simple membership to distributed inventory management and synchronization of supply, production, and distribution schedules. They also support that these problems are inherently distributed, with each organization willing to share only limited information and having its own business goals in conjunction with the overall goal. All the above statements orientate to an agent technology solution.

According to Jennings et al. (1998), considering a virtual enterprise, the domain involves an inherent distribution of data, problem solving capabilities and responsibilities. In addition, the integrity of the existing organizational structure and the autonomy of its sub-parts need to be maintained (Jennings et al., 1998). Moreover, interactions are fairly sophisticated, including negotiation, information sharing, and coordination (Jennings et al., 1998). Besides, the problem solution cannot be entirely prescribed (Jennings et al., 1998). According to Jennings et al. (1998), all the above observations motivate the choice of agents as a technology solution as well.

According to Fox and Gruninger (1998), the entrepreneurial and virtual nature of the agile enterprise coupled with the need for people and information to have a strategic impact entails a greater degree of communication, coordination and cooperation within and among enterprises. In other words, the agile organization must be integrated (meaning by the term integrated the structural, behavioural and information integration of the enterprise) (Fox & Gruninger, 1998). Petersen et al. (2001) support that cooperation is required both to perform work and to adapt the constellation to the varying needs of the environment. They state that goal-oriented and distributed nature of virtual enterprises implies that there is no central control; rather, the control is decentralized. According to their opinion, the distributed and goal-oriented nature of the virtual enterprise provides a strong motivation for the use of agents to model virtual enterprises.

The following parallelism demonstrates remarkable interest. According to Rahwan, Kowalczyk, and Yang (2001) the virtual enterprise creation could be viewed as a Cooperative System design problem. A Cooperative System is a system in which a set of autonomous agents (computational and human) interact with each other through sharing their information, decision making capabilities and other resources, and distributing the corresponding workload among themselves, in order to achieve common and complementary goals (Camarinha-Matos & Afsarmanesh, 1998). The above parallelism motivates as well the agents as a technology solution.

The nature of agents, by definition, enables decentralized control of the enterprise, which is desirable in a dynamic and flexible environment, and the behavior of the complete enterprise emerges as a result of the behaviors of the individual agents (Petersen et al., 2001).

Another strong point in favor of the adoption of agents is their versatility (Petersen et al., 2001). They can play two main roles (Petersen et al., 2001). First, they provide a flexible means of modeling the virtual enterprise in terms of cooperative work among the agents (Petersen et al., 2001). Second, they can be used to provide active support to the members of the virtual enterprise (Petersen et al., 2001). Thus, agents being computational entities, the resulting model provides an easy and efficient passage to the computational support that is required by virtual enterprises (Petersen et al., 2001).

According to Marík and McFarlane (2005), MASs and relevant technologies consider each company as an agent able to carry out specific (usually quite complex) functions. The agents are registered with a certain platform and communicate in a standard agent communication language (Marík & McFarlane, 2005). Virtual enterprise formation, as well as the joint planning and scheduling activities, is based on jointly known negotiation rules and scenarios (Marík & McFarlane, 2005). These are very similar (or identical) to protocols or auctions in the MAS domain (Marík & McFarlane, 2005). The highly specialized members of a virtual enterprise, such as brokers or professional network organizers, can easily find their counterparts in the MAS community—for example, various middle agents and brokers (Marík & McFarlane, 2005). The negotiation and brokering algorithms that have proven useful for the MAS domain can serve to formalize (and later automate) the corresponding virtual enterprise processes (Marík & McFarlane, 2005). Specialized agents called meta-agents could also serve as tools both to help detect the network's less efficient parts or bottlenecks and to provide advice supporting the virtual enterprise's self-evolution in the desired direction (Marík & McFarlane, 2005). Virtual enterprise creation is analogous to coalition formation in the MAS domain (Marík & McFarlane, 2005).

They also support that MAS concept of knowledge sharing, which classifies knowledge as public, private, and semiprivate, has high potential for virtual enterprises. Requirements for keeping agents' knowledge confidential and preventing knowledge disclosure, as well as specific security principles used with MASs, can be reused for virtual enterprises (Marík & McFarlane, 2005).

Current Research Activity Focusing on Agents in Virtual Enterprises (VE)

Virtual enterprises have recently received increasing attention. Due to the advancement of distributed information technology and the changing needs of the business community, enterprises are expected to be more agile and responsive (Petersen et al., 2001). Many current developments in multi-agent systems (MAS) are more and more focused on the production of robust development environments (Camarinha-Matos, 2002). Considerable efforts are also being put on standardization of architectures and communication languages, which are important requirements for the industrial application of the paradigm (Camarinha-Matos, 2002). We have observed that there is a remarkable body of literature that studies the application of agent technology to virtual enterprises as researchers pay enough attention to this scientific area of activity. In continuance of the study, some prominent research efforts follow.

According to Yonghe and Biqing (1999), decision and control processes within the domain of virtual enterprises have not received deserved attention till now. Based on agent technology, they bought up architecture for control and decision-making during the dynamic creation and operation of a virtual enterprise. An approach for integrating different business units is presented (Yonghe & Biqing, 1999). Prototype software simulating the design of a new product in a virtual enterprise is developed (Yonghe & Biqing, 1999).

Petersen, Jinghai, and Matskin (2003) present the virtual enterprise formation process as an agent interaction protocol and an approach to its implementation. They have focused on the selection of partners within the formation process in order to understand these interactions and the contents of the messages that are exchanged between the agents. Based on this, they describe how the AGORA multi-agent architecture can be used to support the formation of a virtual enterprise.

Gou, Huang, Liu, and Li (2001) propose an agent-based virtual enterprise model and provide the agent collaboration mechanisms under the model, thereby achieving the agent based virtual enterprise modeling and operation control. Their agent-based approach achieves distributed control over the whole business process execution of the virtual enterprise.

According to Fankhauser and Tesch (1999), negotiations encourage agents to reason about the interests of their opponents. Thus, negotiations suffer from counter speculations (Fankhauser & Tesch, 1999). Auctions apply to asymmetric trading only; they either favor the auctioneer or the bidders (Fankhauser & Tesch, 1999). Both mechanisms do not promote agents to tell the truth (Fankhauser & Tesch, 1999). Therefore, they propose to use a trust-broker to mediate between the agents. They introduce three symmetric, negotiation free one-step protocols to carry out a sequence of decisions for agents with possibly conflicting interests. The protocols achieve substantially better overall benefit than random or hostile selection, and they avoid lies (Fankhauser & Tesch, 1999). They analyze the protocols with respect to informed vs. uninformed lies, and with respect to beneficial vs. malevolent lies, and show that agents are best off to know and announce their true interests.

Gong and Wang's (2000) research is a contribution to the model of multi-agent system (MAS) for supporting the dynamic enterprise model (DEM). It separates the business process from the organizational structure (organizational structure tier and business process tier), models each of them as MAS, and coordinates agents by the "yellow page" mechanism (Gong & Wang, 2000). This model not only can regulate itself in terms of DEM, but also is centered on the coordination strategies between agents composing it (Gong & Wang, 2000). It is believed that the model of MAS is a practical way to build flexible enterprise information system (Gong & Wang, 2000).

Chrysanthis, Znati, Banerjee, and Shi-Kuo (1999) view the establishment of a virtual enterprise as a problem of dynamically expanding and integrating workflows in decentralized, autonomous and interacting workflow management systems. They focus on the idea of mobile agents called adlets and their use in establishing virtual enterprises that involves advertising, negotiating and exchanging control information and data as well as its management.

Szirbik, Aerts, Wortmann, Hammer, and Goossenaerts (2000) propose a systematisation of the monitoring and control aspects in a virtual enterprise. As an instrument, they use the mobile agent paradigm, defining the concept of a mobile agent web (MA-web). According to them, one of the roles of the agents in this environment is to mediate negotiations between the parties of the virtual enterprise. They make some assumptions about the new behavior and code of conduct in the MA-web, such as the willingness to share data and knowledge.

Based on the analysis of why agent-based mechanism is suitable and only suitable for cross-domain cooperation of virtual enterprise, Zhang et al. (2004) propose a framework to implement it. In their framework, there is a service information supply-demand center that is in charge of service information management, and agent is responsible for cooperative partner selecting before cooperation and interaction during cooperation. The relevant key strategies and basic interaction models are also described (Zhang et al., 2004).

Ouzounis and Tschammer (2001) discuss concepts and technologies that are considered to satisfy key requirements of dynamic virtual enterprises, and propose DIVE, a framework for the specification, execution and management of shared business processes in dynamic virtual enterprises.

Suh et al. (2005) describe an open and flexible infrastructure to support dynamic collaboration among companies through the entire lifecycle of the virtual enterprise. The proposed approach is an agent-enhanced architecture on which the conversation model is grafted (Suh et al., 2005). The collaboration among enterprises is modelled by a collaboration policy, which is a machine-readable specification of a pattern of message exchange among agents participating in the collaboration (Suh et al., 2005).

FUTURE TRENDS

Luck, McBurney, and Gonzalez-Palacios (2006) stated a thorough and outstanding approach about the future of multi-agent systems. As we consider their point of view extremely prominent, we appose at this point of the chapter some parts of their findings (for a more complete investigation consult (Luck et al., 2006)). Luck et al. (2006) extrapolated future trends in multi-agent systems by classifying them into four broad phases (current, short-term future, medium-term future and long-term future) of development of multi-agent system technology over the next decade.

At first phase, multi-agent systems are typically designed by one design team for one corporate environment, with participating agents sharing common high-level goals in a single domain (Luck et al., 2006). These systems may be characterized as closed (Luck et al., 2006). The communication languages and interaction protocols are typically in-house protocols, defined by the design team prior to any agent interactions (Luck et al., 2006). Design approaches, as well as development platforms, tend to be ad hoc, inspired by the agent paradigm (Luck et al., 2006). There is also an increased focus on taking methodologies out of the laboratory and into development environments, with commercial work being done on establishing industrial-strength development techniques and notations (Luck et al., 2006).

In the short-term future, multi-agent systems will increasingly be designed to cross corporate boundaries, so that the participating agents have fewer goals in common, although their interactions will still concern a common domain, and the agents will be designed by the same team, and will share common domain knowledge (Luck et al., 2006). Standard agent communication languages will be used, but interaction protocols will be mixed between standard and nonstandard ones (Luck et al., 2006). Development methodologies, languages and tools will have reached a degree of maturity, and systems will be designed on top of standard infrastructures such as Web services or Grid services, for example (Luck et al., 2006).

In the medium term future, multi-agent systems will permit participation by heterogeneous agents, designed by different designers or teams (Luck et al., 2006). Any agent will be able to participate in these systems, provided their (observable) behavior conforms to publicly stated requirements and standards (Luck et al., 2006). However, these open systems will typically be specific to particular application domains (Luck et al., 2006). The languages and protocols used in these systems will be agreed and standardized (Luck et al., 2006).

In the long-term future, we will see the development of open multi-agent systems spanning multiple application domains, and involving heterogeneous participants developed by diverse design teams (Luck et al., 2006). Agents seeking to participate in these systems will be able to learn the appropriate behavior for participation in the course of interacting, rather than having to prove adherence before entry (Luck et al.,

2006). Selection of communications protocols and mechanisms, and of participant strategies, will be undertaken automatically, without human intervention (Luck et al., 2006).

The above-mentioned aspect about future is enhanced with the AOSE Technical Forum Group's (2004) perception of the future trends in the area of agent-oriented software engineering. According to AOSE Technical Forum Group (2004), the research in the area of agent-oriented software engineering is still in its early stages, and several challenges need to be faced before agent-oriented software engineering becoming a widely accepted and a practically usable paradigm for the development of complex software systems. One possible way to identify and frame the key research challenges in the area of agent-oriented software engineering is to recognize that such challenges may be very different depending on the "scale of observation" adopted to model and build a software system (AOSE Technical Forum Group, 2004).

At one extreme, the micro scale of observation is that where the system to be engineered has to rely on the controllable and predictable behavior of (a typically limited number) individual agents, as well as on their mutual interactions (AOSE Technical Forum Group, 2004). There, the key engineering challenges are related to extending traditional software engineering approaches toward agent-oriented abstractions (AOSE Technical Forum Group, 2004). Brand new modeling and notational tools, as well as possibly brand new software process models may be needed (AOSE Technical Forum Group, 2004).

At the other extreme, the macro scale of observation is the one where a multi-agent system is conceived as a multitude of interacting agents, for which the overall behavior of the system, rather than the mere behavior of individuals, is the key of interest (AOSE Technical Forum Group, 2004). In this case, a discipline of agent-oriented software engineering should focus on totally different problems, and should be able to develop novel "systemic" approaches to software engineering, possibly getting inspiration from areas such as complex systems sciences and systemic biology (AOSE Technical Forum Group, 2004).

In between, the meso scale of observation is where the need of predictability and control, typical of the micro scale, clashes with the emergence of phenomena typical of the macro scale (AOSE Technical Forum Group, 2004). Therefore, any engineering approach at the meso scale requires accounting for problems that are typical of both the micro and the macro scale, and possibly for new problems specific to the meso scale (AOSE Technical Forum Group, 2004). These include: identifying the boundaries of a systems—which may be challenging in the case of open multi-agent systems; electing trust as a primary design issue; identifying suitable infrastructures for multi-agent systems support (AOSE Technical Forum Group, 2004).

As concerns the virtual enterprises' scientific domain, we believe that agent technology has much to offer with respect to the formation and the operation of a virtual enterprise. According to Camarinha-Matos (2002), several challenges remain open for MAS requiring further research, such as support for the full life cycle of the virtual enterprise, adoption of contract-based coordination models, necessary integration of MAS with several other paradigms, interoperation with legacy systems and enterprise applications, inclusion of specialized protocols and standards, and support of robust safety mechanisms.

There is a need to integrate ACL with mechanisms for safe communications (cryptography, digital signature, certification, etc.) that have been developed for virtual enterprises and e-commerce (Camarinha-Matos, 2002). The development of advanced simulation tools to support planning, optimization, and assessment of operation of virtual enterprises and distributed business processes is another open challenge that can benefit from a MAS approach (Camarinha-Matos, 2002).

Finally it is important to stress that in order to be accepted by the industrial community, MAS applications need to be successfully demonstrated in complex real world pilot systems (Camarinha-Matos, 2002).

CONCLUSION

The area of software agents is vibrant and rapidly developing. A number of fundamental advances have been made in the design and the implementation of software agents as well as in the interaction between software agents. In this brief chapter, we have tried to convey some of the key concepts of the active field of software agents and make a reference point to a large body of literature outlining essential issues. We were limited to enumerate our findings of our survey regarding software agent technology, instead of judging them, aiming to provide a synoptic review of the basic aspects. It is up to the reader to judge how successful we have been in meeting our goal in this chapter. In addition, we have argued the issue of applying the agent technology to virtual enterprise. Our purpose was to offer a brief introduction of the application of agent technology to virtual enterprises and to provide some useful hints for further studying concerning the above-mentioned theme.

REFERENCES

Agent-Oriented Software Engineering. *Research Area Examination* (2005). Retrieved from http://www.deg.byu.edu/proposals/ResearchAreaExamMuhammedJM.pdf

Alonso, E. (2002). AI and agents: State of the art. *AI Magazine, 23*(3), 25-29.

AOSE Technical Forum Group (2004). *AL3-TF1 Report*. Retrieved January 31, 2007, from http://www.pa.icar.cnr.it/~cossentino/al3tf1/docs/aose_tfg1_report.pdf

Bracho, A., Matteo, A., & Metzner, C. (1999). A taxonomy for comparing distributed objects technologies. *CLEI Electronic Journal, 2*(2).

Bradshow, J. M. (1997). An introduction to software agents. In J. M. Bradshow (Ed.), *Software agents.* Cambridge: MIT Press.

Bussink, D. (2004). A comparison of language evolution and communication protocols in multi-agent systems. In *Proceedings of the 1st Twente Student Conference on IT, Track C—Intelligent_Interaction.* Retrieved January 31, 2007, from http://referaat.ewi.utwente.nl/

Camarinha-Matos, L. M. (2002). Multi-agent systems in virtual enterprises. In *Proceedings of AIS2002—International Conference on AI, Simulation and Planning in High Autonomy Systems,* Lisbon, Portugal (pp. 27-36).

Camarinha-Matos, L. M., & Afsarmanesh, H. (1998). Cooperative systems challenges in virtual enterprises. In *Proceedings of CESA'98—IMCAS Multiconference on Computational Engineering in Systems Applications,* Nabeu—Hammamet, Tunisia.

Chira, C. (2003). *Software agents.* (IDIMS Report). Retrieved January 31, 2007, from http://pan.nuigalway.ie/code/docs/agents.pdf

Chrysanthis, P. K., Znati, T., Banerjee, S., & Shi-Kuo, C. (1999). Establishing virtual enterprises by means of mobile agents. In *Proceedings of the Ninth International Workshop on Research Issues on Data Engineering: Information Technology for Virtual Enterprises* RIDE-VE '99 (pp.116-123).

Cernuzzi, L., Cossentino, M., & Zambonelli, F. (2004). *Process models for agent-based development.* http://www.pa.icar.cnr.it/~cossentino/paper/eaai_zambonelli_draft.pdf

Creative Science Systems (CSS). Retrieved from http://www.creativescience.com/Products/soa.shtml

DCOM Technical Overview, Microsoft Corporation. (1996). Retrieved from http://msdn.microsoft.com/library/default.asp?url=/library/en-us/dndcom/html/msdn_dcomtec.asp

Do, V., Halatchev, M., & Neumann, D. (2000). A context-based approach to support virtual enterprises. In *Proceedings of the 33rd Hawaii International Conference on System Sciences.*

Etzioni, O., & Weld, D. S. (1995). Intelligent agents on the Internet: Fact, fiction and forecast. *IEEE Expert, 10*(4), 44-49.

Faculty Science Unitn. University of Trento. *AOSE Methologies.* (n.d.) Retrieved from http://www.science.unitn.it/~recla/aose/

Fankhauser, P., & Tesch, T. (1999). Agents, a broker, and lies. In *Proceedings of the Ninth International Workshop on Research Issues on Data Engineering: Information Technology for Virtual Enterprises* RIDE-VE '99 (pp.56-63).

Fox, M. S., & Gruninger, M. (1998). Enterprise modelling. *AI Magazine,* 109-121.

Franklin, S., & Graesser, A. (1996). Is it an agent, or just a program?: A taxonomy for autonomous agents. In *Proceedings of the Third International Workshop on Agent Theories, Architectures and Languages.*

Freitas Mundim, A. P., Rossi, A., & Stocchetti, A. (2000). SME in global markets: Challenges, opportunities and threats. *Brasilian Electronic Journal of Economics, 3*(1).

Gijsen, J. W. J., Szirbik, N. B., & Wagner, G. (2002). Agent technologies for virtual enterprises in the one-of-a-kind-production industry. *International Journal of Electronic Commerce, 7*(1), 9-26.

Goodwin, R. (1993). *Formalizing properties of agents* (Tech. Rep.) Pittsburgh, PA: Carnegie-Mellon University, School of Computer Science.

Gong, B., & Wang, S. (2000). Model of MAS: Supporting dynamic enterprise model. In *Proceedings of the 3rd World Congress on Intelligent Control and Automation* (pp. 2042-2046).

Gou, H., Huang, B., Liu, W., & Li, Y. (2001). Agent-based virtual enterprise modeling and operation control. In *Proceedings of the 2001 IEEE International Conference on Systems, Man, and Cybernetics* (pp. 2058-2063).

Green, S., Hurst, L., Nangle, B., Cunningham, D. P., Somers, F., & Evans, D. R. (1997). *Software agents: A review* (Tech. Rep. No.TCS-CS-1997-06). Trinity College Dublin, Broadcom Éireann Research Ltd.

Hayes, C. C. (1999). Agents in a nutshell: A very brief introduction. *IEEE Transactions on Knowledge and Data Engineering, 11*(1), 127-132.

Horn, E., Kupries, M., & Reinke, T. (1999). Properties and models of software agents and prefabrication for agent application systems. In *Proceedings of the International Conference on System Sciences (HICSS-32), Software Technology Track*

Iglesias, C. A., Garijo, M., & Gonzalez, J. C. (1999). A survey of agent-oriented methologies. In *Proceedings of the Fifth International Workshop on Agent Theories, Architectures, and Languages (ATAL-98)* (pp. 317-330).

Java.sun.com. The Source for Java Developers. Retrieved from http://java.sun.com/products/jdk/rmi/

Jennings, N. R., Norman, T. J., & Faratin, P. (1998). ADEPT: An agent-based approach to business process management. *ACM SIGMOD Record, 27*(4), 32-39.

Jennings, N. R., Sycara, K., & Wooldridge, M. (1998). A roadmap of agent research and development. Autonomous Agents and Multi-Agent Systems Journal, *1*(1), 7-38.

Jennings, N., & Wooldridge, M. (1996). Software agents. *IEE Review,* 17-20.

Katz, B. R., & Schuh, G. (1999). The virtual enterprise. Retrieved January 31, 2007, from http://portal.cetim.org/file/1/68/KatzySchuh-1999-The_virtual_enterprise.pdf

Kostakos, V., & Taraschi, C. (2001). Agents. Retrieved January 31, 2007, from http://www.cs.bath.ac.uk/~vk/files/agents.pdf

Luck, M., McBurney, P., & Gonzalez-Palacios, J. (2006). *Agent-based computing and programming of agent systems* (LNCS 3862, pp. 23-37). Springer.

Marík, V., & McFarlane, D. C. (2005). Industrial adoption of agent-based technologies. *IEEE Intelligent Systems, 20*(1), 27-35

Nwana, H. S. (1996). Software agents: An overview. *Knowledge Engineering Review, 11*(3), 1-40.

Nwana, H., & Ndumu, D. (1996). A brief introduction to software agent technology. In *Proceedings of the Unicom Seminar on "Real-World Applications of Intelligent Agent Technology"* (pp. 278-292).

Nwana, H., & Wooldridge, M. (1996). Software agent technologies. *BT Technology Journal, 14*(4), 68-78.

Odell, J. (2000). Agents: Technology and usage (Part 1). *Executive Report, 3*(4).

Oliveira, E., Fischer, K., & Stepankova, O. (1999). Multi-agent systems: Which research for which applications. *Robotics and Autonomous Systems, 27*, 91-106.

OMG Agent Working Group (2000). *Agent technology.* Green paper, OMG Document ec/8/1/00, (1).

Ouzounis, V. K., & Tschammer, V. (2001). An agent-based life cycle management for dynamic virtual enterprises. In *Proceedings of the Sixth International Conference on Computer Supported Cooperative Work in Design* (pp. 451-459).

Petersen, S. A., Divitini, M., & Matskin, M. (2001). An agent-based approach to modeling virtual enterprises. *Production Planning & Control, 12*(3), 224-233.

Petersen, S. A., Jinghai, R., & Matskin, M. (2003). Virtual enterprise formation with agents: An approach to implementation. In *Proceedings of the IAT 2003, IEEE/VVIC International Conference on Intelligent Agent Technology* (pp. 527-530).

Putnik, G. D. (2004). Virtual Enterprise as a "flow" enterprise. In *Proceedings of the Fourth Annual Meeting of the European Chaos and Complexity in Organisations Network ECCON - ECCON 2005.*

Rahwan, I., Kowalczyk, R., & Yang, Y. (2001). Virtual enterprise design: BDI agents vs. objects. *Advances in artificial intelligence* (LNCS 2112, pp. 147-157).

Serenko, & Deltor, B. (2002). *Agent toolkits: A general overview of the market and an assessment of instructor satisfaction with utilizing in the classroom* (Working Paper No. 455). Retrieved January 31, 2007, from http://www.business.mcmaster.ca/msis/profs/detlorb/nserc/McMaster_Working_Paper_455.pdf

Sycara, K. P. (1998). Multi-agent systems. *AI Magazine, 19*(2), 79-92.

Sycara, K. P. (1998). The many faces of agents. *AI Magazine, 19*(2), 11-12.

Szirbik, N., Aerts, A., Wortmann, H., Hammer, D., & Goossenaerts, J. (2000). Mediating negotiations in a virtual enterprise via mobile agents. In *Proceedings of the Academia/Industry Working Conference on Research Challenges* (pp. 237-242).

The Object Management Group. (n.d.). *CORBA® BASICS*. Retrieved from http://www.omg.org/gettingstarted/corbafaq.htm

The Object Management Group. (n.d.). Retrieved from http://www.omg.org

The CORBA Object Group Service. *A Service Approach to Object Groups in CORBA, № 1867*. (1998). Retrieved from http://lsrwww.epfl.ch/OGS/thesis/

Tuukka Vartiainen, Java Beans, and Enterprise Java Beans. (n.d.). Retrieved from http://www.cs.helsinki.fi/u/campa/teaching/tukka-final.pdf

Weiß, G. (2002). Agent orientation in software engineering. *Knowledge Engineering Review, 16*(4), 349-373.

Wooldridge, M. (1998). Agent-based computing. *Interoperable Communication Networks, 1*(1), 71-97.

Wooldridge, M. (1999). Intelligent agents. In G. Weiss (Ed.), *Multi-agent systems*. MIT Press.

Wooldridge, M., & Ciancarini, P. (2000). Agent-oriented software engineering: The state of the art. In P. Ciancarini & M. Wooldridge (Eds.), *Proceedings of the First International Workshop on Agent-Oriented Software Engineering* (pp. 1-28).

Wooldridge, M., & Jennings, N. R. (1995). Intelligent agents: Theory and practice. *The Knowledge Engineering Review, 10*(2), 115-152.

Yan, Z., Meilin, S., & Shaohua, Z. (2004). An agent-based framework for cross-domain cooperation of virtual enterprise. In *Proceedings of the 8th International Conference on Computer Supported Cooperative Work in Design* (pp. 291-296).

Yonghe, L., & Biqing, H. (1999). Virtual enterprise: An agent-based approach for decision and control. In *Proceedings of the IEEE SMC '99 International Conference on Systems, Man, and Cybernetics* (pp. 451-456).

Zambonelli, F., Jennings, N., & Wooldridge, M. (2003). Developing multiagent systems: The Gaia methology. *ACM Transactions on Software Engineering and Methodology, 12*(3).

Chapter II
Web Services Technology:
An Overview

Fani A. Tzima
Aristotle University of Thessaloniki, Greece

Pericles A. Mitkas
Aristotle University of Thessaloniki, Greece

ABSTRACT

This chapter examines the concept of service-oriented architecture (SOA) in conjunction with the Web services technology as an implementation of the former's design principles. Following a brief introduction of SOA and its advantages, a high-level overview of the structure and composition of the Web services platform is provided. This overview covers the core Web services specifications as well as features of the extended architecture stack, which together form a powerful and robust foundation for building distributed systems. The chapter concludes with a discussion of the scope of applicability of SOA and Web services. The overall goal of this chapter is to portray the key assets of the presented technologies and evaluate them as tools for handling adaptability, portability and interoperability issues that arise in modern business environments.

INTRODUCTION

Nowadays, organizations are facing a highly dynamic and challenging environment, characterized by a rising demand for customized, high quality services and products in several segments of business and industry. This environment, combined with the pace of technological innovation and the globalization of economy, has triggered the development of new value-creating economic paradigms, where the concept of the virtual enterprise (VE) has a central position. Sets of economic actors are combining their resources, forming temporary enterprise alliances (VEs), to effectively respond to the shifts of market demand, identify new opportunities and minimize organizational costs through cooperative and dynamic solutions.

The need to realize new forms of collaboration has forced organizations to shift their focus from intra- to inter-enterprise system and process integration. However, most enterprises have made extensive investments in system resources over the course of years and own an enormous amount of data stored in legacy enterprise information systems (EIS). Since it is impractical to discard existing EIS, there is a constant effort to evolve and enhance them. Thus, IT professionals are currently faced with the challenge of capturing and controlling legacy technology in a way that transcends organizational boundaries and heterogeneities, but also promotes system evolution. In this direction, service oriented architecture (SOA) provides a cost-effective solution, with Web services being a promising implementation, intended to enable the construction of interoperable components that can be assembled and deployed in a distributed environment (Estrem, 2003).

SERVICE-ORIENTED ARCHITECTURE (SOA)

Service-Oriented Architecture Overview

A service oriented architecture (SOA) is a design principle intended for the construction of reliable distributed systems that deliver functionality as services, with an additional emphasis on loose coupling between interacting services (Srinivasan & Treadwell, 2005). In this context, services are typically characterized by the following properties (Orchard, Ferris, Newcomer, Haas, Champion, Booth & McCabe, 2004):

- **Logical view:** The service is an abstracted, *logical* view of an actual business-level operation, defined as an implementation-independent interface. Services may be completely self-contained, or they may depend on the availability of other services,

or on the existence of specific resources such as a database.

- **Message orientation:** A service communicates with its clients by exchanging messages and is formally defined in terms of the message exchange patterns it supports. The internal structure of the provider and requester agents is deliberately abstracted away in the SOA, in order to maintain control of which aspects of an endpoint are revealed to external services.

- **Description orientation:** A service is described by machine-processable metadata. This description only exposes information important for the use of the service, such as its capabilities, interfaces, policies and supported protocols. Further, the description documents, directly or indirectly, the semantics that will govern the interaction between the requester and provider agents.

- **Granularity:** Services tend to use a small number of operations with relatively large and complex messages. However, various levels of granularity are possible, as services may be individually useful, or they can be integrated to provide higher-level services. Among other benefits, this promotes re-use of existing functionality.

- **Network orientation:** Services tend to be oriented toward use over a network. This property emphasizes the need for services to be automatically discoverable.

- **Platform neutrality:** Messages are delivered through the interfaces using a platform-neutral and standardized format, such as XML.

Additionally, services can participate in a workflow, where the order in which messages are exchanged affects the outcome of the operations performed by a service. This notion is defined as a "service choreography" and is actually a model of the sequence of operations, states and conditions that control the interactions involved in the participating services. The interaction prescribed by a choreography results in the completion of some useful function.

Figure 1 illustrates the interaction cycle of a service. This interaction cycle follows the "find-bind-execute" paradigm and begins with service providers advertising their service (1) through a public registry, used by consumers to look-up available services. A potential client (consumer), that may or may not be another service, queries the registry (2) for a service that matches certain criteria. The registry returns a (possibly empty) list of suitable services along with their endpoint addresses, and the client selects one and passes a request message to it, using any mutually recognized protocol (3). The service may respond (4) either with the result of the requested operation or with a fault message.

The above described interaction cycle, of course, covers only the simplest case. In a real-world setting, such as a commercial application, the process may be significantly more complex—protocol configuration, user authorization, interaction patterns and transaction control are only a few of the issues that may arise and need to be resolved.

Benefits of a SOA

A key feature of SOA is that it promotes loose coupling between software components. The interacting entities (services and/or other software components) have no built-in knowledge of each other and discover the information necessary for their interaction on-the-fly, when needed. This notion of loose coupling, imposed by the architecture, is exactly what turns services into valuable reusable "building blocks" and, more importantly, enables the creation of new services from existing assets and IT infrastructure. In other words, SOA promises to deliver interoperability between heterogeneous applications and technologies.

Clearly, the above benefits are of great value in a dynamic distributed environment. However, SOA also provides an unprecedented level of flexibility, as the benefits of service-oriented development also include the following (Srinivasan & Treadwell, 2005):

- **Flexibility:** Prospective clients can always locate (or relocate) a service, as long as the service registry entry is maintained.

Figure 1. Service interaction cycle in a SOA

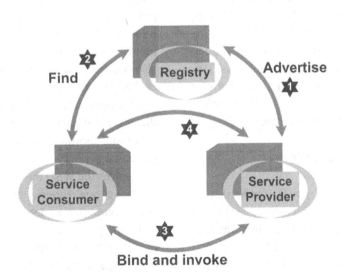

- **Scalability:** Services can be added and removed according to the variations of demand.
- **Replaceability:** Service implementations may be updated or completely altered—provided that the original interfaces are preserved—without any disruption to clients.
- **Fault tolerance:** Clients can always query the registry for alternative services providing the required functionality. In this way, uninterrupted operation is ensured, irrespective of the availability of independent services.

The real value of SOA, though, comes in later stages of development when new applications can be developed entirely, or almost entirely by composing existing services (Newcomer & Lomow, 2005). This may require significant investment in initial service development, but once this point has been reached, the best value for effort can be realized: new applications can be assembled out of a collection of existing, reusable services, with low cost and in fast times, thus resulting in substantial return of investment.

WEB SERVICES

Web services are a promising implementation of the service-oriented architecture, intended to provide a standard means of interoperating between different software applications, running on a variety of platforms and/or frameworks. This interoperability is gained through the use of a set of XML-based open standards for defining, publishing and using Web services.

Web Services: Definitions

A *Web service* is defined by W3C (Orchard et al., 2004, p. 7) as "a software system designed to support interoperable machine-to-machine interaction over a network. It has an interface described in a machine-processable format (specifically

WSDL). Other systems interact with the Web service in a manner prescribed by its description using SOAP messages, typically conveyed using HTTP with an XML serialization in conjunction with other Web-related standards."

It should be pointed out that, according to W3C (Orchard et al., 2004), a Web service should be perceived as an abstract notion, whose implementation is realized by use of a concrete *agent*. In this context, the agent is a basic entity, responsible for the exchange of messages and encapsulating the service, while the service itself is the resource abstractly defined by the provided functionality.

The purpose of a Web service is to provide some functionality on behalf of its owner—a person or organization, such as a business or an individual. The *provider entity* is the person or organization that provides an appropriate agent to implement a particular service. On the other hand, a *requester entity* is a person or organization that uses a *requester agent* to exchange messages with the provider entity's agent, in order to make use of the latter's Web service.

The message exchange between the requester and provider agents conforms to certain rules documented in a *Web service description* (WSD). The WSD is written in Web service description language (WSDL) and provides a machine-processable specification of the Web service's interface. Starting with the invocation address (network location) of the provider agent, the WSD also defines supported message formats, message exchange patterns, data types, transport protocols and transport serialization formats. In essence, the service description represents the contract governing the mechanics of interaction with a particular service.

Besides the WSD though, there is also a need for the service requester and provider entities to share a common understanding of the purpose and consequences of their interaction. This shared expectation about the behavior of the service constitutes the *semantics of a Web service*, on which the two interacting parties should agree upon. This agreement is not necessarily the product of a negotiation process or a legally expressed consensus and may take the form of an informal or implicit contract.

Web Services Infrastructure

As an implementation of SOA, Web services employ an infrastructure that provides the following: a discovery mechanism to locate Web services, a service description mechanism defining how to use those services and standard wire formats with which to communicate. Using this infrastructure, a requester entity might engage and use a Web service in many ways, but still the interaction cycle of a Web service is compatible with that defined for a SOA. In general, the following broad steps are required (Orchard et al., 2004), as illustrated in Figure 2:

1. *The requester and provider entities become known to each other,* in the sense that whichever party initiates the interaction must become aware of the other party. Typically, the *requester* agent will be the initiator and will obtain the invocation address of the provider agent, through the latter's service description. This description may be available for retrieval from a registry service.

2. *The requester and provider entities agree on the service description (a WSDL document) and semantics that will govern the interaction between the requester and provider agents.* This does not necessarily presuppose communication or negotiation between the requester and provider. A shared understanding of the service description and semantics and a commitment to uphold them is sufficient and can be achieved in various ways, such as:

   a. An explicit agreement through a communication or negotiation procedure.
   b. The service description and semantics being published by the provider entity in the form of a "contract" that the requester entity must accept unmodified as conditions of use.
   c. The service description and semantics (excepting the network address of the particular service) being published by the requester entity in the form of a specification that the provider entity must conform to.
   d. The service description and semantics (excepting the network address of the particular service) being a defined industry standard that both parties

Figure 2. The general process of engaging a Web service

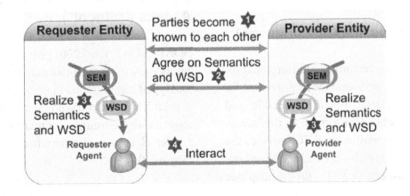

(the requester and provider entities) independently conform to.

3. *The service description and semantics are realized by the requester and provider agents*, in the sense that both the semantics and the service description must somehow be input to, or implemented in, both sides before the two agents can interact.

4. *The requester agent and provider agent exchange SOAP messages on behalf of their owner entities, thus performing some desirable task.*

Some of these steps may be automated, while others may be performed manually.

Core Web Services Specifications

The core of the Web services architecture consists of specifications, such as XML, SOAP and WSDL that support the interaction of a Web service requester with a web service provider. The potential discovery of the web service description may be realized as a universal description, discovery and integration (UDDI) or other type of registry. Though it is clear that a service registry is a required part of the Web services platform, UDDI has not yet been widely accepted by corporations, as most of them are reluctant against the notion of a public registry, due to security and intellectual property concerns.

The technologies considered in this section, in relation to the Web services Architecture, are XML, SOAP, WSDL and UDDI.

XML (eXtensible Markup Language)

XML solves the key technology requirement for the success of Web services: the requirement for a standardized, platform-neutral, flexible and inherently extensible data format. In this sense, the XML initiative within the W3C provides the core standards that Web services are based on. The important aspects of XML, for the purposes

of this architecture, are the core syntax itself, the concepts of the XML Infoset, XML Schema and XML Namespaces.

A Web service message is an XML document information item as defined by the XML Information Set, or Infoset (XML Information Set, 2004). The Infoset is a formal set of information items that comprise an abstract description of an XML and map to the various features in an XML document, such as elements, attributes, namespaces and comments. Each information item has an associated set of properties that provide a more complete description of the item. Infoset's information items along with their associated properties provide for a consistent and rigorous set of definitions that can be used by other specifications when referring to the information in a well-formed XML document.

The abstract data model defined by the Infoset is compatible with the text-based XML 1.0 (extensible markup language (XML) 1.0 Fourth Edition, 2006) and the foundation of all XML specifications: XML Schema (XML Schema, 2004), XML Query (XML Query Working Group Public Page), and XSLT 2.0 (XSL Transformation Version 2.0, 2006). By basing the Web services architecture on the XML Infoset rather than on a specific representation format, both the architecture and its core protocols are compatible with alternative encodings and serialization formats, allowing for broader interoperability between agents in the system.

SOAP (Originally "Simple Object Access Protocol")

SOAP (SOAP 1.1, 2000) provides a simple and lightweight mechanism for exchanging structured and typed messages in a distributed environment. It is an XML-based standard and defines a message as an "envelope" containing an optional header element and a mandatory body element (Figure 3).

Figure 3. Sample SOAP message

```
<?xml version="1.0" encoding="utf-8"?>
<soap:Envelope  xmlns:xsi="http://www.w3.org/2001/XMLSchema-instance"
                xmlns:xsd="http://www.w3.org/2001/XMLSchema"
                xmlns:soap="http://schemas.xmlsoap.org/soap/envelope/">
  <soap:Body>
    <Sub xmlns="http://OnLineMath.com">
        <x> 3 </x>
        <y> 4 </y>
    </Sub>
  </soap:Body>
</soap:Envelope>
```

The envelope is the root element of a SOAP message and specifies its XML namespace and the encoding. The body element is always the last child element of the envelope and acts as a container for the content of the message, intended for its ultimate recipient. Finally, the header element provides a generic mechanism for adding referencing capabilities to SOAP messages. If a header is provided, it extends the SOAP message in a modular way, indicating additional processing that is to be done at an intermediate node, independent of the message's final destination. Typically, the SOAP header is used to convey security-related information to be processed by runtime components.

In addition to the message format described above, SOAP also defines a transport binding framework for exchanging envelopes using a variety of underlying network protocols, including HTTP, SMTP, FTP, RMI/IIOP, or even proprietary messaging protocols. Moreover, there are three optional components to the SOAP specification: (1) a serialization framework defining encoding rules for expressing instances of application-defined data types such as numbers and text, (2) a convention for representing remote procedure calls (RPC) and responses, and (3) a set of rules for using SOAP with HTTP/1.1.

SOAP was originally an acronym for Simple Object Access Protocol, but since SOAP Version 1.2 (SOAP 1.2 Part 0, 2003; SOAP 1.2 Part 1, 2003) it is technically no longer an acronym.

WSDL (Web Service Description Language)

WSDL (WSDL Version 2.0, 2006) is a widely adopted mechanism for describing the basic characteristics of a Web service. A WSDL description is a first step in automatically identifying all characteristics of the target service, starting with the messages that are exchanged between the requester and provider agents. The messages are described abstractly and then bound to concrete physical deployment information to define an endpoint. Typically, messages are bound to the SOAP protocol and the HTTP transport, but these are not the only alternatives. Since the notation that a WSDL file uses to describe message formats is based on XML Schema, the described service interface can be mapped to any implementation language, platform, object model or messaging system.

In addition to describing message contents, a WSDL document uses the following elements in the definition of a web service (Figure 4):

- **Types:** A container for data type definitions using some type system (such as XML Schema Definition, XSD)
- **Message:** An abstract, typed definition of the data being communicated
- **Operation:** An abstract description of an action supported by the service

- **Port type:** An abstract set of operations supported by one or more endpoints
- **Binding:** A concrete protocol and data format specification for a particular port type
- **Port:** A single endpoint defined as a combination of a binding and a network address
- **Service:** A collection of related endpoints

Figure 4. Sample WSDL document

```xml
<?xml version="1.0" encoding="utf-8" ?>
<definitions ...
                targetNamespace="http://OnLineMath.com"
                    xmlns="http://schemas.xmlsoap.org/wsdl/">
  <types>
    <s:element name="Sub">
      <s:complexType>
        <s:sequence>
          <s:element minOccurs="1" maxOccurs="1" name="x" type="s:double" />
          <s:element minOccurs="1" maxOccurs="1" name="y" type="s:double" />
        </s:sequence>
      </s:complexType>
    </s:element>
    <s:element name="SubResponse">
      <s:complexType>
        <s:sequence>
          <s:element minOccurs="1" maxOccurs="1" name="SubResult" type="s:double" />
        </s:sequence>
      </s:complexType>
    </s:element>
  </types>
  <message name="SubSoapIn">
    <part name="parameters" element="s0:Sub" />
  </message>
  <message name="SubSoapOut">
    <part name="parameters" element="s0:SubResponse" />
  </message>
  <portType name="Service1Soap">
    <operation name="Sub">
      <input message="s0:SubSoapIn" />
      <output message="s0:SubSoapOut" />
    </operation>
  </portType>
  <binding name="Service1Soap" type="s0:Service1Soap">
    <soap:binding transport="http://schemas.xmlsoap.org/soap/http" style="document" />
    <operation name="Sub">
      <soap:operation soapAction="http://OnLineMath.com/Sub" style="document" />
      <input>
        <soap:body use="literal" />
      </input>
      <output>
        <soap:body use="literal" />
      </output>
    </operation>
  </binding>
  <service name="Service1">
    <port name="Service1Soap" binding="s0:Service1Soap">
      <soap:address location="http://OnLineMath.com/WSCalc/Service1.asmx" />
    </port>
  </service>
</definitions>
```

UDDI (Universal Description, Discovery and Integration)

The universal description, discovery, and integration protocol (UDDI Executive Overview, 2004) defines a standard method for publishing and discovering services through a common directory of Web service information. It is an open industry initiative (sponsored by OASIS) designed to be interrogated by SOAP messages and to provide access to WSDL documents. Additionally, the specification defines a UDDI schema identifying the types of XML data structures that comprise an entry in the registry for a service.

UDDI registries can be deployed in one of three ways: public, extra-enterprise or intra-enterprise UDDI registries. Intra- and extra-enterprise approaches employ private registries deployed by an organization, or a group of business partners respectively. On the other hand, the UDDI business registry (hosted by a group of vendors led by Microsoft, IBM and SAP) is a public UDDI registry, serving as both a resource for Internet-based Web services and a test bed for Web services developers.

The fundamental goal of UDDI is to enable businesses to register information about the services they provide, in order for prospective clients to locate them easily by consulting a repository. A UDDI business registration consists of three components, commonly referred to as "white pages", "yellow pages" and "green pages" information:

- **White pages** provide basic information about a company, such as the business name, address and contact information. White pages also allow the discovery of services according to unique business identifiers.
- **Yellow pages** describe business services using different categorizations—"taxonomies" in UDDI terminology. This information allows for the discovery of business services based on their categorization.
- **Green pages** provide technical information on the behaviors and supported functions of services hosted by a business. This includes references to specifications for Web services, as well as support for pointers to various file and URL based discovery mechanisms if required. Moreover, green pages in UDDI are not limited to describing XML-based Web services: the technical description is applicable to any service type exposed by a business entity.

UDDI version 2.0 was approved in 2003 and was integrated into the Web Services Interoperability (WS-I) standard as a central pillar of Web services infrastructure. The UDDI Version 3.0 specification (UDDI Version 3.0.2, 2004), approved by the OASIS International Standards Consortium in early 2005, represents another significant milestone in UDDI's evolution, as it provides key capabilities for enterprise-level deployment and is a mature, well-supported standard.

Extended Web Services Specifications

Although the core Web services specifications (XML, SOAP, WSDL and UDDI) comprise an accepted industry-wide basis for interoperability, significant effort has been put in enhancing the scope of the Web services platform and addressing higher-level issues that arise in real-world application domains. In this direction, a wide array of Web services specifications for security, reliability, transactions, metadata management and orchestration have emerged and are currently in their way toward standardization. Figure 5 provides an illustration of some of these technology families.

The extended "architecture stack," depicted in Figure 5, will hopefully provide WS-based solutions with the necessary qualities of service to support enterprise-level projects.

Figure 5. Extended Web services architecture stack

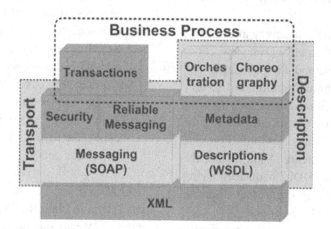

Metadata Management

Metadata management includes the description information about Web services necessary for a service requester to invoke them. In order for this invocation to be successful, the requester needs to effectively construct a message—a message body, including its data types and structures, and message headers—processable by the service provider.

Effective construction of messages depends on the metadata published by the provider and discovered by the requester. Such metadata include not only the data types and structures to be sent, but also the additional qualities of the service provided (if any), such as security, reliability or transactions. The absence of one or more of these features may hinder successful message processing.

Metadata extended specifications include among others:

- **WS-Addressing:** Enables messaging systems to support message transmission in a transport-neutral manner through networks that include processing nodes such as end-point managers, firewalls and gateways. It provides support for endpoint addressing and reference properties associated with endpoints for many of the other extended specifications.

- **WS-Policy:** Provides a general-purpose framework and corresponding syntax to describe and communicate quality of service requirements of a Web service; policy declarations cover various aspects of security, transactions and reliability.

- **WS-MetadataExchange:** Defines request-response message pairs to incrementally retrieve three types of metadata: WSDL files, policy definitions and XML schemata associated with a Web service.

Addressing

SOAP messages must include the endpoint address information within the message, as no directory of Web services endpoint addresses exists on the Web. Proper message routing relies on a common mechanism, which will allow for critical messaging properties to be carried across multiple transports in cases of communication failure or complicated message exchange patterns.

WS-Addressing replaces earlier proposals called WS-Routing, WS-Referral and SOAP routing protocol (SOAP-RP) and promises to provide an effective solution for message transmission problems.

The WS-Addressing (WS-Addressing, 2004) specification specifies how addressing information (typically used for routing) should be conveyed in a SOAP message, by defining common headers such as *message identifiers* and *to* and *from* fields (Figure 6). These headers rely on a WS-Addressing-defined structure called an *endpoint reference* that is an access point of a Web service and bundles together the information needed to properly address a SOAP message.

Policy

An emerging problem in Web services is describing the capabilities and requirements of endpoints, in addition to the data requirements for the messages expressed in the WSDL file. As WSDL does not cover many aspects of a Web service's operation, such as security, transaction or reliability, these aspects have to be specified or negotiated on a point-to-point basis. WS-Policy aims to fill this gap by providing an open framework for the definition of extended requirements, capabilities and configuration issues—together referred to as the policy of a Web service.

WS-Policy provides a machine-readable expression of assertions necessary for achieving interoperability for the extended features. It specifies a base set of constructs that can be used and extended by other Web service specifications to describe a broad range of service requirements and capabilities. For example, WS-PolicyFramework (WS-Policy 1.2 Framework, 2006) describes the overall framework of expressing policy assertions and combining them. WS-PolicyAssertions (WS-Policy Assertions Version 1.0, 2002) defines a set of common message policy assertions, such as document encoding or specification support, that can be specified within a policy. Finally, WS-

PolicyAttachment (WS-Policy 1.2 Attachment, 2006) defines general-purpose mechanisms for associating policies with XML elements, WSDL-type definitions, and UDDI entries.

Acquiring Metadata

WSDL and WS-Policy both define metadata formats, but do not specify mechanisms for acquiring or accessing metadata for a given service. In general, service metadata can be discovered using a variety of techniques—a requester might obtain it using WS-MetadataExchange or another similar mechanism that queries the WSDL and associated policy files directly.

WS-MetadataExchange (WS-MetadataExchange Version 1.1, 2006) is a SOAP-based access protocol for metadata designed to provide information about a Web service description, essentially replacing UDDI that, despite its existence, does not provide the metadata management facilities required to support interoperability requirements at the extended specification level. The WS-MetadataExchange specification, though, ensures that service requesters have all the necessary information to achieve interoperability with providers using extended features.

Security

Security concerns apply at every level of the Web services architecture, involving threats to the host system, the application and the entire network infrastructure. To secure Web services, a range of XML-based security mechanisms are built around encryption, authentication and authorization mechanisms and typically include comprehensive logging for problem tracking. Currently, the industry has achieved consensus around a single specification framework, WS-Security (WS-Security, 2004), although ongoing work is necessary to complete the profiles and additional related specifications.

WS-Security describes enhancements to SOAP messaging to provide quality of protection through message integrity, message confidentiality, and single message authentication. The WS-Security specification supports tokens for common security mechanisms in use today, such as Kerberos tickets and X.509 certificates, and can use XML Encryption and XML Signature technologies for further protecting the message contents. XML-based security tokens also include the security assertion markup language (SAML) (OASIS Security Services TC Webpage).

WS-Security is further extended and complemented by additional specifications, including:

- **WS-SecurityPolicy:** Indicates the policy assertions for WS-Policy, which apply to WS-Security (WS-SecurityPolicy Version 1.1, 2005)
- **WS-Trust:** Defines extensions building on WS-Security to request and issue security tokens (such as Kerberos tickets) and to manage trust relationships (WS-Trust, 2005)
- **WS-SecureConversation:** Defines extensions building on WS-Security to provide secure communication; specifically, it defines mechanisms for establishing and maintaining persistent security contexts, and deriving session keys from security contexts (WS-SecureConversation, 2005).
- **WS-Federation:** Defines mechanisms to bridge multiple security realms into a federated session by allowing and brokering trust of identities, attributes and authentication between participating Web services; the defined mechanisms allow for a Web service to be authenticated only once in order to access all federated Web services (WS-Federation Version 1.0, 2003).

XML-based security technologies are also important for protecting the XML data (metadata or content) in a SOAP message. Such technologies include:

- **XML encryption:** Specifies a process for encrypting data, using a variety of supported encryption algorithms; the encryption result is an XML Encryption element that contains or references the cipher data, ensuring that the contents of the document cannot be intercepted and read by unauthorized persons (XML Encryption Syntax and Processing, 2002).
- **XML signature:** Specifies XML digital signature processing rules and syntax. The specification provides integrity, message authentication and signer authentication services for data of any type, ensuring that documents cannot be altered in transit and are received exactly once (XML Signature Syntax and Processing, 2002).

Reliable Messaging

In any distributed system there are fundamental limits to the reliability of messages sent over a public network. However, in practice there are techniques that can be used to increase the reliability of messages and provide valuable feedback in cases where communication fails. The Web services architecture does not by itself provide specific support for reliable messaging, or for reporting in the event of failure. However, since all messages are structured according to SOAP, overall message reliability can be incorporated within the SOAP message structure.

Though the industry has not yet achieved consensus on a single, unified set of specifications, there are some examples of specifications for an acknowledgement infrastructure that leverage the SOAP extensibility model:

- **WS-Reliability:** An OASIS standard (WS-Reliability 1.1, 2004)
- **WS-ReliableMessaging:** From BEA, IBM, Microsoft and TIBCO (WS-ReliableMessaging, 2005)

Reliable messaging specifications define mechanisms for ensuring that the sending and receiving parties know whether or not a message was delivered. These mechanisms guarantee reliable delivery of SOAP messages, over potentially unreliable networks, with no duplicates, and guaranteed message ordering. Additionally, reliable messaging automates recovery from certain transport-level error conditions, such as in the presence of software component, system or network failures.

In the general messaging area, there are also specifications for message exchange patterns such as event notification and publish/subscribe, which basically extends the asynchronous messaging capability of Web services. Specifications in this area include:

- **WS-Eventing:** Describes how to construct an event-oriented message exchange pattern, allowing Web services to act as event sources for subscribers; it defines the operations required to manage subscriptions to event sources, as well as how the actual event messages are constructed (WS-Eventing, 2006).
- **WS-Notification:** Implements the notification pattern, where a service provider, or other entity, initiates messages based on a subscription or registration of interest from a service requestor; it defines how the "publish/subscribe" pattern can be realized using Web services.;this includes brokered as well as direct "publish/subscribe" patterns, allowing the publisher/subscribers to be decoupled and provides greater scalability (OASIS WSN TC Webpage).

Transactions

Transactions are a fundamental concept in building reliable distributed applications, as they allow multiple operations, usually on persistent data, to succeed or fail as a unit. Traditionally, transactions

have held the following properties collectively referred to as *ACID*:

- **Atomicity:** A transaction allows for the grouping of multiple operations, so that either all of them are performed or none of them is.
- **Consistency:** The application returns to a valid state when the transaction ends, hence the transaction should leave the processing resource in a logical state instead of ambiguity.
- **Isolation:** Operations in a transaction appear isolated from all other operations, until the transaction completes successfully.
- **Durability:** Once a transaction successfully completes, the changes are guaranteed to persist, even in the case of system failure.

Moreover, one of the most important aspects of transaction processing technologies is their ability to recover an application to a known state following an operating system or hardware failure.

A Web service environment may require only the coordination behavior provided by a traditional transaction mechanism to control the operations and outcome of an application. However, it may also require the capability to handle the coordination of processing outcomes or results from multiple services, in a more flexible manner. This requires more relaxed forms of transactions—not strictly abiding to the ACID properties—such as collaborations, workflow, real-time processing and so forth. In this direction, Web services transaction specifications extend the concept of the transaction coordinator, adapt the familiar two-phase commit protocol for Web services, and define new extended transaction protocols for more loosely coupled Web services and orchestration flows.

The specifications in this area include (Newcomer & Lomow, 2005):

- **WS-Transactions family** from BEA, IBM, and Microsoft:

  - **WS-AtomicTransaction:** Provides the definition of the atomic transaction coordination type that is to be used with the extensible coordination framework described in the WS-Coordination specification; the specification defines three specific agreement coordination protocols (completion, volatile two-phase commit, and durable two-phase commit) for short-lived distributed activities that have all-or-nothing semantics (WS-AtomicTransaction 1.1, 2006).

  - **WS-BusinessActivity:** Provides the definition of the business activity coordination type that is to be used with the extensible coordination framework described in the WS-Coordination specification; the specification defines protocols for long-running distributed activities (WS-BusinessActivity 1.1, 2006).

  - **WS-Coordination:** Describes an extensible framework for providing protocols that coordinate the actions of distributed applications (WS-Coordination 1.1, 2006).

- **WS-Composite Application Framework (WS-CAF)** from OASIS that proposes standard, interoperable mechanisms for managing shared context and ensuring business processes achieve predictable results and recovery from failure. WS-CAF has three sub-parts (OASIS WS-CAF TC Webpage):

  - **WS-Context (WS-Context):** Defines a standalone and lightweight context management system (WS-Context, 2006)

  - **WS-Coordination Framework (WS-CF):** A sharable mechanism to manage context augmentation and lifecycle, and guarantee message delivery; a software agent is defined as the coordinator for the basic context specification and the pluggable transaction protocols in the WS-TransactionManagement specification (WS-CF, 2005).

  - **WS-TransactionManagement (WS-TXM):** Comprises three distinct protocols for interoperability across multiple transaction managers and supports multiple transaction models (two phase commit, long running actions and business process flows) (WS-TXM Version 1.0, 2003)

Orchestration and Choreography

Terms such as orchestration and choreography are used to describe the composition of Web services in a process flow. More formally, the term *orchestration* (Peltz, 2003, p. 3) "describes how Web services can interact with each other at the message level, including the business logic and execution order of the interactions. These interactions may span applications and/or organizations, and result in a long-lived, transactional, multi-step process model." On the other hand, the term *choreography* (Orchard et al., 2004, p. 32) "defines the sequence and conditions under which multiple cooperating independent agents exchange messages in order to perform a task to achieve a goal state." In other words, a choreography tracks the sequence of operations, states and messages that may involve multiple parties and multiple sources, interacting for the completion of some useful function.

There is an important distinction between Web services orchestration and choreography. An orchestration refers to a business process that is executed by a single Web service interacting with other parties—both internal and external Web services—but controlling this interaction from its personal perspective. Choreography, on the other hand, is more collaborative in nature, and is typically associated with the public message exchanges that occur between multiple Web services, rather than with a single party's executable business process. In this context, a choreography permits the definition of how several Web services can be composed, how service roles and associations can be established, and how the state, if any, of composed services is to be managed.

Orchestration

The industry has reached a consensus around a single orchestration specification: the business process execution language for Web services (BPEL4WS). BPEL4WS (Business Process Execution Language for Web Services Version 1.1, 2003) is essentially a layer on top of WSDL, with WSDL defining the specific operations allowed and BPEL4WS defining how the operations can be sequenced. More specifically, BPEL4WS includes support for both basic and structured activities, with structured activities managing the overall process flow and specifying which basic activities should be executed and in what order. Moreover, BPEL4WS provides a robust mechanism for handling transactions and exceptions, building on top of the WS-Transactions family of specifications.

It should be pointed out, that BPEL4WS provides support for both executable and abstract business processes. An executable process essentially models a private workflow, while abstract processes—modelled as business protocols—focus more on the choreography of services.

Choreography

W3C's Web services choreography description language (WS-CDL) (Web Services Choreography Description Language Version 1.0, 2005) is the dominant specification in the area of choreography. It is geared towards composing interoperable, peer-to-peer collaborations between any

Figure 6. Sample SOAP message using extended specifications

```
<?xml version="1.0" encoding="utf-8"?>
<soap:Envelope xmlns:xsi="http://www.w3.org/2001/XMLSchema-instance"
               xmlns:xsd="http://www.w3.org/2001/XMLSchema"
               xmlns:soap="http://schemas.xmlsoap.org/soap/envelope/">
  <soap:Header>
    <wsa:ReplyTo>
      <wsa:Address>
        http://MathTutor.com/User17
      </wsa:Address>
    </wsa:ReplyTo>
    <wsa:To>
      http://OnLineMath.com/WSCalc
    </wsa:To>
    <wsa:Action>
      http://OnLineMath.com/WSCalc/Sub
    </wsa:Action>
    <wssec:security>
      <wssec:BinarySecurityToken  ValueType="wssec:x509v3"
                                  EncodingType="wssec:Base64Binary">
        <!--security token content-->
      </wssec:BinarySecurityToken>
    </wssec:Security>
    <wsrm:Sequence>
      ...
    </wsrm:Sequence>
  </soap:Header>
  <soap:Body>
    <Sub xmlns="http://OnLineMath.com">
      <x> 3 </x>
      <y> 4 </y>
    </Sub>
  </soap:Body>
</soap:Envelope>
```

variety of participants, where ordered message exchanges result in accomplishing a common business goal. In this context, WS-CDL provides a standard method for defining, from a global viewpoint, the collaborating parties' common and complementary observable behavior.

Web Services Specification Composability

Composability is a key feature of the Web services architecture stack and has been a guiding principle in the development of all specifications, core or extended. As already mentioned, SOAP and WSDL are designed to support composition inherently. On the other hand, all extended specifications although independently addressing specific concerns, are also designed to work seamlessly with each other in order to provide increasingly powerful functionality.

The composition of Web services specifications is illustrated in Figure 6, by means of a simple SOAP message that contains elements associated with three different specifications: WS-Addressing, WS-Security and WS-ReliableMessaging.

Each of these elements can be used independently of other elements present and without affecting their processing functions. In this way, transactions, security, reliability or any other extended capability can be incorporated into a SOAP message in terms of composable message elements. Moreover, this extension can be implemented incrementally, with necessary assets being added in later stages of development, when the need for new functionality arises.

The practical value of composable Web services is also evident in the case of service consumers seeking to determine to what extend a particular service provides the desired functionality and assurances (Weerawarana et al., 2005). In order for this to be possible, the service must explicitly document its requirements, in terms of its specific support for transactions, security etc. In this direction, WS-Policy provides a flexible mechanism

for Web services to incrementally augment their WSDL and specify the supplementary SOAP elements that are necessary in order to successfully interact with the service.

REALIZING SOA WITH WEB SERVICES

Since 1996 when Service Oriented Architecture was first introduced by Gartner (1996) a lot of effort has been put worldwide in this area. SOA has captured the interest of many software architects and developers but only recently with the advent of Web services, SOA has found its way to real applications. Other technologies have been tried in the mean time, but undoubtedly Web services is the most prominent technology that forms a solid base to develop robust SOA applications.

An important advantage of using Web services as the technology platform for an SOA, is that Web services address a fundamental challenge of distributed computing: to provide a uniform way of describing components or services within a network, locating them and accessing them. The difference between the Web services approach and traditional approaches (for example, distributed object technologies such as the Object Management Group – Common Object Request Broker Architecture (OMG CORBA) or Microsoft Distributed Component Object Model (DCOM)) lies in the loose coupling aspects of the architecture. Instead of building applications that result in tightly integrated collections of objects or components, the Web services approach is much more dynamic and adaptable to change (Weerawarana, Curbera, Leymann, Storey & Ferguson, 2005).

Another key feature (Weerawarana et al., 2005) is that Web services-based software is designed using technology and specifications developed in an open way, utilizing industry partnerships and broad consortia such as W3C and the Organization for the Advancement of

Structured Information Standards (OASIS), and based on standards and technology that are the foundation of the Internet. In fact, Web services "build" on the way in which the World Wide Web achieved its tremendous success (Newcomer & Lomow, 2005), namely with HTML providing a powerful interoperability solution and HTTP an effective and lightweight universal data transfer mechanism. Web services provide the same level of abstraction for IT systems: Web services-based solutions are only required to understand, process and reply to an XML-formatted message received using a supported communications transport.

Despite the apparent benefits of Web services-based solutions, distributed object systems have a number of architectural challenges that apply irrespective of their implementation technology (Orchard et al., 2004). Web services are no less appropriate than the alternatives for building distributed systems, but still they may not add enough benefits to justify their costs in performance. For example, they are not a cost-effective solution for organizations that have relatively small and static application portfolios and do not need to interoperate with other external environments (Weerawarana et al., 2005).

On the other hand, though, SOA and Web services are most appropriate for applications:

- That must operate over the Internet where reliability and speed cannot be guaranteed and high performance is not a primary criterion
- Where there is no ability to manage deployment so that all requesters and providers are upgraded at once
- Where integration of components within heterogeneous environments (e.g., different platforms and vendor products) is at the core of the problem being addressed
- Where an existing application needs to be exposed for use over a network and be made available to various kinds of requesters—this presupposes, however, that the application can indeed be wrapped as a Web service

CONCLUSION

Collaborating companies need their applications and services to interoperate effectively. This is exactly the force driving the industry towards SOA and Web services technologies, which promise significant benefits in terms of adaptability, ease-of-integration, portability and interoperability (Protogeros, 2006).

Projects deployed with Web services and SOA can achieve an important level of business process abstraction. The interoperability and integration issues can successfully be addressed through SOA in a two-step process involving publishing services and orchestrating them. Publishing means making the Web services available through a supported interface/protocol but does not require that all existing systems be "wrapped" with a new XML/SOAP Web service layer. Orchestration means assembling and coordinating these services into a manageable business application.

However, there is work to do, specifically to the wider standards adoptions between medium and small enterprises. The lack of custom and user friendly tools drives developers to manually recode services or provide "glue code" so that they can interconnect with one another. Such painstaking labor deprives SOAs of much of their virtue—namely, rapid integration and composite application.

Wider virtual enterprise models acceptance relies heavily on the ease of integration at the business process level, and this in turn relates closely with SOA acceptance and adoption. BPEL4WS promise for universal remote integration makes us more optimistic about the future of virtual enterprises.

REFERENCES

Business Process Execution Language for Web Services (Version 1.1) (2003, May). Retrieved February 12, 2007, from ftp://www6.software.ibm.com/software/developer/library/ws-bpel.pdf

Estrem, W. A. (2003). An evaluation framework for deploying web services in the next generation manufacturing enterprise. *Robotics and Computer Integrated Manufacturing 19*, 509-519

Extensible Markup Language (XML) 1.0 (Fourth Edition) (2006, August). *W3C Recommendation.* Retrieved February 12, 2007, from http://www.w3.org/TR/2006/REC-xml-20060816/

Newcomer, E., & Lomow, G. (2005). *Understanding SOA with Web services.* Boston: Addison Wesley Professional.

OASIS Security Services (SAML) TC webpage. Retrieved February 12, 2007, from http://www.oasis-open.org/committees/tc_home.php?wg_abbrev=security

OASIS Web Services Composite Application Framework (WS-CAF) TC webpage. Retrieved February 12, 2007, from http://www.oasis-open.org/committees/tc_home.php?wg_abbrev=ws-caf

OASIS Web Services Notification (WSN) TC webpage. Retrieved February 12, 2007, from http://www.oasis-open.org/committees/tc_home.php?wg_abbrev=wsn

Orchard, D., Ferris, C., Newcomer, E., Haas, H., Champion, M., Booth, D., & McCabe, F. (2004, February). Web services architecture. W3C Working Group. Retrieved February 12, 2007, from http://www.w3.org/TR/2004/NOTE-ws-arch-20040211/

Peltz, C. (2003, January). *Web services orchestration: A review of emerging technologies, tools, and standards.* Retrieved February 12, 2007, from

http://devresource.hp.com/drc/technical_white_papers/WSOrch/WSOrchestration.pdf

Protogeros, N. (2006). Service-oriented architectures and virtual enterprises. In M. Khosrow-Pour (Ed.), *Encyclopedia of e-commerce, e-government, and mobile commerce, e-collaboration technologies and applications.* Hershey, PA: Idea Group Reference.

Sculte, R., & Natis, Y. (1996). SSA Research Note SPA-401-068: Service Oriented Architectures, Part 1, Part 2. Garter, Inc.

Simple Object Access Protocol (SOAP) 1.1 (2000, May). *W3C note.* Retrieved February 12, 2007, from http://www.w3.org/TR/2000/NOTE-SOAP-20000508/

SOAP Version 1.2 Part 0: Primer (2003, June). *W3C recommendation.* Retrieved February 12, 2007, from http://www.w3.org/TR/soap12-part0/

SOAP Version 1.2 Part 1: Messaging Framework. (2003, June). *W3C recommendation.* Retrieved February 12, 2007, from http://www.w3.org/TR/soap12-part1/

Srinivasan, L., & Treadwell, J. (2005, November). *An overview of service-oriented architecture, web services and grid computing.* HP Software Global Business Unit.

UDDI executive overview: Enabling service-oriented architecture (2004, October). *OASIS.* Retrieved February 12, 2007, from http://uddi.org/pubs/uddi-exec-wp.pdf

UDDI Version 3.0.2 (2004, October). UDDI spec technical committee draft. Retrieved February 12, 2007, from http://uddi.org/pubs/uddi-v3.0.2-20041019.pdf

Web Services Addressing (WS-Addressing) (2004, August). *W3C member submission.* Retrieved February 12, 2007, from http://www.w3.org/Submission/ws-addressing/

Web Services Atomic Transaction (WS-Atomic-Transaction) 1.1 (2006, August). Public review draft 01. Retrieved February 12, 2007, from http://docs.oasis-open.org/ws-tx/wstx-wsat-1.1-spec-pr-01.pdf

Web Services Business Activity (WS-Business Activity) 1.1 (2006, March). Committee draft 01. Retrieved February 12, 2007, from http://docs.oasis-open.org/ws-tx/wstx-wsba-1.1-spec-cd-01.pdf

Web Services Choreography Description Language Version 1.0 (2005, November). W3C candidate recommendation. Retrieved February 12, 2007, from http://www.w3.org/TR/ws-cdl-10/

Web Services Context Specification (WS-Context). Committee Specification 1.0. Retrieved February 12, 2007, from http://www.oasis-open.org/committees/download.php/19659/WS-Context.zip

Web Services Coordination, Framework Specification (WS-CF). (2005, October). Editor's draft 1.0. Retrieved February 12, 2007, from http://www.oasis-open.org/committees/download.php/15042/WS-CF.zip

Web Services Coordination (WS-Coordination) 1.1 (2006, August). Public review draft 01. Retrieved February 12, 2007, from http://docs.oasis-open.org/ws-tx/wstx-wscoor-1.1-spec-pr-01.pdf

Web Services Description Language (WSDL) Version 2.0 Part 1: Core Language (2006, March). W3C candidate recommendation. Retrieved February 12, 2007, from http://www.w3.org/TR/wsdl20/

Web Services Eventing (WS-Eventing) (2006, March). W3C member submission. Retrieved February 12, 2007, from http://www.w3.org/Submission/WS-Eventing/

Web Services Federation Language (WSFederation) Version 1.0 (2003, July). Retrieved February 12, 2007, from ftp://www6.software.ibm.com/software/developer/library/ws-fed.pdf

Web Services Metadata Exchange (WS-MetadataExchange) Version 1.1 (2006, August). Retrieved February 12, 2007, from http://download.boulder.ibm.com/ibmdl/pub/software/dw/specs/ws-mex/metadataexchange.pdf

Web Services Policy 1.2 - Attachment (WS-PolicyAttachment) (2006, April). *W3C member submission.* Retrieved February 12, 2007, from http://www.w3.org/Submission/2006/SUBM-WS-PolicyAttachment-20060425/

Web Services Policy 1.2 - Framework (WS-Policy) (2006, April). *W3C member submission.* Retrieved February 12, 2007, from http://www.w3.org/Submission/WS-Policy/

Web Services Policy Assertions Language (WS-PolicyAssertions) Version 1.0 (2002, December). Retrieved February 12, 2007, from ftp://www6.software.ibm.com/software/developer/library/ws-polas.pdf

Web Services Reliable Messaging Protocol (WS-ReliableMessaging) (2005, February). Retrieved February 12, 2007, from ftp://www6.software.ibm.com/software/developer/library/ws-reliablemessaging200502.pdf

Web Services Reliable Messaging TC, WS-Reliability 1.1 (2004, November). *OASIS standard.* Retrieved February 12, 2007, from http://docs.oasis-open.org/wsrm/ws-reliability/v1.1/wsrm-ws_reliability-1.1-spec-os.pdf

Web Services Secure Conversation Language (WS-SecureConversation) (2005, February). Retrieved February 12, 2007, from ftp://www6.software.ibm.com/software/developer/library/ws-secureconversation.pdf

Web Services Security: SOAP Message Security 1.1 (WS-Security 2004) (2006, February). *OASIS standard specification.* Retrieved February 12, 2007, from http://www.oasis-open.org/committees/download.php/16790/wss-v1.1-spec-os-SOAPMessageSecurity.pdf

Web Services Security Policy Language (WS-SecurityPolicy) Version 1.1 (2005, July) Retrieved February 12, 2007, from ftp://www6.software.ibm.com/software/developer/library/ws-secpol.pdf

Web Services Trust Language (WS-Trust) (2005, February). Retrieved February 12, 2007, from ftp://www6.software.ibm.com/software/developer/library/ws-trust.pdf

Web Services Transaction Management (WS-TXM) Version 1.0 (2003, July). Retrieved February 12, 2007, from http://developers.sun.com/techtopics/webservices/wscaf/wstxm.pdf

Weerawarana, S., Curbera, F., Leymann, F., Storey, T., & Ferguson, D. F. (2005). *Web services platform architecture: SOAP, WSDL, WS-Policy, WS-Addressing, WS-BPEL, WS-Reliable Messaging, and More.* Upper Saddle River, NJ: Prentice Hall PTR.

XML Encryption Syntax and Processing (2002, December). *W3C recommendation.* Retrieved February 12, 2007, from http://www.w3.org/TR/xmlenc-core/

XML Information Set (Second Edition) (2004, February). *W3C recommendation.* Retrieved February 12, 2007, from http://www.w3.org/TR/2004/REC-xml-infoset-20040204/

XML Query Working Group Public Page. Retrieved February 12, 2007, from http://www.w3.org/XML/Query/

XML Schema Part 0: Primer Second Edition (2004, October). *W3C recommendation.* Retrieved February 12, 2007, from http://www.w3.org/TR/xmlschema-0/

XML-Signature Syntax and Processing. (2002, February). *W3C recommendation.* Retrieved February 12, 2007, from http://www.w3.org/TR/xmldsig-core/

XSL Transformations (XSLT) Version 2.0 (2006, June). *W3C candidate recommendation.* Retrieved February 12, 2007, from http://www.w3.org/TR/xslt20/

Section II
Virtual Enterprise Formation

Chapter III
Virtual Enterprise Formation Supported by Agents and Web Services

Sobah Abbas Petersen
Norwegian University of Science and Technology, Norway

Jinghai Rao
Carnegie Mellon University, USA

Mihhail Matskin
Norwegian University of Science and Technology, Norway

ABSTRACT

This chapter describes the use of software agents and Web services to support the formation of virtual enterprises. The partners of a virtual enterprise are represented as software agents. The AGORA multi-agent architecture is used. The focus of this chapter is on the description of the services provided by each partner and the partner selection process. The concept of agent interaction protocols is used to manage the interactions during the formation of the virtual enterprise. An implementation of the ideas and examples from industrial case studies are used for the validation of the approach and discussions. The use of semantic Web technology and Web services with multi-agent systems is discussed as the future directions for this work.

INTRODUCTION

Recent advances in communication and distributed information technology has changed the way business is conducted. Enabled by technologies such as software agents and electronic commerce, enterprises have gone beyond the geographical and sociocultural boundaries and have become entities that not only compete in the global market, but also draw their resources from an international market. The trend of outsourcing seems to be replaced by strategic alliances, where enterprises or individuals work together towards a common goal and share their responsibilities as well as their profits. The concept of a virtual enterprise (VE) has emerged as a means of dealing with this.

Interest in VEs have grown in the recent years and efforts have been made in several research domains to understand, design, facilitate and support VEs in any possible way. Some of this work is reviewed in the following section. As a result of this focus, the need for technological support of VEs has risen. This chapter describes an agent-based approach to support VEs and a model to describe them. The focus of our work is to support, in particular, the formation phase of the lifecycle of a VE. The formation of a VE is considered within the context of an electronic market place where several parties compete to become partners of a VE. Software agents and Web services are used as solution technologies. Our approach is based on understanding a VE from an organizational perspective and using these ideas to provide technological support. Emphasis has been made to ensure that the work is not technology driven, rather a combination of organizational design ideas as well as an appropriate technology.

The objective of this work is to provide an agent-based model of the VE and a solution technology that meets the needs and challenges of the industry. The work was motivated by the fact that technological solutions will save the industry resources by supporting the automation of some generic operations and processing of information. The aim is not to automate the complete process, rather to support effective decision-making by providing appropriate information to the decision makers. The work described in this chapter has been validated using industrial case studies.

The rest of this chapter is organized as follows: Section 2 provides an overview of related work; Section 3 describes the agent-based model of the VE; Section 4 describes the VE formation process; Section 5 describes the implementation of the approach and the model using a multi-agent architecture; Section 6 presents a validation of the work using industrial case studies; Section 7 discusses the future directions for this work and Section 8 concludes the chapter.

BACKGROUND

This section provides an overview of the literature that is related to this work. The research areas that have been addressed are VEs, intelligent agents, multi-agent systems and Web services and agents and Web services for modelling VEs.

Virtual Enterprises

VEs have received increasing attention during the last decade (e.g., VOSTER, 2003). Due to the advancement of distributed information technology and the changing needs of the business community, enterprises are expected to be more agile and responsive. The concept of a VE is a means of meeting these new expectations. Although a universally accepted definition of the term is still missing, there have been several attempts at defining VEs from different areas of application, for example, from manufacturing (Jagdev & Brown, 1998), organizational design (Davidow & Malone, 1992) and enterprise modelling and integration (Vernadat, 1996). While the definitions address their particular areas of interest, there are some common aspects in these definitions. We have reviewed several definitions of VEs to come up with our working definition of a VE, which is as follows: *A VE is a group of enterprises that collaborate to achieve a specific goal.* The main characteristics of VEs are that it is a temporary network of enterprises, (Jagdev & Brown, 1998), with a limited lifetime, (Fischer et al., 1996), where the partners are distributed geographically and they collaborate (Oliveira & Rocha, 2000); it is goal-oriented, (Petersen, Divitini & Matskin, 2001), and commitment-based (Jain, Aparicio, & Singh, 1999); it is supported by communication and information flow, (Garita & Afsarmanesh, 2001) and the partners share their skills, costs and profits (Byrne, Brandt, & Port, 1993).

The goal-oriented and distributed nature of VEs implies that there is no central control; rather, the control is decentralized. The goals are achieved through complex and varied interactions. The entities that constitute the VE are the partners, who play different roles, and the customer(s). (For example, in a simple manufacturing scenario, the partners can be the supplier and the manufacturer.) As the partners of the VE are distributed, they require some kind of support for their cooperative work. This is achieved by sharing of common goals and knowledge, which can be supported by tools that support collaboration. To deal with the dynamics of the cooperative work context, the partners will need to renegotiate their goals and activities from time to time. Also, as the partners represent different organizations, the information sources are most likely to be distributed and heterogeneous.

VEs are by definition, dynamic and flexible. Unlike traditional enterprises that are established and continue to exist over a long period of time, VEs are established to answer more contingent needs and can have a shorter span of life. Thus, they need to be formed very quickly in order to meet the deadlines of the goals and there is a need to form them often. An important part of the formation is the selection of partners, who are selected on their ability to fulfil the VE's requirements. We focus on the selection of partners for the VE in order to understand the interactions and the contents of the messages that are exchanged between the partners.

Intelligent Agents, Multi-Agent Systems and Web Services

Intelligent agents, similar to VEs, do not have a universally accepted definition. The definition that we have used is one of the most cited and the one that we believe best fits our work. An intelligent agent (also referred to as a software agent or agents) can be defined as a hardware or software-based computer system that is autonomous, reacts to changes in its environment, is pro-active and exhibits goal-oriented behavior and it has social ability to interact and communicate with other artificial and human agents (Wooldridge & Jennings, 1995). Agents communicate using an agent communication language such as FIPA ACL (FIPA-ACL, 2002). An agent that exhibits these characteristics is referred to as a weak agent. A strong notion of agency denotes agents that have mentalistic notions such as knowledge, beliefs and intentions. This notion is favored by the artificial intelligence community, while the weaker notion is more popular among software engineers.

A multi-agent system is a system composed of several agents, collectively capable of reaching goals that are difficult to achieve by an individual agent or a monolithic system. It is concerned with the societal view of agents, where a collection of agents work together and collaborate to solve a problem.

A Web service is a software system identified by a URI, whose public interfaces and bindings are defined and described using extensible markup language (XML). Web services can interact with each other in a manner prescribed by their definitions using XML-based messages conveyed by Internet protocols (W3C, 2004). Web services should be capable of being defined, described and discovered. It is noted that Web services do not merely provide static information, but allow one to affect some action or change in the world, for example, the sale of a product or the control of a physical device.

What makes Web services attractive is the ability to integrate the Web services developed by different organizations together to fulfil a user's requirements. Such integration is based on the common standards of Web service interfaces, regardless of the languages that have been used to implement the Web services and the platforms where the Web services are executed. Industry as well as academia have proposed standard languages for Web services specification, invocation and process description. The industrial standards include universal description, discovery, and integration (UDDI) (Bellwood et al., 2002) for service discovery, Web services description language (WSDL) (Chinnici et al., 2006) for service specification of interfaces, and simple object access protocol (SOAP) (Box et al., 2000) for service invocation. The languages proposed by academia focus on the annotation of the meaning of Web services using semantic Web technologies. The languages from academia include OWL-S, formerly DAML-S, (Martin et al., 2004), WSMO (Bruijn et al., 2005), METEOR-S (METEOR-S, 2005) and WSDL-S (Akkiraju et al., 2005).

Agents and Web Services for Modeling Virtual Enterprises

Based on the properties of VEs described earlier in this chapter, there is a strong motivation to use agents as the solution technology for modeling and realizing VEs. The nature of agents, by definition, enables decentralized control of the enterprise, which is desirable in a dynamic and flexible environment, and the behavior of the complete enterprise emerges as a result of the behaviors of the individual agents.

Several authors have proposed software agents as a means of modeling dynamic organizational forms such as VEs. The first to propose the use of agents in supply chains, (the involvement of companies in the supply chain has been referred to as resembling a set of collaborating partners, (Childe, 1998)) was (Fox, Chionglo, & Barbuceanu, 1993), reported in a survey on using agents for intelligent manufacturing systems (Shen & Norrie, 1999). An agent-based modeling approach to project-oriented organizations engaged in knowledge work is proposed in (Levitt et al., 2001). There have also been attempts at modeling enterprises using computational techniques. An example of this can be seen in (Bernus & Nemes, 1999), where they model an organization as a set of individual, autonomous, cooperative agents maintaining a set of objectives, where the behavior of the entire organization is an emergent property.

In (Petrie & Bussler, 2003), they propose the use of Web services and ideas from multi-agent

system to create "service agents" to create dynamic VEs. They argue that UDDI and WSDL are insufficient to support service discovery and composition and could draw from the ideas of academic multi-agent systems research to develop more sophisticated Web services that could support the formation of VEs. An architecture and a methodology for agent-based Web service discovery and composition using symbolic reasoning is described in (Küngas, Rao, & Matskin, 2004).

Agent-based models that focus on the formation of the VE are described in (Oliveira & Rocha, 2000) and (Rabelo, Camarinha-Matos, & Vallejos, 2000). In a Web services-oriented view, the partners of a VE will provide services to or consume services from each other within an electronic market. Such a view is discussed in (Field & Hoffner, 2002) and (Petersen, Rao, & Tveit, 2002).

MODEL OF A VIRTUAL ENTERPRISE

We consider a VE where individual entities compete to become partners of a VE. The partners of the VE are represented by software agents. The formation of the VE is supported by providing decision support to select the best team of partners for a specific VE. In order to support the rapid formation of VEs, we believe that a model that describes the complete VE in terms of its entities and the relationships among them is important. Using ideas from enterprise modeling, we have developed an agent-based model that shows the different entities that are in the VE and their relationships, see Figure 1.

A VE has a *goal* (or a set of goals) that is/are achieved by a set of *activities* that are performed by *roles* which are filled by *agents*. The agent can be represented by a human being, an organization or software. A role requires a certain set of *skills*. The agent that fills the role meets the skills requirements. Once the VE is formed, relationships can be established between the agent and the goals and activities to indicate the goal(s) of the VE the agent will attempt to fulfil and by performing which activities. Thus, an agent is assigned one or more goals and is assigned to one or more activities.

Goals and activities can be decomposed into subgoals and subactivities. One of the strengths of this model is the fact that the entities are not only described by how they relate to or depend on each other, but also by considering the internal contents of them in terms of attributes. The entities in the model are described using attributes; the relationships among the entities are represented using predicate calculus and a set of rules represent how they can be used. A detailed description of the model is available from (Petersen & Gruninger, 2000).

Although we focus on the contents of the model that are relevant for the formation of a VE, it is important to consider the complete model to be able to understand how the different entities affect one another. For example, how does the selection of a particular agent affect the goals of the VE? Such a question can only be answered if we see

the link from the agent to the goals of the VE. A complete model is also helpful in determining the kind of information that is flowing among the different entities. This in turn helps in designing the agents and the communication and collaboration among the agents.

The agents can be classified as *VE initiator* (who may also be the customer), who takes the initiative to form the VE and *VE partner* (who may also be the VE initiator), who are the people that form the VE. A VE partner evolves from someone that is interested in becoming a part of the VE to someone who is actually a part of the VE.

An agent representing the VE initiator is described by the attributes goals, availability requirements and other requirements such as the skills and cost. Since a VE is a goal-oriented entity that has a time limit and each goal is defined in terms of a deadline and a maximum amount of money, the attributes of the agent representing the VE reflect these. The VE initiator announces a VE and requests for proposals from the interested partners. The VE announcement contains the requirements, (based on the attributes of the VE initiator), that must be met by the agent. Thus, the

Figure 1. Model of VE

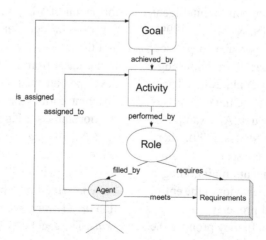

attributes of the agent must match the requirements. A detailed description of the attributes are provided in Petersen and Divitini (2002).

VIRTUAL ENTERPRISE FORMATION

This section discusses the formation of a VE from a lifecycle perspective and describes the VE formation process that we have considered.

Virtual Enterprise Lifecycle

The focus of our work is on the formation of the VE. Hence, it is perhaps interesting to consider the lifecycle of the VE and in particular, the formation phase of the VE. The formation stage of a VE within a lifecycle context is shown in Figure 2. Before a VE is formed, its concepts and goals have to be defined. The requirements from the customer sets the requirements for the VE team and in order for the VE to be able to deliver to its customer, the right team has to be formed. During the formation stage of a VE, the individual entities compete and negotiate to become the partners of the VE. An important aspect of using agents is that ideas from Electronic Commerce and electronic market places can be considered

in bringing together individual entities that want to form a VE (Rocha & Oliveira, 1999). In this respect, the agents can operate within the context of an electronic market during the formation stage of the VE. All the agents that are interested in becoming partners of a VE are at an electronic market, where the VE is announced. They can propose bids as in an auction and the agents that meet the requirements and propose the best bids are then selected. When the VE is formed, the partners that have been selected constitute the VE and work together to deliver to the customer.

The VE formation process that we consider assumes that before a VE is formed, a complete model of the VE is available, that is, its goals, the activities that must be performed to achieve the goals, the roles that perform the activities and the requirements for the roles. During the formation of a VE, a partner evolves from someone who is interested in becoming a partner to someone who is actually a partner in the VE. The partners go through the following stages (see Figure 3 for an illustration of these stages):

- **Interested partner:** One that is interested in becoming a part of the VE and submits a bid for the work

Figure 2. Formation of a VE from a lifecycle perspective

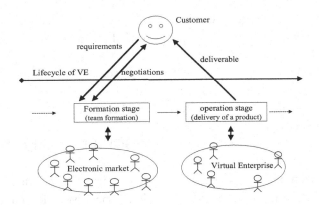

- **Potential partner:** One that is considered for the VE and a contract is negotiated
- **VE partner:** One that is selected as part of the VE team after a process of negotiation

Partner Selection

A VE and an agent are both, by definition, goal-oriented entities. Therefore, an agent that performs an activity in a VE must have its goals aligned with the goals of the VE. Thus, the first step in the selection of partners is to align their goals. Then, the agents are matched against the required skills and availability to select the potential partners. Then, using some evaluation criteria, the potential partners are ranked to identify the best individuals for the VE. This process is illustrated in Figure 3. The best set of individuals can be selected by considering attributes of agents that describe their individual qualities such as their availability, competencies and experiences.

The process illustrated in Figure 3 considers the selection of the best individuals. However, a VE is a *team of partners*. The best set of individuals is not always the best team of partners that collaborate. Thus, it is important to consider the individuals that are selected as a team of partners.

VE Team of Partners

We believe that the concept of a team is an important point in forming a VE as the partners have to collaborate and work as a team to achieve the goals of the VE. The selection of the best team can be based on several criteria and the best team may not always be the team that consists of the highest ranked potential partners. For example, a VE may have constraints such as a total budget that the VE Initiator can pay its partners. There may be other constraints such as the total risk of having the partners in the team. Thus, it is important to consider the selection of the team as a separate subprocess in the selection of the partners and consider the attributes of a team rather than the

attributes of an individual to determine the best team of partners, see Figure 4.

Agent Interaction Protocols

The VE formation process can be considered as a set of interactions between the VE Initiator and the VE Partners. This process can be considered within the context of an electronic market. The VE initiator announces a VE and requests for bids from agents that are interested in becoming partners of the VE. Agents who are interested, propose a bid where the contents of the bid correspond to the requirements expressed in the VE announcement (analogous to an Instructions to Bid document). The VE Initiator then evaluates the bid based on the evaluation criteria. The agents whose bids that do not meet the requirements are informed that their bids are rejected. The VE Initiator then negotiates with the agents whose bids meet the requirements (potential partners). Finally, a contract is awarded to the best potential partner(s).

The interactions among the agents can be shown as an agent interaction protocol, using agent UML (Bauer, Müller, & Odell, 2001), see Figure 5.

IMPLEMENTATION

We have adapted the multi-agent system, AGORA, for modeling VEs. AGORA is an architecture that supports a flexible, conceptual method for modeling cooperative work in a distributed setting (Maktskin et al., 2000; Matskin, Divitini, & Petersen, 1998) and it provides an infrastructure to implement software agents and agent-based market places.

AGORA Multi-Agent Architecture

The central concept is that of an *Agora node*, which is a cooperative node facilitating communication,

Figure 3. Selecting the Best Partners for a VE

Figure 4. Selecting the best VE team

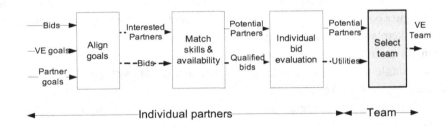

Figure 5. Agent interaction protocol for VE formation

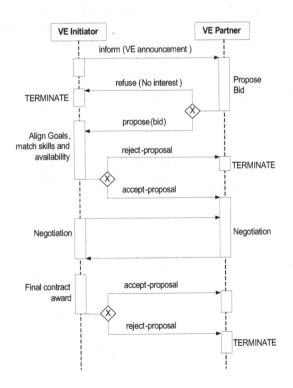

coordination and negotiation among the agents. When an Agora node is created, some agents are created by default and connected to the Agora node automatically. They are the *Agora manager* (for performing general management and match-making functions), *coordinator* (for supporting a coherent behavior among the agents in the node) and *negotiator* (for dealing with conflict resolution via negotiation).

In addition to Agora nodes and default agents, the system also has *registered agents*. The cooperating entities within a VE, that is, the partners, can be represented by agents and registered at the Agora node, see Figure 6.

In a general marketplace scenario, the registered agents can act as either buyers or sellers. The structure of a single agent, either a default agent or a registered agent is illustrated in Figure 7, (Petersen, Rao, & Matskin, 2003). An agent uses the *message proxy* and the *log system* to interact with the outside world, (e.g., the human user that it represents). It communicates with other agents using FIPA ACL, and the FIPA messages are sent and received through the message proxy.

We have used a prolog-based presentation for messages, facts and rules in the *knowledge*

base, implemented using the XProlog system (XProlog, 2002). In order to integrate the FIPA messages with the knowledge base, a *compiler* between FIPA messages and Prolog clauses is implemented.

The *planning unit* decides the agent's next action by a set of explicitly defined rules. In Agora, the plan is specified in a XML-based scripting language. Each step in the plan has an action to be performed and post-conditions. The action refers to an outgoing FIPA message or a method (function) written in Java or Prolog. Post-conditions are described as a reaction of the agent to a communicative act received from another agent.

Model of an Agent

The components of an agent's knowledge base required to support the selection process are its goals, activities and capabilities, which are described by a set of attributes. In addition, an agent has a rule base to support its decision making process and a plan to tell it what to do at any point in time. In our approach, we consider the same agent architecture for both the VE initiator

Figure 6. AGORA multi-agent architecture

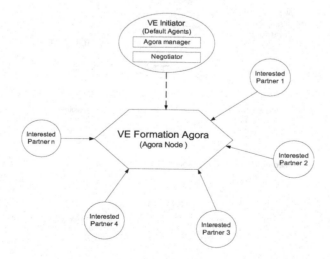

Figure 7. Structure of an agent in AGORA (© 2003 IEEE)

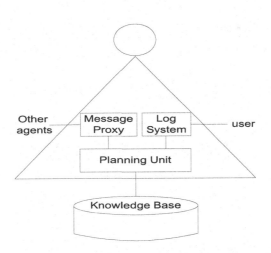

and the VE partners. This is because the VE initiator does not always play the role of a "broker" only, but can also be a partner in the VE. The information that is represented by the goals, the activities and the capabilities of the VE initiator and the VE partners are slightly different and this is summarized in Table 1 (Petersen, Rao, & Matskin, 2003). The requirements of the agents are represented as attributes of the agent (in the VE model).

AGORA for VE Formation

A structure of Agora nodes can be created to support various processes such as the VE formation process and any agent can be registered at one or more Agora nodes. The Agora nodes for VE Formation are presented in Figure 8 (Petersen, Rao, & Matskin, 2003). It contains a general Agora node (VE Formation) for the complete process and separate Agora nodes for each step in the VE formation process. Registered agents (interested partners) can be registered in more than one Agora node. Each Agora node provides the right context for the specific step in the formation process, that is, the right support and a meeting

place for all the participants. Having a separate Agora node for each step ensures information security and privacy, for example, an interested partner whose bid has been refused cannot register at the next Agora node.

Example

In this subsection, we use a simple example to illustrate the VE formation process and the selection of partners by matching agents to roles in a VE. Consider a VE formed to design and create an Intranet for a company. The main goal of the VE, "create an Intranet", can be decomposed into two subgoals, "design Intranet" and "create Intranet". The two subgoals are achieved by performing the activities, "design Intranet" and "create Intranet". The two roles that are required for this VE are an "Intranet designer" and a "Webpage developer". The VE Initiator is looking for two partners that meet the requirements for these roles. In the rest of this section, we will describe how the formation process of this VE is implemented in AGORA.

Table 1. Information represented by the agent model (© 2003 IEEE)

Entity	VE Initiator	VE Partner
Goals	Goals of the VE	Goals of the partner
Activities	Activities that need to be performed to achieve the goals of the VE.	Set of experience of the partner.
Capabilities	Requirements (skills, time, costs, etc.) for the roles of the VE.	Work that the partner is capable of doing.

Figure 8. AGORA structure for VE Formation (© 2003 IEEE)

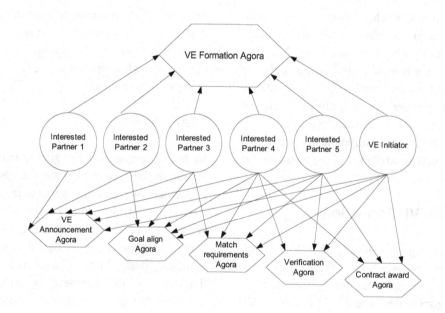

VE Announcement

The VE announcement consists of the main goal of the VE and the set of roles that need to be filled (at VE announcement Agora node). The main goal is defined by the goal, the start date and the maximum cost.

ve_announcement(
goal(create_intranet, 280206,40000),
roles([intranet_designer,
web_program_developer])).

If an agent is interested in performing any of the roles, it requests for more information on that specific role. The VE Initiator will then respond with the requirements for the requested role(s). Table 2 shows the set of requirements and the matching conditions for the role Webpage developer.

The interested partners return bids after receiving the requirements for the roles. In the bids, the Interested partners, (e.g., for the role of Webpage developer), fill their values for required attributes as shown below:

bid_skill(programmer1,
role(Webpage_developer),
attributes(skills([java,xml,html]),
experience_by_year(3),
performance_rating(7),
commitment(8)).

Matching Agent to Roles

The partner's goals are aligned with those of the VE if there is a goal in the VE's goal structure that matches that of the partner's (at the goal alignment Agora node). The matching is based on the attributes of the goal. The requirements for the roles are structured into skills, availability and cost requirements. The matching process consists of matching first the skills, then the availability and finally the costs (at the matching requirements Agora node). If the interested partner meets all the requirements for the role, the interested partner becomes a potential partner. The two best potential partners for the roles can now be selected. The best potential partners can be evaluated using Multi-Attribute Utility Theory and Multi-Attribute

Table 2. VE requirements and matching conditions

Requirements	Range & Matching Conditions
Skills	HTML, JAVA, XML
Min. no. of skills required	>=2
Experience	>=2 years
Availability	Start_date<010106, End_date=<280206, 80% of the time, Matching condition: computed no. of hours =<300
Cost per hour	<60
Performance rating	Range: 1..10, >=7
Commitment	Range: 1..10, >=8

Optimization (Keeney & Raiffa, 1976). Similarly, the best team of Potential partners can also be evaluated using the criteria for the teams and an appropriate utility function. A detailed example of selection of partners for a VE is described in (Petersen & Divitini, 2002).

The VE Initiator can now verify if the selected potential partners actually do have the experience claimed in the bids. Thus, the VE initiator may request for the potential partners' activities or experience structures (at the Verification Agora node). The VE Initiator informs the potential partners whose bids are rejected and a contract is signed with the potential partners whose bids are accepted (at the contract award Agora node).

VALIDATION USING CASE STUDIES

We have validated our approach and the agent-based model of the VE using several industrial case studies. Finding industrial case studies and relevant data from industry was a difficult task as the information that is required for the validation process is sensitive to the business. For these reasons, the companies that have provided us case studies have been kept anonymous.

Case Descriptions

An overview of the cases is provided below:

- **Company A:** This is a private consulting firm that offers all aspects of business, financial, economic and social consulting services. They maintain a database of highly qualified consultants in various fields and draws upon these resources to form the teams that work on their projects. These consultants are analogous to the partners of the VE.
- **Company B:** This is a company that operates in the oil and offshore industry, on a global scale. The particular scenario that

was analyzed was the selection of several groups of students (university level) who will work together as teams during their summer holidays on some projects. Each team, in this case can be considered as a VE.

- **Company C:** This is a company that operates on a global scale in the maritime industry. They are responsible for delivering technical analysis, life-cycle support and knowledge management applications to clients world wide.
- **Company D:** This is a company specialized in project management and selection of contractors in the construction industry. They were hired by a customer to assist them to evaluate bids in the selection of a contractor for the construction of a hospital. They specialize in the selection of the project team or the partners of the VE that will eventually be formed to deliver to the customer. The VEs that they assist to create usually comprise of several organizations and they have to take into consideration the skills of the individuals from each organization that will work in the VE.
- **Company E:** A company that specializes in bid evaluation and selection of contractors for very large scale projects in the off-shore and oil industries. They conduct an evaluation where they focus on the risk management aspects of the project, or VE.

A comparison of the cases is summarized in Table 3.

Validation Process

The case studies were used to validate the approach and the model of the VE as follows:

- **Creating an agent-based model of the case:** Modeling the case using the agent-based model for the VE; this involved identifying

Table 3. Comparison of cases

Characteristic	A	B	C	D	E
Geographical Context	Local	Local (National)	Global	Local (National)	Local (National)
Specialization of skills required for VE	Medium	Low	High	High	High
Level of detail of the VE when the VE is formed	High	High	Low	Low	Low
Duration of the VE	Medium	Short	Long	Long	Long
Consideration of team aspects	Medium	High	High	High	High
Scale of VE: Money	Medium	Small	Large	Large	Large
Complexity of VE	Medium	Low	High	High	High

the goals of the VE, the activities that need to be performed to achieve the goals of the VE, the roles to perform the activities and the requirements for the roles.

- **Comparing the attributes:** Looking at the requirements for the roles and the kinds of attributes that were considered in the case and comparing these to the attributes that have been used in the selection process; this is a comparison of the evaluation criteria.

- **Comparing the selection process:** Comparing the partner selection process that was used in the cases to the selection process that is described in this chapter

- **Identifying negotiation points:** Identifying if and when there is negotiation in the partner selection process in the case; it also involved identifying the issues that were negotiated upon.

Analysis

An overview of the analysis is provided in this section. The VE metamodel was in line with the

way the VEs were designed and implemented. It was possible to model the VEs using the goals, the activities, the roles and the requirements. However, none of the VEs in the cases were explicitly thought in terms of these modeling constructs. Therefore, it was not always possible to obtain all the relevant information to construct a detailed model of the VE. Only a high-level model of the VEs could be developed. The level of detail of the VE varied among the different cases. One observation is that as the size of the project increases, for example companies C, D and E, the level of detail of the VE at the formation stage is low, whereas for smaller projects, it was possible to define the VE in greater detail before it was formed, for example companies A and B.

The generic attributes that we had considered, which represent the partner evaluation criteria, are very simple compared to the cases. All the cases considered the collaborative capabilities of the potential partners in their set of attributes. The complexity of the attributes varied according to the complexity of the VE. For example, company B used a simple set of attributes such as the student's year of study and their work experience, based on a curriculum Vitae. Companies D and E, due to the high risk factor of the VEs that they help form, had very detailed and sophisticated evaluation criteria.

None of the selection processes in the cases considered goal alignment explicitly. They assumed that if two entities have expressed an interest in working together, then their goals must be aligned. The skills and availability matching process was not a one-step process, rather it consisted of several steps. For example, company A first checked if the skills match and considered availability only if the skills matched the requirements. A more advanced process can be considered when the potential partner is invited for an interview or some form of verification of the facts that they have presented in the bid. While our selection process was in line with the selection processes used by the cases, most of the cases had a more detailed process and the processes varied according to the project.

Negotiation among the partners varied; for example company D only negotiated after the selection of partners at the contract signing stage while company B did not negotiate at all as there were more than enough interested partners that bid. All cases considered negotiation as an ongoing process.

The results of the case studies analysis can be summarized as follows: the agent-based model of the VE and the selection process is aligned with the way industry evaluates and selects teams to perform some work. However, a greater level of detail is required to provide full-industry scale support. Thus, there is a need for flexibility in defining the attributes of the partners and the definition of the selection process.

FUTURE TRENDS

The recent trend in the development of solutions such as the one described in this chapter

is the use of semantic Web technology and Web services along with agents and multi-agent systems. Semantic Web service technology makes dynamic enterprise integration more flexible. The interested partners of a VE can be considered as service providers, so that semantic Web services can be used to describe the capabilities of the VE partners, which can be represented by software agents as service provider agents. Similarly, the VE initiator can be represented as a service requester agent. The selection process of the software agents is considered as the matchmaking of the Web services. The Web services and the requests can be specified by a variety of service description languages such as OWL-S or WSDL-S, all of which can be used for dynamic service matchmaking using the service ontologies that include descriptions of the service capabilities and needs of the service consumer. Relying on related languages and inference engines, the matchmaking of semantic Web services aims at matching the machine understandable descriptions of the service capability and the service consumer's goal. The services can be described by information such as: (1) information about the provider of the service, (2) information about the service's functionality and (3) information about nonfunctional attributes. Functional attributes include the service's inputs, outputs, preconditions and effects. Nonfunctional attributes include properties such as competencies, quality of service, price and location. The matchmaking can be precise matching, partial matching or matching based on semantic instance. Many service matchmaking algorithms have been proposed, for example Benatallah et al. (2000) and Constantinescu, Binder and Faltings (2005).

The adaptation of the AGORA multi-agent architecture for agent-based dynamic service discovery and composition, using symbolic negotiation is described in Küngas, Rao, and Matskin (2004). This work is complementary to the work presented in this chapter and is a natural enhancement for supporting the formation of VEs. Using an agent-based approach, the service providers, that is VE Partners are able to play a more proactive role in promoting their service offers. This approach also facilitates easy discovery of services and the automatic composition of services. The default agents at each Agora node provide the support that is necessary for conducting the matchmaking of services, the coordination of the work and negotiation.

The AGORA architecture described in this chapter is a multi-agent architecture inspired by electronic markets. We are currently working on enhancing the AGORA architecture to incorporate aspects of service-oriented architectures (SOA) and Web services in the future (Zhang & Niu, 2006).

Combination of the agent-based approach with semantic Web technology and Web services offers a number of advantages. It supports a means of representing the services uniformly and due to the standardization efforts around Web services, it offers a greater degree of interoperability support when using heterogeneous agents and service providers. In addition, semantic Web technology provides better semantic support in service description and discovery and the use of ontologies is facilitated.

CONCLUSION

This chapter describes an agent-based approach to support VEs and a model to describe them. The focus of our work is to support, in particular, the formation phase of the lifecycle of a VE. Software agents and Web services are used as solution technologies. Our approach is based on understanding a VE from an organizational perspective and using these ideas to provide technological support.

The formation of a VE is considered within the context of an electronic market place where several parties compete to become partners of a VE. A multi-agent architecture provides a meeting place for the software agents that represent the entities that are interested in becoming partners of the VE. The partners are represented by their goals and their competencies, availability as well as other information that is requested by the VE Initiator. Automatic matchmaking and formation of teams of partners are supported by the AGORA multi-agent architecture. Ideas for using Semantic Web technology and Web services along with agents and multi-agent systems for supporting the formation of VEs is proposed as a future direction for this work.

The work was validated using a range of industrial case studies. Case studies were selected from different industry sectors and of varying project sizes. The analysis of the case studies indicated that the agent-based approach and the model of the VE are in line with the work that is conducted in industry in selecting and forming teams of collaborative workers. However, there is a need for flexibility in representing the attributes of the agents that represent the partners and the selection process. Although there are several improvements that are required for supporting VE formation in industry, the model can be used to represent a small percentage of generic attributes and automated matchmaking, which stands to make savings in costs and resources.

REFERENCES

Akkiraju, R., et al. (2005). Web service semantics - WSDL-S technical note version 1.0. Retrieved February 12, 2007, from http://lsdis.cs.uga.edu/library/download/WSDL-S-V1.html

Bauer, B., Müller, J. P., & Odell, J. (2001). *Agent UML: A formalism for specifying multi-agent interaction.* Paper presented at the Agent-oriented Software Engineering.

Bellwood, T. et al. (2002). Universal description, discovery and integration specification (UDDI) 3.0. Retrieved February 12, 2007, from http://uddi.org/pubs/uddi-v3.00-published-20020719.htm

Benatallah, B. et al. (2005). On automating web services discovery. *VLDB Journal, 14*(1), 84-96.

Bernus, P., & Nemes, L. (1999). *Organizational design: Dynamically creating and sustaining integrated virtual enterprises.* Paper presented at the IFAC World Congress, Vol-A, London.

Box, D. et al. (2000). Simple Object Access Protocol (SOAP) 1.1. *W3C note.* Retrieved February 12, 2007, from http://www.w3.org/TR/2000/NOTE-SOAP-20000508/

Bruijn, J. et al. (2005). D2v1.2. Web service modeling ontology (WSMO) final draft. Retrieved February 12, 2007, from http://www.wsmo.org/TR/d2/v1.2/

Byrne, J. A., Brandt, R., & Port, O. (1993). The virtual corporation. *Business Week, 8*, 36-40.

Childe, S. J. (1998). The extended enterprise - A concept of co-operation. *International Journal of Production Planning and Control, 9*(3), 320-327.

Chinnici, R. et al. (2006). Web Services Description Language (WSDL) Version 2.0 Part 1: Core Language. Retrieved February 12, 2007, from http://www.w3.org/TR/wsdl20/

Constantinescu, I., Binder, W., & Faltings, B. (2005). *Flexible and efficient matchmaking and ranking in service directories.* Paper presented at the IEEE International Conference on Web Services (ICWS'05).

Davidow, W. H., & Malone, M. S. (1992). *The virtual corporation: Structuring and revitalising the corporation for 21st century.* Harper Business.

Field, S., & Hoffner, Y. (2002). In search of the right partner. In L. M. Camarinha-Matos (Ed.), *Collaborative business ecosystems and virtual enterprises* (pp. 55-62) Kluwer Academic Publishers.

FIPA-ACL (2002). FIPA agent communication language. Retrieved February 12, 2007, from http://www.fipa.org/repository/aclspecs.html

Fischer, K. et al. (1996). *Intelligent agents in virtual enterprises.* Paper presented at the First International Conference and Exhibition on Practical Applications of Intelligent Agents and Multi-agent Systems (PAAM-96), London.

Fox, M. S., Chionglo, J. F., & Barbuceanu, M. (1993). *The integrated supply chain management system.* University of Toronto, Enterprise Integration Laboratory.

Garita, C., & Afsarmanesh, H. (2001). A study of information management approaches for support infrastructures. *COVE Newsletter, 1.*

Jagdev, H. S., & Brown, J. (1998). The extended enterprise - A context for manufacturing. *International Journal of Production Planning and Control, 9*(3), 216-229.

Jain, A. K., Aparicio, M. IV, & Singh, M. P. (1999). Agents for process coherence in virtual enterprises. *Communications of the ACM, 42*(3), 62-69.

Keeney, R. & Raiffa, H. (1976). *Decisions with multiple objectives: Preferences and value tradeoffs.* John Wiley & Sons.

Küngas, P., Rao, J., & Matskin, M. (2004). *Symbolic agent negotiation for semantic web service exploitation.* Paper presented at the Fifth International Conference on Web-Age Information Management (WAIM'2004), Dalian, China.

Levitt, R. E. et al. (2001). Computational enterprise models: Towards analysis tools for designing organizations. In G. M. Olsen, T. W. Malone, & J. B. Smith (Eds.), *Coordination theory and collaboration technology* (pp. 623-649). Lawrence Erlbaum Associates.

Martin, D., et al. (2004). OWL-S: Semantic markup for web services. Retrieved February 12, 2007, from http://www.w3.org/Submission/OWL-S

Matskin, M., Divitini, M., & Petersen, S. A. (1998). *An architecture for multi-agent support in a distributed informtation technology application.* Paper presented at the Workshop on Intelligent Agents in Information and Process Management, KI'98.

Matskin, M., et al. (2000). *Agora: An infrastructure for cooperative work support in multi-agent systems.* Paper presented at the International Workshop on Infrastructure for Multi-agent Systems, Barcelona, Spain.

METEOR-S (2005). METEOR-S: Semantic web services and processes: Applying semantics in annotation, quality of service, discovery, composition, execution. Retrieved February 12, 2007, from http://lsdis.cs.uga.edu/Projects/METEOR-S/

Oliveira, E., & Rocha, A. P. (2000). Agents' advanced features for negotiation in electronic commerce and virtual organisation formation process. *European Perspectives on Agent Mediated Commerce.* Springer-Verlag.

Petersen, S. A., & Divitini, M. (2002). *Using agents to support the selection of virtual enterprise teams.* Paper presented at the Fourth International Bi-conference Workshop on Agent-oriented Information Systems (AOIS-2002) at AAMAS 2002, Bologne, Italy.

Petersen, S. A., Divitini, M., & Matskin, M. (2001). An agent-based approach to modelling virtual enterprises [Special Issue]. *International Journal of Production Planning & Control, 12*(3), 224-233.

Petersen, S. A., & Gruninger, M. (2000). *An agent-based model to support the formation of virtual enterprises.* Paper presented at the International ICSC Symposium on Mobile Agents and Multi-agents in Virtual Organisations and E-Commerce (MAMA2000), Woolongong, Australia.

Petersen, S. A., Rao, J., & Matskin, M. (2003). *Virtual enterprise formation with agents - An approach to implementation.* Paper presented at the IEE/WIC International Conference on Intelligent Agent Technology (IAT2003), Halifax, Canada.

Petersen, S. A., Rao, J., & Tveit, A. (2002). *Virtual enterprises: Challenges in selecting and integrating computational and human resources.* Paper presented at the Agentcities: Challenges in Open Agent Environments, Bologne, Italy.

Petrie, C., & Bussler, C. (2003, July/August). Service agents and virtual enterprises: A Survey. *IEEE Internet Computing.*

Rabelo, R. J., Camarinha-Matos, L. M., & Vallejos, R. V. (2000). Agent-based brokerage for virtual enterprise creation in the moulds industry. In L. M. Camarinha-Matos, H. Afsarmanesh, & R. J. Rabelo (Eds.), *E-business and virtual enterprises - Managing business-to-business cooperation* (pp. 281-290). Kluwer Academic Publishers.

Rocha, A. P., & Oliveira, E. (1999). Electronic commerce: A technological perspective. *The Future of the Internet.*

Shen, W., & Norrie, D. H. (1999). Agent-based systems for intelligent manufacturing: A state-of-the-art survey. *Knowledge and Information Systems, 1*(2), 129-156.

Vernadat, F. B. (1996). *Enterprise modeling and integration: Principles and applications.* Chapman and Hall.

VOSTER (2003). Virtual organizations cluster. Retrieved February 12, 2007, from http://cic.vtt.fi/projects/voster/public.html

W3C (2004). Web services architecture requirements. Retrieved February 12, 2007, from http://www.w3.org/TR/wsa-reqs

Wooldridge, M. J., & Jennings, N. R. (1995). Intelligent agents: Theory and practice. *Knowledge Engineering Review, 10*(2), 115-152.

XProlog (2002). XProlog. Retrieved February 12, 2007, from http://www.iro.umontreal.ca/~vaucher/XProlog/

Zhang, B., & Niu, X. (2006). *Implementation of agora system*. Unpublished master's thesis, Royal Institute of Technology, Department of Microelectronics and Information Technology, Stockholm.

Section III
Virtual Enterprise Integration

Chapter IV
Adaptive Service Choreography Support in Virtual Enterprises

Adomas Svirskas
Institute Eurécom, France

Bob Roberts
Kingston University, UK

Ioannis Ignatiadis
Kingston University, UK

ABSTRACT

Service oriented architecture (SOA) approach in general and the Web services technology in particular enable creation of business applications from independently developed, deployed and owned components called services. A service captures a distinct business function offering some value independently of its usage context. However, it is not enough to have the business functionality of the partners packaged as (Web) services; there is also a need for business-aligned order of interaction between these services also known as business protocols, which can also be reused. The contribution of the chapter is two-fold: it explores reusability of the applicable business protocols in different business scenarios and it also suggests possible ways to adapt the implementations of the partners' services (end-points) to the changes in the business protocols.

INTRODUCTION

The Web services, as the main realization of the SOA (Hao, 2003) paradigm, imply a significant integration potential at both application and business process levels. These services, being homogeneous in terms of their functional description and advertising mechanisms such as WSDL, UDDI (WSDL, 2006; UDDI, 2006) and the protocols needed to use them (SOAP/HTTP), do not suffer from the usual middleware-level interoperability problems. On the other hand, the services are typically realized as wrappers around the existing or planned business functionality (components, legacy systems, etc.), therefore both types of requirements: heterogeneous infrastructure support and business-aligned discreet functionality are addressed.

A Web service typically exposes a number of operations for clients to invoke and a certain order (agreed by all the involved parties) must be observed to achieve their goals. As an example, the purchasing scenario can be taken, where the customer will need firstly to request a quote, then order the goods, and finally make a payment. In order for the goods to be delivered to the customer, the agreed shipper needs to be informed and provided with the shipment details such as addresses, delivery terms and so forth. In addition, some other players can be brought into the picture, such as financial and/or trade-regulating institutions and so forth.

Such interactions between Web services and their clients are called conversations (Casati, 2004). These conversations need to be governed by the business rules, specifying which conversations are valid and what kinds of data at what point are properly understood by the services. This set of rules is specified as part of the business protocol supported by the service (where the word "business" is used to differentiate it from a communication protocol) (Alonso, Casati, Kuno et al., 2004). Business protocols are examples of why a simple interface description is not enough in Web services. In fact, to completely describe a service, it is necessary to specify not only its interface but also the business protocols that the service supports.

The business protocols, however, are subject to frequent changes and their capability to adapt is crucial for success of participating businesses, which, in turn, need to respond fast to the protocols' changes. In this chapter we present an approach of adaptive business protocol support through dynamic processing of Web services choreography at the partners' end-points and flexible mapping of choreographed message exchanges to the local processes and components.

The rest of this chapter is structured as follows: Section 2 provides some background; Section 3 outlines adaptivity and choreography support requirements; Section 4 describes the main concepts of our approach, followed by Section 5, which concludes the chapter.

THE BACKGROUND

The area of business process modelling, re-engineering and management has been in the focus of attention of IT research and industry for several decades. However in the era of the Internet, SOA and Web services this area is once again getting a lot of attention and in this section we give a brief overview of the latest major efforts in this field.

In the specification of the business protocols there are two aspects that need particular consideration. On the one hand, there is a need to capture the commonality of business rules and the interaction scenarios together with the semantics of business data to be used in the conversations. On the other hand, these protocols need to be described in some declarative machine-readable form for all the prospective collaboration partners to agree upon collectively and enact individually at run-time. Traditionally, each industry sector, for example paper, forest and pulp, and separate "ecosystems" (conglomerates of companies, forming themselves around big vendors) within the individual sectors have their B2B collaboration rules. In order to facilitate the reuse of this knowledge and increase the business-level interoperability, a number of organizations are trying to develop standardized libraries of business collaboration definitions. An example of such an organization is the Open Applications Group (OAGIS, 2006), a nonprofit consortium of enterprise application software developers, formed in February 1995 to create common standards for the integration of enterprise business applications. Member companies are building specifications to standardize integration between enterprise business applications.

There were always a variety of opinions how to model the interactions between the business partners that is, should they be interacting like peers or should some master-slave scheme be put in place. As each of the two approaches has their merits and applicability areas it is important to realize the differences between the two, the purpose of each and, in turn, to apply the right modeling and enactment techniques.

For the first of the two mentioned approaches—peer to peer—it is important to describe the sequence and the format of message exchange between the collaboration participants. These descriptions are known as choreographies. Ross-Talbot (2005) defines choreography as a description of the peer-to-peer externally observable interactions that exist between services. The interactions are described from a global or neutral point of view and not from any one services perspective. Choreography can be used to generate the necessary behavioral contract for each of the peers; further nonobservable logic (code) may be required in order to manifest the full set of service implementations (Vinoski, 2001).

Choreography should not be confused with orchestration, which specifies the behavior of a participant in a choreography by defining a set of "active" rules that are executed to infer what to do next; once the rule is computed, the orchestration runtime executes the corresponding activity(ies). Orchestration assumes existence of an entity, which is the central point of control and governs overall workflow of activities, effectively composing a new service from existing services. Therefore, orchestration corresponds to the master-slave model of interaction.

It is important to emphasize this distinction because in many cases there is certain confusion around the two concepts. For example, IBM Web-Sphere Business Integration products (Kloppman et al., 2005) use the term choreography to refer to the executable scripts coordinating separate Web services. They (Kloppman et al., 2005) also implement a choreography engine, which contradicts the view of many others who believe that declarative choreography, as explained before, is meant to be enacted by peers without an intermediary, at runtime. The choreography description can be used to verify programmatically that all the separate cases (success, failure) of a business scenario are consistent with each other. It is also possible to generate a public interface (Mendling & Hafner, 2005), for example BPEL (2004) or WSDL, Java (Havey, 2006; Pi4SOA, 2006) that can be used to tie in the services of the end-points to support the choreography.

Vinoski (2001) argues that Web services choreographies must take business processes into account. Trivial Web services solve only trivial issues; nontrivial Web services must play a part in business processes. Business-to-business integration (B2Bi) requires standardized choreographies, that is definitions of the "conversations" between cooperating applications that allow them to work together correctly (Vinoski, 2001). Simply put, choreography is a model of the sequence of operations, states and conditions that control the interactions involved in the participating services (WSArch, 2004). The interaction prescribed by a choreography results in the completion of some useful function. Examples include the placement of an order, information about its delivery and eventual payment, or putting the system into a well-defined error state. Gortmaker, Janssen and Wagenaar (2004) have presented an extensive overview of choreography definitions along with a thorough discussion of choreography and orchestration. In this chapter we concentrate on choreographed, that is, peer-to-peer view of services interaction.

Currently there are two major ongoing (coordinated) efforts in choreography modelling and description standardization. One of them is the OASIS ebXML business process (ebBP) Technical Committee (TC) working on ebBP Specification Version 2.0.1 (ebBP, 2006), another the W3C WS Choreography working group, finalising the specification of Web services choreography description language (WS-CDL), (WS-CDL, 2005). Our work is mostly related to the WS-CDL effort due to better support of the Web services technology; however we base some of our ideas on the ebBP work as well.

BUSINESS PROTOCOL SUPPORT ISSUES

There are a number of requirements to be taken into account and satisfied in order to make the idea of commonly agreed business protocol specification and their subsequent enactment viable, let alone efficient, robust, scalable and secure. These requirements arise both from the business and technology domains and represent quite a wide spectrum of issues ranging from the field of activity of a business analyst to that of a software developer involved in business application coding.

Adaptivity in B2B Collaborations

Our chapter aims to contribute to the aspect of adaptivity of business protocol support by collaborating partners. This aspect is a part of a broader issue of adaptivity in the business collaboration domain. Adaptation, which is defined as "*modification of an organism or its parts that makes it more fit for existence under the conditions of its environment*" (Merriam-Webster, 2006), and the speed of it are crucial factors which determine the success and longevity of any business subject or formation in a constantly changing business environment. In the context of B2B collaborations adaptivity has several flavours: adaptivity of the business models to different business requirements and environments (Hofreiter & Huemer, 2005), adaptivity of business protocols in response to business models' changes, adaptivity of the partners' end-point services to the changes in the business protocols descriptions. In addition, the business protocols should be adaptive to the changes of the partners enacting the roles defined in the protocols (both choreography and orchestration should support this). These requirements are contradictory in many cases and cannot be efficiently addressed in isolation: for example, optimization of the work of a business analyst does not necessarily result in scalable implementations

of end-point services and/or their faster time to market. Thus, a holistic approach is needed to business and collaboration modeling, enactment and process management in order to increase overall B2B collaboration adaptivity. Figure 1 depicts the circular dependencies between the main adaptivity dimensions and emphasizes the need for balance between the different views.

This approach puts quite high requirements on the supporting IT infrastructure: not only the business modeling, choreography support, service development and deployment tools and established practices are needed, but also a coherent unifying framework, preferably based on open standards, should be established. Once the choreography definition is created, it needs to be deployed somewhere (SOA suggests use of a registry) and advertised for reuse. It needs to be distributed to (or perhaps, depending on the overall interaction model, discovered by) the appropriate collaboration participants (dynamically chosen to play certain applicable roles) and accepted by each of them as a contract for subsequent interactions. The choreography script is then enacted by the participants' end-point services and this process should be monitored and managed by user and administrative tools. In addition to the basic requirements mentioned above, there are requirements for security and trust (Arenas, Djordjevic, Dimitrakos et al., 2005; Jøsang, Keser, & Dimitrakos, 2005), business-level contract support, adequate levels of quality of service (QoS) and quality of business (QoBiz) by specifying, negotiating, monitoring and enforcement of service level agreements (SLA) (Morsel, 2001). These and some other requirements are defining characteristics for B2B solutions and virtual organizations to be accepted by the corporate world (Svirskas, Wilson, Arenas et al., 2005).

It is therefore clear, that adaptivity in the business protocol support area is a complex issue and depends on many, frequently conflicting, factors. Cherinka, Miller, and Smith (2005) characterize complex adaptive systems as "*dynamically as-*

Figure 1. Relationships between different adaptivity views

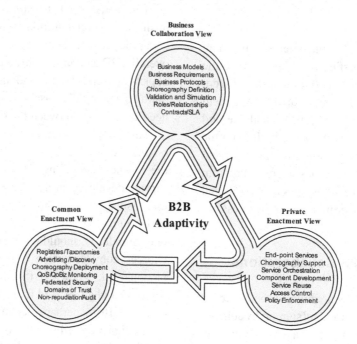

sembled systems characterized by multiple competing stakeholders, fluid requirements, emergent behaviour, and susceptibility to external pressures that can cause change across the entire system". This statement was used to reflect the nature of net-centric operations of the US Department of Defence; however it is applicable to the area of dynamic B2B virtual organizations, which also must accommodate unpredictable external factors that demand rapid response and flexibility to change (Cherinka et al., 2005).

Choreography Requirements

With regard to the service choreography, there were requirements outlined in the Web services choreography requirements document (WS-CHOR, 2004) at the beginning of the work of the W3C Choreography working group. For example, choreography must be independent of implementation technology, be able to describe multiparty

interaction, it must also enable changes to bindings at run time to allow dynamic participation, enable the generation of implementation code and test cases as well as enable the specification of QoS properties and be independent of business semantics (WS-CHOR, 2004).

The result of this Choreography working group effort is WS-CDL language (WS-CDL, 2005), which attempts to address the stated requirements and is the means to define a technical multiparty contract, mentioned above. The same choreography definition (potentially involving any number of parties or processes) needs to be usable by different parties operating in different contexts (industry, locale, etc.) with different software (e.g., application software) (WS-CDL 2005).

The considerations stated above correlate with the adaptivity aspects and support of commonly agreed business protocols helps to raise the overall adaptivity level by promoting reuse of these protocols. However, compliance of the participating services to a common contract might result in the choreography enactment being hard coded into the implementations of the services and/or their composition mechanisms. This approach poses a two-fold problem: it reduces reusability of the services and also makes it difficult to change choreography description without a need for massive programmatic changes at the participating end-points.

Goland discusses these and other issues from a developer's point of view in his contribution to WS choreography requirements (Goland, 2003). He presents a set of use cases, which reveal potential problems of a choreography lifecycle starting from the first attempts to describe choreographies governing interactions between the systems down to the issues of sharing the source code between the participants. Goland also explains the need for generating role-specific code skeletons from the choreography description in order to facilitate faster and more convenient implementation of individual functionality (Goland, 2003). While these skeletons provide a good start for developers to implement choreography compliant end-point implementations, generating a set of skeletons for each of the participants does not solve the problem, which emerges as soon as the choreography descriptions needs to be changed, of how to propagate the changes in the choreography description to the end-points with minimum efforts. Goland advocates usage of a subset of the choreography description language in order for automatic change propagation to be easier (Goland 2003).

An interesting idea expressed in (Goland, 2003) is to deploy a message filter within the end-point implementation. The filter could operate based on the choreography description and the role, which the filtered end-point is supposed to implement. The filter is able to perform both business collaboration message exchanges and monitoring of them for compliance to SLAs, access control and so forth. Our solution, presented in the following section uses similar conceptual ideas.

SUGGESTED APPROACH

As we see from the previous discussion, changes in business protocol and choreography description may be quite costly for the end-points to support, therefore some intelligence is needed to allow smooth and fast propagation of the protocol changes. In this chapter we propose to introduce an application-level gateway between the public business protocol (choreography) and the end-point composite services. This gateway is a part of the implementations of the collaboration participants' end-points. The functions of the gateway range from: virtualization of the business services of the end-point to choreography support via role-based decomposition of it, to mapping of the incoming messages to the appropriate processing entities within the end-point.

In order to organize the structure and the operation of the gateway component in a scalable and efficient manner, it is advisable to follow well-established patterns for such applications. Schmidt (2000) has proposed usage of several patterns (reactor, component configurator, acceptor-connector and other) in application-level gateways. Other patterns, such as chain of responsibility, also apply here.

Inside the gateway there is a set of software components called handlers, which perform distinct tasks, for example, to represent the logic of harmonising public choreographed processes with private functionality of end-point services (as shown in Figure 2). There are two kinds of handlers–application-specific and application-independent (Schmidt, 2000). The latter are reusable across the range of different applications, while the former depend on a particular system. Furthermore, the application-specific handlers are divided into supplier handlers and consumer handlers. Supplier handlers are triggered by the Reactor upon receiving an incoming message, and their task is to find an appropriate consumer handler for the message to be processed. Locating of an appropriate consumer handler may be message content and choreography status based.

Configured with pluggable handlers, choreography support service mediates two-way message exchange between the "outside world" and the local processing entities. Based on the available handlers, various request types and formats can be routed, translated and fulfilled by the business services. Choreography support service can relatively easily be reconfigured, adapted and extended as new processing entities need to be supported. In addition, dynamic selection of processing entities to play the prescribed roles,

policy enforcement, trust and security support and other nonfunctional tasks can be performed by the handlers. The handlers can be implemented as a chain of message filters put in front of processing entities' deployments. Handlers take a choreography definition, the role which processing entity is supposed to play, and map the choreography messages to local operations at run-time.

We call these handlers *business service handlers*, drawing a parallel with the naming used in ebXML framework (ebBP, 2006). The original

Figure 2. Choreography support gateway structure

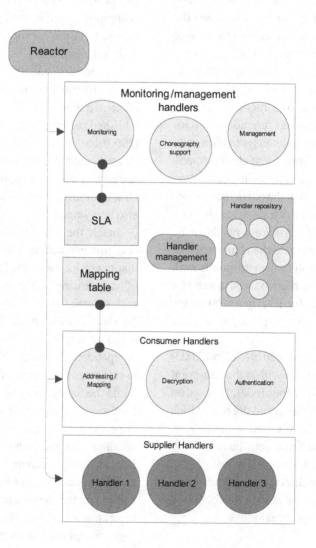

name for these components in ebXML framework was business service interface (BSI), which can be described as a piece of software that handles incoming and outgoing messages at either end of the transport. The ebXML concept of a business transaction and the semantics behind it are central to predictable, enforceable e-business. It is expected that any business service interface (BSI) will be capable of managing a transaction according to these semantics. Dubray (2003) explains the purpose of ebXML BSI in his overview of ebXML:

The business service interface (BSI) should enforce the business collaboration protocol (ebXML BPSS). At any point in time, the BSI is able to determine if a message makes sense from a business perspective (is format correct? did it come on time? in the right sequence? ...). The BSI may be directly communicating with an application, but it is certainly wise to use a broker that will dispatch ebXML requests and responses to and from the business applications.

The ebBP technical specification does not, however, specify how the BSI is implemented. For example, the BSI may be enabled through a BSI-aware business application or through behavior implemented as a part of a message service interface component. The business application may receive business signals that are sent (realized) by the message service handler (ebBP, 2006). Similarly, WS-CDL (WS-CDL, 2005) does not specify how collaborating parties implement/map their services to comply with the common contract. We think that it useful to turn to the ebBP TC work when architecting choreographed Web services solutions, as the ebBP Version 2.0 specification takes Web services into account and explicitly relies on choreographed collaborations (no relation to WS-CDL is defined yet, however, the ebBP TC is working on ebBP and WS-CDL layering).

CONCLUSION

In this chapter we concentrated on the issue of adaptivity of business protocols between the B2B participants. While business protocols are application specific, much of the software required to support such protocols can be implemented as generic infrastructure components. For example, the infrastructure can maintain the state of the conversation between a client and a service, associate messages to the appropriate conversation, or verify that a message exchange occurs in accordance to the rules defined by the protocols (for example WS-CDL). We, therefore have introduced an approach to the issue of choreography support in heterogeneous peer-to-peer business interactions. We base our concepts on the assumption that service choreographies can be mapped to end-point operations using either rich service universal descriptions or end-point specific operation mappings. In both cases it is possible to derive programmatically the configuration artefacts, which can be used to configure the application-level gateway and the business service handlers dynamically at runtime. This possibility is attractive from many points of view, the most important perhaps being clean separation of business services interfaces and business services implementation.

REFERENCES

Alonso, G., Casati, F., Kuno, H. et al. (2004). *Web services concepts, architectures and applications.* Springer-Verlag.

Arenas, A., Djordjevic, I., Dimitrakos, T. et al. (2005).Toward Web services profiles for trust and security in virtual organizations. In *Proceedings of the 6th IFIP Working Conference on Virtual Enterprises*, Valencia, Spain.

Casati, F. (2004). *Web services conversations: Why do they matter and what they mean to you.* Presentation, HP Labs.

Cherinka, R., Miller, R., & Smith, C. (2005). *Beyond Web services: Towards on-demand complex adaptive environments.* MITRE Technical paper.

Dubray, J. J. (2003). ebXML. Retrieved February 12, 2007, from http://www.ebpml.org/ebxml.htm

ebBP (2006). ebXML business process specification schema technical specification (Version 2.0.1) *Public Review Final Draft r03.* OASIS.

Goland Y. Y. (2003). A proposal for W3C Choreography Working Group Use Cases & Requirements. W3C Choreography Working Group.

Gortmaker, J., Janssen, M., & Wagenaar, R. (2004). *SOBI business architectures and process orchestration: Technical overview* (Tech. Report). The Netherlands: Telematica Instituut Enschede.

Hao, H. (2003). *What is service-oriented architecture?* Retrieved Feb. 13, 2007, from http://webservices.xml.com/lpt/a/ws/2003/09/30/soa.html

Havey, M. (2006, January). Modeling Web services choreography with new eclipse tool. *SYS-CON SOA Web services Journal,* 44-48.

Hofreiter, B., & Huemer, C. (2005). Registering a business collaboration model in multiple business environments. In *Proceedings of the OTM Workshop on Modeling Inter-Organizational Systems (MIOS 2005),* Larnaca, Cyprus.

Jøsang, A., Keser, C., & Dimitrakos, T. (2005). Can we manage trust? In *Proceedings of the Third International Conference on Trust Management (iTrust),* Rocquencourt, France.

Kloppman, M., et al. (2005). SOA programming model for implementing Web services, Part 3: Process choreography and business state machines. *IBM developer Works.*

Mendling, J., & Hafner, M. (2005). From interorganizational workflows to process execution:

Generating BPEL from WS-CDL. In *Proceedings of OTM 2005 Workshops. Lecture Notes in Computer Science 3762,* Agia Napa, Cyprus.

Morsel, A. (2001). *Metrics for the Internet age: Quality of experience and quality of business.* Hewlett-Packard Labs Technical Report HPL-2001-179.

Merriam-Webster Online Dictionary (2006). Retrieved February 13, 2007, from http://www.m-w.com

OAGIS (2006). Open Applications Group

Pi4SOA (2006). The official Pi4SOA project site. Retrieved February 13, 2007, from http://sourceforge.net/projects/pi4soa

Ross-Talbot, S. (2005). Orchestration and choreography: Standards, tools and technologies for distributed workflows. In *Proceedings of the NETTAB Workshop - Workflows Management: New Abilities for the Biological Information Overflow,* Naples, Italy.

Schmidt, D. C. (2000). Applying a pattern language to develop application-level gateways. In L. Rising (Ed.), *Design patterns in communications.* Cambridge University Press.

Svirskas, A., Wilson, M., Arenas, A., et al. (2005). Aspects of trusted and secure business oriented VO management in service oriented architectures. In *Workshop Proceedings of Seventh IEEE International Conference on E-Commerce Technology, IEEE Computer Society,* Munich, Germany.

UDDI (2006). UDDI Version 3.0.2, An OASIS Standard,

Vinoski, S. (2001). *The Truth about Web services. Web services and Component Technologies.*

WSArch (2004). Web services Architecture. *W3C Working Group Note.*

WS-BPEL (2004). Web services Business Process Execution Language. OASIS.

WS-CDL (2005). Web services Choreography Description Language Version 1.0. W3C Candidate Recommendation.

WS-CHOR (2004). Web services Choreography Requirements. *W3C Working Draft*.

WSDL (2006). Web services Description Language (WSDL) Version 2.0.

Chapter V
Technologies to Support the Market of Resources as an Infrastructure for Agile/Virtual Enterprise Integration

Maria Manuela Cunha
Polytechnic Institute of Cávado and Ave, Portugal

Goran D. Putnik
University of Minho, Portugal

Joaquim Pereira da Silva
Polytechnic Institute of Cávado and Ave, Portugal

José Paulo Oliveira Santos
University of Aveiro, Portugal

ABSTRACT

The agile/virtual enterprise (A/V E) model is considered a highly dynamic version of the virtual enterprise (VE) model, and its implementation presents several requirements in order to keep the VE partnership aligned with the market, that is, with business. Such requirements include (1) the reduction of reconfiguration costs and effort, and (2) the capability to preserve the firms' private knowledge on products or processes. These must be assured by a specific environment, or, in other words, by organizational infrastructures as a meta-organizational structure for VE design (or integration) and operation, such as the Market of Resources—an environment developed by the authors to cope with the highlighted requirements, and assuring a better performance than the traditional environments such as the Internet search engines or the electronic marketplaces. The chapter describes the functionalities of the Market of Resources and explains how does it supports A/V E integration, and addresses some technologies that could support

A/V E integration within the Market of Resources, namely XML/ebXML and Webservices. The chapter proposes an architecture to support the operation of the Market of Resources, representing a fusion of the peer-to-peer (P2P) architecture with the client-server architecture, as a variant of P2P architecture. Also, a laboratory implementation of the web services for manufacturing is presented too.

INTRODUCTION

Most definitions of virtual enterprise (VE) incorporate the idea of extended and collaborative outsourcing to suppliers and subcontractors, in order to achieve a competitive response to market demands (Webster, Sugden, & Tayles, 2004). As suggested by several authors (Browne & Zhang, 1999; Byrne, 1993; Camarinha-Matos & Afsarmanesh, 1999; Cunha, Putnik, & Ávila, 2000; Davidow & Malone, 1992; Preiss, Goldman & Nagel, 1996), a VE consists of a network of independent enterprises (resource providers) with reconfiguration capability in useful time (or, in other words: in real-time), permanently aligned with the market requirements, created to take profit from a specific market opportunity, and where each participant contributes with its best practices and core competencies to the success and competitiveness of the structure as a whole. Even during the operation phase of the VE, the configuration can change, to assure business alignment with the market demands, traduced by the identification of reconfiguration opportunities and a continuous readjustment or reconfiguration of the VE network, to meet unexpected situations or to keep permanent competitiveness and maximum performance (Cunha & Putnik, 2002, 2005a, 2005b).

A particular model characterized by a high reconfiguration dynamics capability is the agile/virtual enterprise (A/V E) model (Cunha & Putnik, 2005b; Cunha & Putnik, 2006a, 2006b; Putnik, 2001; Putnik, Cunha, Sousa, & Ávila, 2005).

The implementation of the VE model should assure the required reconfiguration dynamics, which, as we will see in the chapter, is dependent on (1) the reduction of reconfiguration ("transaction") costs and effort, that is, requires a balancing between reconfiguration dynamics and reconfiguration time and costs and (2) the capability to preserve the firms' private knowledge on products or processes.

The formation, integration and operation of A/V E relies on the existence of an adequate platform of information and communication technologies. The environment for creation, integration, operation, reconfiguration and dissolution can be implemented under the format of a Market of Resources, an entity conceived to cover the whole A/V E life cycle (Cunha & Putnik, 2005d; Cunha, Putnik, & Ávila, 2004; Cunha, Putnik, Gunasekaran, & Ávila, 2005). The market offers several business models that already provide a reasonable part of the characteristics of the A/V E model and of the Market of Resources. The electronic marketplaces implement several functionalities identified in the Market of Resources, and the emergent technologies that tend to be consolidated in the implementation of electronic marketplaces can be fundamental also in the implementation of the Market of Resources.

In the first part of the chapter we discuss the VE reconfiguration dynamics requirements and present the Market of Resources as the indispensable environment for enabling VE reconfiguration dynamics, that is, as a tool for managing, controlling and enabling networking and dynamics in VE integration, and the related supporting IT platform architecture.

Based on the organization of the Market of Resources, that is, in its general principles, processes, procedures and operation rules, as well as on the current state-of-the-art of electronic marketplaces, an information technologies (IT) architecture to support the Market of Resources was developed. This architecture defines the integration platform for the operation of the Market of Resources in all the phases of the A/VE life cycle. One of the most important elements of the proposed IT architecture is the *middleware* level supporting *Web services*. The supporting IT and the related architecture are presented in the second and third part of the chapter.

In the second part, the chapter addresses some technologies that could support A/V E integration based on the Market of Resources, namely XML/ebXML and *Webservices*, in the integration and automation of processes and services, that is, in the automatic integration of interenterprise business processes and coordination of business transactions.

In the third part, it is proposed a hybrid peer-to-peer (P2P) architecture model to support the Market of Resources, that results of the fusion of the peer-to-peer (P2P) architecture with the client-server architecture, where the characteristics of the first are remarked as a variant of the P2P architecture.

REQUIREMENTS FOR VIRTUAL ENTERPRISE INTEGRATION

A few important trends have been identified in the strongly competitive business environment, which according to several experts will lead to dramatic changes in present and future productivity and approaches. Altogether, the combination of the shorter life span of new products, increasing product diversity over time, rapid technological developments, increased technological complexity, market globalization, frequent changes in demand, uncertainty, strong competition, are the main trends of the actual worldwide economic context.

For the last years, global competition has strengthened the significance of a company's ability to introduce new products, while responding to increasingly dynamic markets with customers rapidly changing needs, and thus claiming for shortening the time required to design, develop and manufacture, as well as for cost reduction and quality improvement. In the past a product could exist without great changes (adaptations, redesigns). Faced with the challenges of today, a product suffers several redesigns in order to be competitive, that is, aligned with the market demands, besides the shorter duration of a product.

These trends requires enterprises the capability to incorporate in their products or processes the best resources available in the market, and to dynamically adjust its interorganizational structure to keep its maximum alignment with the business opportunity.

But the changing business environment requires also the permanent adaptation of the partner organizations (VE), that is, alignment with business opportunities. By alignment, in this context, we mean the actions to be undertaken to gain synergy between business, that is, between a market opportunity, and the delivery of the required product, with the required specifications, at the required time, with the lowest cost and with the best possible return (Cunha & Putnik, 2005a).

Reconfigurability, that is, the ability of fast change of the VE organization (structure) face to the unpredictable changes in the environment (market), is a requirement of the VE to keep the partnership aligned with business requirements and is a consequence of product life cycle dynamics, that is, business and market dynamics. This requirement implies the ability of:

1.   Flexible and almost instantaneous access to the optimal *resources* to integrate in the enterprise

2. Design, negotiation, business management and manufacturing management functions independently from the physical barrier of space
3. Minimization of the reconfiguration or integration time

A VE is defined as a reconfigurable network of independent enterprise, that are partners of the VE, to assure permanent business alignment, in transition between states or instantiations (VE network, or partnership, configurations) along time, as represented symbolically in Figure 1. VE dynamics considers a succession of network's states (physical configurations of the VE) along the time, that is, the network reconfiguration dynamics. Dynamics means precisely the intensity of change the VE is subject of.

MARKET OF RESOURCES: AN ENVIRONMENT FOR VIRTUAL ENTERPRISE INTEGRATION

Value chains have been supported by a wide variety of technologies to communicate, but the pace of competition requires more intelligent and effective information and communication systems and technologies. Literature suggests that "traditional" Internet-based tools (such as WWW search engines, directories, e-mail, electronic marketplaces, etc.), can support some activities of VE integration, helping from procurement processes to the search of partners for a partnership, including electronic automated negotiation, electronic contracting and market brokerage (Cunha & Putnik, 2003a; Dai & Kauffman, 2001; Dogac, 1998; Hands, Bessonov, Blinov, Patel, & Smith, 2000; O'Sullivan, 1998; Wang, 2001).

Khalil and Wang (2002) have proposed ways for information technology to enable the VE model, by providing:

1. Web-based information systems, supporting B2B and B2C applications
2. Sophisticated customer databases, supporting data mining, enhancing business intelligence and decision support
3. Support for organizational learning
4. Groupware supported coordination and decision-making

Figure 1. Networking dynamics considers a succession of network's states along the time (Cunha & Putnik, 2005b)

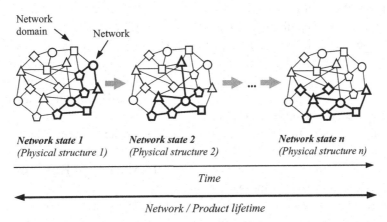

Several authors (Carlsson, 2002; Martin, 1999) refer that the new VE paradigm requires intelligent support for transactions, new effective methods for finding partners, intelligent support to virtual teams, knowledge management support systems, reliable decision support in VE/network design/configuring, effective tools for information filtering and knowledge acquisition, support in the identification of the best alternatives to keep the network aligned with the market, that is, competitive.

Several supporting organizational infrastructures[1] and supporting applications must exist before we can take advantage of the VE organizational model, such as: electronic markets of resources providers, legal platforms, brokerage services, efficient and reliable global and intelligent information systems, electronic contractualisation and electronic negotiation systems and decision support systems and tools.

The Market of resources, is a solution proposed by the authors, to fully support VE implementation, operation and management, which is in details documented in Cunha and Putnik (2005c, 2005d), Cunha and Putnik (2006a, 2006b), Cunha et al. (2000), and Cunha, Putnik, and Gunasekaran (2003).

Virtual Enterprise Integration Using the Market of Resources

The section explains the main activities involved in the VE creation or VE reconfiguration using the Market of Resources. The activities to perform in order to create or reconfigure a VE are the following:

- **VE request:** Request involves the negotiation with the Market of Resources, broker allocation and VE Design. The VE design complexity is function of product complexity and requires time to answer (by the market). There is an amount of resources needed to completely define the VE (creation or recon-

figuration) Project. These resources are broker time, knowledge and effort (human and computational). This VE project consists on a number of instructions and specifications that will drive the search, negotiation and integration, and is associated with a degree of complexity. VE Design is an activity to be undertaken by the client and after validated by the Market of Resources (broker), or in alternative, undertaken interactively by the client (the owner of the VE) and the broker, depending of the request complexity, or of the client ability / knowledge to define the VE project.

- **Resources search, selection and negotiation:** Search, negotiation and selection consists of several steps: the identification of potential resources, separation of eligible resources, negotiation within these to the identification of candidate resources, and finally the selection among these and find the best combination for integration. The identification of the potential resources and, within this set, the separation of the eligible ones is made automatically by the market from its knowledge base, and without intervention of the client (VE owner). In the market, the negotiation can be done using different approaches (automated, reverse auction and direct negotiation). The final selection is a computer-aided activity, controlled by the broker, with an eventual intervention of the VE owner, if necessary.

- **VE integration:** In this activity we will consider only the contractualization aspect. The Market of Resources assures an automated contractualization.

These activities are systematized in Table 1.

The Market of Resources Structure

The Market of Resources is an institutionalized organizational framework and service assur-

Table 1. Description of VE creation/reconfiguration activities

Activity	Activity Description
A/VE Request	
- *Request negotiation*	- Registration of the A/VE owner, specification of the request, broker allocation and contractualization with the Market.
- *A/VE design*	- Computer-aided A/VE design, with specification of the resources requirements and of negotiation parameters; - The selected broker will validate the A/VE Design, or will support the Design, in complex products or when complex negotiation methods are required.
Resources Search and Selection	
- *Eligible resources Identification*	- Identification of the subset of the Market of Resources knowledge base where it is intended to perform the search (Focused domain); - Focused domain filtering – automatically, from the requirements of the VE Design to identify Eligible Resources (eligibility is automatically driven from the catalogues / resources database)
- *Negotiation*	- Computer aided (more or less automated) negotiation with the eligible resources providers, to identify the candidate resources for integration; we distinguish between automatic search, inverse auction and direct negotiation.
- *Selection*	- Computer-aided and broker mediated decision-making for final selection of resources to integrate; sorting of the negotiation results and identification of the best combination of resources providers, followed by confirmation with the selected ones. Depending on the complexity, it involves more or less Broker dedication.
A/VE Integration	
- *Contractualization*	- Automatically, when a selected resources provider confirms its participation; - Selection of the adequate contract from a standardized collection (for request formalization, integration, …); - The Market also offers integration procedures, not considered here.

ing the accomplishment of the competitiveness requirements for VE dynamic integration an-business alignment (Cunha & Putnik, 2005d; Cunha, Putnik, & Gunasekaran, 2002; Cunha et al., 2005). The operational aspect of the Market of Resources consists on an Internet-based intermediation service, mediating offer and demand of resources to dynamically integrate in an VE, assuring low transaction costs (as demonstrated in (Cunha & Putnik, 2003b, 2003c)) and the partners' knowledge preservation.

The services provided by the Market of Resources are supported by (Cunha & Putnik, 2005d; Cunha et al., 2003; Cunha et al., 2005):

• A knowledge base of resources providers and results of their participation in previous VE (historic information)
• A normalized representation of information
• Computer aided tools and algorithms
• A brokerage service
• Regulation, that is, management of negotiation and integration processes, as well as contract enforcement mechanisms (i.e., the services to carry on the judicial processes when needed)

Figure 2. IDEF0 representation of the global process for the creation of a Market of Resources and for VE design, integration and operation (Cunha et al., 2003; Cunha et al., 2005)

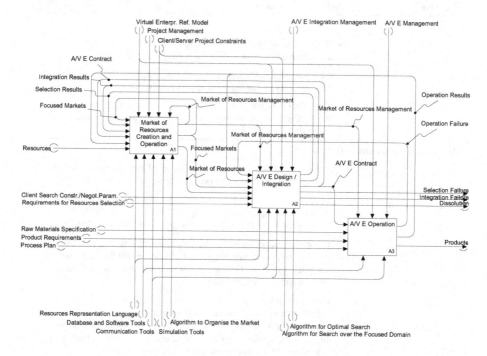

Figure 3. IDEF0 representation of process A.2.—VE design and integration

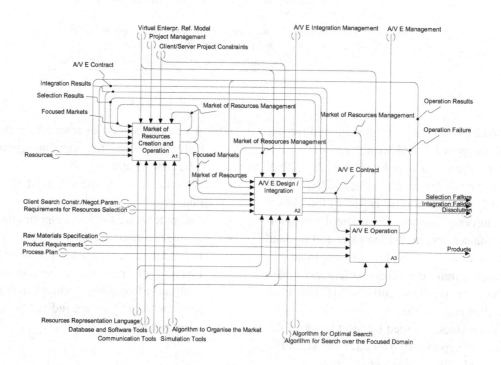

The Market of Resources is able to offer (Cunha & Putnik, 2005d; Cunha et al., 2003):

- Knowledge for VE selection of resources, negotiation and its integration
- Specific functions of VE operation management
- Contracts and formalizing procedures to assure the accomplishment of commitments, responsibility, trust, and deontological aspects, envisaging that the integrated VE accomplishes its objectives of answering to a market opportunity

The overall functioning of the Market of Resources is represented by an IDEF0 diagram[2] in Figure 2. It consists of the creation and management of the Market of Resources itself (process A.1.), as the environment to support the design and integration of the VE (process A.2.) that, under the coordination of the environment, operates to produce a product to answer to a market opportunity (process A.3.). The market offers technical and procedural support for the activities of identifying potential partners, qualifying partners and integrating the VE, as well as coordination and performance evaluation mechanisms. Process A.2. (VE design and integration) is detailed in Figure 3.

This operation is one of the most effort consuming for the user in its interface with the market. The request for VE creation (or reconfiguration or dissolution) is composed by request negotiation, VE design and request formalization.

TECHNOLOGIES TO SUPPORT THE IMPLEMENTATION OF THE MARKET OF RESOURCES

Table 2 lists the main families of technologies to support the main components or processes of the Market of Resources. Virtual enterprise integration is based on the development of technologies able to effective and efficiently handle information

complexity. Several technologies (besides the so-called traditional technologies), such as software agents and Web services are living a period of fast expansion and will impact considerably the way resources providers and virtual enterprises interact and perform.

Web services are the main technology that will support cooperation and integrability. In order to look inside each resources provider, a look inward at their own internal systems, applications and processes is necessary. Several business processes that span across multiple internal applications must be able to communicate dynamically in real-time so that it can communicate with the outside world.

The use of standard XML protocols makes Web services platform, language and vendor independent, and an ideal candidate for use in enterprise application integration solutions and as such, a basis for the Market of Resources. By eliminating the interoperability issues of existing solutions (e.g., CORBA and DCOM), and leveraging open Internet standards, Web services description language (WSDL)—to describe, universal description, discovery and integration (UDDI)—to advertise, simple object access protocol (SOAP)—to communicate and Web services flow language (WSFL)—to define work flows.

But several improvements are to come, with the next generation of functionally and technologically advanced Web services, but this concerns are at moment out of our discussion, as we want to highlight the potential of this universal language and framework to the implementation of an environment to support virtual enterprise integration.

Web services are the most promising technology for business processes integration (webMethods Inc., 2002). The automation of processes, the automatic integration of interenterprise business processes and the coordination of complex business transactions are determinant for obtain high productivity from technology usage and for the creation of dynamic collaboration environ-

Table 2. Technologies to support the main components/processes of the Market of Resources (Cunha & Putnik, 2006a)

Market of resources components /processes	Support technologies and tools
- Market contents: user/buyer **profile**, catalogs, historic, database of resources	- Database management systems - Distributed database management systems - E-Business development platforms - Portals
- Negotiation: request for quotes, auction/reverse auction, optimal selection	- Web services - Software agents - Electronic negotiation tools - Algorithms or protocols - Regulation of negotiation - Intelligent decision making systems - **Workflow** management
- Transactions: payment, contractual-ization	- Web services - Electronic payment - Digital signature - **Certification** - Other security mechanisms
- Management: monitoring, per-formance evaluation, analysis of operation results, decision making, security	- Web services - Simulation tools - **Workflow** technology and collaboration techniques - Regulation - Data analysis and decision support systems - Security systems, digital **certification**, …
- Brokerage: expert advise, monitor-ing and coordination	- Messaging and conferencing - Database management systems, data analysis and decision support systems - Selection algorithms - Management procedures
- Resources providers integration: **file** translation, collaboration,	- Web services - Standards for product/services description - Collaboration tools, - Data translation standards and tools - Communication protocols
- Resources **final** selection (optimal combination)	- Algorithms, heuristics and computer aided tools - Intelligent decision making systems - **Artificial** intelligence - Data analysis and decision support systems

ment. Several specifications were developed to meet that purpose, like business process execution language for Web services (BPEL4WS), electronic business using extensible markup language (ebXML), and business process management language (BPML). BPEL4WS and ebXML are more likely to survive and coexist for the foreseeable future; ebXML will probably dominate a regulated B2B scenario and BPEL4WS is more compliant than a nonregulated B2B/B2C scenario. RosettaNet is the first integration processes standard implemented worldwide in industry, by more then 400 of the world's leading information technology and electronic components companies.

Besides SSL and PKI, supported by all the software platforms, it is required more high level security mechanisms for business processes interenterprise integration, like security assertion markup language (SAML) or XML key management specification (XKMS) for Web services security and management, as well as other basic services to supporting the platform, that is, the WS-security stack of services is required.

INFORMATION TECHNOLOGY ARCHITECTURE AND THE MARKET OF RESOURCES

The organization of the Market of Resources is supported by a communications infrastructure where the electronic processes of business transactions among partners take place. Faced with a plethora of solutions and the permanent development of new technologies, we introduce an IT architecture for the Market of Resources, to guide the selection of the most adequate technologies as well as the development of an integration platform to support the organizational model of the Market of Resources.

There is not yet such architecture. Even SOA architecture when implemented with Web services is distributed, open and presents dynamic characteristics (WSDL and UDDI), which raises its flexibility, lacks an organizational view. The higher layers, such as transactions management, choreography, security or authentication are not yet well established. However, there have been launched recently several specifications by standardization consortia, of which we highlight BPMI and ebXML, to overcome these insufficiencies. The corresponding specifications—*Business Process Modeling Language* (BPML) and *electronic business* XML (ebXML)—focus aspects complementary to the management of electronic commerce processes.

The IT infrastructure must support the functionalities required by the processes list at the first column of Table 2.

Face to the constraints invoked, it is proposed a model of an architecture according to a physical and a logical perspectives.

- **Physical architecture:** Describes the interconnection between the several elements of the system
- **Logical architecture:** Shows the structural composition of the software layers that constitute the system

The Physical Architecture

During the 1970s, the computer was an element of support to enterprise management. At that time, most of the systems were not interconnected and were constituted by one central unit with several terminals for access. Later, at the beginning of the 1980s, the personal computer and Ethernet emerged. Networks within enterprises became common and the hybrid systems emerged, constituted by multi-user systems and personal computers connected in networks. Between the mid-1980s and beginning of the 1990s, it was the apogee of the client/server systems, and the organizations' internal networks were consolidated.

With the World Wide Web explosion in the 1990's, the client/server concept was widened from the organizations' limited universe to the global network.

The recent P2P architecture provides a totally decentralized computation environment. However, functionalities continue to exist that justify the existence of dedicated servers, like for example the management of directories with information about the localization of each node/pair and the services it provides.

The architecture proposed to the support to the Market of Resources operation results from the fusion of the P2P architecture with the client/server

Figura 4. The P2P hybrid network proposed to support the operation of the Market of Resources

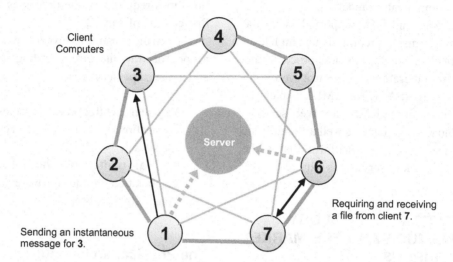

architecture[3], where the characteristics of the first are remarked. This way it is classified by many as a variant of P2P architecture. By its intrinsic characteristics, the hybrid P2P architecture presented in Figure 4 is the one that is best suited to the operation of the Market of Resources, as it offers as key characteristics interoperability and distributivity, fundamental requisites of the A/V E model and its underlying BM_virtual enterprise architecture reference model (BM_VEARM) (Putnik, 2001). P2P platforms have usually objectives of distributed computation, contents sharing and collaboration, which are also the support to the market operation.

The hybrid P2P architecture is based upon two basic entities:

- **Client computers:** The nodes of the network and concern to all the computers that can be clients and suppliers of services/applications of the network
- **Servers:** The computers dedicated to a particular service that perform certain operations of support to the operation of P2P applications

A P2P network can have one or more dedicated servers that support the functions of management and coordination of the network or fundamental services, such as directory of the computers of the network, security and accreditation, business processes management, application server and so forth.

It is a scalable and flexible architecture that allows a fast evolution to be adapted to new requirements. It accomplishes the requisites for the integration infrastructure according to Linthicum (2001):

- Real time answer, which implies the existence of messaging systems and processes automation
- Support to processes and data interconnection, implying the interoperability of processes (BPML, ebXML) and the utilization of open standards for data registry (XML)

- Share of information relevant to all the participating systems

The Logical Architecture

With the introduction of database management systems (DBMS) during the 1970s, business applications focused on the execution of processes and the interface with the users, and laid the functions of data storage and access to the DBMS. This evolution represented an enormous advance towards the easier development and maintenance of applications, as well as in the data security. In the decade of the 1990s, appeared a new paradigm of software applications development with the creation of a third layer referring to the user interface allowing an application of support of a given process that could evolve from one technology to another, or could simultaneously have different interfaces, and only by change of the last layer, the user interface.

We presently assist to a new paradigm, consequence of the need of supporting new processes or to change the processes currently supported by applications, in a short time. Contrarily to the concept prevailing up to now, where the applications were designed according to requisites identified at a given time, being the identified processes integrated in the application structure, the applications to support an A/V E should be independent from the processes. It should exist as a layer of management of business processes, where the active business processes are dynamically configured.

Besides the services of monitoring, management and optimization of interenterprises business processes, it is needed configuration and installation tools. Before being possible the execution of processes in a virtual enterprise, it is needed to specify the relations among the several partners. It is about services of management of extended relationships (XRM—eXtended Relationship Management) that can be configured by the partners themselves to cover the whole virtual enterprise. In this aspect, the concepts of the P2P model inherent to the proposed architecture can perform an important role. Once configured or reconfigured, the A/VE operation can be

Figure 5. Integration platform for the implementation of the Market of Resources (logical architecture).

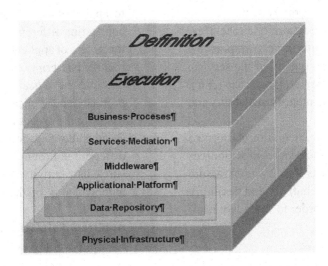

supported by the execution of processes at the superior layer.

The proposed architecture is centered on the interoperability offered by the *middleware* layer of support to *Web services*, as presented in Figure 5.

The architecture of the proposed platform of integration to the implementation of the Market of Resources consists of six layers: (1) business processes, (2) brokerage services, (3) middleware, (4) applicational platform, (5) data repository and (6) physical infrastructure; to assure the necessary interoperability, distributivity and flexibility of the infrastructure to adapt to the A/V E dynamic integration needs.

The processes automation supported by the business processes management allows a high level of flexibility that allows the fast A/V E reconfiguration. The principles of the model driven architecture, rapid development and continuous actualization of applications based on the creation and modification of high level functionalities (UML) are applied in the environments of definition and execution of business processes (BPM).

The layer of business processes (BPM) must contain, besides the current processes definition, a block that stores the business rules (the regulation of the Market of Resources), that the processes must verify and that constitutes a validation tool and the more stable part of the system.

Several types of mediators or brokers exist, supported by adequate servers, responsible by several aspects of the quality of the service: location, availability, performance, capacFity, security, confidentiality, integrity, scalability and maintainability.

The architecture of the integration platform to the implementation of the Market of Resources already introduced consists of six layers that assure the interoperability, distributivity and flexibility of the infrastructure in order to fast adapt itself to changes.

- **Business processes:** This layer defines the management processes of the Market of Resources and of all the processes of the A/V E life cycle. This layer corresponds to the BPM, in which the business processes are defined and executed, assuring traceability of all the processes and defining personalized access to services and contents. The definition of processes is independent of the applications, so it becomes easy to adjust the processes to the requisites of the market.

- **Services brokerage:** The operation of the Market of Resources is based on a set of services provided by this layer, which include the directory of resources, search tools, selection tools, simulation, artificial intelligence, messaging systems, electronic negotiation, security and authentication services, and so forth. In this frame, we can also include the services made available by providers of specific applications or application service providers (ASP), which can include financial management, sourcing and selling management, customers and suppliers relationship management, CAD systems and so forth. This layer allows the available services to locate and know that they are executed by the applicational platform.

- **Middleware:** The protocols, software and interfaces that interconnect BPM systems to applications; it can also be the way of connecting different applications or to allow the access of applications to data. There are included description protocols (UDDI) and execution of *Web services* (SOAP), as well as protocols and application program interface (APIs) to the execution of P2P applications. Besides allowing the operationality between different environments, this layer also assures distributivity and access to resources independently of their geographical location.

- **Applicational platform:** Corresponds to the set of applications available in the Market of

Resources environment, which can be accessed through middleware in the execution of BPM processes or by other applications, local or remote; it includes proprietary applications, legacy systems, P2P applications and ASP applications (applications that can be remotely accessed by accredited users that pay for the service, in alternative to install the applications in a own system). This layer contains the execution of the services indicated in the brokerage layer.

- **Data repository:** The data repository can correspond to different scenarios, from specific of a given application (and only that application can manipulate them), databases (accessible through the respective database management systems) or as data files in standard formats (accessible directly by the file management system). In any case, data can be local, remote or distributed.

- **Physical infrastructure:** Corresponds to computers, networks, operating systems, communications and basic services that assure the operation of all the superior layers; to assure a broader participation of resources providers, this layer must correspond to the Internet.

In each layer there exist two environments: *definition* and *execution*. The *execution* environment is necessary to the operation of processes and application run. It is in the *definition* environment where are defined processes, the available services, the interface with applications and data syntax and structure (metadata); this environment assures interoperability and adaptation to change.

When separating processes from applications, the BPM layer allows an increased agility and fast response to market changes, by an easy processes redefinition. In case of interorganizational processes; it is necessary that the BPM systems verify the WfMC standards to assure its interoperability. However, it is not enough that the process defini-

tion is understood by the partner; it is necessary to negotiate among the diverse partners the process itself and, once accepted a common definition the process should be integrated with other processes active in each organization.

Web services are the other pillar of the proposed architecture. They allow the construction of brokerage and middleware layers, which, under some points of view, can be seen as only one layer. This technology allows to support the interorganizational and distributed business processes, to implement atomic transactions or complete business processes, interconnect heterogeneous applications and to support the operation of P2P applications. They can also be used in interactive applications (standards WSIA e WSRP).

Besides the generalized acceptance of a data representation standard (XML), data are still intrinsically connected to applications, that know their syntax and semantic, which limits interoperability and flexibility. There still exist many problems to overcome in this area, such as data authentication services, product/services description standards, direct access to unknown data (content automatic interpretation, semantics and syntax), management of private and public data, and management of historical data. With the alteration of processes it is also performed the alteration of the data that support them, what poses several difficulties to the storage and interpretation of data concerning processes that are no more supported.

XML is easy and platform independent, but problems remain to be solved, such as storage and management of XML databases. It is missing the implementation of a new database paradigm: a semistructured model, in opposition to the relational model, and object oriented, which are themselves strongly structured (lack of flexibility), that perfectly combines data and metadata, in a way to develop adaptability and perfectly manage historical data.

Table 3. Tools and mechanisms (column 2) and supporting technologies and standards (column 3) proposed for each layer of the architecture

Platform	Supporting Tools and Mechanisms	Supporting Technologies and Standards
Business Processes	- BPM engine, definition and processes interchange	- BPML, ebXML, Wf-XML, BPQL, WSEL
Services brokerage	- Services brokerage, registry and services management, Access control	- UDDI
Middleware – *web services*	- Access to applications and support to services of localization, availability, performance, capacity, security, confidentiality, integrity, reliability, scalability and maintainability, etc.	- SOAP, WSDL, JXTA
Applications	- Electronic catalogues and directories, electronic commerce platforms, tools for resources search and selection, management applications, CAD systems, tools for collaborative development, etc.	- .Net, Java
Data	- Database management systems (DBMS), Distributed DBMS, DOM, etc..	- EDI, XML, cXML, xCBL, STEP
Infrastructure	- Network management and IT infrastructure management	- TCP/IP, http, https, SSL, digital certificates, etc.

Supporting Tools and Mechanisms

Table 3 illustrates as an example some of the supporting tools and mechanisms proposed for each layer (column 2 of Table 3), as well as several supporting standards and technologies—protocolar and technological support (column 3).

The proposed model of architecture focused important functionalities not currently implemented in the electronic marketplaces, such as interoperability, sharing of dedicated applications (P2P) such as CAD systems and artificial intelligence tools, collaboration in processes (P2) and flexibility in business processes (BPM).

AN IMPLEMENTATION

In this section, an example of a laboratory installation that has been implemented at the University of Aveiro (Alvarinhas, 2006) is presented. The example shows how the Web services can be used for the manufacturing services solving real problems.

Figure 6 presents the implementation architecture. This architecture encompasses: the client, the broker, the manufacturer and the UDDI servers. This is a typical "three-level" hierarchy architecture, and the basic architectural pattern as a building block for more complex manufacturing system structures, oriented to the dynamically reconfigurable MS and service architectures (see Putnik, 2001; Putnik & Sluga, 2006; Putnik, Sluga, & Butala, 2006) where Broker (also, resource manager or mediator) is an agent of the reconfiguration dynamics. This architecture implements the market mechanisms as one of the mechanisms for developing an adequate structure that would be the most competitive (for the order considered).

A manufacturer can provide Web services to remotely accept and manufacture client orders in real time. To do so, the manufacturer has to implement Web services on its server. This server interacts with the manufacturer's shop floor machines and with the brokers, around the world, as the intermediators with clients. The manufacturer's server must implement several Web services, for example, to automatically generate budgets and accept contracts through the WEB.

The client, using a usual browser Web, interacts with the broker to define the product specification and the budget criteria sort (by price, by delivery date or others).

The broker automatically will find all manufacturers available in the world, asking for all manufacturers previously registered in UDDI servers (e.g., the IBM or Microsoft UDDI servers).

Using the manufacturer URLs provided by the UDDI servers, the broker automatically asks to all manufacturers their own WSDL files (Web services description language files) where their Web services are described.

Knowing the Web services provided by each manufacturer, the broker is now able to require budgets to all these manufacturers. When the broker receives the manufacturer's responses, with for example the price and the delivery date of the product intended, the broker sorts these responses/budgets and sends a sorted list of budgets, with prices and delivery dates, to the Client. The client chooses one of the budgets and submits them to the broker that in turn sends an order to the chosen manufacturer.

Once ordered and manufactured the products will be sent to the client by regular mail.

Figure 6. Implementation of the inter-enterprise distributed and agile manufacturing system without Market of Resources as an operating environment–basic architectural pattern as a building block for more complex manufacturing system structures (Alvarinhas, 2006)

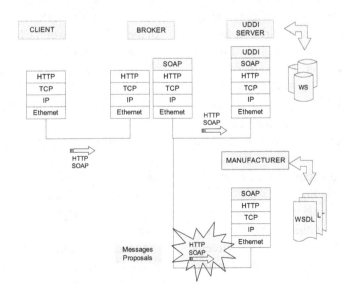

Figure 7. Implementation of the inter-enterprise agile/virtual manufacturing system with Market of Resources as an operating environment

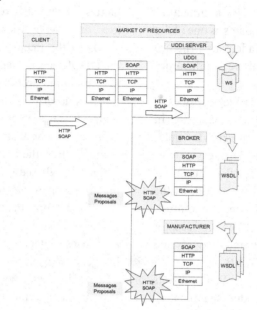

Without using the Market of Resources as the environment for these kinds of services, the architecture is typical, so-called, remote inter-enterprise[4] manufacturing, or, (geographically) distributed manufacturing services.

However, using the Market of Resources, as an indispensable environment for enabling the highest degrees of the interenterprise MS, as well as other types of enterprises, reconfiguration dynamics, the services are monitoring by the Market of Resources. Therefore, all communication has to pass through the Market of Resources.

Further, the Broker is now looking not on all manufacturers available in the world, but on all manufacturers available on the Market of Resources, that is, on the manufacturers that are the members of the Market of Resources. (Of course, they are distributed geographically, around the world). This is shown in Figure 7.

The experimental implementation described above, when performed within the Market of Resources, corresponds to the market of Resources's management process and service: monitor-

ing—which could includes also the performance evaluation, analysis of operation results, decision making, security and others, implemented as Web services (see Table 2, row 4).

The experimental implementation described previously, actually has been tested, or validated. Only the technological aspect of the model through the development and implementation of one particular service and, therefore, only some aspects of the architecture of the Integration platform for the implementation of the Market of Resources. However, further validation should address a more complete set of services, in order to fully validate the architecture and the Integration platform for the implementation of the Market of Resources, as well as other aspects: the organizational aspects, which are in fact the critical ones concerning the application of Web services for the Market of Resources, and integration with other technologies as, for example multi-agent systems (MAS) and grids.

Thus, we could say that the implementation, realized until now and presented earlier, represents the first phase of the model implementation and validation. In the future, the second and the third phases will follow. For these (the second and the third) phases, more complex experimental conditions are necessary that implies establishment of a user network (in order to simulate a VE dynamics and use of the more complete set of services, similar to "real life" conditions). In the second phase, in the future, the "user network" will be constituted of the academic partners and in the third phase industrial partners will be involved. The second phase is already planned for the near future.

CONCLUSION

The proposed information technology architecture model is presented under two specific perspectives (physical and logical). The architecture model works as a guide to the development of architectures with the characteristics intrinsic to the model.

The IT architecture is one of the components of the architecture of an organization. An architecture framework allows developing several architectures in an integrated way and according to objectives of the framework itself. In this chapter we have proposed a model of architecture, with the objective of giving the resultant architectures the ability to support the operation of the Market of Resources as an infrastructure for agile/virtual enterprise integration.

The integration models and the architectures developed are normally based on cutting edge existing technologies. The model presented does not refer technologies in particular, but some technologies are fundamental to the implementation of this model:

- The definition of business processes in high level languages, in a layer above the platform of applications, is the support of adaptability (BPM).

- P2P will be essential to collaboration, from the design to logistics, in particular in the development of new products.
- Web services are the present technology that allows the implementation of this concept and the characteristics of interoperability and distributivity.

The proposed model of architecture promotes interorganizational integration, betting on interoperability, which is a main requisite of market and of organizations. In the same way, it incorporates the identified requisites of the platform of interapplicational integration to support the Market of Resources, and enables interoperability, distributivity, agility and virtuality.

Concerning the model validation, at the moment it is validated only in the technological aspect of the model through the development and implementation of one particular service and, therefore, only some aspects of the architecture of the integration platform for the implementation of the market of resource, described in the section "An Implementation". However, besides the technology, the organizational aspect is critical, too. Future validation will address a more complete set of services, in order to fully validate the architecture and the integration platform for the implementation of the Market of Resources, as well as other aspects: the organizational aspects, which are in fact the critical ones concerning the application of Web services for the Market of Resources, and integration with other technologies as, for example multi-agent systems (MAS) and grids. If the implementation realized could be called the first phase of the model validation, then the future validation will be carried on through the second and the third phase that will involve the network of academic partners and of the industrial partners respectively. The second phase of the validation and development of other Web services, for the network of academic partners, will start in the near future.

REFERENCES

Alvarinhas, H. M. G. (2006) *Locating, negotiating and contracting services on Web.* Unpublished master's thesis, University of Aveiro, Portugal.

Browne, J., & Zhang, J. (1999). Extended and virtual enterprises: Similarities and differences. *International Journal of Agile Management Systems, 1*(1), 30-36.

Byrne, J. A. (1993). The virtual corporation: The company of the future will be the ultimate in adaptability. *Business Week*, pp. 98-103.

Camarinha-Matos, L. M., & Afsarmanesh, H. (1999). The virtual enterprise concept. In L. M. Camarinha-Matos & H. Afsarmanesh (Eds.), *Infrastructures for virtual enterprises* (pp. 3-14). Porto, Portugal: Kluwer Academic Publishers.

Carlsson, C. (2002). Decisions support in virtual organizations: The case for multi-agent support. *Group Decision and Negotiation, 11*, 185-221.

Cunha, M. M., & Putnik, G. D. (2002). Discussion on requirements for agile/virtual enterprises reconfigurability dynamics: The example of the automotive industry. In L. M. Camarinha-Matos (Ed.), *Collaborative business ecosystems and virtual enterprises* (pp. 527-534). Boston: Kluwer Academic Publishers.

Cunha, M. M., & Putnik, G. D. (2003a). Agile/virtual enterprise enablers: A comparative analysis. In D. N. Sormaz & G. A. Süer (Eds.). In *Proceedings of Group Technology/Cellular Manufacturing—World Symposium 2003* (pp. 243-247). Columbus, Ohio: Ohio University.

Cunha, M. M., & Putnik, G. D. (2003b). Market of resources versus e-based traditional virtual enterprise integration - Part I: A cost model definition. In G. D. Putnik & A. Gunasekaran (Eds.), In *Proceedings of the First International Conference on Performance Measures, Benchmarking and Best Practices in New Economy* (pp. 664-669). Guimarães, Portugal

Cunha, M. M., & Putnik, G. D. (2003c). Market of resources versus e-based traditional virtual enterprise integration - Part II: A comparative cost analysis. In G. D. Putnik & A. Gunasekaran (Eds.). In *Proceedings of the First International Conference on Performance Measures, Benchmarking and Best Practices in New Economy* (pp. 667-675). Guimarães, Portugal.

Cunha, M. M., & Putnik, G. D. (2005a). Business alignment in agile/virtual enterprise integration. In M. Khosrow-Pour (Ed.), *Advanced topics in information resources management* (Vol. 4, pp. 26-54). Hershey, PA: Idea Group Publishing.

Cunha, M. M., & Putnik, G. D. (2005b). Business alignment requirements and dynamic organizations. In G. D. Putnik & M. M. Cunha (Eds.), *Virtual enterprise integration: Technological and organizational perspectives* (pp. 78-101). Hershey, PA: Idea Group Publishing.

Cunha, M. M., & Putnik, G. D. (2005c). Market of resources—A knowledge management enabler in virtual enterprises integration. In E. Coakes & S. Clarke (Eds.), *Encyclopedia of communities of practice in information and knowledge management*. Hershey, PA: Idea Group Publishing.

Cunha, M. M., & Putnik, G. D. (2005d). Market of resources for agile/virtual enterprise integration. In M. Khosrow-Pour (Ed.), *Encyclopedia of information science and technology* (pp. 1891-1898). Hershey, PA: Idea Group Publishing.

Cunha, M. M., & Putnik, G. D. (2006a). *Agile/virtual enterprise: Implementation and implementation management.* Hershey, PA: Idea Group Publishing.

Cunha, M. M., & Putnik, G. D. (2006b). Identification of the domain of opportunities for a Market of Resources for virtual enterprise integration. *International Journal of Production Research, 44*(12), 2277-2298.

Cunha, M. M., Putnik, G. D., & Ávila, P. (2000). Towards focused markets of resources for agile/ virtual enterprise integration. In L. M. Camarinha-Matos, H. Afsarmanesh, & H. Erbe (Eds.), *Advances in networked enterprises: Virtual organisations, balanced automation, and systems integration* (pp. 15-24). Berlin: Kluwer Academic Publishers.

Cunha, M. M., Putnik, G. D., & Ávila, P. (2004). Virtual enterprises' extended life cycle. In *Proceedings of SymOrg 2004—IX International Symposium* (pp. 85-99). Belgrade, Serbia (June 6-10). University of Belgrade, Faculty of Organisational Sciences.

Cunha, M. M., Putnik, G. D., & Gunasekaran, A. (2002). Market of resources as an environment for agile/virtual enterprise dynamic integration and for business alignment. In A. Gunasekaran (Ed.), *Knowledge and information technology management in the 21st century organisations: Human and social perspectives* (pp. 169-190). Hershey, PA: Idea Group Publishing.

Cunha, M. M., Putnik, G. D., & Gunasekaran, A. (2003). Market of resources as an environment for agile/virtual enterprise dynamic integration and for business alignment. In A. Gunasekaran & O. Khalil (Eds.), *Knowledge and information technology management in the 21st century organisations: Human and social perspectives* (pp. 169-190). Hershey, PA: Idea Group Publishing.

Cunha, M. M., Putnik, G. D., Gunasekaran, A., & Ávila, P. (2005). Market of resources as a virtual enterprise integration enabler. In G. D. Putnik & M. M. Cunha (Eds.), *Virtual enterprise integration: Technological and organizational perspectives* (pp. 145-165). Hershey, PA: Idea Group Publishing.

Dai, Q., & Kauffman, R. (2001). Business models for internet-based e-procurement systems and B2B electronic markets: An exploratory assessment.

Paper presented at the 34th Hawaii International Conference on Systems Science, Maui.

Davidow, W. H., & Malone, M. S. (1992). *The virtual corporation—Structuring and revitalising the corporation for the 21st century*. New York: HarperCollins Publishers.

Dogac, A. (1998, March). *A survey of the current state-of-the-art in electronic commerce and research issues in enabling technologies*. Paper presented at the Euro-Med Net 98 Conference, Electronic Commerce Track, Cyprus.

Hands, J., Bessonov, M., Blinov, M., Patel, A., & Smith, R. (2000). An inclusive and extensible architecture for electronic brokerage. *Decision Support Systems, 29*, 305-321.

Khalil, O., & Wang, S. (2002). Information technology enabled meta-management for virtual organizations. *International Journal of Production Economics, 75*(1), 127-134.

Linthicum, D. S. (2001). *B2B application integration: E-business enable your enterprise*. Boston: Addison-Wesley.

Martin, C. (1999). *Net future*. New York: McGraw-Hill.

O'Sullivan, D. (1998). Communications technologies for the extended enterprise. *International Journal of Production Planning and Control, 9*(8), 742-753.

Preiss, K., Goldman, S., & Nagel, R. (1996). *Cooperate to compete: Building agile business relationships*. New York: van Nostrand Reinhold.

Putnik, G. D. (2001). BM_virtual enterprise architecture reference model. In A. Gunasekaran (Ed.), *Agile manufacturing: 21st century manufacturing strategy* (pp. 73-93). Oxford, UK: Elsevier Science Publishing.

Putnik, G. D., Cunha, M. M., Sousa, R., & Ávila, P. (2005). BM virtual enterprise - A model for dynamics and virtuality. In G. D. Putnik & M.

M. Cunha (Eds.), *Virtual enterprise integration: Technological and organizational perspectives* (pp. 124-144). Hershey, PA: Idea Group Publishing.

Putnik G.D., & Sluga A. (2006) Reconfigurability of manufacturing systems for agility implementation – Part I: Requirements and principles. In P. F. Cunha (Ed.), In *Proceedings of the 3rd International CIRP Conference on Digital Enterprise Technology—DET 2006*, Setúbal, Portugal.

Putnik G. D., Sluga A., & Butala P. (2006). Reconfigurability of manufacturing systems for agility implementation – Part I: Two architectures. In P. F. Cunha (Ed.), In *Proceedings of the 3rd International CIRP Conference on Digital Enterprise Technology—ET 2006*, Setúbal, Portugal.

Wang, C. X. (2001). Supply chain coordination in B2B electronic markets. In *Proceedings of the 32nd Annual Meeting of the Decision Sciences Institute*, San Francisco.

webMethods Inc. (2002). Demystifying web services. webMethods Inc. Retrieved February 13, 2007, from http://www.webmethods.com

Webster, M., Sugden, D. M., & Tayles, M. E. (2004). The measurement of manufacturing virtuality. *International Journal of Operations & Production Management, 24*(7), 721-742.

ENDNOTES

[1] The infrastructures referred are not information but organizational, meaning that there is a need for a super-, or meta-organizations that enable higher performances of the business processes. Exactly, the Market of resources is one of these meta-organizational infrastructures for the dynamic reconfigurable VE. In fact, this Chapter is about web services as supporting technology for functioning of the Market of resources, i.e. of these meta-organizational infrastructures in general.

[2] IDEF stands for ICAM DEFinition methodology (ICAM—Integrated Computer-Aided Manufacturing). IDEF diagrams illustrate the structural relations between two processes and the entities present in the system. The processes (represented as boxes) transform the *inputs* into *outputs* (respectively the left and the right arrows of a process), using the *mechanisms* for the transformation (the bottom arrows of a process) and constrained by *control information or conditions* under which the transformation occurs (the top arrows).

[3] Other solutions may be adequate too. E.g., it is suggested that SOA could solve the problem too. Concerning a detailed evaluation of a particular approach, at the moment it would is considered as an issue of the future research.

[4] In the case of the interenterprise environment, the Broker wouldn't be necessary (as, in reality, the Brokers do not exist within a "traditional" "monolithic" enterprise).

Chapter VI
The Utilization of Semantic Web for Integrating Enterprise Systems

Dimitrios Tektonidis
ALTEC S.A., Greece

Albert Bokma
University of Sunderland, UK

ABSTRACT

Integrating enterprise system has become an issue of sharing information rather than transforming information due to the increasing complexity and the heterogeneity of the applications. The transition from application centric to integration centric enterprise application integration (EAI) requires methods and technologies that will enable and facilitate the definition of shared information. The use of ontologies semantic Web and technologies can improve the existing EAI methods by providing a framework capable to define shared information. Ontologies-based enterprise application integration (ONAR) framework utilizes semantic Web technologies to define shared information among heterogeneous systems. The present chapter presents the utilization of ontologies for the formation of ONAR framework and its application for service oriented application integration (SOAI)

INTRODUCTION

The integration of enterprise application such as enterprise resource planning (ERP) systems due to their internal complexity, has lead many EAI solution vendors to create solutions based on the structure and the semantics of the application. Nowadays the problem of integration is confronted with technologies (like Enterprise Java Beans) that provide sophisticated and advanced techniques for technical interfaces.

The most recent orientations in enterprise application integration (henceforth EAI) present new techniques that provide methods to define and exploit semantics of complex application. Still this definition is application centric and it cannot be shared among other heterogeneous applications. Tektonidis, Vontas, Hess, and Meschonat (2002) have stressed the problem of integration as a problem of information sharing not as a problem of adaptation that is very common case for ERP systems.

In the technological level, service oriented application integration (SOAI), as it is presented in Linthicum (2004), exploits the capabilities for the functional description of Web services that are used for the actual integration. This section focuses on the creation of an integration framework based on SOAI that utilizes semantic Web technologies (W3C, 2006) in order to enrich the semantics of the exchanged information.

The approach used follows the ontologies based enterprise application integration (ONAR)

approach presented by Tektonidis et al. (2005) that utilizes Web ontologies to create semantic conceptualizations of the business concepts that exist inside an application. This conceptualization is used for the creation and the registration of the Web services in a UDDI based registry.

UTILIZING SEMANTIC WEB FOR ENTERPRISE APPLICATION INTEGRATION

The need for the utilization of semantic Web derives from the requirement for sharing information instead of exchanging information. The adaptation

Figure 1. The difference between data transformation and semantic integration (Source: Capgemini)

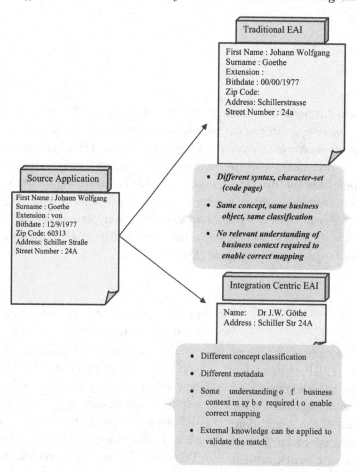

of ontologies for software engineering extends further than the semantic definition of a domain. Liu and Halper (1999) and Chiang (2001) proved that the utilization of the ontologies requires certain modifications in the principals of the frame-based ontologies languages. The utilization of ontologies in order to define concepts for application integration involves also characteristics of the system that are integrated. However in order to avoid definition of concepts based on the structure and the logic of the applications we have defined two layers for the definition of concepts and the association to the application resources.

The semantic definition of the concepts is based on the integration requirements. This implies the concepts and their relation define the information need to be exchanged. This "integration centric" approach follows the principals of modern enterprise application integration (EAI) specification (Linthicum, 2004) contrary to traditional integration approaches that aim to improve the definition based on the semantics of the applications. Figure 1 presents the difference between traditional EAI (data transformation) and integration-centric approach.

The formation of an integration centric information definition EAI methodology required the

utilization and the adaptation of semantic Web technologies. ONAR methodology utilizes ontological definitions for the definition of semantic and uses association techniques in order to associate concepts with the information repositories of the applications.

Integration Centric Semantics

The main objective of our research is to define the integration semantics based on the integration centric approach. The integration centric approach presented in Tektonidis, Bokma, Oatley, and Salampasis (2005) aims to orient the design and development of the integration semantics and components to the specific requirements of the integration case.

The statement that integration centric approach is based on the specific requirements is a claim made in comparison with existing techniques and methodologies. As integration requirements, we imply the information to be shared between the heterogeneous applications.

Figure 2 presents in a simplified example of how information about an Order is shared between four different applications. For the financial system, the "order" concept consists of

Figure 2. Sharing information between heterogeneous applications

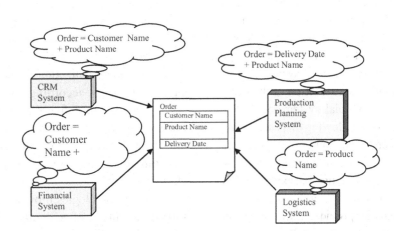

the "customer name", the "product name" and the "delivery date" property. However the other three systems do not have internally the same definition about "order" but they can understand all the concepts (order) and properties (customer name, product name, delivery date) even if they can not process them because there not a shared conceptualization of the order that every application can "understand".

The definition of the order is not based on a specific system but on the need to integrate these four different systems when a new order is submitted to the financial system. The definition of the concept "order" varies from case to case. For example the integration between the production planning system and the production system (plant automation system) would include further information regarding the machines and the personnel that should be involved excluding all financial information.

Therefore, according to the integration case the definition of a concept changes. The problem is confronted today with two main approaches that are (a) application centric approach and (b) shared vocabulary approach. Application centric approach provides techniques, mechanisms and tools that facilitate the adaptation from one system to another. In the previous example the three applications would be adopted to the logic of the financial system in order to retrieve information regarding the submitted order. Technically, this is accomplished with an application programming interface (API) that the financial system offers to external applications. This interface follows the application logic of the financial system and its utilization is actually an adaptation of the other applications to the financial system logic. The definition of semantics following this case would be defined based on the semantics of one system. The reduction to one "central" system semantics, however, exclude the semantics that exists to other systems and not to the central application.

Shared vocabularies provide a common definition of all concepts that appear in all applications

that constitute the integrated system. Therefore in the previous example the definition of the concept "order" would be more descriptive (having all the attributes of all applications) and one for all the possible integration cases. This would complicate the conceptualization of the concept "order" including semantics that in most of the integration case would not be used.

Thus instead of defining the semantics based on one application semantics or to the aggregation of all application semantics we propose that the definition of integration case semantics should be defined based on the requirements of the integration. The application centric approach defines differently the concepts according to the integration case. Following the example of Figure 3 the order concept should have different conceptualization according to the integration case. Thus in a case where the CRM system requires information regarding the consuming habits of a customer from the financial system then the order conceptualization would contain only information about the customer name and the product name while the integration between the production planning system and the financial system would include only the delivery date and the product name.

For the previous simplified example, it is stressed that although inside an application the definition of a concept is univocal inside an integrated system the concept may have different hypostasis according to the integration case.

The requirement is how ontologies would improve the multiple definition of a concept enable different conceptualization for each integration case. Ontologies according to Fensel (2004) are not created to define data but to represent knowledge. The knowledge of a domain does not follow the strict and precise definition of data structure that is found in E-R diagrams or UML class diagrams.

Although ontologies provide an explicit and formal definition of a domain this definition may be divided in different level of abstraction.

In the previous chapter, domain ontologies enabled different levels of ontologies based to their abstraction. An integration case in order to be complete may be very detailed in the concepts that is based on and abstract to the rest of the concepts that are only to be defined for reasons of completion. In the example of Figure 3, for and integration case between the financial system and the CRM system information regarding the customer purchasing habits may be very detailed while other concepts like its order delivery date to be abstract. The abstract part of the ontology is part that the application is not able to process while the detailed part is data that the application uses in the integration case. Thus ontologies are not meant to define the data to be exchanged, but their semantics.

The following section presents how ontologies have been used as modeling technique to define semantic conceptualizations.

SHARING INFORMATION USING OWL ONTOLOGIES: THE ONAR METHODOLOGY

ONAR methodology follows the frame-based logic that modern ontology languages use in order to define conceptualizations. During our research, Tektonidis et al. (2003) has found that languages like the Web ontology (W3C, 2006) are capable in providing us with formal definitions for business concepts as OWL classes.

In comparison with UML class diagrams, OWL is more descriptive enabling the definition of semantics for the business concepts and their attributes. The entities inside the ONAR conceptualization methodology inherit all the features of the OWL classes. However OWL as an ontology based language often permits the abstract definition of domains. For EAI that can lead to the definition of conceptualizations that cannot be reflected to real data since information systems need to formalize abstract concepts into data structures.

The venture of having an ontology language for defining information that is exchange between information systems has been confronted with the definition of a restricted usage of OWL. In this attempt, graphical environment was developed in order the definition of the OWL ontologies to be constrained by certain rules that would prevent from the false usage of OWL. ONAR concepts and services designer (ONAR, 2006) enables the creation of conceptualization ontologies (OWL) providing the business consultant a reduced OWL-Lite ontology (W3C, 2005).

Figure 3 presents the conceptualization of the summary of Deed of Incorporation document used in public administration applications. This ontology contains all the concepts (OWL classes) and their properties (OWL datatype properties) as well as their relation (OWL object properties). The conceptualization is not based on the information system of the participating local authorities (Prefecture, Chamber of Commerce), but on an ontology that is common for all authorities.

It can be argued that the graph does not represent a formal OWL structure since for example there are properties (OWL data-types) like the property "ID" that is presented more that once in the graph. Our framework uses OWL-Lite as ontology language however for reasons of presentation based on the end users feedback we support that this kind of ontology representation is more convenient and less complex to users that are not familiar to ontology engineering.

Summarizing the conceptualization capabilities of our framework we are using the OWL-Lite and more precisely:

1. Inheritance is permitted allowing some class features to be inherited from one class to another. The relation between the parent class and child classes follows the same rules that both object-oriented engineering and frame-based logic supports, however multiple inheritance is not permitted. This constraint is due to the fact that in complex

Figure 3. The graph of a conceptualization ontology produced by ONAR concepts and services designer

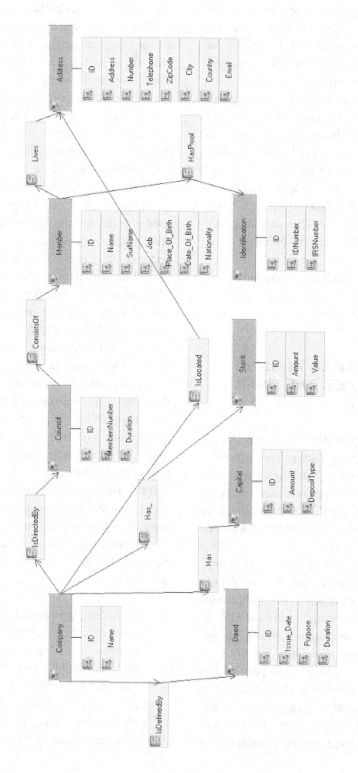

information system polymorphism of some concepts will unduly increase the complexity of conceptualization.

2. Entities are allowed to have properties that correspond to OWL datatype properties. A property can belong to more than one entity and is contrary to the usual principles of object oriented modeling. This principle derives from the frame-based logic of OWL ontologies and extends the object oriented engineering where a property belongs to only one class.

3. Relations between concepts can be defined using

    a. **Functional property:** Defines the "one to many" relation between the instances (objects) of two concepts

    b. **Inverse functional property:** Complementary to functional property in order to facilitate lexical descriptions

c. **Symmetric property:** Symmetric properties are used to declare the one to one elation between the instances (objects) of two concepts.

d. **Transitive properties:** Contrary to the definition of OWL in ONAR framework Transitive properties are used for the division of complex concepts. For example the concept "material" can have properties regarding its financial features (prize, cost), logistics features like (size, weight, quantity) and so forth. Using transitive properties the concept can be divided to more than one concept according to its semantic.

However we have to limit the syntax of OWL, which permits the existence in a relation of more than one concept as ranges and domains. In our approach (in a relation) if the domains contain more than one concept then the range should be

Figure 4. The generic structure of the association ontology

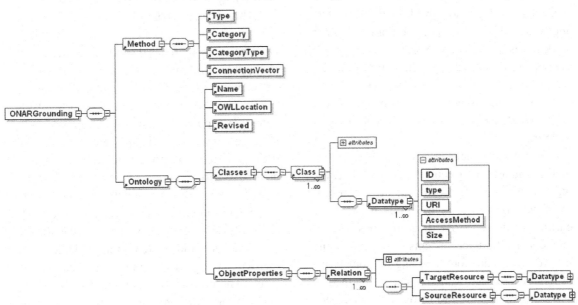

defined from only one concept and vice versa. This ensures that in the association of the logical model to the system resources will not create indeterminism.

Both entities and properties are enriched with (a) notional properties like lexical descriptions, (b) the ability to define the inverse of a concept and (c) the ability that a property can potentially be derived from another property. These enrichments are used to increase the inference for the semantics of the concepts and their properties inside a model following the OWL principles.

The most important reason for the utilization of ontologies is the capability to define semantic relations between the concepts of a domain. Mecella and Batini (2000) introduced the concept of application wrapper as metalayer enables the redefinition of concepts of the application in order to be used from other heterogeneous applications. The lack of the inclusion of semantics limits the capabilities of EAI approaches like application wrappers and object oriented middleware (OOM) techniques.

Defining information using data definition methods like UML class diagrams or entity relation (E-R) schemas the produced conceptualizations unavoidably follow the data structure of an application. This is the actual limitation that our work needs to overcome. Software engineering methods have limited capabilities for semantics definition. For example, the semantics in the relation between two concepts that both in UML or in E-R schemas do not have formal methods to define.

Our work has focused on creating semantics in the relations between concepts. The existing semantics of relations that are expressed in object oriented class diagrams in UML or entities relations (E-R) diagrams pose limits to the semantic two concepts may have at the logical level. Therefore adapting the four types of relations (object relations) that are defined in OWL we are achieved to increase the inference capabilities of the conceptualizations. The rela-

tion between concepts in this level represents semantic relation between the concepts. These concepts may have a syntactic relation, however this is not requisite. This detaches the definition of the concepts from their data realizations. Thus the definition of the concepts is based to the integration requirements.

Concepts relations are defined based on their domain and their range. The domain is consisted of set of concepts that subject of the relation. The range for a relation is the object or the objects of the relation. According to Wache, Vögele, Visser, Stuckenschmidt, Schuster, and Neumann (2001) the definition of information based on ontologies can be unlimited regarding the number of concepts that consist of a domain and the range. However in our research based on e-business (Tektonidis et al., 2002), e-government (Tektonidis et al., 2005) and e-health (Tektonidis & Bokma, 2005) use cases the simultaneous existence of multiple domain and range ontology created problems regarding the comprehension of the ontology as well as in the association of the concepts to the repository of the information system.

Mapping Conceptualizations to System Repositories

Developing an approach that is independent from the application logic of each application necessitate the existence of mechanisms and technique to associate logical conceptualizations (OWL ontologies) to the real application repository. In addition, our approach is independent also from the type of the repository (whether is a RDBMS or an application server).

In our attempt to enrich OWL with elements that would enable as to associate the conceptualization to the system we have discovered that these enrichments would create a complex ontology file that will carry both semantic and syntactic elements. Another important issue was the portability of the ontologies from different kind of systems. Therefore we have created an association ontology that enables the mapping of the conceptualization ontology to the system repository.

The association ontology is related to the system structure and associates the concepts of one conceptualization ontology to the system repository. The ontology enables the definition of the:

1. **Category of repository:** Category of the repository defines level of the repository (e.g., whether is a flat file system or an RDBMS or an application server)
2. **Type of repository:** Defines the technology of the repository (e.g. DCOM application server or JavaBeen application server)
3. **OWL ontology location:** The conceptualization that the association ontology is related
4. **Mapping information:** Information that relates every logical concept to the resources of the repository like the access method or technical information like the data type and the size

With the disassociation of the conceptualization from the repository of the system and the usage of the association ontology we have achieved:

1. **To increase the reusability of the conceptualizations ontologies:** The same conceptualization ontologies can be used to different information system.
2. To reduce cost of maintainability when changes happened in to the application repository
3. To enable the creation of common vocabularies that can be shared between heterogeneous applications

In our work so far we have achieved the application of the ONAR framework to relational databases, ODBC compliant repositories and application server based on Web services (WSDL). In the near future we aim to include other type of repositories.

Figure 5. ONAR integration methodology

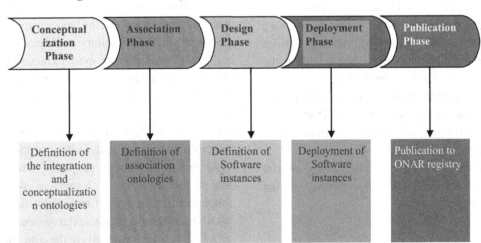

APPLICATION INTEGRATION BASED ON SEMANTIC WEB SERVICES

ONAR Integration Process

The ONAR integration methodology has been developed during this research as the proposed procedure for integrating application following the ONAR approach based on the prototype system. The methodology guides integrators that are not familiar with the ONAR approach, ontologies or the technological and technical issues of the prototype system.

Figure 5 presents the phases of the integration process that are the following:

1. **Conceptualization phase:** In this phase the requirements of the integration are defined. The integrator defines the concepts and their relations that comprise the integration ontology. During this phase also the integrator defines the conceptualization ontologies based on the applicable semantics for each application. The ontologies development is based on the principals of the development phase of the methontology (Gòmez et al., 1997) in order to define the ontologies.

2. **Association phase:** The conceptual schema (conceptualization ontology) is associated to the legacy system resources (data).

3. **Design phase:** The definition of the software instance takes place. The integrator defines the input and the output list based on the conceptualization ontologies.

4. **Deployment phase:** Where the software instance is deployed (creation of the service model) and becomes an integration component.

5. **Publication phase:** The profile of the software component is published in the registry.

The definition, once in every integration case, the integration ontology and the fact that the conceptualization ontologies derived from the initial integration ontology facilitate the insertion of new applications to the integrated system (Tektonidis et al., 2005). Thus the prototype system should automate the procedure in order the development of the software instance to be leveraged in terms of complexity and maintainability.

Designing Web Services Based on the Conceptual Schema

The entire Web services development cycle including the design, the deployment and registration of the Web services to the universal description, discovery and integration (UDDI) registry is related to the conceptualization ontology. The design of the software instance is the process where elements of a conceptualization are used to define the input and the output of the Web service. The design of a Web service consists of its syntactic definition and its semantic description.

The syntactic definition defines the input and the output as well as the behavior of the Web service. This definition is based one conceptualization of the conceptual schema. Starting from one basic entity the Web service designer can use all the concepts that are necessary for his definition. The syntactic definition (ONAR service model) of the service contains all the semantic and syntactic relations between the basic entity (primary concept) and the secondary concepts.

The ONAR service model (Figure 6) is an XML document contains the functional description of the service based on the conceptualization ontology.

The reason for having a new definition document for the syntactic definition of the service, apart from maintenance purposes, is to increase the portability of the Web services. We have to implement the necessary functionality that enables us to automatically generate the source code (C#) of a Web service based only to the conceptualiza-

Figure 6. ONAR service model

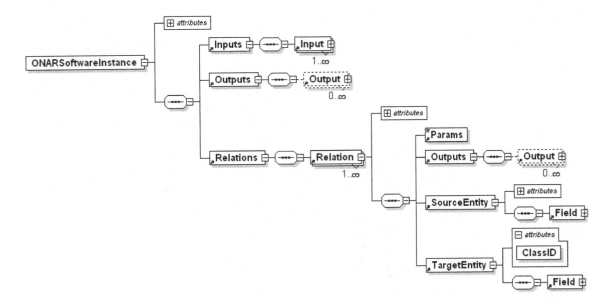

tion ontology the association ontology and the ONAR service model. Therefore, if two applications share the same conceptualization ontologies but have different structures (different association ontologies) they can exchange Web services.

ONAR Framework Architecture

The requirement and the objective that have been set in the previous sections required the development of several components that comprise ONAR framework architecture, presented in Figure 7.

ONAR framework implementation was based on the methodology and in the existing state-of-the-art technologies. The selection of the technologies that materialize the conceptual components of the architecture and it is not unique since other technologies may substitute them.

However the conceptual components role and the architecture materialized into a framework the ONAR methodology. A summary of the role and functionality of the components are the following:

1. **Concepts and services designer:** The graphical environment that enables the integrator to design and develop of the software instances and enables the administrator to remotely administer and maintain the ONAR server

2. **ONAR deployment server:** The component that undertakes the administrative tasks of the ONAR server

1. **ONAR publication server:** The component that enables the administration of the ONAR repository (enriched UDDI)

2. **ONAR repository:** The semantically enriched UDDI based service repository

3. **Semantic repository:** The pool of derived ontologies (integration and conceptual) used inside an integrated system

Additional information for the ONAR prototype components regarding technologies and specifications is included in the ONAR Web site. The following sections analyse the tools and components of the ONAR framework.

Figure 7. ONAR prototype system architecture

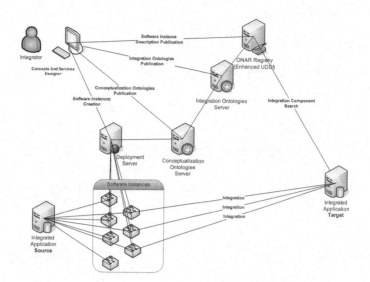

ONAR Ontology Design Tools

The definition of the integration and conceptualization ontologies required a design tool that would enable the design of the ontologies. During the research we have reviewed several ontology design environments and tools like Protégé and WebODE.

As aforementioned, integration and conceptualization ontologies follow a specialized version of OWL Lite. In addition, the facilitation of the creation of association ontology required an environment that would simplify the procedures in the association phase. Therefore, we have developed a graphical environment that integrates the five phases of the ONAR integration methodology.

ONAR concepts and services designer (Figure 8) enables:

a. The graphical design and syntactical validation of the integration conceptualization ontologies

b. The development of the association ontologies and the necessary repository validity checking

c. The design and deployment of the software instances

d. The design and publication of the software instances profiles

We present in the following sections some of the features of the integrated environment however further information can be found in the project Web site: http://research.altec.gr/ONAR.

Ontology Representation

One of the most important issues in order ONAR framework to facilitate the creation of ontologies was the representation of ontology. OWL is a frame-based language however according to the W3C definition data type properties do not belong to one class but to a collection of classes.

A graphical representation of this principal would complicate the design and representation of the ontology. During our research (Tektonidis et al., 2005) the representation that is closer to the UML class diagram than the ontological representation used from other tools (Protégé

Figure 8. ONAR concepts and services designer

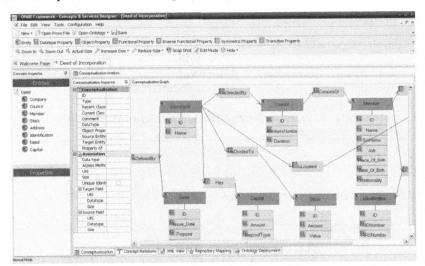

Figure 9. Ontology representation using ONAR concepts and services designer

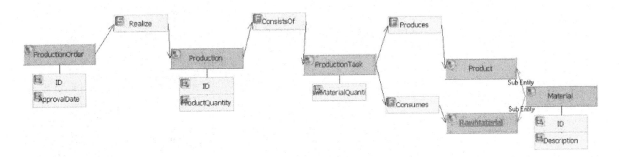

OWL plug-in) simplified the representation of the ontology.

Every class (⬤) in Figure 9 appears to have a set of properties (🔳) that belong only to the class. For example, the "ID" property that appears in "production order", "production" and "material" is one datatype property that has as domain the three classes (Figure 10).

It can be argued that the proposed ontology representation is closer to the UML class diagram; however it provides a simplified view of the ontology without limiting its capabilities.

Software Instance Creation

Software instances are the software components that realize integration rules based on ontological definition of the integration case. For the ONAR prototype system software instances are materialized using Web service technology. The selection of Web services over other technologies (like CORBA, DCOM or EJB) has been based to the fact that Web services follow the message-oriented logic. There are many pros and cons to this selection, however it remains a technological issue and the evolution of technologies may in the future provide better solutions.

Figure 10. The definition of the "ID" property

```
owl:DatatypeProperty rdf:ID="ID">
    <rdfs:domain rdf:resource="#Production" />
    <rdfs:domain rdf:resource="#Material" />
    <rdfs:domain rdf:resource="#ProductionOrder" />
    <rdfs:range
rdf:resource="http://www.w3.org/2001/XMLSchema#integer" />
    </owl:DatatypeProperty>
```

Figure 11. ONAR software instance service model

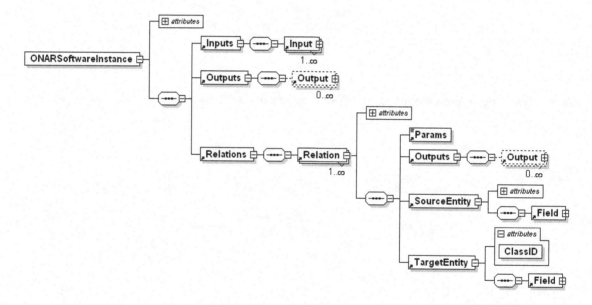

The software instance is divided in two parts:

1. **The software instance profile** (informative part) that contains the semantic description for the use of the software instance based on the integration ontology. The structure of the software instance profile follows the principal of OWL-S profile ontology. The OWL-S profile has been extended in order to be integrated with the repository that follows the UDDI standard that is described later on.

2. **The service model** (performative part) that includes information regarding the functionality of the software instance. The service model (Figure 11) includes the parts of the conceptualization ontology that are related to the software instance as well as their association with the repository of the application. The service model has XML structure and it can be transferable (Tektonidis & Bokma, 2005) to applications that contain the conceptions in their conceptualization ontology. This way the

Figure 12. The portability of the software instances

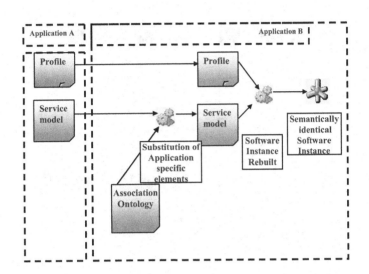

heterogeneous applications can also share software instances with the same semantics. The transfer of the service model (and thus a software instance) is accomplished with the substitution of the association ontology element of the source application with the elements of the target application. Figure 12 presents the process than enables the transport of a software instance between two heterogeneous applications.

ONAR Repository

ONAR prototype system has a service oriented architecture (henceforth SOA) therefore in order to leverage the capability of this technologies required a repository that would enabled the publication of the software instance descriptions. Although ONAR repository is not directly associated to research issues, it is a core component because it serves internal purposes of the framework by reducing the effort needed for the discovery of the appropriate software instance. ONAR framework internal architecture is service oriented and the

existence of a UDDI based repository is considered mandatory for the description and discovery of the software instance (Web services).

To this respect Paulocci, Kawamura, Payne, and Sycara (2001) integrated the ontological service representation definition of OWL-S profile with UDDI. The UDDI has been enriched with a set of TModel in order to include the concepts of OWL-S profile ontology (Figure 13). The enriched UDDI enables semantic descriptions of the services.

ONAR framework used as base the work of Paulocci et al. (2001) in order to create a semantic repository to register the services. ONAR repository is an UDDI based repository that utilizes the semantics of OWL-S profile ontology. However in order to exploit the advantage of the semantic description of the software instance ONAR repository includes more detailed descriptions of the inputs and outputs of the services.

Figure 14 presents the extensions of the OWL-S profile in order to support the semantics of the ONAR framework. More specifically OWL-S input and OWL-S output classes have been en-

Figure 13. Integration of the OWL-S profile ontology with UDDI (Paulocci et al., 2001)

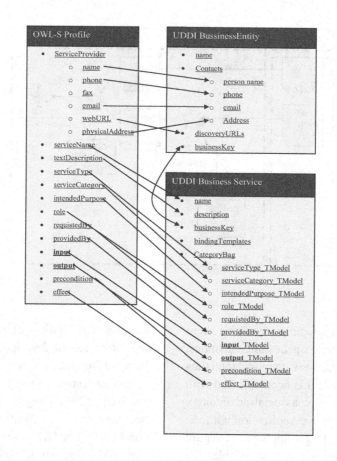

riched with four characteristics namely (a) domain (b) range (c) sub property of and (d) cardinality in order to be able to include the semantics of the software instances.

Thus ONAR repository based on the discovery mechanisms enables semantic searches of the necessary software instances that can be used in complex integration cases.

CONCLUSION AND FURTHER WORK

The utilization of ontologies for the conceptualization of existing system based on an integra-

tion centric approach requires validation and evaluation of our framework. Thus we aim first to validate whether ONAR framework can be applied to a wide variety of Information system. In this direction over this last year, we have been collecting feedback from the registered user of the framework. Currently we have examined e-business e-health (Artemis, 2005) and e-government (EU-Publi.com, 2005) integration cases.

In addition, we aim to create an evaluation framework that will enable us to evaluate ONAR to existing approaches based on its (a) maintainability, (b) complexity, (c) portability and (d) adaptability in order to assess quantitatively its performance to other integration frameworks.

Figure 14. Extensions in OWL-S profile (Source: Tektonidis et al., 2006)

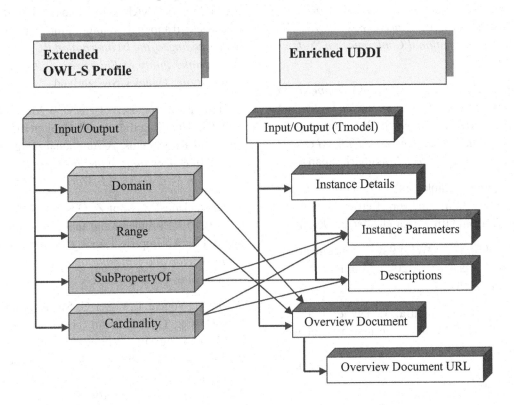

Finally, we are currently working on technical improvements and enrichments of the framework mainly for its adaptability feature in order for ONAR to be used from different information systems.

REFERENCES

Artemis IST-Project (2005). *A Semantic web service-based P2P infrastructure for the interoperability of medical information systems.* Retrieved February 13, 2007, from http://www.srdc.metu.edu.tr/webpage/projects/artemis/

Chiang, C. (2001). Wrapping legacy systems for use in heterogeneous computing environments. *Information and Software Technology, 43*(8), 497-507.

Corcho, O., Fernández-López, M., & Gómez-Pérez, A. (2003). Methodologies, tools and languages for building ontologies. Where is their meeting point? *Data & Knowledge Engineering, 46*(1), 41-64.

Dogac, A., Kabak, Y., & Laleci, G. (2004). Enriching ebXML registries with OWL ontologies for efficient service discovery. In *Proceedings of the 14th International Workshop on Research Issues on Data Engineering*, Boston.

Eu-Publi.com IST-Project (2005). *Facilitating cooperation amongst European public administration employees.* Retrieved February 13, 2007, from http://www.eu-publi.com

Linthicum, D. (2004). *Next generation application integration: From simple information to web services.* Addison-Wesley.

Liu, L., & Halper, M. (1997). *Incorporating semantic relationships into an object oriented database system.* In *Proceedings of the 32nd Hawaiian International Conference on Systems Science.*

Mecella, M., & Batini, C. (2000) *Cooperation of heterogeneous legacy information systems: A methodological framework.* In *Proceedings of the 4th International Enterprise Distributed Object Com-puting Conference*, Makuhari, Japan.

ONAR (2006). Ontologies based enterprise application integration framework. Retrieved Februaty 13, 2007, from http://research.altec.gr/ONAR

OWL (2006). W3C OWL 1.0 syntax specification. Retrieved February 13, 2007, from http://www.w3.org/TR/owl-ref/

Paolucci, M., Kawamura, T., Payne, T. R., & Sycara, M. (2002). Semantic matching of web services capabilities. In *Proceedings of the International Semantic Web Conference (ISWC)* (pp. 333-347).

Ratnakar, V., & Gil, Y. (2002). A comparison of (Semantic) mark-up languages. In *Proceedings of the 15th International FLAIRS Conference, Special Track on Semantic Web*, Pensacola, Finland.

Tektonidis, D., & Bokma, A., (2005). The utilization of ontologies for e-health systems integration. In *Proceedings of the 10th International Symposium on Health Information Management Research*, Thessaloniki, Greece.

Tektonidis, D., Bokma, A., Oatley, G., & Salampasis, M. (2005). ONAR: An ontologies-based service oriented application integration framework. In *Proceedings of the 1st International Conference on Interoperability of Enterprise Software and Applications*, Geneva, Switzerland.

.Tektonidis, D., Vontas, A., Hess, U., & Meschonat, J. (2002). Handling the shop-floor of an industry through ERP systems: A functional integration model. In *Proceedings of the International Conference on E-business & E-Work 2002*, Prague.

Themistocleous, M., Irani, Z., O'Keefe, R., & Paul, R. (2001). ERP problems and application integration issues: An empirical survey. In *Proceedings of the 34th Hawaiian International Conference on Systems Science*, Big Island.

Wache, H., Vögele, T., Visser, U., Stuckenschmidt, H., Schuster, G., Neumann, H., & Hübner, S. (2001). Ontology-based integration of information: A survey of existing approaches. In *Proceedings of the IJCAI-01 Workshop: Ontologies and Information Sharing*, Seattle, Washington.

W3C (2006). Semantic Web description. Retrieved February 13, 2007, from http://www.w3.org/2001/sw/

Chapter VII
A Recommender Agent to Support Knowledge Sharing in Virtual Enterprises

Renata S. S. Guizzardi
Fondazione Bruno Kessler, Italy

Pablo Gomes Ludermir
University of Twente, The Netherlands

Diego Sona
Fondazione Bruno Kessler, Italy

ABSTRACT

To remain competitive, virtual enterprises depend on effective knowledge management (KM). On the other hand, KM is deeply affected by the virtualization of modern organizations. As a result, KM systems need to be reshaped to adapt to these new conditions. This chapter presents KARe, a multi-agent recommender system that supports users sharing knowledge in a peer-to-peer environment. In this way, KARe reflects the intrinsically distributed nature of virtual enterprises. Supporting social interaction, the system allows users to share knowledge through questions and answers. This chapter focuses on KARe's recommendation algorithm, presenting its description and evaluation.

INTRODUCTION

The evolvement of information technology inaugurated new ways of structuring the organization and executing work. Many organizations became partially or completely virtual, processes gained a more dynamic and distributed nature and static and hierarchical structures shifted to increasingly adaptable and flexible ones. In this realm, *virtual*

enterprises can be defined as "distributed organizations and teams of people that meet and work together online. Group members rely on support systems to help gather, retrieve, and share relevant knowledge" (O'Leary, 1997). From this definition, one immediately concludes that it is paramount for these organizations to invest money and effort in finding effective solutions for collecting and sharing knowledge.

Focusing on these matters is the knowledge management (KM) research area, which deals with the creation, integration and use of knowledge, aiming at improving the performance of individuals and organizations. Advances in this field are mainly motivated by the assumption that organizations should focus on *knowledge assets* (generally maintained by the members of an organization) to remain competitive in the information society's age (Nonaka & Takeuchi, 1995). However, KM practices and systems are also affected by the virtualization of modern organizations. Merali and Davies (2001), for instance, mention three trends that have considerably added to the complexity of KM problems:

- The move towards flexible work practices, resulting in the geographical dispersion of people who would be normally co-located
- The increasing importance of cross-functional and inter-organizational collaborative work practices
- The need to provide quick and innovative organizational responses to changes in the environment

KM systems and practices should consequently be reshaped to adapt to these new conditions. Nevertheless, the current landscape concerning KM systems shows that most initiatives still rely on central repositories and portals, which assume standardized vocabularies, languages and classification schemes (Liao, 2002). Consequently, employees' lack of trust and motivation often lead to dissatisfaction (Merali & Davies, 2001; Pumajera, Bondarouk, & Sikkel, 2003). In other words, workers resist on sharing knowledge, since they do not know who is going to access it and what is going to be done with it.

Workers dissatisfaction many times leads the KM system to be abandoned, while people continue relying on their natural ways of finding knowledge, such as asking for the help of colleagues that are part of their circle of trust. The work described in this chapter aims at improving these natural processes by imitating in a virtual environment, the social processes that are involved in knowledge sharing. Instead of taking a centralized view, we rely on the distributed KM paradigm (Bonifacio & Bouquet, 2002), providing autonomous and locally managed knowledge sources organized in a peer-to-peer community. Peer-to-peer technology supports the horizontal relationship between people, seeing them as both consumers and providers of knowledge (Tiwana, 2003). Each peer controls personal knowledge artifacts and exchanges knowledge with other peers based on, for example, their common interests, roles, expertise and trust.

In this work, we present knowledgeable agent for recommendations (KARe), a socially aware recommender system that recommends artifacts to organizational members based on their natural language questions. KARe (Guizzardi, 2006) is designed and implemented as a multi-agent system, where agents cooperate to organize and search knowledge artifacts on behalf of their users, interacting in a peer-to-peer network. In order to look for the answers to the users' questions, we propose an algorithm based on information retrieval techniques that associate semantic information to the queries and to the artifacts being searched. This semantic information allows us to decrease the computational complexity of the algorithm, at the same time as providing less noisy results.

The remainder of this chapter is organized as follows: section 2 presents some background information on relevant research areas composing the scope of this work and how they relate to the domain of virtual enterprises; section 3 describes the proposed system; section 4 presents the description and evaluation of the recommendation algorithm; section 5 focuses on the developed prototypes of the KARe system; section 6 discusses some related work; and section 7 concludes this chapter.

THE SCOPE OF THIS WORK

This work is based on developments of four research areas, namely *intelligent agents, peer-to-peer communities, recommender systems* and *taxonomies*. This section summarizes each area, describing how they are applied in KARe and presenting their connections with the domain of focus of the present book.

Intelligent Agents

Intelligent agents are frequently proposed as appropriate entities to enable the analysis and design of complex systems, made up of several entities that behave autonomously and interact with each other in order to achieve a common objective (i.e., the system's overall functionality) (Jennings, Sycara, & Wooldridge, 1998). These characteristics are common to environments of virtual enterprises, which are generally composed of several autonomous agents working on behalf of one or more organizations that must cooperate on the pursuit of common goals (Cole & Gamble, 1997). The social and cognitive characteristics of agents are their main strength, turning them into promising constructs to emulate human interaction and rational behavior. Using them as modeling metaphor enables the analysis of the current social structures embedded in the organization, hence leading to more appropriate system proposals.

Especially in KM scenarios, agents may be found as appropriate building blocks for system development, for providing knowledge both *reactively* and in a *proactive* fashion (Merali & Davies, 2001). In other words, by taking into account the users' preferences and by monitoring their tasks, agents are both able to react to incoming knowledge requests, and to anticipate specific needs of the users, consequently delivering knowledge appropriately.

KARe explores the use of intelligent agents both as (a) a development metaphor, being modeled as a set of artificial agents interacting with human and organizational agents that are part of the enterprise's overall environment and (b) technological building blocks, being implemented on the basis of the Java Agent Development Framework (Bellifemine, Caire, Poggi, & Rimassa, 2003), a middleware containing the basic infrastructure to support agents' to locate and communicate with each other.

Peer-to-Peer Communities

The distributed nature of peer-to-peer networks reflects the naturally distributed character of knowledge and expertise within virtual enterprises (Tiwana, 2003). In virtual enterprises, knowledge and expertise exist sparsely in the members' understanding of each other's knowledge, and in the behavioral and cognitive similarities among individual users. In this respect, KARe aims at uncovering and making salient some of these hidden characteristics so that users might become more aware of the existing organizational knowledge.

Let us consider a virtual enterprise comprised of two or more organizations. The nodes of peer-to-peer network may change or even be completely removed; much in the way partnerships between different organizations may be created and dissolved, having in mind particular objectives and tasks. During the period of partnership, the members of the involved organizations have the opportunity to share knowledge and experience. Consequently, useful pieces of knowledge exchanged before they depart are likely to stay in both organizations, thus peer-to-peer networks function as a self-organizing environment motivating cross-fertilization, so valued in KM settings.

Central to this work is the recognition that social interaction is the driving force behind the creation of knowledge (Nonaka & Takeuchi, 1995). The members of KARe's peer-to-peer community exchange the knowledge artifacts maintained in their personal collection. In other words, KARe aims at imitating the social processes commonly applied when one has a particular problem to solve during one's daily work. Instead of consulting manuals and documentations, the worker is motivated to get involved in a dialog with workmates, which may lead the worker to grasp more than procedures, the values and tacit strategies adopted in the organization.

Recommender Systems

Managing information overload has been frequently mentioned as one of the challenges in environments surrounding virtual projects and enterprises (Cole & Gamble, 1997; Katzy, Evaristo & Zigurs, 2000; Merali & Davies, 2001). Recommender systems support users in selecting items of their interest or need from a big set of items, helping users to overcome the overwhelming feeling when facing a vast information source, such as the Web, an organizational repository or the like.

Recommendations may be differentiated by (Montaner, Lopez & de la Rosa, 2003): the items they recommend (e.g., movies, Web pages, etc.); the nature of the user models they use to guide the recommendations (e.g., history of items accessed by the user, topics indicating user interest, etc.); the recommendation techniques (mainly, how the user model is represented, what kinds of relevance mechanisms are used to update the user model, and which algorithm is used to generate recommendations); and the recommendation trigger, that is, whether the recommendation is started by the user or by the proactive behavior of the system. Section 3 describes how KARe deals with each of these aspects.

Taxonomies

Taxonomies and *ontologies* are two types of conceptual models which can be applied to describe a domain of discourse, modeling it as a set of concepts and relations. Although also applied in the past, the semantic Web has recently increased the interest on using such conceptual models to explicitate the semantics regarding knowledge artifacts (Davies, Fensel, & van Harmelen, 2003a). A taxonomy can be seen as a simplified ontology. On one hand, both conceptual models are identical regarding the use of concepts. However, while taxonomies focuses on hierarchical relations between concepts, ontologies may exhibit more complex relation types, such as part-of and associations. The choice of using taxonomies instead of ontologies in KARe is motivated by the DKM philosophy (Bonifacio & Bouquet, 2002), which defends that rather than sharing a unique conceptualization, each organizational member has a view of the work domain. Thus, each user builds a conceptual model. As ontologies are generally considered complex and time consuming to be built (Davies et al., 2003a), we consider taxonomies as a more realistic model for the common user to create. In a sense, many workers already create directory classifications of this kind, both for physical or digital file systems.

KARE: KNOWLEDGEABLE AGENT FOR RECOMMENDATIONS

KARe is a multi-agent system that recommends artifacts to meet the user needs based on questioning and answering. When we have a real problem at work, we often rely on asking a question to a colleague with whom we share the office, or to someone who is considered an expert in a subject related to our problem. If this is easy in an environment where workmates are collocated, it becomes more challenging when collaboration is virtual. Thus, KARe offers a solution to virtual enterprises, reflecting their intrinsically distributed nature while supporting social interaction among its members.

Asking and answering to questions is an interactive process. The questioner finds a suitable colleague and poses the doubt. Usually, this choice is based on the questioner's assumption that the colleague knows about the targeted subject, besides feelings of trust and comfort towards the responder. The responder, is likely to help the questioner, provided that the trust between them is mutual. The responder will then use the responder's own language and knowledge to provide the answer to the questioner. Besides solving the problem at hand, having the answer gives the questioner the ability to share this new knowledge with other colleagues.

KARe facilitates the questioning and answering process by using a peer-to-peer infrastructure. Each user (a peer) is able to organize knowledge assets (typically, working documents) according to the domain conceptualization, using a *taxonomy*. After defining meaningful concepts and their inter-relationships the user distributes the artifacts according to the "matching" concepts in the hierarchy. Figure 1 shows the organization of the personal knowledge assets of three users, connected by a peer-to-peer network.

KARe allows the user to pose natural language questions, searching in other peers' collection for answers among their stored artifacts. The answer can be found among *documents* or *messages* sent by other peers responding previous similar questions. In case no response is found, the system indicates a suitable peer (based on peer's user models) to provide the answer to that specific question. Having received a suitable answer from the indicated peer, the questioner now has this answer classified in the questioner's own taxonomy and stored in the questioner's system, so that the questioner can be consulted by others regarding the same subject. These processes are illustrated in Figure 1.

Figure 1(a) shows how KARe behaves when a user submits a question, manually contextualizing it by assigning it to a concept in the user's own taxonomy (in this case, the "Premium" concept). The system submits the question to a peer whose user model seems to describe a suitable responder. The user answers to the question submitting it through the system to the questioner. Note that the contextualization of the question may help the responder to understand more about the questioner's doubt. For instance, suppose that this is an insurance company and that Mike's question is "What measures should we take when a client is late with his payment for

Figure 1. Using KARe for asking and answering to questions

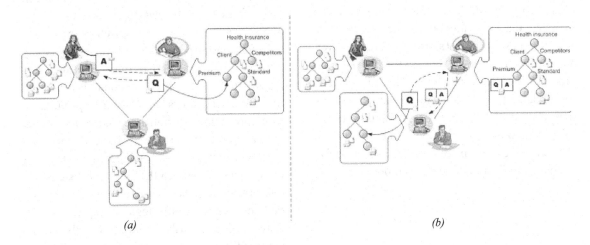

(a)   (b)

the acquired services?" Some information is not expressed in Mike's question, for instance: what kind of service is he talking about? However, this information is explicitated by the contextualization of the question, since it is classified under "Health insurance-Clients-Premium" in Mike's taxonomy. Besides clarifying the type of service (health insurance), this contextualization also indicates the type of client Mike is referring to (in this case, premium), which may have some impact in the responder's answer.

In Figure 1(b), Mike has already received the answer to his question, which was then classified under the concept he previously indicated. In this way, Mike now stores the answer for his own future reference and for sharing it with peers in need. The figure shows the case in which Joey requests similar information, by posing a question similar to Mike's. In this case, Mike does not need to personally answer the question, as the system has already found it in his computer, subsequently sending it to Joey.

By storing the same question/answer pair in different peers, we increase the possibility that this knowledge will remain in the organization even when some members are not available anymore. Considering that these peers will be involved in continuous interactions, the knowledge considered "useful" to the community (i.e., information and documents they need for their daily work) is likely to remain in the community, even if the members that originally owned them leave.

If the questioner is not satisfied with the answer automatically retrieved by KARe, the system provides the questioner with a list of possible responders. Responders are chosen based on their characteristics: expertise, reliability, trust, role, collaborative level and availability. These characteristics are maintained in user models, explained in detail in Guizzardi (2006).

RECOMMENDATION ALGORITHM DESCRIPTION AND EVALUATION

The core of the KARe system consists in mediating the question and answering process. An important part of handling this process comprises the automatic recommendation of existing answers to users' questions. The main focus of this chapter regards the description and assessment of this algorithm, which is based on information retrieval (IR) techniques (Baeza-Yates & Ribeiro-Neto, 1999).

In KARe, the knowledge items stored by a peer are not viewed as a flat collection of documents. Instead, the set of documents are structured by a taxonomy which classifies each of these items under a concept of the tree (both leaves and internal nodes). The choice of using taxonomies to classify knowledge artifacts provides the system peers with a contextualized view of knowledge artifacts (as seen in section 3). However, this is just part of the reason behind this choice. Another strong claim we make is that such information may be helpful in aiding our recommendation agents to automatically find knowledge on behalf of the system users.

In a traditional IR system, items are all considered to be part of a unique collection, which should be completely searched when a retrieval request is issued by the user. In KARe, however, taxonomies are used to classify documents. Consequently, the system is able to search for the answer only considering particular nodes of the taxonomy where the answer is most probably located. Besides diminishing computational complexity, this approach allows the system to profit from user knowledge, previously encoded in personal taxonomies, to retrieve related knowledge.

The search process is triggered when a user asks a question, which the user first assigns to a concept (node) in the taxonomy. Hence, a question (or knowledge request) is logically represented not only by the keywords it contains but also by the keywords representing the concept which classifies it. For finding an appropriate answer, KARe must first match two distinguishing taxonomies, analogously to (Avesani, Giunchiglia, & Yatskevich, 2005; Bouquet, Serafini, & Zanobini, 2003). More precisely, when receiving a knowledge request from the questioner, the system must find in the responders' taxonomies which concepts are more likely to contain artifacts that satisfy this request, subsequently retrieving it.

Although our assumption about the gains of applying taxonomies seems reasonable, it can only be proven by testing our algorithm using real datasets. Thus, besides describing the applied techniques, this chapter shall also present empirical data to validate them. The assessment was based on two existing datasets which simulate well the problem at hand, and the evaluation was based on measures of recall and precision of the proposed algorithm in comparison with a standard approach. Notice that a KARe user can also manage the artifacts with a nonstructured approach, that is, having only a flat collection of items. This only influences the quality of results but not the system functioning.

Information Retrieval Modeling

The approach to retrieve the information is a framework that models the documents and queries into their logical forms, and a ranking function that orders the document set according to queries. Thus, the IR models may be represented as a quadruple $\{D, Q, F, R(q_i, d_j)\}$ where (Baeza-Yates & Ribeiro-Neto, 1999):

- $D = \{d_1,..., d_n\}$ is the set of documents
- Q is the representation of the user query
- F is the framework to model documents, queries, and their relationships into a logical form
- $R(q, d_j)$ is a function to rank documents $d_i \in D$ according to a particular query $q \in Q$.

There are different ways to approach the modeling "framework" and the "ranking function". This results in different IR models, such as: the Boolean model, the probabilistic model and the vector space model. In this work, we use the vector space model, thus describing it in detail.

A collection of text documents is generally represented by a vocabulary, that is, a small set of index terms determined as representative of such collection. In the vector space model, documents and queries are treated as real algebraic vectors where the dimension of the vectors is determined by the size of a vocabulary. Therefore, once the vocabulary is determined (i.e., the text is preprocessed, determining the index-terms) all documents are represented by vectors. Each dimension of the vectors is calculated based on the frequency of each index term in each document itself. Having this vectorial representation, it is possible to calculate the similarity between couples of documents or between a document and a query.

In Figure 2, the depicted vectors are the abstraction of a query q and a document d_j from a set of documents D, and the angle θ indicates how close these vectors are. There are several measures for vectors similarity, and one of the most used in text documents retrieval, also adopted here, is the cosine of the angle θ formed by the two vectors.

Each dimension value of the vectors describing the documents is computed using the frequency of the corresponding index term in the document itself. There are several ways to compute these dimensions, and this process is called *index term weighting*. In our algorithm, we adopted the *TF/IDF* representation, which is one of the most used. This method computes the weights in two steps. First, given a document $d_i \in D$, the *term frequency* (TF) f_k is computed for each index term t_k in the vocabulary. Second, the resulting term frequency is weighted multiplying it by the *inverse document frequency* (IDF), which mea-

Figure 2. The cosine function is used to compute the similarity between a query q and a document d_j

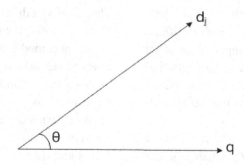

sures the fraction of documents that contain the corresponding index term as follows:

$$d_{i,k} = f_k * \log \frac{N}{n_k} \qquad (1)$$

where N is the total amount of documents in the collection, and n_k is the number of documents containing the index term t_k.

The aim of using both *TF* and *IDF* in the weight calculation is on one hand, to increase the weight if a term is very popular in a document and on the other hand, to penalize the weight (i.e., to decrease its value) if the term is present amongst many documents. In this way, the terms of a document, which are both representative and discriminant, have stronger weight when computing the similarity to a query.

Algorithm Description

As previously outlined, to find relevant documents in a collection, the standard vector space approach computes the similarity between a query of the user and all the documents in the given collection. Then, the most similar documents are selected as the winners. This approach, however, disregards any knowledge that users may have about the structure of the concepts related to the artifacts being searched. This can lead to noisy or not relevant search results. For instance, trying to search for the word "agents" in a standard search engine (e.g., Google, Yahoo, Looksmart, etc.) result in documents about several different kinds of agents (e.g., chemical agents, software agents, real state agents, travel agents, etc.).

In KARe, the user is allowed to classify the documents according to a personal taxonomy, which represents a personal view of the domain of interest. In this way, similar documents are grouped by the user under the same concept as in the taxonomy tree. In addition to that, before submitting the question, the user contextualizes the query, assigning it to a specific concept in the taxonomy. By doing this, the user gives to the system an extra hint on the query's content. Aiming at reducing the noise of the search (not relevant or wrong documents), our algorithm exploits the taxonomic information supplied by the user to determine the region of the search space where the required information is more likely to be found. Besides providing more accurate results, this approach also reduces the computational complexity of the algorithm in comparison with the standard approach. This happens due to the fact that the standard approach needs to search the whole documents collection (complete search space) for an answer. Conversely, following our algorithm, KARe only searches particular regions of the search space.

To illustrate our approach, we go back to the example earlier presented in section 3. Consider two users, Mike and Joey, whose taxonomies are depicted in Figure 3. The taxonomies classify the user's personal documents and also serve to contextualize the user's question. Suppose now that Joey submits the following question as query: "How should we deal with clients' late payment?" contextualizing it in the "policies" concept of his taxonomy. Referring back to the previous example, we know that Mike had a similar doubt in the past (i.e., he previously asked "What measures should we take when a client is late with his payment for the acquired services?") whose answer is now classified under the concept "premium". But how can KARe know about that?

Our algorithm should be able to identify which concept in Mike's taxonomy is more similar to the "policies" concept, where Joey's question is contextualized. Then, the answer can be searched within this concept. Essentially, each of the concepts of the user taxonomy has a vectorial representation, which is an instance on the reference vocabulary containing the weights of the index terms that appears in the documents classified under the concept. Figure 4 illustrates a short vocabulary index and a vector representing

a given concept C, which contains the index terms "client", "insurance" "pay" and "health", but does not contain the terms "life" and "customer". In this figure, the used weights are Boolean (i.e., "1" indicates the presence of an index term, while "0" indicates its absence). Conversely, as previously outlined, in our approach the weights are given by the *TF/IDF* representation. For finding the most similar concept to a given concept C, the algorithm calculates the similarity between the vector representing C and the vector of each of the concepts in the responder taxonomy.

Given a concept C_i, the corresponding reference vector c_i is calculated with basis on the vectors representing the documents classified under that concept. Besides the documents' keywords, the concept label l_i is also considered in the vector calculation. In fact, not only the label of the concept itself, but in addition also the labels of the ancestors of the given concept are taken into account, as has been earlier proposed in (Adami, Avesani, & Sona, 2003). More precisely, this is achieved by including the labels of all concepts of the taxonomy in the collection's vocabulary.

Figure 3. Taxonomies of Mike and Joey contextualizing documents and questions

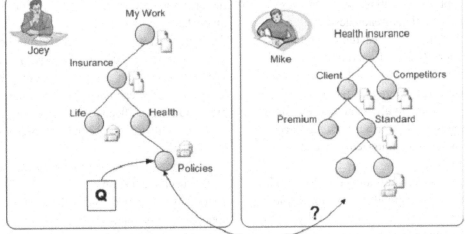

Figure 4. A short vocabulary index and a vector representation for a concept C in the user taxonomy

Vocabulary index					
client	insurance	pay	health	life	costumer
Vector of Concept C					
1	1	1	1	0	0

Consequently, the label of the concept along with the label of the concept's ancestors is considered in the concept's vector calculation. The determination of the concept reference vectors follows the Equation 2.

$$c_{i,j} = \sum_{a \in A_i} l_{a,j} + \frac{\sum_{k \in D_i} d_{k,j}}{|D_i|} \quad (2)$$

where $A_i = \{j \mid C_i \text{ is ancestor of } C_j\}$ indicates the ancestors of concept C_i, $l_{a,j}$ stands for the index term t_j in the label for concept C_a, $D_i = \{k \mid d_k \text{ is classified under concept } C_i\}$ is the set of indexes of documents classified under concept C_i, and $|A_i|$ and $|D_i|$ indicate the dimension of the two sets respectively.

Here, $c_{i,j}$ stands for the weight of the term t_j on the concept C_i. The above equation uses the *TF/IDF* representation already described in section 4.1, both for the document representation and for the concept labels $l_{a,j}$. Equation 2 is basically an average formula, which calculates concept vector c_i based on an average of the weight of the keywords pertaining to all documents classified under concept C_i. This term is then regularized according to the prior knowledge encoded into the concept labels.

We call the process of finding the best matching concept in the responder's taxonomy *query scope reduction*. This is the main novelty of our approach. In summary, the query scope reduction can be seen as a reduction in the *search space* before we retrieve information from it, based on the fact that the required information is more likely to be found in a specific region of this space. Adding this process prior to the execution of the query, we aim to increase the quality of our search, resulting in a less noisy result set, thus recommending mostly pertinent documents to the users. In addition to that, it considerably reduces the computational complexity of the algorithm since it diminishes the set of documents to be searched.

It is important to note that each user's taxonomy uses a different vocabulary, that is, the vectors of the concepts in each taxonomy are created based on different sets of index terms. Consequently, the first step on the query scope reduction is to project the concept vector coming from the questioner in the new space of the responder. This is made by calculating the intersection between the index vector of the questioner and the index vector of the responder. In this way, the concept vector coming from the questioner may be projected into the vocabulary of the responder. This projection is specifically targeted at the problem of coping with different semantic representations of a domain.

After the query scope reduction, the answer to the user's question is searched within the documents classified under the best matching concept(s). For that, all keywords of the user's query are taken into account to select the artifacts of the given concept. In addition to the query's

Listing 1. An excerpt of KARe's recommendation algorithm

```
procedure answer(concVectA, peerQuest, questioner)

//step 1: search the best matching concept for the scope reduction
projConceptVectorA := intersect(concVectA, indexB)

for each (concept on the user B context) {
              s := similarity(currentConceptVectorB, projConceptVec-
torA)

              if (s > maxSimilarity) {

              bestConcept := currentConceptB

              maxSimilarity := s
              }
}

//step 2: search among the documents in the bestConcept
queryVector := createQueryVector(peerQuest, indexB)

for each (doc in bestConcept)
  docList.add(doc,similarity(queryVector,docVector))
  docList.sortBySimilarity()

//step 3: send the answer back to the questioner
sendAnswer(docList, questioner)
```

terms, the labels of the concept classifying the query and its ancestors are attached to the query (as extra terms). In this way the query is embedded with enriched contextualized information. The documents are then ranked in a descending order according to the similarity with the query, and the result set is finally sent to the questioner. Our recommendation algorithm is summarized in the pseudo-code shown in Listing 1.

Case Study

The theory behind our algorithm seems to be consistent, however in order to prove that it actually brings any gains in the efficiency and accuracy of our search, it is advisable to assess it through a case study using real data. The ideal situation would be to experiment our algorithm against two taxonomies classifying real questions and answers. However, as such dataset is not available at the moment, we simulated this dataset using two taxonomies that classify scientific papers in a case study. The question is simulated by the title of a paper, and the paper's body provides the answer.

This seems reasonable because a question is usually short, providing us with a few keywords for the search. The answer, on the other hand, tends to be a longer piece of text. For performing the case study, we used two existing taxonomies: the questioner's taxonomy was created by a Ph.D. student to collect papers of her interest, while the one of the responder is taken from the ACM computing classification system (http://www.acm.org/class/). Table 1 presents some statistics regarding these two taxonomies.

The case study may be divided into two main phases: preparation of the taxonomies, and execution of the assessment. In the first phase, the following activities were performed:

- A set of papers to be used as queries were selected. These papers should be classified by both taxonomies so that we know which is the contextualizing concept in the questioner's taxonomy and the concept the algorithm should find in the responder's taxonomy.

- All the selected papers were then subtracted from the questioner's taxonomy to avoid bias (i.e., the keywords of the selected papers should not be used to compute the concept vectors in the questioner's taxonomy).
- The titles of all the selected papers were subtracted from the papers classified by both taxonomies to avoid bias (i.e., the title keywords should not be used to compute the concept and document vectors in both taxonomies), as they were to be used as queries.
- All papers and titles were preprocessed removing the stop-words and stemming the resulting terms to common roots, then a vocabulary was created for each taxonomy taking the frequent and discriminative terms, and finally, all papers were encoded using the vocabulary of the corresponding taxonomies.

The second part of the case study (i.e., the process carried out to execute the assessment) is illustrated in Figure 5. The first step is to manually contextualize the query, by assigning it to a concept in the questioner's taxonomy. In fact, the information regarding which concept should contextualize the query was already known, since the queries were extracted from papers classified under both taxonomies. Next, the query (i.e., a paper title) is preprocessed removing stop-words and stemming, and is then submitted to the responder's taxonomy along with the contextualizing concept's vector. The

algorithm then searches for a "similar" concept in the responder's taxonomy (query scope reduction). After the targeted concept is found, the answer to the query is retrieved from the documents within this concept. Finally, we analyze the result set, verifying whether the algorithm is able: (a) to find in the responder's taxonomy the *concept* that correctly classifies the paper whose title is the query; and (b) to retrieve from the responder's taxonomy, the *specific paper* corresponding to the title used as query.

The case study is, thus, defined as the analysis of the proposed algorithm to evaluate its information retrieval performance measures in comparison with a standard vector model approach. We compared the results of our algorithm with the standard approach based on the vector model (i.e., without the query scope reduction step). Concerning our approach, we considered two options: (1) to reduce the search space to the best matching concept only; and (2) to reduce the search space to a small subset of concepts that best matched the query (two and three concepts). We evaluated these approaches in terms of *recall* (i.e., the fraction of relevant documents retrieved) and *precision* (i.e., the fraction of retrieved documents that are relevant). Then, the harmonic mean *F1* of recall and precision was calculated and used to compare our results:

$$F1 = \frac{2 * precision * recall}{precision + recall} \qquad (3)$$

Table 1. Some statistics regarding the taxonomies

	Questioner Taxonomy	Responder Taxonomy
Number of Documents	250	315
Number of Concepts	28	15
Average Documents/Concepts	9	21

Figure 5. A schema of the process used to perform the assessment

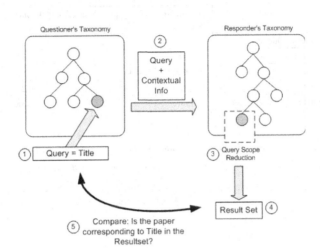

Our hypothesis is that our algorithm should, on average, produce better precision and recall results and take less effort than the standard vector model approach. We identified as parameter factors for the case study the number of concepts selected in the responder taxonomy and the question itself. The dependent variables analyzed are the *F1 measure* and the *computational effort* (i.e., number of comparisons between keywords).

Discussion

We performed 75 queries over our taxonomies, and the results are shown in Table 2. The first column of the table shows the results of the standard approach. The second, third and fourth columns show the results of our approach when returning documents from one, two and three concepts respectively.

As previously illustrated in Figure 5, our assessment considers two important results: the ability to retrieve the correct document and the ability to map the query to the correct concept. Hence, *F1* was correspondingly calculated based on two quantities: (1) the number of times the algorithm finds the specific document whose title

is being searched (F1-doc); and (2) the number of retrieved documents related to the one being searched, which is the number of documents that are classified under the concept being searched (F1-concept). The second measure is determined counting for each query the number of relevant papers among the best-ranked 20 papers.

Observing the number of documents found and the corresponding F1-doc measure it is clear that the standard approach (i.e., search the documents crawling all the papers) is much more effective than our approach (reduced search space). This is particularly true when only the best matching concept is used to limit the search space. Conversely, when searching for related papers, it is evident that our approach gives better results (see the F1-concept measure). In addition to that, our approach considerably reduces the number of comparisons needed to reach a result (see that for 1 concept, it is one order of magnitude faster that the standard approach).

Our approach with varying number of best matching concepts to reduce the search space is worth further discussion. Actually, it is easy to see that, in general, when we increase the number or searched concepts, we increase the chance of

Table 2. Results of the case study

	Standard Approach	**1 concept**	**2 concepts**	**3 concepts**
Number of Queries	75			
Documents Found	69	25	37	43
F1-doc	0.920	0.333	0.493	0.573
F1-concept	0.175	0.243	0.238	0.206
Number of Comparisons	158K	21K	33K	43K

The graphics depict the recall measure for all 75 queries made with the standard approach and our proposed approach using respectively 1 concept (graphic A), 2 concepts (graphic B), and 3 concepts (graphic C).

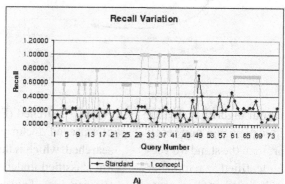

A)

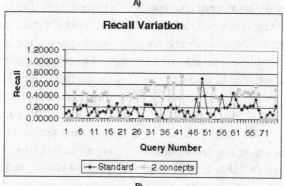

B)

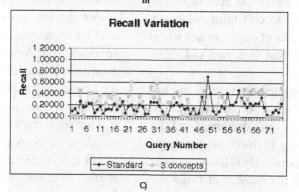

C)

finding the specific paper we look for, but we also end up having a result set with more noise. Moreover, the number of required comparisons is also increased. Hence there is a trade-off between different elements that must be taken into account when implementing our approach for a specific application.

Our approach has the disadvantage of not finding the right concept many times. This becomes apparent by the comparison of the graphics exhibited by Figures 6. These graphics exhibit comparisons between the standard approach and each variation of our algorithm. Notice however, that in general there is a correlation between the standard approach and our approach. Actually, we observe that when our approaches have low recall, the standard approach tends to have low recall as well. Conversely, a high recall in the standard approach also coincides with a high recall in our models.

In summary, the results show that the best solution requires the right balance between the probability of finding very specific information and the ability of retrieving related information. It is also important to note that increasing the probability of finding specific information also increases the number of comparisons the algorithm should perform, thus turning the algorithm more computational complex. The results also appoint

in which direction our work should proceed, that is, to enhance the ability of the algorithm of finding the right concept. Hence, our future solution will combine both finding specific and related information at once, while also keeping the computational complexity very low.

PROTOYPES

Two prototypes of the KARe system were implemented: a desktop computer version, and a prototype for access in a handheld device.

The main purpose of the *desktop system* is to allow organizational members to exchange knowledge while organizing their personal knowledge items locally (Ludermir, 2005). Figure 7 shows a screenshot of the desktop prototype. On the left part of the window, the figure depicts a user's taxonomy, showing in a tree of concepts, how the user structured the knowledge. On the top, there is a text box where the user enters the question, followed by a "Search" button. Having inserted the question, the user may press this button to trigger the searching mechanism. The results of the search are shown in the right side of the screen, classified by peer (the peer from which the artifact was retrieved), and ordered by the similarity of the artifact regarding the question submitted by the user.

Figure 7. A screenshot of the desktop prototype

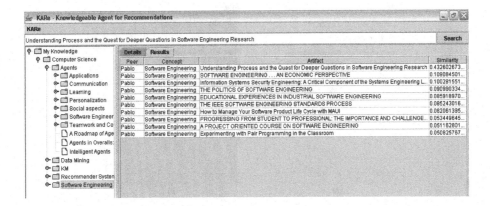

The KARe *handheld prototype* (Ludermir 2005) is based on the assumption that suitable responders to a specific question can be selected based on their geographical proximity to the questioner. This assumption comes from the realization that people usually share spaces with individuals with whom they share interests, for example, workmates within an organization, researchers in a conference and classmates in an educational institution.

By changing user's location, the recommendation is likely to change as well. In contrast, if you try to get a recommendation from the desktop system, the result is the same until the document index is updated. This happens because the KARe's desktop system searches for knowledge artifacts by broadcasting the knowledge request to all peers connected to the network. Thus, such design is slightly modified to accommodate the new search mode. After receiving a request from the user, a search is triggered when the system senses the presence of other peers in the vicinity. Figure 8 (A) shows the resulting screen in the handheld after identifying the devices that run KARe. The request is then submitted solely to these peers. In this way, the handheld prototype also avoids the problems of scaling the system to a great number of peers, which still remains to be

targeted in the desktop version. Finally, KARe notifies the user in case new recommendations were provided by the contacted peer, as seen in Figure 8 (B).

The desktop prototype was developed as two integrated components: recommender agents component and information retrieval component. The recommendation agents component was implemented using the JADE framework. JADE works as a middleware for the agents communication. To enable their communication, an ontology was developed using the Protégé Ontology Editor (http://protege.stanford.edu/), and implemented in Java classes using the Beangenerator Protégé plug-in (http://acklin.nl/page.php?id=34/). The implementation of the *information retrieval* component is based on the use of the Java Lucene library (http://lucene.apache.org/). Lucene is a search engine library that contains implementations of well-known algorithms, such as: the inverted file index, a stopword remover and the stemming algorithm. Persistence of the relevant metadata regarding knowledge artifacts was achieved with the use of XML files. The taxonomy is also represented in an XML file, structured as prescribed in a particularly developed XML schema.

The development of the handheld prototype added an extra component on top of the two

Figure 8. Screenshots of the handheld prototype

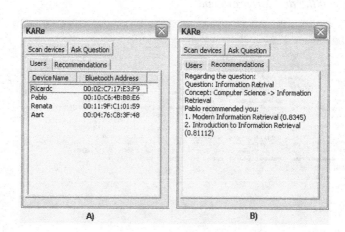

components just described. The interface between the new *peer discovery* component and the *recommendation agent* component is achieved by wrapping up outputs of the former into agent communication language messages that are then sent to the latter. As in the desktop version, the agents are arranged in a peer-to-peer fashion composing a recommender system running on desktop computers. The *recommendation agents* and *information retrieval* components are practically intact. However, a different GUI was developed to run in the iPAQ handheld device. To overcome problems with the limited resources on such devices, the recommendation service was kept in the desktop. This application communicates with the iPAQ through a wireless link to receive the user's inputs and sends back recommendations. The GUI was implemented using the personal profile API implementation of the Java 2 Micro Edition version (J2ME). Finally, the *peer discovery* component was implemented using the Interconnect architecture (Uiterkamp, 2005), developed to enable HTTP communication between service hosts and nomadic service components.

RELATED WORK

This section discusses some work related to KARe. Section 6.1 presents a comparison of KARe with other KM systems, while section 6.2 focuses on related approaches to the proposed recommendation algorithm.

KARe vs. Other KM Systems

Currently, many systems were developed with the purpose of supporting KM. Here, we do not try to be exhaustive, but simply to describe three of them that we believe are more related to KARe.

KEEx (Bonifacio, Bouquet, Mameli, & Nori, 2004) allows users to share knowledge in a peer-to-peer fashion. Similarly to KARe, the users of KEEx contextualize their documents using taxonomies called contexts. Then, they are allowed to search for other documents by keyword or by context similarity. While sharing some features with KEEx, such as the use of taxonomy and the adoption of a peer-to-peer model, KARe's main difference is that it provides recommendations based on questions and answers, thus simulating electronically the natural processes of knowledge sharing.

The work proposed by Vassileva (2002) proposes a peer-to-peer system to support the exchange of messages between students. A student needing help can request it through an agent, which finds other students to respond to it. As in KARe, there is a centralized matchmaker service, which maintains models of the users competences and matches them to incoming help-requests. In comparison with this work, KARe basis the choice for the best responder on a more complete set of social and cognitive characteristics, such as expertise, interest, trust, reliability, collaborative level and organizational role (Guizzardi, 2006).

OntoShare (Davies, Duke, & Stonkus, 2003b) creates a content management system used by organization's members to classify and share knowledge artifacts based on a shared ontology. Differently than KARe, however, this system adopts a client-server approach, and presupposes the existence of a shared conceptualization (ontology) among the members of the community.

KARe Recommendation Algorithm vs. Other Approaches

The most distinguishing feature of KARe is given by the consideration of taxonomic information to recommend knowledge artifacts. We have no knowledge of other initiatives that apply taxonomies to aid the process of questioning and answering, adding to the user's query the contextual information provided by the concept to which this query is assigned. Other than this, KARe's distinction is materialized in the query scope reduction stage of the recommendation algorithm, in which a concept of the questioner's taxonomy is matched with concepts from the responder's taxonomy. Matching taxonomies has been targeted before, having gained considerable strength in the last few years, especially boomed by developments in the semantic Web. In this section, we cite two initiatives more closely related to ours.

There are mainly two ways of conciliating two different taxonomies, A and B. One focuses on mapping labels associated with a concept of taxonomy A into concept labels of taxonomy B. Among the works that adopt such technique, some simply match keywords while others go beyond this, considering semantic information about the labels, usually supported by a dictionary or thesaurus. This is the case of the CtxMatch algorithm (Bouquet et al., 2003), a linguistic-based approach which adopts WordNet (http://wordnet.princeton.edu/w3wn.html) lexical reference system to disambiguate and stem labels. The problem with this kind of technique is that it usually results in low recall. Although the used dictionary or thesaurus provides valuable additional information about the labels, this is hardly enough and a match in the responding taxonomy is rarely obtained (Avesani et al., 2005).

Our algorithm adopts a different approach of matching taxonomies, by considering not only the labels representing the concepts of the taxonomy but also the keywords of all documents classified under the concept. This adds information to the concept representation, usually improving the algorithm's performance at least in terms of recall. A similar approach is adopted by (Avesani et al., 2005). However, this work tries to identify the semantic relationship between the two corresponding nodes, while our approach limits itself to finding one or a few most similar nodes in the responder's taxonomy. Another difference is that the approach of (Avesani et al., 2005) requires the two taxonomies to share documents, as the simi-

larity between them is calculated on the basis of this redundancy. Our algorithm does not require such duplication, working well even if there is no redundant information.

CONCLUSION AND FUTURE WORK

Here we presented KARe, an agent-oriented recommender system that simulates the natural social processes involved in knowledge sharing in virtual enterprises. The suitability of KARe for virtual enterprises can be justified by the fact that the system reflects the natural distribution of this kind of environment. Hence, different organizations can partner and exchange knowledge in a peer-to-peer network. When these organizations depart, the exchanged knowledge remains in all participant organizations, enriching their knowledge flow.

The core of the system is an information retrieval algorithm that was the focus of this chapter. Besides describing such algorithm, this chapter presents empirical results to confirm the algorithm's efficiency, and discusses the system's prototypes. The results of the algorithm assessment showed considerable gains in the recommendation quality are achieved by using the proposed approach. In the future, we aim at confirming this conclusion by evaluating the algorithm against different and larger datasets. Improvements in our evaluation approach can be achieved by experimenting KARe with real users. This would provide us with taxonomies classifying a representative sample of papers, besides unbiased queries. It is however essential to count on several people during a large period of time to have results with statistical confidence

To enhance the query scope reduction performance, we plan the experimentation with the smoothing technique presented in Sona, Veeramachaneni, Avesani, and Polettini (2004) to improve the representation of the taxonomic concepts. Smoothing is a technique targeted at situations in which there are many nodes classifying only a few knowledge artifacts. Thus, such technique is suitable for initial stages of system use, when KARe peers are starting to collect their documents and exchange questions and answers.

In addition to this, scalability issues must be targeted before KARe can become a real product. This issue particularly regards our desktop prototype, which broadcasts knowledge requests to all other peers in the network. We foresee two possibilities to overcome this problem: (a) calculating beforehand the nearest neighbor peers to answer to requests on specific subjects, thus informing system which of them are more likely to have the answer it seeks; and (b) setting up a similarity threshold, limiting the number of documents exchanged between peers to reduce network traffic.

REFERENCES

Adami, G., Avesani, P., & Sona, D. (2003). Clustering documents in a web directory. In *Proceedings of the 5th ACM International Workshop on Web Information and Data Management* (pp. 66-73).

Avesani, P., Giunchiglia, F., & Yatskevich, M. (2005) A large scale taxonomy mapping evaluation. In Y. Gil et al. (Eds.), *International Semantic Web conference* (pp 67-81). Berlin: Springer-Verlag.

Baeza-Yates, R., & Ribeiro-Neto, B. (1999) *Modern information retrieval*. Addison-Wesley.

Bellifemine, F., Caire, G., Poggi, A., & Rimassa, G. (2003). JADE a whitepaper. Retrieved February 13, 2007, from http://jade.tilab.com/papers/2003/WhitePaperJADEEXP.pdf

Bonifacio, M., & Bouquet, P. (2002). Distributed knowledge management: A systemic approach. In G. Minati & E. Pessa (Eds.), *Emergence in complex, cognitive, social and biological systems*. New York: Kluwer Academic/Plenum Publishers.

Bonifacio, M., Bouquet, P., Mameli, G., & Nori, M. (2004). Peer-mediated distributed knowledge management. In L. van Elst, V. Dignum, & A. Abecker (Eds.), *Agent-mediated knowledge management* (pp. 31-47). Heidelberg: Springer-Verlag.

Bouquet, P., Serafini, L., & Zanobini, S. (2003). Semantic coordination: A new approach and an application. In *Proceedings of the Second International Semantic Web Conference* (pp. 130-145). Berlin: Springer-Verlag.

Cole, D. (1997). Application of knowledge based systems to virtual organizations. In *Workshop on Using AI in Electronic Commerce, Virtual Organizations and Enterprise Knowledge Management to Reengineer the Corporation*, AAAI Workshop.

Davies, J., Fensel, D., & van Harmelen, F. (Eds.). (2003a) *Towards the Semantic Web: Ontology-driven knowledge management*. West Sussex, UK: Wiley.

Davies, J., Duke, A., & Stonkus, A. (2003b). *OntoShare: Evolving ontologies in a knowledge sharing system*. In Davies et al. (2003a), pp. 161-177.

Guizzardi, R. S. S. (2006). *Agent-oriented constructivist knowledge management*. Unpublished doctoral thesis, University of Twente, The Netherlands.

Jennings, N. R., Sycara, K. P., & Wooldridge, M. (1998). A Roadmap of Agent Research and Development. *Journal of Autonomous Agents and Multi-Agent Systems*, *1*(1), 7-36.

Katzy, B., Evaristo, R., & Zigurs, I. (2000). Knowledge management in virtual projects: A research agenda. In *Proceedings of IEEE 33rd Hawaii International Conference on System Sciences*.

Liao, S. (2002). Knowledge management technologies and applications: Literature review from 1995 to 2002. *Expert Systems with Applications, 25*, 155-164.

Ludermir, P. G. (2005). *Supporting knowledge management using a nomadic service for artifact recommendation.* Unpublished master's dissertation, University of Twente, The Netherlands.

Merali, Y., & Davies, J. (2001). Knowledge capture and utilization in virtual communities. In *Proceesings of the First International Conference on Knowledge Capture*, Canada.

Montaner, M., Lopez, B., & de la Rosa, J. L. (2003). A taxonomy of recommender agents on the internet. *Artificial Intelligence Review, 19,* 285-330.

Nonaka, I., & Takeuchi, H. (1995). *The knowledge-creating company: How Japanese companies create the dynamics of innovation.* New York: Oxford University Press.

O'Leary, D. E. (1997). The internet, intranets, and the AI renaissance. *IEEE Computer, 30*(1), 71-78.

Pumareja, D., Bondarouk, T., & Sikkel, K. (2003). Supporting knowledge sharing isn't easy: Lessons learnt from a case study. In *Proceedings of the Information Resource Management Association International Conference*, Philadelphia.

Sona, D., Veeramachaneni, S., Avesani, P., & Polettini, N. (2004). Clustering with propagation for hierarchical document classification. In *Proceedings of the ECML Workshop on Statistical Approaches to Web Mining* (pp. 50-61).

Tiwana, A. (2003). Affinity to infinity in peer-to-peer knowledge platforms. *Communications of ACM, 46*(5), 76-80.

Uiterkamp, E. S. (2005). *Nomadic positioning services for a mobile service platform.* Unpublished master's dissertation, University of Twente, The Netherlands.

Vassileva, J. (2002). Supporting peer-to-peer user communities. In R. Meersman & Z. Tari (Eds.), *CoopIS/DOA/ODBASE 2002* (pp. 230-247). Berlin: Springer-Verlag.

Chapter VIII
Framework of Agent–Based Intelligent System for Distributed Virtual Enterprise Project Control

Yee Ming Chen
Yuan Ze University, Taiwan, ROC

Shih-Chang Wang
Lung-Hwa University of Science and Technology, Taiwan, ROC

ABSTRACT

Virtual enterprise-oriented projects need the support of a distributed project management system, which concerns the collaboration of different departments and enterprises. In this chapter, we propose a multi-agent system with negotiation strategies for project schedule control—a collaborative system framework wherein a distributed project can be scheduled dynamically by agents in the virtual enterprise environment. A prototype of the multi-agent systems with the negotiation strategies is implemented by Java, JADE, FIPA-ACL, and the negotiation strategies are experimentally validated. It successfully demonstrates on the online coordination and resolution of scheduling dynamically while encountering unexpected events to meet each project participant's requirements.

INTRODUCTION

Recent developments on environments for computer supported collaborative work, distributed knowledge management and software agents for sharing resources and computational services have lead to an increased interest in what has been termed virtual enterprises. The companies engaged in a virtual enterprise share their knowledge, their competencies and business relationships in order to perform the virtual enterprise's task. This combination of forces is to enable the companies to reach global markets with products and solutions that each of them could not have accomplished on its own. The increasing globalization and flexibility required by companies generated new issues relating to the management of large-scale projects and the cooperation between enterprises within geographically distributed virtual enterprises. Virtual enterprises are established in order to be able to flexibly react to the opportunities of highly dynamic global markets. The globalization of markets leads to the formation of spatially distributed production and logistics services. In a distributed global enterprise project, as the project participants have the characteristics of independence, specialty and distribution by nature, and are always situated at different locations. In contrast, the traditional control mechanism of the project by the general contractor seems to be more often centralized. In current, highly competitive and changeable environments, the traditionally centralized mechanism of the project scheduling control technique for a distributed global enterprise project can easily encounter various difficulties. The major one is that the centralized control mechanism of the general contractor may lose efficacy (Kim, 2001). Although a general contractor conventionally takes the majority of the responsibility of coordinating all of project participants, due to the project participants' characteristics of independence, specialty and distribution, and some of them may not have directly contractual relationships with the general contractor. Accordingly, most project participants still have to monitor schedule progress and to solve difficulties on their own as much as possible (Kim, Paulson, Levitt, Fischer, & Petrie, 2003). Also, various interface problems can occur during a project execution stage because of the general contractor's lack of specialized expertise, shortage of manpower and slow responses (Al-Hammad, 2000; Hinze & Tracey, 1994).

Software agents provide the technology necessary to dynamically negotiate, select and utilize the appropriate services required in today's highly dynamic virtual enterprise. With the emergence and rapid development of multi-agent systems

(MAS), these problems then become solvable in timely manner, and have been the focus of active research in recent years. Multi-agent systems represent an appropriate approach to take unexpected event into account in distributed virtual enterprise project control. Therefore, if project participants were offered an assistance of distributed and real-time multi-agent system that can automatically coordinate activities and resources, while also encouraging intraproject cooperation without the intervention of a general contractor during the project execution phase, then some potential difficulties such as resource discrepancies, interface problems, inarticulate communications and delays could be predicted and resolved earlier by the project participants involved. Such assistance could be important for the success of a distributed virtual enterprise project control.

Virtual enterprises enable the deployment of distributed business processes among different partners in order to shorten development and manufacturing cycles, reduce time to market and operational costs, increase customer satisfaction and operate on global scale. The dynamic property is the most outstanding characteristic of virtual enterprise. It is usually organized according to the demand of the market, and it exists with the emergence of the project begins and disappears with the end of the project. Therefore, the success of a virtual enterprise depends on whether the virtual enterprise project is completed perfectly or not. Virtual enterprise oriented projects need the support of distributed project management system which concerns the collaboration of different departments and enterprises. Many scholars have studied the distributed project management system and some valuable and practical implementation schemes were proposed. For example: Bourgault et al. (2002) proposed project management system supporting distributed product development, and Lin et al. (2003) suggested a distributed project management model based on ASP. Many enterprises developed their own distributed project management software, such as P3 of Primavera (Wang et al., 2004). These systems can support the management of distributed project very well, but it is not fit for virtual enterprise project management. When applied in the cooperation of multicompany, the distributed project management system cannot adapt the situation entirely. Especially, the sharing and visiting of project information among the companies are limited. And the control to the project is weakened. Given the characteristics of distributed project management, we consider the most natural way to model the distributed virtual enterprise project control is as a collection of autonomous distributed problem solving intelligent agents (or multi-agent system). Several studies have addressed multi-agent systems, a branch of distributed artificial intelligence, which can be satisfactorily applied to such problems (Archimede & Coudert, 2001; Chun & Wong, 2003; Tserng & Lin, 2003; Yan, Kuphal, & Bode, 2000). Chun and Wong (2003) introduced a generalized agent-based framework, which uses negotiation to achieve a dynamic scheduling of conflict events. The framework consisted of a user preference model, an evaluation function and a negotiation protocol called Nstar, Tserng and Lin (2003) developed an electronic acquisition model for project scheduling called e-AMPS. The model was based on the ontology defined by the eXtensible markup language schema for scheduling (XSS), the data acquisition language for scheduling (DALS), the hierarchy searching algorithm (HAS), and an automatic mechanism called message transfer chain (MTC). In this model, each project participant is equipped with a message agent serving as a unique information window, to automatically acquire external information and provide other participants with rescheduling information for schedule conflicts. Kim, Paulson, Levitt, Fischer, and Petrie (2003) introduced a framework in which a distributed virtual enterprise project can be rescheduled dynamically by any of the concerned project participants. He also presented a formalized negotiation methodology for distributed virtual enterprise project

rescheduling optimization which allows agents to transfer utility to others. The methodology uses compensation of disadvantageous agreements through a multi-linked negotiation process. Yen (2002) addressed a communication infrastructure to handle connection and communication among distributed Internet rescheduling systems for distributed applications. He presented an agent model of distributed rescheduling systems where agents can communicate and coordinate activities with each other via an agent communication language for rescheduling. It also defined the syntax and semantics for the agent communication language and a negotiation mechanism. Yan et al. (2000) used multi-agent systems to support project management in a distributed environment. They presented methods to reschedule activities and resolve resource conflicts by message exchanging and negotiation among agents.

ISSUES OF DISTRIBUTED PROJECT CONTROL AND VIRTUAL ENTERPRISE

Problem Statements

The goal of a project is mainly to complete all of the activities in the project on schedule and within the budget while observing established requirements of quality, safety and specifications. Since specialty can increase project quality and reduce costs for practical execution, the activities organized by the general contractor will commonly be subcontracted to various specialized distributed project participants. In order to fulfill special expertise, manpower, deadline and so forth, activities subcontracted by some project participants may also be subcontracted to further downstream project participants. Project participants in the distributed project can be referred to as first-tier project participants, second-tier project participants and so forth. A distributed project defined in this context is a project whose project participants are composed of various independent, specialized and distributed project participants; they subcontract one or more project activities performing independent specialized field functions to their subcontracted activities. The activities have fixed work logic and precedence relationships.

During the project execution stage in dynamic virtual enterprise environments, the distributed project can encounter various difficulties inducing the project to falter, or even worst, to fail, as follows:

1. The traditionally centralized project control mechanism of the distributed projects is inefficiency.

The significant difficulty is that the traditionally centralized project control mechanism of the distributed projects performed by a general contractor loses efficiency (Kim, 2001). In most distributed projects, regardless of contract types, 80-90% of tasks are commonly performed by project participants, but only 40% of project participants can be regularly coordinated by the general contractor during the project execution stage (Tserng & Lin, 2003). Although the general contractor conventionally takes the major responsibility to coordinate all of project participants involved, due to project participants' characteristics of independence, specialty and distribution and some of them may not have contractual relationships with the general contractor, accordingly, most project participants still have to monitor their activities and schedules on their own, and solve problems by themselves as much as possible while encountering difficulties (Kim, 2001).

The project execution among project participants occurred from unforeseen events can hardly be resolved immediately if they are self-interested and noncooperative individuals. Although the general contractor should take the responsibility to coordinate such conflicts among project participants during the project execution stage, in

reality the problem is always beyond the capability of the general contractor to solve due to a lack of specialized expertise, shortage of manpower, slow response and so forth (Al-Hammad, 2000; Hinze & Tracey, 1994). In practice these situations generally made difficulties to the project control in a dynamic execution environment, where unforeseen events can quickly invalidate the predictive schedule of the project and bring into question the continuing validity of the scheduled activities. The lifetime of the project control tends to be very short and hence its optimizing advantages generally will not be realized.

Also, various interface problems and inarticulate communications among project participants can easily occur during the execution of the distributed project. Project participants are often self-interested, specialized and competitive by nature and cannot be simply coordinated by the general contractor in nature. The coordination of various conflicts in a large complex distributed project is more difficult for a general contractor, due to the lack of specialized expertise, shortage of manpower, and slow responses (Al-Hammad, 2000; Hinze & Tracey, 1994). Consequently, he has less incentive to accommodate the project participants' requests and wishes to solve their conflicts. This traditionally centralized project control mechanism in virtual enterprise environments stems from a mismatch between the centralized control techniques and current project practice employed more and more distributed project participants.

2. Schedule conflicts among project participants usually occur during the project execution stage.

Another significant obstacle is schedule conflicts among project participants induced by unpredicted events usually occur during a project execution stage. There is always something unexpectedly happening during the execution stage of a project, causing the developed schedule is seldom stable. Unpredicted events in a distributed project may arise from several sources: accidental machine breakdown, unanticipated resource discrepancy, sudden changes in executing environments, stumbles in forecasted durations of activities and so forth. O'Brien, Fischer, and Jucker (1995) indicated that discrepancies between the needed resources for activity executions and the resources available to project participants are a major cause of schedule change and are usually occur in a distributed virtual enterprise project. Resource discrepancies will occur when the timing of activities is not well matched with the available resources. Although the general contractor awards project participants according to the master schedule, they will be forced to change schedules under pressure, as resource discrepancy can cause additional costs either through over-utilizing currently available resources or importing new resources (O'Brien & Fischer, 2000).

Schedule changes are likely to causing conflicts among project participants because any move can affect activity progress and resource profiles of succeeding project participants in a tightly coupled schedule. If the general contractor cannot coordinate with related project participants to ease the difficulties in time, they will vary the schedules and resource allocations of the project activities, cause various unexpected events to the project, and even induce the project as a whole to falter or to fail. But the general contractor has less incentive and capability to solve these conflicts for project participants. Most of them still have to resolve difficulties on their own as much as possible in current practical project environments (Kim, 2001).

In theory, the resolution of schedule conflicts is traditionally the problem of resource reallocations or activity rescheduling that has been regarded as a combinatorial optimization problem. Most of the problems belong to the class of NP-complete problems (Garey & Johnson, 1979), which means the problem needs exponential time in the problem-solving process as the scale of the problem increases. Yen (2002) indicated that most optimization algorithms for the problems are very costly, time-consuming and too idealistic for practical applications, especially in a distributed, large-scale, highly dynamic and online required virtual enterprise project control. Besides, in order to determine an optimal solution, various restrictions have to impose upon the problem (e.g., on the number of machines, manpower, etc.) makes the solution difficult in applying it to real-world practice, or even impossible, because most of the restrictions and constraints in current, highly dynamic and changeable environments cannot be well-performed, especially varying a number of activities and resources on the project to apply the solution.

Due to the complications of finding an optimal solution in theory for practical use, instead, in many project practices the real-world problem-solving of the schedule conflicts among project participants is performed by negotiations, which concern the determination of negotiation agreements regarding the benefits, preferences and acquaintances of related project participants involved. Very important in multi-agent systems for this endeavor is that autonomous agents are able to behave, to distinguish and to resolve these difficulties by means of automated negotiations. Several agent-based automated negotiation models have been addressed to the resolutions by using the problem-specific intelligence of agents in multi-agent systems, as previous section mentioned.

Objectives

To the resolution of these problems, there are objectives in the context, described as follows:

1. Proposing an agent-based intelligent system for the coordination of a distributed virtual enterprise project.

To overcome the practical defects of distributed virtual enterprise project control about the traditionally centralized project control mechanism losing efficacy, interface problems and inarticulate communications among project participants, introducing a collaboration mechanism among project participants by multi-agent systems technology is helpful to the resolution of these problems. For this part, a collaborative framework of an agent-based intelligent system for a distributed virtual enterprise project is proposed that can automatically coordinate the difficulties for project participants through the agents involved without the intervention of the general contractor. In addition, as modern computing systems and information environments possess distributed, large, open, and heterogeneous characteristics, computers are no longer stand-alone systems, but have become closely connected with each other and with their users. Thus, the multi-agent system not only can perform interoperability, but also can be established complying with industrial standards in the current agent world for practical purpose and for future extension and development. In order to ensure interoperability of the system in the agent world, some essential components in the system are discussed with promising industrial standardizations in current agent world. Plus, some distinguishing differences and characteristics with current popular commercial software in project management are also compared.

2.   Implementation and validation of the agent-based intelligent system

To validate the feasibility of that the multi-agent system can be applicable to agent practice, a prototype system followed by various active technologies and industrial standards in current agent engineering is implemented. We choose Java and JADE (2005) which is open source providing Java-based agent infrastructure for building multi-agent systems in compliance with FIPA (2005) industrial standardizations as the

agent development tools. Also, two industrial standard languages, FIPA agent communication language (FIPA-ACL) and semantic language (SL), are adopted as the agent communication language and the content language respectively for the agents' interactions. Also, a distributed virtual enterprise project case and an evolutionary compensatory negotiation approach discussed in researches customized by Matlab are employed for the validation of the prototype system.

FRAMEWORK OF AGENT-BASED INTELLIGENT SYSTEM FOR DISTRIBUTED VIRTUAL ENTERPRISE PROJECT SCHEDULING CONTROL

In order to overcome the practical difficulties of traditionally centralized project control mechanism in distributed virtual enterprise project management such as the general contractor losing efficacy, interface problems among project participants, the general contractor's lack of specialized expertise for project control, and slow responses and so forth, a collaborative mechanism of a distributed project for coordinating the independent, specialized and distributed project participants involved by multi-agent systems technology is suggested to these problems solving. In this section, we propose a collaborative framework of an agent-based intelligent system for the distributed virtual enterprise project control, which can automatically handle the intraproject difficulties for project participants through the intelligent agents involved without the intervention of the general contractor. In Subsection 3.1, a comprehensive description of the collaborative framework of the distributed agent-based intelligent system as a whole with related logical and physical components involved are addressed. Then a project operation subsystem named the project participant system, which is the control kernel of the project work for respective participant in a distributed virtual enterprise environment, is discussed in Subsection 3.2. In Subsection 3.3, to ensuring the interoperability of the system in the agent world, some important constituents and issues concerning the promising industrial standardization in current agent world with the system are discussed. Besides, the distinguishing characteristics of the popular commercial software with the system in the domain of project management and control are also analyzed.

The Agent-Based Intelligent System

To the resolution of the aforementioned difficulties, a collaborative framework of an agent-based intelligent system for a distributed virtual enterprise project control is proposed, depicted in Figure 1. The system not only can provide a flexible mechanism to handle a distributed project, but also can help participants in a distributed virtual enterprise project monitoring and managing their activity work through the assistance of agents situated in the system. The system consists of various logical and physical components, described as follows:

1. **Naming agent:** The naming agent can provide supervisory management over access to and use of the agents situated in different locations. There is only one naming agent deployed in the system which offers "white pages" services to other agents based on the directory of agent identifiers it maintains, and contains transport addresses for running of agents. Each agent situated in the distributed system has to register with the agent in order to obtain a valid agent identifier to activate.

2. **Directory agent:** The directory agent provides supervisory control over services that other agents can provide in the system. There can be more than one directory agents deployed in the system while needed, which support "yellow pages" services that agents have been registered with them in the system. Other agents can query the directory agent to find out what services can be required in the system. Each of agents has to register with the directory agent in order to offer services that other agents need for cooperation in the distributed project.

3. **Message transport service:** The message transport service can provide articulate

Figure 1. Framework of the agent-based intelligent system

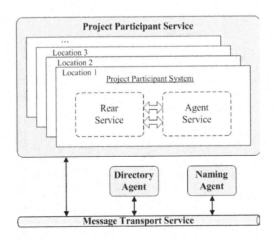

communications among agents. It offers the networking control mechanism by physical and logical elements for message transport among agents situated at different locations in the distributed virtual enterprise environment.

4. **Project participant service:** The project participant service exerts the major control over operating and monitoring activity work for respective project participant in the distributed virtual enterprise environment. The service consists of several project participant systems that each of which is deployed on the host situated at the location of a project participant. Through the connection of network, collaborative and supervisory functionalities of the project works can be provided by the host. Each project participant system comprises two kinds of logical services: the agent service and the rear service, both of which offer various agents and supports to control and to manage project work managed and subcontracted by a project participant in a distributed virtual enterprise project.

The Project Participant System

The project participant systems are the control kernel of project work in the agent-based intelligent system. The related work of a project participant can be performed and supervised through the agents and supports provided by the system. The agents in the project participant system can collaborate and cooperate with each other or with agents situated at other project participant systems to resolve difficulties while encountering various difficulties during the project execution phase. The framework of the project participant system is shown in Figure 2, which comprises two kinds of operating components, as follows:

1. **Agent service:** The agent service consists of several kinds of agents endowed with specialized capabilities to serve on different works for a project participant. If any problem occurs during the project execution phase, the agents can collaborate and communicate with others to deal with the problem. Based on different kinds of services that the agents can provide, there are four kinds of agents distinguished in the service:

Figure 2. Framework of the project participant system

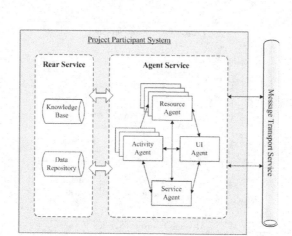

a. **Activity agent:** The activity agent can provide the supervisory control on related inputs and outputs associated with an activity subcontracted by a project participant. Each activity agent handles one activity and behaves specialized abilities to keep the activity running smoothly and successfully.

b. **Resource agent:** The resource agent can handle the utilization of resources that a project participant maintains. These resources can be material, machinery, manpower and so forth, and each kind of resource is supervised by one resource agent depending on the consideration of resource attributes. The agent can also provide supervisory management for its resource, such as consuming, reusing, dispatching and so forth.

c. **User interface agent:** The user interface agent maintains inputs and outputs of the system interacting with the project participant. It provides several graphic user interfaces for system configuring, reporting, diagramming, system alarming and so forth. Only one user interface agent is equipped to fulfill all interactive tasks in a project participant system.

d. **Service agent:** The service agent dominates all of the internal system tasks to assure consistency and performance of the system. Not only can it supervise the system works such as tracking, logging, process control, system backup, data maintenances and so forth, but also the agent can interact with other service agents resided in different project participant

Figure 3. Integrated operation of the agent-based intelligent system

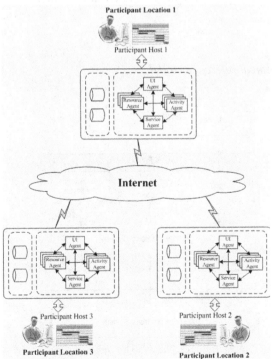

systems for information sharing and data exchanging. Each system equips one service agent to perform these works.

2. **Rear service:** The rear service is used to support all of the agents performing their related tasks in the system. These services such as decision-making, domain knowledge, data access control and so forth, can be offered by the following components deployed and operated in the background of the project participant system.

    a. **Knowledge base:** There are two kinds of knowledge modules organized in the knowledge base. One kind of knowledge module is rule modules used to provide the decision-making and reasoning capabilities of the application domain for agents. Through the module agents can make a precise decision while facing various kinds of problems and situations. The other kind is application ontology which provides the abstract view of the application domain for agents in the system. Many key concepts and interrelationships are organized in it. From the support of the application ontology, agents can make articulate communications with each other or with other agents situated at different location through the shared and common understanding of the application domain.

    b. **Data repository:** The data repository consists of various databases and data files installed in the system. Not only is it used to keep track of system events, operations and agents in the system, but it also stores and maintains information of concerned activities and resources associated with the participant.

In the project participant system, each agent is endowed with specialized capabilities and goals to perform project work for its owner. The integrated operation of the agent-based intelligent system,

Figure 4. FIPA agent management reference model

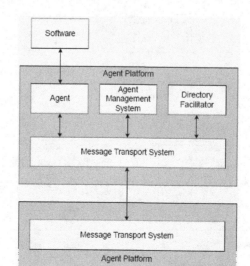

constructed with an example of three project participants, is depicted in Figure 3.

Interoperability and Comparisons of the System

The proposed framework of the agent-based intelligent system containing distributed control and applicable entities that can dynamically collaborate to satisfy control of virtual enterprise project work by means of various agents for project participants in a distributed project environment. The agents are capable of addressing both knowledge processing and control specific actions simultaneously in a real-time distributed virtual enterprise environment. The system can integrate data acquisition and the control components for a distributed project in the multi-agent environment. It can be equipped with the ability to cope with the dynamic reconfiguration of the distributed virtual enterprise project control in real time manner by auto-generating or specializing specific control agents whenever new resources or activities are added.

In current, open, flexible, distributed, multi-agent operation environment, the need of industrial standard and specifications are essential for ensuring interoperability of the autonomous agents around agent world. FIPA (FIPA, 2005), Foundation for Intelligent Physical Agents, is considered the most promising standardization effort in the software agent world. FIPA specifications establish a logical reference model named FIPA agent management reference model, as shown in Figure 4, was chosen to provide the normative framework within which agents can be deployed and operate in our system for the creation, registration, location, communication and retirement of agents. The FIPA standards and specifications do not attempt to prescribe the internal architecture of agents nor how they should be implemented, but it specifies the interface necessary to support interoperability between various agent systems or platforms. Our framework of the agent-based

distributed virtual enterprise project control environment can be realized complying with the FIPA specified implementations in the mechanisms of the mandatory components and normative agents to the agent platform of the reference model, as seen in Figure 4.

In FIPA agent management reference model, an agent management system (AMS) is mandatory which provides agent name services performed "white pages" mechanism, and maintains an index of all agents which currently are registered with the agent platform. It exerts supervisory control over access to and the use of an agent platform in a system. In our system, the mechanism of the AMS can be formalized and interchangeable to the normative agent called naming agent, which is responsible for these functionalities in our agent-based environment.

The directory facilitator (DF) in the FIPA agent management reference model can also be formalized and served as an agent in our system, named directory agent, which provides "yellow pages" services to other agents in the agent platform. Agents may register their services with the DF or query the DF for information on other agents. An agent platform can have multiple DF providing the variety of creating communities or domains of agents. A DF can register with each other among various agent platforms forming a federation of application domains.

The agent communication channel in FIPA agent management reference model is the message transport system, which controls all the exchanges of messages in the platform, as well as message to and from remote platforms. This mechanism consists of logical and physical networking components that can also be performed by the message transport service sketched in our framework.

Finally, the control kernel of the distributed virtual enterprise operations for individual project participant is the project participant system. It provides supervision and management of all the project works through various customized autonomous agents and supports performed in the system. All of these agents and components form the distributed project execution mechanisms in the framework of the multi-agent system.

On the other part, in comparison with popular commercial software commonly used in the application domain of project management and control such as Microsoft Office Project 2003 (2005), Milestones (2005) and Schedule (2005), some distinguishing differences and characteristics between these popular commercial package suites and our system framework are addressed and compared, as follows:

These commercial package suites commonly consist of three key components: a centralized database that holds all the information about the project work, spreadsheet tools that calculates and maintains the costs and resources required for each activity and scheduling tools that can schedule and charts activity works in Gantt or PERT. Also, reporting and multi-project supporting are common functions and they all integrate hands-on management tools into the graphic user interface. E-mail reception is supported in order to collect information from other team member. Data and results can also be reported and published in Web pages.

These kinds of popular commercial software are mainly centralized. That is, they all need centralized database for keeping data and cen-

tralized decision-making tools for supporting the problem solving of project difficulties that make them difficult to apply to the distributed and dynamic circumstances in the distributed project control. Hands-on management tools make more human errors than agent technology in information processing that can bring more mistakes and unexpected events to project control as a whole. Although many useful mathematical algorithms in rescheduling and resource reallocation have been proposed, most of them are not integrated in these commercial software packages.

In short, they are difficult to provide a distributed scheme that supports local decision-making power, problem-solving capability and autonomous information processing, to avoid human errors and increase efficiency and flexibility.

IMPLEMENTATION AND VALIDATION

To evaluate the feasibility and capability of that the collaborative framework of the agent-based intelligent system can be applicable to the practical agent application, certain works on the implementation of the system framework are elaborated and analyzed in this section. They are categorized into following two sequential stages: (1) the implementation sketch and (2) the architectural design.

Figure 5. The designed infrastructure of the prototype system

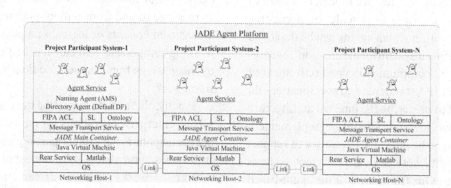

In the implementation sketch, an implementing scheme of a prototype of the system framework with a case of a distributed project is addressed. Representations of the implementing architecture and work-flows in the prototype system with a compensatory negotiation approach discussed in researches (Chen & Wang, in press) are elaborated in the architectural design stage.

Implementation Sketch

In order to validate that the collaborative framework of the multi-agent system can be realized and applicable to practical agent applications, a prototype of the system framework discussed in deep technologies and detailed infrastructure is revealed in this section. As Java is an outstanding language for programming multi-agent systems which possesses good properties in openness, flexibilities, platform independence, integrated network ability and so forth, we choose Java as the programming language for the prototype system. We also employ Java agent development framework (JADE) (Burbeck, Garpe, & Nadjm-Tehrani, 2004; JADE, 2005) as the middleware infrastructure of the prototype system, which is open source and a famous multi-agent development platform in compliance with Java and FIPA (2005) standard specifications, letting the extension of the implemented prototype can easily put into practice and meet the industrial standards in the practical agent world. Also, for the agents' interactions in the prototype system, two industrial standard languages, FIPA agent communication language (FIPA-ACL) and semantic language (SL), are adopted as the agent communication language and the content language respectively. The power tool of Matlab is also employed to the implementation of the evolutionary compensatory negotiation approach in the prototype system. The framework of the designed infrastructure of the distributed agent-based intelligent prototype system is depicted in Figure 5.

In the designed infrastructure, the prototype of the distributed multi-agent system is constructed by several project participant systems. Each of the project participant systems associated with related agent service and rear service is established and deployed on each networking host situated at respective project participant's location. The JADE distributed agent platform is used to provide runtime support and collaboration to the distributed agents which can be performed according to the properties of the weak notion of agency (Wooldridge & Jennings, 1995) and FIPA standards. JADE largely impact on the research and development of multi-agent systems exceeds the ones of other contributions. Almost every agent technology idea can be constructed by JADE, especially in industrial standards of the agent software engineering. JADE is a Java framework for developing FIPA-compliance agent applications, making FIPA standard assets available to programmers through object-oriented abstractions. It provides two system service mandated by FIPA, available in two system agents: the first system agent is called agent management system (AMS) which provides white page service associating logical agent identifiers to status and address information, and whose responsibility is to manage the life cycle of all agents situated in the platform. We realize the functionality of the naming agent in our system framework by the agent; the second system agent is called directory facilitator (DF) providing yellow page service with basic matchmaking capabilities. A special instance of the agent named the default DF must be available in FIPA compliance that is realized as the directory agent in our system framework. Our prototype system conforms to FIPA by automatically starting an AMS and a default DF agent during startup. The extensions of the two system agents play an important role providing significant and essential functionalities to be the naming agent and the directory agent in our prototype system, letting us can concentrate more

Figure 6. The subcontractual relationships among the project participants

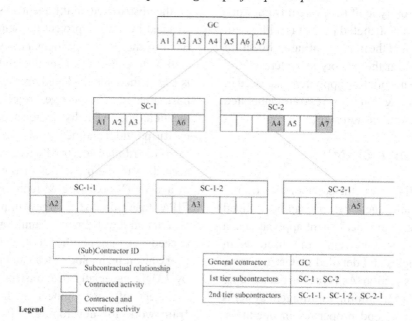

on the detailed implementing works in the agent behavior formulation, the agent's interactions, and the compensatory negotiation model.

To a project participant system in the distributed virtual enterprise environment, Java virtual machine is mandated and deployed on each networking host connected via Internet. Each of the project participant systems must implement a program called agent container which can activate more than one agent. There is a key agent container called main container essential to host the whole agent platform organized by more than one agent containers. This agent-operating environment of the prototype system can result in a very flexible association among agent realizations, operating systems, and networking nodes for interoperability. An agent is the fundamental actor in the prototype system accounts for the basic autonomy requirement, can be implemented as a Java Active object running within its own threads of control. It is capable of bringing a number of capabilities

together to form a unified and integrated execution model that can access to external software, human users and communication facilities. In social support for industrial standards among these agents, the agent communication language named FIPA-ACL defined by the FIPA specification is chosen for the agents' interactions in the prototype system. FIPA-ACL messages embed in a content expression within them expressed in a suitable content formulation. FIPA also provides a content language library called semantic language (SL) we selected too. The agent communication language, FIPA-ACL, the content language, SL and customized negotiation ontology are built for the main operations of the compensatory negotiation model in the prototype system.

Case Example

On the validation of the feasibility and the capability of the agent-based intelligent system, a

Figure 7. The Gantt chart of the project schedule

No	Activity ID	Subcontractor ID	Earliest Start	Earliest Finish	Duration	Slack Time	3/1/2004
1	A1	SC-1	2004/3/1	2004/3/5	5	0	
2	A2	SC-1-1	2004/3/6	2004/3/18	12	0	
3	A3	SC-1-2	2004/3/6	2004/3/13	8	4	
4	A4	SC-2	2004/3/18	2004/3/25	8	2	
5	A5	SC-2-1	2004/3/18	2004/3/27	10	0	
6	A6	SC-1	2004/3/18	2004/3/24	7	3	
7	A7	SC-2	2004/3/28	2004/3/31	4	0	

distributed virtual enterprise project case discussed in this research. The case is a distributed virtual construction project whose subcontractual relationships among project participants and Gantt chart of the project schedule are shown in Figure 11 and Figure 13 respectively. The participants in the project are composed of various independent, specialized and distributed project participants who subcontract one or more activities and perform specialized field functions to their subcontracted activities. Each of them may in turn sub-subcontract one or more subcontracted activities to others for practical consideration. Project participants can be referred to as first-tier project participants, second-tier project participants and so forth. The goal of the distributed virtual enterprise project control is mainly to complete all of activities in the project on schedule and within budget while observing established requirements of quality, safety and specifications. The schedules of these planed activities have fixed work logic and precedence relationships.

In the distributed virtual enterprise project, the general contractor (GC) is a prime contractor who contracts an assignment from a client, organizes it into seven required and specialized activities (A1 to A7) as a project formulation. As specialization can increase quality and reduce cost for the project, the activities in the project are then subcontracted to various specialized project participants by the general contractor for meeting the project's requirements. The general contractor subcontracts them out to two first-tier project participants, SC-1 (for activities A1, A2, A3, A6) and SC-2 (for A4, A5, A7). Also, under the two project participants' practical considerations in fulfilling specialized requirements, manpower demands, deadlines and so forth, these activities subcontracted by the first-tier project participants may also be successively subcontracted to other project participants. They subcontract some of their activities to three second-tier project participants, SC-1-1 (for A2 from SC-1), SC-1-2 (for A3 from SC-1) and SC-2-1 (for A5 from SC-2), and perform the remaining activities by themselves (SC-1 for A1, A6; SC-2 for A4, A7). Each project participant in the project performs field functions to the subcontracted activities within a specialized scope and subcontracted schedule.

In this kind of the distributed virtual enterprise project, each of the project participants in practical sense is a self-interested individual possessed different expertise and resources performing its subcontracted works. The project participants may be competitors lacking any business relationship with each other or with the general contractor, for example, SC-1-1 and SC-2-1 in Figure 6. As these activities in the project have fixed work logic and precedence relationships, a schedule delay of an activity caused by unforeseen events may affect

Figure 8. The online deployment of the agents in the prototype system

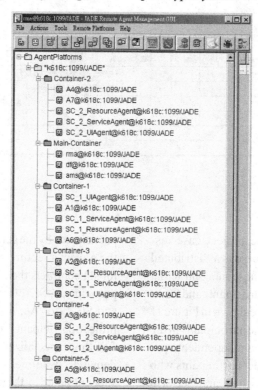

Figure 9. Main frame of the project participant system

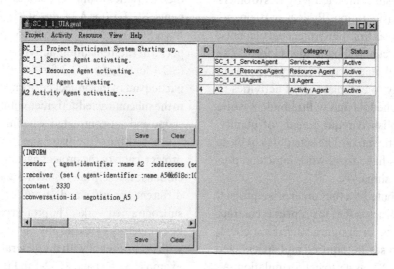

Figure 10. The snapshot of resource configuration

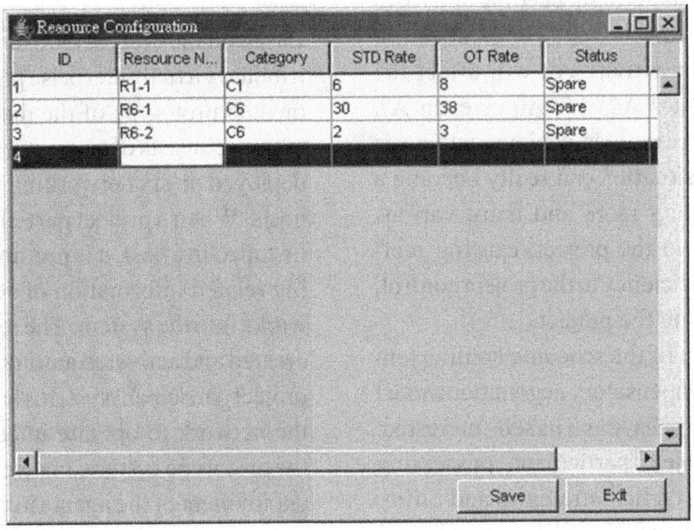

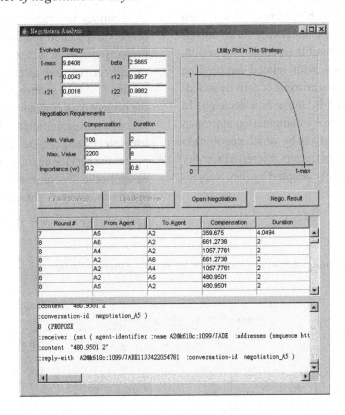

Figure 11. The snapshot of negotiation analysis

the schedules of other activities, or even further affect all of the schedules of succeeding activities in the tightly coupled schedule. For example, in Figure 7, a delay of activity A2 will affect the schedules of activities A4, A5, A6 or even A7, varying their resource profiles, deployments, costs and so forth. This situation can really become a fountainhead deriving more and more various unexpected events to the project, causing ineffectiveness and inefficiency to the project control, or even worse, failing the project.

To the resolution of the schedule conflicts, in the evolutionary compensatory negotiation model an activity agent can behave as if its self-interested, noncooperative project participant, possessing various negotiation tactics, strategies and utility functions in negotiations. If any delay event occurs to an activity which cannot be resolved by other related agents while encountering unexpected events during the activity execution phase, an activity agent associated with the activity will take the major responsibility to coordinate with succeeding activity agents seeking for an appropriate decision on possible rescheduling action, opening negotiations with related succeeding activity agents whose start-time of activity schedules will be affected by the action decision. In addition, an evolutionary computation approach is also applied respectively by which negotiation tactics and strategies of the self-interested activity agents can be optimally adopted by their subjective preference.

Architectural Design

Based on the designed infrastructure and the distributed virtual enterprise project case, the implemented prototype of the distributed multi-agent system consists of six project participant systems deployed on six networking and Windows-based hosts. When a project participant system is being installed in a host, it is prompted to ask for assigning related information of subcontracted project works into the system. The related agents are then created and activated automatically, and all of the project participant systems are connected through the network to operate integrally. This initiates the prototype system. Figure 8 sketches an online deployment of the agents in the prototype system by way of the remote monitoring agent, which is a tool with graphical user interface allows controlling the life cycle of the agent platform and of all the registered agents, provided by JADE and packed as an agent formulation. Each agent is an autonomous individual working for the agent's owner on specified goals in the background of the project participant system without a user interface except for the user interface agent. Figure 9 to Figure 11 depict snapshots of the main frame of the project participant system, resource configuration, and negotiation analysis displayed by the user interface agent. During the system operating phase, the service agent associated with a system can periodically communicate with other service agents to retrieve shared information such as

Table 1. The agents' negotiation requirements for two negotiation issues

	min_{comp}	max_{comp}	min_{dur}	max_{dur}	w_{comp}	w_{dur}
A1 (IAA)	100	1000	2	6	0.2	0.8
A2 (PAA-1)	150	600	1	4	0.6	0.4
A3 (PAA-2)	200	700	1	5	0.7	0.3

Box 1. Function derivation and details (Source: Chen & Wang , in press)

$$U_i^{IAA}(x_i) = \begin{cases} 1 - \dfrac{x_i - \min_i^{IAA}}{\max_i^{IAA} - \min_i^{IAA}} & \text{for the compensation issue} \quad\quad 1a) \\[2em] \dfrac{x_i - \min_i^{IAA}}{\max_i^{IAA} - \min_i^{IAA}} & \text{for the duration issue} \quad\quad 1b) \end{cases}$$

$$U_i^{PAA}(x_i) = \begin{cases} 1 - \dfrac{x_i - \min_i^{PAA}}{\max_i^{PAA} - \min_i^{PAA}} & \text{for the compensation issue} \quad\quad 2a) \\[2em] \dfrac{x_i - \min_i^{PAA}}{\max_i^{PAA} - \min_i^{PAA}} & \text{for the duration issue} \quad\quad 2b) \end{cases}$$

$$U^a(x) = \sum_{i=1}^{2} w_i^a U_i^a(x_i) = w_{comp}^a U_{comp}^a(x_{comp}) + w_{dur}^a U_{dur}^a(x_{dur}) \quad\quad 3)$$

$$x_i = \begin{cases} \min_i^a + \alpha_i^a(t)(\max_i^a - \min_i^a) & \text{if } U_i^a \text{ is decreasing} \quad\quad 4a) \\[1em] \min_i^a + (1 - \alpha_i^a(t))(\max_i^a \; \min_i^a) & \text{if } U_i^a \text{ is increasing} \quad\quad 4b) \end{cases}$$

$$\alpha_i^a(t) = \left[\frac{\min(t, t_a^{max})}{t_a^{max}} \right]^{\frac{1}{\beta}} \quad\quad 5)$$

$$\alpha_i^a(t) = e^{-\max(0, t_a^{max} - t)} \quad\quad 6)$$

$$\Gamma = \begin{bmatrix} \gamma_{11} & \gamma_{12} \\ \gamma_{21} & \gamma_{22} \end{bmatrix} \quad\quad 7)$$

schedules, progress, resource allocations and so forth, and displayed by the user interface agent.

The scenario of the distributed virtual enterprise project employed for the resolution of schedule conflicts among agents is as follows: when activity agent A1 perceives delay events which cannot be resolved by related agents situated in associated project participant system while encountering unexpected events during its activity execution phase, in order to consider which advantageous action decision should best be made to solve the predictive conflicts, the agent A1 will then request for negotiations in a possible

schedule adjustment with the succeeding activity agents whose schedules will be affected by the possible decision of delay action the agent is going to make, preparing for compensatory negotiations with them. To exhibit the many-issue and the mutual influencing effects of alternating offers in the one-to-many-party compensatory negotiation model, we choose two negotiation issues, each for one kind of issues: the one is the issue of the compensation of schedule adjustment for the kind of the comprehensive issue; the other is the issue of the duration of schedule adjustment for the kind of the incomprehensive issue. Through the rear

Table 2. The values of the parameters in the evolutionary computation approach

Parameter	Value
Population size (N)	20
Tournament size (T)	2
Elite individuals (E)	2
Crossover probability (P_c)	0.8
Crossover children (C)	14
Mutation scale (M_{SC})	1
Mutation shrink (M_{SH})	1
Mutation children (M)	4
Stalling generation (G_S)	100
Maximum generation (G_M)	250

Table 3. Each agent's evolved values of parameters of the evolutionary strategies

	t^{max}	β	γ_{11}	γ_{12}	γ_{21}	γ_{22}
A1 (IAA)	9.531	0.3791	0.9948	0.0052	0.9985	0.0015
A2 (PAA-1)	9.9764	0.2291	0.9985	0.0015	0.9724	0.0276
A3 (PAA-2)	9.79	0.4684	0.9989	0.0011	0.9995	0.0005

service of the project participant system the agent situated, some negotiation requirements for the both negotiation issues can be prepared, depicted in Table 1. As the negotiation requirements of agent A1 on the duration issue is 2-6 min-max unit delays, which will affect the start-time of the succeeding activity A2 and A3, the agent A1 then requests agent A2 and A3 to open the compensatory negotiations following the negotiation protocol. After receiving agree messages responded by these agents, the negotiation requirements of agent A2 and A3 for both negotiation issues can also be derived and prepared, as depicted in Table 1, also. The appropriate negotiation tactics and strategies associated with respective self-interested agents are simultaneously evolving to prepare for the

negotiations, and then the compensatory negotiations among these agents are initiated.

Note that in this case of the two-issue, one-to-two-party compensatory negotiation, the agent A1 behaves as initiating activity agent (IAA) and the agents A2 and A3 as participating activity agent (PAA), having opposite interests and utilities to the negotiation issues. As less compensation and more duration of delays are advantageous and expected by agent A1, the agent possesses monotonically decreasing utility to the value of the compensation issue, and monotonically increasing utility to the value of the duration issue in the negotiations; the agents A2 and A3 have utilities in the opposite way to the values of these issues against agent A1. The scoring functions of an issue *i* dominated

Table 4. Communication messages between agents

```
(propose
 :sender (agent-identifier :name A1@server-1-1:1099/JADE)
 :receiver (set (agent-identifier :name A2@server-2:1099/JADE))
 :content "(
     (action (agent-identifier :name A1@server-1-1:1099/JADE)
         (propose (offer-description
                 :name (agent-identifier :name A1@server-1-1:1099/JADE)
                 :compensation (52.12)
                 :duration (5.94)
     ))"
 :reply-with  A2@server-2:1099/JADE1084244665828
 :language  fipa-sl0
 :ontology  compensation-ontology
 :protocol  compensation-negotiation
 )
```

```
(propose
 :sender (agent-identifier :name A2@server-2:1099/JADE)
 :receiver (set (agent-identifier :name A1@server-1-1:1099/JADE))
 :content "(
     (action (agent-identifier :name A2@server-2:1099/JADE)
         (counterpropose (counteroffer-description
                 :name (agent-identifier :name A2@server-2:1099/JADE)
                 :compensation (594.33)
                 :duration (1.04)
     ))"
 :reply-with  A1@server-1-1:1099/JADE1084244666875
 :language  fipa-sl0
 :ontology  compensation-ontology
 :protocol  compensation-negotiation
 )
```

Table 5. Alternating offers in the negotiation

Rounds / Item	1st Comp	Dur	2nd Comp	Dur	3rd Comp	Dur	4th Comp	Dur	5th Comp	Dur	6th Comp	Dur
Counteroffers to A2 and A3 proposed by A1												
A1's accumulated offer	100.00	6.00	112.92	5.94	162.20	5.72	256.74	5.30	409.92	4.63	611.00	3.74
A1 to A2	50.00	6.00	52.12	5.94	74.48	5.72	115.41	5.30	176.35	4.63	244.14	3.74
A1 to A3	50.00	6.00	60.80	5.94	87.72	5.72	141.33	5.30	233.57	4.63	366.86	3.74
Offers to A1 proposed by A2 and A3 respectively												
A2 to A1	599.99	1.00	594.33	1.04	571.38	1.18	525.61	1.47	448.48	1.97	244.14	3.74
A3 to A1	700.00	1.00	699.99	1.00	699.71	1.00	696.13	1.03	673.92	1.21	371.32	3.63

by the both kind of agents, IAA and PAA, in the negotiations are represented in equation (1) and equation (2), and an agent a's scoring function for a negotiation contract is shown in equation (3). The information for each agent about the offer formulation of an issue, the concession behavior function of time-dependent tactics, the concession behavior function of resource-dependent tactics, and negotiation strategy is denoted from equation (4) to equation (7) respectively. The derivation and details of these functions are provided in Chen & Wang (in press) (see Box 1).

Also, the values of the parameters used by the evolutionary computation approach for evolving negotiation strategies are shown in Table 2. One negotiation strategy is derived at the beginning of the negotiations and is used through the process of the negotiations for respective agent. Each agent's evolved values of the parameters of the negotiation strategies are shown in Table 3.

In the evolutionary compensatory negotiations, offers are alternating by the agent communication language at each negotiation rounds between the two parties. Two communication messages of agent A1 and A2 in a negotiation round are expressed in Table 4. The negotiations continue until the offers converge on mutually acceptable contracts by these agents or anyone opts out from the negotiations. After six rounds of alternating offers within 10 seconds, the compromises have been achieved among these agents based on the assessment of the behavior function of agent A1, as shown in Table 5. It is agreed that agents A2 and A3 will be paid 244.14 and 371.32 units of currency respectively for compensation from agent A1 to make delays in their start-time of activity schedules for activity A1's delay of 3.63 units of days (the minimum duration of delays in 3.74 and 3.63). The utilities of the offers of agents A1, A2, and A3 to the achieved contracts are 0.1983, 0.55 and 0.3889 respectively.

Figure 12. The utility plot of negotiations using the random strategy

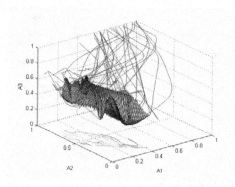

Figure 13. The utility plot of negotiations using the evolutionary strategy

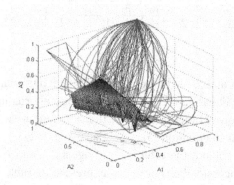

Figure 14. The utility plot of negotiations using the collaborative strategy

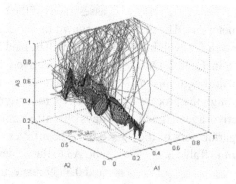

Table 6. Negotiation outcomes in the experimental simulations

Strategy / Item	Random Strategy	Evolutionary Strategy	Collaborative Strategy
Mean Utility of A1	0.3020	0.3474	0.2586
Mean Utility of A2	0.5475	0.5141	0.7176
Mean Utility of A3	0.6110	0.6491	0.7633
Average	0.4868	0.5035	0.5798
Standard Deviation	0.1632	0.1511	0.2791
Mean Joint Utility	1.4505	1.5106	1.7395
Successes	27	46	48
Achieving Rate	54%	92%	96%

As a further validation of the feasibility and the capability of the proposed distributed virtual enterprise project scheduling control, the three agents' negotiation requirements of the negotiation issues are depicted in Table 1. The experiments involve selecting three particular negotiation strategies for the agents' interactions that are called: (1) the random strategy (each agent's parameters of negotiation tactics and strategies are randomly selected without the use of the evolutionary computation approach), (2) the evolutionary strategy (each agent's parameters of which are computed by the evolutionary computation approach respectively), and (3) the cooperative strategy (all of the agents' parameters of which are calculated together by the evolutionary computation approach. The negotiation outcomes by using the strategy can be approached to the Pareto optima of the negotiation context in the model, generating a range of experimental simulations, and then allowing the agent to negotiate using the chosen strategy against its opponent who employs the same strategy. Various statistical measures related to the utilities of achieved agreements for each agent are then recorded and compared.

To produce statistically meaningful results, each of the experimental outcomes in Table 6 are processed and averaged over 50 runs of negotia-

tions in simulations under each chosen strategy in the negotiation context. Figure 12 to Figure 14 depict the utility plots of achieved agreements together with the utility paths during negotiations based on the random strategy (Figure 12), the evolutionary strategy (Figure 13), and the collaborative strategy (Figure 14) respectively, generated from 50 runs of negotiations for each strategy. In these three-dimension figures, offers proposed by each agent in each round of a negotiation are transformed to each agent's utilities measured from each agent's scoring function for a negotiation contract. From these utility paths, we can experience the trade-offs and the mutually influencing effects of the compensatory negotiations on each strategy. The statistical measures of these experimental results are exhibited in Table 6.

At this experimental simulations, there are some distinguishing findings in experimental outcomes depicted in Table 6, described as follows:

1. In the measure of the achieving rates, the value of which agents using the collaborative strategy superior to the use of evolutionary strategy for each agent self-interested, and largely greater than that using the random strategy.

2. With the use of the collaborative strategy by each agent, the value of the mean joint utility is greater than that with the use of the evolutionary strategy. It could show that with the use of the collaborative strategy in the negotiation issue for each agent, the whole benefit and efficacy in achieved agreements are more advantageous than that the use of the evolutionary strategy and the random strategy.

3. In the measure of the standard deviation of mean utilities, with the use of the evolutionary strategy the value of which is smaller than that using other strategies, which could mean that the mean utility of agreements achieved by each agent with the use of the evolutionary strategy are more even than that of using other strategies.

CONCLUSION

This research is mainly focus on the coordination of conflicts in a distributed virtual enterprise project while encountering unexpected events during the execution stage of the project, in order to overcome the defects of the distributed project practice about the centralized control mechanism losing efficacy, interface problems, shortage of manpower and expertise, slow response and so forth. We have proposed a distributed collaborative framework of an intelligent system by using the approach of multi-agent systems with negotiation strategies for project schedule control. The system can automatically coordinate the intra-project difficulties for project participants through the intelligence and the knowledge of agents involved without the intervention of general contractor. Also, for practical purpose and for future extension and development, the system framework not only can perform interoperability but also can be established complying with industrial standards in current agent world. Besides, a prototype system followed by FIPA-ACL and SL industrial stan-

dards with a distributed project case discussed in researches has been implemented and validated. It is suitable for practical agent applications and potentially useful to the application of a distributed virtual enterprise project in the resolution of online rescheduling with unforeseen event to meet each project participant's requirements. From practical viewpoint, this collaborative framework of a distributed virtual enterprise project control may effectively handle the requirements of autonomy and collaborative fashion and can provide the satisfactory solutions.

REFERENCES

Al-Hammad, A.-M. (2000). Common interface problems among various construction parties. *Journal of Performance of Constructed Facilities, 14*(2), 71-74.

Archimede, B., & Coudert, T. (2001). Reactive scheduling using a multi-agent model: the SCEP framework. *Engineering Application of Artificial Intelligence, 14*, 667-683.

Burbeck, K., Garpe, D., & Nadjm-Tehrani, S. (2004). *Scale-up and performance studies of three agent platforms.* Paper presented at the International Workshop on Middleware Performacne (IWMP 2004), Phoenix, Arizona.

Chen, Y. M., & Wang, S. C. (2004). *An agent-based collaborative framework for distributed project dynamic scheduling.* Paper presented at the International Summer Workshop on the Economic, Financial and Managerial Applications of Computational Intelligence (EFMACI2004), Taipei, Taiwan, ROC.

Chen, Y. M., & Wang, S. C. (2007). Framework of agent-based intelligence system with two-stage decision-making process for distributed dynamic scheduling. *Applied Soft Computing, 7*(1), 229-245.

Chen, Y. M., & Wang, S. C. (in press). An agent-based evolutionary strategic l for dynamic scheduling. *International Journal of Advanced Manufacturing Technology.*

Chun, H. W., & Wong, Y. M. (2003). N*: An agent-based negotiation algorithm for dynamic scheduling and rescheduling. *Advanced Engineering Informatics, 17*(1), 1-22.

FIPA (2005). Foundation for Intelligent Physical Agents. Retrieved February 14, 2007, from http://www.fipa.org./

Garey, M. R., & Johnson, D. S. (1979). *Computers and intractability: a guide to the theory of NP-Completeness.* San Francisco: W. H. Freeman.

Hinze, J., & Tracey, A. (1994). The contractor-subcontractor relationship: the subcontractor's view. *Journal of Construction Engineering and Management, 120*(2), 274-287.

JADE (2005). Java Agent DEvelopment Framework. Retrieved February 14, 2007, from http://jade.cselt.it/

Kim, K. (2001). *Distributed coordination of project schedule changes: An agent-based compensatory negotiation approach.* Stanford University.

Kim, K., Paulson, B., Levitt, R., Fischer, M. A., & Petrie, C. (2003). Distributed coordination of project schedule changes using agent-based compensatory negotiation methodology. *Artificial Intelligence for Engineering Design, Analysis and Manufacturing, 17*, 115-131.

Microsoft Office Project 2003 (2005). Microsoft Corporation. Retrieved February 14, 2007, from http://www.microsoft.com/office/project/prodinfo/default.mspx

Milestones (2005). KIDASA Software, Inc. Retrieved February 14, 2007, from http://www.kidasa.com/

O'Brien, W., & Fischer, M. A. (2000). Importance of capacity constraints to construction cost and schedule. *Journal of Construction Engineering and Management, 126*(5), 366-373.

O'Brien, W., Fischer, M. A., & Jucker, J. V. (1995). An economic view of project coordination. *Construction Management and Economics, 13*(5), 393-400.

Schedule, F. (2005). AEC Software, Inc. Retrieved February 14, 2007, from http://www.aecsoft.com/

Tserng, H. P., & Lin, W. Y. (2003). Developing an electronic acquisition model for project scheduling using XML-based information standard. *Automation in Construction, 12*, 67-95.

Wang, S. C., & Chen, Y. M. (2005, June 8-10). *Framework of agent-based two-stage decision-making process for distributed dynamic scheduling.* Paper presented at the International Conference on Technology and Accreditation (ICTA2005), Taoyuan, Taiwan, ROC.

Wooldridge, M., & Jennings, N. R. (1995). Intelligent agents: Theory and practice. *The Knowledge Engineering Review, 10*(2), 115-152.

Yan, Y., Kuphal, T., & Bode, J. (2000). Application of multi-agent systems in project management. *International Journal of Production Economics, 68*, 185-197.

Yen, B. P.-C. (2002). Communication infrastructure in distributed scheduling. *Computers & Industrial Engineering, 42*, 149-161.

Chapter IX
Sharing Views, Information, and Cross–Enterprise Culture in the Corporate Situation Room

Bob Roberts
Kingston University, UK

Adamantios Koumpis
ALTEC S.A., Greece

ABSTRACT

A major challenge for virtual organizations is the integration of their various corporate organizational and information assets, as well as their communication infrastructures and personnel. There also remains a need for greater understanding of how such virtual enterprises will operate in a "shared data / information / knowledge environment", through distributed working approaches and based on the paradigm of using the situation room metaphor as the core paradigm for carrying out joint operations. In this chapter, we present a methodology for modelling corporate interactions using the concept of the situation room (SR) as a supporting paradigm. Such an approach enables a way to model interactions of a virtual enterprise nature by means of a information and knowledge auction market that is concerned with the communications and interactions within a virtual enterprise (VE). This forms part of a wider research in defining a methodological framework for situation room analysis (SRA), and its deployment for complex corporate intelligence systems study.

INTRODUCTION

In this chapter, we present a methodology for modeling corporate interactions using the concept of the situation room (SR) as a supporting paradigm. Such an approach enables a way to model interactions of a virtual enterprise nature by means of a information and knowledge *auction market* that is concerned with the communications and interactions within a virtual enterprise (VE). This forms part of a wider research in defining a methodological framework for situation room analysis (SRA), and its deployment for complex corporate intelligence systems study.

Using this approach we propose the use of ontologies as a powerful means to support the implementation of multiparty collaboration and decision-making activities that build on the paradigm of a situation room (SR).

The approach is characterized as top-down in that the SR paradigm is conceptualized through three related models: the situation room model (SRM), the information management model (IMM) and the situation analysis model (SAM). The ontology-based approach includes the semantic features of the exchanged auction-related information thus offering the integration of the SRA framework with existing corporate decision-making grids (Ankolekar, Burstein, Hobbs, Lassila, Martin, & McIlraith, 2001).

From the viewpoint of the architecture of the SRA-based auction system, Web services are used as a means for organizing the interactions amongst the SR participants, and the latter may assign their tasks (e.g., look up, identify and classify, relevance check, etc.) to them.

In this respect, SRA-based auction services can be divided into three general groups:

- **Information retrieval services:** A particular Web service is designed to support its "owner" in finding data or locating documents within the corporate Intranet environment. It searches structured (e.g., auction profile) and semistructured (e.g., auction-related support documentation) data, extracts information, processes it and filters it. Such a service is expected to "know" the desires and interests of its "owner" or its "invoker". It knows where to look for this data and needs no assistance by the user. The autonomy is the main reason why someone should use such a service.
- **Cooperation services:** These are used to solve more complex problems. The cooperation Web service interacts and cooperates therefore with other Web services, its environmental resources and the users. Generally the cooperation service is more intelligent than the information retrieval

service because the ability of collaboration demands complex algorithms and functions. (Imagine for instance an SRA-based auction for a subject that needs involvement of experts from two different disciplines; in the simple case where no cooperation services exist, no initiative for a joint action could be taken.)

- **Transaction-related services:** These are used in the distributed SRA-based auction environment and are mainly assigned responsibility of carrying out valuation transactions to / from the participating (sub)systems or applications with a defined level of security. It is easy to understand that this third level of services can be treated as a black box, without causing any loss of the generality of the provided solution.

A focus aspect is the number of VE users, that is, the SR members to populate such a system. If just a few people participate in the SRA sessions, the resulting outcome is of marginal benefit with respect to the costs related for establishing and operating the system. The appropriateness of the proposed approach therefore lends itself to the case of larger VE organizations and schemes where there is an actual need to support multiparty decision-making with use of asynchronous session-based interactions. The individual SR members would be asked then to provide their individual views and contribute to parts of a global problem or issue, and coordinate their (individual) information appropriately through an *auction process*.

For instance, it is a totally different exercise to employ a thematic relevance check procedure for an amount of 10,000 documents with an average of circa 15 separate thematic keywords in each one of them, than it is to use it for a base of 1,000 documents with a complicated (nested) average of 15 keyword items for each document. Similar limitations to the appropriateness of the solution apply for the amount of involved parties.

In the conclusions of this chapter we provide explicit answers for two important questions:

- Why is the situation room appropriate for virtual environments?
- Why can our proposed approach (as an auction engine for corporate information and knowledge exchange) be extended beyond the traditional cooperative groupware environments?

ARCHITECTURE COMPONENTS

In this chapter we address implementation aspects in terms of describing an overall IT architecture, its modules and interfaces, its information flows, and its transfer into a tool-based environment for decision support. Furthermore, we define rules, mechanisms and operational guidelines for its components, and particular attention is paid to conceptual design and alternatives for update routines.

The IEEE STD 610.12, as extended slightly by the information architecture plan (IAP) of the integration task force (ITF), defines *"archi-tecture"* as *"the structure of components, their relationships, and the principles and guidelines governing their design and evolution over time."* (IEEE, 1990) However, it is important to note the difference between an architecture *description* and an architecture *implementation*; while the former is a representation or "blueprint" of a current or postulated "real-world" configuration of resources, rules and relationships, it is only once the blueprint enters the design, development and acquisition process, that the architecture description is transformed into a real *implementation*. It should be noted that it is neither in the scope of this chapter nor of the study to address this blueprint-to-implementation transformation process.

There are three major perspectives, that is, views, which logically combine to describe the SRA framework architecture. These three archi-tecture views are related to the operational, the systems, and the technical views respectively, in full conformance to the C4ISR Architecture Framework, for "Command, Control, Communications, Computers, Intelligence, Surveillance, and Reconnaissance" (C4ISR, 1997). The latter was intended to ensure that the architectures developed by the geographic and functionally unified commands, of military services for example, are *interrelatable* between and amongst the various organizations' operational, systems and technical architecture views, and are *comparable* and *integratable* across organizational boundaries. This is also close to our aim (Roberts & Koumpis, 2005) for a powerful infostructure based on the metaphor of a situation room in which actions are included to improve coordination towards the harmonization and standardization of each party's individual ontologies and sophisticated metadata architectures. Each of the three architecture views has implications on which architecture characteristics are to be considered, though there is often some degree of redundancy in displaying certain characteristics from one view to another.

In the paragraphs that follow, the essential components of the different architectural views are described. For most of them, a generic template is shown that illustrates the basic format of the component. In many cases, existing, real-world examples are provided.

Situation Synopsis

The situation synopsis facility addresses essential aspects of a situation considered by means of providing answers to questions related to Who? What? When? Where? How? of a particular situation under consideration.

In this respect, it may facilitate the initial phases of planning. It is easy to recognize the need for it to be provided in a consistent form that will allow quick reference and comparison amongst other situations, thus disabling error proneness with respect to links with the "wrong" situations.

It is upon the situation synopsis that indexing and retrieval operations will be based.

It is time-dependent, that is, as time goes by it may change—after the completion of a situation, it is still important that this has been appropriately documented in the Situation Synopsis.

The following apply when providing the situation synopsis:

- **Identification:** Provide a unique descriptive name for the situation, identify the person responsible for its handling (the "Account" manager for that particular situation), identify involved units and so forth.
- **Purpose:** Explain why the SRA is needed, what it is intended to achieve, the types of analysis expected to be applied to it, who is expected to perform the analysis, what decisions are expected to be made on the basis of that analysis, who is expected to make those decisions and what actions are expected to result from the architecture.

It is highly possible that the answers to these questions cannot be given from the beginning – it is however imperative that the person responsible for the situation will try to provide answers.

Of course, a situation that was initially identified to be related with a cause X might be attributed to cause Y; and the interactions with some other entities may have been initially erroneously attributed to some reasons Z. But it is in any case essential that the synopsis will enable enrichments and further—continuous updates.

- **Scope:** Identify the situation views and implications and its particular temporal nature, such as the time frame covered, for example whether by specific years or by designations such as "as-is", "to-be", "transitional" and so forth.
- **Context:** Describe the interrelated conditions that compose the setting in which the situation exists. Include such things as doctrine, relevant goals and vision statements, concepts of operation, scenarios and environmental conditions. Identify the tasking that led to the architecture's development, and known or anticipated linkages to other situations.

Document-specific assumptions and constraints regarding the situation analysis effort, and identify authoritative sources for the rules, criteria and conventions that were followed in developing the particular syllogisms.

- **Findings:** State the findings and recommendations that have been developed based on the aformentioned. Examples of findings include recommended actions, identification of shortfalls or successful implementations and opportunities for reaction.
- **Tools and file formats:** Identify the tool suites to be used to support the SRA exercise. Identify the system and file names, and location of the data and appropriate resources including also humans.

Integrated Situation Dictionary

There is considerable textual information in the form of definitions and metadata (i.e., data about an item) associated with the various situations encountered.

The Integrated Situation Dictionary provides a central source for all these definitions and metadata, including those that may be provided for convenience within another architectural component as well. At a minimum, the Integrated Situation Dictionary is a glossary with definitions of terms used in a given situation description. The Integrated Situation Dictionary makes the set of components capable of standing alone and allows a set of situation related documents to be read and understood without reference to other documents.

Each labeled item (e.g., terms, phrase or acronym) in the situation literature should have a corresponding entry in the Integrated Situation Dictionary. For instance, when we speak about a Sales downsizing—whatever this may mean—the ISD provides a unique explanation for this. The same also when speaking about a Sales downscaling—whatever this may mean also. By using specific terminology, actions and reactions can be standardized and this saves time, decreases error rates and so forth.

The type of metadata included in the Integrated Situation Dictionary for each type of item will depend on the type of the component from which the particular service item is 'taken'. For example, the metadata about a labeled input/output connector from an activity model will include a textual description of the type of input/output information designated by the label.

The contents for the Integrated Situation Dictionary entries for each component type should be regarded as evolving—as it is the case for any dictionary of a natural language. SR participants should use standard terms where possible (i.e., terms from existing, approved situation dictionaries). However, in some cases, new terms and/or modified definitions of existing terms may be needed. This can happen when new concepts are devised. In those cases, the *new terms contained in a given architecture's Integrated* Situation *Dictionary should be submitted to the maintainers of the SR for approval.* All definitions that originate in existing dictionaries should provide a reference to show the source, which may be the first situation in which a particular term was used. Furthermore, indicative references to a term may be used for helping the comprehension of the particular term(s).

In this respect, the terms sales downsizing and sales downscaling might have been used for first time in situations ABC and XYZ respectively, while the "best" example for conceiving their notion may be situations ABC and XYZ respectively.

Indexes and thesauri that provide support for synonyms, or other type of processing the particular semantics of a term are not considered as part of the Integrated Situation Dictionary.

Situation Concept

The situation concept is the most general of the architecture-description components and the most flexible in format. Its main utility is as a facilitator of human communication, and it is intended for presentation to SR participants and decision makers. This kind of diagram can also be used as a means of orienting and focusing detailed discussions.

A possible template may show generic icons that can be tailored as needed and used to represent various classes of players in a particular situation under consideration. The icons could also be used to represent missions or tasks. The lines connecting the icons can be used to show simple connectivity, or can be annotated to show what information is exchanged.

How the template is tailored depends on the scope and intent of the implementation, but in general a Situation Concept should be capable to communicate to interested parties some basic information regarding causality and time dependencies, as well as interactions amongst the various involved actors.

Information Supply Chain Node Connectivity Description

The main features of information supply chain (ISC) node connectivity description are the operational nodes and elements, the necessary links between them, and the characteristics of the information exchanged for a particular situation (Vontas, Koutsakas, Athanasopoulou, Koumpis, Hatzaras, & Manolopoulos, 2002).

Each information exchange is represented by an arrow (indicating the direction of information flow), which is annotated to describe the characteristics of the data or information (e.g., its substantive content, other operational requirements and environmental parameters, security or classification level, timeliness, and requirements for information system interoperability. Information-exchange characteristics can be shown selectively in diagrammatic form, or more comprehensively in a matrix format).

The information illustrated in the information supply chain node connectivity description can be used to make decisions about which systems are needed to satisfy the needs related with the situation under consideration. However, it is the conduct of operations that is illustrated, not supporting systems.

In the operational architecture view it is not required to name real physical facilities as nodes; it can instead focus on "virtual" nodes, which could be based on operational roles. Thus, operational nodes would not always be directly integratable with real (physical) nodes from other architectures, but they could provide insight as to which real nodes might be able to assume the roles portrayed.

It should be noted that what constitutes an operational node can vary from one situation to another, including, but not limited to, representing a role, an organizational entity and so forth. The notion of node will likewise vary depending on the level of detail addressed by the architecture effort.

To emphasize the focus of the analysis and to ensure comparability and integratability across different situations, it is important therefore that each SRA implementation carefully documents its use of the operational node concept.

The activities associated with a given information exchange should be noted in some way to provide linkages between each node and the activities performed there; this is especially true if no formal activity model is developed. (An ISC

node connectivity description, in effect turns the activity model inside out, focusing first-order on the nodes and second-order on the activities. An activity model, on the other hand, places first-order attention on activities and second-order attention on nodes, which can be shown as mechanisms.) Activities may be associated with the node.

Situation Information Exchange Matrix

Using the defined activities as a basis, information exchange requirements express the relationship across the basic entities of a particular situation with a focus on the specific aspects of the information flow. More specifically, they identify *who* exchanges *what* information with *whom*, *why* the information is necessary and in *what* manner.

This is essential both for the examination of the situation per se, as well as for the identification of interactions amongst the SR participants, during the SRA exercise.

The emphasis in this product is on the logical and operational characteristics of the information (e.g., what information is needed by whom, from whom and when).

The nature of the operational description lends itself to being described as a matrix. However, the number of information exchanges associated with an architecture may be quite large. Also, in order to understand the nature of the information exchanges, the SRA developers and users of the architecture may want to see the data sorted in multiple ways, such as by task, by node or by attribute. Consequently, using a matrix to present that information is limiting and frequently not practical. Due to its highly structured format, the situation info exchange matrix lends itself readily to a spreadsheet or a relational database. In practice, additional hardcopy versions could be limited to high-level summaries or highlighted subsets of particular interest.

It is easy to see that an SRA implementation should encompass features expected to dominate in distributed service provision environments, which will adopt a decentralized approach in all aspects related to the service design, the provision and the lifecycle management.

The starting point for the design of the access to service environment relates to the following:

- An SRA e-service is regarded as an aggregate formed by fundamental service elements, which are implemented by means of corresponding components.
- The IT-realisation of a generic SRA e-service is platform independent and uses common components. A service agent infrastructure may be used to "route" SRA e-service elements intelligently, and carry out other key information supply-related operations.
- The SRA e-service agent infrastructure thus supports the decentralized process execution that is so essential to the dynamic character of an efficiently networked inter-organizational infrastructure like the SRA implementation.
- In the context of the aforementioned, the e-service agent "navigation" aspect deals with the interconnection of the various service flow scenarios of the SRA implementation that involve the static, or structural characteristics of the service pathway elements amongst the particularly involved entities (i.e., the SR participants and the various systems connected to).

More specifically, e-services are described as combined work and information flows, which we call in the context of the study *service flows*. An indicative service flow is depicted next, according to which:

- The overall service flow involves inclusion of several info supply chain "nodes".
- The service agents are enabling the service flow between the various nodes by means

of transferring both data and metadata information amongst them.

Upon the reception of an e-service, then given the particular scenario under execution as well as specifics related to service agent permissions and access rights, as these are specified by the relevant service data elements, the SRA agent execution may commence according to three alternative modes:

1. Immediate scenario execution, which forms the case of an *executor*
2. By means of presenting a user interface entity informing the particular node / user about the event, and delegating the latter for choosing whether to, for example, resume execution at that moment, to redirect the execution to another user or to decide inclusion into a waiting list. This forms the case of a *controller*.
3. No information is communicated to the particular node user and the service agent is immediately included in a waiting list; this forms the case of a *coordinator*, where the user's decision is expected for enabling the scenario execution or whether the service agent may be relocated elsewhere for execution (i.e., moved further to another node).

Information describing the services in terms of service flows, service elements and service pages is depicted in the service database (see Figure 2).

As seen in the Figure 2, the scheme can be augmented for inclusion of billing information. Even in the case that the SRA is given for free to corporate management, it is essential for an assessment of the particular utility and valuation that someone may attribute to a particular situation information exchange matrix.

Figure 1. Changes in the route of a service flow and reuse of service components

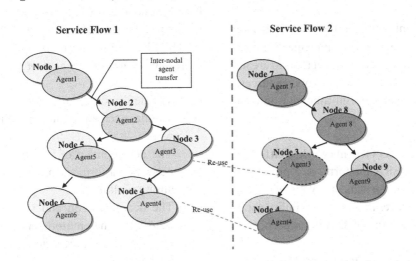

Figure 2. View of a service database schema

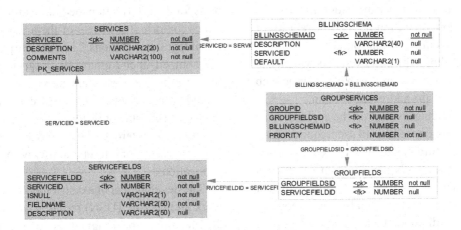

THE RUN-TIME ENVIRONMENT

On the implementation side the SRA run-time environment will focus on the implementation of the distributed Architecture and of tools to create and manage shared corporate network resources. More specifically, the SRA run-time environment will comprise:

- **Distributed service network platform:** Namely the SRA platform, as a prototype solution based on semantic Web technologies, to achieve maximum flexibility for a wider applicability of SRA in the corporate world
- **Seamless semantic interoperability toolkit:** Will enable corporate as well as external content and service providers and SRA users to communicate and transact through the SRA run-time environment

The above-mentioned technical objectives will be based on an information mediation architecture that will allow the semantic interoperability of heterogeneous information sources.

Figure 3 shows the improvements, which can be gained by using the approach of semantic Web technologies in the addressed domain.

Today, if changes occur on the application or service level or on the level of user requirements, the data structure has to be changed and often manually adjusted to the new situation. Developers mostly implement proprietary solutions, which fit their current needs. The overall view is missing. This model will allow the automatic adaptation of the data structures to changing situations according to the rules and specifications defined in the SRA ontologies and the aggregation, exchange and synthesis of services in different levels.

The SRA run-time environment key objective is to deliver the semantic tools, components and guidelines in order to satisfy a series of representative situation room sessions as well as the underlying business cases, which cover data exchange, and service provision and synthesis based on content sharing between various corporate participants and resource "servers".

The SRA run-time environment tools mentioned above are the key achievements:

- The definition of an open, distributed and seamless semantic interoperability framework
- The development of a distributed service network platform and a semantic interoperability toolkit
- The demonstration and validation of the SRA run-time environment developments by executing test scenarios of the examined business cases

The Distributed Service Network Platform and the Seamless Semantic Interoperability Toolkit

Ontology technologies are adopted as the technical basis for the information mediation architecture, which conforms to the state-of-the-art in information integration solutions. The platform provides a harmonized, open framework for services where multiple business partners as well as content providers and service providers can exchange data ensuring not only the syntactic, but also the semantic interoperability. Furthermore, the platform caters for interoperability with existing applications.

The development of a distributed service network architecture (DSN) requires two software architectures to be designed: a network architecture and an application architecture.

The network architecture, accounts for how systems in the DSN should know and understand each others. At present the following kinds of system are envisaged:

- SRA client nodes, using services
- SRA supplier nodes, providing services

Figure 3. Improvement in using semantics in the addressed domain

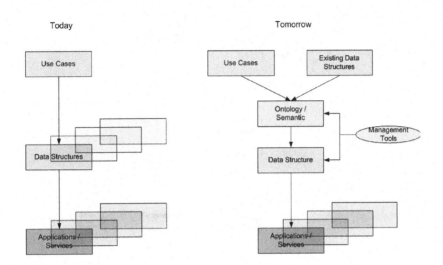

- SRA directories, providing a list of supplier nodes together with the offered services
- SRA devices (handheld user devices, workstations, servers and so forth), normally supported by client nodes

Protocols such as SOAP and UDDI (or ebXML) belong to this picture of the architecture, as well as "semantic enablers" suited for these protocols.

Seamless Semantic Interoperability Toolkit (SSIT)

The seamless semantic interoperability environment will be used as a base platform to create a toolkit for interconnecting content and service providers to the SRA run-time environment. SSIT consists of interfaces and utilities for users within the SRA scope of execution, and namely for publishing content, discovering and composing Web services. This environment forms an integral part of the overall interoperability environment that includes common data formats for information exchange and service interactions.

The toolkit uses an ontology-based approach to connect individual content providers with their own data formats to the SRA run-time environment. Corporate learning, based on the notion of the situation room, domain related ontology is used as a base for the toolkit and will be extended and generalized to cover the SRA run-time environment services.

By utilizing the developed toolkit, service and content providers are able to join the SRA run-time environment network and interface their content and services with the network and other providers. SSIT is comprised of the following components:

- **Semantic Context designer** creates context based on ontologies and registers this as publishable content to the context server. The latter graphically annotates semantic-defined information which flows with the various client request messages as part of the particular services.
- **Service oriented application integration module (SOAI)** facilitates the creation of a

Figure 4. The SRA run-time environment network architecture

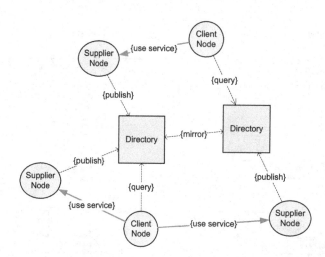

service-oriented infrastructure that wraps the provider legacy system functionality. The SOAI module uses semantic conceptualization of the legacy system that can be defined by a composer and generates the set of Web services that are responsible for the integration of the legacy system to the SRA run-time environment platform.

- **Semantic registry configuration module** facilitates the registration of the services provided by the provider. Using OWL profiles the module enables the registry administrator to enrich Web service descriptions with semantic information.

In its practical application, SRA addresses the needs for a solid technological basis for online recommendations and for corporate value creation through recommendations by an application orientation that will provide:

- The transfer of technology and expertise based on a lightweight web mining infrastructure for recommendations and
- The establishment of the corresponding recommendation services that go beyond

the conventional model of exploiting the preferences of corporate users.

In Figure 5 we provide an estimate of the gross system performance based on a simulation we have run for a set of more than 4,600 different cases. It should be noted that the reliability for the border values is rather low (< 1,7), signifying a possibly reduced adequacy of the approach for such extreme cases.

For determining gross performance we used the weighted average sum of parameters including amongst others user recall, connectedness of thematic items, retrievability and relevance.

From the trace results, we see that higher numbers indicate better performance as it is also the "natural" expectation, though it is apparent that the performance peak exhibits abnormalities; for example, for 10 themes and 100 users the system behavior is close to this shown for 10,000 users, while there is a decline in performance in between for 1,000 users.

This anomaly is easier to understand when we look back to the correlation amongst the different parameters that have been considered but further

Figure 5. Simulation-based estimation of SRA-based auction performance

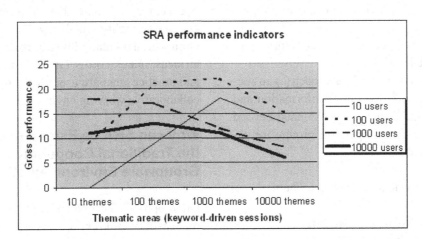

discussion and exploration of these aspects is beyond the scope of this particular chapter.

CONCLUSION

In the world of business, changes in the working environment of enterprises are now driven by the needs of industry to respond in an agile manner to market forces, such as customer demands, increased competition and shifting patterns of global trade and so forth. This also requires a clear identification and redeployment of traditional business functions. A major challenge for virtual organizations in that respect is the integration of their various corporate organizational and information assets, as well as their communication infrastructures and personnel. There also remains a need for greater understanding of how such virtual enterprises will operate in a "shared data / information / knowledge environment", through distributed working approaches and based on the paradigm of using the situation room metaphor as the core paradigm for carrying out joint operations.

The fast growth of innovations in the last 20 years (coming mainly from the proliferation of the distributed computing and services area) exposes companies and their shareholders to varied risks and different types of risk that may be difficult to quantify. Though extended report-centric infrastructures have been established (with companies investing several thousands of Euros on them on an annual basis, many of which are simply wasted and misspent) these often result in extensive, yet largely meaningless statements, enumerating every possible risk yet still exhibit insufficient specific risk disclosures.

The concept of situation room analysis (SRA) is proposed as a means of achieving the expected level of integration, thus closing the gap between the (envisaged) functionality and the (supporting) semantics of any particular VE integration process and especially the one related with intangible goods such as information and knowledge. Activities related to both the preparatory actions needed for establishing a session within the SR as well as for organizing information management and processing within it, can make apparent the fact that there are plenty of infinite regress problems and that we need to disaggregate the concept of information before we can get a better understanding of the arguments.

In the introduction of this chapter we promised to provide answers to two important questions:

- Why is the situation room appropriate for virtual environments?
- Why can our proposed approach (as an auction engine for corporate information and knowledge exchange) be extended beyond the traditional cooperative groupware environments?

It is now time to answer each of them.

Why is the Situation Room Appropriate for Virtual Environments?

Virtual environments have been treated in the literature either as extensions of the "real" environment, or as operational spaces that support—see for instance a representative collection of research approaches in Camarinha-Matos (2002).

In our approach we employ the situation room (SR) concept as a central metaphor of the virtual collaborative working environment (CWE) of the future, supporting personal and corporate requirements, work and management practices, organizational issues and emerging enabling technologies.

The metaphors and the various conceptual schemes and mental representations that people use for carrying out most types of work tasks and job assignments, spanning from what we call "simple" and "everyday" to those we tend to regard as more abstract or sophisticated, and which work and the learning process in general are part of, have a great significance to the way tasks are carried out and work practices are developed for carrying out these tasks. By the use of such a nonmaterial or intangible culture (Lakoff & Johnson, 1980), which is inherent to any specific job assignment, being able to "serve" it and to sufficiently express its characteristics, it is often

possible to improve substantially the way a task is executed, no matter how abstract, complex, detailed or sophisticated may this be. That same nonmaterial or intangible culture also consists of all ideas, values, norms, interaction styles, beliefs and practices that are used by the members of a collaborative working environment (CWE).

Why can SRA be Extended Beyond the Traditional Cooperative Groupware Environments?

Our proposed approach for organizing a situation room as an auction engine for corporate information and knowledge exchange lies in the overall area of design schemes for cooperative groupware environments. The question focus is on why does SRA go *beyond* the traditional environments.

First of all, an SRA implementation may build either on existing "traditional cooperative groupware environments" or not. It does not concentrate on the functions of a groupware application; its focus rather lies on the processes related to the actual group activities, their nature and their relative positioning within the value system of the company (it is therefore that we talk about sharing *views*, *information* and *culture* within the corporate situation room). And it is in this respect that different classes of *macro* and *microprocesses* can be organized to serve the particular needs of the company. One could name SRA as an umbrella model that can accommodate various cooperative groupware environments—or alternatively call for the need to organize the application of situation room Analysis as a metamodel to guide the application of a specific type or instance of a cooperative groupware environment. In all cases, this is still the subject of novel interaction approaches that need to be explored and which shall draw their paradigms from crossdisciplinary research.

REFERENCES

Ankolekar, A., Burstein, M., Hobbs, J. R., Lassila, O., Martin, D. L., McIlraith, S. A., Narayanan, S., Paolucci, M., Payne, T., Sycara, K., & Zeng, H. (2001). DAML-S semantic markup for web services. In *Proceedings of the First Semantic Web Working Symposium* (SWWS '01).

C4ISR (1997). Architecture working group. *C4ISR Architecture Framework* (Version 2.0).

Camarinha-Matos L. M. (Ed.) (2002). Collaborative business ecosystems and virtual enterprises. In *Proceedings of the IFIP TC5/WG5.5 Third Working Conference on Infrastructures for Virtual Enterprises (PRO-VE'02)*, Sesimbra, Portugal.

Lakoff, G., & Johnson, M. (1980). *Metaphors we live by*. University of Chicago Press.

Roberts, B., & Koumpis, A. (2005). Use of ontologies to support the situation room metaphor as an auction engine for corporate information and knowledge exchange [Electronic version]. *International Journal of Electronic Commerce & Business Media, 15*(1).

Vontas, A., Koutsakas, F., Athanasopoulou, C., Koumpis, A., Hatzaras, P., Manolopoulos, Y., & Vassilakopoulos, M. (2002). Integrating mobile agents infrastructures in operational ERP systems. In *Proceedings of the 4th International Conference on Enterprise Information Systems*, Ciudad Real, Spain.

Chapter X
Multi–Agent Systems Integration in Enterprise Environments Using Web Services

Eduardo H. Ramírez
Tecnológico de Monterrey, Mexico

Ramón F. Brena
Tecnológico de Monterrey, Mexico

ABSTRACT

In this paper we present a decoupled architectural approach that allows software agents to interoperate with enterprise systems using Web services. The solution leverages existing technologies and standards in order to reduce the time-to-market and increase the adoption of agent-based applications. We present case studies of applications that have been enhanced by our proposal.

INTRODUCTION

Software agents (Jennings & Wooldridge, 1996) and Web services (W3C, 2003b) have become key research areas for a growing number of organizations and they are expected to bring a new generation of complex distributed software systems (Jennings, 2000). Even if Agent tech-nology is finding its way little by little into the mainstream, Web services have been adopted much more widely and rapidly (Barry, 2003).

Several authors have pointed out some over-lapping areas between agents and Web services semantic capabilities (Hunhs, 2002; Preece & Decker, 2002). However, issues regarding how they may be competing or complementary technologies remain open (Petrie, 1996). Because of that, research involving agents and Web services is mainly focused on building improved semantics (Dickinson & Wooldridge, 2003; Hendler, 2001), communication languages and interaction protocols (Labrou et al., 1999).

We assume that in order to impact real-world organizations, a greater emphasis should be made on interoperability between agent-based applications and enterprise information systems. Moreover, we believe that the adoption of agent technologies will grow by leveraging existing industry standards and technologies. Therefore he problem we address is an instance of "the legacy software integration problem" (Nwana & Ndumu, 1999; Genesereth & Ketchpel, 1994).

In this work we present a decoupled architectural approach and design principles, called "embedded Web services architecture" (EWSA), that allows agent-based applications to be integrated into enterprise application environments (Peng et al., 1998) using Web services, thus allowing them to interoperate with robust conventional systems such as:

- Web-applications, portals and content management systems (CMS)
- Enterprise resource planning (ERP)
- Manufacturing execution systems (MES)
- Workflow engines and business process management systems (BPMS)

This integration allows agents to publish XML (W3C, 2000) Web services (W3C, 2003b) or standard HTML providing thus a convenient interface for other distributed components. The Web service architecture is widely understood as "a software system" designed to support interoperable machine-to-machine interaction over a network. It has an interface described in a machine-processable format (specifically WSDL (W3C, 2001)). Other systems interact with the Web service in a manner prescribed by its description using SOAP-messages (W3C, 2003a), typically conveyed using HTTP with an XML (W3C, 2000) serialization in conjunction with other Web-related standards" (W3C, 2003b).

Regarding the external behavior of the agent based application, our approach fits into the design paradigm identified as service oriented architecture (SOA). The SOA foundation ideas were introduced by Arsajani (Arsanjani, 2001); he defines SOA as: "the architectural style that supports loosely coupled services to enable business flexibility in an interoperable, technology-agnostic manner." SOA consists of a composite set of business-aligned services that support a flexible and dynamically re-configurable end-to-end business processes realization using interface based service descriptions (Borges et al., 2004).

This paper also discusses the kind of agent-based applications we have found to be suitable for this approach and the nature of Web Services that agents can provide. The rest of the paper is organized as follows. In the next section, we provide an overview of our solution approach. Specifically, we discuss the proposed embedded Web server architecture for integrating agent-based applications and enterprise applications and its implementation. Then, we discuss its evaluation and application to some example domains. Finally, the paper concludes with some expected business results.

SOLUTION OVERVIEW

Instead of making an agent-based application look "different" compared to other applications from the outside, which is indeed a "religious" point of view frequent in the agent research community, we intend to hide the *agentness* of a group of agents from the outside.

We contend that agents should solve problems for which they are well suited for, and should relate to other software components just as another software component. This is especially true when a set of technologies for gluing software components are maturing, such as Web services and service-oriented architectures. So, our approach relies much more on *hiding* the agents than on exposing them to the outside world.

Architecture

As shown in Figure 1, the underlying metaphor used to determine the design strategy is the aim to create a "black-box" in which agents can live and perform complex tasks. The main architectural principle consists of decoupling agent-based applications through the exposure of Web service interfaces. Enterprise applications should not be aware that a service is provided by agents if the system offers a standard SOAP endpoint as interface, appearing to the world as a conventional Web service or application.

An agent based application which exposes Web interfaces requires the interoperability of Web components and agents and their respective containers, as they are built on different programming models, each following different sets of specifications. The relevant components and containers in a system combining agents and servlets would be:

- **Web container:** Also called the "servlet container," it is the application that provides the execution environment for the web components and implements the Java

Servlet API in conformity with the JSR-154 specification (Sun Microsystems, Inc., 2003). Web containers are usually built within web servers and provide network services related with HTTP request processing.

- **Web component:** Servlets are the standard user defined web components written in Java. JSR-154 defines them as "A Java technology-based web component, managed by a container that generates dynamic content" (Sun Microsystems, Inc., 2003). They follow a synchronous processing model as they are designed to handle the content of the HTTP requests. The dynamic content delivered in the request may be HTML for web pages or XML (W3C, 2000) for Web services.

- **Agent container:** The execution environment for the agents provided by the agent platform in conformity with FIPA (FIPA, 2002) specifications.

- **Web service agent:** A Java thread that periodically executes a set of behaviors containing the agent tasks. For the purposes of this work we could say that an agent is a "Web service agent" if it receives and processes requests formulated by a human user or an application in collaboration with a Web component. The requests may be synchronous or asynchronous.

Figure 1. Decoupled architecture top-level view

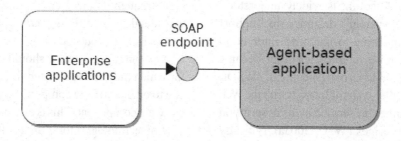

Figure 2a. EWSA decoupled architecture (component view)

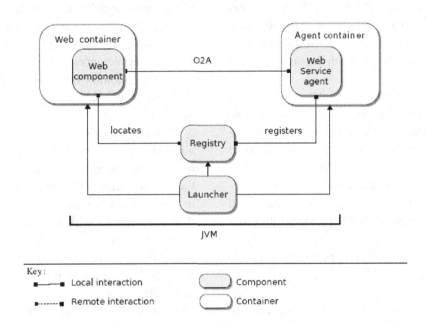

Figure 2b. EWSA decoupled architecture (execution model)

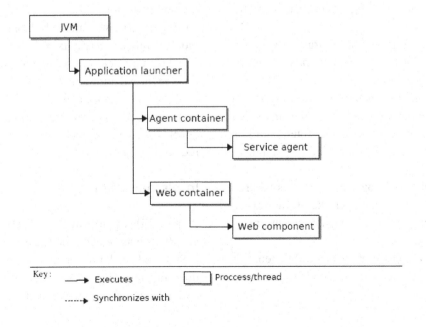

Our proposed solution (Figure 2(a)) is designed around the idea of embedding a Web container into the agent-based application. This approach makes it easier to communicate with both containers because they are placed in the same memory space.

When the agent and web containers are started on the same Java virtual machine operating system process, agents and web components may communicate by sharing object references in a virtual object-to-agent (O2A) channel. The resulting execution model is shown in Figure 2(b).

As an intermediate result, the embedded Web server architecture (EWSA) provides intra-container integration and allows the agent-based application to process HTTP petitions in a simple and efficient way.

However, in order to leverage the achieved integration, it is necessary to provide some additional artifacts to simplify the interactions between the agents and the web components, namely:

- An **agent registry:** Where all the agents with web services capabilities register in order to be located for web component invocations
- A **platform launcher:** A boot system that initializes and configures the main containers

Moreover, from the structural view of the architecture as well as the behavioral or dynamic perspective, we notice that when the agents and web components exist in the same space, synchronization becomes an issue. So, in the embedded architecture, the complexity of interactions is handled by two core framework components:

- A **call monitor** object that serves as a shared memory space between the agent and the web component, and handles synchronization among them
- A **service behavior** object used by agents for exposing internal tasks as Web Services

The call monitor is a simple implementation of the classic synchronization construct (Hoare, 1974), used to encapsulate the concurrent access to shared resources. In the EWSA framework, when a web component requires an agent service, a call monitor object is created to handle the agent response, which may be synchronous or asynchronous.

When a synchronous web service is invoked, a web component attempts to access the agent results (the shared resource in this case) calling the monitor entry method *getResult*, then the monitor makes the caller wait until the agent thread finishes its work and releases the monitor through the exit method *setResult*. In the case of asynchronous invocations to agent services, the call monitor releases the web component process immediately. As the synchronization may involve a busy wait time, the monitor can optionally handle a maximum invocation timeout. Details of these interactions are shown in Figure 4(a).

On the other hand, as the agent request processing is asynchronous by nature, the service behavior allows agents to unqueue received message objects (each containing a monitor) and transparently translate them into internal service method invocations. In the case of synchronous requests, that is, when the web component remains blocked until agent results are calculated, the service behavior object is responsible of delivering them to the call monitor object and thus releasing the lock. The service behavior object also implements a round robin service discipline within the agent, allowing it to serve many web component requests simultaneously.

Implementation

Among FIPA platforms, JADE (Bellifemine et al., 1999) was selected because it is considered well suited for large scale deployments mainly due to its thread-per-agent programming model and the support of "virtual channels" that allow agents to interact with regular Java components (Rimassa, 2003).

In this particular implementation, the "Launcher" program, initializes and starts an instance of the JADE platform besides an embedded version of the Tomcat Web server (Jakarta Project—The Apache Software Foundation, 2003). The aforementioned "Registry" is nothing but a data structure that holds references to the running service agents, implemented as a Singleton pattern (Gamma et al., 1995).

Access to the agent's source code is required as they need to be recompiled to include the Web Service capability, which is encapsulated in a platform specific library. In JADE's particular case, agents are enhanced with a custom behavior class, which only requires the addition of one line of code.

The architecture is applicable to FIPA platforms other than Jade; however, it would be necessary to port the framework components (Registry and Launcher) using its particular libraries and program interfaces and to add missing components provided by the platform like virtual channels between objects and agents.

Evaluation and Comparison

Our proposal is not the first solution that allows agents to interoperate with web based components. In fact such an architecture was defined by developers (Berre and Fourdrinoy, 2002) of the Jade platform and later implemented on the WSAI Project (Whitestein Technologies, 2003) as a contribution to AgentCities initiative (Dale et al., 2002).

The WSAI solution assumes the existence of two agent containers - one standalone, which we may call the "main container", and another one contained within the web container. Each container is executed in a separate JVM system process. WSAI introduces the concept of "Gateway Agent" as an agent living in the "web container", responsible of translating HTTP requests into ACL messages. The general gateway architecture components are shown in Figure 3(a).

One of the major drawbacks of the approach resides in the existence of several processes that should synchronize using remote method invocations even if both of them are deployed on the same machine. The synchronization problem is addressed by instantiating the "gateway agents" and "caller" objects on a request basis. "Callers" implement the Java synchronization and time out handling, as shown in Figure 4(a). Additional complexity comes from the fact that it is able to interoperate with any running FIPA compliant agent platform (even non Java-based ones) without access to its source code.

An alternative interesting proposal by Cowan and Griss (2002) is BlueJADE, a connector that allows the management of a JADE platform by a Java application server, and therefore its interaction with the enterprise applications deployed inside it. BlueJADE's main strengths are manifested at the container level. Although the containers are running separately, the connector eliminates the need for remote calls which enables the use of the object-agent channels. However, BlueJADE does not define any interaction model for the components inside the application and is highly dependant on the particular application server product running the applications.

We believe that in order to build enterprise-class agent-based applications, it is not critical to provide web-interoperability to an indefinite number of FIPA platforms. Therefore, we trade-off this flexibility in favor of good integration with the chosen agent platform, even though the architectural principles remain useful for them. As a result, our framework implementation is simple and provides good performance.

In the EWSA framework, interactions are reduced to a minimal subset which does not require any remote method invocation. The model shown in Figure 4(b) considers interactions similar to the ones in the gateway architecture until the HTTP request is delivered to the gateway agent.

Figure 3a. Gateway architecture (component view)

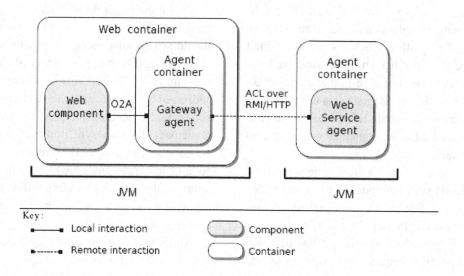

Figure 3b. Gateway architecture (execution model)

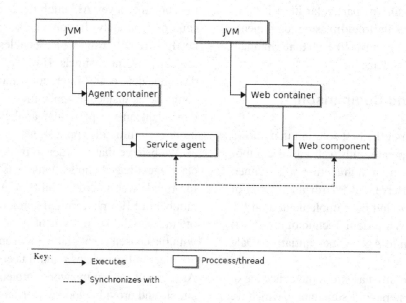

Figure 4a. Interactions sequence diagrams (WSAI interactions)

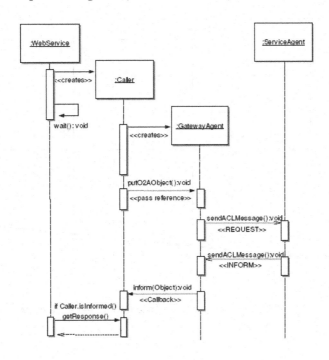

Figure 4b. Interactions sequence diagrams (EWSA interactions)

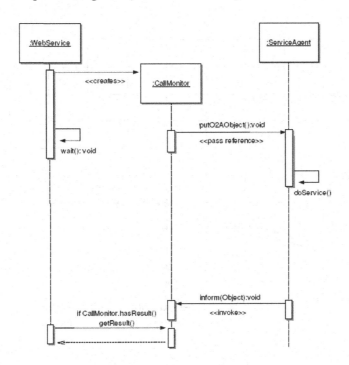

Figure 5a. Mean service time for concurrent requests (EWSA vs. WSAI)

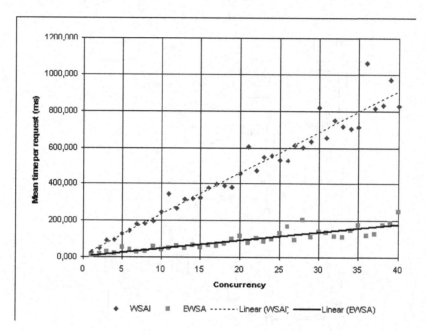

Figure 5b. Mean service time for concurrent requests (EWSA vs. non-agent service)

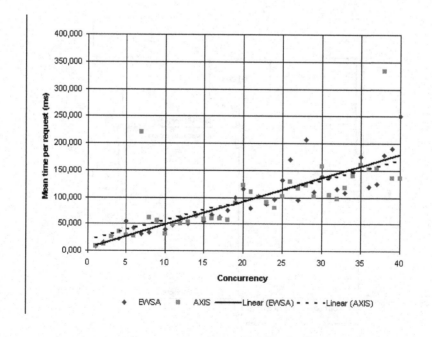

In a benchmark comparison between WSAI and the EWSA decoupled architecture, an important performance and scalability gain was observed. A currency exchange Web service is provided in the WSAI platform. The service implementation is trivial as it only consists of a simple mathematical conversion performed by an agent. As shown in Figure 5(a) we may notice that not only EWSA's response times are better, but that they increase at a slower rate with respect to the number of concurrent requests which leads to better scalability. The performance gain in the embedded architecture can be interpreted as an effect of the elimination of network calls overhead between agents and web components.

A complementary experiment was performed in order to measure the relative performance overhead of the agent based architecture against a non-agent based solution implemented as a regular Axis Web service. Results shown on Figure 5(b) indicate that using the embedded architecture, the performance of the agent system follows a behavior pattern close to that of the pure Java solution. As a preliminary conclusion we may state that the embedded architecture solves the potential performance limitations for using agents in simple scenarios.

Additionally, by means of simple metrics we could show some of the desirable properties of the proposed architecture. As seen in Table 1, a functional implementation for embedding Web services into agent based applications is several times smaller than the implementation of a gateway framework from the WSAI Project.

Although the number of classes is not an absolute metric of software complexity, from the interaction models we can deduce that the interactions present in the embedded model (Figure 4(b)) are nothing but a subset of the interactions required in a gateway approach (Figure 4(a)). Consequently, the internal complexity of the embedded Web services architecture (EWSA) is not significantly different from the gateway architecture. In the embedded architecture only one abstract class is provided as an extension point for service developers, which consequently simplifies the agent and Web service implementation as shown in Table 2.

This comparison is provided as a reference resulting from the programming models. Considering that even if a code generation tool could actually simplify the development process, the additional interactions remain with a significant performance penalization.

Table 1. Integration framework size comparison

Package	Total Classes	Abstract	Concrete
Embedded	6	1	5
Gateway	52	6	46

Table 2. Example implementation size comparison

Package	Total Classes	Abstract	Concrete
Embedded	2	0	2
Gateway	4	1	3

APPLICATIONS

In general, we believe that the proposed integration model is useful to allow agent-based applications to provide knowledge-intensive services, such as:

- Search and automatic classification
- User profile inference
- Semantic-based content distribution

Web-enabled agent systems may serve in a variety of domains. As presented in the just-in-time information and knowledge (JITIK) case study, they are well suited to support knowledge distribution in enterprise environments.

Just-in-Time Information and Knowledge

The proposed model has been successfully implemented for the just-in-time information and knowledge (JITIK) environment that may be defined as a web-enabled agent-based intelligent system capable of delivering highly customized notifications to users in large distributed organizations (Brena et al., 2001). JITIK is aimed to support collaboration within organizations by delivering the right knowledge and information to the appropriate people just-in-time. JITIK is designed to interoperate with enterprise systems in order to retrieve and distribute contents in a flexible way.

The JITIK agent model is shown in Figure 6. Personal agents work on behalf of the members of the organization. They filter and deliver useful content according to user preferences. Personal agents are provided with information by the site agent who acts as a broker between them and service agents. For the purposes of this work, the most relevant agents of JITIK are the so called service agents which collect and detect information and knowledge pieces that are supposed to be relevant for someone in the organization. Examples of service agents are the Web service agents that receive and process external requests, as well as monitor agents which are continuously monitoring sources of information and knowledge (web pages, databases, etc.).

The ontology agent contains the knowledge about the interest areas of the members of the organization and about its structure (Brena &

Figure 6. JITIK and enterprise systems interaction

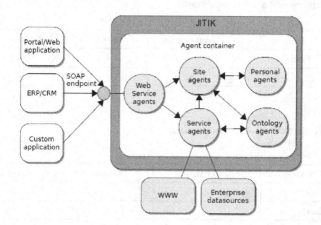

Ceballos, 2004). This knowledge is hierarchically described in the form of taxonomies, usually one for interest areas and one describing the structure of the organization. For example, in an academic institution, the interest areas could be the science domains in which the institution is specialized in, and the organizational chart of the institution gives the structure of the organization.

JITIK Web Services

JITIK is an example of an agent-based application able to provide knowledge intensive services which may be grouped as follows:

- **Recommendation services:** A user's profile is represented by a set of points in the taxonomies, as each user could have many interests and could be located at different parts of the organizational structure. As JITIK keeps track of user interests and preferences, it is able to recommend content to users on demand. Recommended content may be used in Portals or Web applications.
- **Content search and classification:** One of the main difficulties for web users is obtaining relevant information. In normal conditions people waste a lot of time searching for documents on the web because the user must examine the documents in detail to determine if they are really relevant for the search purpose. In the context of JITIK, a service agent that searches the most relevant documents on the web can be constructed. The knowledge that guides the search is handled by the ontology agent where the keywords with which the search engine is invoked are defined. The documents obtained by the search are qualified by a fuzzy system and then the best ones are presented to the user.
- **Subscription services:** JITIK allows users to subscribe to changes in specific areas. Also, users may customize the media and

frequency of JITIK notifications using simple web-based interfaces. Rules may be defined so that messages relative to certain topics are handled with higher priorities. A rule may state that several alerts may be sent to their cell-phone via SMS, and also define that interest-area messages be sent as a weekly summary via email. Organization managers may set high-level distribution rules.
- **Content distribution services:** Enterprise applications may deliver content to the system using its semantic-based content distribution services. When new content is received, it is classified and distributed to users who may be interested. Users receive the notifications of new content as specified by their own rules.

As shown above, the EWSA decoupled architecture allows an agent-based application like JITIK to provide enterprise communities with a number of knowledge oriented Web services, especially useful in large organizations where performance and scalability attributes become critical.

Implementation of a Recommendation Service

Standard collaborative applications could be enhanced by agent-based web services, for example, consider the simple scenario in which a user joins a workgroup using the collaborative application interface. After this event, the system will send recommendations about documents related to the group activity and interests on a daily basis. Some of the internal services interaction needed to fulfill this case are:

- Once the user joins the group, the collaborative application will invoke the agent-based service using a standard coarse-grained interface.

Figure 7: Recommendation service detailed view

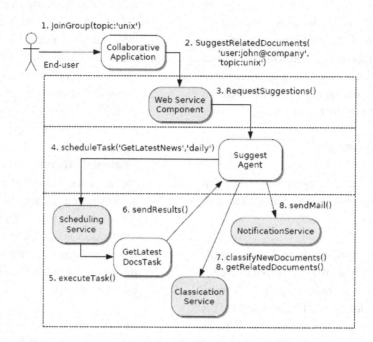

- Periodical updates to the document base will be programmed to be triggered upon certain conditions using the agent-platform scheduling service.
- Information gathered from data sources and repositories will be classified and filtered against the interests of the relevant groups using the semantic processing and classification services.
- Relevant information will be distributed to users using the agent-based notification services; the system may leverage the use of several distribution media (Email, SMS) to alert users of new documents and other application events according to its relevance.

The components and services interactions for the use-case are shown in detail in Figure 7. It should be noted that the use of generic services for scheduling, notification and classification allows the task specific code (read documents, send mail) to be encapsulated in the lower layers of the

system, thus enhancing the abstraction level for the agent layer.

Implementation of a Classification Service

Another use case that serves as an example to our integration approach is a news delivery and classification service. Interaction between agents and services causes the flow of events between services and agents, as shown in Figure 8. The sequence of interaction is as follows:

- Once the user of the content management system (CMS) publishes a new article, it triggers a notification to the JITIK service. The CMS application will invoke the content-distribution service using a standard coarse-grained interface.
- After that, the classification service will attempt to match a set of topics for the article,

Figure 8. Classification service detailed view

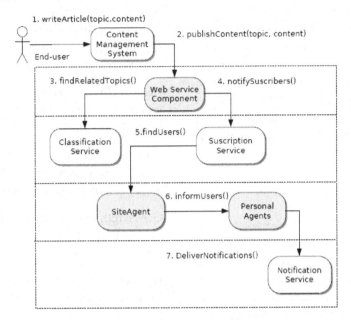

according the contents of the ontology of the organization.

- When the content is classified, the request is passed onto the agent-layer where agents determine the set of content receivers considering their interest profiles and personal preferences.
- Finally, relevant information will be delivered to users through the internal notification services; the system may leverage the use of several distribution media (Email, SMS) to alert users of new documents and other application events.

CONCLUSION

We have presented an architectural approach aimed to allow integration of multi-agent systems as Web Services components. Besides its simplicity, the advantage of this approach is that it provides an efficient way of interoperating agent-based subsystems with web-centric loosely-coupled systems. We think that this solution is a good compromise given the current status of technology, and it allows rapid integration of modular systems conforming to open standards. As expected business results, we hope the solution to be helpful to:

- Reduce the time to market of agent-based applications
- Deliver good performance for large volume of users
- Improve the code base maintainability

It is to be noted that our solution assumes that the agent and web component source code is available. With respect to the architectures presented in the literature, this solution mostly trades-off flexibility in favor of simplicity and maintainability.

We have presented experimental evidence to support our claim of efficiency. We have also presented a case study, which is the application of our architecture to the JITIK system. It is a multi-agent system to deliver information items to a distributed community of users.

In the near future we intend to test our architecture with other real-world systems integrating agents in a web-based framework. We are currently studying the methodological issues to guide the development of hybrid agent-web systems, as current agent development methodologies need to be strongly enhanced in order to suite our architecture.

REFERENCES

Arsanjani, A. (2001). A domain-language approach to designing dynamic enterprise component-based architectures to support business services. In *39th International Conference and Exhibition on Technology of Object-Oriented Languages and Systems, TOOLS 39* (pp. 130-141).

Barry, D. K. (2003). *Web services and service-oriented architectures: The savvy manager's guide.* Morgan Kaufmann.

Bellifemine, F., Poggi, A., & Rimassa, G. (1999). JADE-A FIPA-compliant agent framework. In *the Proceedings of PAAM'99*, London.

Borges, B., Holley, K., & Arsanjani, A. (2004). *Service-oriented architecture.* http://webservices.sys-con.com/read/46175.htm.

Berre, D. L., & Fourdrinoy, O. (2002). *Using JADE with Java Server Pages.* In JADE documentation. Available at http://sharon.cselt.it/projects/jade/doc/tutorials/jsp/JADE4JSP.html

Cowan, D., & Griss, M. (2002). *Making Software Agent Technology available to Enterprise Applications.* Technical Report HPL-2002-211, HP Labs. Available at http://www.hpl.hp.com/techreports/2002/HPL-2002-211.pdf

Dale, J., Willmott, S., & Burg, B. (2002). *Agentcities: Building a global next-generation service environment.* 10 June.

Dickinson, I., & Wooldridge, M. (2003). Towards practical reasoning agents for the Semantic Web. In *Proceedings of the Second International Joint Conference on Autonomous Agents and Multiagent Systems* (pp. 827-834). ACM Press.

FIPA (2002). *FIPA abstract architecture specification.* Available at http://www.fipa.org/specs/fipa00001/SC00001L.html

Gamma, E., Helm, R., Johnson, R., & Vlissides, J. (1995). *Design patterns: Elements of reusable object-oriented software.* Addison-Wesley.

Genesereth, M. R., & Ketchpel, S. P. (1994). Software agents. *Communication of the ACM, 37*(7), 48-55.

Hendler, J. (2001). Agents and the Semantic Web. *IEEE Intelligent Systems, 16*(2), 30-37.

Hoare, C. (1974). Monitors: An operating system structuring concept. *Communications of the ACM, 17*(10):549 - 557.

Hunhs, M. (2002). Agents as Web services. *IEEE Internet Computing, 6*(4), 93-95.

Jakarta Project - The Apache Software Foundation (2003). The Tomcat Web Server v. 4.1.

Jennings, N., & Wooldridge, M. (1996). Software agents. *IEE Review, 42*(1), 17 -20.

Jennings, N. R. (2000). On agent-based software engineering. *Artificial Intelligence, 177*(2), 277-296.

Labrou, Y., Finin, T., & Peng, Y (1999). Agent communication languages: the current landscape. *IEEE Intelligent Systems, 14*(2), 45 -52.

Nwana, H. S., & Ndumu, D. T. (1999). A Perspective on Software Agents Research. *The Knowledge Engineering Review, 14*(2), 1-18.

Peng, Y., Finin, T., Labrou, Y , Chu, B., Long, J., Tolone, W. J., & Boughannam, A. (1998). A multi-agent system for enterprise integration. In

Proceedings of the 3rd International Conference on the Practical Applications of Agents and Multi-Agent Systems (PAAM98) (pp. 155-169). London.

Petrie, C. J. (1996). Agent-based engineering, the Web and intelligence. *IEEE Expert, 11*(6), 24-29.

Preece, A., & Decker, S. (2002). Intelligent Web services. *IEEE Intelligent Systems, 17*(1), 15-17.

Rimassa, G. (2003). *Runtime support for distributed multi-agent systems.* PhD Thesis, University of Parma.

Sun Microsystems, Inc. (2003). JSR-000154 Java(TM) Servlet 2.4 Specification (Final release).

W3C (2000). Extensible Markup Language (XML) 1.0 (Second Edition). Available at http://www.w3.org/TR/2000/REC-xml-20001006

W3C (2001). *Web Services Description Language (WSDL)1.1.* Available at http://www.w3.org/TR/2001/NOTE-wsdl-20010315

W3C (2003a). *Simple Object Access Protocol (SOAP)1.2.* Available at http://www.w3.org/TR/soap12-part1/

W3C (2003b). *Web services glossary, Working Draft.* Available at http://www.w3.org/TR/2003/WD-ws-gloss-20030808/

Whitestein Technologies, A.G. (2003). Web Services Agent Integration Project.

An earlier summarized version of this work was published in ICEIS'05 conference selected papers book titled "Enterprise Information Systems VI," ISBN: 1-4020-3674-4, Springer, 2006.

Chapter XI
Web Service Discovery and Composition for Virtual Enterprises

Jürgen Dorn
E-Commerce Competence Center, Austria

Peter Hrastnik
E-Commerce Competence Center, Austria

Albert Rainer
E-Commerce Competence Center, Austria

ABSTRACT

One main characteristic of virtual enterprises are short-term collaborations between business partners to provide efficient and individualized services to customers. The MOVE project targets at a methodology and a software framework to support such flexible collaborations based on process oriented design and communication by Web services. MOVE's framework supports the graphical design and verification of business processes, the execution and supervision of processes in transaction-oriented environment, and the dynamic composition and optimization of processes. A business process may be composed from a set of Web services, deployed itself as Web service and executed in the framework. The composition of processes from Web services is implemented with methods from AI-planning. We apply answer set programming (ASP) and map Web service descriptions and customer requests into the input language of the ASP software DLV. Composition goals and constraints guide a composition challenge. We show the performance of our program and give some implementation details. Finally we conclude with some insights.

INTRODUCTION

A *virtual enterprise* is a business model (with many variants) in which different legally independent companies cooperate electronically (mainly by means of the Internet) to offer better services to customers that cannot be offered by one single member. The configuration of new services for customers is faster and more flexible than in traditional business models because a cooperation is initiated electronically.

Since one of our industrial partners comes from the tourism sector and another partner is an Austrian mobile communication provider, we use scenarios from the tourism sector extended with mobile communication features. In the tourism sector, partners in a virtual enterprise are for instance airlines, taxi drivers, hotels and others. In particular, the better coordination of services (e.g., flight arrival, luggage transport, taxi drive and hotel check-in) is an advantage for customers achieved by sophisticated information and communication technology in a virtual enterprise. Moreover, the possibility to contact the customer anytime and anywhere by means of mobile communication can result in continually better services. Of course, there are also benefits for single members of the virtual enterprise (e.g. the taxi driver), because they can schedule their workload better.

Mainly small enterprises exist in the tourism sector. These can participate in the development of larger products—so called *dynamic holiday packages* with the virtual enterprise concept. In contrast to actual business practices between tour operators and hotels, the virtual enterprise concept leads to more flexibility in defining such packages. A small enterprise can define a new service, announce it in the virtual enterprise and a customer can select this service immediately.

It is assumed that the cooperation is often short-term because the collaboration is established only for one individual service. Thus, the establishment of a collaboration must be achievable very easily without great organizational or financial efforts, but it must conform to certain standard behavior in order to guarantee high quality. For example, let us consider that the luggage of an airline customer is automatically transported to the hotel by taxi without requiring the customer to take care of it. Since the virtual enterprise has all required data, the taxi is already waiting for the customer and the luggage is immediately transported from the aircraft to the taxi. This process has to be controlled and supervised electronically to avoid the luggage loss. An architecture based on standardized Web services is a promising technique for achieving the required flexibility as well as the quality. The interfaces between members of the virtual enterprise (i.e., the data transmitted) are implemented on basis of international standards, especially those based on XML. Furthermore, open source software is reused as much as possible in the Move-project. Hrastnik (2004) and Rainer (2004) describe these infrastructure aspects in more detail.

Members of a virtual enterprise do not commit themselves to any financial or legal obligations. However, each member has to express which services it will supply under which conditions to the virtual enterprise and for the end customer in a transparent way. Some central decision support system to enable fast and flexible reactions to customer queries has to exist. The ideal solution would be an automatic decision based on centrally stored knowledge as well as knowledge distributed over all partners accessible through electronic communication. However, there may also be problems that require human expert knowledge. There will be a variety of commitments from members to such a decision support system.

Given a Web services based architecture, we can define a planning component as one Web service that obtains the customer query as input and produces a document containing several proposals as output. If the user selects one proposal, a second Web service can reserve and book this proposal. The first Web service calls further Web services to obtain the customer's profile data and preferences stored somewhere in the Internet. The second Web service may store an adapted version of the customer's preferences.

The planner may search for resources in the Internet by querying further Web services published in repositories or other sources. Thus, the planner may find available rooms in hotels and seats in aircrafts. If the customer searches for complex services (dynamic holiday packages), the following prototypical process steps are executed:

1. **Configuration step:** Define which basic services / parts (including certain attributes) should be part of the final service / product
2. **Coordination step**: Coordinate and refine the parts (temporal, geographical or qualitative fitting)
3. **Resource instantiation step:** Check the availability of resources and assign resources to services
4. **Reservation step:** Resources are reserved to enable a consistent complex product
5. **Customer feedback step:** Ask customer for acceptance (or rejection)
6. **Booking step**: Book the accepted services, if desired
7. **Adaptation step:** Sometimes a booking change is desired

In order to define the basic services, the system requires some basic model, which describes the concept *holidays* or *travel*. Such a model describes required and optional parts. The customer may select from several alternative models. We assume the customer has made the first specification of his request, such as "family winter holiday over Christmas". In general, the exact period for the holidays is not fixed by hard constraints. Sometimes hotels are available only for a shorter duration or a flight ticket might be cheaper on a certain day. In these cases the system must be able

to propose solutions fitting the customer's general specification in the best possible way. Perhaps, the customer has filled out additionally a questionnaire about his profile (address, gender, etc.). This is not part of the planning process. Further, he may have specified explicit preferences (e.g. likes sports, likes theatre, etc.). Finally, a record of earlier bookings may suggest some implicit preferences (e.g. cheap holidays or high quality, etc.). A destination can be proposed from customer's preferences and hence, the transportation may be derived from the customer's home address and the proposed destination. Further, the system may propose special events in accordance with the customer's preferences (e.g. a golf tournament). Often, customers do not want to book such events so early. However, it may be that the customer will stay longer, if such an event takes place and he will be able to get a reservation.

After finding some basic services, those found services must be refined and coordinated with each other. The proposed destination must be reachable by means of proposed transportation and the proposed events must take place during the holiday period. Those events have to be reachable in a comfortable way. The coordinated proposal may be shown to the customer now without checking availability. If desired by the customer, the system could also make alternative proposals. If the customer selects one of the proposals, it could happen, that no reservations could be made which would lead to some frustration.

Therefore, it would be better to first check for availabilities. One possibility to check for availability is to ask individual resource providers. We propose Web services to make such queries. However, this may lead to large search trees and a long processing time. Alternatively, we could store availabilities in a central database. This would contradict the idea of openness of the virtual enterprise and moreover, there would be a problem of consistent modeling of real availability. A solution often applied is to give a certain contingent of available rooms to a booking portal.

In this case, however, the remaining resources cannot be used by the virtual enterprise.

A mechanism for improving the efficiency is a central data pool describing availabilities on an abstract level and a two step checking procedure. The system may determine that during a certain period in a certain region there will be no availability problem and the proposal will be shown to the customer immediately. If the customer has such requirements whose availability cannot be estimated easily, two sub-processes can be distinguished. The system can supply uncertain ranked offers in a short time. After customer's evaluation of these offers, the system may check the availability. The second way would be to check all availabilities first and to show only available solutions. This would also mean that the system checks solutions the customer is not interested in. This discussion shows that an intelligent reasoning dependent on season, customer preferences and other aspects must be designed for finding a user-friendly booking behavior.

If the user selects a booking solution, the system has to book several basic services. The customer's acceptance message can be interpreted as a contract with the virtual enterprise. When the virtual enterprise has booked the first resource, it is possible that the second resource has become unavailable. Since getting only one proposed service is not acceptable to the customer, the booking of the entire proposed package is defined as one transaction which either succeeds or fails. Therefore, the virtual enterprise will first reserve all resources and if this was successful, it will finally ask the customer for a definitive booking decision. This decision must be taken before a set deadline, derived from the deadlines of the single resource providers. If the customer accepts the final proposal, the booking will be processed.

We are developing a framework to support such dynamic planning tasks in virtual enterprises. We have used the actual version of the framework to implement a system to participate in the first competition on Web service discovery and composition (Blake et al., 2005). In the next section, we describe the basic applied technology and short overview on work in the planning community. In the third section we present in detail the planning approach based on answer set programming and results of our system for the given benchmarks of the contest. Finally we conclude and stress the advantages of our approach.

BASICS AND RELATED WORK

In recent research related to Web services, several initiatives provide means to support integration of heterogeneous systems by defining languages, methods, or platforms. A Web service is a collection of protocols and standards used for exchanging data between applications. Software applications written in various programming languages and running on various platforms can use Web services to exchange data over computer networks like the Internet in a manner similar to inter-process communication on a single computer.

The Web service description language WSDL (Booth and Liu, 2005) is a standard to describe Web services. It encompasses the definition of the messages and the message exchange protocol between a requester and provider agent as well as the definitions of operations and of bindings to a network protocol. The messages themselves are described abstractly and then bound to a concrete network protocol and message format. Web service definitions can be mapped to any implementation language, platform, object model, or messaging system. As long as both, sender and receiver, agree on the service description, (i.e. the WSDL document), the implementation behind the Web service can be any kind of software that is able to deliver the described service.

The definition of process languages such as BPEL (Andrews et al., 2003) or XPDL (WfMC, 2005) and the extension of Web service descriptions by OWL-S (Martin et al., 2004) aim towards static processes with a priori knowledge of all possible execution paths. In order to achieve dynamic processes to be composed during run-time, we need AI methods to compose services on-the-fly for an individual service requester.

Coping with Web services (or services in general) leads to the fundamental tasks of discovery, i.e., to find the appropriate services for a certain customer request, of composition, i.e., to bundle single or complex services to complex products, and of invocation and monitoring, i.e., to enact and supervise (complex) services. Additionally, with respect to composition, at least three other tasks are of interest:

- To specify goals for a composite
- To specify constraints that have to be respected
- To provide means that help to analyze and to compare possible solutions against each other

This work presents an approach that uses techniques from Answer Set Programming to solve some of the tasks required to build reliable and optimal compositions. In particular, we address the problem of finding and selecting an appropriate service, and the problem of limiting solution candidates to those that solve the goals and obey the restrictions imposed by the constraints. We demonstrate our work by using the challenges as well as the data format that has been specified for the Web Service Composition Contest (Blake et al., 2005).

The following WSDL document (taken from the composition contest) shows the data format and operation signature used for our work. It has a single operation with request/response protocol and simple data types - just a list of string properties.

```
<?xml version="1.0" encoding="utf-8"?>
<definitions name="interopLab" xmlns="...">
<message name="findCloseHotel_Request">
  <part name="custStreetAddress" type="xsd:
```

string"/>
  <part name="custCityAddress" type="xsd: string"/></message>
<message name="findCloseHotel_Response">
  <part name="hotelName" type="xsd:string"/>
  <part name="hotelStreetAddress" type="xsd: string"/></message>
<portType name="findCloseHotel"> <operation name="findCloseHotel">
    <input message="findCloseHotel_Request"/>
  </operation> </portType> </definitions>

Since XML is verbose we use the following simplified textual notation to describe a Web service:

```
(findCloseHotel //operation
  (custStreetAddress custCityAddress ...) //request
message
  (hotelName hotelStreetAddress ...)) //response
message
```

Web Service Composition as Planning Problem

Dynamically composing complex products (or services) is a research topic in the AI world since a long time. The first well-known system was STRIPS the Stanford Research Institute Planning System that planned actions for a mobile robot in the research lab (Fikes and Nilsson, 1971). Theoretical investigations into this program have identified some drawbacks of the planner. First, there could be planning problems where the solution of one subgoal would destroy another subgoal. This led to the definition of the non-linear planning strategy. Moreover, the original algorithm was not able to handle parallel actions. Partial order planning or POP for short is a planning strategy that solves both problems (Weld, 1994). Instead of searching for a linear plan, required sequences between actions are identified first. Nevertheless, the original problem formulation with action that have pre- and post-conditions is still applied in modern planning systems.

So, not surprisingly, a survey of composition approaches for Web services conducted by Rao et al. (2004) revealed that typically AI methods from the planning domain are applied to the problem.

In general, a planning problem can be described as a five-tuple (S, S_0, G, A, Γ), where S is the set of all possible states of the world, $S_0 \subset S$ denotes the initial state of the world, $G \subseteq S$ denotes the goal state of the world, A is the set of actions the planner can perform, and the transition relation $\Gamma \subseteq S \times A \times S$ defines the precondition and effect for the execution of each action.

In terms of Web services, S_0 and G are the initial states and the goal states that are specified in the requirements of a service request. In the notation of the composition contest the initial state corresponds to a provided element and the goal state corresponds to the resultant elements of an XML document.

```
<Challenge><CompositionRoutine
name="bookTrip">
<Provided>custStreetAddress,custCityAddress,
... </Provided>
<Resultant>itineraryURL,...</Resultant>
</CompositionRoutine> ...</Challenge>
```

Again, a simplified notation helps to overcome the problem of verbose XML:

```
((problem bookTrip
  (provided custStreetAddress custCityAddress
...)
  (resultant itineraryURL ...)) ...)
```

Answer Set Programming with DLV

Answer set programming (ASP) is a form of declarative programming oriented towards difficult combinatorial search problems. It has been applied, for instance, to plan generation and product configuration problems in AI and to graph-theoretic problems arising in VLSI design. The original definition of answer sets for disjunctive logic programs was given by Gelfond and Lifschitz (1988, 1991).

Syntactically, ASP programs look like Prolog programs, but the computational mechanisms used in ASP are different: they are based on the ideas that have led to the development of fast satisfiability solvers for propositional logic. A main difference between Prolog and ASP programs is that ASP programs are strictly declarative, while Prolog programs have a procedural aspect. In Prolog, the order of rules as well as the order of subgoals in a rule matters while in ASP this makes no difference.

Datalog with disjunction (DLV) is a powerful deductive database system (Leone et al., 2002). It is based on the declarative programming language Datalog, which is known for being a convenient tool for knowledge representation. With its disjunctive extensions, it is well suited for all kinds of non-monotonic reasoning, including diagnosis and planning. DLV was developed in cooperation between the University of Calabria and the Vienna University of Technology. More information about DLV is available at http://www.dbai.tuwien.ac.at/proj/dlv.

Datalog is a declarative (programming) language. This means that the programmer does not write a program that solves some problem but instead specifies what the solution should look like, and a Datalog inference engine (or Deductive Database System) tries to find the way to solve the problem and the solution itself. This is done with rules and facts. Facts are the input data, and rules can be used to derive more facts, and hopefully, the solution of the given problem. Disjunctive Datalog is an extension of Datalog in which the logical "or"-expression (the disjunction) is allowed to appear in the rules - this is not allowed in basic Datalog. A disjunctive Datalog program consists of an arbitrary number of facts, rules, and constraints. A rule takes the form:

head :- body

which can be read as "if the body is true, the head must also be true". The head can contain one or more disjunctive literals while the body can contain zero or more conjunctive literals. A fact is a special form of a rule in which the body is empty and thus is always true. The other special form of a rule, in which the head is empty, is called a constraint. The body of a constraint must not become true, because the head can never become true.

The Guess/Check/Optimize Methodology

The core language of DLV can be used to encode problems in a declarative fashion following a Guess/Check/Optimize (GCO) paradigm.

Given a set F_I of facts that specify an instance I of some problem **P**, a GCO program P for **P** consists of the following three main parts:

- **Guessing part:** The guessing part $G \subseteq P$ of the program defines the search space, such that answer sets of $G \cup F_I$ represent "solution candidates" for I.
- **Checking part:** The (optional) checking part $C \subseteq P$ of the program filters the solution candidates in such a way that the answer sets of $G \cup C \cup F_I$ represent the admissible solutions for the problem instance I.
- **Optimization part:** The (optional) optimization part $O \subseteq P$ of the program allows to express a quantitative cost evaluation of solutions by using weak constraints (Buccafurri et al., 2000). It implicitly defines an objective function $f: AS(G \cup C \cup F_I) \to \Re+$ mapping the answer sets of $G \cup C \cup F_I$ to (positive) real numbers. The semantics of G

$\cup C \cup F_I \cup O$ optimizes f by filtering those answer sets having the minimum value.

In general, both G and C may be arbitrary collections of rules, and it depends on the complexity of the problem at hand which kind of rules are needed to realize these parts. In the next section some examples will illustrate the GCO paradigm.

SOLUTION

A Web service repository contains a set A of services. Each service maps to a WSDL operation with input and output parameters that represent preconditions and effect of this service. From the composition request two artificial services are created, named *start* (the service that provides the initial data) and *end* (the service that requires the goal data). The repository and the two additional services are depicted in Figure . The repository contains the services *a0-a9*. The arrows denote disjunctive ordering constraints, for instance, service *a5* can be scheduled after service *a2 or a3*.

In order to reduce the search space simple filtering is applied. Only those services are selected for further processing which may play a role in a solution:

- **Forward reduction:** In the first step, breadth first forward search beginning at the *start* service is applied to reduce the set of services by such services that will in no case be invoked since their preconditions are never satisfied (cf. Figure 2).
- **Backward reduction:** In the second step, using the (possibly) reduced set from step one, breadth first backward search starting from the *end* service is applied in order to remove services whose effects are never used. (cf. Figure 3).

Figure 1. Services a0-a9 in a repository, extended with artificial services start, end

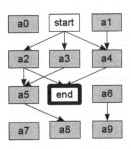

Figure 2. Services after forward reduction

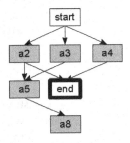

Figure 3. Services after backward reduction

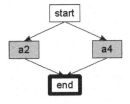

Mapping Domain Model to DLV

The algorithm for mapping the services to the input of DLV:

For each service a from the set of services A (the repository) select the set P of services from A that have as an effect one of the preconditions s required by a. For each of the services in P one disjunctive entry in the body of the rule will be created. In other words, each service is represented as a formula in conjunctive normal form (CNF).

$$((a_0 \vee a_1 \vee...\vee a_j)_1 \wedge (a_0 \vee a_1 \vee.. \vee a_j)_2 \wedge ... \wedge ((a_0 \vee a_1 \vee...\vee a_j))_i)$$

with j being the services that are providers for the precondition i.

So for example, the requesting services in Figure 4 have the formulæ:

1. *(a0 ∧ a0)*
2. *((a0 ∨ a1) ∧ (a2 ∨ a3))*
3. *((a0 ∨ a1) ∧ (a1))*

Reduction for formulæ is as usual:

$(x \wedge x) \to x$ and $(X \wedge Y) \to X$ if $X \subseteq Y$.

In the example, the first formula becomes *(a0)*, the second remains unchanged, and the last is reduced to *(a1)*.

These formulæ are the input for the DLV solver. Each conjunction maps to one rule with the service name as body of the rule and the disjunctive part of the formula as the head of the rule. For instance, Figure 4 *(2)* yields two rules:

a0 v a1 :-a4.
a2 v a3 :-a4.

If the fact *a4* is present in the database, DLV computes four models, each being a solution (a plan) for the given problem:

{a4, a1, a3}
{a4, a0, a3}
{a4, a1, a2}
{a4, a0, a2}

Constraints

Constraints are means to reduce the result set either to answers that do not violate a (hard) constraint, or to limit the answer set to the cheapest answers. A constraint takes the form of a rule having no head. If the body becomes *true* the constraint is applied. The following example shows the layered structure of a program that follows the GCO para-

Figure 4. Reduction of preconditions

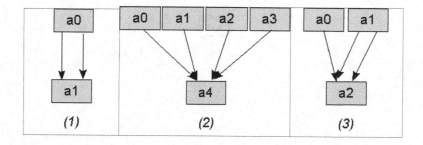

digm. The guessing part consists of disjunctive rules that guess a solution candidate, the checking part consists of integrity constraints that check the admissibility of the candidate, and the optimization part consists of weak constraints.

```
a4. %fact
% disjunctive rules -> guess
a0 v a1 :-a4.
a2 v a3 :-a4.
% hard constraint -> check
:-a2,a0.
% weak constraints -> optimize
:~a0.[1:1] :~a1.[1.3:1] :~a2.[1:1] :~a3.[1:1]
```

This example shows weak constraints denoting the costs to invoke a service. Service *a1* has cost *1.3* while all other services have cost 1 associated. The second part of the cost array is used for the level the cost belongs to. The last line is a hard constraint that does not allow answers that have service *a0* as well as service *a2* in the result set. DLV comes up with a single answer in the result:

```
Best model: {a4, a0, a3}
Cost ([Weight:Level]): <[2:1]>
```

Plan Construction for DLV Input

The input for DLV is constructed by transforming the CNF representation for each service to rule(s).

The literals in the head are the links from the providing service to the requesting service. Theses links express the ordering constraints between services. The body for each rule is the requesting service. The (artificial) *end* service denoting the goal is added as initial fact. This forms a graph with nodes *n(service)* representing services and links *l(from-service, to-service)* representing causal relationships. Searching is done backwards beginning at the goal, i.e. the *end* service.

Ordering constraints: Services can have cyclic dependencies between preconditions and effects, i.e. one service, e.g. service *a1* may have as a predecessor service *a0*, which in turn has *a1* as its predecessor. To avoid such answers (which are valid models but not valid plans) a constraint is applied that computes the path between nodes and becomes true if a node has been already visited.

A sample program: Input: a problem *p1* and services *s0-s5* with preconditions and effects.

```
((problem p1(provided s)(resultant u v w)))
((s0(s)(a))
(s1(s)(b))
(s2(s)(c))
(s3(a)(u b))
(s4(b)(a c v))
(s5(c)(b w)))
```

Figure 5. Example problem with cyclic dependencies

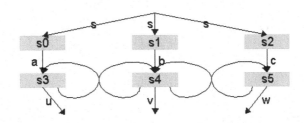

A graphical representation of services and their dependencies is shown in Figure 5.

Transformation of this problem and services to the input format of DLV yields the following GCO program:

```
%the goal
n(end).
%service dependencies
l(s5,end) :- n(end).
l(s4,end) :- n(end).
l(s3,end) :- n(end).
l(s0,s3) v l(s4,s3) :- n(s3).
l(s5,s4) v l(s1,s4) v l(s3,s4) :- n(s4).
l(s2,s5) v l(s4,s5) :- n(s5).
%add node
n(X):-l(X,_).
%compute path
r(X,Y) :-l(X,Y).
r(X,Z) :-r(X,Y),l(Y,Z).
%check admissibility
:-r(X,Y),X==Y.
%cost
:~ n(s0).[1:1] :~ n(s1).[1:1] :~ n(s2).[1:1]
:~ n(s3).[1:1] :~ n(s4).[1:1] :~ n(s5).[1:1]
```

Description of the program:

- The first part is the representation of services and their dependencies, with one fact *n(end)*, i.e., the goal.

- The second part n(X):-l(X,_)adds a node for a selected link to the database (X is a variable and _ is an anonymous variable).

- The third part computes the path for any two nodes.

- The fourth part is a hard constraint. This constraint prohibits answers that contain a path from a node to itself from being included in the result set.

- The final part are the cost constraints, each service costs 1 unit.

The following code shows a single answer from the result set of the domain and problem above. It contains the selected services (as nodes n(service)), the ordering constraints (as links l(from,to)), and the cost for of the selected services.

```
{l(s5,end), l(s4,end), l(s3,end), n(s5), n(end),
n(s4),
n(s3), l(s0,s3), l(s3,s4), l(s4,s5), n(s0)}
Cost ([Weight:Level]): <[4:1]>
... other answers (the problem has 8 answers,
3 are optimal in terms of costs)
```

From the eight solutions generated for the problem above two plans are shown in the following table: the cheapest answer (left) is constructed from four services, ordered sequentially and concurrently (requires 3 time steps). The

Table 1. Two solutions

Cheapest Plan		Fastest Plan	
(1)		(1)	s2
s1		(1)	s0
(2)		(1)	s1
s4		(2)	s5
(3)		(2)	s4
s5		(2)	s3
(3)			
s3			

Figure 6. Visualized cheapest plan

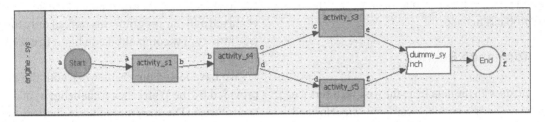

most expensive answer (right) with eight services ordered in three parallel sequences (requires two time steps).

The following figure shows the resulting XPDL process for the first plan. The XPDL source code is given in the appendix of the paper.

Problem Relaxation

Composition as described above results in totally ordered plans, i.e., every step is ordered with respect to every other step, and partially ordered plans, i.e., steps can be unordered with respect to each other.

Search space can become very large when many alternative services are available. So, for instance, when two services, (s1(a)(b c)) and (s2(b)(a d)), and data a b are available and c d is a (sub)goal, then the answer will contain three compositions having the same costs:

s1 → s2, s2 → s1 and s1 && s2.

The symbols → and && denote sequence and concurrency, respectively.

The problem can be relaxed when search is done beginning at the start node, again using the GCO paradigm. The idea is that in the "guessing" part a service whose preconditions are satisfied is either selected (service is true) or not selected (service is false). When it is selected, the effects of the service are added to the facts which in turn may guess other services. The constraint is that an

answer must contain the *end* node, i.e., the goal. Optimization is as usual with soft constraints.

```
%data available
a. b.
% Guess - either service is true or false
n(s2) v ~n(s2) :-b.
n(s1) v ~n(s1) :-a.
n(goal):-c,d.
% Check constraint - prunes illegal branches
:-not n(end).
% rules for adding effects of services
a :- n(s2). d :- n(s2).
b :- n(s1). c :- n(s1).
% Soft constraints, i.e. costs
:~n(s2).[1:1] :~n(s1).[1:1]
```

Running this program with DLV results in the single solution:

{a, b, n(s2), n(s1), d, c, n(end)}.

This solution has no ordering constraints, it contains just the selected services, the services that are not selected (none for this example) and the data elements added by selected services.

To gain an ordered solution we combine the two approaches: In a first step, guess and check is employed to find the cheapest solution candidates quickly. In the second step, starting backwards with the goal yields ordered plans from the un-ordered solution candidates as described above. Considering only services that are members of a solution found in the first step may reduce the search space extremely, but this may depend on the problem instance.

Performance Results

First tests with the data from the first Web service discovery and composition competition performed very well since the supplied data sets were rather small. Data sets for the second competition were larger and consequently in the temporal comparison to other programs drawbacks of our approach occurred and our program was ranked only third (see http://www.comp.hkbu.edu.hk/~ctr/wschallenge/).

We have tested our framework with the data provided by the Web service challenge syntactic repositories. The structure of these challenges is as follows: each repository contains several thousand WSDL files, each file has a single operation

Table 2. Results for the benchmarks

Instance	WSDL docs	Challenges	Parse time (sec)	Composition time (sec)
composition1-20-4	2156	11	13.98	1.59
composition1-20-16	2156	11	15.93	1.73
composition1-20-32	2156	11	24.84	2.02
composition1-50-4	2656	11	24.86	1.86
composition1-50-16	2656	11	27.36	1.98
composition1-50-32	2656	11	29.40	2.12
composition1-100-4	4156	11	44.40	2.31
composition1-100-16	4156	11	40.00	2.65
composition1-100-32	4156	11	52.10	2.76
composition2-20-4	3356	11	33.00	134.20
composition2-20-16	6712	11	91.30	136.30
composition2-20-32	3356	11	38.70	135.60
composition2-50-4	5356	11	61.81	135.70
composition2-50-16	5356	11	66.03	138.90
composition2-50-32	5356	11	71.25	136.60
composition2-100-4	8356	11	125.45	138.70
composition2-100-16	8356	11	130.00	138.00
composition2-100-32	8356	11	102.00	139.00

(i.e., the service) and a single portType element. A repository is associated with a single challenge file that has around ten challenges that refer to data elements from the WSDL descriptions. Each challenge can be solved with a fixed number of services in various defined combinations. For instance, a challenge named composition2-20-16-5 has as solution a sequence of seven services and each of the steps in the sequence can be performed by one of four services, resulting in $47 = 16384$ possible solutions (since all services are distinctive). In order to reflect the fact that parsing WSDL documents is a substantial part of the overall composition time we have split the total composition time for a set of challenges in two parts; one part for parsing the documents and constructing a memory representation and the other part that represents the time for composition of services.

The results show that parsing the WSDL files and construction of a repository in memory takes a lot of time for several thousand WSDL files. This is due to the fact that processing XML documents requires generally a lot of resources and also has to do with the Java implementation which is slower compared, for instance, with an C++ implementation.

The tests were performed on a PC with an Intel Pentium 2 GHz processor with 1 Gigabyte Memory and Windows 2000 operating system.

The measurements show clearly that our program has problems with large Web service repositories where the compositions have many solutions. One reason is the time and space required to parse these with standard Java libraries. Another reason is of course our attempt to produce all solutions.

We believe, however, that it is not realistic that there exist so many possible solutions that are also even good.

Implementation Details

We have implemented the composition within the MOVE framework. MOVE is a framework for designing and execution of processes in virtual enterprises. The framework is based on Java, open-source components and the Eclipse development environment. The main focus of the MOVE framework is laid on Web service integration. Processes are modeled graphically and transformed into XPDL. Such XPDL processes are executed with a workflow engine whereas each activity in an XPDL process may represent a Web service call. Moreover, there are specialized Web services called infrastructure Web services. Infrastructure Web services provide frequently used services in a Web service integration framework. Such common infrastructure Web services include for example the transformation of XML documents

Figure 7. Architecture

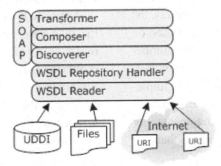

and the discovery of Web services at process run-time. The composition of Web services from discovered Web services also represents an infrastructure Web service and was implemented in this manner.

The composition Web service consists of several components shown in Figure 7. These components have fixed interfaces and can be substituted at run-time in a flexible way when required. Thus, Web services can be discovered at different sources, different solvers can create different compositions, and different transformers can transform results to different data formats.

The WSDL reader component processes WSDL documents and converts them into a Java data structure. Depending on the WSDL reader's implementation, any source of WSDL document is possible: Files on a local file system, documents on remote servers, documents in an XML database or in some registry, and so on. How WSDL information is transformed to a Java data structure is arbitrary, too. Our implemented WSDL reader uses WSDL4J to transfer WSDL information to a Java data structure and is able to process WSDL documents residing in the local file system or in the Internet via http protocol. WSDL4J is a library that complies with the JWSDL standard. JWSDL provides a standard for Java APIs that can be used for representing, manipulating, reading and writing WSDL. Future implementations of the WSDL reader may consider registry sources for WSDL documents like UDDI and may use specialized SAX parsers instead of the extensive WSDL4J library for performance reasons.

To provide unified, comfortable and flexible access to a set of Java WSDL data structures, the WSDL repository component is used. Based on certain environment variables like the number or sources of WSDL documents, different performance enhancement strategies may be implemented. Our implementation provides solutions for different numbers of WSDL documents. For a small number, the WSDL repository handler loads all WSDL documents at program start a priori. For a large number of WSDL documents that is likely to change, another implementation lazy-loads WSDL documents just before they are needed. Also caching strategies may be considered in future implementations. When WSDL sources are prone to provide slow and unreliable access like it is the case with WSDL documents in the Internet, caching will provide a significant performance and reliability improvement.

The discoverer component provides searching capabilities for discovering Web services that fulfill certain requirements. Such requirements could be based on the currently available set of input data and the expected output data. Web services whose needed input data does not exceed the available input data set and whose output satisfies the expected output data could be searched and discovered. In addition, semantic Web service concepts could be implemented here to enable semantic search and discovery of suitable Web services.

The composer component is responsible for building complex services. Apart from applying the DLV solver other planning and optimization software may be used.

The transformer component can be used to manifest service compositions into different representations. Translating service composites to an executable software like a Java algorithm or a Web service orchestration such as XPDL or BPEL(4WS) are options as well as creating DLV input files from WSDL documents. Furthermore, visual representations of the composition using e.g. SVG may be worthwhile manifestations.

Not only the Composer component, but also the discoverer and transformer may represent reasonable infrastructure services. Thus, as shown in Figure 7, these components publish their functionality via SOAP interfaces also and can be used in the MOVE framework as infrastructure services to discover services or to transform compositions.

SUMMARY AND OUTLOOK

We have presented briefly a general framework for developing virtual enterprises and in detail an approach to construct business processes from basic Web services using AI-techniques. Service descriptions given in WSDL are mapped into a rule-based language that allows to search a repository efficiently and to build solutions that solve a goal with respect to soft and hard constraints. In contrast to other solutions, we generate all possible solutions for a given problem.

In our contribution to the Web service composition contest (Dorn et al., 2004) we have shown the usefulness of our approach. The strength of our approach is that it provides all solutions for a given problem despite the costs in computation time and space. Our tool has performed best in finding solutions for a given set of problems in the first competition. The tool was also used to analyze the randomly generated data for the second composition contest in Beijing in October 2005. Finding all possible solutions helps to control the complexity of the challenges. Additionally, having all solutions computed ensures that solution claims from competitors can be verified. In the second contest, our program was ranked only third. One reason for this is that the required time for finding a solution was the selective criteria. Since our tool is implemented in Java and uses Java libraries for standard functions the speed is restricted in contrast to other programming languages.

Nevertheless, our solution exhibits some strong benefits that shall be stressed here. Due to the nonlinear planning strategy our solution detects also which Web services may be executed in parallel. This would result in a shorter execution of the whole set of Web services. Moreover, we support a soft evaluation of solutions. This means we can attribute costs to single Web services, aggregate them for a solution and rank the found solutions by means of a cost function. Finally, our solution is part of larger framework. The found solution can be mapped into a process language

such as XPDL and executed in the framework. Generic solutions could also be deployed as a new Web service. In this case no planning has to be performed again.

In related work, other methods from the planning domain are applied. For instance, Peer (2004) maps WSDL documents to PDDL (McDermott 2000) a language defined for planning competitions. A planner may then process the resulting PDDL statements. This is similar to our approach. However, a number of researchers see plain WSDL as too limited to express preconditions and effects of services and they propose a richer syntax and semantic for service descriptions. As an example, Sirin and Parsia (2004) propose to annotate Web services with semantic information expressed in OWL-S. They show how a reasoner for description logics (DL) in combination with a planner can be applied to compose services. However, they claim that using DL may cause performance problems.

The current solution is performing very well in a rather simple domain. We see a number of possible extensions for our framework to cope with "real world" requirements. First of all, the message format is very simple and may be enriched with complex data types or ontological information, for instance, OWL (Bechhofer et al., 2004) expressions. We think that a logic reasoner like DLV fits very well the needs imposed by Description Logics. Second, services in a repository may have a control flow already defined and the challenge is to generate solutions that combine different processes. Again, we think that such requirements can be solved efficiently within our framework, but this needs more clarification. Third, using a simple cost function such as plainly adding service costs may be not suitable to distinguish solution candidates and may be replaced by a complex utility function that represents better the requirements of a single service request. Finally, the contest assumption that all Web services are already known is not a realistic point of view.

ACKNOWLEDGMENT

This reported work is performed in the MOVE project supported by ec3, the E-Commerce Competence Center in Vienna, its industrial partners as well as the Austrian Government. The authors would like to thank also the organizers of the Web service contests M.B. Blake, W.K. Cheung, K.C. Tsui, and A. Wombacher for providing services and problem instances as input data. This helped to verify the correctness of the results of the composition tool as well as insight in requirements for our framework.

REFERENCES

Andrews, T., et al. (2003) Business Process Execution Language for Web Services. 2nd public draft release, Version 1.1

Bechhofer, S., et al. (2004) OWL Web Ontology Language Reference.http://www.w3.org/TR/owl-ref/.

Blake, M.B., Tsui, K.C., & Wombacher, A. . (2005) The eee-05 challenge: A new Web service discovery and composition competition. In *Proceedings of the 2005 IEEE International Conference on e-Technology, e-Commerce and e-Service (EEE'05)*, Washington, DC (pp. 780-781). IEEE Computer Society.

Booth, D., & Liu, C.K. (2005) *Web Services Description Language (WSDL)*. Version 2.0. http://www.w3.org/2002/ws/desc/

Buccafurri, F., Leone, N., & Rullo, P. (2000) Enhancing disjunctive datalog by constraints. *Knowledge and Data Engineering 12*, 845-860

Dorn, J., Hrastnik, P., & Rainer, A. (2005) Web service discovery and composition with move. In *Proceedings of the 2005 IEEE International Conference on e-Technology, e-Commerce and e-Service (EEE'05)*, Washington, DC (pp. 791-792). IEEE Computer Society.

Gelfond, M., & Lifschitz, V. (1988) The stable model semantics for logic programming. In R. A. Kowalski & K. Bowen (Eds:), *Proceedings of the Fifth International Conference on Logic Programming* (pp. 1070-1808). Cambridge, MA: The MIT Press.

Fikes, R. E., & Nilsson, N. (1971).STRIPS: A new approach to the application of theorem proving to problem solving. *Artificial Intelligence, 5*(2), 189-208.

Gelfond, M., Lifschitz, V. (1991). Classical negation in logic programs and disjunctive databases. *New Generation Computing, 9*, 365-386

Hrastnik, P. (2004) Execution of business processes based on Web services. *Int. J. Electronic Business, 2*(3).

Leone, N., Pfeifer, G., Faber, W., Calimeri, F., Dell'Armi, T., Eiter, T., Gottlob, G., Ianni, G., Ielpa, G., Koch, C., Perri, S., & Polleres, A. (2002) The dlv system. In *JELIA '02 Proceedings of the European Conference on Logics in Artificial Intelligence*, London (pp. 537-540). Springer-Verlag.

Martin, D., et al. (2004) *OWL-S: Semantic Markup for Web Services*. http://www.daml.org/services/owl-s/1.1.

McDermott, D. (2000) The 1998 AI Planning Systems Competition. *AI Magazine, 2*(2), 35-55

Peer, J. (2004) A pddl based tool for automatic Web service composition. In H.J. Ohlbach & S. Schaffert (Eds.), *PPSWR. Volume 3208 of Lecture Notes in Computer Science* (pp. 149-163). Springer.

Rainer, A. (2004). Web-centric business process modelling. *Int. J. Electronic Business, 2*(3).

Rao, J., & Su, X. (2004) A survey of automated Web service composition methods. In J. Cardoso & A.P. Sheth (Eds.), *SWSWPC. Volume 3387 of Lecture Notes in Computer Science* (pp. 43-54). Springer.

Sirin, E., & Parsia, B. (2004). *Planning for Semantic Web services.* In Semantic Web Services Workshop at 3rd International Semantic Web Conference (ISWC2004).

W3C. (2003) *Simple Object Access Protocol (SOAP) 1.2.* http://www.w3c.org/TR/2003

Weld, D.S. (1994). An introduction to least-commitment planning. *AI Magazine, 15*(4), 27-61.

WfMC (2005). *XML Process Definition Language (XPDL) 1.09.* http://www.wfmc.org

This work was previously published in the International Journal of Web Services Research, Vol. 4, No. 1, edited by L. J. Zhang, pp. 23-39, copyright 2007 by IGI Publishing, formerly known as Idea Group Publishing (an imprint of IGI Global).

Chapter XII
Achieving Agile Enterprise Through Integrated Process Management:
From Planning to Work Execution

Ali Bahrami
Boeing Phantom Works, USA

ABSTRACT

Project management tools are used to manage projects from time as well as from resource leveling perspectives. Workflow management systems guide users through processes by driving the processes based on formal process definitions also called workflow types. This paper describes integrated process management system that will integrate project management, business process modeling, simulation and workflow technologies in order to support scheduled workflow execution. The target will be achieved by utilizing a tool for modeling work processes which can semi automatically generate workflow processes based on scheduling tool and then exported it to workflow engine via web services using XML process definition language (XPDL). Addition of simulation capability allows testing workflows before deployment.

INTRODUCTION

Coordinating a large program such as new airplane design is a big challenge, and improving coordination would save time and money. Coordination relies on frequent meetings and discussions to understand the current and planned activities of all the programs' participants. We need to make faster, more informed decisions—communicating and collaborating immediately and effectively no matter where employees are located. We need to better understand and serve our customers globally and seamlessly interact with suppliers and distributors to take advantage of market opportunities faster than our competitors. We need to be more efficient than ever. In short, we need business agility to succeed.

Scheduling and project management tools provide support for determining task sequencing, dependencies, and resource loading, and once the schedule is established, its status is updated and reviewed in meetings. The work within each scheduled task is coordinated by people communicating with one another: Managers talking to IPT leads, and the leads talking to their team members. There is little automated support to ensure that work is done in accordance with a specified process. Process owners lack the tools required to describe their processes at the level of detail required for workflow automation, and there is no integration of workflow management tools with scheduling and project management tools.

An integrated process management environment supports coordination of program tasks, reducing the time required to perform these tasks and the costs of coordinating them. Process owners or their designees construct executable models that define the task elements, the roles responsible for each task element, and the rules that determine task element sequencing. Tasks are initiated automatically in accordance with the program schedule by alerting the individuals responsible for performing the work. As each person completes a task element, the work is automatically routed in accordance with the established process to the next person, who may be selected from an available pool of people based on resource loadings. The status of all current tasks is visible and updated automatically as task elements are completed.

This vision can be achieved through integration of project management, workflow management, simulation and business process modeling technologies. The workflow template designer provides a low-cost method for business process owners to create and view their processes and for workflow modeling experts to generate the details required by the workflow engine. Its development requires leveraging workflow standards to enable information exchange between dissimilar workflow engines (such as PTC Windchill and Enovia workflow engines) and process modeling tools. To enable distributed workflows that accomplish downstream deployment of work packages, the template designer will support standards such as the Workflow Management Coalition (WfMC) XML process definition language (XPDL).

The interface between scheduling and workflow management systems will support rollup of workflow data to support workflow plans, schedules, status, and critical chain analysis. We have developed an interface between Primavera P3e (project management) and PTC Windchill (workflow engine) utilizing web services as a means of integration.

ENTERPRISE REPOSITORY OF BUSINESS PROCESSES

Within an enterprise, business process knowledge is an asset of critical importance. The primary objective in building the proposed system is to develop integrated process management that can capture process knowledge in a repository of business processes, thereby allowing for coordination of program tasks, reducing the time required to perform these tasks and the costs of coordinating them.

Creating and managing this knowledge motivates the organization to address challenges in designing and implementing an information system, including:

- Suitability for many levels and types of access
- Adaptability for strategic, long-term use
- Customizability to support innovation
- Use of legacy information
- Acceptance and compliance by process constituents

Significant benefits can be realized by using the proposed system via a corporate repository. The repository of executable models that can be used across organization to assist in standardization of processes. For example, a model that has been constructed for a specific department can be reused when designing new one. A history of modeling process metrics, results of experiments, etc. can be maintained for analysts, users, and managers. With a corporate history of process improvement, knowledge gained through modeling and simulation can contribute to managing future change.

MULTIPLE USERS, VARYING NEEDS

Any business, production, service, or other kind of process has a wide array of interested parties, each with different perspectives and needs. In most organizations, many "models"—whether process, data, or descriptive—are used to capture knowledge about the process. Maintaining all of this information and coordinating the dissemination of changes can be costly.

An integrated organization requires a common repository for process knowledge that can be presented and modified using different methodologies and standards. Process designers need mechanisms for laying out relationships among activities, composing models from subsystem components, and capturing and communicating business rules. Business users require analysis tools for comparing process alternatives, measuring and predicting process costs and performance, and reviewing models for consistency with business objectives. Process performers need a clear, concise tool for understanding their role and its relationship to other activities. Others in the organization may provide process metrics and other data, review process designs, or obtain workflow descriptions.

STRATEGIC, LONG-TERM USE

An enterprise process modeling tool must maintain long-term use as the company and its needs change. However, at any point in time, an organization cannot anticipate all possible new requirements or the business environment of the future.

To position the process knowledge system for longevity, the core data repository must allow for growth and change in standards to be employed based on its contents. Rather than planning to build new monolithic applications more rapidly as replacements for outdated systems [1], an open architecture approach that supports widely accessible "best-of-breed" tools that can easily adapt to emerging standards.

RESPONSIBLE INNOVATION

Progressive organizations recognize that supporting responsible innovation fosters an environment of continuous process improvement. Process modeling and simulation can help innovators to measure and understand the value of their ideas to the organization.

The methods and tools used to capture process knowledge need to be customizable so that new models, data, and reports can be created "in the field." These models can encourage innovation and support responsible experimentation to drive process improvements without the risk of trying new ideas on the system itself.

EXPLOITING CURRENT INFORMATION

Except in unusual circumstances, a company deploys process knowledge systems in an environment where there are already existing databases, models, drawings, and other information systems. This legacy information can be valuable, particularly in supplying process metrics and ad hoc business rules.

USABILITY AND ACCEPTANCE

The best-designed and architected information system is of little use if it's not used properly and maintained with great integrity. To invite process constituents to use the knowledge system, use of familiar tools (i.e., commercial, off-the-shelf applications) and interfaces that are personalized for various users can ease the change to the new approach.

PROCESS MANAGEMENT

Enterprise-wide process management implementations are similar to a large program from the standpoint of size, scalability, and performance issues. Enterprise-wide processes are those that cross programs and/or business units. Examples may include processes associated with employee benefits or payroll, travel expense processing, general purchasing, and similar corporate wide processes.

Typically, these processes are controlled at a corporate level—with modifications based on special classes of activities. For example, a health insurance benefits process may actually be several different processes based on a person's status—union represented, salaried, hourly, etc. In each case the process is likely "owned" or controlled by a corporate group. In a large enterprise these types of implementations require workflow systems that are scalable, have high performance, and are available in a widely distributed environment. In addition, loads on the system may be very variable depending on a wide variety of circumstances. Some level of surge capability is needed so that performance

is relatively consistent across a broad range of user access loads.

The user interface must be user friendly and deployable without needing large new support or training infrastructures. The system must be highly reliable, as business critical processes will be executed.

BUSINESS PROCESS MODELING

A business process is a set of one or more linked procedures or activities that collectively realize a business objective or policy goal, normally within the context of an organizational structure defining functional roles and relationships [2, 3].

Modeling allows the user to visualize processes. This increases the understanding of relationships and effects among activities and, as a common communications tool for a wide array of individuals, makes the task of validating a process easier [4].

Because modeling can take place on many levels and models can serve many needs, a flexible, tailorable, widely accessible and more importantly based on industry standards is required.

SIMULATION AND ANALYSIS

While modeling allows the user to visualize processes, simulation brings them to life. Dynamic simulation allows users to analyze what-if scenarios, obtain cost and performance predictions, and validate processes more easily. The animation of a process enhances the buy-in of process performers, business managers, and others [5]. Simulation also provides a rigor to modeling that can be useful in optimizing business processes. It enables making better decisions, such as how to allocate work to resources, whether to consolidate processes, what shift schedules to operate, and which business rules to employ.

As with the models themselves, it is critical that the information supplied by the system for supporting business decisions be appropriate for each of the user needs.

The proposed system provides a mechanism and environment for collecting process metrics; recording problems such as bottlenecks, inaccurate information, etc.; and providing solutions for each step of the process. In the pilot project, we allowed employees to access their processes and provide the system with metrics. The Integrated process management enables a collection of reference information to support key decisions. This is done by establishing a query and search function on existing processes and by generating various forms of reports that are accessible throughout the organization.

System enables a reusable and repeatable way to capture processes. Furthermore, it offers a reusable and repeatable means for modeling, simulation, and performance measurement.

WORKFLOW TEMPLATE DESIGNER

Modeling, simulation and management system (MS)2 developed at the Boeing phantom works by author allows the designer of business processes to define a static view of these processes using the extended unified modeling language (UML) activity diagram [6].

The (MS)2 is written in Java and integrates a number of commercial off-the-shelf software tools (COTS) in a single comprehensive tool by utilizing the open architecture of all of the components involved. The heart of the tool is a sharable repository (any ODBC/OLE DB database such as Microsoft jet engine™, SQL Server™, or other suitable information repository) for storing process models and various process information, such as class diagrams, activity diagrams, use case diagrams as well as their associated data and modeling objects and attributes. Furthermore, the modeling systems allows for reusability and

creation of common process libraries via "Process Component." The repository makes it possible to perform search and query on the processes. For data entry and reporting, the system can interface with Microsoft productivity tools such as Excel™.

The web publishing capability of the tool provides an easy way of publishing and viewing the process information on the web. Furthermore the tool is capable of exporting the content of the repository into an XML document. For simulating the activity diagrams, (MS)2 uses the Arena Business Edition (ABE)™ from Rockwell Software. The simulation capability of the tool allows users to perform a dynamic simulation of the business processes in order to collect process performance statistics, to validate the processes and to analyze "what-if" scenarios.

Modeling in (MS)2 is also done by using the Visio™ engine for creating and editing graphical models. These models are a collection of customized (MS)2 modeling objects. Users can define static view of processes using the extended UML activity diagram, and if the user chose to simulate the processes all is required is to provide the necessary information (e.g., resources, duration, or distribution probability, etc.) on the same model for a dynamic simulation study of the processes. The (MS)2 representation language is based on the three UML diagrams:

- UML class diagram for modeling objects defined within processes as well as data modeling
- UML use-case diagram for expressing how actors (e.g. people, departments) and systems interact to accomplish a portion of the business (or system)
- UML activity diagram for modeling workflows, business process definitions, simulation, and workflow execution

Using these basic concepts further modeling is possible to meet specialized needs. Thus, the modeling is supported on different levels by the same integrated modeling tool which allows capturing cross-organizational processes with zooming functionality into each single activity and its attributes and objects.

Research is being done to make extending (MS)2 easier by allowing users to perform meta-modeling or extending the tool modeling objects. We believe this will be a very powerful capability which enables the tool to be very adaptable for various organizational environments and modeling activities.

Workflow template designer uses (MS)2 to define activities and associate these activities with attributes and objects. Because (MS)2 is based on UML, the models it creates provide support for software development and system design. The web functionality of (MS)2 supports cooperative modeling across organizational boundaries.

The process designer may simulate a process by providing dynamic data such as resources, duration, and distribution probability. This dynamic information is added to the static process model and used by the Arena simulation engine to simulate the process. (MS)2 uses UML diagrams and a representation language based on use cases, sctivities, and class diagrams as illustrated in Figure 1 and listed below:

- UML class diagrams model objects defined within processes as well as data modeling
- UML use-case diagrams express how actors (e.g. people, departments, or applications) and systems interact to accomplish a portion of the business (or system)
- UML activity diagrams model workflows and business process definitions for simulations and workflow execution

A process designer can represent processes at varied levels of detail ranging from step-by-step tasks performed by a single user to highest-level business processes that span enterprises. Because the process models are hierarchical, the designer can shift between these different perspectives while maintaining overall consistency. The appropriate level of detail in the activity diagrams depends on the intended use of the model. The finest (lowest) level of detail describes the activities of people who actually perform the individual tasks, e.g., machinists, fabricators etc. The coarsest (highest) level of detail may be more appropriate for higher level of management.

(MS)2 is a work modeling tool, but not a workflow management system. Windchill and other workflow management systems include their own tools for modeling work processes graphically, but these modeling tools lack the analysis, simulation,

Figure 1. UML based business process modeling tool supports industry standards

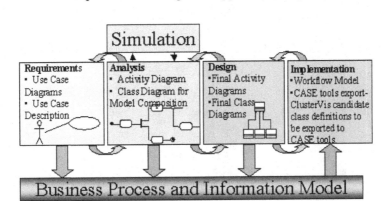

and more importantly cross tools interoperability especially for model exchange.

PROJECT MANAGEMENT

Numerous models exist for managing projects, but each includes a similar set of basic phases: project definition, project planning, performance tracking and project closure.

During project definition one establishes the framework for the project, including the following:

- Project scope, describing the work to be done, defining objectives and clarifying them against other organizational priorities
- Resources, identifying the people, equipment and materials you will need
- Project limits, describing project assumptions, determining constraints such as cost or schedule, and clarifying risk

An effective plan provides the direction for a project, maintaining information about scope, resources and schedule in one place. Developing a project plan involves the following steps:

- Work breakdown, identifying project tasks and determining the skills required to accomplish each one
- Time estimates, determining the time involved, or duration of each task
- Task dependencies, establishing how tasks relate to each other and the order in which they must be completed
- Task constraints, identifying specific task issues, such as schedule constraints or lack of certain people or skills

Tracking mechanisms help you evaluate your project's progress by analyzing performance against specific criteria. By regularly reviewing results, you can better direct and refine the project. Tracking performance involves the following:

- **Comparing actual progress against planned estimates:** Comparing where you are with where you planned to be can pinpoint areas that may put your project at risk, such as slower-than-expected progress.
- **Identifying issues:** Identifying issues as they arise helps ensure that you are aware of potential problems that may affect the project scope, resources or schedule.

Figure 2. (MS)2 user Interface easily provides access to the breadth of the functionalities

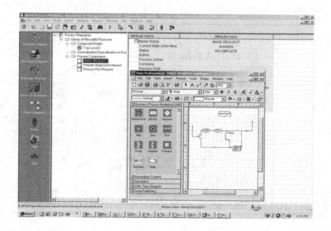

- **Reviewing resource and schedule requirements:** Overloading one or more members of the project team is one of the most common causes for schedule delays.

WORKFLOW MANAGEMENT

Workflow is the automation of a business process, in whole or part, during which documents, information, or tasks are passed from one participant to another or among business partners for action, according to a set of procedural rules. Workflows also represent the order in which individual activity steps are to be executed, the conditions for the activation of an activity, the tools for the execution of an activity, the people resources and other applications that may be needed for the activity execution, among other things [7].

A workflow management system (WfMSs) defines, creates, and manages the execution of workflows through the use of software, running on one or more workflow engines, which is able to interpret the process definition, interact with workflow participants and, where required, invoke the use of information technology tools and applications. Workflow management systems (WfMSs), in general, are used to coordinate and streamline workflows and hence business processes [8]. WfMS include tools for workflow definition and design, workflow instantiation and control, external applications integration to execute individual activities and workflow administration and monitoring. WfMSs assign individual activities using mechanisms such as worklists for execution of activities that include user interaction—the user need not necessarily be aware of the higher level workflow to which the activity belongs. Addition of simulation capability allows testing workflows before deployment.

A commonly used analogy that positions WfMSs in the computing domain is as follows. While databases guarantee the safe storage and easy access to massive amounts of data, workflow management systems are intended as the basic support for the business/process flows in those same environments where databases are used. The successful incorporation of WfMSs into a business workplace greatly depends on the ability to make workflows a technology as mature and resilient as existing databases (following the same evolutionary track of today's widely prevalent relational DBMSs) [9].

For effective productivity improvement, best practices implementation, supply chain linkage, and process based management there is a fundamental need to focus on automating the assortment of manual activities executed among enterprises. The genesis of this opportunity comes from the reality that business activities among enterprises today are still typically performed manually. For effective productivity improvement, best practices implementation, supply chain linkage, and process based management there is a fundamental need to focus on automating the assortment of manual activities executed among enterprises. Major benefit of WfMS is that they allow the "automation" of business processes. Automation does not mean to "control" or to "force" a user to perform in a certain way [10, 11]. Automation means that business process steps and their dependencies (data, control, etc.) are specified formally and that a WfMS can support the user based on this formal specification. For example, a WfMS can deliver documents, alert the user of priorities and deadlines, and can route information according to company policies. WfMS are not only targeted to human user environment.

They are also able to implement processes between software systems not requiring user communication but perform by invoking software services directly. Furthermore, since WfMS automates a business process as a repeatable sequence of subtasks, it makes each process explicit and well defined in the information technology infrastructure. This makes it amenable to monitoring and change in a way that is not possible when a process is simply built into specific application code.

Workflow technology typically involves integrating other information technologies (such as document management, product data management, and collaboration technologies) to support the management and execution of business processes [12].

BENEFITS OF INTEGRATED PROCESS MANAGEMENT

The benefits of modeling the best practices not only derived from the automation of time-consuming administrative tasks (such as tracking, monitoring, and notification), but also by the detailed, on-line documentation of those processes, which increases their visibility and reusability throughout the enterprise.

In order to realize these benefits, the business processes managed by workflow technology should be amenable to being understood, modeled (i.e., represented as sequential flows of tasks), executed (i.e., carried out by a identifiable participants), monitored (i.e., identifiable as having being started and completed), coordinated, (i.e., having some sequential constraints on the order of subtasks), shared (i.e., having subtasks that may be carried out by different participants), repeated (i.e., executed many, separate times in an organization), and, in some cases, simulated (i.e., able to estimate performance metrics). If a business process meets these criteria, then the level of benefit from workflow management often depends on the degree to which the business process can take advantage of the other information technologies that are integrated with the particular workflow manager.

The key benefits of integrated process management are as follows:

- **Tool/vendor neutral workflow process definition:** Define once, execute anywhere

- Reusing library of process components and knowledge captured in the PM; enabling fast workflow development in accordance with PM and vise-versa.
- Workflows are executed according to schedule—no arbitrary workflow execution
- **Schedule changes reflected in WFMS:** Real work execution affected
- **Ad-hoc changes in WFMS reflected in schedule:** Additions / deletions / modifications sent to schedule
- Schedule shows always correct status and history
- **Improved efficiency:** By the detailed model of long running processes one can find clues to process inefficiency. Furthermore, automation of business processes results in the elimination of time-consuming, manual steps, such as routing documents between subtask participants.
- **Better process control:** Improved management of business processes results from standardizing the subtasks involved in a process and in the availability of audit trails.
- **Improved visibility and documentation:** Participants are better able to monitor upcoming tasks and to understand their interfaces with the participants of other subtasks.
- **Flexibility:** Using software to manage business processes enables their re-design with changing business needs and the tracking of any ad hoc modifications to the processes.
- **Business process improvement:** Design and simulation tools facilitate the modeling of coherent, efficient business processes.

INTEGRATED PROCESS MANAGEMENT ARCHITECTURE

The integrated process management architecture addresses integration of scheduling systems (such as Primavera P3e) with workflow management systems (implemented using a tool such as PTC Windchill or Enovia) and process modeling tool—(MS)2.

Scheduling and workflow systems both manage the flow of work, but they emphasize different aspects of the work. Scheduling systems emphasize analyzing the dependencies between tasks and using those dependencies to plan the human and temporal resources required to perform the work. These systems enable management to determine what resources will be required, when they will be required, and how long it will take to complete a project. The systems may also provide a prioritized activity list or work list to the people responsible for performing the work. Workflow management systems emphasize the implementation of the work via the process flow, including conditional branches and loops in the process. These systems provide management with visibility of the current status of every process instance and assurance that the work is done in accordance with the process. Workflow management systems alert the people who must do the work of the tasks assigned to them, and they also provide a work list of these tasks. Workflow systems are generally well integrated with the work objects, and they provide links from an item in a work list to the relevant data objects. For example, a task to review a design in Enovia would include a link to the design.

The target will be achieved by utilizing a tool for modeling work processes which can semi automatically generate workflow processes based on scheduling tool and then exported it to workflow engine via web services using XML process definition language (XPDL) as it is shown in Figure 3. Run time architecture allows for synchronization of workflow and project management resources during process instantiation and workflow execution. See Figure 4.

Workflow management systems require and enable the definition of business processes, typically via a process-modeling tool. A process definition includes the rules, constraints, attributes, and relationships of the activities, participants, roles, and informational items (such as documents) instrumental to the workflow. Because different business process management server implement workflow modeling in different ways, trying to run a workflow model created for one vendor's

Figure 3. Integrated process management design time architecture

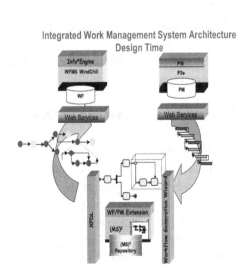

Figure 4. Integrated process management run time architecture

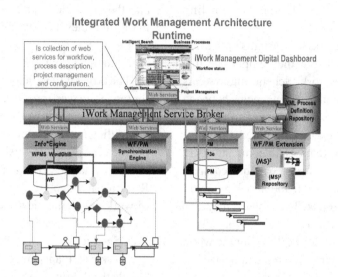

product on another BPM server is unlikely to be successful. The WfMC has been working on a standard interface specification to enable process definitions to be passed from modeling tools to workflow engines in a vendor-neutral way. In late 2002 WfMC released version 1 specification for a process definition language based on extensible markup language (XML) schema referred to as XPDL. XPDL provides a basic foundation for a vendor neutral, standard interface between process modeling tools and workflow engines. Similarly group of vendors including Microsoft, IBM and others have defined the Business Process Execution Language (BPEL). Now being standardized under auspices of OASIS, BPEL is also an XML-based language for defining interaction via web services.

XML has emerged as the standard syntax for representing and exchanging information when independent, computing applications are involved. So it is a natural choice to base a standard workflow process definition language on XML. However, adequately representing the complex semantics of business process definitions is beyond the scope and purpose of the core XML specifications. Information modeling grammars can be used to extend the XML syntax by prescribing how complex statements can be formed using simple elements.

We have developed capability to output XPDL from (MS)2 process models. The hope is in very near future every workflow management system that complies with the WfMC standards (or other industry standards such as BPEL) should be able to support XML representation of processes. However, currently most workflow management systems does not support mentioned standards. For example, Windchill support only comma separated value or CSV. We have built the translator that take XPDL and convert it to CSV for Windchill consumption.

WORKFLOW GENERATION

Once the project plan has been established based on Critical chain analysis, workflow model can be generated based on scheduled tasks. See Figure 2. The workflow generation wizard will then assist designer in generating workflow (see Figure 5).

There appear to be three options for generating workflow from project management tasks:

Figure 5. Workflow auto generation tool

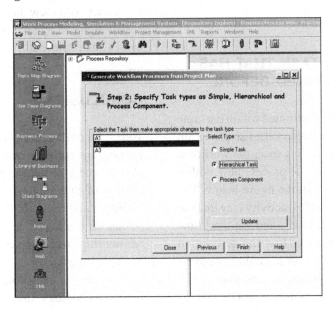

\

Figure 6. Hierarchical task composed of several sub tasks corresponds to a scheduled task

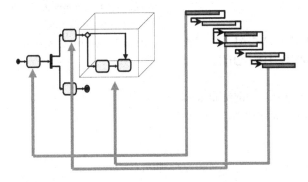

1. **Simple task:** The scheduling activities and workflow management tasks could be in one-to-one correspondence

2. Hierarchical task composed of several sub tasks corresponds to a scheduled task that has not been designed before

3. **Process component:** Same as step 2 but hierarchical task has been deigned before

Simple Task-One-to-One Correspondence

The workflow tasks and scheduled activities could be in one-to-one correspondence. Both the schedule representation and the workflow representation contain the same tasks/activities. The workflow template could be initialized from this description of steps, but it is likely that it would have to be augmented by descriptions of decisions and loops.

HIERARCHICAL TASK THAT HAS NOT BEEN DESIGNED BEFORE

These tasks may all be performed within the same functional area and correspond to steps within a scheduled activity. In this case, the workflow model would represent the process flow within one activity, as shown in the figure below. The description of a hierarchical activity may include a sequence of sub activities, and the workflow template could be initialized from this description of steps, but it is likely that it would have to be augmented by descriptions of conditionals and loops, as shown. The scheduling tool defines all the resources responsible for carrying out the total activity, and somehow these must be allocated to the individual steps.

PROCESS COMPONENT-HIERARCHICAL TASK HAS BEEN DESIGNED BEFORE

Workflow management is often used for processes such as engineering change management that oc-

cur many times and involve many short duration tasks such as review and approval tasks. In this case design can reused previously designed processes and retrieve it from process repository.

CONCLUSION

Today, an onslaught of business imperatives is pushing enterprises to automate the highly complex business or exchange activities occurring outside of any single participating enterprise. To thrive and remain competitive, it will be essential for businesses to automate and optimize relationships with partners throughout the entire business lifecycle.

The key to achieving enterprise agility is fusing technology that supports coordination of program tasks, reducing the time required to perform these tasks and the costs of coordinating them. Providing services that integrate project and resource management tools with workflow management systems can enable efficient process automation across the large, complex, and distributed businesses.

Figure 7. Process component refers to processes that have been defined and in the library of business processes for reusability

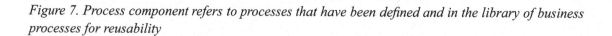

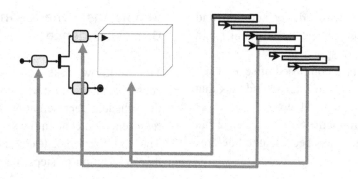

REFERENCES

Appleton, D.S. (1995). Business reengineering with business rules. In V. Grover & W. J. Kettinger (Eds.), *Business process change: Reengineering concepts, methods and technologies* (pp. 291-329). Idea Group Publishing.

Bahrami, A. (2002). *Modeling and simulation management system (MS)2 user's guide.* The Boeing company Version 2, November.

Basu, A., & Kumar, A. (2002). Research commentary: Workflow management issues in e-business. *Information System Research, 13*(1), 1-14.

Denna, E. L., Jasperson, J., & Fong, K. (2000). Reengineering and REAL business process modeling. In V. Grover & Fischer (Eds.), *The Workflow Handbook 2001,* in association with the Workflow Management Coalition (WfMC).

Huckvale, T., & Ould, M. (1995). *Process modeling—who, what and how: Role activity diagramming.* In V. Grover & Kettinger (Eds.), *Business process change: Reengineering concepts, methods and technologies* (pp. 291-329). Idea Group Publishing.

Lin, F.-r., Yang, M.-c., & Pi, Y.-h., (2002). A generic structure for business process modeling. *Business Process Management Journal, 8*(1), 19-41.

Mayer, R.J., Benjamin, P.C., Caraway, B.E., & Painter, M. (1995). A framework and a suite of method for business process reengineering. In V. Grover & W. J. Kettinger (Eds.), *Business process change: Reengineering concepts, methods and technologies* (pp. 245-290). Idea Group Publishing.

Profozich, D. (1998). *Managing change with business process simulation.* Upper Saddle River, NJ: Prentice-Hall PTR.

Swiss Bank Corporation, Switzerland; e-Workflow.org, Gold Award, Workflow, Europe (1998). Nominated by Eastman Software, Inc. with integration by Systor AG.

Taylor, D. (1995). *Business engineering with object technology.* New York: John Wiley & Sons.

Wang, S. (1994). OO modeling of business process. *Information System Management,* 36-43.

Wooldridge, M., & Jennings N.R. (1995). Agent theories, architectures, and languages: A survey. In M. Wooldridge & N.R. Jennings (Eds.), *Intelligent agents* (pp. 1-22). Berlin: Springer-Verlag.

Section IV
Virtual Enterprise Operation

Chapter XIII
Agents and Multi-Agent Systems in Supply Chain Management:
An Overview

Pericles A. Mitkas
Aristotle University of Thessaloniki, Greece

Paraskevi Nikolaidou
Aristotle University of Thessaloniki, Greece

ABSTRACT

This chapter discusses the current state-of-the-art of agents and multi-agent systems (MAS) in supply chain management (SCM). Following a general description of SCM and the challenges it is currently faced with, we present MAS as a possible solution to these challenges. We argue that an application involving multiple autonomous actors, such as SCM, can best be served by a software paradigm that relies on multiple independent software entities, like agents. The most significant current trends in this area are shown, focusing on potential areas of further research. Furthermore, the authors believe that a clearer view on the current state-of-the-art and future extension will help researchers improve existing standards and solve remaining issues, eventually helping MAS-based SCM systems to replace legacy ERP software, but also give a boost on both areas of research separately.

INTRODUCTION

This chapter discusses the current state-of-the-art of agents and multi-agent systems in supply chain management (SCM). The growing complexity of the supply chain has increased the need for effective supply chain management, which may raise profit and reduce stock at a minimal cost. However, SCM is a complex problem of distributed nature and it often involves sensitive data that companies may be reluctant to reveal. Multi-agent systems (MAS) appear to be an ideal solution to this problem, as they can handle complex and distributed processes in an effective way. Considerable ongoing research efforts on MAS have yielded a wide variety of prototypes and applications although the adoption of agents by the software industry proceeds at a cautious pace. Agent-based solutions for the SCM problem abound in the literature underlining the significant interest in this approach and its huge potential.

Section 1 provides a general description of SCM and explains the reasons that make effective SCM critical, both within a single company and across the chain. Section 2 discusses the main problems that SCM is currently faced with and section 3 explains the reasons why MAS are an ideal solution to this problem. Section 4 describes the various approaches and current trends and focuses on current problems that arise and areas that need further research. Finally, section 5 presents the main conclusions.

Current Trends in SCM

According to Stanfield (2002), "supply chain management deals with the management of materials, information and finance in a network consisting of suppliers, manufacturers, distributors and customers" (p.11). Practically, according to Kim, Tannock, Byrne, Farr, Cao, and Er (2004), "the activities involved in the material flow are to deliver to the end-user via procurement of raw materials, manufacturing, distribution and customer service" (p.10). All these activities must be managed using suitable information flows. This is easily illustrated in Figure 1.

The above factors cause increasing emphasis to be placed on integrating, optimizing and managing the entire supply chain from component sourcing, through production, inventory management and distribution to final customer delivery. Recent technological advances have facilitated this job, replacing approximate estimations by human experts by more precise calculations, as managing the supply chain is a complex task with increased sensitivity on small changes.

Increasing competition has emphasized the need for more flexible, robust and powerful supply chain management. The current trend in production is changing "from mass-production to customisation, and from technology and product-driven to market and customer-driven" (Kim et al., 2004, p.9). Bielli and Mecoli (2005) state that "current scenario in production and logistics fields must accomodate globalization, needs for increasing quality of goods, rapid changing in market demand, customer-service policies, flexibility of production processes, e-business and e-commerce" (p.147).

Many companies see the need for complete visibility into their supply chain as the starting point for managing them and many solutions are already implemented in this area. The next stage is to go further and implement solutions that are designed to change business practices and make supply chains more efficient.

Figure 1. Flows in the supply chain (Adapted from Speckman, Kamauff, & Myhr, 1998)

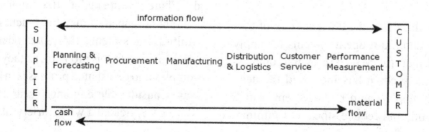

SCM PROBLEMS

Managing the supply chain is an extremely complicated task, which requires correct coordination of distributed heterogeneous information. Each part of the chain plays a different role in the functionality of the entire chain and it is difficult to conceive a suitable model, especially when the latter is designed to be more generic rather than to describe a particular chain. "The speed and accuracy required to increase the company's profit, as well as the current trends for customisation and flexibility, require the adoption of 'just-in-time' practices" (Stanfield, 2002, p.11). However, these practices not only require a totally transparent chain, but also increase its sensitivity on real-world problems, such as delays, specification changes and compromises. The most important problems of SCM are discussed below.

Bullwhip Effect

As explained by Kombrough, Wu, and Zhong (2001), a very well-known phenomenon in SCM is the so-called bullwhip effect, where the variance of orders amplifies upstream the supply chain.

Figure 2 illustrates this effect.

Such results are commonly observed in real-life situations. Small fluctuations on one end of the chain often become surprisingly large on the other end, hindering the flawless functionality that one would expect from a well-designed supply chain. As a result, there is a growing interest in efforts to eliminate the bullwhip effect, or at least minimize it.

Kombrough et al. (2001) state that the bullwhip effect can be minimized under the assumption that all divisions of the supply chain work as a team. Yung and Yang (1999) claim that information sharing and, more generally, coordinating information and planning along the supply chain can minimize the bullwhip effect. Ganapathy and Narayanan (2003) suggest simulation methodologies to lower demand amplification, but this, of course, requires extensive collaboration between the different levels of the supply chain system.

Coordination

It is also necessary to discuss the importance of correct timing and coordination in SCM. The most immediate consequence of incorrect coor-

Figure 2. The bullwhip effect

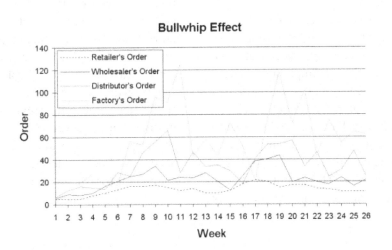

dination is a bottleneck effect, where products are accumulated in one part of the chain, while there is a shortage at its end. This can lead to products eventually becoming useless, or can force a modification of the manufacturing and supplying process, with immediate impact on product quality, cost and competition.

Ganapathy and Narayanan (2003) present time delay, added together with delays from other levels, as the major cause of the bullwhip effect. Chan and Chan (2004) state that one common weakness is the assumption of deterministic demand. Facing uncertain demand, retailers prefer to place an order late in most cases in order to gather enough time to collect more information. However, this leads to insufficient production times and hence increased production cost.

MAS AS A SOLUTION

Generally speaking, the best way to define software agents and distinguish them from other software entities is to do so based on some common attributes that they have. As stated by Ta, Chai, and Liu (2005), agents' main characteristics are autonomy, sociability, capacity for cooperation, capacity for reasoning, adaptive behavior and trustworthiness. One can easily understand that all of these capabilities are, not only necessary, but also vital to SCM.

However, there is still not a commonly accepted definition on what an agent might be. Wan (2004) states that an agent is merely an object with initiative. Of course, initiative is an important feature of an agent, but one can easily understand that there's more in an agent than initiative. Other authors, such as Caglayan and Harrison (1997), define an agent as "a software entity that accomplishes a specific task, usually on the Internet, according to the user's requirements". This definition, though commonly used, is also too vague and does not give a complete picture of agents.

A multi-agent system (MAS) is a system, in which many agents communicate and interact. This interaction may be either cooperative or selfish. According to Sycara (1998), the main characteristics of a MAS are:

- Each agent has incomplete information or capabilities to solve the problem
- There is no global control on the system
- Data is distributed
- Computations are asynchronous

As explained earlier, SCM is a problem of distributed nature, which requires processing of heterogeneous data in an intelligent way. Resource allocation is crucial to the supply chain's functionality and negotiation and cooperation between the parts of the supply chain are necessary. This shows that MAS are an ideal solution to this problem, since they are designed for distributed problem solving and negotiating.

According to Wu, Ulieru, Cobzaru, and Norrie (2000), since SCM is fundamentally concerned with coherence among multiple, globally distributed decision makers, a multi-agent modeling framework based on explicit communication between constituent agents (such as manufacturers, suppliers, retailers and customers) seems very appealing.

"Agent technology may facilitate the integration of the entire supply chain as a networked system of independent echelons, each of which utilizes its own decision-making procedure" (Jiao, You, & Kumar, 2006). Ulieru and Cobzaru (1999) argue that "agents are suitable for integrating supply chain functions because they can extend applications like production, distribution and inventory management functions across supply chains spanning various organisations without the need for additional interfaces, especially when a common infrastructure is used."

STATE-OF-THE-ART

MAS are still a new research area, not yet fully adopted by industry. As a result, the agent-based solutions for SCM to be found today are relatively limited. A simplistic approach would be to merely simulate the supply chain by substituting each part of it by an agent, as in Figure 3. This solution increases the chain's performance, but it does not totally exploit the huge potential of agents and MAS.

Various Approaches

Negotiation and Cooperation

The most common approach on agent-based SCM is negotiation and cooperation. Many people, like Kaihara (2001, 2000), have discussed bidding mechanisms. One strategy (2001) is based on market-oriented programming, whose mechanism is shown in Figure 4. *Pt(S)* is the price of resource *s* at time *t*, while *ftms* and *gtns* represent the supply function of supplier *m* and the demand function of demander *n* on resource *s* at time *t*.

Agent activities in terms of products required and supplied are defined so as to reduce an agent's decision problem to evaluate the trade offs of acquiring different products in market-oriented

programming. Kaihara defines several functions that formulate agents' strategy for the resource allocation in SCM, taking into account the budget constraints of each agent.

Kaihara (2000) discusses the advantages of double-auction mechanisms. He formulates supply chain as a discrete resource allocation problem with supply/demand agents and demonstrates the applicability of economic analysis. Finally, he introduces an agent-based double auction algorithm based on market mechanisms and demonstrates that it can provide several advantages on resource allocation.

Lou, Zhou, and Chen (2005) give a definition of *agile SCM* and discuss coordination mechanisms for both self-interested and cooperating agents. "The *agile supply chain* is an operational strategy focused on inducing velocity and flexibility in a supply chain" (p. 171). The two differences between an agile supply chain and a normal supply chain are (a) speed, which is the ability to respond quickly to the changing of customers' requirements, and (b) flexibility, namely the ability of reconfiguring quickly according to changing. The coordination mechanism in ASCM is shown in Figure 5.

The main doctrine of the coordination mechanism for cooperating agents is "as decentralized as possible, as centralized as necessary", and the reasoning process is shown in Figure 6.

Figure 3. Simplistic MAS modeling of a supply chain

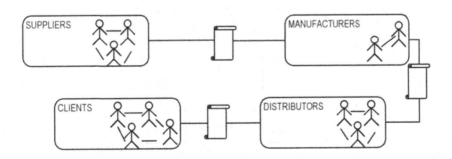

Figure 4. The bidding mechanism proposed by Kaihara (Adapted from Kaihara, 2001)

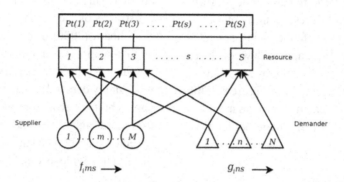

Figure 5. Coordination mechanism in multi-agent based ASCM

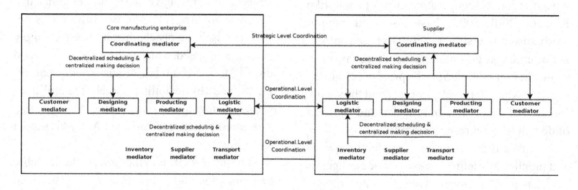

Figure 6. Reasoning process for cooperating agents

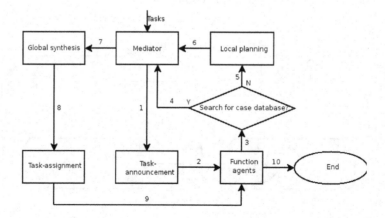

As shown in Figure 5, coordination for self-interested agents is done at two levels, namely strategic-level coordination and operational-level coordination.

Chan and Chan (2004) introduce a coordination framework for distributed supply chains by using the distributed constraints satisfaction problem (DSCP). They propose a coordination framework by adopting the DSCP philosophy for distributed supply chains, which are modeled by MAS, subjected to uncertainties. In their simulation, they demonstrate that the proposed mechanism outperforms traditional stochastic modeling.

Chan and Chan (2005) perform a comparative analysis of negotiation-based information sharing in agent-based supply chains. They model a distributed make-to-order (MTO) manufacturing supply chain as a MAS. In this case, information can only be exchanged through negotiation in the agent-based framework. In their simulation results, they show that partial information sharing has comparable performance in terms of total cost and fill rate against full information sharing based on negotiation. Considering the associated cost and limitations to achieve full information sharing, they prove that partial information sharing is more practical in real applications.

Sauer and Appelrath (2003) present an approach using teams of cooperating agents in a hierarchical as well as heterarchical way. Traditional hierarchical implementations lack incorporation of feedback from lower levels and possibilities of reactive scheduling, so the authors use a hierarchical and heterarchical approach. To simplify the generation of such a hierarchy of agents, they develop and describe a framework for scheduling agents and they use an example to illustrate how it is used to build teams of cooperating agents.

Distributed Optimisation / Resource Allocation

SCM is also often seen as a *distributed optimisation* and *resource allocation* problem. Schnee-weiss (2003) describes a unified approach on distributed decision-making (DDM) by providing a general theoretical framework for it and characterizing the main directions or approaches in DDM in view of the general features of such a framework. He classifies DDM settings as shown in Figure 7 and discusses a general coordination scheme, showing how it might be specialized for particular DDM problems.

Silva, Sousa, Sa da Costa, and Runkler (2004) use ant colony optimization (ACO) for the supply chain. This algorithm builds a so-called "pheromone matrix", an indirect record of the optimization steps, that is manipulated at all times during the optimization process. This concept is presented for a supply chain system with a logistic, a supplying and a distribution subsystem. After describing the general ACO framework, they implement the algorithm for each of the optimization problems and then they introduce the framework for the multi-agent platform, where the communication protocol is based on pheromone matrices updating.

Frey, Stockheim, Woelk, and Zimmermann (2003) discuss a MAS architecture based on production planning and control. They are integrating many individual projects: DISPOWEB for SCM scheduling, KRASH, IntaPS and FABMAS for shop floor production planning and control, and ATT/SCC for proactive tracking and tracing services. The integration is made by providing interfaces and gateways between these systems, as shown in Figure 8.

Smirnov, Sheremetov, Chilov, and Cortes (2004) use genetic algorithms (GA) for resource allocation. The proposed approach considers configuring as: (1) coalition formation and (2) product and resource allocation tasks in a multi-agent environment. Their first approach uses GA to find a suboptimal solution applying the theory of games with fuzzy coalitions. Their second approach uses genetic algorithms directly and constraint satisfaction problem solving for resource

Figure 7. Classifications of DDM systems (Adapted from Schneeweiss, 2003)

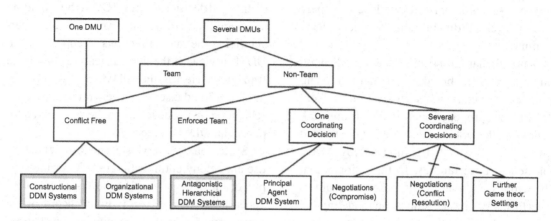

Figure 8. Integration of the MAS projects by Frey et al. (2003)

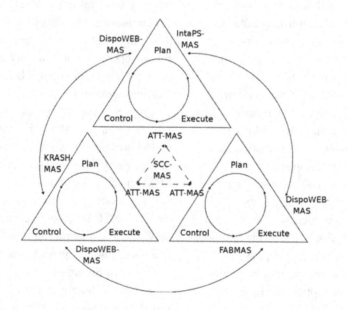

allocation tasks. They use FIPA-compliant agents using ontologies for task description.

Moyaux, Chaib-draa, and D'Amours (2004) use game theory to analyze collaborative strategies in a forest supply chain. They use collaboration in an attempt to reduce the bullwhip effect, under the assumption that each company is one single agent using one of three ordering schemes,

where each ordering scheme represents a level of collaboration. They run a simulation to evaluate each company's inventory holding and backorder costs and use the outcome of this simulation to build a game in the normal form, which is then analyzed using Game Theory. They identify two Nash equilibria incurring the minimum cost of the supply chain, both of which include collaboration between companies: collaborating companies have no incentive to stop collaboration.

Symeonidis, Kehagias, and Mitkas (2003) describe a multi-agent SCM system that acts mostly as a recommendation engine. It uses data mining techniques to discover new customer trends and dynamically incorporate the extracted knowledge into the company selling policy. Agents can be periodically retrained to improve their knowledge. In the paper, the architecture and development details of this system are presented and their application is demonstrated on a real test case.

Simulation of the SCM / Particular Assumptions

Another area of research is simulation of the SCM and/or particular frameworks. Web services, for example by Mi, Jianjun, Zunping, Yinsheng, and Binyu (2005) or by Hassan and Soh (2005), is a very commonly used technology. Mi et al. (2005) define a strategy for aggregating the agents, both normal and mobile agents, into the Web service architecture and the functionalities for them to control the business conducts. They also devise a UDDI ranking frame based on analysis of supply chain activities, deploying Web Service-oriented technologies and protocols for modeling, managing and executing business-oriented functionalities. Their framework is illustrated in Figure 9.

Hassan and Soh (2005) propose an agent structure to provide more agility to the supply chain in an attempt to overcome its traditional problems. They focus on two aspects of SCM: removing inefficiencies in supply chains by real-time knowledge sharing and automated supply chain configuration by negotiating methods being used by agents. They argue that Web services are not only easier to implement, but also take care of the problems of legacy application connectivity. Figure 10 shows how an agent is structured and placed in the supply chain net.

Web services are also examined by Maximilien and Singh (2005). The authors present a multiagent framework for dynamic Web services selection. Based on their trust model (2005) and on their architecture for autonomic Web service selection (2003), they provide a basis that incorporates providers' offering advertisements and consumers' preferences, but also enables the gathering and sharing of ratings of services. Based on the requirement that "trust should be self-adjusting", their application uses a service agent, which selects the suitable implementation of a particular service, according to the customer's policy. Their results show that the agents' trust assignments are dynamically adjusted, enabling agents to select the best policies, according to consumers' needs.

Qing and Renchu (2001) provide a review of modeling methodologies and model a distribution system in a supply chain. They consider the following approaches to modeling supply chain systems: (a) simulation-based method, (b) network design method and (c) rough-cut method. However, these traditional models are based on mathematical and statistical tools and rely on the assumption of linearity, while many phenomena in a supply chain are of non-linear nature. They model a distribution system based on a MAS, with agents configured as manufacturer, distributor, transporter, retailer and customer interconnected through the network.

Schieritz and Groessler (2003) perform a study integrating agent-based and system dynamic modeling and make a distinction between the macro and micro level of a supply. Their approach discusses the strengths and weaknesses of system dynamics and discrete agent-based modeling and integrates these two methodologies. They model a supply chain with two levels of aggregation, as shown in Figure 11.

The macro level shows a network of agents that are potential supply chain participants, while the micro level shows the internal structure and functionality of each agent.

Giorgini, Kolp, and Mylopoulos (2006) propose architectural styles for MAS, which adopt

Figure 9. UDDI-based Web service framework

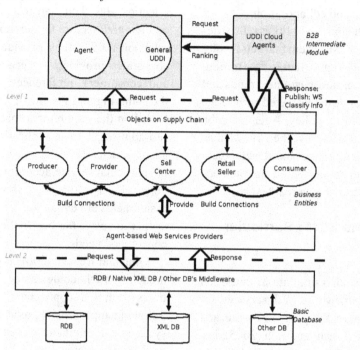

Figure 10. Structure of an agent as proposed by Hassan and Soh (2005)

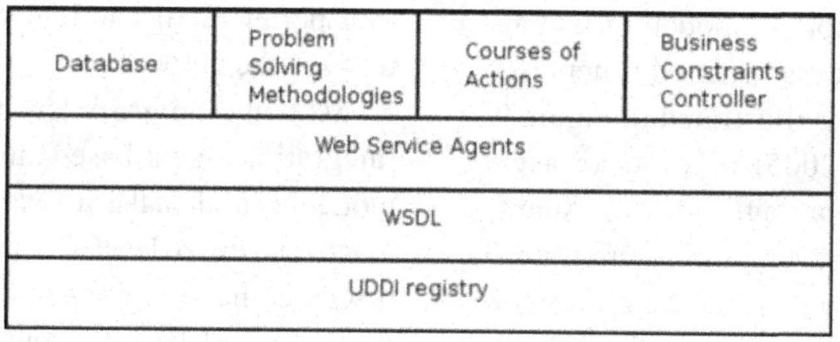

Database	Problem Solving Methodologies	Courses of Actions	Business Constraints Controller
Web Service Agents			
WSDL			
UDDI registry			

Figure 11. Macro and micro level of supply chain

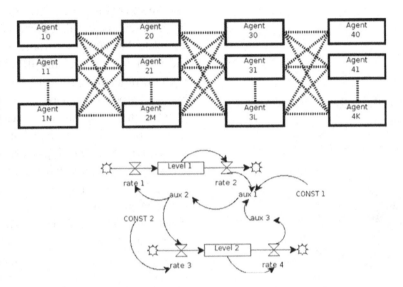

concepts from organizational theories. They start by presenting organizational styles identified in Organization Theory and in Strategic Alliances. They detail the structure-in-5 and the joint venture as organizational structures and present four case studies, two for each structure. Each case study describes an existing company. They continue by presenting the software qualities that characterize MAS architectures and demonstrate the application of the two organizational styles they described using the classical mobile robot case study. They conclude by presenting a framework to select architectural styles with respect to their identified software quality attributes, based on a requirements-driven methodology.

Li and Feng (2003) propose a J2EE-based multi-agent platform, decomposing each function of the supply chain into groups of various agent types. In their platform, each group is formed by a scheduling agent which supervises several vertex agents. The enterprise's internal supply chain behavior is simulated by interaction among groups, while behaviors of different enterprises are

coordinated by interaction among platforms. They think of their platform as "an effective tool for building the virtual organization of enterprises", designed to meet businesses' requirements for project information sharing, process integration and coordination of decisions.

Nissen (2000) proposes a set of techniques and tools, aiming to integrate agent design for the supply chain into e-commerce. He models the enterprise supply chain process at user, supplier and contractor levels and designs the agents structure from above using Grafcets. Subsequently, he analyzes the supply chain of an operational enterprise and deploys a supply chain agent federation to demonstrate its effective performance along the supply chain. He states that his work facilitates the process of agent development, giving end users the potential to develop their own agents in an e-commerce context.

Goh and Gan (2005) construct a framework based on the requirement to enable dynamic interoperation of units within a supply chain. They argue that effective coordination of ac-

Figure 12. The framework proposed by Goh and Gan (2005)

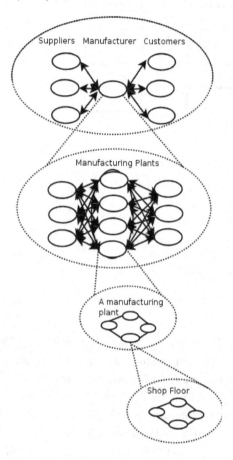

tivities within the supply chain is inevitable for manufacturing excellence. To address this need, they identify the core requirement for activity coordination and construct a framework based on the requirement to enable dynamic interopera- tion of units within a supply chain for successful global manufacturing. Figure 12 illustrates their proposed framework.

Decision Making and Learning

Another approach on agent-based SCM is *decision making and learning*. Sheremetov and Rocha-Mier (2004) deal with collective intelligence as a frame-

work for SCM. They consider a large multi-agent system where there is no centralized control and communication, but also, there is a global task to complete. Their proposed framework is focused on the interactions at local and global levels with the agents in order to improve the overall supply chain business process behavior. Learning consists of adapting the local behavior of each entity with the aim of optimizing a given global behavior. They use reinforcement learning algorithms at the local level and a Q-neural algorithm to optimize the global behavior. Their work demonstrates that the SCM problem is a good experimental field for the investigation and application of the Collective Intelligence theory.

Guo and Mueller (2004) use knowledge models with historical and context information. Their approach is threefold: first, they develop a multi- agent architecture and learning algorithms that enable us to combine background models learned from history data with context-related knowledge about the current situation. Second, they use a large real data set to show that adding situated knowledge actually improves the performance of a supply chain decision support system. Third, for their settings they evaluate the degree to which agent-assisted decision support is actually usable/ sufficient to improve human decision-making and to support automated decision-making in dynamic supply network management scenarios.

Simek, Albayrak, and Korth (2004) use rein- forcement learning (RL) algorithms for procure- ment agents. They use the well-known Q learning algorithm of reinforcement learning in evaluating production orders within a SCM framework and making decisions. They introduce their SCM model and show that RL performs better than traditional tools for dynamic problem solving in daily business, but also show some cases where RL fails to perform efficiently.

Kwon, Im, and Lee (2005) use optimization and case-based reasoning (CBR) models on a Web services-based platform. They think that, despite the advancement of optimization techniques,

Figure 13. MAS with CBR models on a web services-based platform

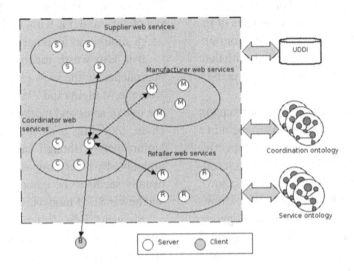

Figure 14. Decision support system for partner choice

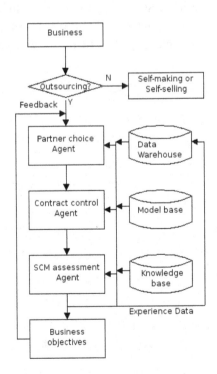

this approach has not been fully extended to addressing more complicated problems such as revenue maximization and stochastic dimension. They compare the performance outcomes of the prototype system, which uses linear programming and mixed integer programming, with their optimization model shown in Figure 13 using a variety of scenarios.

Zhang and Xi (2005) discuss a decision support system for partner choice and measurement in a supply chain. Their study presents a perspective and technical framework based on decision support system and agents. This framework is shown in Figure 14. The model they propose exhibits basic characteristics of agents, that is, intelligence, flexibility, integration and collaboration, and it provides a technical support on partner choice decision and assessment.

Agent-Based SCM for Particular Supply Chains

Many researchers have modeled agent-based SCM systems for a particular supply chain, or under other particular assumptions. For example, Liu,

Zhang, and Hu (2005) discuss a supply chain for a motorcycle corporation, Xue, Shen, and Wang (2005) present a framework for construction supply chains, and Yi, Kim, and Kim (2002) use a MAS simulation for a harbor supply chain.

It is also worth mentioning some different approaches on the view of the supply chain. For example, Mangina and Vlachos (2005) emphasize the role of sales and marketing on a food supply chain, modeling it as illustrated in Figure 15. Unfortunately, though sales and marketing is undoubtedly a very important factor in SCM, it usually seems to be ignored in most traditional and newer SCM models.

Shuwang, Ren, Zhifeng, and Guangfu (2003) introduce the concept of a green supply chain, aiming to reduce or eliminate environmental impacts of products in their life cycle by preventing excess consumption of resources. The green supply chain is shown in Figure 16.

Bonura, Corradini, Merelli, and Romiti (2004) emphasize quality control, an important aspect that again seems to be missing from most supply chain models in bibliography. More precisely, they define the extended supply chain, to take quality

Figure 15. A food supply chain according to Mangina and Vlachos (Adapted from Mangina & Vlachos, 2005)

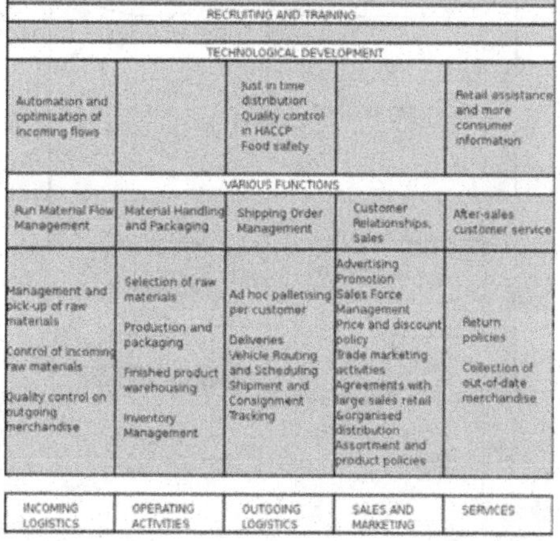

Figure 16. The green supply chain

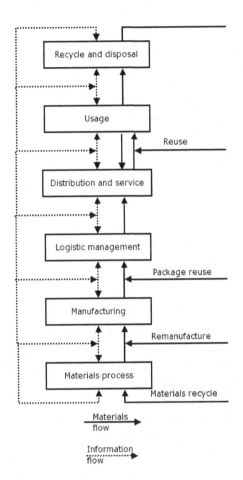

Materials
flow →

Information
flow →

control into account, as shown in Figure 17.

Failures in assembled products may be detected at many points of the product life, therefore an early diagnosis could depend on the retrieval of all significant information recorded along the extended supply chain. The basic idea proposed in this work is to define a society of Autonomous Agents created to support the traceability of components information in a federated enterprises environment.

Trading Agent Competition

Finally, the trading agent competition for SCM (SCM TAC) has given an important boost on SCM research. As described by Kiekintveld and Wellman (2005), in the TAC/SCM scenario, "six agents representing PC assemblers operate in a common market environment over a simulated year. The environment constitutes a supply chain, in that agents trade simultaneously in markets for supplies (PC components) and the market for finished PCs. Agents may assemble for sale 16 different models of PCs, defined by the compatible combinations of the four component types: CPU, motherboard, memory, and hard disk."

Figure 18 diagrams the basic configuration of the supply chain. The six agents (arrayed vertically in the middle of the figure) procure components from the eight suppliers on the left, and sell PCs to the entity representing customers,

Figure 17. The extended supply chain

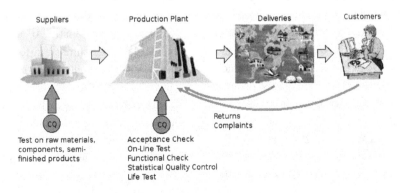

Figure 18. The TAC SCM game

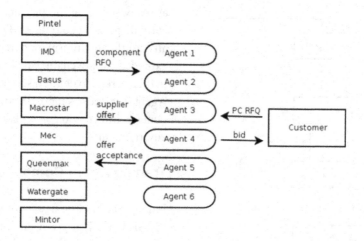

on the right. Trades at both levels are negotiated through a request-for-quote (RFQ) mechanism, which proceeds in three steps:

- Buyer issues RFQs to one or more sellers
- Sellers respond to RFQs with offers
- Buyers accept or reject offers; an accepted offer becomes an order

Arunachalam and Sadeh (2004) provide a description of the 2003 SCM TAC, while Zhang and Zao (2004) discuss an economic model for it. They consider that the most important issues in the TAC SCM game are "daily production, product pricing and market-clearing price prediction" (p. 63), then differentiate the quantity competition (defined as a variation of Cournot model) and price competition (extension of Bertrand game). They argue "the results of their paper provide the solution to the decision-making problem of TAC SCM" (p.63).

Kiekintveld and Wellman (2005) analyze the 2004 SCM TAC, discussing differences in agents' behavior and strategic interactions, as well as the different ways that the agents responded, as these are the most important factors that shaped market prices and determining agents' classification in the competition.

Jordan, Kiekintveld, Miller, and Wellman (2006) compare the results of the 2005 competition to the games played in previous years by considering market efficiency, sales competition, and the bullwhip effect. They present a way to measure and compare market efficiency in the game to find "statistically significant increases in intra-tournament market efficiency, whereas agents are generally decreasing in manufacturer market power" (p. 99).

Borghetti, Sodomka, Gini, and Collins (2006) present a way to evaluate TAC SCM agents' performance, using benchmarking tools that manipulate market environments based on market pressure. They claim that these tools can be used to inspect agents' behavior and check for possibly unwanted behaviors under special conditions, and use them for their agent MinneTAC.

Of course, many publications have been made about specific TAC agents, for example MinneTAC by Gini, Ketter, Kryzhnyaya, Damer, McGillen, Agovic, and Collins (2004), Botticelli by Tschantz, Benisch, Greenwald, Grypari, Lederman, and Naroditskiy (2004), or TacTex05 by Pardoe, Stone and VanMiddlesworth (2006). Toulis, Kehagias, and Mitkas (2006) present their agent Mertacor, which participated in the 2005 TAC and finished third in the final round. This agent is based on "a combination of OR, statistic and heuristic modeling techniques" (p. 1198). Its main advantages are its robust inventory management system and flexible learning models that correctly captured the dynamics of the TAC market, while heuristics also played an important role.

Overall Problems

According to Goh and Gan (2005), the fundamental issue of a supply chain, namely "interoperation among suppliers, manufacturers and customers" (p. 330), is still not addressed. Smooth negotiation and coordination mechanisms, optimization to generate optimal solutions, developing adaptive systems and emphasizing on a real-time information sharing and updating are significant, but not sufficient to enable global manufacturing when the fundamental issue is not addressed.

Jiao et al. (2006) observe that "most current MAS approaches assume that a fixed number of entities share a common target in a closed environment" (p. 239). However, on a real-case global manufacturing supply chain, this is not always the case. Not only each supply chain entity has its own interests, but also there is no obligation for any company to remain within the supply chain for a certain period of time. Moreover, all agents should be loosely coupled and not coordinated by any central controller.

However, even after having considered the aforementioned problems, the huge potential of agents and MAS is still not exploited. Agents are powerful decision-making entities, capable of taking over complex tasks. On the other hand,

when it comes to SCM, their usage is still mostly limited to recommendation rather than autonomous functionality.

Another area of research on SCM MAS can deal with evaluating and increasing the agents' intelligence. Very little research has been done on intelligence itself (Sheremetov & Rocha-Mier, 2004) and nobody has addressed the issue of possibly evaluating it, even in specific environments or benchmarks. The trading agent competition is a benchmark only for single agents. It evaluates their performance under very particular conditions, which are quite distinct from real-life situations. On the other hand, SCM requires intelligent solutions, as it deals with critical and complex problems.

The supply chain can be so sensitive that even very small deviations or fluctuations on one part can badly influence, not only this particular part, but also the whole chain. Current solutions have limited capability to learn from their past (especially in an unsupervised way), which is essential in an efficient MAS. Apart from this, efficiency is usually evaluated in terms of increased profit, which might be the desired result and an easily measurable quantity, but it is a rather short sighted approach and can only relate to the structure and the essence of the MAS by experimenting or trial-and-error. The real problem, however, is the agents' intelligence itself, as well as the intelligence of the whole MAS. This issue is usually not faced and the MAS intelligence, or even its performance, is hardly evaluated in depth. As a result, one can easily see the need for research on this topic.

CONCLUSION

Current trends in SCM demand customization, high quality, flexibility and customer-service policies in a highly competitive environment. This has emphasized the need for more flexible, reliable and powerful SCM systems. Agent-based technology, with its inherent capabilities for distributed problem solving, flexibility and handling large amounts of data, provide an ideal solution to this problem. However, this technology is still a large area of research, which shows the lack of not only a commonly deployed system, but also of a unified approach on this area.

The most important areas of research today are negotiation and cooperation, distributed optimization and resource allocation, decision making and learning, as well as particular frameworks and simulation. Many researchers have modeled SCM systems based on a particular supply chain or suggested enhancements to the supply chain, such as the green supply chain or, more commonly, the agile supply chain.

However, most SCM products today are designed to be used in only one company, and they are designed for recommendation rather than making their own decisions. On the other hand, no evaluation is made on the agents' performance and intelligence. This indicates a large potential for future research on this area, promising fruitful results.

REFERENCES

Arunachalam, R., & Sadeh, N.M. (2004). The supply chain trading agent competition. *Electronic Commerce Research and Applications, 4*, 63-81.

Bielli, M., & Mecoli, M. (2005). Trends in modelling supply chain and logistics networks. In *Proceedings of the 10th Meeting of the EURO Working Group Transportation* (pp. 147-152).

Bonura, D., Corradini, F., Merelli, E., & Romiti, G. (2004). FarMAS: A MAS for extended quality workflow. In *13th IEEE International Workshops on Enabling Technologies: Infrastructure for Collaborative Enterprises (WETICE'04)* (pp. 435-440). IEEE Computer Society.

Borghetti, B., Sodomka, E., Gini, M., & Collins, J. (2006). A market-pressure-based performance evaluator for TAC-SCM. In *Trading Agent Design and Analysis and Agent Mediated Electronic Commerce (TADA/AMEC) Joint International Workshop* (pp. 193-196). Springer.

Caglayan, A., & Harrison, C. (1997). *Agent sourcebook*. John Wiley & Sons.

Chan, H.K., & Chan, F.T.S. (2004). A coordination framework for distributed supply cChains. In *2004 International Conference on Systems, Man and Cybernetics* (pp. 4535-4540). IEEE Press.

Chan, H.K., & Chan, F.T.S. (2005). Comparative analysis of negotiation based information sharing in agent-based supply chains. In *3rd International Conference on Industrial Informatics* (pp. 813-828). IEEE Press.

Frey, D., Stockheim, T., Woelk, P.-O., & Zimmermann, R. (2003). Integrated multi-agent-based supply chain management. In *12th International Workshops on Enabling Technologies: Infrastructure for Collaborative Enterprises* (pp. 24-29). IEEE Computer Society.

Ganapathy, S., & Narayanan, S. (2003). Decision support for supply chain analysis. In *2003 International Conference on Systems, Man and Cybernetics* (pp. 2077-2082). IEEE Press.

Gini, M., Ketter, W., Kryzhnyaya, E., Damer, S., McGillen, C., Agovic, A., & Collins, J. (2004). MinneTAC sales strategies for supply chain TAC. In *Third International Joint Conference on Autonomous Agents and Multiagent Systems (AAMAS'04)* (pp. 1372-1373). IEEE Computer Society.

Giorgini, P., Kolp, M., & Mylopoulos, J. (2006). Multi-agent architectures as organizational structures. In *Journal of Autonomous Agents and Multi Agent Systems, (AAMAS'06) 13*(1), 3-25.

Goh, W.T., & Gan, J.W.P. (2005). A dynamic multi-agent based framework for global supply chain. In *2ⁿᵈ IEEE International Conference on Service Systems and Services Management* (pp. 981-984). IEEE Computer Society.

Guo, Y., & Mueller, J.P. (2004). A multiagent approach for logistics performance prediction using historical and context information. In *Proceedings of the Third International Joint Conference on Autonomous Agents and Multiagent Systems - Volume 3* (pp. 1164-1171). IEEE Computer Society.

Hassan, U., & Soh, B. (2005). Web service intelligent agent structuring for supply chain management (SCM). In *2005 IEEE International Conference on e-Technology, e-Commerce and e-Service (EEE'05)* (pp. 329-332). IEEE Computer Society.

Jiao, J., You, X., & Kumar, A. (2006). An agent-based framework for collaborative negotiation in the global manufacturing supply chain network. *Robotics and Computer-Integrated Manufacturing, 22*(3), 239-255.

Jordan, P.R., Kiekintveld, C., Miller, J., & Wellman, M.P. (2006). Market efficiency, sales competition, and the bullwhip effect in the TAC SCM Tournaments. In *Trading Agent Design and Analysis and Agent Mediated Electronic Commerce (TADA/AMEC)*. Joint International Workshop (pp. 99-111). Springer.

Kaihara, T. (2000). Agent-based double auction algorithm for global supply chain system. In *26ᵗʰ Annual Conference of Industrial Electronics Society* (pp. 678-683). IEEE Press.

Kaihara, T. (2001). Supply chain management with market economics. *International Journal of Production Economics, 73*(1), 5-14.

Kiekintveld, C., & Wellman, M.P. (2005). An analysis of the 2004 supply chain management trading agent competition. In *2005 Annual Meeting of the North American Fuzzy Information Processing Society* (pp. 257-262). IEEE Press.

Kim, C.-S., Tannock, J., Byrne, M., Farr, R., Cao, B., & Er, M. (2004). *State-of-the-art review: Techniques to model the supply chain in an extended enterprise* (VIVACE WP2.5). Nottingham, UK: University of Nottingham, Operations Management Division.

Kombrough, S. O., Wu, D.J., & Zhong, F. (2001). Computers play the beer game: Can artificial agents manage supply chains? In *34ᵗʰ Hawaii International Conference on System Sciences* (pp. 1-10). IEEE Computer Society.

Kwon, O., Im, G., & Lee, K.C. (2005). MACE-SCM: An effective supply chain decision making approach based on multi-agent and case-based reasoning. In *Proceedings of the 38th Annual Hawaii International Conference on System Sciences (HICSS'05)* (pp. 82-91). IEEE Computer Society.

Li, T., & Feng, Z. (2003). A system architecture for agent based supply chain management platform. *IEEE CCECE 2003, Canadian Conference on Electrical and Computer Engineering, 2*(2), 713-716.

Liu, J., Zhang, S., & Hu, J. (2005). A case study of an inter-enterprise workflow-supported supply chain management system. *Information & Management, 42*(3), 441-454.

Lou, P., Zhou, Z.D., & Chen, Y.P. (2005). Study on coordination in multi-agent-based agile supply chain management. In *4ᵗʰ International Conference on Machine Learning and Cybernetics* (pp. 171-185). IEEE Press.

Mangina, E., & Vlachos, I. P. (2005). The changing role of information technology in food and beverage logistics management: Beverage network optimisation using intelligent agent technology. *Journal of Food Engineering, 70*(3), 403-420.

Maximilien, E.M., & Singh, M.P (2003). Agent-based architecture for autonomic Web service selection. In *Second International Joint Conference on Autonomous Agents and Multiagent Systems (AAMAS '03)*. ACM.

Maximilien, E.M., & Singh, M.P. (2005). Agent-based trust model involving multiple qualities. In *Fourth International Joint Conference on Autonomous Agents and Multiagent Systems (AAMAS '05)* (pp. 519-526). ACM.

Maximilien, E.M., & Singh, M.P. (2005). Multiagent system for dynamic Web services selection. In *Workshop on Service-Oriented Computing and Agent-Based Engineering (SOCABE '05)*. Springer.

Mi, Z., Jianjun, X., Zunping, C., Yinsheng, L., & Binyu, Z. (2005). A Web service-based framework for supply chain management. In *Eighth IEEE International Symposium on Object-Oriented Real-Time Distributed Computing (ISORC'05)* (pp. 316-319). IEEE Computer Society.

Moyaux, T., Chaib-draa, B., & D'Amours, S. (2004). Multi-agent simulation of collaborative strategies in a supply chain. In *Third International Joint Conference on Autonomous Agents and Multiagent Systems (AAMAS'04)* (pp. 52-59). IEEE Computer Society.

Nissen, M.E. (2000). Supply chain process and agent design for e-commerce. In *Proceedings of the 33rd Annual Hawaii International Conference on System Sciences* (pp. 1-8). IEEE Computer Society.

Pardoe, D., Stone, P., & VanMiddlesworth, M. (2006). TacTex-05: An adaptive agent for TAC SCM. In *Trading Agent Design and Analysis and Agent Mediated Electronic Commerce (TADA/AMEC)* Joint International Workshop (pp. 85-98). Springer.

Qing, Z., & Renchu, G. (2001). Modeling of distribution system in a supply chain based on multi-agent. In *2001 International Conferences on Info-Tech and Info-Net* (pp. 94-99). IEEE Press.

Sauer, J., & Appelrath, H.J. (2003). Scheduling the supply chain by teams of agents. In *36th Hawaii International Conference on System Sciences* (pp. 81-92). IEEE Computer Society.

Schieritz, N., & Groessler, A. (2003). Emergent structures in supply chains: A study integrating agent-based and system dynamic modeling. In *Proceedings of the 36th Annual Hawaii International Conference on System Sciences (HICSS'03)* (pp. 94-102). IEEE Computer Society.

Schneeweiss, C. (2003). Distributed decision making: A unified approach. *European Journal of Operational Research, 150*(2), 237-252.

Sheremetov, L., & Rocha-Mier, L. (2004). Collective intelligence as a framework for supply chain management. In *Proceedings of the 2004 2nd International IEEE Conference on Intelligent Systems* (pp. 417-422). IEEE Computer Society.

Shuwang, W., Ren, Z., Zhifeng, L., & Guangfu, L. (2003). Construction of dynamic green supply chain based on agent. In *IEEE International Symposium of Electronics and the Environment* (pp. 30-35). IEEE Press.

Silva, C.A., Sousa, J.M.C., Sa da Costa, J.M.G., & Runkler, T.A. (2004). A multi-agent approach for supply chain management using ant colony optimization. In *2004 International Conference on Systems, Man and Cybernetics* (pp. 1938-1943). IEEE Press.

Simek, B., Albayrak, S., & Korth, A. (2004). Reinforcement learning for procurement agents of the factory of the future. In *2004 Congress on Evolutionary Computation* (pp. 1331-1337). IEEE Press.

Smirnov, A. V., Sheremetov, L. B., Chilov, N., & Cortes, J. R. (2004). Soft-computing technologies for configuration of cooperative supply chain. *Applied Soft Computing, 4*(1), 87-107.

Speckman, R. E., Kamauff, J., & Myhr, N. (1998). An empirical investigation into supply chain management: A perspective on partnerships. Reprinted from *Internatinal Journal of Physical Distribution and Logistics, 28*(8), 53-67.

Stanfield, J. (2002). Agents in supply chain management. *AgentLink News, 9,* 11-12

Sycara, K. (1998). Multiagent systems. *AI Magazine, 19*(2), 79-92.

Symeonidis, A.L., Kehagias, D.D., & Mitkas, P.A. (2003). Intelligent policy recommendations on enterprise resource planning by the use of agent technology and data mining techniques. *Expert Systems with Applications, 25*(4), 589-602.

Ta, L., Chai, Y., & Liu, Y. (2005). A multi-agent approach for task allocation and execution for supply chain management. In *2005 International Conference on Networking, Sensing and Control* (pp. 65-70). IEEE Press.

Toulis, P., Kehagias, D., & Mitkas, P. (2006). Mertacor: A successful autonomous trading agent. *Fifth International Joint Conference on Autonomous Agents and Multiagent Systems* (pp. 1191-1198). ACM.

Tschantz, M., Benisch, M., Greenwald, A., Grypari, I., Lederman, R., & Naroditskiy, V. (2004). Botticelli: A supply chain management agent. In *Third International Joint Conference on Autonomous Agents and Multiagent Systems (AAMAS'04)* (pp. 1174-1181). IEEE Computer Society.

Ulieru, M., & Cobzaru, M. (1999). Building holonic supply chain management systems: An e-logistics application for the telephone manufacturing industry. *Transactions on Industrial Informatics, 1*(1), 18-29.

Wan, G. (2004). Joint production and delivery scheduling in two-level supply chains: A distributed agent approach. In *2004 IEEE International Conference on Systems, Man and Cybernetics* (pp. 1522-1526). IEEE Press.

Wu, J., Ulieru, M., Cobzaru, M., & Norrie, D. (2000). Supply chain management systems: state of the art and vision. In *9th International Conference on Management of Innovation and Technology* (pp. 759-764). IEEE Press.

Xue, X., Li, X., Shen, Q., & Wang, Y. (2005). An agent-based framework for supply chain coordination in construction. *Automation in Construction, 14*(3), 413-430.

Yi, D.W., Kim, S.H., & Kim, N.Y. (2002). Combined modeling with multi-agent systems and simulation: Its application to harbor supply chain management. In *35th Annual Hawaii International Conference on System Sciences (HICSS'02)* (pp. 70-79). IEEE Computer Society.

Yung, S.K., & Yang, C.C. (1999). A new approach to solve supply chain management problem by integrating multi-agent technology and constraint network. In *32nd Hawaii International Conference on System Sciences* (pp. 1-10). IEEE Computer Society.

Zhang, D., & Zhao, K. (2004). Economic model of TAC SCM game. In *IEEE/WIC/ACM International Conference on Intelligent Agent Technology* (pp. 273-280). IEEE Computer Society.

Zhang, Z.Q., & Xi, B. (2005). Research on framework of decision support system for partner choice and measurement in supply chain. In *Proceedings of 2005 International Conference on Machine Learning and Cybernetics* (pp. 378-382). IEEE Press.

Chapter XIV
A Conceptual Framework for Business Process Modeling in Virtual Organizations

Dimitris Folinas
University of Macedonia, Greece

Tania Pavlou
City University (London), UK

Bill Karakostas
City University (London), UK

Vicky Manthou
University of Macedonia, Greece

ABSTRACT

Among different approaches in business processes modeling procedure are those in virtual and dynamic organizational environments. In this chapter, a conceptual framework for modeling business processes in virtual organizations is suggested, by introducing Web services technology. Web services can be the business enabler for the new organizational form, which is particularly well suited to meet the demands arising from today's turbulent changes in the firms' environment. The proposed framework consists of several steps in a bottom-up approach, aiming to support the modeling and coordination of the complex and shared business processes in the examined environment.

INTRODUCTION

As Internet reduces interaction costs between enterprises and the establishment of partnerships is considered a mean to achieve short-term economic benefits and to gain long-term competitive advantages, the demands for creating virtual organizations are increasing. A virtual organization (VO) is a temporary or permanent association of geographically dispersed organizations communicating with each other and / or triggering services that carry out some complex workflow of transactions (Browne & Zhang, 1999; Bultje & Ja-coliene, 1998; Camarina-Matos & Afsarmanesh, 1999; Palmer & Speier, 1997; Papazoglou, Ribber, & Tsalgatidou, 2000; Pfohl & Buse, 2000; Timmers, 1999; Van Aken, 1998). VO is more than collaboration between organizations. It integrates the core competencies and special abilities of its members in order to respond rapidly both to the global market and customer requirements (Huang, 2004) and has unique characteristics: lack of geographical boundaries, the absence of informational barriers, form fluidity, cooperative and instant partnerships capability, exceptional speed and agility and a unity of appearance.

Researchers and practitioners both in conventional and virtual environments are describing business entities in terms of processes rather than functional hierarchies. Generally, a business process can be defined as a set of one or more linked and partially ordered activities, which collectively realize a specific business goal (Davenport & Short, 1990). According to Scheer (1993) a business process is the occurrence of some duration that is triggered by an event and results into another event. In a VO virtual environment business processes are distributed and shared (Folinas, Manthou, & Vlachopoulou, 2003; Huang, 2004). The basic implication of this characteristic is that all network partners have a common realization of interenterprises business processes, in order to ensure the seamless materials, information and financial flows of transactions. Thus, the concept of VO refers to the activities of procurement, order fulfilment, product design and development, distribution, delivery, shipping and customer service, planned, executed and controlled by two or more separate organizations aiming to fulfil customers' orders.

Business process modeling is considered an effective tool for designing and managing an enterprise. Luo and Tung (1999) have classified process modeling objectives into three main categories: (1) communication among partners by achieving common understanding and representation of shared business processes, (2) identification, analysis and improvement of existing business processes, and (3) control and monitoring of business processes. Furthermore, Hammer, and Champy, (1993), and Grover, Fiedler, and Teng (1994), argued that three well-known and widely accepted strategic approaches are based on process modeling: Business process reengineering, enterprise integration and enterprise engineering.

During the last decades many approaches to support business process modeling have introduced initially for a single enterprise, such as IDEF0 (Mayer, Benjamin, Caraway, & Painter, 1995), IDEF1, IDEF1X, IDEF3 (Mayer et al., 1995), RAD, REAL, Dynamic Modeling, Object-Oriented Modeling, MAIS, CIMOSA, as well as, in virtual environments (Camarinha-Matos & Pantoja-Lima, 2001; Chang-Ouk & Nof, 2000; Dong & Chen, 2001; Jensen, 1994; Van der Aalst, 1999; Van der Aalst & ter Hofstede, 2000). Lin et al. (2002), have presented process-modeling methods in the literature and compared them in different dimensions. While there is a rapidly growing body of literature in process modeling techniques only few studies have been proposed to support new and innovated practices and technologies (Presley, Sarkis, & Liles, 2000). We suggest that Web services have the potential to become an effective approach to support the modeling and coordination of the complex and shared business processes in VO.

The advantageous properties of a VO depend on the modeling of business processes, which defines the form of the interpretation of messages/documents and services passing through VO partners. To achieve this goal certain heterogeneity difficulties need to be overcome. Integrating business partners requires integration between their business activities defining a formal way to express business objects and data vocabularies. Additionally, different operating systems and information platforms need to be connected and enabled to communicate.

In this chapter, a Web services-based conceptual framework to model VO's distributed business processes and interaction relations among them are proposed. The proposed framework consists of several steps in a bottom-up approach aiming to support the design, development and deployment of shared interenterprise business processes in a virtual environment. It can be used in many dynamic business fields especially in those that the need for the sharing of skills and information is a critical success factor to achieve the ultimate goal of meeting customer's expectations at a lower cost.

WEB SERVICES AND BUSINESS PROCESSES

Based on the paradigm of software as service, Web services are reusable software components that can be remotely accessed over the Web or any other network. By exploiting open Internet standards and protocols Web services can interact with each other eliminating interoperability issues and integrating different operating systems and platforms (Papazoglou & Georgakopoulos, 2003). The description and the basic operations of the services (publish, discover, invoke) are based on the WSDL/SOAP/UDDI suite. The Web services definition language (WSDL) is an eXtensible markup language (XML) "grammar" that describes the interface of the Web services and provides information about them. This information refers to what the Web Service does; it's location and the way it is invoked (Cristensen, Curbera, Meredith, & Weerawarana, 2001). Interactions between Web services are accomplished with the use of the simple object access protocol (SOAP). SOAP is a standard which using XML enables the exchange of structured and typed information between peers in a decentralized, distributed environment (Box, Ehnebuske, Kakivaya, Layman, Mendelsohn, & Nielsen, 2000).

The operations of discovery and invocation are supported by the universal description discovery and integration (UDDI) protocol. UDDI provides a common "ground" on which information about the services can be published (Tsalgatidou & Pilioura, 2002).

Web services are based on open architecture and on widely accepted protocols and standards (Crauldwell, 2003). This factor makes the creation of a lock-in-vendor solution difficult and hence minimizes the risk of excluding small partners in a VO. The main characteristic of Web services is that they manage to overcome interoperability issues. This is a factor that when exploited appropriately sets the basis for communication and data exchange between different operating systems. For example, a company can receive stock information from its partner overcoming incompatibilities in data formats and storage systems. Additionally Web services leverage existing systems by utilizing legacy applications, as they are reusable software components. Web services can be either a complete application or a functional component of a larger solution, which affects the flexibility of their use in supply chain software systems (Freeman & Jones, 2003).

Different projects have been proposed to increase operational efficiency and achieve process integration between partners. Different technologies are utilised such as Web services, intelligent agents and radio-frequency identification (RFID). An early attempt to integrate Web services in a network of business processes was the supply chain management sample application architecture (Werden, Evans, & Goodner, 2002). This solution has been developed by the Web Services Interoperability Organization in order to illustrate the way Web services can be modeled in simple supply chain operations. The supply chain management Sample Application Architecture is to assist developers to incorporate architecture of interoperable Web services to implement e-logistics solutions. The architecture is based on the

Web services Stack, which consists of three layers each one representing one of the fundamental functional areas of a Web service instance, namely the data layer, the SOAP message layer and the transport layer. The WS-I organization defined Web services that were related to warehouse operations, such as availability control. The sample application was based on a simple range of supply chain operations and doesn't reflect the reality of supply chain activities. Despite the fact that the sample application is not widely applicable, it has set the basis for the incorporation of Web services in managing business processes.

A Web services model supporting distributed e-business applications was developed by Nagarajan, Lam, and Su (2004). It is part of a larger project which views business processes as series of events and aims to explore techniques that enhance the Web services model in business processes. The user is allowed to choose the methods that will be exposed as a Web service and the events to be installed on the event server. This information is deployed to create a Web service wrapper that posts the installed events and additionally a WSDL document is created. When an operation is invoked the appropriate method is triggered and the wrapper posts the event to initiate the selected business rules from the event directory.

The model is an interesting approach to how Web services can be utilized when realising business processes. It enables the communication between business processes but is based on the event driven paradigm and goes beyond the scope of this document.

Examining the current literature and related projects derives the need to investigate Web services as an enabling technology for business process integration, as a business enabler. Thus it is essential to establish a strategic framework that will identify and model business processes and map them using a supporting technology.

A CONCEPTUAL FRAMEWORK FOR BUSINESS PROCESS MODELING

In order to model business processes in virtual environment new information technology (IT) approaches are required. These approaches need to support the dynamic operation of VO by creating clear standards between partners, specifying the information to be exchanged and the steps to be taken in this exchange of data.

The proposed framework presents a roadmap for modeling and integrating business processes and information in VO following a four-step approach (Figure 1):

- **Step 1: Common ICT standards:** Creating of a common ground for the ICT operation
- **Step 2: Common business applications logic and data:** Identification and modeling of the exchanged business data / information among VO partners
- **Step 3: Common workflows activities:** Identification and modeling of shared workflows activities among VO partners
- **Step 4: Common Web services:** Identification and modeling of shared Web-services that integrates shared business processes among VO partners

Step 1: Creating a Common Ground for the ICT Operation

The first task is the determination and the establishment of the technical and communications standards for data transmission among two or more partners in VO nodes, as well as, safety mechanisms, to ensure availability, confidentiality and integrity. Ensuring the above objectives in the VO context is quite challenging due to a number of factors. One of the main problems is that there

Figure 1. Proposed methodology for modeling and integrating business processes in VO

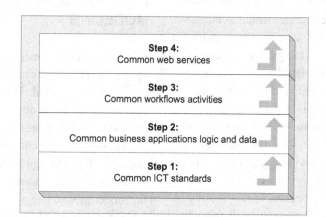

is a gap in terms of economic size, structure and access on ICT applications among VO members. In addition, a problem exists regarding the increased heterogeneity of the technology platforms used (incompatible information systems).

This level consists of the selection of transfer protocols and the mechanisms for the messages management. In both cases the basic idea is the connection of systems in a synchronous or asynchronous manner. Synchronous communication requires a private channel installation between sender and receiver, whereas asynchronous communication allows a more loosely connection without requiring continuous connection between them. Message queuing mechanisms are good candidates in asynchronous connection. They operate as intermediaries administrating and auditing data flows, supporting loosely coupled integration and providing the freedom to change the sender's or receiver's view of the message format in minor ways, without having to recompile or re-link other senders or receivers (especially when using self describing message formats such as XML).

Step 2: Identification and Modeling of the Exchanged Business Data

This step consists of two main sub-steps: (a) modeling of the exchanged business data / information in the VO, and (b) modeling and sharing VO's enterprises' applications business logic and rules.

Initially, it is significantly critical, for VO players to exchange information and data in real or near real-time manner, through messages that could be written, processed and finally easily transmitted, non costly and in a user friendly format. Thus, there is the need to standardize both the structure and the semantics of the exchanged data with the use of common business vocabularies. It is also essential to establish an environment that permits information transparency across the VO. Information and data exchange could be essentially divided in three parts: the first part refers to the basic information of every product (e.g., code, title, producer ID etc.), the second part has to do with information and data regarding business processes and the relevant performances, and the third with quality aspects of the products. The quality aspects of the products can be defined as a set of certain parameters, such as: product attributes, handling details, shipment conditions and so forth.

The process of the above business information identification and modeling in a virtual environment consists of four phases: determination, analysis, design of business information requirements and finally the creation of business vocabularies. Initially, the problem must be described and the requirements have to be registered for the accomplishment of the various business transactions. This phase consists of the specification of collaborative objectives and common processes determining the various roles (business entities or systems) and their relationships (Carlson, 2001). For this purpose, unified modeling language (UML) diagrams are used for modeling business integration and information requirements. These diagrams are used to communicate the business logic behind the complicated business processes between people with technical and nontechnical knowledge. Therefore, Use Case Diagrams are used to model the interdependence between them and the roles of involved business entities. For each use case diagram, an activity diagram will be created on demand that describes the assigned functions. In the second phase the analysis of requirements is performed. It can be accomplished with the determination and the initial planning of the business objects or classes. The integration requirements according to the proposed model are: the integration of data / processes with the adoption or creation of messages, and the modeling of process flows that includes a series of exchanged messages. Hence, interactions of objects (exchanged messages) must be constructed using activity diagrams that demonstrate the interaction of objects in specific period of time. Activity diagrams are used to communicate the behaviour of a system, at different levels of abstraction depending on the target audience (Arlow & Neustadt 2002). They model the nature and the dynamics of the system as different activities change the state of the classes in the system. The reason for

modeling the information exchange using activity diagrams is because they are object-oriented flowcharts that can capture decisions and concurrency through the activities. The main objective of design is to implement a realistic system of static models in practice, which were created during analysis. In this phase, the vocabularies of business messages are developed with the use of class diagrams, which represent the basic elements, their relationships and the restrictions of the system. Furthermore, in this phase the creation of state diagrams is required in order to represent the state of every object and the various events that lead to every objects state. During the final phase the business vocabularies (XML schemas) from UML diagrams are developed. These XML schemas are used for the creation and the validation of the messages. Generally, XML schemas technologies have gained ground in becoming a standard in terms of transport of business information and encode product information. The transformation from diagrams to schemas is the research subject of many projects (Booch, Christerson, Fuchs & Koistinen, 1998; Conrad, Scheffner & Freytag, 2000; Folinas et al., 2003; Routledge, Bird & Goodchild, 2002). Practically an intermediate stage between the conceptual models (corresponding classes) and natural models of XML schemas is applied to all of the approaches. This can be achieved by extending UML diagrams with the use of stereotypes, which can describe more complicated business rules, in order to capture all the functionalities provided by the XML schemas.

Furthermore, during this step another objective is to model and share VO's enterprises' applications business logic and rules. Sharing business logic among the various enterprises applications is achieved by the design and construction of specific components, which at first encapsulate the applications business logic, and then they call remote methods of other applications in order to implicate specific services or functions. The components interaction is achieved under the platform of Internet, which is anticipated as the most cost effective supporting infrastructure. The development and sharing of business applications logic in the examined environment, is a demanding task, since VO's members may be hesitant to modify their application software modules. In addition, integration issues may arise, as a result of incompatible systems, and of the complexity of applications. Web services technology is proposed for the deployment of this sub-step. The approach to integrate Web services in VO is by identifying a way to communicate business processes using Web services. The first step is the requirements specification both in terms of industrial and technical needs. Web services are identified as task coordinators that enable the communication across heterogeneous platforms between VO participants. Modeling the interactions of Web services with business processes is achieved using the event process chain (EPC) notation. The use of the EPC notation enables the examination of the examined business processes at a task level picturing all inputs and outputs required to perform business operations (Curran & Lad, 1999).

Step 3: Identification and Modeling of Shared Workflows Activities Among VO Partners

A business process can be defined as a set of one or more linked activities, which collectively realize a specific business objective. There is a need to automate business processes across all the VO partners and ensure transactions flow quickly. Every transaction is determined as the sequential exchange of business documents / messages, resulting in the transition to a new state for the partners. The objective is the development and use of common business vocabularies that describe the structure and the semantics of the exchanged messages. Thus, the third level defines organizational and collaboration rules for the involved partners in the form of modeling and integration of the shared business processes.

This level aims to achieve a common understanding of businesses, as well as, to a common business operation, by modeling and sharing business processes and workflow activities. Furthermore, the whole process of business exchanges between VO members must be unanimously agreed (i.e., main functions and transmission protocols of message management, application functionality, and legal matters subjects). The main difficulty in this level is that some of the VO members (small and medium size firms) do not have structured processes and workflow activities according to business standards (ISO, HACCP, etc.).

Step 4: Identification and Modeling of Shared Web Services

The proposed framework is based on a Web services architecture, where process functionality is exposed as a service and shared within the VO partners. One of the main advantages is that current applications can be utilized, as Web services are re-usable software components, thus design and implementation time and cost factors could be potentially reduced. However, before moving into the design stage the exposed services need to be modeled and mapped on the VO's business processes.

Identification and modeling of Web services consists of three tasks where business processes are modeled and connect step 3 with step 4, illustrating the activity areas where Web services can be incorporated. The second task is the creation of Web services' patterns reflecting the main functionalities that need to be exposed. Finally, information is gathered from steps 1-3 which is used for semantics analysis and workflow mapping.

The initial three steps of the proposed methodology need to be mapped and integrated in the Web services' design process. Figure 2 describes the way the conceptual framework is integrated with the Web services paradigm dividing the

Figure 2. Integration of conceptual framework with the Web services paradigm

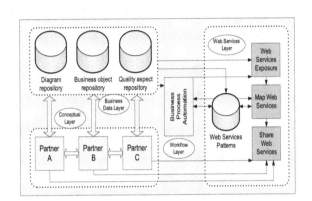

methodology into four layers, relating to the four steps described in the framework. Partner integration is achieved defining ICT standards and protocols, communication information is structured and standardized vocabularies are established. This information is transmitted to the repository layer, which is a dynamic database constantly updated about business objects and their qualitative aspects and business process activity. These activities enable Web services semantics design and establish communication standards between partners.

After the formal definition of a structured way for information exchange, process workflow modeling illustrates the areas where Web services are incorporated in the process and automation hubs between partners are established. This task receives input from the Web services pattern repository, which contains the main patterns of Web services that can be mapped on a process. Web services pattern description includes the shared functionality between the VO's partners and are customized based on industrial and company requirements. Finally, application exposure information is integrated both with workflow modeling and semantic vocabularies resulting in shared Web services that can be consumed by VO partners.

Web services identification and modeling is an iterative process which receives input as the VO expands and new applications need to be exposed. The main concept behind the designed framework is the communication between applications and processes within the partners, which is achieved in the workflow layer. Business process automation is the intermediate layer where Web services are conceptually mapped on business processes.

Figure 3 shows models a redesigned business processes incorporating the Web services patterns that are mapped on the VO business processes. The proposed notation to illustrate Web services in business functions is using the EPC notation. EPC models clearly indicate all functions and tasks that are performed during a business process and the analyst can determine the level of detail. Additionally, EPC models portray all resources and information required to perform a particular task. An example of a process incorporating Web services is given in Figure 4 where Web services are pictured in the right side of certain functions as task coordinators / enablers.

Figure 3 portrays a sales process that is coordinated by Web services. In the current example five Web services are identified that communicate the process between different partners of the VO.

Figure 3. Web services in the sales process

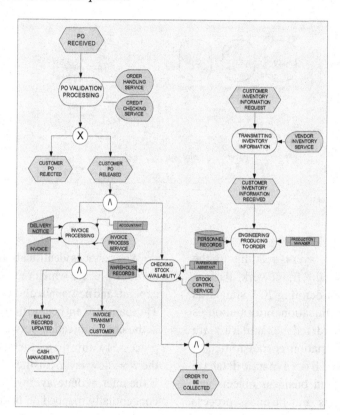

CONCLUSION

Building the appropriate framework for business process modeling in virtual environments is a real challenge, since it must satisfy the needs of all network members. However, the requirements of VO members may not always be the same, and as a result the critical point when building a framework, is to address the common needs. The design of a framework for process modeling should always take into consideration the new, innovative and standard Web-based technologies. In this chapter, a framework is introduced, in order to set the basic guidelines and directions for actions for the effective design, development and deployment of shared inter-enterprise business processes in a virtual environment by using the Web services approach.

The proposed framework provides a complete description of the analysis stage when implementing a VO system based on Web services. The next step is the design of the architecture and the technical requirements analysis to implement Web services. However, although Web services address the need for message exchange through firewalls and interoperability between diverse systems they are not a remedy for every remote application integration issue. The adoption of Web services requires further analysis in terms of standardizing data and developing common semantics for partner communication. This feature is feasible in a VO environment however it requires attention when exposing services to external business partners.

One of the most important limitations in Web services architecture is the security implications deriving from the use of the Internet as a based technology. Concerns about Web services usage, rise in terms of data confidentiality and data integrity, as well as, partner authentication and authorization and service availability (Turban, 2002). In the move to integrate separate applications an important aspect is the integration of current security systems, as enforcing a security system across diverse information systems is required when working over heterogeneous systems. Also, one of the major parameters is performance that is affected by the limitations of the protocols supporting message exchange. Performance is a parameter that is affected by lengthy calls and reduces time efficiencies. The main impact of reduced performance is reflected on architectures that require performance intensive activities and each transaction is interpreted as an exchange of several messages. Excess network traffic is an issue that is very common particularly when SOAP is used for message exchange.

Analyzing the suitability of the proposed four-step conceptual framework on real world business processes can further enhance its applicability. Further research can be carried out for the application of the proposed framework in specific virtual domains, in order to justify this framework in different business environments.

REFERENCES

Arlow, J., & Neustadt, I. (2002). *UML and the Unified Proces.* London: Addison Wesley.

Booch, G., Christerson, M., Fuchs, M., & Koistinen, J. (1998). *UML for XML schema mapping specification.* Retrieved February18, 2007, from http://www.rational.com/media/uml/resources/media/uml_xml schema33.pdf

Box, D., Ehnebuske, D., Kakivaya, G., Layman, A., Mendelsohn, N., Nielsen, H., Thatte, S., & Winer D. (2000). *Simple object access protocol (SOAP) 1.1.* Retrieved February 18, 2007, from http://www.w3.org/TR/SOAP/

Browne, J., & Zhang (1999). Extended and virtual enterprises: Similarities and differences. *International Journal of Agile Management Systems, 1*(1), 30-36.

Bultje, R., & Jacoliene, Van W. (1998). Taxonomy of virtual organizations, based on definitions, characteristics and typology. *VoNet - Newsletter, 2*(3).

Camarina-Matos, L., & Afsarmanesh, H. (1999). *Virtual enterprises: Life cycle supporting tools and technologies.* European Esprit PRODNET II project.

Camarinha-Matos, L. M., & Pantoja-Lima, C. (2001). Cooperation coordination in virtual enterprises. *Journal of Intelligent Manufacturing, 12*(2), 133-150.

Carlson, D. (2001). Modeling XML applications with UML, practical e-business applications. *Object technology series.* Addison-Wesley.

Chang-Ouk, K., & Nof, S. Y. (2000). Investigation of PVM for the emulation and simulation of a distributed CIM workflow system. *International Journal of Computer Integrated Manufacturing, 13*(5), 401-409.

Conrad, R., Scheffner, D., & Freytag, J. (2000). XML conceptual modeling using UML. In *Proceedings of the International Conceptual Modeling Conference.*

Crauldwell, P. (2003). *Professional XML Web services.* Wrox, Birmingham, 18-50.

Cristensen, E., Curbera, F., Meredith, G., & Weerawarana, S. (2001). *Web services description language (WSDL) 1.1.* Retrieved February 18, 2007, from http://www.w3.org/TR/wsdl

Curran, L. (2000). *SAP R/3 business blueprint* (2ⁿᵈ ed.). New York: Prentice Hall.

Davenport, T. H., & Short, J. E. (1990). The new industrial engineering: Information technology and business process redesign. *Sloan Management Review, 31*(4), 11-27.

Dong, M., & Chen, F. F. (2001). Process modeling and analysis of manufacturing supply chain networks using object-oriented petri nets. *Robotics and Computer Integrated Manufacturing, 17*(1-2), 121-129.

Folinas, D., Manthou, V., & Vlachopoulou, M. (2003). Modeling business information in virtual environment. In *Proceedings of 10ᵗʰ International Conference on Human-Computer Interaction*, Irakleion, Greece.

Freeman, A., & Jones, A. (2003). *Microsoft.net XML Web services*. Microsoft Press.

Grover, V., Fiedler, K. D., & Teng, J. T. C. (1994). Exploring the success of information technology enabled business process reengineering. *IEEE Transactions on Engineering Management, 41*(3), 276-84.

Hammer, M., & Champy, J. (1993). *Reengineering the corporation*. New York: Harper Collins.

Huang, S. (2004). *Computers & Industrial Engineering, 47*, 61-76.

Jensen, C. K. (1994). *An introduction to the theoretical aspects of colored petri nets* Tech. Rep. Aarhus University, Denmark, Computer Science Dept.

Luo, W., & Tung, A. (1999). A framework for selecting business process modeling methods. *Industrial Management & Data Systems, 99*(7), 312-319.

Mayer, R. J., Benjamin, P. C., Caraway, B. E., & Painter, M. K. (1995). A framework and a suite of methods for business process reengineering. In V. Grover & W.J. Kettinger (Eds.), *Business process change: Reengineering concepts, methods, and technologies* (pp. 245-290). Idea Group Publishing.

Nagarajan, K., Lam, H., & Su, S. (2004). Integration of business event and rule management with the web services model. *International Journal of Web Services Research, 1*(1), 41-57.

Palmer, W., & Speier, C. (1997). A typology of virtual organizations: An empirical study. In *Proceedings of the Association for information systems 1997 Americas' Conference*, Indianapolis, Indiana.

Papazoglou, M., Ribber, R., & Tsalgatidou, A. (2000). Integrated value chains and their implications from a business and technology standpoint. *Decision Support Systems, 29*, 323-342.

Papazoglou, M. P., & Georgakopoulos, D. (2003). Service-oriented computing. *Communications of the ACM, 46*(10), 25-28.

Pfohl, H. C., & Buse, H. P. (2000). Inter-organizational logistics systems in flexible production networks: An organizational capabilities perspective. *International Journal of Physical Distribution & Materials Management, 30*(5), 388-408.

Presley, A., Sarkis, J., & Liles, D. H. (2000). A soft-system methodology approach for product and process innovation. *IEEE Transactions on Engineering Management, 47*(3), 379-92.

Routledge, N., Bird, L., & Goodchild, A. (2002). UML and XML schema. In *Proceedings of the Thirteenth Australasian Database Conference (ADC2002)*, Melbourne, Australia. In Xiaofang Zhou (Ed.), *Conferences in research and practice in information technology: Vol. 5.*

Scheer, A. (1993). Architecture of integrtaed information systems (ARIS). In H. Yoshikawa & J. Goosenaerts (Eds.), *Information infrustructure systems for manufacturing*. North Holland, Amsterdam.

Timmers, P. (1999). *Electronic commerce: Strategies and models for business-to-business trading.* John Wiley & Sons.

Tsalgatidou, A., & Pilioura, T. (2002). An overview of standards and related technology in Web services. *Distributed and parallel databases* (pp. 135-320). The Netherlands: Kluwer Academic Publishers.

Turban, E. (2002). *Electronic commerce: A managerial perspective.* Upper Saddle River, NJ: Prentice Hall.

Van Aken, E. (1998). The virtual organization: A special mode of strong inter-organizational cooperation. *Managing strategically in an interconnected world* (pp. 301-320). Chichester: John Wiley & Sons.

Van der Aalst, W. M. P., & ter Hofstede, A. H. M. (2000). Verification of workflow task structures: A petri-net-based approach. *Information Systems, 25*(1), 43-69.

Van der Aalst, W. M. P. (1999). Formalization and verification of event-driven process chains. *Information and Software Technology, 41*(10), 639-50.

Werden, S., Evans, C., & Goodner, M. (2002). *WS-I usage scenarios.* Retrieved February 18, 2007, from http://www.wsi.org/SampleApplications/SupplyChainManagement/2002-11/UsageScenarios-1.00-CRD-02a.mht

Chapter XV
Towards a Virtual Enterprise Architecture for the Environmental Sector

Ioannis N. Athanasiadis
Dalle Molle Institute for Artificial Intelligence (IDSIA), Switzerland

ABSTRACT

This chapter introduces a virtual enterprise architecture for environmental information management, integration and dissemination. On a daily basis, our knowledge related to ecological phenomena, the degradation of the natural environment and the sustainability of human activity impact, is growing and as a consequence raises the need for effective environmental knowledge exchange and reuse. In this work, a solution among collaborating peers forming a virtual enterprise is investigated. Following an analysis of the main stakeholders, a service-oriented architecture is proposed. Technical implementation options, using Web services or software agents, are considered and issues related to environmental information management, ownership and standardization are discussed.

INTRODUCTION

On Service-Orientation

Service oriented approaches attract the broad interest of the scientific community, investing on the added value for the digital world of tomorrow. The promising point of service orientation is the synergy of computer science with artificial intelligence theories and computer networks practices. The primitives of distributed computing, the semantic Web, human-computer interaction, software engineering and agent computing are put together in order to design and deploy open, complex yet intelligent and adaptive computer systems that are based on simple agents of fine granularity, which, in turn, provide services in virtual enterprise (VE) environments.

Virtual enterprise architectures could be valuable for efficient information processing and open, loosely coupled service integration, not only in business-related sectors, from where they originate, but also in non-for-profit sectors. For example, consider these sectors related with public domain data and citizen-centered services in the context of e-government, e-health, e-agriculture, e-environment, e-science and so forth. In such a setting, the notion of a virtual enterprise is rather decoupled from its narrow business context, and extended to a broader scheme that accommodates constellations of cooperating service-providers. Service orientation became quite fashionable lately in several implementation variations, as those of software agents, Web services or grid computing. Each one of the technical solutions has advantages and disadvantages that make it more suited in some types of applications. For example, software agents are considered to be active entities, able to take initiatives, in contrast with Web services, which are required to be invoked, that is, operate in a passive way. In this respect, agents are well suited in competitive environments, as those of knowledge brokering and auction-like environments, while Web services are typically used for integrating heterogeneous components in open environments. Finally, grid computing seems more appropriate for computationally-intense applications. Whatever the application case or the suitable technical approach might be, unarguably, service orientation and virtualization remain a critical characteristic that aims in extending sytem capabilities through the composition of fine-granularity service elements with the ultimate goal of providing added-value services in dynamic environments.

This chapter explores the potential of formulating virtual enterprises for the environmental sector. Firstly, the background is set by introducing concepts related to environmental management information systems (EMIS) and the major challenges for environmental information processing and dissemination. Next, a virtual enterprise architecture for environmental information management is introduced and specifies the operational fashion of such a virtual enterprise. Finally, it summarizes latest developments on the field, and discusses the potential for wide-range adoption of virtual enterprises in the environmental sector.

ENVIRONMENTAL INFORMATION AND CHALLENGES

Environmental Data

Environmental data, although considered as public domain, have not been treated as such so far. Environmental information, either collected by public institutes, private industries or generated as a result of scientific computations in academia, has been kept for long in nonreusable, legacy systems and reports. Therefore the vision for enabling access to information and the provision of value-added services that will benefit from the information society initiatives, technologies and tools, often referred as e-environment, or e-agriculture applications, is still in infancy. Nowadays, there are ongoing efforts on defining standards for sharing data about the natural environment, including these published by the US Environmental Data Standards Council in January 2006 (EDSC, 2006) along with the standards developed gradually since 1994 by the european environment information and observation network (EIONET, 1994) and the guidelines (on vegetation plots and classifications) of the Ecological Society of America (VEGBANK, 2006). Also, Food and Agriculture Organization (FAO) of the United Nations has recently made its thesaurus of food and agricultural terms, publicly available through the AGROVOC Web services (AGROVOC, 2006). This task is part of FAO's activities for establishing agricultural information management standards. Significant is the contribution of the OpenGIS specifications by the Open Geospatial Consortium (OGC, 1994) for the standardization of geo-referenced data, which are very common in environmental applications.

However, it is still a long way to go for disseminating effectively environmental information, as there still are problems of data availability and quality that need to be addressed. As Dave Swayne underlined:

the problems of data quality and availability in environmental systems are areas of research that continue to require support" and that "the advances in database technology are not uniformly available in the environmental domain. (Swayne, 2003)

Common practice has proven that environmental data are usually stored in nonreusable raw formats, situated in sparse locations and managed by different authorities, which ultimately raise obstacles in making environmental information accessible. With the growing concern of the public for the sustainability of the planet and the degradation of the natural environment, environmental information, data acquisition management and processing and dissemination, becomes a key element for the sound justification of environmental studies, integrated assessment and policy making. A second issue related to environmental studies has to do with the scaling complexity and reuse of prior studies and models in new application areas. Open services for both data and model access and reuse are one of the important components that can boost future developments in the field. This chapter argues that service orientation and the formulation of virtual enterprises can be utilized for overcoming both of these two obstacles.

Environmental Management Information Systems

Environmental management information systems (EMIS) is a broad term that we use as an umbrella for a range of IT systems related to natural resources data management, varying from environ-

mental databases, simulation packages, reporting tools or visualization applications, geographical information systems (GIS), to extremely complex systems such as environmental decision support systems, or integrated assessment toolkits. An environmental management information system can be considered as an enterprise information system that provides efficient and accurate access to knowledge elements related to information about the natural environment. Collections of data sources and databases, simulation algorithms and environmental models, or decision support modules can be parts of an environmental management information system, which packages them together for addressing complex problems.

Among the challenges that modern environmental management information systems have to face is the documentation and dissemination of their results, ultimately via the provision of information services. Significant efforts are required for providing environmental information services to broad audiences, through the exploitation of digital technologies. Modern environmental management information systems are required to broaden their system goals and core requirements for encapsulating open dissemination e-services. Traditionally, environmental management information systems were developed for specific case studies, therefore the generalization of the approach and the potential reuse of the tools was a very seldom situation. This is partially an intrinsic characteristic of environmental systems, as model configuration and adaptation to local conditions is required. However, the disadvantages of EMIS development that do not confront to (any) common specifications become evident to the environmental community. Knowledge sharing, in any forms from raw data to sophisticated environmental model implementations, has become an increasingly important aspect of sound environmental management. As a consequence, the need for modular, service-oriented approaches rises to prominence.

This chapter investigates the potential of creating virtual enterprises for managing and disseminating environmental information, and summarizes recent developments towards this direction. Given the diversity of standards, formats and practices in collecting, managing and storing environmental data, alongside with the emerging need for sharing and disseminating environmental information to wide-ranging audiences, modular service-centered approaches, which form loosely-coupled synergies in open environments, can be the medium for overcoming the existing problems and meeting the requirements.

VIRTUAL ENTERPRISES FOR ENVIRONMENTAL INFORMATION

The Main Users

Day by day natural resources, the physical environment, and sustainability attain the interest of our society. As a result, the community of stakeholders asking for environmental information, from raw measurements to model simulation results or other kind of studies, is growing rapidly. In this respect, there is an emergent need for sharing environmental information, among diverse and cross-disciplinary audiences. This is one of the major challenges that environmental management information systems are facing today: disseminating environmental information across a broad spectrum of potential end–users.

The major stakeholders involved in the lifecycle of environmental information are illustrated in Figure 1. They consist of the scientific community, governmental bodies and institutions, industry and the business sector, nongovernmental organizations and the wide public. Obviously, each one of them has its own perceptions, goals, objectives and interests on the environment and natural resources, which signifies the conflicting perspectives on environmental data interpretations. The main stakeholders and their involvement

in the lifecycle of environmental information are summarized as follows:

a. **Environmental institutes:** Mainly occupied with the collection and the analysis of environmental data

b. **Scientific community:** Responsible for the study of the natural phenomena involved; note that both environmental institutes and the scientific community are proposing policy options (alternatives) to the governmental bodies.

c. **Industry and the business sector:** Required to monitor the environmental effects of their activities, as a result of legal obligations, or even of their marketing strategies (as for example the ISO19000 family standards (ISO TC 211, 2004), the Eco-label products (ECO-LABEL, 1994), EMAS certifications (EMAS, 1995-2001), green technology campaigns, etc.)

d. **Government and governmental bodies:** Have the main responsibility of decision making and enforcing regulatory policies.

e. **Nongovernmental organizations:** Exist for a variety of purposes related to the preservation of the natural environment, and have very strong interests in accessing environmental information; NGO's participate in consultation procedures for policy-making and influence policy-makers to adopt environmental-friendly options.

f. **Public:** Generally interested in the preservation of the physical environment, natural resources and biodiversity, as a significant factor of every-day quality of life

From the description above, it becomes quite evident that there are significant disagreements among stakeholders' interests, which result to clashing interpretations of environmental data, as the basis for justifying policies, business-activity orientation and the expenditure of natural resources. Even if the various interpretations of environmental data are subjective, conflicting or overlapping, and raw environmental measurements often suffer from low reliability, there is a common, emergent need for *sharing environmental data.* In Figure 1, we illustrate the main stakeholders involved in environmental information management, as players around a cloud of environmental information, which they want to contribute in its creation, have effective access to it, and ultimately share.

On Virtualization of Environmental Information

In a collaborative setting that involves all the abovementioned users, environmental data need to be shared and re-used in different contexts and for divergent purposes. The virtualization of a collaborative environment is essential for treating environmental information as a common asset that is shared among peers, instead as a resource in scarcity that peers strive for. Environmental information is required to become a *virtual resource* that is manipulated by all virtual organization peers. In such a setting, the members of a virtual enterprise are enabled to construct scientific workflows for combining original data sources, with environmental models, reporting tools and consequently achieve their own goals.

The virtualization of environmental information, though, raises two very important issues: one is data standardization, and the second is related to data ownership and rights of disclosure. Related to the first one, XML documents associated with ontologies defining scientific data observations and measurements could be the way for resolving issues related to standardization. The success stories from several business sectors (i.e., in e-publishing, or in business-to-business services) are showing the way for similar development in environmental data management. Consider for example the contribution of ISBN/ISSN numbering system in the development of publishing business in a global scale, or the ebXML business standards. (See related the Organization for the Advancement of Structured Information Standards (OASIS) specifications available at: www. ebxml.org). Similar approaches for standardization of environmental data are required to be established, as those initiatives discussed earlier. A second aspect relates to issues of ownership and disclosure. On this front, the digital rights management frame could be followed. Although free access to environmental data is still mandated by the public's right to know about human health and environmental issues, there are often conflicts with other interests. For example, industrial patent protection, intellectual property rights

Figure 1. Main stakeholders to environmental information

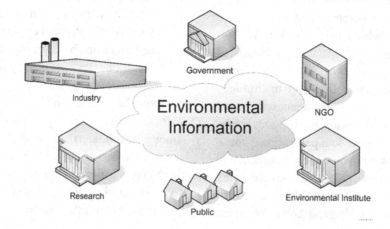

or private information and privacy issues often conflict with the amount of information available. Also, note that even if in many countries there is a legal obligation for environmental reporting and dissemination, the frequency and scale of reporting is an issue of dispute among peers. Such issues of scale and access rights need to be handled effectively within a virtual enterprise for environmental data processing.

A FUNCTIONAL VIRTUAL ENTERPRISE FRAMEWORK ARCHITECTURE

Abstract Agent Roles in a Virtual Enterprise

To realize the requirements for making environmental data as commonly available as virtual resources, an abstract virtual enterprise architecture is presented which accommodates common stakeholders' needs and the requirements of sharing public domain data. Within the virtual enterprise, stakeholders can be represented, as agents that could potentially realize three roles (also discussed in Athanasiadis, 2006).

a. **Contribution agents:** These agents act as data fountains of the system and implement the appropriate interfaces to grant access to raw collections of environmental information. Contribution agents could be located in geographically remote locations. Contribution agents provide data gathering, and preprocessing services, including activities like filtering, standardization and normalization.

b. **Data management agents:** These agents are responsible for data fusion and processing. Data management agents operate as knowledge brokers, and are occupied with orchestration, and synthesis and querying activities and the calculation of environmental indicators.

c. **Distribution agents (DA):** These agents are the marketplace of environmental information, as they are occupied with publishing data to the final audiences. Distribution agents deliver the final data implement custom interfaces to the end-user applications.

These three roles are considered as agents to underline their proactive behavior within a virtual organization. To shed some light on this argument, contribution agents are not considered simply as a Web service or portal-like function that can retrieve environmental information upon request, that is, in a passive way, rather they have the responsibility to make available online resources. In this way, contribution agents take the initiative and make environmental information available to the virtual enterprise. In a similar fashion, data management agents capture information as it becomes available and exploit it appropriately. This could mean that, for example, that they run simulation models or execute environmental assessment toolkits as soon as the required inputs become available. Consequently, distribution agents are constantly updating end-user applications as environmental data and indicators are offered. In such a situation, a virtual enterprise for environmental information management and processing operates as a vigorous virtual organization that intentionally delivers tasks, instead of responding to final-audience requests. Agency of the three roles has the meaning of purposive action and proactiveness, as opposed to passive invocation of available services, rather than implying a technical restriction on the implementation side.

Integration and Demonstration

The integration of the previously discussed agent roles in a generic service-oriented architecture is presented in Figure 2. The main stakeholders involved in environmental data processing can engage services of three agent roles, based on their needs, interests or priorities. However, it must be pointed out that such an architecture requires that all agents in the virtual enterprise should adhere common semantics and standards in environmental data representation, as for example the ISO19100 family of spatial information standards. Ontologies could play a vital role in the definition of a general cognition within the virtual enterprise, that is, for specifying shared terms, vocabularies and data constructs. They could also be used for the integration/mediation of data with dissimilar semantics.

In Figure 2, an example virtual enterprise architecture is presented: we assume that industry, research, NGO and environmental institutes employ (several) contribution agents for "registering" their data and making them available within the virtual enterprise. Similarly, government, NGO, research and the public employ their distribution agents for granting access to the environmental information services available. Knowledge brokering and mediation is performed through the management agents which fuse data coming from contribution agents, process and combine services and ultimately make them available to distribution agents. Note that in this example the roles employed by each stakeholder are indicative. A

detailed design of such a virtual enterprise may vary, depending on the technical solutions selected for deployment. Nevertheless it should include functionalities that support an open architecture, where agents of generic types may register and operate. In this respect, the requirements for extensibility and reusability are achieved, along with main objective for service composition and orchestration. Also, it should be pointed that each stakeholder could employ more than one agent, of the same or dissimilar types, according to their needs. Agent communication and service composition is an intrinsic characteristic of the proposed system.

Implementation Considerations

The implementation of the system could rely either on Web services or software agent implementations, acting as service providers in an open, virtual, collaborative environment, which undertakes environmental information management tasks. In this way, a virtual enterprise is formulated that can both tackle the obstacles of legacy systems, data noise and redundancy, lack of data standardization and variety of data formatting and aggregation, and to (semi) automate

Figure 2. An example virtual enterprise for environmental information management

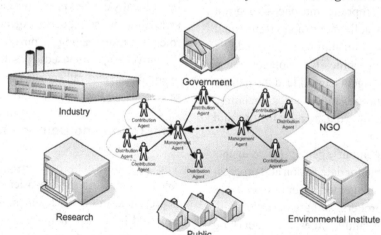

the environmental data review processes by incorporating decision support capabilities (i.e., see Athanasiadis & Mitkas, 2004). Virtual enterprises for managing environmental data can ultimately come out with solutions for providing advanced information services to a wider user group. The need for conducting scientific workflows and the integration of environmental models, integrated assessment tools or raw environmental datasets can be also achieved within a virtual enterprise. In this way, future environmental studies could be built using existing components that are available as services from the peers of the virtual enterprise. Data sources, simulation or optimization models, and dissemination platforms are made available within the enterprise and can be reused for building up new services.

Overcoming the Obstacles of Standardization and Ownership

Some could consider that the development of virtual enterprises in the environmental sector is unrealistic, given the poor solutions available related to problems of environmental information standardization and ownership. However, a more positive reading of the situation reveals that even by investigating the virtualization of environmental information had brought forth these problems, essential to environmental data management, modeling and software development. Therefore, the virtualization of environmental information should be considered as a motivation to tackle such problems, and as a part of their remedy. The adoption of service-orientation in environmental software, along with the virtualization of environmental information will eventually lead to solutions of these data-related problems. In the presented architecture, we consider environmental information to be provided in the virtual enterprise through the contribution agents. Let a contribution agent *a* be responsible for providing access to some data source. Through its proactive behavior, Agent *a* can require from the potential

"consumers" that request portions of the date, to show credentials of their rights for accessing the data. Agent *a* may contact other services of the systems for verifying the credentials. A procedure for digital rights certification will essentially mandate the decision of agent *a,* whether to respond to a request or not, and in case it will, to decide how detailed this response should be (in terms of resolution, frequency, scale, units, etc). Such kind of negotiation among the peers within a virtual enterprise can resolve issues of data ownership, so that dissemination can be modularized, follow some rules, instead of the common situation of obscuring environmental data.

DISCUSSION

Related Work

A couple of applications reported in the literature drive towards the direction of virtual enterprises for environment information integration, management and sharing. For example, environmental data exchange network for inland water (EDEN-IW) aims to provide citizens, researchers and other users with existing inland water data, acting as a one-stop-shop (Felluga, Gauthier, Genesh, Haastrup, Neophytou, & Poslad, 2003). EDEN-IW exploits the technological infrastructure of Infosleuth system (Nodine, Fowler, Ksiezyk, Perry, Taylor, & Unruh, 2000; Pitts & Fowler, 2001), in which software agents execute data management activities and interpret user queries on a set of distributed and heterogeneous databases. Also, InfoSleuth agents collaborate for retrieving data and homogenizing queries, using a common ontology that describes the application field.

A quite analogous system that uses software agents for accessing environmental data is New Zealand distributed information system (NZDIS). NZDIS (Cranefield & Purvis, 2001, Purvis, Cranefield, Ward, Nowostawski, Carter, & Bush, 2003) has been designed for managing environmental metadata in order to service queries to heterogeneous data sources.

The Australian Bureau of Meteorology reports (Dance, Gorman, Padgham, & Winikoff, 2003) the development of forecast streamlining and enhancement project (FSEP), where agents are utilized for detecting and using data and services available in open, distributed environment. In FSEP agents manage weather monitoring and forecasts data.

Efforts towards the use of distributed architectures for environmental data integration and service provision have been given in the followings work also:

- **The Bremen University semantic translator for enhanced retrieval (BUSTER):** Utilizes ontologies for retrieving information sources and semantic translation into the desired format (Neumann, Schuster, Stuckenschmidt, Visser, & Vögele, 2001); BUSTER prototype is to be redesigned using software agents
- **The multi-agents-based diagnostic data acquisition and management in complex systems (MAGIC):** Even if it does not target only environmental applications, its objective is to develop a flexible multi-agent architecture for the diagnosis of progressively created faults in complex systems, by adopting different diagnostic methods in parallel. MAGIC has been demonstrated in an automatic industrial control application (Köppen-Seliger, Ding, & Frank, 2001). A similar application, developed by the same team is the DIstributed Architecture for MONitoring and Diagnosis (DIAMOND) architecture, which adopts an agent-based architecture for distributed monitoring and diagnosis (Albert, Laengle, Woern, Capobianco, & Brighenti, 2003). DIAMOND will be demonstrated for monitoring of the water-steam cycle of a coal fire power plant.

- **The Rilevamento dati Ambientali con Interfaccia DECT (RAID):** This system deals with pollution monitoring and control in indoors environments. *RAID* exploits the general architecture of *Kaleidoscope* that uses "entities" for the dynamic integration of sensor (Micucci, 2002).

Towards the direction of virtual enterprises for the environmental sector fall our prior experiences in developing environmental information management systems in distributed agent-based architectures. The O_3RTAA system (Athanasiadis & Mitkas, 2004) utilizes a community of intelligent software agents for assessing urban air quality. O_3RTAA agents share a domain-ontology for capturing information from air quality monitoring sensors, assess air quality and ultimately disseminate alarms to the public. A follow-up generic middleware system called AMEIM (Athanasiadis, Solsbach, Mitkas, & Gómez, 2005) has been developed that enables a configurable community of software agents to adjust dynamically behavior by introducing new services dynamically, based on already existing ones.

Future Trends

Previous experiences in the above-mentioned applications give a clear indication that the technological infrastructure for realizing complex, distributed architectures that manage environmental data, are available. Building upon these experiences, this chapter proposed a virtual enterprise formulation that exploits a distributed, service-oriented architecture for efficient environmental data fusion. A new paradigm for future EMIS design and development is established. However, inborn properties of environmental information make things much harder in real world, large-scale implementations. The lack of standardization in environmental data management, or to rephrase it more precisely: the poor penetration of standards in the every day environmental data collection and management practices has already led to a Babel of environmental information. Sound and semantically consistent integration of these data is a critical requirement for knowledge sharing. Virtualization of environmental information is the mean for overcoming problems (as those mentioned previously), but also for maximizing reusability, open access and easy integration of environmental software services. Finally, the role of ontologies for environmental data annotation and modeling is essential in future work in virtual enterprises for the environmental sector.

REFERENCES

AGROVOC (2006). The AGROVOC multilingual dictionary of the United Nations Food and Agriculture Organization. Retrieved February 18, 2007, from www.fao.org/agrovoc/

Athanasiadis, I. N., & Mitkas, P. A. (2004). An agent-based intelligent environmental monitoring system. *Management of Environmental Quality, 15*(3), 238-249.

Athanasiadis, I. N., Solsbach, A. A., Mitkas, P., & Gómez, J. M. (2005). An agent-based middleware for environmental information management. In L. Filho, et al. (Eds.), *Second international ICSC symposium on information technologies in environmental engineering* (pp. 253-267). Osnabrück, Germany: Shaker-Verlag.

Athanasiadis, I. N. (2006). An intelligent service layer upgrades environmental information management. *IEEE IT Professional, 8*(3), 34-39.

Albert, M., Laengle, T., & Woern, H. (2002). Development tool for distributed monitoring and diagnosis systems. In M. Stumptner & F. Wotawa (Eds.), In *Proceedings of the 13th International Workshop on Principles of Diagnosis*, Semmering, Austria.

Albert, M., Laengle, T., Woern, H., Capobianco, M., & Brighenti, A. (2003). Multi-agent systems for industrial diagnostics. In *Proceedings of 5th IFAC Symposium on Fault Detection, Supervision and Safety of Technical Processes*, Washington DC.

Cranefield, S., & Purvis, M. (2001). Integrating environmental information: Incorporating metadata in a distributed information systems architecture. *Advances in Environmental Research, 5*, 319-325.

Dance, S., Gorman, M., Padgham, L., & Winikoff, M. (2003). An evolving multi agent system for meteorological alerts. In *Proceedings of the 2nd international joint conference on Autonomous Agents and Multiagent Systems, AAMAS-03.*

ECO-Label. (1994). The European ECO-label certification scheme for distinguished environmental friendly products. Retrieved February 18, 2007, from www.eco-label.com

EDSC (2006). Environmental data standards council data standards. Retrieved February 18, 2007, from www.envdatastandards.net

EIONET (1994). European environment information and observation network. Retrieved February 18, 2007, from www.eionet.europa.eu

EMAS (1995-2001). The eco-management and audit scheme (EMAS) registry of acknowledged organizations that improve their environmental performance on a continuous basis. Retrieved February 18, 2007, from http://ec.europa.eu/environment/emas

Felluga, B., Gauthier, T., Genesh, A., Haastrup, P., Neophytou, C., Poslad, S., Preux, D., Plini, P., Santouridis, I., Stjernholm, M., & Würtz, J. (2003). *Environmental data exchange for inland waters using independent software agents* (Report 20549 EN). Institute for Environment and Sustainability, European Joint Research Centre, Ispra, Italy.

ISO TC 211 (2004). The ISO technical committee 211 ISO19000 standards series on geographic information/geomatics. Retrieved February 18, 2007, from www.iso.org

Köppen-Seliger, B., Ding, S. X., & Frank, P. M. (2001). European research projects on multi-agents-based fault diagnosis and intelligent fault tolerant control. *Plenary Lecture IAR Annual Meeting*, Strasbourg.

Micucci, D. (2002). Exploiting the kaleidoscope architecture in an industrial environmental monitoring system with heterogeneous devices and a knowledge-based supervisor. In *Proceedings of the 14th international conference on Software Engineering and Knowledge Engineering.*

Neumann, H., Schuster, G., Stuckenschmidt, H., Visser, U., & Vögele, T. (2001). Intelligent brokering of environmental information with the BUSTER system. In L. M. Hilty & P. W. Gilgen (Eds.), *International symposium informatics for environmental protection* (Vol. 30) (pp. 505-512). Metropolis, Zurich, Switzerland.

Nodine, M. H., Fowler, J., Ksiezyk, T., Perry, B., Taylor, M., & Unruh, A. (2000). Active information gathering in InfoSleuth. *International Journal of Cooperative Information Systems, 9*(1-2), 3-28.

OGC (1994). The open geospatial consortium. Retrieved February 18, 2007, from http://www.opengeospatial.org

Pitts, G., & Fowler, J. (2001). InfoSleuth: An emerging technology for sharing distributed environmental information. *Information systems and the environment* (pp. 159-172). National Academy Press.

Purvis, M., Cranefield, S., Ward, R., Nowostawski, M., Carter, D., & Bush, G. (2003). A multi-agent system for the integration of distributed environmental information. *Environmental Modelling & Software, 18*, 565-572.

VEGBANK (2006). The vegetation plot database of the Ecological Society of America. Retrieved February 18, 2007, from www.vegbank.org

Chapter XVI
Using VO Concept for Managing Dynamic Security Associations

Yuri Demchenko
University of Amsterdam, The Netherlands

ABSTRACT

This chapter discusses how the virtual organisation (VO) concept can be used for managing dynamic security associations in collaborative applications and for complex resource provisioning as possible components of the agent-based virtual enterprises. The chapter provides an overview of the current practice in VO management at the organizational level and its support at the security middleware level. It identifies open issues and basic requirements to the VO security functionality and services and suggests possible directions of further research and development, in particular, VO management concept, VO security services operation, and basic VO operational models. The author hopes that understanding the VO concept and current practice in Grid of using VO for managing security associations will help developers effectively use Gird technologies and middleware for building distributed security infrastructure for virtual enterprises.

INTRODUCTION

Business and production/enterprise virtualization is a vital need and a condition for competitiveness in modern world. The advantages of the virtual enterprises (VE) include (Alexakis, Koelmel, & Heep, 2004): increased flexibility, broader scope of products, participation in wider nomenclature of orders, access to external knowledge and involv-ing remote experts and specialists, cost reduction and flexible planning, international presence and faster partners search.

Using multi-agent systems (MAS) for VE was always a topic for industry oriented and scientific research. This allowed a few MAS platforms to be developed that are capable to model some of prospective VE processes and infrastructural components. But until now, MAS remain rather narrowly focussed and close technologies using specific operational environment. MAS security model remains client-server based that maintains security context between communicating hosts/systems, in contrary to service-oriented and document-based security model used in grid and Web services that can provide end-to-end security and better mobility.

At the same time, needs of the highly technological industry were strong driving force for rapid developments of the collaborative technologies that intended to solve the same problem of the high-tech workforce mobility, unique equipment and expertise access and sharing. Traditional collaborative technologies are developing in the direction of adopting more dynamics and architectural openness to reduce implementation and deployment time. Grid and Web services provide a good platform for interoperability and also standard framework for security middleware infrastructure.

Multi-agent systems are seen as a natural way to develop in the direction of autonomous intellectual systems that can be easily integrated into the VE environment.

However, such important components of the distributed collaborative infrastructure, such as security association management, still remain unsolved for the dynamic virtualized environment. Currently, even companies widely using virtual laboratories (VL) as a collaborative environment between cooperative members still rely on the traditional enterprise identity management systems.

Virtual organizations (VO) as a concept was initially introduced and currently being developed in the grid community. It is evolving currently from the specifically project oriented to more general mean for managing dynamic security associations of users and resources. There are few works focused on the VO conceptual (Demchenko, 2004; Demchenko, Gommans, de Laat, Steenbakkers, Ciaschini, & Venturi, 2006) and technology issues (Ciaschini, 2006). Most of the

VO related developments are originated from the large grid infrastructure projects where the VO membership attributes are used for the VO related authorization. In general, grid applications provide quite a strong experience and a good example of how the VO can be used in (worldwide) distributed collaborative infrastructure. VO management support is a component of the grid infrastructure and currently available in the grid middleware. But actually the VO concept and real practice remains unknown and quite new outside of the grid community.

On other hand, there are few works that are evaluating current VE experience and looking into using the VO concept for building highly dynamic VE infrastructure and environment (Marik & Pechoucek, 2004; Marik & Pechoucek, 2004a).

The goal of this work is to provide extended information about current state of art and current practice in using the VO in grid based applications. This should provide an initial reference basis for considering VO use in VE and MAS applications. The chapter itself intends to contribute to further development of the VO conceptual model and its application to typical collaborative applications and complex resource provisioning in open service oriented environment.

The proposed approach and solutions are based on current experience in the two major grid infrastructure projects Enabling Grid for E-sciencE (EGEE) (EGEE, 2006). The analysis and proposed conceptual model can also be used for other use cases that require creation of dynamic security association or interorganizational trust management and may also provide a basis for further development of the VO management services and tools. Implementation suggestions are given for complex resource provisioning (CRP) and open collaborative environment (OCE) (Demchenko, Gommans, de Laat, Oudenaarde, Tokmakoff, & Snijders, 2005) and potentially can be used for virtual enterprise that are built using grid and Web services.

USE CASE FOR THE VIRTUAL ORGANIZATION

VO and Grids

Virtual organization (VO) and resource virtualization are among the key concepts proposed in the grid. According to the initial definition in one of the grid foundational papers the "Anatomy of the Grid (Foster, Kesselman, & Tuecke, 2001), grid systems and applications aim to integrate, virtualise, and manage resources and services within distributed, heterogeneous, dynamic 'virtual organizations' ".

The more detailed grid definition includes such main components as distributed infrastructure, dynamics, virtualization, and user-defined security—the components that provide a framework for coordinated collaborative resource sharing in dynamic, multi-institutional virtual organizations (Foster, Kesselman, Nick, & Tuecke, 2002; Foster et al., 2006).

Resources and services virtualization together with provisioning are two major concepts in the open grid services architecture (OGSA) (OGSA, 2006). OGSA security is built around VO concept and targeted for the security policies enforcement within a VO as an association of users and resources. VO provides a framework for interorganizational and interdomain *trust managements*. VO allows overcoming the problem of accessing by external users the enterprise/provider internal network without affecting integrity of enterprise security perimeter protected by the firewall. VO may run its own security services, for example, credential validation service, trust service, authorisation service and attributes service but still many other services will remain in member domains and their authority needs to be translated into VO domain through established trust relations and shared semantics.

Although presenting a basic approach to understanding security services interaction in virtualized grid environment, the VO definition in OGSA needs to be extended with the more conceptual model and basic operational models describing such typical use cases like project based collaboration, members' resource sharing or dynamic provisioning of complex multidomain distributed resources in general. At least, those VO operational models should describe existing and prospective use cases.

Current VO concept and existing practice lack a common theoretical foundation and as a result cause different understand of the VO concept and functionality by different groups of potential adopters and users. In particular, the OGSA's vision of the VO and virtualization is not provided with more detailed description of the VO functionality and operation required to support services and resources virtualization and dynamic provisioning.

The following issues with the VO conceptual definition and current rather narrow practice in grid projects remain controversial:

- Virtualization and how it's related to dynamics
- **Dynamics:** Current VO model well suited for creating dynamic security associations
- **Trust management:** With the potentially dynamic nature of the VO, how the trust inside VO and between member organizations are maintained
- **Setup and configuration:** What are foundational components for the VO creation and deployment given the current VO management practice is not automated and human driven, first of all in negotiating and signing agreement and configuring trust infrastructure.

The VO conceptual model and its application to typical collaborative applications and complex resource provisioning in open service-oriented environment discussed in this research intends to clarify some the mentioned controversial issues based on the generic VO definition as mechanism of creating dynamic security association and currently available experience in major grid projects.

Collaboration and Complex Resource Provisioning and Required VO Functionality

Basic VO security services and functionality discussed in this section are defined based on two major use cases that benefit from using basic grid middleware services and infrastructure: access to complex experimental equipment in open collaborative environment and optical light path provisioning as an example of the general complex resource provisioning.

Effective use of advanced and unique experimental equipment for research and for production work requires complex infrastructure and the involvement/collaboration of many specialists that may be distributed and span multiple organizations. Computer grids and Web services technologies provide a relevant platform for building a virtual collaborative environment.

Typical OCE use cases requires that the collaborative environment:

- Is dynamic since the environment can potentially change from one experiment to another
- May span multiple trust domains
- Can handle different user identities and attributes/privileges that must comply with different policies (both experiment and task specific)

Security services are an important component of grid-based collaborative infrastructure to provide a reliable and secure operational environment that is capable of managing customers' and providers' resources. Collaborative applications require a sophisticated, multidimensional security infrastructure that manages secure operation of

user applications between multiple administrative and trust domains associated with the particular experiment.

Proposed in (Demchenko et al., 2005) the Job-centric security model uses the Job description as a semantic document, created on the basis of a signed order (or business agreement). The document contains all the information required to run the analysis, including the job ID, assigned users and roles, and a trust/security anchor(s) in the form of the resource and additionally the customer's digital signature. In general, such approach allows binding security services and policies to a particular job and/or resource and provides customer-controlled security environment with the root of trust defined by a user/subject (i.e., their identity or private key).

Job-centric security model is logically integrated with other stages and components of the collaborative (virtual) organization managing the experiment stages. These stages include the initial stage of order creation and the main experimental stage that requires secure access to the instrument or resource.

OLPP is another important component of the distributed collaborative environment when a dedicated high-speed communication channels are required for the experiment that may last from few hours to few months. OLPP provides a good business model with current widely deployed optical network and dark optical cables. Further in the chapter, the OLPP use case will be referred to as a complex resource provisioning as a more general definition.

OLPP and complex resource provisioning in general require creation of dynamic user-controlled resource allocation that may span multiple administrative and security domains. In comparison to the job-centric OCE security model where trust relations and consequently security associations are defined by an agreement or job, in OLPP user/customer may have agreement or business and consequently trust relations with only one, usually home, network provider. However, the provisional model must ensure that finally provisioned lightpath/resource is securely associated with the user credentials of trust domain.

Typically provisioning process comprises of four steps: resource lookup, complex resource composition (including options), reservation of individual resources and their association with the reservation ID/ticket and finally provisioning/delivery. Reservation ID/ticket created at the reservation stage actually defines a security association between user/customer and service provider(s) that will exist for all periods when the complex resource is used/consumed. It is logical to suggest that the (dynamic) VO model can be used here for creation and managing dynamic security association.

In both cases, the VO model and framework are suggested as a relevant approach to provide the following security functionality for the dynamic collaboration and provisioning:

1. **Dynamic trust management:** VO as a security association created dynamically at the reservation/negotiation stage will provide a security context for other security operations such as Authentication (AuthN) and Authorisation (AuthZ) and also for general session management.
2. **Attributes and metadata resolution and mapping:** Correct policy evaluation and combination in multidomain scenario requires either use of common attributes and metadata format and namespace or mapping between used formats and namespaces. Actual attribute and metadata mapping can be provided by authoritative/trusted identity providers (IdP) and/or attribute authority (AA) services belonging to the VO or VO trust domain.
3. **Policy combination and aggregation:** VO can provide a framework for the multiple policies combination that may be defined and managed by the VO common or federated/associated policy. This may be especially

important when individual policies may have conflicts at different levels and in different domains; in this case the VO association policy should defined how these conflicts can be resolved.

VIRTUAL ORGANIZATIONS IN GRID APPLICATIONS: CURRENT PRACTICE

Virtualization and Virtual Organizations in Grid

Resources and services virtualization together with provisioning, are two key concepts in grid and OGSA (OGSA, 2006). OGSA Security is built around virtual organization (VO) concept and targeted for the enforcement of the security policies within a VO as an association of users and resources. VO provides a framework for inter-organizational and inter-domain trust managements. VO allows to overcome the problem of accessing by external users the enterprise/provider internal network protected by firewall without affecting integrity of enterprise security perimeter protected by the firewall.

Figure 1 illustrates the conceptual model for VO security services and their interaction with VO members' security services. VO may run its own security services, for example, credential validation service, trust service, authorization service and attributes service as shown in Figure 1. But still many other services will remain in member domains and their authority needs to be translated into VO domain through established trust relations and shared/translated semantics.

Although presenting basic approach to understanding security services interaction in virtualized a grid environment, the model in Figure 1 needs to be extended with basic operational models describing such use cases like project based collaboration, members' resource sharing or OLPP (or dynamic provisioning of complex multidomain

Figure 1. Security services in a virtual organization setting (OGSA, 2006)

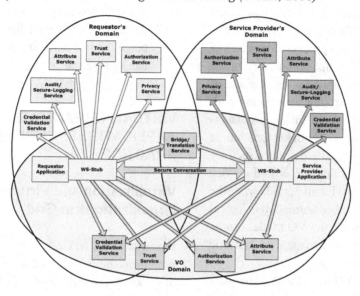

distributed resources in general). At least, those VO operational models should describe existing and prospective use cases. Such attempt is undertaken in the section 4: Conceptual VO model and basic operational models.

The Virtual Organization Membership Service (VOMS)

The Virtual Organization Membership Service (VOMS) has been developed in the framework of EU project EDG and DataTAG and is currently being developed in the framework of the EGEE project (Ciaschini, Venturi, & Cecanti, 2006; VOMS, 2006). VOMS goal is to solve the problems of granting users authorization to access the resources at VO level, providing support for group membership, roles and capabilities.

In VOMS design, a VO is represented as a complex, hierarchical structure with groups and subgroups (Ciaschini et al., 2006) what is required

to clearly separate VO users according to their tasks and home institutions. From an administrative point of view, the management of each group can be independently delegated to different administrators. The administrators of each group can create subgroups and grant administration rights to these subgroups; they cannot modify memberships in any other subgroup. A group is basically a set of users, which may also contain other groups. In general a user can be a member of any number of groups contained in the VO hierarchy.

Every user in a VO is characterized by the set of his attributes defining their group membership, roles and capabilities in the scope of the VO that can be expressed in a form of 3-tuples (group, role, capability). The combination of all 3-tuple values forms unique attribute, the so-called "fully qualified attribute name" (FQAN). In general an FQAN has the following form (Ciaschini, Venturi, & Cecanti, 2006a):

Figure 2. VOMS system architecture

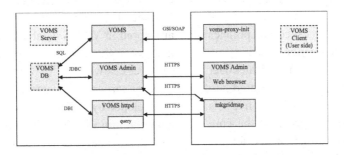

/VO[/group[/subgroup(s)]]][/Role=role][/Capability=cap]

For example, the FQAN corresponding to the role of administrator in the group "Nerds" of the VO campus.example.org is:

/c a m p u s . e x a m p l e . o r g / N e r d s / Role=Administrator

The VOMS system consists of the following parts (see Figure 2) (VOMS, 2006):

- **User server:** Receives requests from client and returns information about the user
- **User client:** Contacts the server presenting a user's certificate and obtains a list of groups, roles and capabilities of the user
- **Administration client:** Used by VO administrator to add users, create new groups, change roles
- **Administration server:** Accept the request from the admin client and updates the database

In grid user or service request authorisation is based on user VO credentials or attributes that are defined by the VOMS attribute certificate. In the basic scenario, user obtains VOMS certificate via user client, which is embed it into their proxy certificate (ProxyCert) (RFC 3820, 2004)

and sends it together with the service request to the grid service or resource where it is used for user authorization. The procedure includes the following steps (see Figure 3):

1. The user and the VOMS server authenticate each other using their certificates (via the standard Globus API).
2. The user sends a signed request to the VOMS Server.
3. The VOMS server verifies the user's identity and checks the syntactic correctness of the request.
4. The VOMS server sends back to the user the required information (signed by itself);
5. The user checks the validity of the information received.
6. The user optionally repeats this process for other VOMS's to collect membership information in other VO's.
7. The user creates the proxy certificate containing all the information received from the VOMS server in a (noncritical) extension.
8. The user may add user-supplied authentication information (e.g., Kerberos tickets).

VOMS server returns user X.509 attribute certificate (AC) that contains information about user VO and optionally about user group and role (Ciaschini et al., 2006). Future version of VOMS server is claimed to support SAML attribute assertion format. At the resource, the authorization information provided by VOMS needs to be extracted from the user's proxy certificate and evaluated against the local access control policies in order to make the authorization decision.

The administration server communicates over SOAP protocol and can be easily integrated into WS-based Globus Toolkit. It consists of five sets of routines grouped into services: (1) the core which provides the basic functionality for the clients; (2) the admin which provides the methods to administrate the VOMS database; (3) the history which provides the logging and auditing functionality (the database scheme provides full audit records for every changes); (4) the request which provides an integrated request handling mechanism for new users and for other changes; and (5) the compatibility, which provides a simple access to the user list for the mkgridmap utility. Two administrative interfaces (Web and command line) are available.

VOMS infrastructure suggests that VO may have few VOMS servers with synchronized membership databases, however one VOMS server can serve multiple VO's. Central/main member-

ship database is maintained by a VO and must contain information/attributes for all registered VO members. Currently, only user attributes are stored in VOMS database. There is ongoing discussion about providing VO credentials to the resources as well.

User server and clients (core VOMS system) is developed by INFN, administration server and client (admin interface) is developed at CERN. VOMS is available as open source software under EGEE license.

Privacy Enhanced VO Attributes Management with GridShib Profile

GridShib is an NSF middleware initiative (NMI) project that intends to integrate GT/grid security infrastructure and Shibboleth to form a robust attribute infrastructure for campus environments to enable secure verification of user attributes for interinstitutional grid users (GridShib, 2006). This project will deliver over 2005-2006, a framework that allows participants in multiorganizational collaborations to control the attribute information that they want to publish, share and reveal

Figure 3. Interaction between VOMS server and user client when obtaining VOMS attribute certificate that is further presented in the service request by user

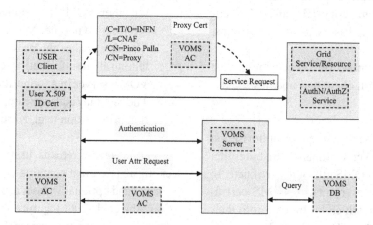

to other parties according to common attribute release policy. Pseudonymous interactions will be supported through the use of anonymous public key credentials that are mapped to the client's identity at the client's own discretion.

The project substantially leverages on, and extends existing technologies, primarily Internet2's Shibboleth and the Globus Alliance's Globus Toolkit (GT4) (GT4, 2006) and MyProxy (MyProxy Online Credential Repository, 2006) based GridLogon service. The framework will use Shibboleth attribute authority service (SAAS) (Shibboleth Project, 2006) and its attribute release policies to restrict the attributes communicated to other parties. GridShib will enable Web services access to Shibboleth services by using GT4 application integration tools. To enable pseudonymous deployment, a module will be developed for the GridLogon service to allow authenticated users to obtain public key credentials that do not reveal their identity, yet are fully compatible with the Grid Security Infrastructure. Formats and protocols will be developed and implemented to express, publish, share and match attribute-related policies and capabilities.

In summary, GridShib will produce a Shibboleth implementation for nonWeb-based applications, so-called GridShib profile. GT4 and Shibboleth integration will be based on Shibboleth attributes management/access model and will focus on the following attributes handling/providing/requesting models:

1. Basic Globus-Shibboleth integration without anonymity using attributes requested/pulled by the resource from the trusted SAAS
2. Basic Globus-Shibboleth integration without anonymity using attributes provided by the requestor which are previously obtained from the trusted SAAS
3. Globus-Shibboleth integration with anonymity and attributes requested by the resource from the trusted SAAS that is can release attributes based on user pseudonym or authentication confirmation credentials.

4. Globus-Shibboleth integration with anonymity using attributes provided by the requestor which are previously obtained from the trusted SAAS for the user pseudonym or anonymous authentication confirmation credentials (Authentication/identity token)

Interaction between the Shibboleth enabled client and the resource in the GridShib profile will consists of four major steps:

1. The Grid Client POSTs a SOAP request to the Grid service together with user credential in the form of user ProxyCert.
2. The Grid service, if user authentication is passed, POSTs a SAML SOAP message to the attribute authority (AA) at the identity provider (IdP). Information about AA may be included by the requestor into its proxy credential, or the service may use preconfigured list of trusted AA's.
3. The AA returns an attribute assertion to the grid dervice based on provided user identity (both real and pseudonymous providing identity mapping if necessary).
4. The Grid service performs request evaluation based on received attributes and access control policy and proceeds with the requested operation and returns a response to the Grid client.

It is essential that the described attribute-based authorization scenario require an initial security configuration that includes:

1. The grid user and the grid service each possess an X.509 credential that uniquely identifies them.
2. The grid user is enrolled with a Shibboleth identity provider (IdP), and correspondently with IdP's AA.
3. The IdP is able to map the grid user's X.509 subject DN to one and only one user in its security domain.

4. The IdP and the grid service each have been assigned a unique identifier called a providerID.

5. The grid client application has access to the grid user's X.509 certificate and the IdP providerID. This information is used to create proxy cert that will contain IdP providerID and signed by the user private key.

6. The grid service has a set of certificates identifying IdP/AAs that it trusts to provide attributes suitable for use in authorization decisions.

7. The grid service and the IdP rely on the same metadata format and exchange this metadata out-of-band.

8. It is assumed that all X.509 end-entity certificates (EEC) issued by CAs are trusted by all parties mentioned in this document.

VO Management in the EGEE Project

Current VO management practice in the EGEE Project provides a good example of the instant implementation of the VO concept, which is however project based and project oriented. They have well-defined VO registration procedure, basic Security Policy, and simple acceptable use policy. major VO membership management tool is VOMS which supports user registration procedure with the VOMS Admin server automated workflow.

The following documents define VO management framework in EGEE:

Virtual organization registration procedure (Dimou & Neilson, 2006) lists the necessary steps a virtual organization (VO) should take in order to get registered, configured and integrated in the EGEE infrastructure. Before following this procedure, the VO managers should follow the instructions of the virtual organization security plicy document and prepare their VO acceptable use policy (AUP).

Note: The complete life-cycle of a VO, including its wrap-up procedure, is not discussed in this document. The operational responsibilities during the life of the VO, for example, regular membership expiration and re-registration, nonreplication of personal user data across sites and so forth are defined in the user registration and virtual organisation membership management requirements document (Dimou, 2004).

EGEE virtual organisation security policy (Neilson, 2006) defines a set of responsibilities placed on the members of the VO and the VO as a whole through its managers. It aims to ensure that all grid participants have sufficient information to properly fulfil their roles with respect to interactions with a Virtual Organization (VO).

VO acceptable use policy (AUP) (UAP, 2006) is a statement which, by clearly describing the goals of the VO, defines the expected and acceptable usage of the grid by the members of the VO. By requiring that all members of the VO who participate in the grid agree to act within the constraints of the VO AUP the VO manager defines a community of responsible users with a common goal. This definition enables Site Managers to decide whether to allow VO members to use their resources.

Several decisions and steps need to be taken in the process of a VO creation and registration:

1. **Naming the VO:** Recommended VO naming style suggests that VO name should resemble project and/or team. It also includes appropriate DNS host aliases (or even dedicated domain name) and host certificates, when necessary, in order to prepare a properly managed system environment for VO-related data, scripts, Web pages and transactions.

2. **Request VO integration into existing EGEE infrastructure** from the designated project body such as EGEE generic applications advisory panel (EGAAP). During the request processing EGAAP will estimate required resources (computing power and load, storage size, etc.) and propose possible VO applications hosting and resources allocation between candidate hosting sites and grid regional centers (RC) and also fix requirement to RC to participate in the VO. As a result of this stage (but not limited to) a VO manager is appointed and a core infrastructure centre (CIC) appointed to provide VO user management service to the new VO.

3. **Setting-up a VO:** The VO management selects a site where to run the VO database (VODB) server and the registration service/database (where the acceptance of the grid usage rules by the user is registered). There can be few options for particular implementations of the VO services.

4. **Populating a VO:** Candidate entries in the VODB are passed through successful registration process and Registration database additions. Suggested mechanisms to bootstrap and update a VODB depends on the selected technology and may be use LDAP based solution or integrated Registration and VODB solution based on VOMS

5. **Integrating VO into existing infrastructure:** As soon as a VO is configured, the VODB contents must be propagated to the grid sites in order to be matched to the users' credentials at job submission time. This is done currently with the grid-map file or LCMAPS that reside on resource side and are supported by RC mapping system. In addition to the VO Registration server and VODB, two other grid infrastructure components must be VO-aware: A resource broker service, that is at least a resource broker (RB) and its associated BDII, and

a replica manager service, that is a replica manager (RM) and a replica catalog.

6. **Organising support structure for the VO:** This requires designated group of people to manage VO procedures both registration and user support, including VO-wide security Incident response. A VO support manager is responsible for building this structure and becomes a member of the EGEE support task force.

There are many different valid options for some of these steps. They depend on many parameters like the technology (LDAP or VOMS) and the location where the VO database (VODB) resides.

Summary on VO Functionality for Complex Resource Provisioning

Current VO concept and existing practice lack a common theoretical foundation and as a result cause different understand of the VO concept and functionality by different groups of potential adopters and users. The following can be considered as a reason of this confusion and misunderstanding:

- OGSA's vision of the VO and virtualization is not supported by more detailed description of the VO functionality and operation
  ○ First of these confusions is relations between virtualisation and VO which presumably could be resolved with the definition of the VO management functionality including VO foundation/agreement and life cycle
  ○ Second issue to be clarified is relation between VO and dynamic associations: which part of the VO concept is static (like PKI certification authority CA/PMA and attribute authority) and which can support dynamic associations (and dynamic trust management).

- Current VO implementation in EGEE needs more conceptual/higher-level definition to be aligned with (yet to be developed) OGSA VO concept.
  - ○ There is still no clear definition of the VO Agreement and VO policy in EGEE. Current use of the VO is directly associated with two projects, and therefore VO is managed under the project administration. (Using in this case generic word VO adds to the confusion around VO concept itself).

The following issues should be taken into account when considering VO use for dynamic resource provisioning:

- VO setup is a complex long-time procedure; therefore VO cannot be used in first row for the global ad-hoc dynamic trust establishment.
- VO management and VOMS infrastructure is rather designed for long-term collaborative projects. However, VOMS provides all necessary functionality for creating ad-hoc dynamic VO association. The issue remains how to consistently manage trust and authority in such a dynamic VO. One of possible solution is to combine/add attribute management functionality being developed in the framework of Internet2 Grouper and Signet projects that are specially oriented to support user attribute management in SAAS (Shibboleth, 2006). This is in addition to suggested use of the GridShib profile for SAAS integration into the VO management.
- VOMS server attribute certificate is based on X.509 AC for authorisation and currently well defined. However, its use for grid authorisation (e.g., with the GT4 AuthZ service) suggests using proxy certificate.

- VOMS client-server protocol is not clearly defined. Formalization of the VOMS client-server protocol will facilitate wider VOMS adoption and better understanding
- Current VOMS implementation do not have flexible attribute namespace management (and corresponding procedure and policy)
- VOMS requires user ID and therefore does not provide (user) controlled privacy protection (in contrary to Shibboleth).
  - ○ It is expected that currently being developed GridShib profiles will provide a framework for combing well-developed Shibboleth attribute management solutions and VOMS functionality, currently a standard-de-facto for VO management in grid.
- There is an obvious benefit in interoperability between VOMS and SAAS and presumably will be achieved with the GridShib profile, which targets for providing SAAS integration into Grid/GT environment/infrastructure. Although VOMS and SAAS both serve as Attribute Authorities, there are minor differences in their operation on the user/client and service/resource sides:
  - ○ In VOMS the user first needs to obtain VOMS AC by requesting particular VOMS server, and next include it into newly generated proxy cert and send request to the service
  - ○ In SAAS the user sends request to the Shib-aware service and it may include a particular IdP reference, otherwise service will poll trusted AA/IdP's based on preconfigured list of trusted providers.
- Existing EGEE VO registration procedure allows actually using DNSSEC (RFC4034, 2005) for populating VO together with its (secondary) public key that can be used for initial trusted introduction of the VO and secure session request by the requestor.

Note: DNSSEC has limited space for putting the key information because of DNS/DNSSEC response message allows only one nonfragmented package of size 1220 bytes for standard DNS message and 4000 bytes for special DNSSEC extension (RFC4035, 2005). Note: In DNSSEC, it is suggested that domain's (in our case VO's) record and key is signed by upper layer domain's key, and therefore DNSSEC trust tree must be compatible with the application oriented trust domain.

CONCEPTUAL VO MODEL

VO and Dynamic Security Associations

This section attempts to review current VO concept and provide multilevel approach and model to understand how the VO as an abstract concept and as a practical implementation can be used for federated and/or dynamic trust management. In other words, we will discuss relations between VO and dynamic associations: which part of the VO organization and operation is static (like CA/PMA and AttrAuth) and which can support dynamic associations (and dynamic trust management).

First of all, we need to clarify one widely used misunderstanding between VO as virtual entity, and dynamic processes and associations. To do it consistently, we need to look at different types of security associations and their dynamics (or lifetime characteristics). In relation to this we can build the following list:

- **Session:** This establishes security context in the form of session key that can be a security token or simple UID bound to secure credential or session ticket. The session may associate/federate users, resources and actions/processes.

- **Job/workflow:** This may be a more long-lived association and include only a few sessions. Job or workflow is built around a specific task that is defined either by contract to perform some work or deliver product, or business process unit that also deliver some service and provides orchestration of many other processes. They may need to associate a more distributed collection of users and resources for longer time required to deliver a final product or service. Job and workflow may contain decision points that switch alternatively between flows and processes. Security context may change during workflow execution or Job lifetime. Job description, as it is used in the Job-centric security model (8), may contain both user and resource lists, and also provide trust anchor(s) (TA) and security policy. Job TA is derived from the requestor and the service trust relations established on the base of the contract to perform some job. Workflow TA can be implicitly derived from the parent process.

- **Project or mission oriented cooperation:** This type of association is established for long-time cooperation (involving people and resources) to do some research, development or production but it still has some well-defined goals and area of activity and often criteria of mission fulfilment. This is actually the area of currently existing VO associations.

- **Interorganizational association or federation:** This type of association is built on long-term (often indefinite) cooperation agreements and may have a wide scope of cooperative areas. This is the area of interuniversity associations which examples include InCommon or InQueue, and Shibboleth (18) is especially designed to support this kind of federations.

Comparing two last types of associations, we can suggest that for the VO type of federation the central/single membership service is typical and essential. However, its implementation can be either centralized like in VOMS or distributed like it is intended in the GridShib profile.

Proposed in the aforementioned classification, allows us to assume that all identified types of associations will have its place and use in the future responding to different goals and tasks. Another suggestion that can be done from the earlier discussion in the context of user-controlled service provisioning (UCSP) is that job-centric/VO-based associations may scale to each other and consequently use each other's technical infrastructure and tools by adopting the dynamics to their specific tasks.

Now we will try to identify possible VO operational models depending on more detailed analysis of the major service provisioning use cases. Introducing VO concept/functionality into dynamic service provisioning will bring flexibility to the problem of dynamic trust management

When considering the use of VO for trust and attributes management, we should refer to the conclusion made in the VO overview section (section 3.5) that VO creation is quite a complicated and bureaucratic/formal procedure. VO creation is normally initiated by one organizational or business/project entity and has a specific goal and mission. VO can be created for the project-based collaboration, members' resource sharing or dynamic provisioning of complex multidomain distributed resources in general. VO concept can be also used for general-purpose user association.

VO attribute or membership service is used for trusted attributes brokering between (member) organizations when requesting resources or services from the VO members or their associates. However, VO operation will differ depending on what are the VO associated members and how the VO membership service is used in VO related activities or services.

In this context three basic and one additional VO operational models can be defined:

- User-centric VO (VO-U) that manages user federation and provide attribute assertions on user (client) request
- Resource/Provider centric VO (VO-R) that supports provider federation and allows SSO/access control decision sharing between resource providers
- Agent centric VO (VO-A) that provides a context for interdomain agents operation, which process a request on behalf of the user and provide required trust context to interaction with the resource or service
- Project centric VO (VO-G) that combines user centric and provider centric features what actually corresponds to current VO use in grid projects

This classification helps to understand how major security services operate in each of the different types of VO.

User-centric VO-U manages user federation and provides attribute assertions on user (client) request. For this purpose, VO-U maintains VOMS or user Attribute Authority that receives requests from user clients and provides VO member attribute certificates or other type of attribute assertion. VOMS/AA can also validate user credentials on request from services. However, this is the user who presents attribute credentials to the service in order to obtain access control permission. In this sense, VO-U actually implements pull model for the access control decision. VO Attribute service is the central service for this type of VO. This can be considered as current operational model for the VOMS in grid application. GridShib profile will allow decentralisation of attributes management.

Resource/Provider centric VO-R supports provider federation and allows SSO and access control decision sharing between VO members, that is, resource providers. In this respect, VO-R may run own VO-wide AuthN and AuthZ services and correspondently VO-wide access control policy. It is logical that all services in the VO-R association can accept the VO AuthZ service decision once issued for the user on their request. If the user wants to access multiple services in the VO-R the user can use obtained access granting ticket as a SSO credential, however services may need to validate presented credentials/ticket with the VO AuthZ and AuthZ services.

Agent centric VO-A provides a context for interdomain agent operation. In this model/profile agent acts as a representative and a broker of the trust and other services for the specific domain. Agents are considered more independent in the VO-A than users or providers in other models VO-U and VO-R. Agents may have central attribute or certificate service but in more specific for the VO-A model case they will maintain mutual trust relations (which initial establishment for a time being is out of scope for this study).

Project centric VO-G (as originated from a grid projects) can be introduced to reflect typical use case when a VO is established to support user cooperation in the framework of the long-running project and to overcome existing/legacy organizational boundaries. VO-G associates both users and resources, and actually combines two identified earlier models VO-U and VO-R. It maintains central VO membership/attribute service and may run also VO-wide security services such as AuthN/IdP/SSO and AuthZ.

There may not be a clear difference in real life VO implementations and to which operational model they adhere, but proposed abstraction will help to more flexibly design supporting security services. For example, it can be suggested that current VOMS based VO in Grid will evolve from currently used VO-U model to a more appropriate VO-G model.

One open issue that should be resolved by practice in ongoing implementations is to which operational model we should ascribe a resource/service attributes assignment/management if we need to provide mutual user/requestor and resource/service AuthN or AuthZ.

The major motivation behind defining basic VO operation models is to define possible profiles for the VO security services as well as suggested gateway services to interact with different/external security models.

Benefit of using VO based trust and attribute managing/brokering is that VO can be created and used as a dynamic association for wide range of duration given the VO as a concept that can potentially combine virtualization and dynamic.

What was proposed in earlier classification and definitions could also help in achieving better understanding between grid-originated customers and traditional infrastructure providers (in particular, network/OLP providers) in situations when attempting to match their traditional operational security models. For example, a grid customer comes to network/LP provider on behalf of the VO and wants to order LP connectivity on-demand. The question for the customer is how it can present its VOMS credential normally used inside VO to the external service; the question for the provider is how it must handle VOMS credentials to consistently adhere to its corporate security model and policy.

VO Management Framework

Virtual organization is defined in OGSA as a key concept for operation and managing grid services (Foster et al., 2006). VO supplies a context to associate users, resources, policies and agreements when making and processing requests for services related to a particular VO.

VO management service should provide the following functionality (Demchenko et al., 2006; Foster et al., 2006): (a) registration and association of users and groups with the VO; (b) management of user roles; (c) association of services with the VO; (d) associating agreements and policies with the VO and its component services.

Implementing and using VO concept requires a mechanism to reference the VO context and associate it with the user request. VO membership service establishes and manages relationship of entities to the VO. These entities can be users, groups, other VO's or grid resources. VO creation is initiated by establishing agreement between VO members that, among others, may include service providers and customers. In this way VO follows the same procedure as a real organization and in case of business-oriented VO, this stage may require relevant legal basis for establishing and operating such a VO. WS-Agreement (WS-Agreement, 2004), WS-Trust (WS-Trust, 2005), WS-Policy (WS-Policy, 2006), and WS-Federation (WS-Federation, 2003) can provide the initial technological platform for dynamic VO creation.

VO membership service (VOMS*) is supported by the VO Database (VODB) that contains authoritative information about the entities and services associate with the VO, or VO's associated with the particular entity or user, and may also contain or reference user credentials and other related information. Although VO reference can be included into the request by the requestor, processing of the request may require obtaining authoritative information from the VOMS*. VOMS* should support different queries on any VO attribute or component, and also provide propagations of digest information between other VOMS*.

In order to securely process requests that traverse between members of a VO, it is necessary for the member organizations to have established trust relations. These trust relations may be direct or mutual, or established via intermediaries like VO trust management service.

In wider VO and grid infrastructure there may be a need to establish a VO registry service that will provide a VO reference/ID registration and resolution and can also keep VOMS public credentials. Current EGEE VO naming and registration procedure actually allows using

DNSSEC (RFC4034, 2005) for populating VO together with its public key that can be used for initial trusted introduction of the VO and secure session request by the requestor.

VO Security Services and Operation

VO can be established according to a well-defined procedure and based on common agreement between member organizations to commit their resources to the VO and adhere common policy that may be simple enough but not to contradict to the local security policies at member institutions. VO security policy cannot be more restricted than the local policies. This means that if some specific enforcement is required by a specific VO, it should be also supported by local policies. Otherwise VO should provide direct individual membership for users which home organization (HO) credentials cannot be used or not trusted.

VO establishes its own virtual administrative and security domains that may be completely separate, or simply bridge VO members' security domains. This is required to enable secure service invocations across VO security domain but also requires coordination with the security policies in member organizations.

The following security services and related functionalities are required for VO:

1. Identity Management Service, normally provided by the identity provider (IdP) and may also include Identity Federation service that provides federated identity assertions for users or resources, including pseudonymous services as a particular case.
2. Attribute authority (like VOMS) that issues attributes bound to user or resource identity that primary can be used for authorization decision when accessing VO resources or services.
3. Authorization service to enforce access control to the resource or service based on

entity's attributes/roles and authorisation policies

4. Policy authority to provide VO-wide policies related to authorization, trust management, identity federation, mapping of identities, attributes and policies

5. Trust management service that may include CA and associate PKI management services, and Security Token Services as defined by WS-trust; VO Agreement provides initial base for building trust relation inside VO

VO can also have other services, which are important for it's functioning such as logging, accounting, auditing/nonrepudiation and so forth. Physically, all VO services may be provided by member organizations on behalf of the VO and be distributed.

VO is normally created for a specific task, which however may be long lived. A VO life-cycle includes stages of creation, operation and termination. Initial stage of VO forming, after its establishing, also includes the following steps:

1. Establishing VO trust domain that defines trust relationships between VO members
   o VO Agreement provides initial basis for the trust relations between VO members
   o VO trust domain may be established on the base of PKI; two options are possible: VO can establish root cer-tifications authority (VO-rootCA) to maintain hierarchical trust relations inside VO, or provide bridge CA (VO-bridgeCA) function/service for member CA's

2. Establishing and/or configuring VO basic services, particularly: Identity management service, authorisation service, attribute authority, policy authority. This work is normally performed by the VO administra-tor.

It is perceived that an initial VO is created by individuals or organizations (in fact, real or virtual, depending on agreement and policy) on the base of the agreement between all member organizations that also defines a set of policies that VO must adhere. The following implies:

- VO may be created as a "close" VO with explicitly defined members however with the possibility to be extendable on base of individual participation, or as an "open" VO which membership is defined by specific roles or functions. As an example, in the first case, VO creates a special task-oriented infrastructure for cooperative use of the resources and services belonging to and provided by VO members; in the second case, VO may be created for providing some service or group of services that have already established infrastructure.

- VO agreement forms VO administrative domain

- Basic VO services are created at the ini-tialization stage and may include identity management service, authorization service, attribute authority, policy authority, however all are subject to VO agreement.

- Policies will drive all further steps of form-ing VO infrastructure, including adding and resigning new members, and defining its operation.

- VO's may create hierarchical structure and create another VO's, however, first or "initial" VO still must be created by human principal or real organizations. As such ,VO foundation elements like agreements and policies are human-crafted.

- The VO administrator's role is created at the initialization stage and will have all privileges to form the initial VO structure and administer VO operation in the future. The VO administrator will use available ad-ministration tools for the particular runtime environment, of which most administrative

Figure 4. Virtual organization structure and relationship with member organizations

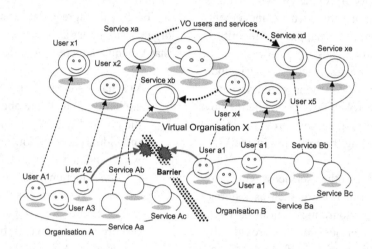

Figure 5. Interaction of the VO security services when processing a request inside VO

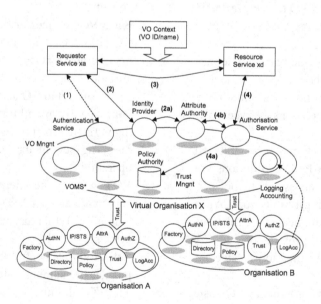

functions and interfaces are expected to be standardized in OGSA and consequently automated to be run by authorized entities.

Figure 4 illustrates relationship between virtual organization X and two member organizations, A and B, which can be either real or virtual. VO X has been created to perform some task or provide some service(s) for designated group of users that constitute VO user community. VO established its own administrative and trust domain. Some of the users of organizations A and B may become the members of the virtual organization; some of the services provided by member organizations may become VO services. Based on their VO identity or attributes, the VO users and services can interact in the trusted manner using VO security services.

Figure 5 shows basic services representing VO security infrastructure that provides reliable, secure and accountable VO operation, and illustrates in details how the request from the service xa (that actually represents service Aa from the member organization A to the service xd (representing service Bb from the member organization B is handled using VO context. To become an active entity in the VO, services or users must authenticate themselves to the VO authentication service (step 1). Then, the requestor service requests a security token from the identity service (step 2), this step may also include obtaining specific attributes for the service xd from the attribute authority (step 2a). Now the security token together with the obtained attributes may be presented to the target service xd (step 3). It is suggested that the resource will the trust security token issued by the VO's identity service, otherwise it may verify presented credentials with the identity service. Before granting or denying access, the resource may request VO authorization service to evaluate user request and presented credentials against access control policy that may be obtained from the policy authority step 4, 4a, 4b).

CONCLUSION AND SUMMARY

Information presented in this chapter is targeted both at traditional grid community and potentials users of the VO concept as a way of managing dynamic security associations in other areas, in particular MAS and VE communities.

It is important to notice that the VO is a genuine grid technology, and if grid infrastructure and applications are to be used by other applications they need to support VO based credentials and authorization.

On the other hand, MAS and VE researchers may need to recreate compatibility with the grid and the VO management infrastructure in their own operational environment using discussed here, using grid-oriented VO operational model as a basis. Using grid middleware as a platform for developing/creating problems oriented MAS and VE, will also benefit from the global grid trust management infrastructure that provides strong assurance security services.

The chapter provides an overview of current practice with the VO management at the organizational level and its support at the grid security middleware level. It identifies the open issues and basic requirements to the VO security functionality and services, and discusses possible areas of research and development, in particular, related to the VO management model, dynamic interdomain trust management for user-controlled applications, multi-domain policy decision and user attributes management.

Based on suggested VO definition as a framework for managing dynamic security associations of users and resources in service oriented environment, the chapter identifies a few basic VO operations models depending on what the VO primary goal is to associate users, resources, or agents as active business intermediaries.

The proposed conceptual VO model addresses VO management issues and VO security services operation and can be used as a conceptual basis for developing VO management tools to support required creation, management and termination of dynamic security associations. Practical implementations of the proposed VO management and security models can consider using Shibboleth attribute authority service or WS-trust security token service (STS) for managing user attributes in dynamically created VO-based security associations.

REFERENCES

Alexakis, S., Koelmel, B., & Heep, T. (2004). VO in industry: State of the art. In L.M. Camarina-Matos & H. Afsarmanesh (Eds.), *Collaborative networked organisations: A research agenda for emerging business models* (pp. 15-26). Kluwer Academic Publishers.

Ciaschini, V., et al. (2006). An integrated framework for VO-oriented authorization, policy-based management and accounting. In *Proceedings of CHEP06 - Computing in High Energy and Nuclear Physics*, Mumbai, India.

Ciaschini, V., Venturi, V., & A. Cecanti (2006). The VOMS attribute certificate format. Open Grid Forum Draft. Retrieved February 17, 2007, from http://forge.gridforum.org/sf/docman/do/downloadDocument/projects.ogsa-authz/docman.root.attributes/doc13797/2

Demchenko, Yu. (2004). Virtual organisations in computer grids and identity management. *Elsevier Information Security Technical Report, 9*(1), 59-76.

Demchenko, Y., Gommans, L., de Laat, C., Steenbakkers, M., Ciaschini, V. &, Venturi, V. (2006). VO-based dynamic security associations in collaborative grid environment. In *Proceedings of the 2006 International Symposium on Collaborative Technologies and Systems* (pp. 38-47)

Demchenko, Y., Gommans, L., de Laat, C., Oudenaarde, B., Tokmakoff, A., & Snijders,

M. (2005). Job-centric security model for open collaborative environment. In *Proceeding of the 2005 International Symposium on Collaborative Technologies and Systems* (pp. 69-77)

Dimou, M. (Ed.). (2004). *User registration and VO membership management requirements*. Retrieved February 17, 2007, from https://edms.cern.ch/document/428034

Dimou, M., & Neilson, I. (Eds.). (2006). *Virtual organisation registration procedure*. Retrieved February 17, 2007, from https://edms.cern.ch/document/503245/

Enabling Grid for E-sciencE (EGEE) Project (2006). Retrieved February 17, 2007, from http://www.eu-egee.org/

Foster, I., et al. (2006). The open grid services architecture, Version 1.5. Global Grid Forum. Retrieved February 17, 2007, from http://www.ggf.org/documents/GFD.80.pdf

Foster, I., Kesselman, C., & Tuecke, S. (2001). The anatomy of the grid: Enabling scalable virtual organizations. *International Journal of Supercomputer Applications, 15*(3), 200-222.

Foster, I., Kesselman, C., Nick, J., & Tuecke, S. (2002). *The physiology of the grid: An open grid services architecture for distributed systems integration*. Globus Project, 2002. Retrieved February 17, 2007, from http://www.globus.org/alliance/publications/papers/ogsa.pdf

Globus Toolkit Version 4.1 (GT4) (2006). Retrieved February 17, 2007, from http://www.globus.org/toolkit/

GridShib—A Policy Controlled Attribute Framework. Retrieved February 17, 2007, from http://grid.ncsa.uiuc.edu/GridShib/

LCG/EGEE Acceptable Use Policy (2006). Joint security policy group. Retrieved February 17, 2007, from https://edms.cern.ch/document/428036

Marik, V., & Pechoucek. M. (2004). Agent technologies for virtual organisation. In L.M. Camarina-Matos & H. Afsarmanesh (Ed.), *Collaborative networked organisations: A research agenda for emerging business models* (pp. 245-252). Kluwer Academic Publishers.

Marik, V., & Pechoucek. M. (2004a). Agent technology. In L.M. Camarina-Matos & H. Afsarmanesh (Eds.), *Collaborative networked organisations: A research agenda for emerging business models* (pp. 193-206). Kluwer Academic Publishers.

MyProxy Online Credential Repository. Retrieved February 17, 2007, from http://grid.ncsa.uiuc.edu/myproxy/

Neilson, I. (Ed.). (2006). *LCG/EGEE virtual organisation security policy.* Version 1.1. Retrieved February 17, 2007, from https://edms.cern.ch/document/573348/

RFC 3820 (2004). Standard track, internet X.509 public key infrastructure (PKI) proxy certificate profile. Retrieved February 17, 2007, from ftp://ftp.isi.edu/in-notes/rfc3820.txt

RFC4034 (2005). Resource records for the DNS security extensions. Retrieved February 17, 2007, from http://www.rfc-archive.org/getrfc.php?rfc=4034

RFC4035 (2005). Protocol modifications for the DNS security extensions. Retrieved February 17, 2007, from http://www.rfc-archive.org/getrfc.php?rfc=4035

Shibboleth Project (2006). Retrieved February 17, 2007, from http://shibboleth.internet2.edu/

Virtual Organization Membership Service (VOMS) (2006). Project homepage. Retrieved February 17, 2007, from http://infnforge.cnaf.infn.it/voms/

Web Services Agreement Specification (WS-Agreement) (2004). Retrieved February 17, 2007, from https://forge.gridforum.org/projects/graap-wg/document/WS-AgreementSpecification/

Web Services Federation Language (WS-Federation) Version 1.0 (2003). Retrieved February 17, 2007, from http://msdn.microsoft.com/ws/2003/07/ws-federation/

Web Services Policy Framework (WS-Policy). Version 1.2 (2006). Retrieved February 17, 2007, *from* http://msdn.microsoft.com/ws/2002/12/Policy/

Web Services Trust Language (WS-Trust) (2005). Retrieved February 17, 2007, from ftp://www6.software.ibm.com/software/developer/library/ws-trust.pdf

Chapter XVII
Interoperability Middleware for Federated Business Services in Web–Pilarcos

Lea Kutvonen
University of Helsinki, Finland

Toni Ruokolainen
University of Helsinki, Finland

Janne Metso
University of Helsinki, Finland

ABSTRACT

Participation in electronic business networks has become necessary for the success of enterprises. The strategic business needs for participating multiple networks simultaneously and for managing changes in these networks are reflected as new requirements for the supporting computing facilities. The web-Pilarcos architecture addresses the needs of managed collaboration and interoperability of autonomous business services in an inter-organisational context. The web-Pilarcos B2B middleware is designed for lowering the cost of collaboration establishment and to facilitate management and maintenance of electronic business networks. The approach is a federated one: All business services are developed independently, and the B2B middleware services are used to ensure that technical, semantic, and pragmatic interoperability is maintained in the business network. In the architecture and middleware functionality design, attention has been given to the dynamic aspects and evolution of the network. This paper discusses the concepts provided for application and business network creators, and the supporting middleware-level knowledge repositories for interoperability support.

INTRODUCTION

The globalisation of business and commerce makes enterprises increasingly dependent on their partners; competition takes place between supply chains and networks of enterprises. In this competition, the flexibility of enterprise information systems becomes critical. The IT systems and development teams should be able to respond timely to the requirements rising from the changing co-operation networks and their communications needs.

At present, development and research is directed towards autonomous enterprises with sovereign services and loosely-coupled, contract-governed business networks formed between them. In this kind of environment, several strategical, process-related and technological needs must be attended by the business network management:

- Formation of new business networks that provide added value services for clients.
- Joining multiple networks at the same time without unnecessary restrictions on technologies or operational policies.
- Taking up new business processes and services with relatively low cost.
- Moving existing business networks to new phases of life-cycle so that new collaboration forms can be used
- Monitoring the progress and correctness of the collaborative processes
- Automating some collaboration establishment and correction events
- Protecting local services and computing solutions from the changes and failures of the collaboration partner services and solutions

To address these management needs, we need to use concepts and operations for forming electronic business networks, eCommunities, and managing their life-cycle by eContracts. The business services themselves should not be burdened, but these facilities are to be introduced as generic B2B middleware.

Thus, from the computing infrastructure side, the enter-prise's needs can be addressed by an architecture where business level services, B2B middleware, and abstract communication services are clearly separated from each other, and the relationships between collaboration life-cycle, B2B middleware, and software engineering tools are changed from the traditional approach.

Traditionally, inter-enterprise collaboration has required integration of enterprise computing systems or applications. The topical integration techniques vary from new generation ERP systems, and process-orientation to distributed workflow management systems. A significant amount of research is currently focusing on virtual-enterprise approaches. Virtual enterprises are joint ventures of independent enterprises joining a shared collaboration process. In many projects (like PRODNET (Afsamanesh, Garita, Hertzberger, & Santos Silva, 1997), MASSYVE (Rabelo, Camarinha-Matos, & Vallejos, 2000), FETISH-ETF (Camarinha-Matos & Afsarmanesh, 2001) and WISE (Lazcano, Alonso, Schuldt, & Schuler, 2000; Alonso, 1999)) the support environment consists of a breeding environment and operational environment. The breeding environment provides facilities for negotiating and modelling the collaboration processes; the operational environment controls the enactment of the processes. Many of the virtual enterprise support environments use a unified architecture approach: there is a shared abstract model to which all enterprises have to adapt their local services.

In contrast to this, the approach in the web-Pilarcos project is federated: enterprises seek out partners that have services with which they are able to interoperate (within the strategically acceptable limits). A collaboration model (business network model, BNM) is used for explicitly expressing what kind of collaboration is wanted and comparison of BNMs is used as a semantic interoperability verification tool. Enactment of services and local business processes, either by applications or a local workflow management system are required features of the service management facilities of each local computing system. This design choice has been made in order to make the evolution of BNMs and business networks themselves more flexible. Changes in the model to follow require that the model is explicitly available at the operational time, and that there is a synchronisation and negotiation mechanism for partners to reach a safe point where new rules can be adopted.

The web-Pilarcos architecture and services address the infrastructure requirements and solutions for bridging the gap between enterprise-level business considerations and the corresponding service management at the computing platforms. The global infrastructure services, transparently used by B2B middleware services at each enterprise, comprise partner service selection support, eContract management facilities, eCommunity life-cycle management, breach detection by business-rule-aware monitors, and interoperability support facilities for technical, semantic, process-aware, and pragmatic aspects.

This paper concentrates on the breeding environment facilities for checking interoperability of business services for the purposes of forming an eCommunity, and the connection between business-level aspects and enterprises' computational services. Section 2 discusses interoperability challenges in the context of eCommunity management, and Section 3 briefly describes the web-Pilarcos B2B middleware services and repositories. Section 4 addresses the meta-information and corresponding public repositories presented by the web-Pilarcos middleware. Section 5 describes the mechanisms and processes used to guarantee interoperability in eCommunities.

MANAGEMENT OF eCOMMUNITIES AND INTEROPERABILITY

The web-Pilarcos architecture proposes a model of inter-enterprise collaborations as eCommunities consisting of independently developed business services. Business service denotes a set of functionalities provided by an enterprise to its clientele and partners, and that is governed by the enter-prise's own business rules and policies, as well as by business contracts and regulatory systems controlling the business area. Furthermore, as the business service is realised by software, the service is also defined by the computing, information representation, and communication facilities used and required.

As the eCommunities indeed are formed by software services implementing tasks of strategical business needs, the high level architecture shows the bridges between business needs and technical solutions. The web-Pilarcos architecture has been developed in interaction with RM ODP (reference model of open distributed processing (IS10746, 1996)) and is founded on many of the principles also visible in current SOA (service oriented architecture (Papazoglou & Georgakopoulos, 2003)) trend. Shared foundations include the strong encapsulation of business services into autonomous units, introduction of meta-information services for service discovery and selection, and loose coupling of services for composites or collaborations.

The inter-enterprise collaboration management concepts supported by the web-Pilarcos architecture include those of:

- An eCommunity that represents a specific collaboration, its operation, agreements and state; the eCommunities carry identities and are managed according to their eCommunity contract information
- Electronic business services that are provided by enterprises, used as members

in eCommunities, and are made publicly available by exporting service offers.

The functionalities supported by the B2B middleware include:

- A set of B2B middleware services for establishing, modifying, monitoring, and terminating eCommunities, or looking from the business service point of view, operations for joining and leaving an eCommunity either voluntarily or by community decision
- A set of repositories for storage of meta-models for communities, ontologies of service types, and services, to support interoperability validation

The business service providers are responsible to provide describing metainformation to the B2B middleware repositories, but are otherwise freed of implementing any of the eCommunity life-cycle management. Instead, they are expected to use local middleware services for it.

The eCommunity life-cycle is mainly controlled in an eCommunity contract. The contract comprises of the business network model, BNM (to define the network structure), information about the member services at each role, some overview state information about the progress of the external business processes, and methods for changing the contract itself.

In the eCommunity establishment process (and operational time management) the eContract is used to gather together all relevant information about both the business and the technical level details for the eCommunities. Figure 1 illustrates how contractual information derived from different sources becomes part of the eCommunity contract and is used to govern a computational service in order to bring it up to represent the intended business service. In the following, these steps are discussed in more detail.

The strategical requirements of a business network are expressed as a meta-level model that defines a set of external business processes (right side of Figure 1). We call this business network

Figure 1. Source of business-level and technical-level information to control software behaviour to fulfil the business service commitments and restrictions

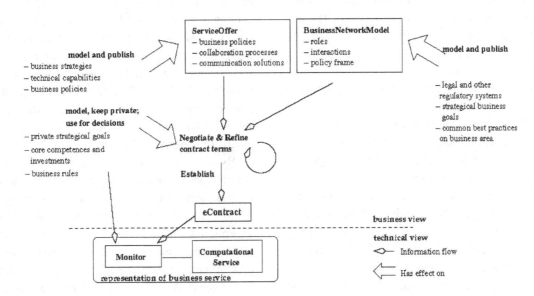

model, BNM. The structure is defined in terms of roles and interactions between the roles. For each role, assignment rules define additional requirements for the service offer that can be accepted to fulfil it, and conformance rules determine limits for acceptable behaviour during the eCommunity operation. The explicit use of such a model allows comparison and matching of strategical and pragmatic goals of members in the network by giving a working structure for comparable and negotiable service offers. The business network models should take into consideration all relevant legal and regulatory systems on the application area.

An enterprise that is able to run a computational service, i.e., a constellation of software components providing interfaces for functionalities of a business service, can make it available for other parties by publishing its interface and property information (left side of Figure 1). In addition, we expect the service offer to be considered as a binding offer to provide the service with the identified properties, terms, and conditions. The information elements required in the service offer are determined by two aspects: first, by the requirements of the B2B middleware concepts, and second, by the mandatory properties defined for the service type in question (will finally match the business network role requirements). The service offers and the structuring effect of service types is further discussed in Section 3. Essential for the offer structure is that the contract terms relevant for the business area become represented in a way that allows comparison.

The contracting process between the business services is governed by the selected business network model. The business service basic properties become defined by the service offer, although the mechanism does not technically enforce the offer to be truthful or the service implementation to conform to the offer. However, in business terms, the enterprise loses credibility by false offers, and increased certainty levels can be acquired by external conformance testing and certifications.

The process of enforcing enterprises to provide accurate service offers is mainly an organisational issue not fully addressable by computing solutions. Computationally, it is possible to control that exporters of service offers are authorised by their organisations for making external commitments, and that there are technical facilities to follow the thread of delegations and negotiations for determining the responsible party for each commitment.

The resulting contract object contains both business network regulations and the agreed constraints for joint behaviour. This context information is configured (in suitable phases) to the monitor object governing all service requests passing in or out the computational services interface. Thus the business rules and terms are passed to the monitor for controlling that the actual business service behaviour is not violated by the computational service that is capable of more varied behaviours.

Because the business services are provided by autonomous service providers, there is no inherent guarantee that they would form an interoperable eCommunity. Therefore, special functionality for interoperability checking takes place when establishing an community, or entering a new service into an existing community. The applications themselves need only to concentrate on the local business logic, implemented on their local computing platform. For the eCommunity management functionality, it is necessary that the underlying B2B middleware is able to evaluate interoperability of business services based on their service offers and to monitor the interoperability during the operational time.

By interoperability, or capability to collaborate, we mean effective capability of mutual communication of information, proposals and commitments, requests and results (including exceptions). Interoperability covers technical, semantic and pragmatic interoperability. Technical interoperability means that messages can be transported from one application to another.

Semantic interoperability means that the message content becomes understood in the same way by the senders and the receivers. This may require transformations of information representation or messaging sequences. Finally, the pragmatic interoperability captures the willingness of partners for the actions necessary for the collaboration. The willingness to participate involves both capability of performing a requested action, and policies dictating whether the potential action is preferable for the enterprise to be involved in.

The interoperability validation process is further discussed in Section 5, based on the interoperability-related meta-information that is made available through the middle-ware repositories discussed in Section 4.

The web-Pilarcos eCommunity management approach is directed towards loosely-coupled business networks consisting of autonomous business services. The strategical processes for enterprises involved are:

- Defining and publishing suitable business network models for relevant business areas and allowing those to affect the provision of new business services on open service markets
- Implementing and publishing services to become part of business networks
- Managing eCommunities, especially the negotiation process between potential network partners and maintaining interoperability

The B2B interoperability middleware presented in this paper aims for automating these processes as far as possible, especially the negotiation process. However, it is not the intent that all collaboration decisions would be automated; aspects such as trust between potential partners limit the applicable area. The main benefits come from the agility on changes and reusability of verified interoperability results: New business network models, new service types, and new services can be easily adopted, without causing a cascading change requirement through the business network.

THE WEB-PILARCOS B2B MIDDLEWARE ARCHITECTURE

To map the above business-driven management needs, the required functionality from the B2B-middleware platform includes:

- Advanced service discovery functionality, i.e., a breeding environment where it is possible to fill in roles of a given BNM by suitable service offers and ensure interoperability by using meta-information repositories from the middleware
- Contract-based management of collaboration between autonomous services
- Proactive local monitoring of contract conformance
- Repositories that present the knowledge base required for B2B interoperability support; these repositories get role in collaboration modelling, software engineering, and service deployment processes too.

These main functional elements can be seen Figure 2. The upper part represents the breeding environment services, including populator, service offer repository, business network model repository and type repository. These services can be placed on public domain to be used by any enterprise. Breeding environment services like populators and type repositories are not required from all sites, but can be provided as infrastructure services as a business on its own right.

For the support of the populator, the BNM design process involves the introduction and verification of new models to be stored into the repositories. Implementation of new services or introduction of legacy applications involves interaction with the type repository. New business services are published for use by exporting service offers to the corresponding repositories. Deployment processes are naturally augmented with service offer exports. These processes feed in meta-level knowledge of potential participants in communities to be formed. The feeding processes are independent of each other, even withdrawing or deprecating information may take place.

The two lower parts of Figure 2 represent two autonomous enterprises. By autonomy we mean the potential for control over the private computing systems, and moreover on strategic business processes and policies. Each site or administrative domain, representing an autonomous ICT system, is expected to run a business process management agent. The lower part of the figure also shows the network management agents (NMAs) and eContracts as the major players of the operational environment. As discussed in the previous section, the eCommunity contract captures shared meta-information about the collaboration. At operational time, reflective methods

are used to keep the real system at each involved computing site correspondent with this meta-information. At each administrative computing domain, there is a local agent for management of knowledge about locally deployed services. The local management interfaces are homogenised by a protocol for requesting the system to prepare for running a service (resourcing), querying about communication points, releasing the service, etc. Likewise, all relevant changes in the real system are notified and thus change the meta-information accordingly. The eCommunity contract is an active object itself, and includes logic that may react to changes in the meta-information and request local sites for further negotiations or changes in the system state.

As this paper focuses on the breeding environment functionality and requirements, the following paragraphs will give an overview of the main agents. The populator theme is then extended further by the following sections with

Figure 2. Service agents of the operational environment; arrows represent communication relationships, boxes are active agents, and cylinders data stores.

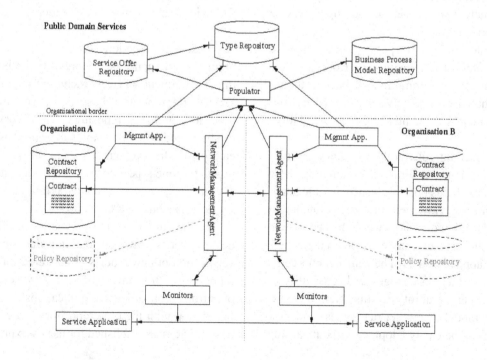

information about the related repositories and meta-information, and then, about interoperability verification.

The *Populator* uses a given BNM for ensuring the pragmatic interoperability of partners to an eCommunity; it also uses a set of compulsory aspects in service offers to determine service types, communication channel requirements, and non-functional aspects to be agreed on for the eCommunity. The populator represents a breeding process where services are selected for eCommunity roles. The population process is a constraint satisfaction challenge between candidates' attribute value spaces and constraints given for roles in the business network model. The service type definitions dictate the attributes and attribute value sets necessary to describe the service, and the actual values for each published service is found in the service offer repository. As there is dependencies between selected offers in interacting roles (on channels and NFA), the process is complex. The populator provides its clients with a set of interoperable communities from which to choose during negotiations. Replacement of partners in an existing community, or one partner changing to a significantly different service implementation are also situations where interoperability preconditions need to be checked.

The eCommunity management is performed in cooperation with *network management agent (NMA)* and the *contract* object. The NMA agents are responsible for managing the inter-organisational coordination and management protocols. while the contract object is responsible for making decisions regarding the eCommunity it represents. The NMA agents are located so that there is a agent acting as a representative between the eCommunity and the local service-providing system at each administrative domain. The contract object is made available across all involved domains; redundancy is required for availability can be ensured also in most common failure situations. The NMA agents provide three interfaces. For the

local administrator, there is a eCommunity management interface for triggering renegotiations on conditions and memberships. Between themselves the agents have a protocol for notifications of task completions and contract breaches, and another interface for for negotiation and commitment protocols for joint contract changes. For communication with the local monitors, the NMAs provide an interface for receiving notifications of contract breaches and task completion and another for feeding monitoring instructions to the monitor. The protocols are described in detail in (Metso & Kutvonen, 2005). It is essential for the NMA role that it acts on behalf of the administrative domain it represents, and is able to access relevant policy information private for the enterprise. Based on local policies and guidelines, the NMA is able to enforce decisions, for example, on the significance of the breach notifications received from the monitors, and the subsequently decide on which protocol to trigger between the NMAs.

The *eCommunity contract* itself is a key element in the architecture, because it makes aspects from different lev-els/viewpoints of the business network available at operational time. The community contract describes technical, semantic, (external business) process-related, and pragmatic aspects. Technical information includes service types and related behaviour descriptions, binding types between services, implementation-specific messages or function parameters, and policies used in the eCommunity. The structuring element of the contract is the BNM used for the eCommunity: each role is supplemented with information from the participant's service offer, each binding with connector parametrisation information. Semantic aspects cover information representation formats in messages exchanged. The pragmatic aspects covered include functional description of business processes, policies constraining roles, and non-functional aspects. The non-functional aspects govern features like trust, security, QoS that are traditionally considered additional platform-level service solutions required. In addition, non-func-

Figure 3. Information contents of the eContract

```
        o       Reference to the business network model
        o       Information about the epoch in which the network is
        o       Process for changing epoch
    •   For each role:
        o       Assignment rules that specify the requirements on
        o       Service type
        o       Nonfunctional aspect
        o       Restrictions on identity, participation in other business networks, etc.
        o       Conformance rules that are used for determining conformance to the role which the assigned component
                is in the role; similar as above;
    •   For each interaction relationship between roles:
        o       Channel requirements
        o       Locations of the channel endpoints
        o       QoS agreement; security agreement
        o       Information presentation formats
    •   For each policy that governs the choices between alternative behaviour patterns in the business network model
    •   Acceptable values or value ranges:
        o       References to alternative breach recovery processes
        o       Objective of the business network as business rules
```

tional aspects related to business process models capture more business-oriented features, like business rules (captured as policies and monitoring rules here). These main elements of the eContract are captured in Figure 3.

The structure of the contract is directly determined by the business network model in use. Most of the contract structure is a copy of the associated business network model. The business network model lacks identification of the business services as members, and only gives acceptable ranges for some negotiable policies. The business network model is also independent of the bindings (interaction support) the business services need to deploy between themselves.

Monitors are part of the communication channel between participating services. A monitor has a generic sensor element that can be configured to filter traffic by classifying it to expected and unexpected event sequences (task started / completed, unacceptable traffic or lack of expected traffic). The network management agents provide each monitor with a behaviour automaton to follow, based on the service choreographies described for the corresponding role. The monitors can be used both to monitor the behaviour of the roles provided by its own organisation and the roles of the other organisations. Monitoring reports can be acted on in various ways, scaling from post-operational auditing to proactive prevention of unwanted events. In web-Pilarcos, the intent is to allow major breaches on agreed behaviour or policies to be acted on during the eCommunity operation, and allowing automatic recovery processes to be started. In this respect, the web-Pilarcos approach differs from related projects (like Neal et al., 2003) that otherwise use similar techniques. Because the definition of "severe breach" and the appropriate methods of potentially replacing misbehaving partners are specific to each application domain, those rules and process definitions are compulsory parts of BNMs.

The most important task of the monitors is to provide a method for enforcing the business-level policies and enterprise-wide operational policies onto the computational service constellations. In the operational environment, the monitor and the computational service constellation together form a representation of the business service.

INTEROPERABILITY KNOWLEDGE IN THE GLOBAL MIDDLEWARE

The three meta-information repositories in the B2B middleware—business network model repository, service type repository, and service offer repository—have a central role in establishing a knowledge base that allows interoperability tests on to be made. Essential target concepts are service types, service offers, and business network models. Each repository is distributed for scalability and improved accessibility. Due to different types of load, the good distribution styles differ (Kutvonen, 1998).

Service types and BNMs have separate life-cycles as this provides isolation layers that keep local changes from involving the whole eCommunity and minimises the effects of BNM enhancements to local services. Furthermore, each model requires only a reasonably narrow expertise to create. In addition to direct relationships between models, the repositories store transformation rules and components for improved transformer/interceptor re-usability (Kutvonen, 1998).

The service elements of the web-Pilarcos breeding environment address the need of joining four important processes:

- Introduction of BNMs to the model repository, and introduction of supporting service types to the type repository
- Software engineering processes to provide implementations that correspond to the known service types and thus are applicable for the known BNMs
- Deployment of services and export of corresponding service offers to traders, effectively making a commitment to keep the service consistent with the service offer
- eCommunity establishment process using the provided information

These processes are only loosely interleaved. Business network models and the actual business services can be developed independently from each other; indeed, their development form quite a separate profession. In the platform, these concepts have to meet at the service description level.

Type and Service Offer Repositories

The *type repository* provides a structured storage for type information related to services and their access interfaces. Operations are provided for publishing new types, comparing types, and creating relationships between types.

Service types are abstract descriptions of business service functionality. Service descriptions are used to ensure technical connectivity, semantic interoperation and behavioural compatibility in possibly heterogeneous environments. Service descriptions do not expose internal properties of business services as this decreases the possibilities of reuse and evolution of services. Implementation-specific information, such as binding of a service into a specific communication protocol or address, is not covered by service type. Service type is like a contract, which an actual service must implement.

Service types are XML-based descriptions which define interface signatures, service attributes and an interface protocol. Interface signature in web-Pilarcos is described using a WSDL description without technical binding information (see (WSDL, 2001). Each service supports only one kind of behaviour; different behaviour implies different service type. We refer to the definition of service behaviour as *interface protocol* which is a behavioural description defining externally visible behaviour at one endpoint of a bilateral communication. Interface protocols in web-Pilarcos are based on session types (see (Takeuchi, Honda, & Kubo, 1994; Gay & Hole, 1999)). For behavioural descriptions we have a simple XML-based process description language. Semantic interoperability of services is supported by binding ontological concepts to the exchanged documents. XML-based ontology description languages, such as general purpose description languages RDF(S) and OWL (RDF-S, 2004; OWL, 2004) or more specialised XML-based ontologies such as RosettaNet, can be used (RosettaNet Consortium, 2004). The rules of the type system are based on behavioural session types, structural matching of syntactic information and semantic relations based on description logic (Takeuchi et al., 1994; Jha, Palsberg, & Zhao, 2002; Nardi & Brachman, 2002). Subtyping-like relationships that support service evolution are also important (Di Cosmo, Pottier, & Rémy, 2005; Gay & Hole, 1999; Nardi & Brachman, 2002).

The type discipline in the web-Pilarcos platform is strictly managed. Every type definition must be contained by a type repository. Each type name, i.e. URI, must also identify the type repository responsible for managing the corresponding namespace and its type definitions. Without strict management of typing information it would be impossible to ensure that types are unambiguously named, persistently stored, verified to be correct, and relationships between types verified and intact (Kutvonen, 1998). Type repositories can also be organised into a hierarchy for partitioning of namespaces.

Service types are published by institutions responsible for a business domain or by enterprises willing to promote use of new kinds of services. Standardisation of a new service type is however not necessary because the applicability and adoption of the service type is determined by peer acceptance.

The relationships of interest for the type repository users are: no match, similar types (equality of text or reference, subtyping), and interoperable with interception. The comparison and judgement is not fully automated and cannot be made (due to performance issues) at the time of query. Instead, the service type publication process involves verification of the type, comparison to other named types, and verification of the type relationships. The process of creating interceptors (i.e., transformers that change the inputs and outputs of one interface type so that they become suitable for another) is external to the type repository. The service types can thus be matched with each other in a more relaxed way, only limited with an interoperability requirement. As an enhancement, the cost of connection can be added to direct users to choose "native" types instead of transformed connections.

The initial Pilarcos type repository was designed and developed during the work on the ODP type repository function standard (IS14746, 1999), and OMG MOF specification (MOF, 2002). Although there are certain differences, most interfaces are similar. Thus the type repository offers operations (Kutvonen, 1998) for:

- Publishing realisations of abstract types
- Checking whether two type realisations are conformant and interchangeable
- Retrieving subtypes or supertypes of a type realisation
- Retrieving templates for a given abstract type
- Translating one type realisation to another
- Retrieving names for abstract types and type realisations in other type domains

Figure 4. Structure of service offers in Web-Pilarcos

- Interface syntax and protocol; either IDL or WSDL specification for the service interface, and partial ordering rules of operations
- Schema for information elements
- List of nonfunctional aspects, such as QoS offers (acceptable range for QoS), trust requirements, or name for security mechanism to be used
- Requirements for platform
- Requirements for communication channel service level

The *service offer repository* refers to services (like UDDI (Belwood & et al., 2004) and ODP trading service (IS13235, 1995)) for locating services that are published using structured meta-information description of the service. We consider these descriptions as binding offers for the service. When a new service offer is published, type repository functionality is used to validate the conformance between the offer and the corresponding service type.

Given a service type and a service offer, the conformance validation algorithm verifies if the service offer corresponds to the behavioural and structural properties of the corresponding service type. Concerning behaviour, each communication action described in the service offer has to be matched with the communication behaviour defined in the service type. Both substitutability and compatibility relationships can be used as a behavioural matching criteria. For structural properties, similarity between the document structures used in the service offer and document types declared in the service type must be matched.

Functional properties of the type checking algorithm are characterised by the service-typing rules which are based on the session typing discipline (Takeuchi et al., 1994; Gay & Hole, 1999). The session typing discipline provides formal characterisations for service substitutability and compatibility which are based on the notions of session subtyping and duality (Vallecillo, Vas-

concelos, & Ravara, 2003). The algorithm for validating session subtyping is syntax-driven and is expected to be efficient in practise (Vallecillo et al., 2003); however, no formal validation of this claim has yet been given.

If the conformance validation is successful, the service offer is published into a service offer repository with the claimed service type. The service offer publishing process requires predefined service types. In the web-Pilarcos architecture, we expect service types to mandate properties for expressing issues affecting technical, semantic, and pragmatic interoperability. This is reflected by the structure required by service offers, as illustrated in Figure 4.

Business Network Model Repository

The BNM repository provides interfaces for publishing models, verifying their properties, comparing and querying: models for population or software engineering processes.

The structure (topology) and properties of a business network are defined by its BNM that explicates the roles of partners and the interactions between roles that are needed for reaching the objective of the eCommunity. A BNM comprises a collection of roles, a set of connectors and a set of architecture-specific non-functional properties. The approach combines ideas from the ODP enterprise viewpoint language (IS15414,

Figure 5. Contents of business network models

> - A set of named business process models each presented in terms of named roles with:
>   - role assignment rules for guiding the populator to retrieve suitable service offers from the offer repository
>   - Role conformance rules for guiding the monitors to notify its BNA about all deviations from these rules
>   - Interaction pattern expected at each communication channel; may be simple invocation, announcement or full session specification
>   - Name for the breach recovery process to be used
>   - Role association requirements expressing how a business service is required to simultaneously act in named roles of named business process models; this allows functional slicing of the model for reuse and design purposes
>   - Policy rules overarching the business network model; these policies provide invariants that need to be fulfilled
>   - Breach recovery process name and type (type for example "dissolving", "restarting" or "continuable with sanctions")

2003) and those of separating functional units and their interconnection into distinct concepts of components and connectors (Allen & Garlan, 1994).

A role represents a logical business service or entity in an administrative domain. The role definition expresses the functional and non-functional properties required. Role functionality is described as a composition of service types and role-specific synchronisation patterns. Synchronisation patterns express causal relationships between actions in distinct services of a role (by setting preconditions for interactions using terms before, after etc).

Interaction relationships between roles are described by bilateral connectors between service interfaces. Connectors may define other communication-related properties, such as control or data adaption, eCommunity coordination and nonfunctional properties of communication.

Non-functional properties are managed as named values that are used for selecting the right technical configurations from the underlying platform. Some properties are used for dynamic branching of behaviour at operational time. These decisions stem from the business level, but the negotiation and commitment protocols needed are preferably transparent to the business services.

The elements of the business network model descriptions required are captured into Figure 5.

Life-Cycles of the Contents in B2B Repositories

The meta-information repositories' contents are interdependent. A verified business network model acts as a template for the eCommunity. The model to be used as a contract template is first negotiated between the potential partners, involving comparison and matching of strategical, pragmatic goals of members in the network. As the matching of network models is too hard a problem to solve by an automated process in general cases for a heterogeneous modelling environment, we require a single shared model to be agreed on at the eCommunity establishment. Checking that all parties expect the same business network model is one of the pragmatic interoperability aspects.

Within the business network models, service types are used as means to define requirements for role players. Again, the matching problem is too hard in a general theoretical sense, and therefore we have focused on practical goals: grouping of similar models, and identifying suitable transformers or adapters available when similar models need to be mapped together.

The service type repository is used for holding such a relationships between models and the transformation information associated. The actual adapters are produced in a separate process starting from the service type descriptions (Kutvonen, 2004b) for configuring a communication channel between peers so that the information exchange becomes understood correctly and there is no known deadlock in the sequence of message exchanges. The adapters can address modifications at multiple levels of interoperability, such as data representation modifications, and changing the communication pattern (for example, splitting a request of a task to a set of requests for subtasks from the peer).

Figure 6 illustrates the various processes involved: publication of a) service types and b) business network models, c) service offers, and d) eCommunity population and negotiation processes. These processes are inter-related but not tightly dependent; for example new service types can be published without a business network model using them.

The service publication functionality is similar to the UDDI (Belwood & et al., 2004) or the ODP trading mechanisms (IS13235, 1995); the type management system resembles the ODP type repository function (IS14746, 1999) and enforces a typing discipline to follow over service offer repositories. The BNM repository is a shared storage of business collaboration information that enable enterprises to share business transaction models, such as the ebXML repository (Kotok & Webber, 2001), although with more automated and repeatable breeding process. The notations used are not discussed here, but they resemble the ODP enterprise language and use XML-style notations (see (Kutvonen, 2004a) and (Kutvonen, Ruoko-

Figure 6. Repository usage during eCommunity life-cycle

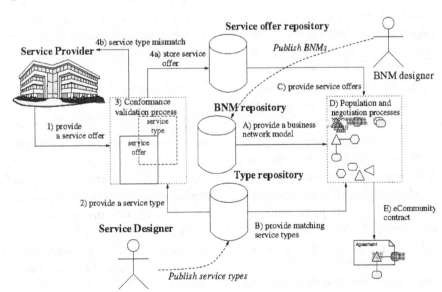

lainen, Metso, & Haataja, 2005)). In the service publication process (step 1), service providers send service offers to the service offer repository, to state claims about the type and properties of the services. A service offer describes functional and non-functional properties of the service to be published: the actual service interface signature, service behaviour, requirements for technical bindings (e.g. transport protocol), and attributes such as service quality and trust-related commitments. The service offer repository then initiates a conformance validation process. For this purpose, a service type corresponding to the claimed service type is retrieved from the type repository (step 2). The service type defines syntactical structures for service interface signature and messages, externally visible service behaviour and semantics for exchanged messages (Kutvonen, Ruokolainen, et al., 2005). Conformance validation is executed by the service type repository holding the corresponding service type (step 3). Only after a successful validation, the service offer is published (step 4a), otherwise a service typing mismatch is reported between the service offer and its claimed type (step 4b).

In Figure 6, the eCommunity establishment process is also shown: it is initiated by a willing partner, the corresponding business network model is first fetched from the BNM repository (step A). The population process (step D) provides a set of interoperable eCommunity proposals where roles of the BNM are filled with potential partners. For this purpose, the type repository is consulted for providing service types matching the requirements of the business network model (step B), after which the service offer repository can be used to provide the corresponding service providers (step C). After population, and the subsequent negotiation, the eCommunity contract is received (step E) and distributed to every participant.

The service interoperability and correct operation of the community assumes that the meta-level information on BNMs, service types, and service offers is correct. Therefore, we find

it necessary to collect the meta-information into repositories, where the trustworthiness of the information source can be controlled, and the quality of the information can be validated by the repository management actions. These aspects must be weaved into the tasks involved with eCommunity establishment, such as service publication or discovery (Ruohomaa, Viljanen, & Kutvonen, 2006).

VERIFICATION AND OBSERVATION OF INTEROPERABILITY

The web-Pilarcos middleware aims for maintaining correct collaborative behaviour in eCommunities, involving several aspects of interoperability requirements. The requirements cover technical, semantic, and pragmatic aspects, i.e., awareness of collaborative behaviour and policies. Traditional verification and static analysis methods are complemented by dynamic observation of behaviour conformance against the contracted BNM and policies.

The research and prototype building in the web-Pilarcos project focuses on interoperability and eCommunity management problems at the business service level, i.e. at the level of eCommunity, its participants, behaviour and life-cycle. As we presume that services are implemented or wrapped using Web Services technology, technical interoperability at the lower protocol levels is well provided by a service-oriented technical middleware layer.

Interoperability problems in software systems stem mainly from components' implicit and incorrect assumptions about behaviour of their surrounding environment (Garlan, Allen, & Ockerbloom, 1995). Every aspect of service and eCommunity functionality must be made explicit using unambiguous notations. Concepts of compatibility and substitutability are key issues in integration of autonomous services into communities; descriptions of services and communities must be founded on a formal basis.

When an eCommunity is established, we ensure *sufficient* conditions for interoperability of services during service discovery and population. Conditions for an interoperable eCommunity are fulfilled by three solutions. First, the use of a verified BNM as a basic structuring rule for the eCommunity; the various business process models intertwined into the network model can be verified to be for example deadlock-free and complete by traditional protocol-verification tools. Second, the use of constraint matching for accepting service offers to fulfil roles in the BNM. Previously verified compatibility and substitutability relationships between service types, provided by the type repositories, and validated conformance claims between service offers and corresponding services types are utilised in this process. Third, the augmentation of the constraint matching process by the interference of further constraints arising from the selected offers for neighbour roles.

Behavioural interoperability is considered in the extent of verifying that service offers and role requirements for service behaviour match. In large, this is accomplished by utilising the already verified correspondences between service offers and services types. However, roles may also impose additional constraints for the behavioural patterns of the contained services, such as obligations to perform specific transactions. Other relevant issues in role-related constraints cover interface syntax with behaviour descriptions, syntax of documents to be exchanged, semantic aspects of control and information flows, and nonfunctional aspects like trust and business policies that further restrict the behaviour. The role specific constraints are validated during the design of the BNM (verifying that the constraints imposed by the role do not conflict with the properties of the corresponding service types), and during the operation of the community (verifying that the service implementations actually conform to these constraints). These validation procedures can be implemented using model checking techniques.

To promote evolution and flexible use of syntactic structures utilised by the services, we will adopt principles of by-structure matching instead of by-name matching for service interface comparisons (Ruokolainen, 2004). Using structural typing constructors for WSDL and XML-Schema definitions we can decide if two WSDL interface descriptions are structurally equal. This interface matching is done using an approach similar to (Palsberg & Zhao, 2001; Jha et al., 2002). Service selection and matching based on semantic concepts is not addressed in the present version of the web-Pilarcos platform but it will be implemented in future versions. Matching of semantic concepts shall be implemented using standard theories and tools, similarity to (Peer, 2002; Sriharee & Senivongse, 2003).

We do not even seek to completely prove that an eCommunity behaves correctly, as this would need verification of behaviours between every possible participant in an eCommunity during its establishment process. Even in theory, a complete pre-operational verification of an eCommunity behaviour would be impossible, because of dynamic changes in the system, such as evolving business policies. Instead, service types are considered as contracts, and the subtyping of session types as proof of conformance. Inevitable behaviour and policy conflicts are observed and acted on during operational time by the monitoring system.

During runtime, however, participants of an eCommunity may behave incorrectly due to outdated service descriptions, changed business policies or technical problems. To overcome, or at least identify, interoperability problems during operation of communities we have adopted an approach based on runtime monitoring of eCommunity contracts.

The monitoring system can be given a fairly free set of rules to monitor passing message traffic, different informational and behavioural aspects are fairly straightforward to monitor (Kutvonen, Metso, & Ruokolainen, 2005). The monitoring system reports detected situations (task started, completed, unacceptable traffic or lack of expected traffic). In monitoring, the challenges lie in the performance of the communication system, the design of monitoring rules, and decision engine.

Some breaches that can be detected by monitoring include a) messages from parties not partners in the eCommunity; b) transactions that are not acceptable in the current state of the eCommunity life-cycle or not fulfilling precedence requirements; c) information contents are not allowed to be exchanged (e.g., private documents, unknown structure); d) the expected flow of information is broken; and e) obligatory transactions are not performed.

Each administrative domain can have their own decision method on how critical a breach is considered. The eCommunity contract provides methods for NMAs to invoke in case of breaches, either for information only, or for the removal of the partner in fault. The eCommunity contract carries these rules for deciding which recovery or sanction processes to use.

RELATED WORK

The B2B middleware developed in web-Pilarcos provides support for autonomously administered peer services that collaborate in a loosely coupled eCommunity. The eCommunity management by design excludes the need for distributed enactment services, but in contrast provides facilities for ensuring interoperability at the semantic and pragmatic level. In this respect the federated approach has a different focus from those in most other P2P community management systems, such as ADEPT (Reichert & Dadam, 1998) or METEOR (Aggarwal, Verma, Miller, & Milnor, 2004), and contract-driven integration approaches, such as ebXML (Kotok & Webber, 2001). Even most virtual enterprise support environments, such as CrossFlow (Grefen, Aberer, Hoffner, & Ludwig, 2000) and WISE (workflow-based internet ser-

vices) (Lazcano et al., 2000), rely on models for distributed business process enactment. However, the web-Pilarcos approach leaves enactment as a local business processing task, concentrating on interoperability monitoring.

The web-Pilarcos concept of eContracts ties together ICT-related viewpoints of ODP (Open Distributed Processing reference model (IS10746, 1996)), also ranging to some features of business aspects. The ODP-RM introduces information, computational, engineering and technical viewpoints. Each of these present interrelated but somewhat independent aspects of the collaboration features and their composition using more basic computing services. The web-Pilarcos contract structure captures these aspects in its BNMs, binding requirements, and behavioural and non-functional monitoring rules (Kutvonen, 2004a). The initial Pilarcos type repository was developed during the work on the ODP type repository function standard (IS14746, 1999), and OMG MOF specification (MOF, 2002). In other projects, like BCA (Milosevic, Linington, Gibson, Kulkarni, & Cole, 2004), contracts have legal and business level focus and detect contract breaches post-operatively (Quirchmayr, Milosevic, Tagg, Cole, & Kulkarni, 2002). The web-Pilarcos aims for more real-time intervention.

In the web-Pilarcos middleware, the eCommunity life-cycle is built to be collaboration-process-aware. The architecture model acts on two abstraction layers, the upper layer involved with the abstract, external business process describing the collaboration requirements; the lower layer comprising actual services bound to the eCommunity dynamically. In this kind of environment, static verification of models and interoperability cannot be complete. In the B2B middleware provided by the web-Pilarcos project, we find it necessary to develop control environments for monitoring and reflectively restructuring the operational eCommunities, besides a breeding environment. The goals are similar to other projects, but the solution methods differ. While ADEPT supports direct modification of the workflow control structures, web-Pilarcos uses negotiated policy-values to choose between predefined behaviour alternatives. The web-Pilarcos solution even requires that well-formed contracts include suitable recovery processes that involve whole communities. In contrast to METEOR-S, the web-Pilarcos platform has no central tool for making the whole of an interoperability analysis, but partial static verification is done at the meta-data repositories, and monitoring is used to detect further problems.

The B2B middleware is in some extent comparable to agent-based approaches, such as MASSYVE (Rabelo et al., 2000). The main difference seems to be the separation of business services and B2B middleware services from each other. The web-Pilarcos middleware agents do not provide workflow execution, but expect local application management to play that part. In contrast to (Daskalopulu, Dimitrakos, & Maibaum, 2002), the middleware agents are responsible for semantic verification and failure resolution, and use separate monitors to help and report.

CONCLUSION

The web-Pilarcos architecture provides a B2B middleware layer that supports management of virtual organisations. The management facilities are based on a shared vision of meta-information captured into a eContract. Changes in the contract are locally reflected to the enterprise computing system; and correspondingly, relevant progress and breach reports are delivered to partners through the eContract.

The architecture follows a federated approach: participating services are independent and pre-existing, and the collaborative behaviour model is used only for watching conformance. Enforcement of the contract is reached through the independent monitoring facilities at each participant. Those monitors basically react to events that should not take place at that service or resource interface. Those self-protective reactions are then used as triggers for corrective actions for the benefit of the whole virtual organisation.

The web-Pilarcos approach supports autonomous services to form federated communities. A federated approach means that there is no overarching shared collaboration model from which the services would be derived. Instead, the services stand on their own and interoperability from the collaboration process, semantic and technical view must be maintained explicitly by B2B middleware. From the BNM, it would be possible to use the popular model-driven approach and generate applications but those are not resistant for evolution needs. This is further discussed in (Kutvonen, 2004b, 2004a).

The provision of the web-Pilarcos architecture requires further development of business process modelling techniques. The collaboration of business processes or workflows should be modelled without unnecessary revealing of local processing steps. Instead, only the collaborative part (external view) should be agreed on and monitored. Work has already been started by the component-driven approach on splitting workflows into Web Services. The structural needs of business process models are also widened by the requirements of incorporating reusable sanctioning, recovery, and compensation processes into eCommunity contracts. Furthermore, shared ontologies and repositories for business process models should be made available. Such facilities would improve the potential for reaching interoperability in an environment where service components are truly developed independently from each other. More fundamentally, ontologies and repositories would create a facility for checking semantic similarity of a business process model as part of the interoperability tests during eCommunity establishment.

The federated approach has been criticised for the lack of advice for service elements to be developed. However, making existing business network models globally available and thus exposing repeating patterns of roles -i.e., expected local business processes -gives the required guidance. Such publishing has already taken place with RosettaNet etc; our solution is to provide a repository for external process descriptions that can be augmented on demand, and that will provide an element of evolution support. These model definitions can be added to the repositories at will, without interfering with already operational communities. Existing models can be frozen so that new communities are no more formed using them, but are not actually removed automatically. The verification and matching hierarchies within the repositories may depend on them, and of course, operational communities may do references.

Another criticism frequently arising is the performance penalty of the eCommunity interoperability checking. From our earlier prototype on the populator process, we can judge that the cost of the process and its scalability are acceptable (Kutvonen & Metso, 2005). The scalability of the open-ended search for potential partners from service offer repositories indicates a large search space; the matching process is further complicated by the interdependencies between selected partners in terms of available communication solutions and policies. The populator algorithms address the potentially exponential growth of the search space by limiting the resources used for the search, at the cost of the completeness of the results.

Specific features of the web-Pilarcos breeding environment include the level of automation expected, the relaxed matching of service types aimed for, and the use of explicit business network model repositories.

The level of automation in eContracting has to be considered carefully. Enterprises are generally not ready to allow automated agents to take business-level decisions. Therefore, the automatically acceptable commitments have to be guarded by enterprise policies, and to be directed towards routine decisions. The main impact on the web-

Pilarcos facilities is in providing control over technological and evolution-involved problems, not in the aggressive enhancement to new business partners. The major development on the architecture, however, is the trust management, on which we have started a separate development project (Ruohomaa et al., 2006).

The federated type repository service is an essential element of a B2B middleware that supports the establishment of new business networks, or in a more simple case, connection between independently administered clients and servers. The role of the type repository is to provide a trustworthy source of service type information, and furthermore, provide transformation services for communication between almost similar interfaces. The service types can thus be matched with each other in a more relaxed way, only limited with the interoperability requirement. As an enhancement, the cost of connection can be added to direct users to choose "native" types instead of transformed connections. The service type matching approach supports evolution of services in a heterogeneous environment, where independent actors create new items, and where market forces has an effect on the usability of items, in addition to the verifiable correctness properties. Furthermore, the approach gives a natural tool for managing one type of transformation components needed in the current component-based, model-driven networking environment.

The use of explicit business network model repository is an ontology-defining tool that allows dynamic development and quick publication of new collaboration models. This is one of the key elements in the trial of developing evolution support for dynamic, inter-enterprise networks.

ACKNOWLEDGMENT

This article is based on work performed in the Pilarcos and web-Pilarcos projects at the Department of Computer Science at the University of Helsinki.

The Pilarcos project was funded by the National Technology Agency TEKES in Finland, Nokia, SysOpen and Tellabs. In web-Pilarcos, active partners have been VTT, Elisa and SysOpen. The work integrates much with RM-ODP standards work, and recently has found an interesting context in the INTEROP NoE collaboration.

REFERENCES

Afsamanesh, H., Garita, C., Hertzberger, B., & Santos Silva, V. (1997). Management of distributed information in virtual enterprises: The PRODNET approach. In *ICE'97. International Conference on Concurrent Enterprising*.

Aggarwal, R., Verma, K., Miller, J., & Milnor, W. (2004, September). Contstraint driven Web service composition in METEOR-S. In *IEEE International Conference on Services Computing (SCC'04)* (pp. 23-30). Los Alamitos, CA: IEEE Society Press.

Allen, R., & Garlan, D. (1994). Formalizing architectural connection. In *ICSE '94: Proceedings of the 16th international conference on Software engineering* (pp. 71-80). Los Alamitos, CA: IEEE Computer Society Press.

Alonso, G. (1999). WISE: Business to business e-commerce. In *9th workshop on research issues on data engineering (RIDE-VE'99)*. Sydney.

Belwood, T., et al. (2004). *UDDI version 3.0*. Retrieved September 1, 2005, from http://uddi.org/pubs/uddi_v3.htm

Camarinha-Matos, L. M., & Afsarmanesh, H. (2001, November). Service federation in virtual organisations. In *Prolamat'01*. Budabest, Hungary.

Christensen, E., Curbera, F., Meredith, G., & Weerawarana, S. (2001, March). *Web Services Description Language (WSDL) 1.1*. Retrieved September 1, 2005, from http://www.w3c.org/TR/wsdl

Daskalopulu, A., Dimitrakos, T., & Maibaum, T. (2002). Evidence-based electronic contract performance monitoring. *The INFORMS Journal of Group Decision and Negotiation*. (Special Issue on Formal Modelling in E-Commerce)

Di Cosmo, R., Pottier, F., & Rémy, D. (2005, April). Subtyping recursive types modulo associative commutative products. In P. Urzyczyn (Ed.), *7th International Conference on Typed Lambda Calculi and Applications (TLCA 2005)* (Vol. 3461, pp. 179-193). Berlin, Heidelberg, Germany: Springer-Verlag.

Garlan, D., Allen, R., & Ockerbloom, J. (1995). Architectural mismatch or why it's hard to build systems out of existing parts. In *ICSE '95: Proceedings of the 17th International Conference on Software Engineering* (pp. 179-185). New York: ACM Press.

Gay, S. J., & Hole, M. (1999). Types and subtypes for client-server interactions. In *ESOP '99: Proceedings of the 8th European Symposium on Programming Languages and Systems* (Vol. 1576, pp. 74-90). London: Springer-Verlag.

Grefen, P., Aberer, K., Hoffner, Y., & Ludwig, H. (2000). Cross-flow: Cross-organizational workflow management in dynamic virtual enterprises. *International Journal of Computer Systmes Sciences and Engineering, 15*(5), 277-290.

Information Technology—*Open Distributed Processing—Reference Model—Enterprise Language*. (2003). (IS15414)

Information Technology—*Open systems interconnection, data management and open distributed processing*. ODP Trading Function. (1995). (IS13235)

Information Technology—*Open systems interconnection, data management and open distributed processing*. Reference Model of Open Distributed Processing. (1996). (IS10746)

Information Technology—Open Systems Interconnection, Data Management and Open Distributed Processing. Reference Model of Open Distributed Processing. ODP Type repository function. (1999). (IS14746)

Jha, S., Palsberg, J., & Zhao, T. (2002). Efficient type matching. In *FoSSaCS '02: Proceedings of the 5th International Conference on Foundations of Software Science and Computation Structures* (pp. 187-204). London: Springer-Verlag.

Kotok, A., & Webber, D. R. R. (2001). *ebXML: The new global standard for doing business over the Internet.* Boston: New Riders.

Kutvonen, L. (1998). *Trading services in open distributed environments.* Department of Computer Science, University of Helsinki. PhD Thesis. A-1998-2.

Kutvonen, L. (2004a). Challenges for ODP-based infrastructure for managing dynamic B2B networks. In A. Vallecillo, P. Linington, & B. Wood (Eds.), *Workshop on ODP for Enterprise Computing (WODPEC 2004)* (pp. 57-64). Málaga, Spain: University of Málaga.

Kutvonen, L. (2004b, September). Relating MDA and inter-enterprise collaboration management. In D. Akehurst (Ed.), *Second European Workshop on Model Driven Architecture (EWMDA)* (pp. 84-88). Canterbury, UK: University of Kent.

Kutvonen, L., & Metso, J. (2005, September). Services, contracts, policies and eCommunities – Relationship to ODP framework. In P. Linington, A. Tanaka, S. Tyndale-Biscoe, & A. Vallecillo (Eds.), *Workshop on ODP for enterprise computing (WODPEC 2005)* (pp. 62-69). Málaga, Spain: University of Málaga.

Kutvonen, L., Metso, J., & Ruokolainen, T. (2005, November). Inter-enterprise collaboration management in dynamic business networks. In R. Meersman & Z. Tari (Eds.), *OnTheMove 2005 DOA, ODBASE and CoopIS vol.1* (Vol. 3760). Berlin, Heidelberg: Springer-Verlag.

Kutvonen, L., Ruokolainen, T., Metso, J., & Haataja, J. (2005, December). Interoperability middleware for federated enterprise applications in web-Pilarcos. In *Interoperability of Enterprise Software and Applications.* Springer-Verlag.

Lazcano, A., Alonso, G., Schuldt, H., & Schuler, C. (2000). The WISE approach to electronic commerce. *Computer Systems Science and Engineering, 15*(5), 345-357.

Meta Object Facility (MOF) Specification: Version 1.4. (2002, April). Retrieved September 1, 2005, from http://www.omg.org/docs/formal/02-04-03.pdf

Metso, J., & Kutvonen, L. (2005, September). Managing virtual organizations with contracts. In *Workshop on Contract Architectures and Languages (CoALa2005).* Enschede, The Netherlands.

Milosevic, Z., Linington, P. F., Gibson, S., Kulkarni, S., & Cole, J. B. (2004). Inter-organisational collaborations supported by e-contracts. In W. Lamersdorf, V. Tschammer, & S. Amarger (Eds.), *Building the E-Service Society: E-Commerce, E-Business, and E-Government. IFIP 18th World Computer Congress TC6/TC8/TC11 4th International Conference on E-Commerce, E-Business, E-Government (I3E 2004)* (pp. 413-429). Kluwer.

Nardi, D., & Brachman, R. (2002). The description logic handbook. In F. Baader, D. Calvanese, D. L. McGuinnes, D. Nardi, & P. Pate-Schneider (Eds.), (pp. 5-44). Cambridge, UK: Cambridge University Press.

Neal, S., Cole, J. B., Linington, P. F., Milosevic, Z., Gibson, S., & Kulkarni, S. (2003). Identifying requirements for business contract language: A monitoring perspective. In *7th International Enterprise Distributed Object Computing Conference (EDOC 2003)* (pp. 50-61). Los Alamitos, CA: IEEE.

OWL Web Ontology Language Guide. (2004, February). W3C Recommendation 10 February 2004. Retrieved September 1, 2005, from http://www.w3.org/TR/owl-guide/

Palsberg, J., & Zhao, T. (2001). Efficient and flexible matching of recursive types. *Information and Computation, 171*(2), 364-387.

Papazoglou, M. P., & Georgakopoulos, D. (2003). Introduction. *Communications of the ACM, 46*(10), 24-28.

Peer, J.(2002). Bringing together Semantic Web and Web services. In *ISWC '02: Proceedings of the First International Semantic Web Conference on The Semantic Web* (pp. 279-291). London: Springer-Verlag.

Quirchmayr, G., Milosevic, Z., Tagg, R., Cole, J., & Kulkarni, S. (2002). Establishment of virtual enterprise contracts. In *Database and Expert Systems Applications: 13ᵗʰ International Conference* (Vol. 2453, pp. 236-248). London: Springer-Verlag.

Rabelo, R. J., Camarinha-Matos, L. M., & Vallejos, R. V. (2000). Agent-based brokerage for virtual enterprise creation in the moulds industry. In *Proceedings of the IFIP TC5/WG5.3 Second IFIP Working Conference on Infrastructures for Virtual Organizations: Managing Cooperation in Virtual Organizations and Electronic Busimess towards Smart Organizations* (pp. 281-290). Deventer, The Netherlands: Kluwer, B.V.

RDF Vocabulary Description Language 1.0: RDF Schema. (2004, February). W3C Recommendation 10 February 2004. Retrieved September 1, 2005, from http://www.w3.org/TR/rdf-schema/

Reichert, M., & Dadam, P. (1998). ADEPTflex—Supporting dynamic changes of workflow without losing control. *Journal of Intelligent Information Systems, 10*(2), 93-129. (Special Issue on Workflow Management)

RosettaNet Consortium.(2004). *RosettaNet Implementation Framework: Core Specification V02.00.00.* Retrieved September 1, 2005, from http://www.rosettanet.org/

Ruohomaa, S., Viljanen, L., & Kutvonen, L. (2006, March). Guarding enterprise collaborations with trust decisions: The TuBE approach. In *Proceedings of the First International Workshop on Interoperability Solutions to Trust, Security, Policies and QoS for Enhanced Enterprise Systems (is-tspq 2006).*

Ruokolainen, T. (2004). *Component interoperability.* University of Helsinki, Department of Computer Science. MSc thesis C-2004-42. In Finnish

Sriharee, N., & Senivongse, T. (2003, November). Discovering Web services using behavioural constraints and ontology. In J.-B. Stefani, I. Demeure, & D. Hagimont (Eds.), *Distributed Applications and Interoperable Systems: 4ᵗʰ IFIP WG6.1 International Conference (DAIS 2003)* (pp. 248-259). Springer-Verlag.

Takeuchi, K., Honda, K., & Kubo, M. (1994). An interaction-based language and its typing system. In *PARLE '94: Proceedings of the 6ᵗʰ International PARLE Conference on Parallel Architectures and Languages Europe* (pp. 398-413). London: Springer-Verlag.

Vallecillo, A., Vasconcelos, V. T., & Ravara, A. (2003). Typing the behavior of objects and components using session types. *Electronic Notes in Theoretical Computer Science, 68*(3). (Presented at FOCLASA'02)

This work was previously published in the International Journal of Enterprise Information Systems, Vol. 3, No. 1, pp. 1-21, copyright 2007 by IGI Publishing, formerly Idea Group Publishing (an imprint of IGI Global).

Chapter XVIII
Web–Based Template–Driven Communication Support Systems:
Using Shadow netWorkspace to Support Trust Development in Virtual Teams

Herbert Remidez, Jr.
University of Arkansas at Little Rock, USA

Antonie Stam
University of Missouri, USA

James M. Laffey
University of Missouri, USA

ABSTRACT

Teams whose interactions might be mediated entirely via Internet-based communication, virtual teams, are emerging as commonplace in business settings. Researchers have identified trust as a key ingredient for virtual teams to work effectively (Aubrey & Kelsey, 2003; Beranek, 2000; David & McDaniel, 2004; Iacono & Weisband, 1997; Jarvenpaa, Knoll & Leidner, 1998). However, researchers have not identified scalable methods that consistently promote trust within virtual teams. Improved interface design for communication support systems used by virtual teams may contribute to solving this problem. Interface cannot solve the problem of members trusting each other, but it can support the type of activities that do. This paper describes the development and some initial experiences with a web-based, template-driven, asynchronous communication support tool and how this system can be used to support trust development in virtual teams and performance goals of virtual teams. This article presents the capabilities and features of the communication support system. More detailed findings from an experimental study of this system's use can be found in another publication (Remidez, 2003).

INTRODUCTION

Communication support tools mediate an increasing amount of communication in work settings. In particular, communication support systems are critical to the functioning of virtual teams, as the systems often times mediate all interactions (Powell, Piccoli, & Ives, 2004). Although the importance of the systems in the communication process continues to grow, they do not provide support for constructing messages. They do not support creating a good introduction message or other key communication actions researchers have found to be characteristic of high functioning teams. This lack of support presents a problem for workers but at the same time an opportunity for system designers and researchers.

The use of templates is a framework for designing systems that engage forms of communication that support trust development. An example of a successful use of templates to support communication can be found in Microsoft Word. A Microsoft Word user who has no experience creating a professional letter can choose to create a new document based on the "Professional Letter" template available in the system. By using this template, a novice user can take advantage of the knowledge and experience of the publisher and is more likely to succeed in creating a professional letter. Similar templates are available for supporting the creation of brochures, resumes and memos. These templates no doubt have helped many workers communicate more effectively; similarly, we suggest message templates in online communication systems can facilitate successful collaborative work.

Trust has been identified as a key, yet challenging, ingredient for the effectiveness of virtual teams (Aubrey & Kelsey, 2003; Beranek 2000; Coppola et al., 2004; David & McDaniel, 2004; Iacono & Weisband, 1997; Jarvenpaa et al., 1998; Jarvenpaa et al., 2004). Researchers have not developed scalable methods that consistently promote trust within virtual teams. Given that virtual teams often interact entirely via communication support systems, part of the solution to promoting trust might lie in the design of the communication support systems these teams utilize. For a discussion of the multifaceted nature of virtual teams see Dubé and Paré (2004). Semi-structured message templates have been found to be helpful in designing a variety of computer-based communication and coordination systems (Malone et al., 1987) and might be a basis for designing communication systems that support trust. Specifically, Malone et al. (1987) conclude that semi-structured messages can serve as aids for composing messages to be sent; selecting, sorting, and prioritizing messages that are received; responding automatically to some messages and suggesting likely responses to other messages. Researchers have found that one key characteristic of high-trusting teams is the inclusion of affective statements early in the teams' lifecycle, suggesting that message templates of appropriate affective statements might be a useful means by which computers could support the inclusion of such statements and indirectly promote the development of trust. Te'eni (2001) proposed the use of message templates to promote the inclusion of affective statements in his discussion of a new model of organizational communication, cognitive-affective model of organizational communication (CAMOC), which he used as the basis for suggesting design principles for future communication support systems. CAMOC takes into consideration the impact of the communication strategy, task inputs, message form, and medium selection on cognitive and affective goals of the sender.

This chapter focuses on the design of the communication support tool itself. We present the flexibility of the tool, in terms of the user interface and interaction, the design and nature of the message templates and how they are organized. Our motivation for presenting details of the communication tool is that journal articles reporting on experimental studies often lack the space to detail the specifics of the tools used. In our case, this is unfortunate, because—in contrast to the vast majority of systems used in other research studies—the system we used is custom-designed with a number of special features; moreover, as we will detail below, the system is available free of charge to anyone in the research community.

Throughout this article we strive to keep the focus on the tool, because we believe that understanding how tools can be developed to match with organizational goals has value for the IS community. The purpose of this paper is not to present a tool that can be used to investigate trust development per se. Instead, by keeping the focus on the tool, and using the investigation of trust development as an illustration of the tool's capabilities, we hope to promote the development and use of tools for use in the investigation of multiple phenomena (team cohesion, decision quality, shared mental model development, the use of message labels to promote information processing, etc.).

We next review the importance of trust in virtual teams, followed by the development and implementation of a web-based template-driven asynchronous communication support tool that we have used in several ongoing experimental research projects in which we investigate how systems like ours can be used to support trust development in virtual teams. Findings from our customized system implementation in three such experiments are summarized, and we explain how our particular choice of template structure is rooted in the existing theory on trust in virtual teams and empirical results generated by Jarvenpaa and her colleagues (1998, 1999).

TRUST IN VIRTUAL TEAMS

We have long known that forcing people to cooperate requires expensive and constant surveillance; in addition, it engenders distrust, and can have various negative effects (Kelman, 1958). This is especially true in today's organizations, where traditional controls based on authority have been replaced with self-directed teams and empowered workers (Golembiewski & McConkie, 1975; Jarvenpaa et al., 1998; Larson & LaFasto, 1989). The phenomenon that the control mechanisms work against the development of trust appears to hold true even in virtual team settings. A recent study by Piccoli and Ives (2003) encouraged participants to employ behavioral controls within virtual teams. For example, team members were to prompt a tardy member to participate. Unfortunately, in this study teams using the behavioral control mechanisms reported lower levels of trust than the teams that did not use the control mechanisms.

A large and expanding body of literature demonstrates the importance of trust in facilitating cooperation (Krackhardt & Stern, 1988; Mayer, Davis, & Schoorman, 1995), a more productive free flow of information (Hart & Saunders, 1997; Nelson & Cooprider, 1996), communication (Dore, 1983; Griffin, 1967; Williamson, 1975), collaborative relationship performance (David & McDaniel, 2004), leadership (Atwater, 1988), self-managed work teams (Lawler, 1992; Claus, 2004), the improvement of organizations' abilities to adapt to complexity and change (Korsgaard, Schweiger & Sapienza, 1995; McAllister, 1995), collective learning, knowledge sharing, and creative problem solving (Argyris, 1999; Reina & Reina, 1999; Senge, 1990), and the design, implementation and evaluation of trust-supporting components in virtual communities (Ebner & Krcmar, 2005).

Given what we know about forcing people to work together and the benefits of trust, promoting trust appears to be the more productive option. However, organizations might find it difficult to promote trust between people who hardly ever meet (Handy, 1995). As a result of little physical interaction, communication support systems will play a greater role in promoting "not only task-oriented goals, but also relationship-oriented goals" (Te'eni, 2001). Communication support systems can influence not only how a message is delivered but also the effect of the message on both task-oriented and relationship-oriented goals. Designers of communication support systems now face the task of developing systems that stimulate more effective communication by changing the medium and attributes of the message depending on the goal or goals of the user.

TRUST TEMPLATES

Although Te'eni (2001) suggested that message templates might be used to encourage the inclusion of affective statements, he did not suggest the format or content of such templates. A comprehensive study by Jarvenpaa et al. (1998) found several characteristics of high-trusting teams: getting started early, early positive interactions, high levels of activity, communication about communication strategies, expressions of time orientation, robust feedback, and confrontation of slackers or other areas of conflict. This section explains how Jarvenpaa et al.'s (1998) and Jarvenpaa et al.'s (1999) work provided the empirical basis for the contents of a set of message templates.

In Jarvenpaa et al. (1998), the interactions of 75 teams with four to six members per team were analyzed in order to extract communication characteristics that resulted in trust formation or degradation. Team members lived in different countries and worked together for eight weeks. Participants were asked to conduct two voluntary exercises and were required to complete a third exercise. Based on their findings, Jarvenpaa et al. (1998) suggested strategies like encouraging "proactive behavior, empathetic task communication, positive tone, rotating team leadership, task goal clarity, role division, time management, and frequent interaction with acknowledged and detailed responses to prior messages" (p. 60), that virtual teams might employ to reinforce trust and improve team process outcomes. They also found that the initial interactions between team members are critical to trust development and the team's overall functioning. This finding is consistent with other studies (Beranek, 2000; Chidambaram, 1996; Clear & Daniels, 2001; Huff et al., 2002; Iacono & Weisband, 1997; Meyerson et al., 1996).

In another paper, Jarvenpaa and Leidner (1999) reported that communication that rallies around the project and tasks, social communication that complements rather than substitutes for task communication, meaningful and timely responses, and members explicitly verbalizing their com-

Table 1. Characteristics of high trusting teams and template titles

Characteristics of High Trusting Teams (Jarvenpaa et al. 1998;1999)	Templates
Positive initial interactions	Introduction
Early starters	Getting Started
Discussed communication plans	Communication Issues
Time and goal oriented	Time management/ Milestones
Provided robust feedback	Feedback
Addressed and managed conflict	Issue/Conflict
Task oriented	Task completion/ Questions

mitment, excitement, and optimism are behaviors that strengthen trust. As an example of how we implemented Jarvenpaa et al.'s (1998) concepts in our studies, we outline in Table 1 how we aligned the templates used in our research studies with the activities identified by Jarvenpaa et al. (1998) and Jarvenpaa and Leidner (1999).

We next give descriptions of each of the seven templates. Included in the template descriptions are "Strategy" sections with statements explaining the purpose of the template. The example statements were taken from the statements Jarvenpaa and her colleagues (1998, 1999) selected as representative of communications that promoted trust. For example, "Looking forward very much to working with you all" was identified as an expression of excitement about the forthcoming collaboration. Other examples include "Great job" and "I shall keep in touch soon to congratulate us all on winning." The motivation for each template is summarized in Table 1.

Introduction Template

Introduce yourself. Members of a strong team will get to know each other a little before beginning work. A good introduction includes: 1) information about yourself and your background, 2) your past job experiences, 3) your current focus of study, 4) why you chose to study this subject, and 5) what are your aspirations. In addition, you should address any skills you have that might help your team solve this problem. Also, you should raise any concerns you have about the successful completion of the project.

Strategy: Expressing positive emotions throughout the project will help your team succeed. For example, "I am looking forward to working with you all." would be a good comment to include.

The "Introduction" message template includes several *individual prompts*: "Provide a little in-

formation about yourself and your background," "How often you plan to check the system for new messages (early and often is better)," "Times you will not be available to communicate during the course of this project," and "Address any skills you have that might help your team solve this problem. Also, you should raise any concerns you have about the successful completion of the project." Each of these prompts is followed by fields for users to enter their answer.

Introduction Template

Begin the problem-solving process by sharing your understanding of the goals. Adopt a role that will help your team reach its goal and begin acting the part of that role.

Strategy: It is a good practice to state positive feelings about the project or the work of team members. For example, "Well, done" or "I like this group" are good type of comments to include. In addition, it is best to do what you can to get the project started early and to keep it moving through regular communication with your teammates.

Communication Issues Template

Discuss how often you would like to communicate with your teammates and any other communication practices you would like to see everyone use.

Strategy: Expressions of enthusiasm are always a good thing to include in your messages. For example, "I think we are going to win." or related statements help your teammates feel good about their work.

Time Management/Milestones Template

Time Management/Milestones – Suggest deadlines and milestones for completing the task (*e.g.*, "I think we can get this done by Tuesday.").

Feedback Template

You can use this option to reply to any message that your teammates have posted. Good feedback goes beyond simple statements such as "ok" and "looks good." It includes thoughtful compliments, critiques, edits and additions.

Strategy: Expressions of social greeting and positive statements are good items to include in your feedback statements (*e.g.*, "Hi everyone, I think we can win this.").

Issue/Conflict Template

Use this option to address any concerns about the process being followed or the participation of others. If a team member is not participating and you feel it is hurting the team, it is important to address it in front of the entire team.

Strategy: It is better to address concerns in the open, even if they lead to conflict. For example, if you do not hear from someone, it is good to address it in front to the entire team (*e.g.*, "Where is Joe?").

Task Completion/Questions Template

If you have completed a task or have questions about something, select this option. For example, if you wish to post individual or final team rankings of the items in the problem, this is the option you should choose. You also can take advantage of the ability to compile your results in MS Word or Excel and attach these files to messages.

Strategy: Social greetings included in messages are a good way to keep team members feeling close to each other and to keep your team functioning well (*e.g.*, "I like working in this team"). In addition, expressions of enthusiasm are always a good thing to include in your messages, and they help keep your team working well.

SHADOW NETWORKSPACE (SNS)

The template-driven discussion board application that we will introduce and discuss in the next sections was implemented within Shadow net-Workspace (SNS) (http://sns.internetschools.org) (Laffey, Musser, Remidez, & Gottdenker, 2003). SNS is a web-based work environment originally designed for and extensively tested in education settings. Although SNS was designed with the education environment in mind, the template-driven discussion application we describe was designed to be flexible enough to support discussions in multiple settings. Much like a personal computer's desktop, SNS provides a personal workspace for organizing, storing, and accessing files, and an environment for running applications. SNS also provides the ability to create groups, and for each group to have a "group desktop" for file sharing, communication and collaboration. As such, SNS is capable of supporting a wide variety of virtual collaboration and online communication needs. Our use of SNS to design a virtual team environment that fosters trust is just one of many potential applications. SNS is freely available for downloading from the SNS website to all users under the GNU free software license.

CREATION OF THE TEMPLATE-DRIVEN SYSTEM ENVIRONMENT

This section describes the creation of a template-driven discussion board intended to support trust development. Illustrating the flexibility of the template structure will facilitate the subsequent example of how we have used these types of templates in our experimental studies of trust development in virtual teams. Throughout, we focus on creating template-based discussion boards; however, the application we use to create the template-driven discussion boards can also

Figure 1. Creating a template-driven discussion board

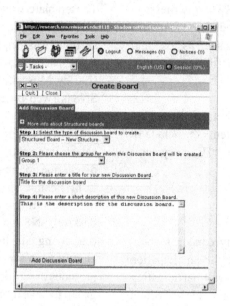

Figure 2. Creating message templates

be used to create a typical non-template driven discussion board. A non-template-driven discussion board shares all the features of the template version except for the ability to choose a message type and view customized message input screens. In addition, a non-template-driven board does not display message type labels and all messages are displayed in a single non-interrupted field, whereas messages created with a customized input screen (e.g. Introduction messages) are displayed in sections corresponding to the input template's sections.

Creating a Board

In order to create a template-driven (i.e., structured) forum, the board creator must enter a title and description for the discussion forum (see Figure 1), define the specific templates (e.g., introduction, time management, issue/conflict, etc.), and specify a name and description for each template (see Figure 2).

After specifying all of the message templates to be available to users of a given discussion board, the next step is optional for the board creator, but allows the creation of an input format for each message template (see Figure 3). For example, in building a specific template-driven discussion board which was intended to promote trust within virtual teams, we specified that all "Introduction" messages should be composed of several different text blocks: (1) a text block (i.e., text area in HTML) with the prompt "Provide a little information about yourself and your background", (2) another single text line for responding to the question "How often do you plan to check the system for new messages (early and often is better)?", (3) a text block with the prompt: "Times you will not be able to communicate during the course of the project," and (4) a text block with the prompt: "Address any skills you have that might help your team address this problem. Also, you should raise any concerns you have about the successful completion of this project."

There is no limit to the number of text blocks or text lines that a single message template can contain. In addition, there is no limit to the number of message templates that accompany a single discussion board or the number of template-driven discussion boards a user can have access to at any one time. If the board creator chooses not to specify the input format for a message template,

Figure 3. Creating the input format for message templates

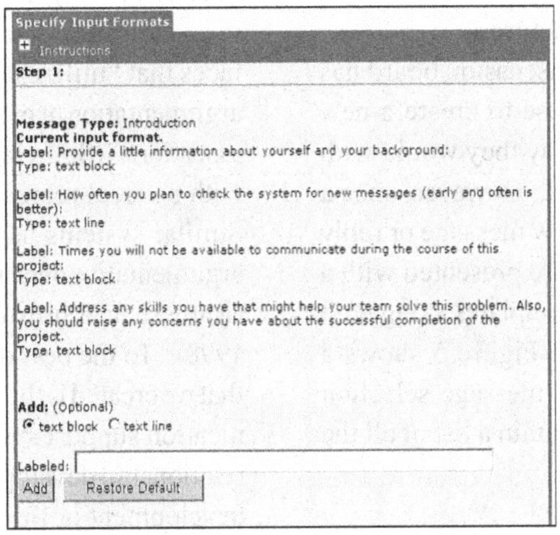

Figure 4. Defining relationships between message templates

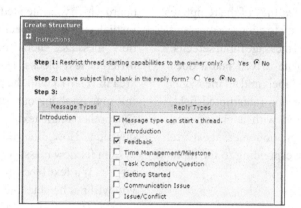

the input screen for that message template will include the familiar subject line and a text block, that are the input means for standard discussion boards.

The next step for the board creator is to specify the relationships between message templates (see Figure 4), by checking which message templates are allowed to respond to other message templates. The resulting hierarchical structure constrains and streamlines users' comments and message response structures. After specifying the relationship the message types can take, the next step is to complete the creation of the board. In addition to supporting the creation of template structures, the system supports the ability to save, load, and share template structures.

Once a template-driven discussion board has been created, users can choose to create a new message in much the same way they would with a traditional discussion board. However, once a user has chosen to create a new message or reply to an existing message they are presented with a list of the available message templates along with their associated description. Figure 5 shows a partial screen capture of the message selection screen. This screen would contain a list of all the available message templates.

After making a selection from the available message templates, the user is then presented with that template's associated input screen (see Figure 6), the format of which was previously specified by the author of the template-driven discussion board (see Figure 3). The message description is restated at the top of the input screen in hopes of providing additional support for the user.

Template-driven communication support systems have been developed to support domain-specific conversations and problem solving (e.g. KIE (Bell & Linn, 1997), CaMILE (Guzdial et al., 1995), the Collaboratory Notebook (O'Neill & Gomez, 1994) and CSILE (Scardamalia & Bereiter, 1994)). Many of these systems are used in an education setting and have graphical interfaces that "utilize node-link graphs representing argumentation or evidential relationships between assertions" (Suthers, 1998, p. 8) and provide users with a visual representation of the conversation. Similar systems have been proposed to support argumentative decision processes in organizations (Ramesh & Whinston, 1994; Bui, Bodart, & Ma, 1998). To the best of our knowledge, the system that we created is the first template-driven communication support system implemented to support relationship development as opposed to cognitive development or information processing.

Figure 5. Users select the type message template to author

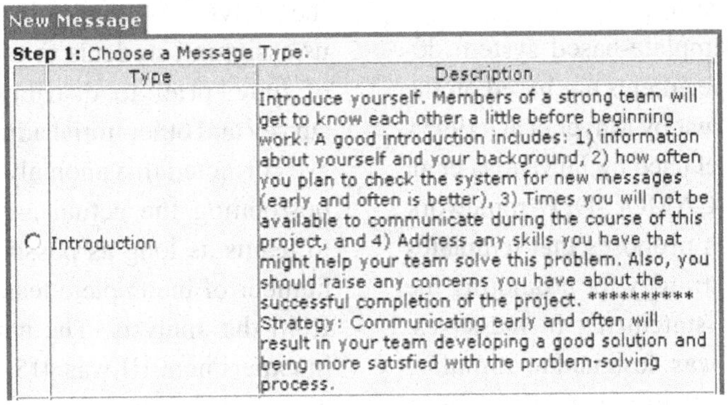

Figure 6. Message input screen for the introduction message template

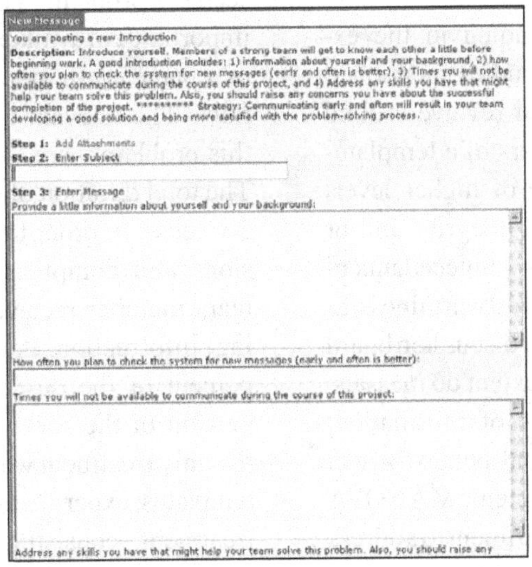

THREE EXPERIMENTAL STUDIES

We tested our template-driven communication support system with the trust templates described in the previous section in several experimental studies. In this section, we highlight the results of three experimental studies that we have conducted using the system. These experiments are part of our ongoing research on template-supported virtual teamwork, and represent a progression of efforts to assess the effectiveness of our approach. Preceding these three studies, several pilot studies were conducted as well, but those merely served to try out and refine different features and screens in the system. With some very minor variations of negligible consequence, the template-based system as described in this paper corresponds to that used in each of the experiments. Although there were slight differences between the experiments, these were very minor. Therefore, the experiments were very similar in nature.

As we used the template-based system described above, our experiments are based on the rational definition of trust by Mayer et al. (1995), build on the trust model used by Jarvenpaa et al. (1998) and extend the CAMOC-DIT framework of Te'eni (2001), which proposes that templates might be an effective strategy for promoting the inclusion of affective statements in messages. Moreover, the system was designed to stimulate the flow of information between team members, and is grounded in the work by Hart and Saunders (1997) and Nelson and Cooprider (1996). These authors found that mutual trust facilitates a freer flow of information.

The research questions studied in the experiments are based on the studies mentioned in the previous paragraph, and revolve around the following issues: (1) do users of a template-driven system show evidence of higher levels of perceived ability, perceived integrity and or perceived benevolence (these are antecedents of trustworthiness) and/or overall trustworthiness, as compared with users of a regular discussion board without templates; (2) to what extent do message templates influence the free flow of information; and (3) how does the situational context affect the use of the template-based system? MANOVA analyses were used in each experiment to address these research questions.

The first experiment, experiment I, involved 40 students in a graduate level MIS course. As discussed below, this experiment yielded quite interesting results (see also Remidez, 2003). However, as the sample size in Experiment I was limited, we conducted a follow-up experiment in a large undergraduate management course involving a total of 432 students. In the analysis we omitted those teams that had at least one member cheating or dropping out, reducing the number of students analyzed substantially. We discovered that in experiment II a number of students dropped out

just after the experiment had started, effectively reducing the sample size suitable for inclusion in the analysis. We determined that this was due to us assigning students to teams at an early point of time, prior to distributing the preliminary survey and other initial administrative activities. We corrected this anomaly in experiment III, by postponing the actual assignment of students to teams as long as possible, thus reducing the number of incomplete teams we had to exclude from the analysis. The number of participants in experiment III was 415. The write-ups of the extended results of experiments II and III are still in process.

Each experiment involved teams of 5 randomly assigned students solving a mountain survival scenario problem. The task was to rank order the importance of available items for use by survivors of a plane crash in a remote, mountainous location. The relevance and the correct solution to this problem were validated by several experts. The total duration of the task was approximately 5 weeks. In order to stimulate the team discussions and complicate the decision task, each team member received partial (but no conflicting) information. Each scenario was missing 10 percent of the descriptive information and 10 percent of the survival items. In experiment I the only treatment was the use (or non-use) of the templates; experiments II and II included a second treatment, consisting of e-mail messages that were sent to students anytime when a teammate posted a note on the discussion board. In addition to the information and descriptive statistics provided directly through the discussion boards, the students filled out pre- and post-test surveys to assess any changes in trust development. These participant surveys closely followed those used by Jarvenpaa et al. (1998). In Experiment II, the Sarker, Valacich and Sarker (2003) trust questionnaire was used as well. In addition, Experiment I included selective post-test interviews to check for undetected problems that might be unique to the context of the experiments.

In Experiment I, we found that both the flow of information (as measured by the number of messages authored and the number of messages viewed) and perceived ability were significantly higher ($p<.05$) for users of the template-driven system, but the other two antecedents of trust, perceived integrity and perceived benevolence were not significantly higher. The increase in information flow may indicate higher levels of mutual trust or be antecedents to trust development. The most interesting finding in Experiment II was that, among those teams that used the template-based system, the teams that also received e-mail notifications exhibited significantly higher levels ($p<.05$) of perceived ability and benevolence than teams that did not receive e-mail notifications. Among teams that used the regular discussion board, no such effect was detected. Experiment III showed strong evidence that template-based systems can enhance overall trustworthiness ($p<.05$), but this result was found only for those teams that also received e-mail notifications. In addition, the number of messages authored, and therefore the flow of information, was significantly enhanced ($p<.05$) for those template-driven teams that received e-mail prompts, again suggesting the possibility that mutual trust did develop.

The variable that improved most consistently through the use of templates and/or e-mail notification in experiments I–III was the flow of information. Although experiments I–III did not yield consistently increased levels for all three antecedents of trust and/or for trustworthiness, each study showed clear effects with respect to some of the variables involved, confirming that template-based systems at least hold significant promise as a means to enhance trust development in the virtual team environment.

Summarizing, we have established that there are significant differences in the interaction patterns and trust development between users of the template-driven system and those using a traditional discussion board. On the negative side, interviews with students suggest that, while most find the message templates helpful, some find them to be distracting. This is not unexpected given previous work in the area of the perceived restrictiveness of decision support systems (Silver, 1988). We are working on making the templates optional much the way that templates in Microsoft Office are optional. We are also learning from others using the system to successfully support classroom discussion (Jonassen & Remidez, 2002).

FUTURE DIRECTIONS

Message templates can be viewed as behavior/process controls because they work to promote team members' conformity to predefined communication strategies (Kirsch, 1997). Behavior controls have been used in colocated and virtual teams with different levels of success. Henderson and Lee (1992) fond that high-performing colocated IS teams exihibited high process control by managers and high outcome control by team members. In a virtual team setting, Piccoli and Ives (2003) found that teams using process controls experienced greater levels of vigilance, increased saliencey of reneging and incongruence, and decreased levels of trust.

Any action to make intentions and obligations more explicit increases the probability that deviations will be detected and viewed negatively by the team. It is possible that by prompting team members to be more explicit about their intentions that messages templates might promote the salience of reneging and incongruence, which was associated with lower levels of trust in the Piccoli and Ives study (2003). One advantage of using message templates to facilitate process control procedures is that, like this set of templates, message templates can be created to help team members address deviations when they are first detected, before they impact team preformance and permanently damange team trust. The ability to embed process support for dealing with infractions is one of the advantages that message templates have over training alone.

Trust, although important, is just one of the many types of affect that might be supported by a template-driven discussion board. In addition, through our experiments we have come to realize that the templates we created emphasize ability and integrity aspects of the conversation. While these are two important antecedents of trust (Jarvenpaa et al., 1998), benevolence is another important antecedent that our templates seem to underemphasize. One future direction might be to develop a template structure specifically designed to promote benevolence.

Moreover, as our studies support the finding by Hart and Saunders (1997) and Nelson and Cooprider (1996) that trust and a freer flow of information are associated, and indeed this flow may be enhanced particularly in the presence of both a template-based system and e-mail notification, one may seek ways to fine-tune the system design in order to optimize the communication patterns. Presumably, these patterns may lead to increased perceptions of ability, integrity and benevolence.

Other types of affect that might benefit from this type of communication support include feelings of satisfaction, cohesion and decision confidence. Each of these types of affect might require different kinds of communication support for them to fully develop in a virtual team setting. The SNS system is very versatile, and with appropriate choice and design of message templates might accommodate some of these needs. The flexibility of this system allows us to easily create and re-use entire sets of message templates and allows us to control the label, description, input format, and relationship of the messages. In effect, we can map a discourse structure onto the conversation, which opens up a new set of possibilities for understanding human computer interactions.

From a research perspective, we face issues of how to control for the effects of the system vs. the effects of the content in the system. For example, would teams benefit just the same if we simply gave them the information in the templates? Also, what is the right number of templates? Too few might have no effect, while too many might cause the user to become frustrated or not accurately use the system. Would making the templates optional, like Microsoft Word templates, be a good idea or not? These are all interesting questions that invite others to investigate along with us.

The experiments that we have conducted to date have been limited to populations of college students. It is certainly worthwhile to study the effectiveness of template-based systems such as ours in a "real world" virtual work environment. One would expect that different types of template-based systems might be more effective in a real-world environment, and that strategies effective in terms of promoting trust in teams of college students might not be useful in real-world work settings, and vice versa.

While the possible combinations of message labels, relationships, descriptions, etc. are limitless. It is important to keep in mind that message templates are inherently restrictive. Their use immediately raises questions about how much support to provide. Support can be limited to requiring students to label incoming and outgoing messages (Hilmer and Dennis, 2001) or as elaborate as forcing users to select message types (Request, Offer, Answer, etc.) and then providing custom templates for each type of message Winograd (1987-1988). A finding by Silver (1988) that different users viewed the same set of supports differently complicates template structure decisions.

Another large area that has yet to be explored is the cultural interpretation of various template sets and their impact on the team development process. For example, some of the included statements would be less natural in a non-US setting (e.g. "Hi everyone, I think we can win this"). For a discussion on cultural effects on virtual teams, see Sarker and Sahay (2004).

One strategy for overcoming the lack of explicit theoretical guidance is to draw from communication models such as Te'eni's (2001) model for guiding the design of IT. His model offers insights into how the use of message templates might impact participants' cognitive and affective load, understanding and relationships. The lack of explicit empirical guidance for designing templates might also be mediated by using software development techniques for ill-structured problems (e.g. rapid prototyping). Only after multiple sets of templates have been developed and employed can the IS community hope to develop a theoretical basis for determining the appropriate amount of support to provide for a given task and setting.

In closing, we emphasize that, in contrast with most other studies of communication support systems, SNS allows for a custom-designed structure and interface, offering ample opportunity for future research involving virtual team work, especially since the software can be downloaded free of charge from the SNS website at http://sns.internetschools.com. It is our hope that researchers will make use of this unique research opportunity.

REFERENCES

Argyris, C. (1999). *On Organizational Learning* (2nd ed.). Mallden, MA: Blackwell.

Atwater, L. E. (1988). The relative importance of situational and individual variables in predicting leader behavior: The surprising impact of subordinate trust. *Group and Organization Studies, 12*(3), 290-310.

Aubrey, B., & Kelsey, B. (2003). Further understanding of trust and performance in virtual teams. *Small Group Research, 34*(5), 575-619.

Bell, P., & Linn, M. C. (2000). Scientific arguments as learning artifacts: Designing for learning from the Web with KIE. *International Journal of Science Education, 22*(8), 797-817.

Beranek, P. (2000). The impacts of relational and trust development training on virtual teams: An exploratory investigation. Paper presented at the *33rd Hawaii International Conference on System Sciences*. Honolulu.

Bui, T., Bodart, F., & Ma, P. C. (1998). ARBAS: A formal language to support argumentation in network-base organizations. *Journal of Management Information Systems, 14*(3), 223-237.

Chidambaram, L. (1996). Relational development in computer-supported groups. *MIS Quarterly 20*(2), 143-163.

Claus, L. (2004). Too much of a good thing? Negative effects of high trust and individual autonomy in self-managing teams. *Academy of Management Journal, 47*(3), 385-400.

Clear, T., & Daniels, M. (2001). A cyber-icebreaker for an effective virtual group? In *6th Annual Conference On Innovation and Technology In Computer Science Education (ITiCSE)*, June 25-27, Canterbury.

Coppola, N., Hiltz, S., & Rotter, N. (2004). Building trust in virtual teams. *IEEE Transactions on Professional Communication, 47*(2), 65-105.

David, P., & McDaniel, R. (2004). A field study on the effect of interpersonal trust on virtual collaborative relationship performance. *MIS Quarterly, 28*(2), 183-227.

Dore, R. (1983). Goodwill and the spirit of market capitalism. *British Journal of Sociology, 34*(4), 459-482.

Dubé, L., & Paré, G. (2004). The multi-faceted nature of virtual teams. In D. J. Pauleen (Ed.), *Virtual teams: Projects, protocols, and processes* (pp. 1-39). Hershey, PA: Idea Group Publishing.

Ebner, W., & Krcmar, H. (2005). Design, implementation, and evaluation of trust-supporting components in virtual communities for patients. *Journal of Management Information Systems, 21*(4), 101-135.

Golembiewski, R. T., & McConkie, M. (1975). The centrality of interpersonal trust in group processes. In C.L. Cooper (Ed.), *Theories of group processes* (pp. 131-185). New York: John Wiley & Sons.

Griffin, K. (1967). The contribution of studies of source credibility to a theory of interpersonal trust in the communication process. *Psychological Bulletin, 68*(2), 104-120.

Guzdial, M., Kolodner, J. L., Hmelo, C., Narayanan, H. Carlson, D. Rappin, N., Hubscher, R., Turns, J., & Newsletter, W. (1996). Computer support for learning through complex problem-solving. *Communications of the ACM, 39*(4), 43-45.

Handy, C. (1995). Trust and the virtual organization. *Harvard Business Review, 73*(3), 40-50.

Hart, P., & Saunders, C. (1997). Power and trust: Critical factors in the adoption and use of electronic data interchange. *Organization Science. 8*(1), 23-42.

Henderson, J. C., & Lee, S. (1992). Managing I/S design teams: A control theories perspective. *Management Science, 38*(6), 757-777.

Hilmer, K., & Dennis, A. (2001). Stimulating thinking: Cultivating better decisions with groupware through categorization. *Journal of Management Information Systems, 17*(3), 93-114.

Huff, L. C., Cooper, J., & Jones, W. (2002). The development and consequences of trust in student project groups. *Journal of Marketing Education, 24*(1), 24-34.

Iacono, C. S., & Weisband, S. (1997). Developing trust in virtual teams. Paper presented at the *30th Annual Hawaii International Conference on System Sciences,* Honolulu.

Jarvenpaa, S., Knoll, K., & Leidner, D. (1998). Is anybody out there? Antecedents of trust in global virtual teams. *Journal of Management Information Systems, 14*(4), 29-64.

Jarvenpaa, S., & Leidner, D. (1999). Communication and trust in global virtual teams. *Organization Science, 10*(6), 791-815.

Jarvenpaa, S., Shadow, T., & Staples, S. (2004). Toward contextualized theories of trust: The role of trust in global virtual teams. *Information Systems Research, 15*(3), 250-267.

Jonassen, D., & Remidez, H. (2002). Mapping alternative discourse structures onto computer conferences. In G. Stahl (Ed.), *Computer support for collaborative learning: Foundations for a CSCL community* (pp. 237-244). Hillsdale, NJ: Erlbaum.

Kelman, H. C. (1958). Compliance, identification and internalization: Three processes of attitude change. *Journal of Conflict Resolution, 2*(1), 51-60.

Kirsch, L. J. (1997). Portfolios of control modes and IS project management. *Information Systems Research, 8*(3), 215-239.

Korsgaard, M. A., Schweiger, D. M., & Sapienza, H. J. (1995). Building commitment, attachment, and trust in strategic decision-making teams: The role of procedural justice. *Academy of Management Journal, 38*(1), 60-84.

Krackhardt, D., & Stern, R. N. (1988). Informal networks and organizational crises: An experimental simulation. *Social Psychology Quarterly, 51*(2), 123-140.

Laffey, J., Musser, D., Remidez, H., & Gottdenker, J. (2003). Networked systems for schools that learn. *Communications of the ACM, 46*(9), 192-200.

Larson, C. E., & LaFasto, F. M. J. (1989). *Teamwork: What must go right/what can go wrong.* Newbury Park, NJ: Sage.

Lawler, E. (1992). *The ultimate advantage: Creating the high-involvement organization.* San Francisco: Jossey-Bass.

Malone, T. W., Grant, K. R., Lai, K.-Y., Rao, R. & Rosenblitt, D. (1987). Semi-structured messages are surprisingly useful for computer-supported coordination. *ACM Transactions on Information Systems, 5*(2), 115-131.

Mayer, R. C., Davis, J. H., & Schoorman, F. D. (1995). An integration model of organizational trust. *Academy of Management Review, 20*(3), 709-734.

McAllister, D. J. (1995). Affect and cognition-based trust as foundation for interpersonal cooperation in organizations. *Academy of Management Journal, 38*(1), 24-59.

Meyerson, D., Weick, K. E., & Kramer, R. M. (1996). Swift trust and temporary groups. In R. M. Kramer & T. R. Tyler (Eds.), *Trust in organizations: Frontiers of theory and research*. Thousand Oaks, CA: Sage Publications.

Nelson, K. M., & Cooprider, J. G. (1996). The contribution of shared knowledge to IS group performance. *MIS Quarterly, 20*(4), 409-432.

O'Neil, D. K., & Gomez, L. M. (1994). The collaboratory notebook: A distributed knowledge building environment for project learning. *Proceedings of ED MEDIA94*. Vancouver B.C., Canada.

Piccoli, G., & Ives, B. (2003). Trust and the unintended effects of behavior control in virtual teams. *MIS Quarterly, 27*(3), 157-180.

Powell, A., Piccoli, G., & Ives, B. (2004). Virtual teams: A review of current literature and directions for future research. *The Data Base for Advances in Information Systems, 35*(1), 6-36.

Ramesh, R., & Whinston, A. (1994). Claims, arguments, and decisions: Formalisms for representation, gaming, and coordination. *Information Systems Research, 5*(3), 294-325.

Reina, D., & Reina, M. (1999). *Trust and betrayal in the workplace*. San Francisco: Berrett-Koehler.

Remidez, H. (2003). *System structure design and social consequence: The impact of message templates on affectivity in virtual teams*. Unpublished doctoral dissertation. University of Missouri, Columbia.

Sarker, S., & Sahay, S. (2004). Implications of space and time for distributed work: an interpretive study of US-Norwegian systems development teams. *European Journal of Information Systems, 13*(1), 3-20.

Sarker, S., Valacich, J., & Sarker, S. (2003). Virtual team trust: Instrument development and validation in an IS educational environment. *Information Resource Management Journal, 16*(2), 35-55.

Scardamalia, M., & Bereiter, C. (1994). Computer support for knowledge-building communities. *The Journal of Learning Sciences, 3*(3), 265-283.

Senge, P. (1990). *The fifth discipline: The art and practice of the learning organization*. New York: Doubleday.

Silver, M. (1988). User perceptions of decision support system restrictiveness: An experiment. *Journal of Management Information Systems, 5*(1), 51-65.

Suthers, D. (1998). Representations for scaffolding collaborative inquiry on ill-structured problems. Paper presented at the *1998 AERA Annual Meeting*. San Diego, CA.

Te'eni, D. (2001). Review: A cognitive-affective model of organizational communication for designing IT. *MIS Quarterly, 25*(2), 251-312.

Williamson, O.E. (1975). *Markets and hierarchies*. New York: The Free Press.

Winograd, T. (1987-1988). A language/action
perspective on the design of cooperative work.
Human-Computer Interaction, 3(1), 3-30.

*This work was previously published in the International Journal of e-Collaboration, Vol. 3, No. 1, pp.
65-83, copyright 2007 by IGI Publishing, formerly Idea Group Publishing (an imprint of IGI Global).*

Chapter IXX
Web Service Design Concepts and Structures for Support of Highly Interconnected E–Health Infrastructures:
A Bottom–Up Approach

Adamantios Koumpis
ALTEC S.A., Greece

ABSTRACT

In this chapter we present organizational aspects that appear when considering the case of interconnecting and integrating different compartments of a modern hospital. While the information and communication technologies provide advanced and powerful means for the creation of coherent information supply services, such as the Web service and ontology technologies, there is a lack of appropriate organizational metaphors that will enable the successful assimilation of these technologies, helping to aid in the improvement of critical cost parameters that concentrate a large part of the hospital's management resources, while also helping to improve the knowledge capital and the intangible and immaterial assets of any particular hospital, which are considered as the most essential and scarce resource. In this paper we presents a technology-based approach for solving interoperability problems at the service level, and we deliberately adopt a problem-solving approach that has successfully been adopted by the European IST Project ARTEMIS.

INTRODUCTION

What we more intensively experience is that the Web is moving from being a collection of pages toward a collection of services that interoperates through the Internet (Paolucci, Kawamura, Payne, & Sycara, 2002). According to the same source:

Web services provide a new model of the web in which sites exchange dynamic information on demand. This change is especially important for the e-business community, because it provides an opportunity to conduct business faster and more efficiently. Indeed, the opportunity to manage supply chains dynamically to achieve the greatest advantage on the market is expected to create great value added and increase productivity. On the other hand, automatic management of supply chain opens new challenges: first, web services should be able to locate automatically other services that provide a solution to their problems, second, services should be able to interoperate to compose automatically complex services. In this paper we concentrate on the first problem: the location of web services on the basis of the capabilities that they provide.

In this chapter our concern is the application of some Web service design concepts and structures in order to support highly interconnected e-health infrastructures; though health for sure constitutes a special application domain with several idiosyncrasies and singular characteristics, there is a great extent of paradigms and analogies that can be drawn from the area of e-business and supply chain management.

We believe that our contribution by means of the work conducted under the European IST project ARTEMIS (ARTEMIS, 2004), which was lead by professor Asuman Dogac of the Middle East Technical University, constitutes a success story that can be followed to form the basis of several VE ventures in the area of e-health as well as in other business domains.

Currently, the majority of the interoperability problems of medical information systems are two-fold (Bicer, Banu Laleci, Dogac, & Kabak 2005a; Bicer, Kilic, Dogac, & Banu Laleci, 2005b):

1. First there are multiple, incompatible, proprietary approaches to connecting disparate applications to clinical networks and information systems. As a result, for example it is not possible to integrate electronically the clinical patient records with critical emergency control information.
2. Secondly, when there are standards to achieve interoperability, there are more than one standard to represent the same information, which in turn creates an interoperability problem. For example, GEHR, CEN 13606

and openEHR are all standards for patient electronic health records.

The proposed model provides the most important entity of the healthcare industry, namely the hospital, with an ideal platform to achieve difficult organizational and technology integration problems. The proposed services as developed in our project ARTEMIS allow for seamless integration of disparate applications representing different and, at times, competing standards, thus allowing for a service to be invoked *on demand* pervasively by business processes, applications or people to fulfil a particular function. The latter forms the most important innovation of the presented work and a tangible contribution towards smarter hospitals that are capable to build dynamic information exchange and sharing infrastructures that might have the form of virtual enterprises. Though from a legal point of view there are many problems and difficulties, it is however important that such a goal will guide the investments in the health industry in Europe.

As will be further described, the innovation of our approach comes to the fact that our approach for design and management of services is implemented in a distributed service infrastructure according to a *preplanned usage of a multiple service actors' scheme*. The term distributed service infrastructure is used for description of an environment with the following characteristics:

1. It consists of a number of service flows that are executed using resources of several sites simultaneously.
2. That service flows communicate with each other by exchanging messages over a commonly agreed network of participants (in our case it is the network of the hospitals or hospital units involved in the provision of a service).

Our efforts may be viewed from within the perspective of building the service flow execution kernel for mobile agent applications that may regarded as the high-end of the foreseen application service providers (ASP) market in terms of *aggregating* functionality requested by the particular differentiated users of the distributed service environment. In this respect, the approach we employ address the following two needs:

1. From an *operational* viewpoint, it focuses on the intersite aspects (timing and security) for remote interoperability of the participating hospital services. Intrasite, it will focus on the dynamic adaptation of the application to changes in the environment of a single hospital (unit).
2. From a *methodological* viewpoint, it focuses on the way to capture and validate dependability requirements and validates these requirements, on the way to derive from requirements the structure of the modeling approach, and on the use of modeling to drive the development and the assessment of the proposed solutions.

The building of the proposed services is based on:

*   **Service elements:** Regarded from the service designer's perspective as these concern reusable elements that may be used for developing new services or enhancing/changing the functionality of existing (operational) ones
*   **Service pages:** Entities upon which the hospital user (i.e., a doctor, a nurse or an administration employee) may regard services either for carrying out customization activities such as personalization of the access-to-service interface for example, for different user categories and different types of usage (data entry, retrieval of data, sophisticated query formulation and processing, etc.)

The approach taken helps in the creation of a significant competitive advantage and market knowledge and creates first-mover advantage in the addressed transition towards *service-oriented architectures*. This know-how is faster transferable from within the operational environment to those key divisions that will be acting as uptakers and adopters. Of course, a key objective has been how to get improved ideas to those who can effectively apply them. The main focus is to gain the technological capabilities and the necessary means (i.e., methods, practices and software components) so that any new services will be affordably priced for a segment of the hospital market that has been *largely unable to afford such services—namely small and medium sized hospitals with fewer than 200 employees such as the case of regional or prefecture-level hospital and / or health centers.*

The access-to-service environment under implementation enables the users of the service platform to:

*   Establish an overall service flow direction, by means of providing linkage to a set of pre-programmed resources that are executed in the distributed (Internet) environment, such as ERP, patient recording applications, and so forth.
*   Acquire resources for a particular service property which may be it a service flow, a service element, or a service "page".
*   Provide "capabilities" to a service flow by means of integrates both structural and behavioral aspects from within a single perspective, which will be utilized to instantiate the actual service delivery at the end user's point.
*   Execute the service flow by means of utilizing resources to accomplish the particularly assigned service scenario.

The last may also be regarded also the "bottom-line" for the actual service delivery by a particular service flow to support the purpose of the latter's establishment (i.e., the reason for existence of that particular service flow in the overall hospital value chain).

The Artemis Project

Medicine is one of the few domains to have some domain knowledge in a computable form which can be exploited in defining the semantics of Web services. This semantic knowledge exists in "controlled vocabularies", or "terminologies". Some vocabularies are rich semantic nets, such as SNOMED-CT while others such as ICPC and ICD are little more than lexicons of terms. Although such vocabularies do not express all the possible semantics of basic concepts—they are generally limited to terms, definitions and some semantic relationships—they offer significant value in terms of expressing the semantic of Web services.

ARTEMIS is a project that runs under the 6th Framework Programme of the European Commission, and aims to develop a semantic Web services based interoperability framework for the health care domain. The interoperability problems of medical information systems are two fold:

- First there are multiple, incompatible, proprietary approaches to connecting disparate applications to clinical networks and information systems. As a result, for example it is not possible to integrate electronically the clinical patient records with billing information.

- Secondly, when there are standards to achieve interoperability, there are more than one standard to represent the same information, which in turn creates an interoperability problem. For example, GEHR, CEN 13606 and openEHR are all standards for patient electronic health records. The CEN 13606 model, for instance, describes a hierarchical representation for all data using the cluster and data_item classes. The GEHR model does the same thing, with its hierarchical_value and hierarchical_group classes.

Figure 1 gives an overview of the ARTEMIS architecture to enable the peer-to-peer networks

Figure 1. An overview of the service-oriented architecture in the ARTEMIS project

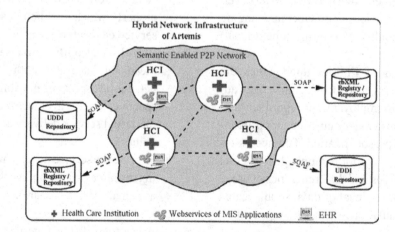

as a platform for publishing, discovering and invoking semantically enriched Web services that wrap Medical Information System Applications based on the semantic Web initiative. To achieve this objective the following basic components will be provided by the ARTEMIS project:

- Semantically enriched and secure P2P Web service environment for medical information systems
- Semantic wrapper for Web service creation and composition that adapts the medical information system applications
- Service-based access layer for electronic health records
- User friendly interfaces for the healthcare organizations, such as for publishing, discovering and composing Web services

These components are presented in more detail in Figure 2.

Furthermore, in our approach we provide a P2P platform that with enhanced capabilities for publishing, discovering and invoking *semantically enriched medical Web services in a highly secure framework.*

This component will be a base for the medical informatics Web services to operate on. The objective of this component is to facilitate the discovery of medical Web services both from the individual peers in a network and also from the public service registries.

However neither existing P2P architectures nor the Web service registries provide facilities for exploiting the semantics of the services, and P2P security models are still emerging mainly in the context of the WS-Security standardization roadmap (Dogac, Bicer, Banu Laleci, Kabak, Gurcan, & Eichelberg, 2006).

In order to achieve an integrated hybrid semantic based infrastructure, this component will be developed in three main steps. In the first step existing Web service registries will be enhanced to store domain specific ontologies, and services based on these ontologies; the second step will be incorporating service semantics in to P2P networks, particularly developing semantic based advertisement and discovery mechanisms for P2P networks. In the final step, semantically enriched service registries will be integrated to the P2P architecture.

Figure 2. ARTEMIS components overview

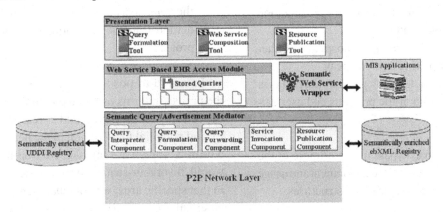

POSITIONING OF THE SYSTEM AND THE APPROACH

Having in mind that some of the most essential problems that users, administrators, developers and vendors of information supply services in the health discipline, as well as in every application and service field, face today may be viewed under the common denominator of "interoperability" problems, the presented approach illustrates possible ways to address these problems. A design goal of the project is to provide a cohesive technological infrastructure independent of any specific implementation pathway and to contain features that are effective and easy to use in a broad range of representative networked service environments which may be subject to variable configurations. For this reason we recognize the following types and broad categories of users:

1. Platform and service vendors (may concern IT companies, content providers or—in case they exhibit competencies in any of them—as a specialization of the broker category)
2. Professional health service providers (as a specialization of the broker category)
3. Service developers (as a specialization of the broker category)
4. Service administrators (as a specialization of the broker category)
5. Service end users (i.e., hospitals—either public or private owned ones)
6. Information technology managers (as a specialization of the previous end user category)

These users participate in one or more of the following four stages in the development and usage of the health-based service infrastructures:

- **Establishment:** Implementing and deploying the presented service approach across the health information "supply chain."

- **Build:** Exercising the service elements to define a baseline service flow configuration (establishing the exchange paths between known service sources and targets as well as the various filtering mechanisms involved).
- **Operation:** Operating the service flow infrastructures.
- **Maintenance:** Exercising the introduced concepts to define changes in the distributed service configuration (e.g., to cover changes as "small" as the addition of new service elements in the overall service configuration and as "large" as merger with or replacement by another configuration such as in the case of replacing a service flow with a group of supplying service flows loosely linked and using a new distributed management scheme); this is a quite complex issue for which description may be regarded as outside the scope of the project. It concerns the "reverse" engineering of a service into a set of constituent services that should be chosen for support of an, for example, localization exercise (a global service gets localized and a set of local service points are now assigned the responsibility for running the service). In the following we present some usage scenarios that illustrate activities in the *build* and *maintenance* steps that clearly demonstrate the value addedness of the approach.

In regard to positioning the added value of the project in terms of linkage with the business opportunity for the project and its real applicability and potential for adoption in the health sector within a supportive uptake environment that would favorably sustain business development in that specific area, we note that there is certain potential in coupling the project work with developments in the application service provider (ASP) market segment. In our context we adopt the usual definition for an application service provider as a

Table 1. Shows the forseen added values to the users

User category	Stage	Problem or need	Tools and repositories	How the system promotes better service utilization
			Foreseen Added Value to the Users	
Platform and Service vendors	Build	Must subscribe to standards for intervendor interconnect	– Web service infrastructure – Common Repository Facility – Tools for modeling, development, deployment and service management	– System provides a common "backplane" for pluggable subsystems. – It may be exploited as a globally usable notation for metaservice exchange protocols which enables flexible distribution of distributed services over a heterogeneous collection of information systems.
Professional Service Providers	Build	Must accumulate and reuse elements from service engagement	Third party and in-house tools that apply metaservices to concrete service-base catalogs and vice versa	Reusable, editable, and extensible metaservice should provide a first-level "asset base" that builds (new) value. This base of reusable elements starts a self-reinforcing feedback loop with continually increasing returns improved by engagement productivity for the users.
Professional Service Providers	Maintenance	Must modify Service process configuration: knowing what and where to modify; knowing dependency closure	Third party or in-house tools to manage reconfiguration editing of a service flow	System exposes the information required to modify a service flow model. Service context definition and self-describing features for the service flows are used to isolate dependency relationships.
Professional Service Providers, Dielemma Service Administrators	Maintenance	Must integrate existing tools and data which adhere to standards other than service flow model into a distributed service configuration environment.	Tools based on ability to incorporate metamodels of services and alternate service definition practices and standards.	System does or can subsume non-service representations. For example, may be elaborated in the future to contain any XML-based service model with a focus to domain-specific characteristics.
Service Administrators	Build	Must establish and manage expressions, relationships, and lineage over multiple service-based schemata.	Tools that use built-in facilities to define schema content, relationships, and lineage.	System design is based on need to manage such information at multiple levels. The basic Web services will have to be designed to allow navigation of metaservices correlated to schemata.
Service Administrators	Maintenance	Must add, subtract, re-partition, reallocate, or merge service resources in deployment configuration.	Service management tools.	System consists of models of metaservices that assist in making such changes and allow impact of these changes to be assessed.

3rd-party service firm which deploys, manages, and remotely hosts a both the various application and service portfolios through centrally-located servers in a "rental" or lease agreement as well as the related business model for operating them. Our work in the project helps a revisit to the topic of ASPs for two main reasons:

• We now see that there is a strong future for ASP related businesses.
• A great deal has changed on the ASP competitive landscape.

Over the past months multiple variations on the basic ASP model have emerged which warrant review and analysis. In addition, the ASP business model is beginning to face serious challenges regarding its viability and broader market acceptance, linking those models to the potential of providing through ASPs the means for operating into a networked enterprise environment.

In its "purest" sense, the ASP model invokes the delivery of software as a service. In exchange for accessing the application, the client renders rental-like payments; in this respect, an ASP facilitates a remote, centrally-managed "rent-an-application" service for the client. The emphasis is placed on the *use and not on the ownership* of the application. The client no longer owns the application or the responsibilities associated with initial and ongoing maintenance. The client, through an Internet browser, accesses remote, centralized computer servers hosting the application. Only the results from the application are managed locally by the client.

Currently the ability of an ASP to sell "mission-critical" solutions to early ASP adopters hinges to a large degree on whether the application being hosted was designed specifically for delivery over the Internet. In point of fact, many of the "mission-critical" packages sold by highly respected vendors were *not* developed for a hosted / services delivery methodology.

Where the added value of our approach comes to the stage relates to the fact that our approach for design and management of services is implemented in a distributed service infrastructure according to planned (actually: envisaged) usage of a multiple actors scheme. The term distributed

Figure 3. Distinction of roles in the operation of the system

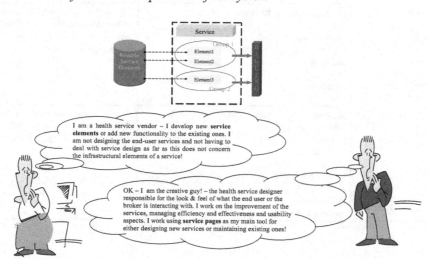

service infrastructure is used for description of an environment with the following characteristics:

1.   It consists of a number of service flows that are executed using resources of several sites simultaneously.

2.   The service flows communicate with each other by exchanging messages over a commonly agreed network of participants (in our case it is the network of the health organizations i.e., hospitals and regional health centers involved).

In this respect our efforts in the project may be viewed from within the perspective of building the service flow execution kernel for mobile agent applications that may regarded as the high-end of the foreseen ASP market in terms of *aggregating* functionality requested by the particular differentiated users of the distributed service environment.

SETTING THE STAGE FOR THE VE BUSINESS DESCRIPTION

According to "The Emerging European Health Telematics Industry" market analysis report (2000), developed by Deloitte (2000) on assignment by the European Commission-Directorate General Information Society, "the healthcare sector represents 6% of the overall current European IT market" and the "consolidation on the supply side" constitutes on the most important "vital conditions" for the market growth.

The ARTEMIS platform can have a significant role in e-health, as it may form the basis for realizing most of the e-services that all health institutions will be providing to their beneficiaries.

The ARTEMIS platform aims at delivering a *semantic Web services based interoperability support* and an associated software engineering methodology specific to the issue of e-health data, systems and service interoperability. The approach

of the ARTEMIS project to the addressed problem is holistic. It targets in satisfying the needs of all stakeholders in the provision of such e-services, namely health sector IT staff (administrators), health sector domain experts (medical experts and doctors), managers of health sector authorities (managers) and patients, businesses that do business with health authorities (e.g., in terms of hospital procurements, etc.) or any other health sector employees (end users). The approach of ARTEMIS also covers all steps and processes involved in the e-health services provision, as it will be demonstrated further on in the project, and shall cover other related parties, such as insurance companies.

In this chapter, the opportunities and drivers for the project are analyzed, the ARTEMIS platform is positioned amongst other relative products and technologies, the available services are outlined, and lastly, the Unique Selling Proposition of the ARTEMIS project is presented.

Business Opportunity: Business Drivers

According to the above mentioned survey the drivers for the provision of e-services as those we are developing in ARTEMIS (2004) include:

*   As the market is made up of hardware, software and services, the role played by services in 1998 was an estimated 26% while the projection for 2002 was for this to raise to 37 %, becoming the largest component in terms of revenue ahead of the other two, and with an incremental pattern
*   "The main trend which can be observed in European hospitals, which presents a challenge in the coming years, consists of integrating the different areas of the HIS (medical, nursing, technical or administrative) into a common architecture.
*   However, when looking more closely at hospital information systems, the picture is

more fragmented. The analysis confirmed that currently there is no architecture which can integrate all modules of the HIS, but they are often run alongside each other in the forms of the clinical patient record, the laboratory information system, the patient administration system, etc." (p. 188).

- "Apart from internal integration of HIS, hospitals are also heading towards external integration on a regional, national and even an international level. Here, the emergence of care networks, involving many different healthcare actors, hopes to optimise patient management" (p. 192).

In the light of the above the main opportunity concerns an apparent need for common service platforms. Furthermore, it was identified that the main need that ARTEMIS aims to fulfill is to enable *otherwise disconnected systems* to communicate *over different standards*. This will result in services of one health institution being available to another, which will carry all users of the ARTEMIS platform to become members of the same domain.

Since ARTEMIS works over standards and enables to map and convert them to each other, it lowers the negotiation cost, when one system is integrated to or with another. As a result, some services which may require huge costs in terms of investment to hardware/staff may be presented to other institutions, resulting in much better *price discrimination* for suppliers, and new service opportunities for consumers of such services.

This service-oriented business model enables implementers of products to have a much larger market by selling / renting them as services over the ARTEMIS "network".

The basic business opportunity for the ARTEMIS project lies in that the health sector spends on integration forms—including cost of designing, management and handling—is massive. Bureaucracy is the inevitable consequence

of the traditional method of handling the extreme volume of information and knowledge derived from them, while the low quality of service is another collateral outcome of this situation.

ARTEMIS aims at capitalizing on this opportunity by offering the means to the health authorities and institutions to reduce involved costs by the implementation of e-services (note: we refer to e-services for simplicity reasons; the correct terms for the ARTEMIS services is "semantically enriched Web services") and associated service management infrastructures. The appropriate design of e-services, according to ARTEMIS approach, will increase cost-efficiency and effectiveness. Moreover, the interaction between the health sector and businesses will be improved when the ARTEMIS tools are combined with best practices. Additionally, the platform is open to enhancements with facilities such as open source development paradigm and self-regulated communities of practice.

Identification of the ARTEMIS Platform

Taking into consideration the various software solutions available to health authorities, it is evident that the market is quite chaotic in the sense that there are no well-established products on the market for healthcare-specific enterprise application integration (EAI), but the rather inflationary estimates we mention previously (have) attract(ed) many vendors. This means that there are many projects, many announcements, but very few results so far. This is where ARTEMIS comes and fills the gap.

Only for Germany, where one of the partners of the ARTEMIS project came from, are two indicative projects to take into consideration, namely:

- The Bit4Health project, a big national initiative to establish a smartcard based PKI for the healthcare sector which would be used for electronic prescriptions, digital signatures (e.g., patient consent) and, at some point in the future) as an "access key" to a national electronic healthcare record, which is, however, totally unspecified at the moment. (http://www.dimdi.de/de/ehealth/karte/bit4health/index.htm)

- The "doctor 2 doctor" (D2D) and "VCS" communication standards, which aim at integration of private practices. While D2D is promoted by an organization representing medical doctors, VCS is promoted by healthcare IT industry. (http://www.kvno.de/mitglieder/d2d/; http://www.vdap.de/html/vcs/vcs.html)

Both projects have at most a few hundred installations so far, which is a very limited success given there are about 130,000 private practices in Germany.

ARTEMIS as a stand-alone product is characterized as a user-friendly service development tool, which can be complementary to the above software solutions. But more importantly, it can be offered as a solution, and furthermore it features a service platform which interacts with the various legacy systems and assists deployment parties in the generation and manipulation of online (transaction-based) services. Using ARTEMIS as a stand-alone product will simplify the development and maintenance of these e-services. On the other hand, using ARTEMIS with another installed IT system will not create any technical or process problems in the integration stage, due to the platform's open architecture.

The ARTEMIS platform constitutes an environment that enables health sector professionals in different levels (administrators, experts / doctors and managers) to develop and maintain services for both their own institution and for other authorities as end users. In this environment an employee with the necessary skills and domain knowledge will be able to use a predefined form template or create a new service in order to implement a new functionality or to edit an existing service.

The employee will be assisted by the ARTEMIS development environment (i.e., the ARTEMIS platform), which will automate parts of the development process. At the end of the development procedure the employee will be able to activate the service even if the connection to the back-end has not been implemented yet. The platform will retain all collected data and once the IT staff implements the connection to the back-end the data will be processed.

The types of the envisaged users of the system can be listed as follows:

- Users should know the backend legacy system.
- Users should know the input output structures of the applications from which the Web services will be created.

Additionally, we can open ARTEMIS certificate programs such as:

- ARTEMIS healthcare ontology engineer
- ARTEMIS healthcare service engineer
- ARTEMIS P2P engineer

Unique Selling Proposition of the ARTEMIS Services

A holistic approach in the management of services in the health sector reveals the Unique selling proposition of the ARTEMIS system. The system's approach to the introduction of semantically enriched Web services in the health sector very much takes into account, that the addressed area is a process and person related issue. It has to involve individual participants from different organizations and with different backgrounds, cultural elements and adopted practices, where continuous and situated elaboration and maintenance of the required knowledge through the involved parties is necessary (actually: a precondition if not a sine qua non). This means a shift from a technology oriented paradigm to an activity oriented paradigm, where involved human beings, administrative processes and technical resources represent the equally eligible units of analysis and where system design follows the concept of socio-technical systems as holistic and dynamic structures.

The ARTEMIS project suggests that by adopting the above *holistic approach* for the introduction of semantically enriched Web services in the health sector, most of the following problems, that health sector stakeholders face can be reduced or even eliminated:

- Complexity in creating e-services and most importantly difficulty in encapsulating domain expertise in them
- Difficulty in interoperability with existing IT systems within the organization and with external IT systems of other organizations
- Lack of user-friendliness for the end-user in the service creation phase
- Lack of mechanisms to encapsulate the knowledge as a whole also by transforming implicit knowledge into an explicit form. ARTEMIS shall provide tools for creating and mapping ontologies; of course, ARTE-MIS aim is not proposing ontologies to the healthcare community, but providing all the necessary technology means so that if ontologies are available, then be also exploited to facilitate semantic interoperability.
- Lack of coherent process models for exploiting the use of "public" e-services within the health sector
- Organizational and cultural barriers, such as health sector employees' fear of new technology and new methods of work.

Target Market: A Dynamic Health Service Market

ARTEMIS supports the concept and the implementation of decentralization in European health care systems thus setting the stage for multiple different types of synergies and ventures to emerge and foster a culture of joining efforts and resources. Though such an exercise may face impediments from the legal environments on the one hand and from the tendency of private organizations to operate on short term profitability plans, it is yet an open challenge for all actors in Europe and internationally.

The concept of decentralization has become a cornerstone of health policymaking in an increasing number of Western European countries. Once confined only to the Nordic region and Switzerland, intergovernmental decentralization has now become a central principle of health policy in Spain and Italy, in a different context in the United Kingdom (to Scotland, Wales and Northern Ireland), and to a lesser degree in France, Portugal and more recently in Greece.

In certain respects, decentralization has become a synonym for a strengthening process of regionalization not just in the health sector, but in broader social as well as political arenas, serving as something of a cultural corrective in a Europe where more and more aspects of national sovereignty are being exercised at the supranational European Union level.

The best-known public administration effort to define decentralization is that of (Rondinelli, 1983), with a four-part, structurally oriented framework of:

- Devolution
- De-concentration
- Delegation
- Privatization

The economic argument in favor of decentralization typically has as its common denominator the belief that decentralization will create competition between different local actors, thus opening the door for local/regional-based small or medium-sized enterprises to innovate and provide cost-efficient services to the health care institutions for both sides (i.e., themselves and the particular health organizations). Not unlike economic assumptions about commodity markets generally, the economic argument here is that decentralization will enable different SMEs to provide different levels of *e*-health-related services, which will generate three economically-"prized" advantages:

- Greater efficiency in the service provision process (same is the case for the service conception, design and delivery processes)
- Greater choice for the health institutions of different alternative services
- Smaller complexity (bureaucracy) reduced times and improved responsiveness in the identification of a need and its fulfillment

Moreover, the complex intergovernmental relations created by the EU single market are seen as an extremely suitable opening to adopt such an economically-driven mechanism.

Of course, the basic and strongest from an economical standpoint argument regarding the disadvantages of decentralization focuses on the inefficiency and duplication of having multiple small service providers.

At this point it is interesting to carry out some type of sensitivity analysis regarding how many customers should an SME afford to have for ARTEMIS customers so that it can operate its business with different levels of profitability and amortization period. (Independently to this, there is also the concern (worry, rather) that such smaller operating units will be managerially weaker than larger ones.)

CONCLUSION

With the approach developed as part of the IST Project ARTEMIS, we provide the healthcare industry with an ideal platform to achieve difficult integration problems while also utilising the VE concept as the underlying basis for all different types of ventures and business partnerships. Our Web service model encapsulates already existing applications and access to documents in a standard way and incorporates service providers, service consumers and service registries.

It should be noted that currently most prominent Web service registries are universal description, discovery, integration (UDDI) and electronic business XML (ebXML). There are also very recent efforts to use peer-to-peer networks based on Web services. However both service registries and P2P architectures available do not provide semantically enriched search capabilities.

Furthermore, in ARTEMIS we provide extensions to these architectures to enable discovery of the Web services based on their semantic descriptions. As mentioned above, medicine is one of the few domains to have some domain knowledge in a computable form, which we exploit in defining the semantics of medical Web services.

The nature of business model research is extremely demanding as an exercise (Afuah, 2003; Alt & Zimmermann, 2001) and in many scientific research projects is not given adequate importance – however the reasoning behind a business model is not the understanding of a phenomenon, rather it is a problem-solution finding approach. In this respect, a particular technology may or may not facilitate the success of a business model; and similar to this, a particular market may or may not support the uptake of a particular solution as result of a more or less appropriate business model.

As a result of the approach taken, virtual enterprises (VEs) may emerge taking the form of joint ventures which will aim to provide operative and highly specialized value added services in all necessary e-health application fronts related to individuals, private companies and public health organizations, such as in the following application fields:

- Single point access to health services using technologies and methodologies developed within the project and which base on the ARTEMIS conceptual architecture and service modeling approach
- Heterogeneous hospital platform integration for support of online one-stop-shop services in various situations
- Design and lifecycle management of integrated hospital or other health care organization services from different back-offices, based on advanced interoperability frameworks and standards for the health sector

ACKNOWLEDGMENT

Work reported was partially funded by the European Commission under the contract IST-1-002103-STP, and under the e-Health priority. The authors would like to thank the European Commission for the generous support provided. More information about the ARTEMIS project the reader can find under in the official project Web site: http://www.srdc.metu.edu.tr/webpage/projects/artemis/.

REFERENCES

Afuah, A., & Tucci, C. (2003). *Internet business models and strategies*. Boston: McGraw Hill.

Alt, R., & Zimmermann, H. (2001). Introduction to special section – Business models. *Electronic Markets Journal, 11*(1).

ARTEMIS (2004). *IST project ARTEMIS: A Semantic Web service-based P2P infrastructure for the interoperability of medical information systems.* Coordinator Middle East Technical University, Software Research and Development Center, Turkey.

Bicer, V., Banu Laleci, G., Dogac, A., & Kabak, Y. (2005, October 19-21). Providing semantic interoperability in the healthcare domain through ontology mapping. In *Proceedings of the E-Challenges 2005 Conference*, Ljubljana, Slovenia.

Bicer, V., Kilic, O., Dogac, A., & Banu Laleci, G. (2005, October). Archetype-based semantic interoperability of Web service messages in the healthcare domain. *International Journal on Semantic Web & Information Systems, 1*(4).

Deloitte (2000). *The emerging European health telematics industry* (Market Analysis Report). European Commission-Directorate General Information Society.

Dogac, A., Bicer, V., Banu Laleci, G., Kabak, Y., Gurcan, Y., Eichelberg, M., & Riesmeier, J. (2006, February 12-16). Untangle the Web: Communicating through the Web services using semantics. In *Proceedings of the 2006 Annual HIMSS Conference*, San Diego, California.

Paolucci, M., Kawamura, T., Payne, T. R., & Sycara, K. (2002). Importing the semantic web in UDDI. In *Proceedings of the E-Services and the Semantic Web Workshop*.

Rondinelli, D. A. (1983). *Decentralization in developing countries*. (Staff Working Paper No. 581). Washington, DC: World Bank.

Compilation of References

Adami, G., Avesani, P., & Sona, D. (2003). Clustering documents in a web directory. In *Proceedings of the 5th ACM International Workshop on Web Information and Data Management* (pp. 66-73).

Afsamanesh, H., Garita, C., Hertzberger, B., & Santos Silva, V. (1997). Management of distributed information in virtual enterprises: The PRODNET approach. In *ICE'97 International Conference on Concurrent Enterprising.*

Afuah, A., & Tucci, C. (2003). *Internet business models and strategies.* Boston: McGraw Hill.

Agent-Oriented Software Engineering. *Research Area Examination* (2005). Retrieved from http://www.deg.byu.edu/proposals/ResearchAreaExamMuhammedJM.pdf

Aggarwal, R., Verma, K., Miller, J., & Milnor, W. (2004, September). Contstraint Driven Web Service Composition in METEOR-S. In *IEEE International Conference on Services Computing (SCC'04)* (pp. 23-30). Los Alamitos, CA: IEEE Society Press.

AGROVOC (2006). The AGROVOC multilingual dictionary of the United Nations Food and Agriculture Organization. Retrieved February 18, 2007, from www.fao.org/agrovoc/

Akkiraju, R., et al. (2005). Web service semantics: WSDL-S technical note version 1.0. Retrieved February 12, 2007, from http://lsdis.cs.uga.edu/library/download/WSDL-S-V1.html

Albert, M., Laengle, T., & Woern, H. (2002). Development tool for distributed monitoring and diagnosis systems. In M. Stumptner & F. Wotawa (Eds.), In *Proceedings of the*

13th International Workshop on Principles of Diagnosis, Semmering, Austria.

Albert, M., Laengle, T., Woern, H., Capobianco, M., & Brighenti, A. (2003). Multi-agent systems for industrial diagnostics. In *Proceedings of 5th IFAC Symposium on Fault Detection, Supervision and Safety of Technical Processes*, Washington DC.

Alexakis, S., Koelmel, B., & Heep, T. (2004). VO in industry: State of the art. In L.M. Camarina-Matos & H. Afsarmanesh (Eds.), *Collaborative networked organisations: A research agenda for emerging business models* (pp. 15-26). Kluwer Academic Publishers.

Al-Hammad, A.-M. (2000). Common interface problems among various construction parties. *Journal of Performance of Constructed Facilities, 14*(2), 71-74.

Allen, R., & Garlan, D. (1994). Formalizing architectural connection. In *ICSE '94: Proceedings of the 16th international conference on Software engineering* (pp. 71-80). Los Alamitos, CA: IEEE Computer Society Press.

Alonso, E. (2002). AI and agents: State of the art. *AI Magazine, 23*(3), 25-29.

Alonso, G. (1999). WISE: Business to business e-commerce. In *9th Workshop on Research Issues on Data Engineering (RIDE-VE'99)*. Sydney.

Alonso, G., Casati, F., Kuno, H., et al. (2004). *Web services concepts, architectures and applications.* Springer-Verlag.

Alt, R., & Zimmermann, H. (2001). Introduction to special section: Business models. *Electronic Markets Journal, 11*(1).

Alvarinhas, H. M. G. (2006) *Locating, negotiating and contracting services on Web.* Unpublished master's thesis, University of Aveiro, Portugal.

Andrews, T., et al. (2003) *Business Process Execution Language for Web Services.* 2nd public draft release, Version 1.1

Ankolekar, A., Burstein, M., Hobbs, J. R., Lassila, O., Martin, D. L., McIlraith, S. A., Narayanan, S., Paolucci, M., Payne, T., Sycara, K., & Zeng, H. (2001). DAML-S semantic markup for Web services. In *Proceedings of the First Semantic Web Working Symposium (SWWS '01).*

AOSE Technical Forum Group (2004). *AL3-TF1 Report.* Retrieved January 31, 2007, from http://www.pa.icar.cnr.it/~cossentino/al3tf1/docs/aose_tfg1_report.pdf

Appleton, D.S. (1995). Business reengineering with business rules. In V. Grover & W. J. Kettinger (Eds.), *Business Process Change: Reengineering concepts, Methods and Technologies* (pp. 291-329). Idea Group Publishing.

Archimede, B., & Coudert, T. (2001). Reactive scheduling using a multi-agent model: The SCEP framework. *Engineering Application of Artificial Intelligence, 14,* 667-683.

Arenas, A., Djordjevic, I., Dimitrakos, T., et al. (2005). Toward web services profiles for trust and security in virtual organizations. In *Proceedings of the 6th IFIP Working Conference on Virtual Enterprises*, Valencia, Spain.

Argyris, C. (1999). *On organizational learning* (2nd ed.). Mallden, MA: Blackwell.

Arlow, J., & Neustadt, I. (2002). *UML and the unified process.* London: Addison Wesley.

Arsanjani, A. (2001). A domain-language approach to designing dynamic enterprise component-based architectures to support business services. In *39th International Conference and Exhibition on Technology of Object-Oriented Languages and Systems. TOOLS* (pp. 130-141).

ARTEMIS (2004). *IST project ARTEMIS: A Semantic Web service-based P2P infrastructure for the interop-erability of medical information systems.* Coordinator Middle East Technical University, Software Research and Development Center, Turkey.

Artemis IST-Project (2005). *A Semantic web service-based P2P infrastructure for the interoperability of medical information systems.* Retrieved February 13, 2007, from http://www.srdc.metu.edu.tr/webpage/projects/artemis/

Arunachalam, R., & Sadeh, N.M. (2004). The supply chain trading agent competition. *Electronic Commerce Research and Applications, 4,* 63-81.

Athanasiadis, I. N. (2006). An intelligent service layer upgrades environmental information management. *IEEE IT Professional, 8*(3), 34-39.

Athanasiadis, I. N., & Mitkas, P. A. (2004). An agent-based intelligent environmental monitoring system. *Management of Environmental Quality, 15*(3), 238-249.

Athanasiadis, I. N., Solsbach, A. A., Mitkas, P., & Gómez, J. M. (2005). An agent-based middleware for environmental information management. In L. Filho, et al. (Eds.), *Second international ICSC symposium on information technologies in environmental engineering* (pp. 253-267). Osnabrück, Germany.

Atwater, L. E. (1988). The relative importance of situational and individual variables in predicting leader behavior: The surprising impact of subordinate trust. *Group and Organization Studies, 12*(3), 290-310.

Aubrey, B., & Kelsey, B. (2003). Further understanding of trust and performance in virtual teams. *Small Group Research, 34*(5), 575-619.

Avesani, P., Giunchiglia, F., & Yatskevich, M. (2005) A large scale taxonomy mapping evaluation. In Y. Gil, et al. (Eds.), *International Semantic Web Conference* (pp 67-81). Berlin: Springer-Verlag.

Baeza-Yates, R., & Ribeiro-Neto, B. (1999) *Modern information retrieval.* Addison-Wesley.

Bahrami, A. (2002). *Modeling and Simulation Management System (MS)2 User's Guide.* The Boeing company Version 2, November.

Barry, D. K. (2003). *Web services and service-oriented architectures: The savvy manager's guide.* Morgan Kaufmann.

Basu, A., & Kumar, A., (2002). Research commentary: *Workflow management issues in e-business. Information System Research, 13*(1), 1-14.

Bauer, B., Müller, J. P., & Odell, J. (2001). *Agent UML: A formalism for specifying multi-agent interaction.* Paper presented at the Agent-oriented Software Engineering.

Bechhofer, S., et al. (2004) OWL Web Ontology Language Reference. http://www.w3.org/TR/owl-ref/

Bell, P., & Linn, M. C. (2000). Scientific arguments as learning artifacts: Designing for learning from the Web with KIE. *International Journal of Science Education, 22*(8), 797-817.

Bellifemine, F., Caire, G., Poggi, A., & Rimassa, G. (2003). JADE a whitepaper. Retrieved February 13, 2007, from http://jade.tilab.com/papers/2003/WhitePaperJADEEXP.pdf

Bellifemine, F., Poggi, A., & Rimassa, G. (1999). JADE: A FIPA-compliant agent framework. In *the Proceedings of PAAM'99*, London.

Bellwood, T., et al. (2002). Universal description, discovery and integration specification (UDDI) 3.0. Retrieved February 12, 2007, from http://uddi.org/pubs/uddi-v3.00-published-20020719.htm

Belwood, T., et al. (2004). *UDDI version 3.0.* Retrieved September 1st, 2005, from http://uddi.org/pubs/uddi_v3.htm

Benatallah, B., et al. (2005). On automating web services discovery. *VLDB Journal, 14*(1), 84-96.

Beranek, P. (2000). The impacts of relational and trust development training on virtual teams: An exploratory investigation. Paper presented at the *33rd Hawaii International Conference on System Sciences.* Honolulu.

Bernus, P., & Nemes, L. (1999). *Organisational design: Dynamically creating and sustaining integrated virtual enterprises.* Paper presented at the IFAC World Congress, Vol-A, London.

Berre, D. L., & Fourdrinoy, O. (2002). *Using JADE with Java Server Pages.* In JADE documentation. Available at http://sharon.cselt.it/projects/jade/doc/tutorials/jsp/JADE4JSP.html

Bicer, V., Banu Laleci, G., Dogac, A., & Kabak, Y. (2005, October 19-21). Providing semantic interoperability in the healthcare domain through ontology mapping. In *Proceedings of the E-Challenges 2005 Conference*, Ljubljana, Slovenia.

Bicer, V., Kilic, O., Dogac, A., & Banu Laleci, G. (2005, October). Archetype-based semantic interoperability of web service messages in the healthcare domain. *International Journal on Semantic Web & Information Systems, 1*(4).

Bielli, M., & Mecoli, M. (2005). Trends in modelling supply chain and logistics networks. In *Proceedings of the 10th Meeting of the EURO Working Group Transportation* (pp. 147-152).

Blake, M.B., Tsui, K.C., & Wombacher, A. (2005). The eee-05 challenge: A new Web service discovery and composition competition. In *Proceedings of the 2005 IEEE International Conference on e-Technology, e-Commerce and e-Service (EEE'05)*, Washington, DC (pp. 780-781). IEEE Computer Society.

Bonifacio, M., & Bouquet, P. (2002). Distributed knowledge management: A systemic approach. In G. Minati & E. Pessa (Eds.), *Emergence in complex, cognitive, social and biological systems.* New York: Kluwer Academic/Plenum Publishers.

Bonifacio, M., Bouquet, P., Mameli, G., & Nori, M. (2004). Peer-mediated distributed knowledge management. In L. van Elst, V. Dignum, & A. Abecker (Eds.), *Agent-mediated knowledge management* (pp. 31-47). Heidelberg: Springer-Verlag.

Bonura, D., Corradini, F., Merelli, E., & Romiti, G. (2004). FarMAS: A MAS for extended quality workflow. In *13th IEEE International Workshops on Enabling Technologies: Infrastructure for Collaborative Enterprises (WETICE'04)* (pp. 435-440). IEEE Computer Society.

Booch, G., Christerson, M., Fuchs, M., & Koistinen, J. (1998). *UML for XML schema mapping specification*. Retrieved February18, 2007, from http://www.rational. com/media/uml/resources/media/uml_xml schema33. pdf

Booth, D., & Liu, C.K. (2005). *Web Services Description Language (WSDL)* Version 2.0 http://www.w3.org/2002/ ws/desc/.

Borges, B., Holley, K., & Arsanjani, A. (2004). *Service-oriented architecture*. http://webservices.sys-con. com/read/46175.htm.

Borghetti, B., Sodomka, E., Gini, M., & Collins, J. (2006). A market-pressure-based performance evaluator for TAC-SCM. In *Trading Agent Design and Analysis and Agent Mediated Electronic Commerce (TADA/AMEC) Joint International Workshop* (pp. 193-196). Springer.

Bouquet, P., Serafini, L., & Zanobini, S. (2003). Semantic coordination: A new approach and an application. In *Proceedings of the Second International Semantic Web Conference* (pp. 130-145). Berlin: Springer-Verlag.

Box, D. et al. (2000). Simple Object Access Protocol (SOAP) 1.1. *W3C note*. Retrieved February 12, 2007, from http://www.w3.org/TR/2000/NOTE-SOAP-20000508/

Box, D., Ehnebuske, D., Kakivaya, G., Layman, A., Mendelsohn, N., Nielsen, H., Thatte, S., & Winer, D. (2000). *Simple object access protocol (SOAP) 1.1*. Retrieved February 18, 2007, from http://www.w3.org/TR/SOAP/

Bracho, A., Matteo, A., & Metzner, C. (1999). A taxonomy for comparing distributed objects technologies. *CLEI Electronic Journal, 2*(2).

Bradshow, J. M. (1997). An introduction to software agents. In J. M. Bradshow (Ed.), *Software agents*. Cambridge: MIT Press.

Browne, J., & Zhang (1999). Extended and virtual enterprises — Similarities and differences. *International Journal of Agile Management Systems, 1*(1), 30-36.

Browne, J., & Zhang, J. (1999). Extended and virtual enterprises: Similarities and differences. *International Journal of Agile Management Systems, 1*(1), 30-36.

Bruijn, J., et al. (2005). D2v1.2. Web service modeling ontology (WSMO) final draft. Retrieved February 12, 2007, from http://www.wsmo.org/TR/d2/v1.2/

Buccafurri, F., Leone, N., & Rullo, P. (2000) Enhancing disjunctive datalog by constraints. *Knowledge and Data Engineering, 12*, 845-860

Bui, T., Bodart, F., & Ma, P. C. (1998). ARBAS: A formal language to support argumentation in network-base organizations. *Journal of Management Information Systems, 14*(3), 223-237.

Bultje, R., & Jacoliene, Van W. (1998). Taxonomy of virtual organizations, based on definitions, characteristics and typology. *VoNet - Newsletter, 2*(3).

Burbeck, K., Garpe, D., & Nadjm-Tehrani, S. (2004). *Scale-up and performance studies of three agent platforms*. Paper presented at the International Workshop on Middleware Performacne (IWMP 2004), Phoenix, Arizona.

Business Process Execution Language for Web Services (Version 1.1) (2003, May). Retrieved February 12, 2007, from ftp://www6.software.ibm.com/software/developer/ library/ws-bpel.pdf

Bussink, D. (2004). A comparison of language evolution and communication protocols in multi-agent systems. In *Proceedings of the 1ˢᵗ Twente Student Conference on IT, Track C—Intelligent_Interaction*. Retrieved January 31, 2007, from http://referaat.ewi.utwente.nl/

Byrne, J. A. (1993). The virtual corporation: The company of the future will be the ultimate in adaptability. *Business Week*, pp. 98-103.

Byrne, J. A., Brandt, R., & Port, O. (1993). The virtual corporation. *Business Week, 8*, 36-40.

C4ISR (1997). Architecture working group. *C4ISR Architecture Framework* (Version 2.0).

Caglayan, A., & Harrison, C. (1997). Agent Sourcebook. John Wiley and Sons.

Camarina-Matos, L., & Afsarmanesh, H. (1999). *Virtual enterprises: Life cycle supporting tools and technologies*. European Esprit PRODNET II project.

Camarinha-Matos L. M. (Ed.) (2002). Collaborative business ecosystems and virtual enterprises. In *Proceedings of the IFIP TC5/WG5.5 Third Working Conference on Infrastructures for Virtual Enterprises (PRO-VE'02)*, Sesimbra, Portugal.

Camarinha-Matos, L. M. (2002). Multi-agent systems in virtual enterprises. In *Proceedings of AIS2002. International Conference on AI, Simulation and Planning in High Autonomy Systems*, Lisbon, Portugal (pp. 27-36).

Camarinha-Matos, L. M., & Afsarmanesh, H. (1998). Cooperative systems challenges in virtual enterprises. In *Proceedings of CESA'98. IMCAS Multiconference on Computational Engineering in Systems Applications*, Nabeu - Hammamet, Tunisia.

Camarinha-Matos, L. M., & Afsarmanesh, H. (1999). The virtual enterprise concept. In L. M. Camarinha-Matos & H. Afsarmanesh (Eds.), *Infrastructures for virtual enterprises* (pp. 3-14). Porto, Portugal: Kluwer Academic Publishers.

Camarinha-Matos, L. M., & Afsarmanesh, H. (2001, November). Service federation in virtual organisations. In *Prolamat'01*. Budabest, Hungary.

Camarinha-Matos, L. M., & Pantoja-Lima, C. (2001). Cooperation coordination in virtual enterprises. *Journal of Intelligent Manufacturing, 12*(2), 133-150.

Carlson, D. (2001). Modeling XML applications with UML, practical e-business applications. *Object technology series*. Addison-Wesley.

Carlsson, C. (2002). Decisions support in virtual organizations: The case for multi-agent support. *Group Decision and Negotiation, 11*, 185-221.

Casati, F. (2004). *Web services conversations: Why do they matter and what they mean to you*. Presentation, HP Labs.

Cernuzzi, L., Cossentino, M., & Zambonelli, F. (2004). *Process models for agent-based development*. http://www.pa.icar.cnr.it/~cossentino/paper/eaai_zambonelli_draft.pdf

Chan, H.K., & Chan, F.T.S. (2004). A coordination framework for distributed supply chains. In *2004 International Conference on Systems, Man and Cybernetics* (pp. 4535-4540). IEEE Press.

Chan, H.K., & Chan, F.T.S. (2005). Comparative analysis of negotiation based information sharing in agent-based supply chains. In *3rd International Conference on Industrial Informatics* (pp. 813-828). IEEE Press.

Chang-Ouk, K., & Nof, S. Y. (2000). Investigation of PVM for the emulation and simulation of a distributed CIM workflow system. *International Journal of Computer Integrated Manufacturing, 13*(5), 401-409.

Chen, Y. M., & Wang, S. C. (2004). *An agent-based collaborative framework for distributed project dynamic scheduling*. Paper presented at the International Summer Workshop on the Economic, Financial and Managerial Applications of Computational Intelligence (EFMACI2004), Taipei, Taiwan, ROC.

Chen, Y. M., & Wang, S. C. (2007). Framework of agent-based intelligence system with two-stage decision-making process for distributed dynamic scheduling. *Applied Soft Computing, 7*(1), 229-245.

Chen, Y. M., & Wang, S. C. (in press). An agent-based evolutionary strategic 1 for dynamic scheduling. *International Journal of Advanced Manufacturing Technology*.

Cherinka, R., Miller, R. &, Smith, C. (2005). *Beyond web services: Towards on-demand complex adaptive environments*. MITRE Technical paper.

Chiang, C. (2001). Wrapping legacy systems for use in heterogeneous computing environments. *Information and Software Technology, 43*(8), 497-507.

Chidambaram, L. (1996). Relational development in computer-supported groups. *MIS Quarterly, 20*(2), 143-163.

Childe, S. J. (1998). The extended enterprise: A concept of co-operation. *International Journal of Production Planning and Control, 9*(3), 320-327.

Chinnici, R., et al. (2006). Web Services Description Language (WSDL) Version 2.0 Part 1: Core Language. Retrieved February 12, 2007, from http://www.w3.org/TR/wsdl20/

Chira, C. (2003). *Software agents.* (IDIMS Report). Retrieved January 31, 2007, from http://pan.nuigalway.ie/code/docs/agents.pdf

Christensen, E., Curbera, F., Meredith, G., & Weerawarana, Chrysanthis, P. K., Znati, T., Banerjee, S., & Shi-Kuo, C. (1999). Establishing virtual enterprises by means of mobile agents. In *Proceedings of the Ninth International Workshop on Research Issues on Data Engineering: Information Technology for Virtual Enterprises RIDE-VE '99* (pp.116-123).

Chun, H. W., & Wong, Y. M. (2003). N*: An agent-based negotiation algorithm for dynamic scheduling and rescheduling. *Advanced Engineering Informatics, 17*(1), 1-22.

Ciaschini, V., et al. (2006). An integrated framework for VO-oriented authorization, policy-based management and accounting. In *Proceedings of CHEP06 - Computing in High Energy and Nuclear Physics*, Mumbai, India.

Ciaschini, V., Venturi, V., & A. Cecanti (2006). The VOMS attribute certificate format. Open Grid Forum Draft. Retrieved February 17, 2007, from http://forge.gridforum.org/sf/docman/do/downloadDocument/projects.ogsa-authz/docman.root.attributes/doc13797/2

Claus, L. (2004). Too much of a good thing? Negative effects of high trust and individual autonomy in self-managing teams. *Academy of Management Journal, 47*(3), 385-400.

Clear, T., & Daniels, M. (2001). *A cyber-icebreaker for an effective virtual group?.* 6th Annual Conference On Innovation and Technology In Computer Science Education (ITiCSE), June 25-27, Canterbury.

Cole, D. (1997). Application of knowledge based systems to virtual organizations. In *Workshop on Using AI in Electronic Commerce, Virtual Organizations and Enterprise Knowledge Management to Reengineer the Corporation*, AAAI Workshop.

Conrad, R., Scheffner, D., & Freytag, J. (2000). XML conceptual modeling using UML. In *Proceedings of the International Conceptual Modeling Conference.*

Constantinescu, I., Binder, W., & Faltings, B. (2005). *Flexible and efficient matchmaking and ranking in service directories.* Paper presented at the IEEE International Conference on Web Services (ICWS'05).

Coppola, N., Hiltz, S., & Rotter, N. (2004). Building trust in virtual teams. *IEEE Transactions on Professional Communication, 47*(2), 65-105.

Corcho, O., Fernández-López, M., & Gómez-Pérez, A. (2003). Methodologies, tools and languages for building ontologies. Where is their meeting point? *Data & Knowledge Engineering, 46*(1), 41-64.

Cowan, D., & Griss, M. (2002). *Making Software Agent Technology available to Enterprise Applications.* Technical Report HPL-2002-211, HP Labs. Available at http://www.hpl.hp.com/techreports/2002/HPL-2002-211.pdf

Cranefield, S., & Purvis, M. (2001). Integrating environmental information: Incorporating metadata in a distributed information systems architecture. *Advances in Environmental Research, 5*, 319-325.

Crauldwell, P. (2003). *Professional XML web services.* Wrox, Birmingham, 18-50.

Creative Science Systems (CSS). Retrieved from http://www.creativescience.com/Products/soa.shtml

Cristensen, E., Curbera, F., Meredith, G., & Weerawarana, S. (2001). *Web services description language (WSDL) 1.1.* Retrieved February 18, 2007, from http://www.w3.org/TR/wsdl

Cunha, M. M., & Putnik, G. D. (2002). Discussion on requirements for agile/virtual enterprises reconfigurability dynamics: The example of the automotive industry. In L. M. Camarinha-Matos (Ed.), *Collaborative business ecosystems and virtual enterprises* (pp. 527-534). Boston: Kluwer Academic Publishers.

Cunha, M. M., & Putnik, G. D. (2003). Agile/virtual enterprise enablers: A comparative analysis. In D. N.

Sormaz & G. A. Süer (Eds.). In *Proceedings of Group Technology/Cellular Manufacturing—World Symposium 2003* (pp. 243-247). Columbus: Ohio University.

Cunha, M. M., & Putnik, G. D. (2003). Market of resources versus e-based traditional virtual enterprise integration - Part I: A cost model definition. In G. D. Putnik & A. Gunasekaran (Eds.), In *Proceedings of the First International Conference on Performance Measures, Benchmarking and Best Practices in New Economy* (pp. 664-669). Guimarães, Portugal

Cunha, M. M., & Putnik, G. D. (2003). Market of resources versus e-based traditional virtual enterprise integration - Part II: A comparative cost analysis. In G. D. Putnik & A. Gunasekaran (Eds.), In *Proceedings of the First International Conference on Performance Measures, Benchmarking and Best Practices in New Economy* (pp. 667-675). Guimarães, Portugal.

Cunha, M. M., & Putnik, G. D. (2005). Business alignment in agile/virtual enterprise integration. In M. Khosrow-Pour (Ed.), *Advanced Topics in Information Resources Management* (Vol. 4, pp. 26-54). Hershey, PA: Idea Group Publishing.

Cunha, M. M., & Putnik, G. D. (2005). Business alignment requirements and dynamic organizations. In G. D. Putnik & M. M. Cunha (Eds.), *Virtual Enterprise Integration: Technological and Organizational Perspectives* (pp. 78-101). Idea Group Publishing.

Cunha, M. M., & Putnik, G. D. (2005). Market of resources for agile/virtual enterprise integration. In M. Khosrow-Pour (Ed.), *Encyclopedia of Information Science and Technology* (pp. 1891-1898). Hershey, PA: Idea Group Publishing.

Cunha, M. M., & Putnik, G. D. (2005). Market of resources—A knowledge management enabler in virtual enterprises integration. In E. Coakes & S. Clarke (Eds.), *Encyclopedia of Communities of Practice in Information and Knowledge Management.* Hershey, PA: Idea Group Publishing.

Cunha, M. M., & Putnik, G. D. (2006). *Agile/virtual enterprise: Implementation and implementation management.* Idea Group Publishing.

Cunha, M. M., & Putnik, G. D. (2006). Identification of the domain of opportunities for a market of resources for virtual enterprise integration. *International Journal of Production Research, 44*(12), 2277-2298.

Cunha, M. M., Putnik, G. D., & Ávila, P. (2000). Towards focused markets of resources for agile/ virtual enterprise integration. In L. M. Camarinha-Matos, H. Afsarmanesh, & H. Erbe (Eds.), *Advances in networked enterprises: Virtual organisations, balanced automation, and systems integration* (pp. 15-24). Berlin: Kluwer Academic Publishers.

Cunha, M. M., Putnik, G. D., & Ávila, P. (2004). Virtual enterprises' extended life cycle. In *Proceedings of SymOrg 2004. IX International Symposium* (pp. 85-99). Belgrade.

Cunha, M. M., Putnik, G. D., & Gunasekaran, A. (2002). Market of resources as an environment for agile/virtual enterprise dynamic integration and for business alignment. In A. Gunasekaran (Ed.), *Knowledge and information technology management in the 21st century organisations: Human and social perspectives* (pp. 169-190). Idea Group Publishing.

Cunha, M. M., Putnik, G. D., & Gunasekaran, A. (2003). Market of resources as an environment for agile/virtual enterprise dynamic integration and for business alignment. In A. Gunasekaran & O. Khalil (Eds.), *Knowledge and information technology management in the 21st century organisations: Human and social perspectives* (pp. 169-190). Idea Group Publishing.

Cunha, M. M., Putnik, G. D., Gunasekaran, A., & Ávila, P. (2005). Market of resources as a virtual enterprise integration enabler. In G. D. Putnik & M. M. Cunha (Eds.), *Virtual enterprise integration: Technological and organizational perspectives* (pp. 145-165). Idea Group Publishing.

Curran, L. (2000). *SAP R/3 business blueprint* (2nd ed.). New York: Prentice Hall.

Dai, Q., & Kauffman, R. (2001). Business models for internet-based e-procurement systems and B2B electronic markets: An exploratory assessment. Paper presented at the 34th Hawaii International Conference on Systems Science, Maui.

Dale, J., Willmott, S., & Burg, B. (2002). *Agentcities: Building a global next-generation service environment.* 10 June.

Dance, S., Gorman, M., Padgham, L., & Winikoff, M. (2003). An evolving multi agent system for meteorological alerts. In *Proceedings of the 2nd international joint conference on Autonomous Agents and Multiagent Systems, AAMAS-03.*

Daskalopulu, A., Dimitrakos, T., & Maibaum, T. (2002). Evidence-Based Electronic Contract Performance Monitoring. *The INFORMS Journal of Group Decision and Negotiation.* (Special Issue on Formal Modelling in E-Commerce)

Davenport, T. H., & Short, J. E. (1990). The new industrial engineering: Information technology and business process redesign. *Sloan Management Review, 31*(4), 11-27.

David, P., & McDaniel, R. (2004). A field study on the effect of interpersonal trust on virtual collaborative relationship performance. *MIS Quarterly, 28*(2), 183-227.

Davidow, W. H., & Malone, M. S. (1992). *The virtual corporation—Structuring and revitalising the corporation for the 21st century.* New York: HarperCollins Publishers.

Davies, J., Duke, A., & Stonkus, A. (2003). *OntoShare: Evolving ontologies in a knowledge sharing system.* In Davies et al. (2003), pp. 161-177.

Davies, J., Fensel, D., & van Harmelen, F. (Eds.) (2003) *Towards the semantic web: Ontology-driven knowledge management.* West Sussex, UK: Wiley.

DCOM Technical Overview, Microsoft Corporation. (1996). Retrieved from http://msdn.microsoft.com/library/default.asp?url=/library/en-us/dndcom/html/msdn_dcomtec.asp

Deloitte (2000). *The emerging European health telematics industry.* (Market Analysis Report). European Commission-Directorate General Information Society.

Demchenko, Y., Gommans, L., de Laat, C., Oudenaarde, B., Tokmakoff, A., & Snijders, M. (2005). Job-centric security model for open collaborative environment. In *Proceeding of the 2005 International Symposium on Collaborative Technologies and Systems* (pp. 69-77)

Demchenko, Y., Gommans, L., de Laat, C., Steenbakkers, M., Ciaschini, V. &, Venturi, V. (2006). VO-based dynamic security associations in collaborative grid environment. In *Proceedings of the 2006 International Symposium on Collaborative Technologies and Systems* (pp. 38-47)

Demchenko, Yu. (2004). Virtual organisations in computer grids and identity management. *Elsevier Information Security Technical Report, 9*(1), 59-76.

Denna, E. L., Jasperson, J., & Fong, K. *Reengineering and REAL business process modeling.* In V. Grover, and W. Di Cosmo, R., Pottier, F., & Rémy, D. (2005, April). Subtyping Recursive Types modulo Associative Commutative Products. In P. Urzyczyn (Ed.), *7th International Conference on Typed Lambda Calculi and Applications (TLCA 2005)* (Vol. 3461, pp. 179-193). Berlin, Heidelberg, Germany: Springer-Verlag.

Dickinson, I., & Wooldridge, M. (2003). Towards practical reasoning agents for the semantic web. In *Proceedings of the Second International Joint Conference on Autonomous Agents and Multiagent Systems* (pp. 827-834). ACM Press.

Dimou, M. (Ed.). (2004). User registration and VO membership management requirements. Retrieved February 17, 2007, from https://edms.cern.ch/document/428034

Dimou, M., & Neilson, I. (Eds.). (2006). Virtual organisation registration procedure. Retrieved February 17, 2007, from https://edms.cern.ch/document/503245/

Do, V., Halatchev, M., & Neumann, D. (2000). A context-based approach to support virtual enterprises. In *Proceedings of the 33rd Hawaii International Conference on System Sciences.*

Dogac, A. (1998, March). *A survey of the current state-of-the-art in electronic commerce and research issues in enabling technologies*. Paper presented at the Euro-Med Net 98 Conference, Electronic Commerce Track.

Dogac, A., Bicer, V., Banu Laleci, G., Kabak, Y., Gurcan, Y., Eichelberg, M., & Riesmeier, J. (2006, February 12-16). Untangle the web: Communicating through the web services using semantics. In *Proceedings of the 2006 Annual HIMSS Conference*, San Diego, California.

Dogac, A., Kabak, Y., & Laleci, G. (2004). Enriching ebXML registries with OWL ontologies for efficient service discovery. In *Proceedings of the 14th International Workshop on Research Issues on Data Engineering*, Boston.

Dong, M., & Chen, F. F. (2001). Process modeling and analysis of manufacturing supply chain networks using object-oriented petri nets. *Robotics and Computer Integrated Manufacturing, 17*(1-2), 121-129.

Dore, R. (1983). Goodwill and the spirit of market capitalism. *British Journal of Sociology, 34*(4), 459-482.

Dorn, J., Hrastnik, P., & Rainer, A. (2005) Web service discovery and composition with move. In *Proceedings of the 2005 IEEE International Conference on e-Technology, e-Commerce and e-Service (EEE'05)*, Washington, DC (pp. 791-792). IEEE Computer Society

Dubé, L. , & Paré, G. (2004). The multi-faceted nature of virtual teams. In D.J. Pauleen (Ed.), *Virtual teams: Projects, protocols, and processes* (pp. 1-39). Hershey, PA: Idea Group Publishing.

Dubray, J. J. (2003). ebXML. Retrieved February 12, 2007, from http://www.ebpml.org/ebxml.htm

ebBP (2006). ebXML business process specification schema technical specification (Version 2.0.1) *Public Review Final Draft r03*. OASIS.

Ebner, W., & Krcmar, H. (2005). Design, implementation, and evaluation of trust-supporting components in virtual communities for patients. *Journal of Management Information Systems, 21*(4), 101-135.

ECO-Label. (1994). The European ECO-label certification scheme for distinguished environmental friendly products. Retrieved February 18, 2007, from www.eco-label.com

EDSC (2006). Environmental data standards council data standards. Retrieved February 18, 2007, from www.envdatastandards.net

EIONET (1994). European environment information and observation network. Retrieved February 18, 2007, from www.eionet.europa.eu

EMAS (1995-2001). The eco-management and audit scheme (EMAS) registry of acknowledged organizations that improve their environmental performance on a continuous basis. Retrieved February 18, 2007, from http://ec.europa.eu/environment/emas

Enabling Grid for E-sciencE (EGEE) Project (2006). Retrieved February 17, 2007, from http://www.eu-egee.org/

Estrem, W. A. (2003). An evaluation framework for deploying web services in the next generation manufacturing enterprise. *Robotics and Computer Integrated Manufacturing 19*, 509-519.

Etzioni, O., & Weld, D. S. (1995). *Intelligent agents on the Internet: Fact, fiction and forecast*. IEEE Expert, *10*(4), 44-49.

Eu-Publi.com IST-Project (2005). *Facilitating cooperation amongst European public administration employees*. Retrieved February 13, 2007, from http://www.eu-publi.com

Extensible Markup Language (XML) 1.0 (Fourth Edition) (2006, August). W3C Recommendation. Retrieved February 12, 2007, from http://www.w3.org/TR/2006/REC-xml-20060816/

Faculty Science Unitn. University of Trento. *AOSE Methologies*. (n.d.) Retrieved from http://www.science.unitn.it/~recla/aose/

Fankhauser, P., & Tesch, T. (1999). Agents, a broker, and lies. In *Proceedings of the Ninth International Workshop on Research Issues on Data Engineering: Information Technology for Virtual Enterprises*, RIDE-VE '99 (pp.56-63).

Felluga, B., Gauthier, T., Genesh, A., Haastrup, P., Neophytou, C., Poslad, S., Preux, D., Plini, P., Santouridis, I.,

Stjernholm, M., & Würtz, J. (2003). *Environmental data exchange for inland waters using independent software agents* (Report 20549 EN). Institute for Environment and Sustainability, European Joint Research Centre, Ispra, Italy.

Field, S., & Hoffner, Y. (2002). In search of the right partner. In L. M. Camarinha-Matos (Ed.), *Collaborative business ecosystems and virtual enterprises* (pp. 55-62) Kluwer Academic Publishers.

Fikes, R. E. & Nilsson, N. (1971). STRIPS: A new approach to the application of theorem proving to problem solving. *Artificial Intelligence, 5*(2), 189-208.

FIPA (2002). *FIPA Abstract Architecture Specification.* Available at http://www.fipa.org/specs/fipa00001/SC00001L.html

FIPA (2005). Foundation for Intelligent Physical Agents. Retrieved February 14, 2007, from http://www.fipa.org./

FIPA-ACL (2002). FIPA agent communication language. Retrieved February 12, 2007, from http://www.fipa.org/repository/aclspecs.html

Fischer L. (Ed.). (2000). The Workflow Handbook 2001, in association with the Workflow Management Coalition (WfMC).

Fischer, K., et al. (1996). *Intelligent agents in virtual enterprises.* Paper presented at the First International Conference and Exhibition on Practical Applications of Intelligent Agents and Multi-agent Systems (PAAM-96), London.

Folinas, D., Manthou, V., & Vlachopoulou, M. (2003). Modeling business information in virtual environment. In *Proceedings of 10th International Conference on Human-Computer Interaction*, Irakleion, Greece.

Foster, I. et al (2006). The open grid services architecture, Version 1.5. Global Grid Forum. Retrieved February 17, 2007, from http://www.ggf.org/documents/GFD.80.pdf

Foster, I., Kesselman, C., & Tuecke, S. (2001). The anatomy of the grid: Enabling scalable virtual organizations. *International Journal of Supercomputer Applications, 15*(3), 200-222.

Foster, I., Kesselman, C., Nick, J., & Tuecke, S. (2002). *The physiology of the grid: An open grid services architecture for distributed systems integration.* Globus Project, 2002. Retrieved February 17, 2007, from http://www.globus.org/alliance/publications/papers/ogsa.pdf

Fox, M. S., & Gruninger, M., (1998). Enterprise modelling. *AI Magazine,* 109-121.

Fox, M. S., Chionglo, J. F., & Barbuceanu, M. (1993). *The integrated supply chain management system.* University of Toronto, Enterprise Integration Laboratory.

Franklin, S., & Graesser, A. (1996). Is it an agent, or just a program?: A taxonomy for autonomous agents. In *Proceedings of the Third International Workshop on Agent Theories, Architectures and Languages.*

Freeman, A., & Jones A. (2003). *Microsoft.net XML web services.* Microsoft Press.

Freitas Mundim, A. P., Rossi, A., & Stocchetti, A. (2000). SME in global markets: Challenges, opportunities and threats. *Brasilian Electronic Journal of Economics, 3*(1).

Frey, D., Stockheim, T., Woelk, P.-O., & Zimmermann, R. (2003). Integrated multi-agent-based supply chain management. In *12th International Workshops on Enabling Technologies: Infrastructure for Collaborative Enterprises* (pp. 24-29). IEEE Computer Society.

Gamma, E., Helm, R., Johnson, R., & Vlissides, J. (1995). *Design patterns: Elements of reusable object-oriented software.* Addison-Wesley.

Ganapathy, S., & Narayanan, S. (2003). Decision Support for Supply Chain Analysis. In *2003 International Conference on Systems, Man and Cybernetics* (pp. 2077-2082). IEEE Press.

Garey, M. R., & Johnson, D. S. (1979). *Computers and intractability: A guide to the theory of NP-Completeness.* San Francisco: W. H. Freeman.

Garita, C., & Afsarmanesh, H. (2001). A study of information management approaches for support infrastructures. *COVE Newsletter, 1.*

Garlan, D., Allen, R., & Ockerbloom, J. (1995). Architectural mismatch or why it's hard to build systems out of existing parts. In *ICSE '95: Proceedings of the 17th international conference on Software engineering* (pp. 179-185). New York: ACM Press.

Gartner, Inc. (1996). SSA Research Note SPA-401-068, "Service Oriented Architectures, Part 1, Part 2".

Gay, S. J., & Hole, M. (1999). Types and subtypes for client-server interactions. In *ESOP '99: Proceedings of the 8th European Symposium on Programming Languages and Systems* (Vol. 1576, pp. 74-90). London: Springer-Verlag.

Gelfond, M., & Lifschitz, V. (1988). The stable model semantics for logic programming. In Kowalski & Bowen (Eds.), *Proceedings of the Fifth International Conference on Logic Programming*, Cambridge, MA, The MIT Press.

Gelfond, M., & Lifschitz, V. (1991) Classical negation in logic programs and disjunctive databases. *New Generation Computing, 9*, 365-386

Genesereth, M. R., & Ketchpel, S. P. (1994). Software agents. *Communication of the ACM, 37*(7), 48-55.

Gijsen, J. W. J., Szirbik, N. B., & Wagner, G. (2002). Agent technologies for virtual enterprises in the one-of-a-kind-production industry. *International Journal of Electronic Commerce, 7*(1), 9-26.

Gini, M., Ketter, W., Kryzhnyaya, E., Damer, S., McGillen, C., Agovic, A., & Collins, J. (2004). MinneTAC Sales Strategies for Supply Chain TAC. In *Third International Joint Conference on Autonomous Agents and Multiagent Systems (AAMAS'04)* (pp. 1372-1373). IEEE Computer Society.

Giorgini, P., Kolp, M., & Mylopoulos, J. (2006). Multi-agent architectures as organizational structures. In *Journal of Autonomous Agents and Multi Agent Systems (AAMAS '06), 13*(1), 3-25.

Globus Toolkit Version 4.1 (GT4) (2006). Retrieved February 17, 2007, from http://www.globus.org/toolkit/

Goh, W.T., & Gan, J.W.P. (2005). A dynamic multi-agent based framework for global supply chain. In *2nd IEEE International Conference on Service Systems and Services Management* (pp. 981-984). IEEE Computer Society.

Goland, Y. Y. (2003). A proposal for W3C choreography working group use cases & requirements. W3C Choreography Working Group.

Golembiewski, R. T., & McConkie, M. (1975). The centrality of interpersonal trust in group processes. In C.L. Cooper (Ed.), *Theories of Group Processes*. New York: John Wiley & Sons.

Gong, B., & Wang, S. (2000). Model of MAS: Supporting dynamic enterprise model. In *Proceedings of the 3rd World Congress on Intelligent Control and Automation* (pp. 2042-2046).

Goodwin, R. (1993). *Formalizing properties of agents* (Tech. Rep.) Pittsburgh, PA: Carnegie-Mellon University, School of Computer Science.

Gortmaker, J., Janssen, M., & Wagenaar, R. (2004). *SOBI business architectures and process orchestration: Technical overview* (Tech. Report). The Netherlands: Telematica Instituut Enschede.

Gou, H., Huang, B., Liu, W., & Li, Y. (2001). Agent-based virtual enterprise modeling and operation control. In *Proceedings of the 2001 IEEE International Conference on Systems, Man, and Cybernetics* (pp. 2058-2063).

Green, S., Hurst, L., Nangle, B., Cunningham, D. P., Somers, F., & Evans, D. R. (1997). *Software agents: A review* (Tech. Rep. No.TCS-CS-1997-06). Trinity College Dublin, Broadcom Éireann Research Ltd.

Grefen, P., Aberer, K., Hoffner, Y., & Ludwig, H. (2000). Cross-Flow: Cross-Organizational Workflow Management in Dynamic Virtual Enterprises. *International Journal of Computer Systmes Sciences and Engineering, 15*(5), 277-290.

GridShib. A Policy Controlled Attribute Framework. Retrieved February 17, 2007, from http://grid.ncsa.uiuc.edu/GridShib/

Griffin, K. (1967). The contribution of studies of source credibility to a theory of interpersonal trust in the communication process. *Psychological Bulletin, 68*(2), 104-120.

Grover, V., Fiedler, K. D., & Teng, J. T. C. (1994). Exploring the success of information technology enabled business process reengineering. *IEEE Transactions on Engineering Management, 41*(3), 276-84.

Guizzardi, R. S. S. (2006). *Agent-oriented constructivist knowledge management.* Unpublished doctoral thesis, University of Twente, The Netherlands.

Guo, Y., & Mueller, J.P. (2004). A multiagent approach for logistics performance prediction using historical and context information. In *Proceedings of the Third International Joint Conference on Autonomous Agents and Multiagent Systems - Volume 3* (pp. 1164-1171). IEEE Computer Society.

Guzdial, M., Kolodner, J. L., Hmelo, C., Narayanan, H. Carlson, D. Rappin, N., Hubscher, R., Turns, J., & Newsletter, W. (1996). Computer support for learning through complex problem-solving. *Communications of the ACM, 39*(4), 43-45.

Hammer, M., & Champy, J. (1993). *Reengineering the corporation.* New York: Harper Collins.

Hands, J., Bessonov, M., Blinov, M., Patel, A., & Smith, R. (2000). An inclusive and extensible architecture for electronic brokerage. *Decision Support Systems, 29*, 305-321.

Handy, C. (1995). Trust and the virtual organization. *Harvard Business Review, 73*(3), 40-50.

Hao, H. (2003). *What is service-oriented architecture?* Retrieved February 13, 2007, from http://webservices.xml.com/lpt/a/ws/2003/09/30/soa.html

Hart, P., & Saunders, C. (1997). Power and trust: Critical factors in the adoption and use of electronic data interchange. *Organization Science, 8*(1), 23-42.

Hassan, U., & Soh, B. (2005). Web Service Intelligent Agent Structuring for Supply Chain Management (SCM). In *2005 IEEE International Conference on e-Technol-*

ogy, e-Commerce and e-Service (EEE'05) (pp. 329-332). IEEE Computer Society.

Havey, M. (2006, January). Modeling web services choreography with new eclipse tool. *SYS-CON SOA Web Services Journal*, 44-48.

Hayes, C. C. (1999). Agents in a nutshell: A very brief introduction. *IEEE Transactions on Knowledge and Data Engineering, 11*(1), 127-132.

Henderson, J. C., & Lee, S. (1992). Managing I/S design teams: A control theories perspective. *Management Science, 38*(6), 757-777.

Hendler, J. (2001). Agents and the Semantic Web. *IEEE Intelligent Systems, 16*(2), 30-37.

Hilmer, K., & Dennis, A. (2001). Stimulating thinking: Cultivating better decisions with groupware through categorization. *Journal of Management Information Systems, 17*(3), 93-114.

Hinze, J., & Tracey, A. (1994). The contractor-subcontractor relationship: the subcontractor's view. *Journal of Construction Engineering and Management, 120*(2), 274-287.

Hoare, C. (1974). Monitors: An operating system structuring concept. *Communications of the ACM, 17*(10), 549-57.

Hofreiter, B., & Huemer, C. (2005). Registering a business collaboration model in multiple business environments. In *Proceedings of the OTM Workshop on Modeling Inter-Organizational Systems (MIOS 2005)*, Larnaca, Cyprus.

Horn, E., Kupries, M., & Reinke, T. (1999). Properties and models of software agents and prefabrication for agent application systems. In *Proceedings of the International Conference on System Sciences (HICSS-32), Software Technology Track.*

Hrastnik, P. (2004) Execution of Business Processes Based on Web Services, *Int. J. Electronic Business,* Vol. 2, No. 3.

Huang, S. (2004). *Computers & Industrial Engineering, 47*, 61-76.

Huckvale, T., & Ould, M. *Process modeling—who, what and how: Role activity diagramming.* In V. Grover, and W. Huff, L. C., J. Cooper & W. Jones. (2002). The development and consequences of trust in student project groups. *Journal of Marketing Education, 24*(1), 24-34.

Hunhs, M. (2002). Agents as Web Services. *IEEE Internet Computing, 6*(4), 93 -95.

Iacono, C. S., & Weisband, S. (1997). Developing trust in virtual teams. Paper presented at the *30th Annual Hawaii International Conference on System Sciences.* Honolulu.

Iglesias, C. A., Garijo, M., & Gonzalez, J. C. (1999). A survey of agent-oriented methologies. In *Proceedings of the Fifth International Workshop on Agent Theories, Architectures, and Languages (ATAL-98)* (pp. 317-330).

Information Technology—*Open Distributed Processing—Reference Model—Enterprise Language.* (2003). (IS15414)

Information Technology—*Open systems interconnection, data management and open distributed processing.* ODP Trading Function. (1995). (IS13235)

Information Technology—*Open systems interconnection, data management and open distributed processing.* Reference Model of Open Distributed Processing. (1996). (IS10746)

Information Technology—Open Systems Interconnection, Data Management and Open Distributed Processing. Reference Model of Open Distributed Processing. ODP Type repository function. (1999). (IS14746)

ISO TC 211 (2004). The ISO technical committee 211 ISO19000 standards series on geographic information/geomatics. Retrieved February 18, 2007, from www.iso.org

JADE (2005). Java Agent DEvelopment Framework. Retrieved February 14, 2007, from http://jade.cselt.it/

Jagdev, H. S., & Brown, J. (1998). The extended enterprise - A context for manufacturing. *International Journal of Production Planning and Control, 9*(3), 216-229.

Jain, A. K., Aparicio, M. IV, & Singh, M. P. (1999). Agents for process coherence in virtual enterprises. *Communications of the ACM, 42*(3), 62-69.

Jakarta Project - The Apache Software Foundation (2003). The Tomcat Web Server v. 4.1.

Jarvenpaa, S., & Leidner, D. (1999). Communication and trust in global virtual teams. *Organization Science, 10*(6), 791-815.

Jarvenpaa, S., Knoll, K., & Leidner, D. (1998). Is anybody out there? Antecedents of trust in global virtual teams. *Journal of Management Information Systems, 14*(4), 29-64.

Jarvenpaa, S., Shadow, T., & Staples, S. (2004). Toward contextualized theories of trust: The role of trust in global virtual teams. *Information Systems Research, 15*(3), 250-267.

Java.sun.com. The Source for Java Developers. Retrieved from http://java.sun.com/products/jdk/rmi/

Jennings, N. R. (2000). On agent-based software engineering. *Artificial Intelligence, 177*(2), 277-296.

Jennings, N. R., Norman, T. J., & Faratin, P. (1998). ADEPT: An agent-based approach to business process management. *ACM SIGMOD Record, 27*(4), 32-39.

Jennings, N. R., Sycara, K., & Wooldridge, M. (1998). A roadmap of agent research and development. *Autonomous Agents and Multi-Agent Systems Journal, 1*(1), 7-38.

Jennings, N., & Wooldridge, M. (1996). Software agents. *IEE Review, 42*(1), 17 -20.

Jensen, C. K. (1994). *An introduction to the theoretical aspects of colored petri nets* (Tech. Rep.). Aarhus University, Denmark, Computer Science Dept.

Jha, S., Palsberg, J., & Zhao, T. (2002). Efficient type matching. In *FoSSaCS '02: Proceedings of the 5th International Conference on Foundations of Software Science and Computation Structures* (pp. 187-204). London, UK: Springer-Verlag.

Jiao, J., You, X., & Kumar, A. (2006). An agent-based framework for collaborative negotiation in the global manufacturing supply chain network. *Robotics and Computer-Integrated Manufacturing, 22*(3), 239-255.

Jonassen, D., & Remidez, H. (2002). Mapping alternative discourse structures onto computer conferences. Gerry Stahl, ed. *Computer Support for Collaborative Learning: Foundations for a CSCL Community.* Hillsdale, NJ: Erlbaum.

Jordan, P.R., Kiekintveld, C., Miller, J., & Wellman, M.P. (2006). Market Efficiency, Sales Competition, and the Bullwhip Effect in the TAC SCM Tournaments. In *Trading Agent Design and Analysis and Agent Mediated Electronic Commerce (TADA/AMEC).* Joint International Workshop (pp. 99-111). Springer.

Jøsang, A., Keser, C., & Dimitrakos, T. (2005). Can we manage trust? In *Proceedings of the Third International Conference on Trust Management (iTrust)*, Rocquencourt, France.

Kaihara, T. (2000). Agent-Based Double Auction Algorithm for Global Supply Chain System. In *26th Annual Conference of Industrial Electronics Society* (pp. 678-683). IEEE Press.

Kaihara, T. (2001). Supply chain management with market economics. *International Journal of Production Economics 73*(1), 5-14.

Katz, B. R., & Schuh, G. (1999). The virtual enterprise. Retrieved January 31, 2007, from http://portal.cetim.org/file/1/68/KatzySchuh-1999-The_virtual_enterprise.pdf

Katzy, B., Evaristo, R., & Zigurs, I. (2000). Knowledge management in virtual projects: A research agenda. In *Proceedings of IEEE 33rd Hawaii International Conference on System Sciences.*

Keeney, R., & Raiffa, H. (1976). *Decisions with multiple objectives: Preferences and value tradeoffs.* John Wiley & Sons.

Kelman, H. C. (1958). Compliance, identification and internalization: Three processes of attitude change. *Journal of Conflict Resolution, 2*(1), 51-60.

Kettinger, J. (Ed.). (1995) *Business process change: Reengineering concepts, methods and technologies.* Idea Group Publishing.

Khalil, O., & Wang, S. (2002). Information technology enabled meta-management for virtual organizations. *International Journal of Production Economics, 75*(1), 127-134.

Kiekintveld, C., & Wellman, M.P. (2005). An Analysis of the 2004 Supply Chain Management Trading Agent Competition. In *2005 Annual Meeting of the North American Fuzzy Information Processing Society* (pp. 257-262). IEEE Press.

Kim, C.-S., Tannock, J., Byrne, M., Farr, R., Cao, B., & Er, M. (2004). *State-of-the-art review: Techniques to model the supply chain in an extended enterprise* (VIVACE WP2.5). Nottingham, England: University of Nottingham, Operations Management Division

Kim, K. (2001). *Distributed coordination of project schedule changes: An agent-based compensatory negotiation approach.* Stanford University.

Kim, K., Paulson, B., Levitt, R., Fischer, M. A., & Petrie, C. (2003). Distributed coordination of project schedule changes using agent-based compensatory negotiation methodology. *Artificial Intelligence for Engineering Design, Analysis and Manufacturing, 17*, 115-131.

Kirsch, L. J. (1997). Portfolios of control modes and IS project management. *Information Systems Research, 8*(3), 215-239.

Kloppman, M., et al. (2005). SOA programming model for implementing web services, Part 3: Process choreography and business state machines. *IBM developer Works.*

Kombrough, S. O., Wu, D.J., & Zhong, F. (2001). Computers play the beer game: Can artificial agents manage supply chains? In 34th *Hawaii International Conference on System Sciences* (pp. 1-10). IEEE Computer Society.

Köppen-Seliger, B., Ding, S. X., & Frank, P. M. (2001). European research projects on multi-agents-based fault diagnosis and intelligent fault tolerant control. *Plenary Lecture IAR Annual Meeting*, Strasbourg.

Korsgaard, M. A., Schweiger, D. M. & Sapienza, H. J. (1995). Building commitment, attachment, and trust in strategic decision-making teams: The role of procedural justice. *Academy of Management Journal, 38*(1), 60-84.

Kostakos, V., & Taraschi, C. (2001). Agents. Retrieved January 31, 2007, from http://www.cs.bath.ac.uk/~vk/files/agents.pdf

Kotok, A., & Webber, D. R. R. (2001). *ebXML: The New Global Standard for Doing Business Over the Internet.* Boston: New Riders.

Krackhardt, D., & Stern, R. N. (1988). Informal networks and organizational crises: An experimental simulation. *Social Psychology Quarterly, 51*(2), 123-140.

Küngas, P., Rao, J., & Matskin, M. (2004). *Symbolic agent negotiation for semantic web service exploitation.* Paper presented at the Fifth International Conference on Web-Age Information Management (WAIM'2004), Dalian, China.

Kutvonen, L. (1998). *Trading services in open distributed environments.* Department of Computer Science, University of Helsinki. (PhD thesis. A-1998-2)

Kutvonen, L. (2004). Challenges for ODP-based infrastructure for managing dynamic B2B networks. In A. Vallecillo, P. Linington, & B. Wood (Eds.), *Workshop on ODP for Enterprise Computing (WODPEC 2004)* (pp. 57-64). 29071 Málaga, Spain: University of Málaga.

Kutvonen, L. (2004, September). Relating MDA and inter-enterprise collaboration management. In D. Akehurst (Ed.), *Second European Workshop on Model Driven Architecture (EWMDA)* (pp. 84-88). Canterbury, Kent CT2 7NF, UK: University of Kent.

Kutvonen, L., & Metso, J. (2005, September). Services, contracts, policies and eCommunities – Relationship to ODP framework. In P. Linington, A. Tanaka, S. Tyndale-Biscoe, & A. Vallecillo (Eds.), *Workshop on ODP for Enterprise Computing (WODPEC 2005)* (pp. 62-69). 29071 Málaga, Spain: University of Málaga.

Kutvonen, L., Metso, J., & Ruokolainen, T. (2005, November). Inter-enterprise collaboration management in dynamic business networks. In R. Meersman & Z. Tari (Eds.), *OnTheMove 2005 DOA, ODBASE and CoopIS vol.1* (Vol. 3760). Berlin, Heidelberg: Springer-Verlag.

Kutvonen, L., Ruokolainen, T., Metso, J., & Haataja, J. (2005, December). Interoperability middleware for federated enterprise applications in web-Pilarcos. In *Interoperability of Enterprise Software and Applications.* Springer-Verlag.

Kwon, O., Im, G., & Lee, K.C. (2005). MACE-SCM: An Effective Supply Chain Decision Making Approach based on Multi-agent and Case-based Reasoning. In *Proceedings of the 38th Annual Hawaii International Conference on System Sciences (HICSS'05)* (pp. 82-91). IEEE Computer Society.

Labrou, Y., Finin, T., & Peng, Y (1999). Agent communication languages: the current landscape. *IEEE Intelligent Systems, 14*(2):45 -52.

Laffey, J., Musser, D., Remidez, H. & Gottdenker, J. (2003). Networked systems for schools that learn. *Communications of the ACM, 46*(9), 192-200.

Lakoff, G., & Johnson, M. (1980). *Metaphors we live by.* University of Chicago Press.

Larson, C. E. & LaFasto, F. M. J. (1989). *Teamwork: What must go right/what can go wrong.* Newbury Park, NJ: Sage.

Lawler, E. (1992). *The ultimate advantage: Creating the high-involvement organization.* San Francisco: Jossey-Bass.

Lazcano, A., Alonso, G., Schuldt, H., & Schuler, C. (2000). The WISE approach to Electronic Commerce. *Computer Systems Science and Engineering, 15*(5), 345-357.

LCG/EGEE Acceptable Use Policy (2006). Joint security policy group. Retrieved February 17, 2007, from https://edms.cern.ch/document/428036

Leone, N., Pfeifer, G., Faber, W., Calimeri, F., Dell'Armi, T., Eiter, T., Gottlob, G., Ianni, G., Ielpa, G., Koch, C., Perri, S., & Polleres, A. (2002) The dlv system. In JELIA '02 *Proceedings of the European Conference on Logics in Artificial Intelligence.* London: Springer-Verlag 537-540

Levitt, R. E., et al. (2001). Computational enterprise models: Towards analysis tools for designing organisations. In G. M. Olsen, T. W. Malone, & J. B. Smith (Eds.), *Coordination theory and collaboration technology* (pp. 623-649). Lawrence Erlbaum Associates.

Li, T., & Feng, Z. (2003). A system architecture for agent based supply chain management platform. *IEEE CCECE 2003, Canadian Conference on Electrical and Computer Engineering 2*(2), 713-716.

Liao, S. (2002). Knowledge management technologies and applications: Literature review from 1995 to 2002. *Expert Systems with Applications, 25*, 155-164.

Lin, F.-r., Yang, M.-c., & Pi, Y.-h., (2002). A Generic Structure for Business Process Modeling. *Business Process Management Journal, 8*(1), 19-41.

Linthicum, D. (2004). *Next generation application integration: From simple information to web services.* Addison-Wesley.

Linthicum, D. S. (2001). *B2B application integration: E-business enable your enterprise.* Addison-Wesley.

Liu, J., Zhang, S., & Hu, J. (2005). A case study of an inter-enterprise workflow-supported supply chain management system. *Information & Management, 42*(3), 441-454.

Liu, L., & Halper, M. (1997). *Incorporating semantic relationships into an object oriented database system.* In *Proceedings of the 32nd Hawaiian International Conference on Systems Science.*

Lou, P., Zhou, Z.D., & Chen, Y.P. (2005). *Study on Coordination in Multi-Agent-Based Agile Supply Chain Management,* In *4th International Conference on Machine Learning and Cybernetics* (pp. 171-185). IEEE Press.

Luck, M., McBurney, P., & Gonzalez-Palacios, J. (2006). *Agent-based computing and programming of agent systems* (LNCS 3862, pp. 23-37). Springer.

Ludermir, P. G. (2005). *Supporting knowledge management using a nomadic service for artifact recommendation.* Unpublished master's dissertation, University of Twente, The Netherlands.

Luo, W., & Tung, A. (1999). A framework for selecting business process modeling methods. *Industrial Management & Data Systems, 99*(7), 312-319.

Malone, T. W., Grant, K. R., Lai, K.-Y., Rao, R., & Rosenblitt, D. (1987). Semi-structured messages are surprisingly useful for computer-supported coordination. *ACM Transactions on Information Systems, 5*(2), 115-131.

Mangina, E., & Vlachos, I. P. (2005). The changing role of information technology in food and beverage logistics management: beverage network optimisation using intelligent agent technology. *Journal of Food Engineering 70*(3), 403-420.

Marik, V., & Pechoucek. M. (2004). Agent Technologies for Virtual Organisation. In Camarina-Matos & Afsarmanesh (Ed.), *Collaborative networked organisations: A research agenda for emerging business models* (pp. 245-252). Kluwer Academic Publishers.

Marik, V., & Pechoucek. M. (2004). Agent technology. In L.M. Camarina-Matos & H. Afsarmanesh (Eds.), *Collaborative networked organisations: A research agenda for emerging business models* (pp. 193-206). Kluwer Academic Publishers.

Martin, C. (1999). *Net future.* New York: McGraw-Hill.

Martin, D., et al. (2004). OWL-S: Semantic markup for web services. Retrieved February 12, 2007, from http://www.w3.org/Submission/OWL-S

Marík, V., & McFarlane, D. C. (2005). Industrial adoption of agent-based technologies. *IEEE Intelligent Systems, 20*(1), 27-35

Matskin, M., et al. (2000). *Agora: An infrastructure for cooperative work support in multi-agent systems.* Paper presented at the International Workshop on Infrastructure for Multi-agent Systems, Barcelona, Spain.

Matskin, M., Divitini, M., & Petersen, S. A. (1998). *An architecture for multi-agent support in a distributed informtation technology application.* Paper presented at the Workshop on Intelligent Agents in Information and Process Management, KI'98.

Maximilien, E.M., & Singh, M.P (2003). Agent-based Architecture for Autonomic Web Service Selection. In *Second International Joint Conference on Autonomous Agents and Multiagent Systems (AAMAS '03)*, ACM.

Maximilien, E.M., & Singh, M.P (2005). Agent-Based Trust Model Involving Multiple Qualities. In *Fourth International Joint Conference on Autonomous Agents and Multiagent Systems (AAMAS '05)* (pp. 519-526). ACM.

Maximilien, E.M., & Singh, M.P. (2005). Multiagent system for Dynamic Web Services Selection. In *Workshop on Service-Oriented Computing and Agent-Based Engineering (SOCABE '05)*. Springer.

Mayer, R. C., Davis, J. H. & Schoorman, F. D. (1995). An integration model of organizational trust. *Academy of Management Review, 20*(3), 709-734.

Mayer, R. J., Benjamin, P. C., Caraway, B. E., & Painter, M. K. (1995). A framework and a suite of methods for business process reengineering. In V. Grover & W.J. Kettinger (Eds.), *Business process change: Reengineering concepts, methods, and technologies* (pp. 245-290). Idea Group Publishing.

McAllister, D. J. (1995). Affect and cognition-based trust as foundation for interpersonal cooperation in organizations. *Academy of Management Journal, 38*(1), 24-59.

McDermott, D. (2000) The 1998 AI Planning Systems Competition. *AI Magazine, 2*(2), 35-55

Mecella, M., & Batini, C. (2000) *Cooperation of heterogeneous legacy information systems: A methodological framework*. In *Proceedings of the 4th International Enterprise Distributed Object Com-puting Conference*, Makuhari, Japan.

Mendling, J., & Hafner, M. (2005). From inter-organizational workflows to process execution: Generating BPEL from WS-CDL. In *Proceedings of OTM 2005 Workshops. Lecture Notes in Computer Science 3762*, Agia Napa, Cyprus.

Merali, Y., & Davies, J. (2001). Knowledge capture and utilization in virtual communities. In *Proceesings of the First International Conference on Knowledge Capture*, Canada.

Merriam-Webster Online Dictionary (2006). Retrieved February 13, 2007, from http://www.m-w.com

Meta Object Facility (MOF) Specification—Version 1.4. (2002, April). Retrieved September 1st, 2005, from http://www.omg.org/docs/formal/02-04-03.pdf

METEOR-S (2005). METEOR-S: Semantic web services and processes: Applying semantics in annotation, quality of service, discovery, composition, execution. Retrieved February 12, 2007, from http://lsdis.cs.uga.edu/Projects/METEOR-S/

Metso, J., & Kutvonen, L. (2005, September). Managing Virtual Organizations with Contracts. In *Workshop on Contract Architectures and Languages (CoALa2005)*. Enschede, The Netherlands.

Meyerson, D., K. E. Weick and R. M. Kramer. (1996). Swift trust and temporary groups. In R. M. Kramer & T. R. Tyler (Eds.), *Trust in Organizations: Frontiers of Theory and Research*. Thousand Oaks, CA: Sage Publications.

Mi, Z., Jianjun, X., Zunping, C., Yinsheng, L., & Binyu, Z. (2005). A Web Service-based Framework for Supply Chain Management. In *Eighth IEEE International Symposium on Object-Oriented Real-Time Distributed Computing (ISORC'05)* (pp. 316-319). IEEE Computer Society.

Microsoft Office Project 2003 (2005). Microsoft Corporation. Retrieved February 14, 2007, from http://www.microsoft.com/office/project/prodinfo/default.mspx

Micucci, D. (2002). Exploiting the kaleidoscope architecture in an industrial environmental monitoring system with heterogeneous devices and a knowledge-based supervisor. In *Proceedings of the 14th international conference on Software Engineering and Knowledge Engineering*.

Milestones (2005). KIDASA Software, Inc. Retrieved February 14, 2007, from http://www.kidasa.com/

Milosevic, Z., Linington, P. F., Gibson, S., Kulkarni, S., & Cole, J. B. (2004). Inter-Organisational Collaborations Supported by E-Contracts. In W. Lamersdorf, V. Tschammer, & S. Amarger (Eds.), *Building The E-Service Society: E-Commerce, E-Business, and E-Government -IFIP 18th World Computer Congress TC6/TC8/TC11 4th International Conference on E-Commerce, E-Business, E-Government (I3E 2004)* (p. 413-429). Kluwer.

Montaner, M., Lopez, B., & de la Rosa, J. L. (2003). A taxonomy of recommender agents on the internet. *Artificial Intelligence Review, 19*, 285-330.

Morsel, A. (2001). *Metrics for the Internet age: Quality of experience and quality of business.* Hewlett-Packard Labs Technical Report HPL-2001-179.

Moyaux, T., Chaib-draa, B., & D'Amours, S. (2004). Multi-Agent Simulation of Collaborative Strategies in a Supply Chain. In *Third International Joint Conference on Autonomous Agents and Multiagent Systems (AAMAS'04)* (pp. 52-59). IEEE Computer Society.

MyProxy Online Credential Repository. Retrieved February 17, 2007, from http://grid.ncsa.uiuc.edu/myproxy/

Nagarajan, K., Lam, H., & Su, S. (2004). Integration of business event and rule management with the web services model. *International Journal of Web Services Research, 1*(1), 41-57.

Nardi, D., & Brachman, R. (2002). The description logic handbook. In F. Baader, D. Calvanese, D. L. McGuinnes, D. Nardi, & P. Pate-Schneider (Eds.), (pp. 5-44). Cambridge CB2 2RU, UK: Cambridge University Press.

Neal, S., Cole, J. B., Linington, P. F., Milosevic, Z., Gibson, S., & Kulkarni, S. (2003). Identifying requirements for Business Contract Language: a Monitoring Perspective. In *7th International Enterprise Distributed Object Computing Conference (EDOC 2003)* (pp. 50–61). Los Alamitos, CA, USA: IEEE.

Neilson, I. (Ed.). (2006). *LCG/EGEE virtual organisation security policy.* Version 1.1. Retrieved February 17, 2007, from https://edms.cern.ch/document/573348/

Nelson, K. M., & Cooprider, J. G. (1996). The contribution of shared knowledge to IS group performance. *MIS Quarterly, 20*(4), 409-432.

Neumann, H., Schuster, G., Stuckenschmidt, H., Visser, U., & Vögele, T. (2001). Intelligent brokering of environmental information with the BUSTER system. In L. M. Hilty & P. W. Gilgen (Eds.), *International symposium informatics for environmental protection* (Vol. 30) (pp. 505-512). Metropolis, Zurich, Switzerland.

Newcomer, E., & Lomow, G. (2005). *Understanding SOA with Web services.* Addison Wesley.

Nissen, M.E. (2000). Supply Chain Process and Agent Design for E-Commerce. In *Proceedings of the 33rd Annual Hawaii International Conference on System Sciences* (pp. 1-8). IEEE Computer Society.

Nodine, M. H., Fowler, J., Ksiezyk, T., Perry, B., Taylor, M., & Unruh, A. (2000). Active information gathering in InfoSleuth. *International Journal of Cooperative Information Systems, 9*(1-2), 3-28.

Nonaka, I., & Takeuchi, H. (1995). *The knowledge-creating company: How Japanese companies create the dynamics of innovation.* New York: Oxford University Press.

Nwana, H. S. (1996). Software agents: An overview. *Knowledge Engineering Review, 11*(3), 1-40.

Nwana, H. S., & Ndumu, D. T. (1999). A Perspective on Software Agents Research. *The Knowledge Engineering Review, 14*(2), 1-18.

Nwana, H., & Ndumu, D. (1996). A brief introduction to software agent technology. In *Proceedings of the Unicom Seminar on "Real-World Applications of Intelligent Agent Technology"* (pp. 278-292).

Nwana, H., & Wooldridge, M. (1996). Software agent technologies. *BT Technology Journal, 14*(4), 68-78.

O'Brien, W., & Fischer, M. A. (2000). Importance of capacity constraints to construction cost and schedule. *Journal of Construction Engineering and Management, 126*(5), 366-373.

O'Brien, W., Fischer, M. A., & Jucker, J. V. (1995). An economic view of project coordination. *Construction Management and Economics, 13*(5), 393-400.

O'Leary, D. E. (1997). The internet, intranets, and the AI renaissance. *IEEE Computer, 30*(1), 71-78.

O'Neil, D. K. & Gomez, L. M. (1994). The collaboratory notebook: A distributed knowledge building environment for project learning. *Proceedings of ED MEDIA 94.* Vancouver B.C., Canada.

O'Sullivan, D. (1998). Communications technologies for the extended enterprise. *International Journal of Production Planning and Control, 9*(8), 742-753.

OAGIS (2006). Open Applications Group

OASIS Security Services (SAML) TC webpage. Retrieved February 12, 2007, from http://www.oasis-open.org/committees/tc_home.php?wg_abbrev=security

OASIS Web Services Composite Application Framework (WS-CAF) TC webpage. Retrieved February 12, 2007, from http://www.oasis-open.org/committees/tc_home.php?wg_abbrev=ws-caf

OASIS Web Services Notification (WSN) TC webpage. Retrieved February 12, 2007, from http://www.oasis-open.org/committees/tc_home.php?wg_abbrev=wsn

Odell, J. (2000). Agents: Technology and usage (Part 1). *Executive Report, 3*(4).

OGC (1994). The open geospatial consortium. Retrieved February 18, 2007, from http://www.opengeospatial.org

Oliveira, E., & Rocha, A. P. (2000). Agents' advanced features for negotiation in electronic commerce and virtual organisation formation process. *European Perspectives on Agent Mediated Commerce.* Springer-Verlag.

Oliveira, E., Fischer, K., & Stepankova, O. (1999). Multiagent systems: Which research for which applications. *Robotics and Autonomous Systems, 27,* 91-106.

OMG Agent Working Group (2000). *Agent technology.* Green paper, OMG Document ec/8/1/00, (1).

ONAR (2006). Ontologies based enterprise application integration framework. Retrieved Februaty 13, 2007, from http://research.altec.gr/ONAR

Orchard, D., Ferris, C., Newcomer, E., Haas, H., Champion, M., Booth, D. & McCabe, F. (2004, February). Web services architecture. W3C Working Group. Retrieved February 12, 2007, from http://www.w3.org/TR/2004/NOTE-ws-arch-20040211/

Ouzounis, V. K., & Tschammer, V. (2001). An agent-based life cycle management for dynamic virtual enterprises. In *Proceedings of the Sixth International Conference on Computer Supported Cooperative Work in Design* (pp. 451-459).

OWL (2006). W3C OWL 1.0 syntax specification. Retrieved February 13, 2007, from http://www.w3.org/TR/owl-ref/

OWL Web Ontology Language Guide. (2004, February). (W3C Recommendation 10 February 2004, Retrieved September 1st, 2005, from http://www.w3.org/TR/owl-guide/)

Palmer, W., & Speier, C. (1997). A typology of virtual organizations: An empirical study. In *Proceedings of the Association for information systems 1997 Americas' Conference*, Indianapolis, Indiana.

Palsberg, J., & Zhao, T. (2001). Efficient and flexible matching of recursive types. *Information and Computation, 171*(2), 364-387.

Paolucci, M., Kawamura, T., Payne, T. R., & Sycara, K. (2002). Importing the Semantic Web in UDDI. In *Proceedings of the E-Services and the Semantic Web Workshop.*

Papazoglou, M. P., & Georgakopoulos, D. (2003). Introduction. *Communications of the ACM, 46*(10), 24-28.

Papazoglou, M., Ribber, R., & Tsalgatidou, A. (2000). Integrated value chains and their implications from a business and technology standpoint. *Decision Support Systems, 29,* 323-342.

Pardoe, D., Stone, P., & VanMiddlesworth, M. (2006). TacTex-05: An Adaptive Agent for TAC SCM. In *Trad-*

ing *Agent Design and Analysis and Agent Mediated Electronic Commerce (TADA/AMEC)* Joint International Workshop (pp. 85-98). Springer.

Peer, J. (2004) A pddl based tool for automatic Web service composition. In H.J. Ohlbach & S. Schaffert (Eds.), *PSWR*. Volume 3208 of Lecture Notes in Computer Science (pp. 149-163). Springer.

Peer, J. (2002). Bringing together Semantic Web and Web services. In *ISWC '02: Proceedings of the First International Semantic Web Conference on The Semantic Web* (pp. 279-291). London: Springer-Verlag.

Peltz, C. (2003, January). Web services orchestration: A review of emerging technologies, tools, and standards. Retrieved February 12, 2007, from http://devresource. hp.com/drc/technical_white_papers/WSOrch/WSOrchestration.pdf

Peng, Y., Finin, T., Labrou, Y., Chu, B., Long, J., Tolone, W. J., & Boughannam, A. (1998). A multi-agent system for enterprise integration. In *Proceedings of the 3rd International Conference on the Practical Applications of Agents and Multi-Agent Systems (PAAM98)* (pp. 155-169). London.

Petersen, S. A., & Divitini, M. (2002). *Using agents to support the selection of virtual enterprise teams.* Paper presented at the Fourth International Bi-conference Workshop on Agent-oriented Information Systems (AOIS-2002) at AAMAS 2002, Bologne, Italy.

Petersen, S. A., & Gruninger, M. (2000). *An agent-based model to support the formation of virtual enterprises.* Paper presented at the International ICSC Symposium on Mobile Agents and Multi-agents in Virtual Organisations and E-Commerce (MAMA 2000), Woolongong, Australia.

Petersen, S. A., Divitini, M., & Matskin, M. (2001). An agent-based approach to modeling virtual enterprises. *Production Planning & Control, 12*(3), 224-233.

Petersen, S. A., Jinghai, R., & Matskin, M. (2003). Virtual enterprise formation with agents: An approach to implementation. In *Proceedings of the IAT 2003, IEEE/VVIC International Conference on Intelligent Agent Technology* (pp. 527-530).

Petersen, S. A., Rao, J., & Tveit, A. (2002). *Virtual enterprises: Challenges in selecting and integrating computational and human resources.* Paper presented at the Agentcities: Challenges in Open Agent Environments, Bologne, Italy.

Petrie, C. J. (1996). Agent-Based Engineering, the Web and intelligence. *IEEE Expert, 11*(6), 24-29.

Petrie, C., & Bussler, C. (2003, July/August). Service agents and virtual enterprises: A Survey. *IEEE Internet Computing.*

Pfohl, H. C., & Buse, H. P. (2000). Inter-organizational logistics systems in flexible production networks: An organizational capabilities perspective. *International Journal of Physical Distribution & Materials Management, 30*(5), 388-408.

Pi4SOA (2006). The official Pi4SOA project site. Retrieved February 13, 2007, from http://sourceforge. net/projects/pi4soa

Piccoli, G. & Ives, B. (2003). Trust and the unintended effects of behavior control in virtual teams. *MIS Quarterly, 27*(3), 157-180.

Pitts, G., & Fowler, J. (2001). InfoSleuth: An emerging technology for sharing distributed environmental information. *Information systems and the environment* (pp. 159-172). National Academy Press.

Powell, A., Piccoli, G. & Ives, B. (2004). Virtual teams: A review of current literature and directions for future research. *The Data Base for Advances in Information Systems, 35*(1), 6-36.

Preece, A., & Decker, S. (2002). Intelligent web services. *IEEE Intelligent Systems, 17*(1), 15-17.

Preiss, K., Goldman, S., & Nagel, R. (1996). *Cooperate to compete: Building agile business relationships.* New York: van Nostrand Reinhold.

Presley, A., Sarkis, J., & Liles, D. H. (2000). A soft-system methodology approach for product and process innovation. *IEEE Transactions on Engineering Management, 47*(3), 379-92.

Profozich, D. (1998). *Managing change with business process simulation*. Upper Saddle River, NJ: Prentice-Hall PTR.

Protogeros, N. (2006). Service-oriented architectures and virtual enterprises. In M. Khosrow-Pour (Ed.), *Encyclopedia of e-commerce, e-government, and mobile commerce, e-collaboration technologies and applications*. Hershey, PA: Idea Group Reference.

Pumareja, D., Bondarouk, T., & Sikkel, K. (2003). Supporting knowledge sharing isn't easy–Lessons learnt from a case study. In *Proceedings of the Information Resource Management Association International Conference*, Philadelphia.

Purvis, M., Cranefield, S., Ward, R., Nowostawski, M., Carter, D., & Bush, G. (2003). A multi-agent system for the integration of distributed environmental information. *Environmental Modelling & Software, 18*, 565-572.

Putnik G. D., Sluga A., & Butala P. (2006). Reconfigurability of manufacturing systems for agility implementation – Part I: Two architectures. In P. F. Cunha (Ed.). In *Proceedings of the 3rd International CIRP Conference on Digital Enterprise Technology. ET 2006*, Setúbal, Portugal.

Putnik, G. D. (2001). BM_virtual enterprise architecture reference model. In A. Gunasekaran (Ed.), *Agile manufacturing: 21st century manufacturing strategy* (pp. 73-93). UK: Elsevier Science Publishing

Putnik, G. D. (2004). Virtual Enterprise as a "flow" enterprise. In *Proceedings of the Fourth Annual Meeting of the European Chaos and Complexity in Organisations Network ECCON. ECCON 2005*.

Putnik, G. D., Cunha, M. M., Sousa, R., & Ávila, P. (2005). BM virtual enterprise - A model for dynamics and virtuality. In G. D. Putnik & M. M. Cunha (Eds.), *Virtual enterprise integration: Technological and organizational perspectives* (pp. 124-144). Idea Group Publishing.

Qing, Z., & Renchu, G. (2001). Modeling of distribution system in a supply chain based on multi-agent. In *2001 International Conferences on Info-Tech and Info-Net* (pp. 94-99). IEEE Press.

Quirchmayr, G., Milosevic, Z., Tagg, R., Cole, J., & Kulkarni, Rabelo, R. J., Camarinha-Matos, L. M., & Vallejos, R. V. (2000). Agent-based brokerage for virtual enterprise creation in the moulds industry. In L. M. Camarinha-Matos, H. Afsarmanesh, & R. J. Rabelo (Eds.), *E-business and virtual enterprises - Managing business-to-business cooperation* (pp. 281-290). Kluwer Academic Publishers.

Rabelo, R. J., Camarinha-Matos, L. M., & Vallejos, R. V. (2000). Agent-based brokerage for virtual enterprise creation in the moulds industry. In *Proceedings of the IFIP TC5/WG5.3 Second IFIP Working Conference on Infrastructures for Virtual Organizations: Managing Cooperation in Virtual Organizations and Electronic Busimess towards Smart Organizations* (pp. 281-290). Deventer, The Netherlands: Kluwer, B.V.

Rahwan, I., Kowalczyk, R., & Yang, Y. (2001). Virtual enterprise design: BDI agents vs. objects. *Advances in Artificial Intelligence* (LNCS 2112, pp. 147-157).

Rainer, A. (2004) Web-centric business process modelling. *Int. J. Electronic Business, 2*(3).

Ramesh, R., & Whinston, A. (1994). Claims, arguments, and decisions: Formalisms for Representation, Gaming, and Coordination. *Information Systems Research, 5*(3), 294-325.

Rao, J., & Su, X. (2004). A survey of automated Web service composition methods. In J. Cardoso & AP Sheth (Eds.), *SWSWPC*. Volume 3387 of Lecture Notes in Computer Science., Springer43-54

Ratnakar, V., & Gil, Y. (2002). A comparison of (Semantic) mark-up languages. In *Proceedings of the 15th International FLAIRS Conference, Special Track on Semantic Web*, Pensacola, Finland.

RDF Vocabulary Description Language 1.0: RDF Schema. (2004, February). (W3C Recommendation 10 February 2004. Retrieved September 1st, 2005, from http://www.w3.org/TR/rdf-schema/)

Reichert, M., & Dadam, P. (1998). ADEPTflex—Supporting dynamic changes of workflow without losing control.

Journal of Intelligent Information Systems, 10(2), 93-129. (Special Issue on Workflow Management)

Reina, D., & Reina, M. (1999). *Trust and betrayal in the workplace.* San Francisco: Berrett-Koehler.

Remidez, H. (2003). *System structure design and social consequence: The impact of message templates on affectivity in virtual teams.* Unpublished doctoral dissertation. University of Missouri, Columbia.

RFC 3820 (2004). Standard track, internet X.509 public key infrastructure (PKI) proxy certificate profile. Retrieved February 17, 2007, from ftp://ftp.isi.edu/in-notes/rfc3820.txt

RFC4034 (2005). Resource records for the DNS security extensions. Retrieved February 17, 2007, from *h*ttp://www.rfc-archive.org/getrfc.php?rfc=4034

RFC4035 (2005). Protocol modifications for the DNS security extensions. Retrieved February 17, 2007, from http://www.rfc-archive.org/getrfc.php?rfc=4035

Rimassa, G. (2003). *Runtime support for distributed nulti-agent systems.* PhD Thesis, University of Parma.

Roberts, B., & Koumpis, A. (2005). Use of ontologies to support the situation room metaphor as an auction engine for corporate information and knowledge exchange [Electronic version]. *International Journal of Electronic Commerce & Business Media, 15*(1).

Rocha, A. P., & Oliveira, E. (1999). Electronic commerce: A technological perspective. *The Future of the Internet.*

Rondinelli, D. A. (1983). *Decentralization in developing countries.* (Staff Working Paper No. 581). Washington, DC: World Bank.

RosettaNet Consortium.(2004). *RosettaNet Implementation Framework: Core Specification V02.00.00.* Retrieved September 1st, 2005, from http://www.rosettanet.org/

Ross-Talbot, S. (2005). Orchestration and choreography: Standards, tools and technologies for distributed workflows. In *Proceedings of the NETTAB Workshop - Workflows Management: New Abilities for the Biological Information Overflow,* Naples, Italy.

Routledge, N., Bird, L., & Goodchild, A. (2002). UML and XML schema. In *Proceedings of the Thirteenth Australasian Database Conference (ADC2002),* Melbourne, Australia. In Xiaofang Zhou (Ed.), *Conferences in research and practice in information technology: Vol. 5.*

Ruohomaa, S., Viljanen, L., & Kutvonen, L. (2006, March). Guarding enterprise collaborations with trust decisions—The TuBE approach. In *Proceedings of the first international workshop on interoperability solutions to trust, security, policies and qos for enhanced enterprise systems (is-tspq 2006).*

Ruokolainen, T. (2004). *Component interoperability.* University of Helsinki, Department of Computer Science. MSc thesis C-2004-42. In Finnish

S. (2001, March). *Web Services Description Language (WSDL) 1.1.* (Retrieved September 1st, 2005, from http://www.w3c.org/TR/wsdl)

S. (2002). Establishment of Virtual Enterprise Contracts. In *Database and Expert Systems Applications : 13th International Conference* (Vol. 2453, pp. 236–248). London, UK: Springer-Verlag.

Sarker, S., & Sahay, S. (2004). Implications of space and time for distributed work: an interpretive study of US-Norwegian systems development teams. *European Journal of Information Systems, 13*(1), 3-20.

Sarker, S., Valacich, J. & Sarker, S. (2003). Virtual team trust: Instrument development and validation in an IS educational environment. *Information Resource Management Journal, 16*(2), 35-55.

Sauer, J., & Appelrath, H.J. (2003). Scheduling the Supply Chain by Teams of Agents. In *36th Hawaii International Conference on System Sciences* (pp. 81-92). IEEE Computer Society.

Scardamalia, M. & Bereiter, C. (1994). Computer support for knowledge-building communities. *The Journal of Learning Sciences, 3*(3), 265-283.

Schedule, F. (2005). AEC Software, Inc. Retrieved February 14, 2007, from http://www.aecsoft.com/

Scheer, A. (1993). Architecture of integrtaed information systems (ARIS). In H. Yoshikawa & J. Goosenaerts (Eds.), *Information infrustructure systems for manufacturing.* North Holland, Amsterdam.

Schieritz, N., & Groessler, A. (2003). Emergent structures in supply chains—A study integrating agent-based and system dynamic modeling. In *Proceedings of the 36ᵗʰ Annual Hawaii International Conference on System Sciences (HICSS'03)* (pp. 94-102). IEEE Computer Society.

Schmidt, D. C. (2000). Applying a pattern language to develop application-level gateways. In L. Rising (Ed.), *Design patterns in communications.* Cambridge University Press.

Schneeweiss, C. (2003). Distributed decision making—a unified approach. *European Journal of Operational Research, 150*(2), 237-252.

Senge, P. (1990). *The fifth discipline: The art and practice of the learning organization.* New York: Doubleday.

Serenko, & Deltor, B. (2002). *Agent toolkits: A general overview of the market and an assessment of instructor satisfaction with utilizing in the classroom.* (Working Paper No. 455). Retrieved January 31, 2007, from http://www.business.mcmaster.ca/msis/profs/detlorb/nserc/McMaster_Working_Paper_455.pdf

Shen, W., & Norrie, D. H. (1999). Agent-based systems for intelligent manufacturing: A state-of-the-art survey. *Knowledge and Information Systems, 1*(2), 129-156.

Sheremetov, L., & Rocha-Mier, L. (2004). Collective intelligence as a framework for supply chain management. In *Proceedings of the 2004 2nd International IEEE Conference on Intelligent Systems* (pp. 417-422). IEEE Computer Society.

Shibboleth Project (2006). Retrieved February 17, 2007, from http://shibboleth.internet2.edu/

Shuwang, W., Ren, Z., Zhifeng, L., & Guangfu, L. (2003). Construction of dynamic green supply chain based on agent. In *IEEE International Symposium of Electronics and the Environment* (pp. 30-35). IEEE Press.

Silva, C.A., Sousa, J.M.C., Sa da Costa, J.M.G., & Runkler, T.A. (2004). A multi-agent approach for supply chain management using ant colony optimization. In *2004 International Conference on Systems, Man and Cybernetics* (pp. 1938-1943). IEEE Press.

Silver, M. (1988). User perceptions of decision support system restrictiveness: An experiment. *Journal of Management Information Systems, 5*(1), 51-65.

Simek, B., Albayrak, S., & Korth, A.(2004). Reinforcement Learning for Procurement Agents of the Factory of the Future. In *2004 Congress on Evolutionary Computation* (pp. 1331-1337). IEEE Press.

Simple Object Access Protocol (SOAP) 1.1 (2000, May). W3C note. Retrieved February 12, 2007, from http://www.w3.org/TR/2000/NOTE-SOAP-20000508/

Sirin, E., & Parsia, B. (2004) *Planning for semantic Web services.* In Semantic Web Services Workshop at 3ʳᵈ International Semantic Web Conference (ISWC2004).

Smirnov, A. V., Sheremetov, L. B., Chilov, N., & Cortes, J. R. (2004). Soft-computing technologies for configuration of cooperative supply chain. In *Applied Soft Computing 4*(1), 87-107.

SOAP Version 1.2 Part 0: Primer (2003, June). W3C recommendation. Retrieved February 12, 2007, from http://www.w3.org/TR/soap12-part0/

SOAP Version 1.2 Part 1: Messaging Framework. (2003, June). W3C recommendation. Retrieved February 12, 2007, from http://www.w3.org/TR/soap12-part1/

Sona, D., Veeramachaneni, S., Avesani, P., & Polettini, N. (2004). Clustering with propagation for hierarchical document classification. In *Proceedings of the ECML Workshop on Statistical Approaches to Web Mining* (pp. 50-61).

Sriharee, N., & Senivongse, T.(2003, November). Discovering Web Services Using Behavioural Constraints and Ontology. In J.-B. Stefani, I. Demeure, & D. Hagimont (Eds.), *Distributed Applications and Interoperable Systems: 4ᵗʰ IFIP WG6.1 International Conference (DAIS 2003)* (pp. 248-259). Springer-Verlag.

Srinivasan, L. & Treadwell, J. (2005, November). An overview of service-oriented architecture, web services and grid computing. HP Software Global Business Unit.

Stanfield, J. (2002). Agents in Supply Chain Management. *AgentLink News, 9*, 11-12

Sun Microsystems, Inc. (2003). JSR-000154 Java(TM) Servlet 2.4 Specification (Final release).

Suthers, D. 1998. Representations for scaffolding collaborative inquiry on ill-structured problems. Paper presented at the *1998 AERA Annual Meeting.* San Diego, CA.

Svirskas, A., Wilson, M., Arenas, A. et al. (2005). Aspects of trusted and secure business oriented VO management in service oriented architectures. In *Workshop Proceedings of Seventh IEEE International Conference on E-Commerce Technology.* IEEE Computer Society, Munich, Germany.

Swiss Bank Corporation, Switzerland; e-Workflow.org, Gold Award, Workflow, Europe (1998) Nominated by Eastman Software, Inc. with integration by Systor AG.

Sycara, K. P. (1998). Multi-agent systems. *AI Magazine, 19*(2), 79-92.

Sycara, K. P. (1998). The many faces of agents. *AI Magazine, 19*(2), 11-12.

Symeonidis, A.L., Kehagias, D.D., & Mitkas, P.A. (2003). Intelligent policy recommendations on enterprise resource planning by the use of agent technology and data mining techniques. In *Expert Systems with Applications, 25*(4), 589-602.

Szirbik, N., Aerts, A., Wortmann, H., Hammer, D., & Goossenaerts, J. (2000). Mediating negotiations in a virtual enterprise via mobile agents.In *Proceedings of the Academia/Industry Working Conference on Research Challenges* (pp. 237-242).

Ta, L., Chai, Y., & Liu, Y. (2005). A Multi-agent Approach for Task Allocation and Execution for Supply Chain Management. In *2005 International Conference on Networking, Sensing and Control* (pp. 65-70). IEEE Press.

Takeuchi, K., Honda, K., & Kubo, M. (1994). An Interaction-based Language and its Typing System. In *PARLE '94: Proceedings of the 6th International PARLE Conference on Parallel Architectures and Languages Europe* (pp. 398-413). London, UK: Springer-Verlag.

Taylor. D. (1995). *Business engineering with object technology.* New York: John Wiley & Sons.

Te'eni, D. (2001). Review: A cognitive-affective model of organizational communication for designing IT. *MIS Quarterly, 25*(2), 251-312.

Tektonidis, D., & Bokma, A. (2005). The utilization of ontologies for e-health systems integration. In *Proceedings of the 10th International Symposium on Health Information Management Research*, Thessaloniki, Greece.

Tektonidis, D., Bokma, A., Oatley, G., & Salampasis, M. (2005). ONAR: An ontologies-based service oriented application integration framework. In *Proceedings of the 1st International Conference on Interoperability of Enterprise Software and Applications*, Geneva, Switzerland.

Tektonidis, D., Vontas, A., Hess, U., & Meschonat, J. (2002). Handling the shop-floor of an industry through ERP systems: A functional integration model. In *Proceedings of the International Conference on E-business & E-Work 2002*, Prague.

The CORBA Object Group Service. *A Service Approach to Object Groups in CORBA, N° 1867.* (1998). Retrieved from http://lsrwww.epfl.ch/OGS/thesis/

The Object Management Group. (n.d.). *CORBA®BASICS.* Retrieved from http://www.omg.org/gettingstarted/corbafaq.htm

The Object Management Group. (n.d.). Retrieved from http://www.omg.org

Themistocleous, M., Irani, Z., O'Keefe, R., & Paul, R. (2001). ERP problems and application integration issues: An empirical survey. In *Proceedings of the 34th Hawaiian International Conference on Systems Science*, Big Island

Timmers, P. (1999). *Electronic commerce: Strategies and models for business-to-business trading*. John Wiley & Sons.

Tiwana, A. (2003). Affinity to infinity in peer-to-peer knowledge platforms. *Communications of ACM, 46*(5), 76-80.

Toulis, P., Kehagias, D., & Mitkas, P. (2006). *Mertacor: A successful autonomous trading agent*. Fifth International Joint Conference on Autonomous Agents and Multiagent Systems (pp. 1191-1198), ACM.

Tsalgatidou, A., & Pilioura, T. (2002). An overview of standards and related technology in web services. *Distributed and parallel databases* (pp. 135-320). The Netherlands: Kluwer Academic Publishers.

Tschantz, M., Benisch, M., Greenwald, A., Grypari, I., Lederman, R.. & Naroditskiy, V. (2004). Botticelli: A Supply Chain Management Agent. In *Third International Joint Conference on Autonomous Agents and Multiagent Systems (AAMAS04)* (pp. 1174-1181). IEEE Computer Society.

Tserng, H. P., & Lin, W. Y. (2003). Developing an electronic acquisition model for project scheduling using XML-based information standard. *Automation in Construction, 12*, 67-95.

Turban, E. (2002). *Electronic commerce: A managerial perspective*. Upper Saddle River, NJ: Prentice Hall.

Tuukka Vartiainen, Java Beans, and Enterprise Java Beans. (n.d.). Retrieved from http://www.cs.helsinki.fi/u/campa/teaching/tukka-final.pdf

UDDI (2006). UDDI Version 3.0.2, An OASIS Standard,

UDDI executive overview: Enabling service-oriented architecture (2004, October). OASIS. Retrieved February 12, 2007, from http://uddi.org/pubs/uddi-exec-wp.pdf

UDDI Version 3.0.2 (2004, October). UDDI spec technical committee draft. Retrieved February 12, 2007, from http://uddi.org/pubs/uddi-v3.0.2-20041019.pdf

Uiterkamp, E. S. (2005). *Nomadic positioning services for a mobile service platform*. Unpublished master's dissertation, University of Twente, The Netherlands.

Ulieru, M., & Cobzaru, M. (1999). Building holonic supply chain management systems: An e-Logistics application for the telephone manufacturing industry. In *Transactions on Industrial Informatics, 1*(1), 18-29.

Vallecillo, A., Vasconcelos, V. T., & Ravara, A. (2003). Typing the behavior of objects and components using session types. *Electronic Notes in Theoretical Computer Science, 68*(3). (Presented at FOCLASA'02)

Van Aken, E. (1998). The virtual organization: A special mode of strong inter-organizational cooperation. *Managing strategically in an interconnected world* (pp. 301-320). Chichester: John Wiley & Sons.

Van der Aalst, W. M. P. (1999). Formalization and verification of event-driven process chains. *Information and Software Technology, 41*(10), 639-50.

Van der Aalst, W. M. P., & ter Hofstede, A. H. M. (2000). Verification of workflow task structures: A petri-net-based approach. *Information Systems, 25*(1), 43-69.

Vassileva, J. (2002). Supporting peer-to-peer user communities. In R. Meersman & Z. Tari (Eds.), *CoopIS/DOA/ODBASE 2002* (pp. 230-247). Berlin: Springer-Verlag.

VEGBANK (2006). The vegetation plot database of the Ecological Society of America. Retrieved February 18, 2007, from www.vegbank.org

Vernadat, F. B. (1996). *Enterprise modelling and integration principles and applications*: Chapman and Hall.

Vinoski, S. (2001). The truth about Web services. *Web Services and Component Technologies*.

Virtual Organization Membership Service (VOMS) (2006). Project homepage. Retrieved February 17, 2007, from http://infnforge.cnaf.infn.it/voms/

Vontas, A., Koutsakas, F., Athanasopoulou, C., Koumpis, A., Hatzaras, P., Manolopoulos, Y., & Vassilakopoulos, M. (2002). Integrating mobile agents infrastructures in operational ERP systems. In *Proceedings of the 4th*

International Conference on Enterprise Information Systems, Ciudad Real, Spain.

VOSTER (2003). Virtual organizations cluster. Retrieved February 12, 2007, from http://cic.vtt.fi/projects/voster/public.html

W3C (2000). Extensible Markup Language (XML) 1.0 (Second Edition). Available at http://www.w3.org/TR/2000/REC-xml-20001006

W3C (2001). *Web Services Description Language (WSDL)1.1*. Available at http://www.w3.org/TR/2001/NOTE-wsdl-20010315

W3C (2003). *Simple Object Access Protocol (SOAP)1.2*. Available at http://www.w3.org/TR/soap12-part1/

W3C (2003). *Web Services Glossary, Working Draft*. Available at http://www.w3.org/TR/2003/WD-ws-gloss-20030808/

W3C (2004). Web services architecture requirements. Retrieved February 12, 2007, from http://www.w3.org/TR/wsa-reqs

W3C (2006). Semantic web description. Retrieved February 13, 2007, from http://www.w3.org/2001/sw/

Wache, H., Vögele, T., Visser, U., Stuckenschmidt, H., Schuster, G., Neumann, H., & Hübner, S. (2001). Ontology-based integration of information: A survey of existing approaches. In *Proceedings of the IJCAI-01 Workshop: Ontologies and Information Sharing*, Seattle, Washington.

Wan, G. (2004). Joint production and delivery scheduling in two-level supply chains: A distributed agent approach. In *2004 IEEE International Conference on Systems, Man and Cybernetics* (pp. 1522-1526). IEEE Press.

Wang, C. X. (2001). Supply chain coordination in B2B electronic markets. In *Proceedings of the 32ᵈ Annual Meeting of the Decision Sciences Institute*, San Francisco.

Wang, S. C., & Chen, Y. M. (2005, June 8-10). *Framework of agent-based two-stage decision-making process for distributed dynamic scheduling*. Paper presented at the International Conference on Technology and Accreditation (ICTA2005), Taoyuan, Taiwan, ROC.

Wang, S. (1994). OO modeling of business process. *Information system Management*, 36-43

Web Services Addressing (WS-Addressing) (2004, August). W3C member submission. Retrieved February 12, 2007, from http://www.w3.org/Submission/ws-addressing/

Web Services Agreement Specification (WS-Agreement) (2004). Retrieved February 17, 2007, from https://forge.gridforum.org/projects/graap-wg/document/WS-AgreementSpecification/

Web Services Atomic Transaction (WS-AtomicTransaction) 1.1 (2006, August). Public review draft 01. Retrieved February 12, 2007, from http://docs.oasis-open.org/ws-tx/wstx-wsat-1.1-spec-pr-01.pdf

Web Services Business Activity (WS-Business Activity) 1.1 (2006, March). Committee draft 01. Retrieved February 12, 2007, from http://docs.oasis-open.org/ws-tx/wstx-wsba-1.1-spec-cd-01.pdf

Web Services Choreography Description Language Version 1.0 (2005, November). W3C candidate recommendation. Retrieved February 12, 2007, from http://www.w3.org/TR/ws-cdl-10/

Web Services Context Specification (WS-Context). Committee Specification 1.0. Retrieved February 12, 2007, from http://www.oasis-open.org/committees/download.php/19659/WS-Context.zip

Web Services Coordination (WS-Coordination) 1.1 (2006, August). Public review draft 01. Retrieved February 12, 2007, from http://docs.oasis-open.org/ws-tx/wstx-wscoor-1.1-spec-pr-01.pdf

Web Services Coordination, Framework Specification (WS-CF). (2005, October). Editor's draft 1.0. Retrieved February 12, 2007, from http://www.oasis-open.org/committees/download.php/15042/WS-CF.zip

Web Services Description Language (WSDL) Version 2.0 Part 1: Core Language (2006, March). W3C candidate recommendation. Retrieved February 12, 2007, from http://www.w3.org/TR/wsdl20/

Web Services Eventing (WS-Eventing) (2006, March). W3C member submission. Retrieved February 12, 2007, from http://www.w3.org/Submission/WS-Eventing/

Web Services Federation Language (WS-Federation) Version 1.0 (2003). Retrieved February 17, 2007, from http://msdn.microsoft.com/ws/2003/07/ws-federation/

Web Services Federation Language (WSFederation) Version 1.0 (2003, July). Retrieved February 12, 2007, from ftp://www6.software.ibm.com/software/developer/library/ws-fed.pdf

Web Services Metadata Exchange (WS-MetadataExchange) Version 1.1 (2006, August). Retrieved February 12, 2007, from http://download.boulder.ibm.com/ibmdl/pub/software/dw/specs/ws-mex/metadataexchange.pdf

Web Services Policy 1.2 - Attachment (WS-PolicyAttachment) (2006, April). W3C member submission. Retrieved February 12, 2007, from http://www.w3.org/Submission/2006/SUBM-WS-PolicyAttachment-20060425/

Web Services Policy 1.2 - Framework (WS-Policy) (2006, April). W3C member submission. Retrieved February 12, 2007, from http://www.w3.org/Submission/WS-Policy/

Web Services Policy Assertions Language (WS-PolicyAssertions) Version 1.0 (2002, December). Retrieved February 12, 2007, from ftp://www6.software.ibm.com/software/developer/library/ws-polas.pdf

Web Services Policy Framework (WS-Policy). Version 1.2 (2006). Retrieved February 17, 2007, *from* http://msdn.microsoft.com/ws/2002/12/Policy/

Web Services Reliable Messaging Protocol (WS-ReliableMessaging) (2005, February). Retrieved February 12, 2007, from ftp://www6.software.ibm.com/software/developer/library/ws-reliablemessaging200502.pdf

Web Services Reliable Messaging TC, WS-Reliability 1.1 (2004, November). OASIS standard. Retrieved February 12, 2007, from http://docs.oasis-open.org/wsrm/ws-reliability/v1.1/wsrm-ws_reliability-1.1-spec-os.pdf

Web Services Secure Conversation Language (WS-SecureConversation) (2005, February). Retrieved February 12, 2007, from ftp://www6.software.ibm.com/software/developer/library/ws-secureconversation.pdf

Web Services Security Policy Language (WS-SecurityPolicy) Version 1.1 (2005, July) Retrieved February 12, 2007, from ftp://www6.software.ibm.com/software/developer/library/ws-secpol.pdf

Web Services Security: SOAP Message Security 1.1 (WS-Security 2004) (2006, February). OASIS standard specification. Retrieved February 12, 2007, from http://www.oasis-open.org/committees/download.php/16790/wss-v1.1-spec-os-SOAPMessageSecurity.pdf

Web Services Transaction Management (WS-TXM) Version 1.0 (2003, July). Retrieved February 12, 2007, from http://developers.sun.com/techtopics/webservices/wscaf/wstxm.pdf

Web Services Trust Language (WS-Trust) (2005). Retrieved February 17, 2007, from ftp://www6.software.ibm.com/software/developer/library/ws-trust.pdf

webMethods Inc. (2002). Demystifying web services. webMethods Inc. Retrieved February 13, 2007, from http://www.webmethods.com

Webster, M., Sugden, D. M., & Tayles, M. E. (2004). The measurement of manufacturing virtuality. *International Journal of Operations & Production Management,* *24*(7), 721-742.

Weerawarana, S., Curbera, F., Leymann, F., Storey, T. & Ferguson, D. F. (2005). *Web services platform architecture.* Prentice Hall

Weiß, G. (2002). Agent orientation in software engineering. *Knowledge Engineering Review, 16*(4), 349-373.

Weld, D.S. (1994). An Introduction to Least-Commitment Planning, *AI Magazine, 15*(4) 27-61.

Werden, S., Evans, C., & Goodner, M. (2002). *WS-I usage scenarios.* Retrieved February 18, 2007, from http://www.wsi.org/SampleApplications/SupplyChainManagement/2002-11/UsageScenarios-1.00-CRD-02a.mht

WfMC (2005) *XML Process Definition Language (XPDL) 1.09*, http://www.wfmc.org.

Whitestein Technologies, A.G. (2003). Web Services Agent Integration Project.

Williamson, O.E. (1975). *Markets and hierarchies*. New York: The Free Press.

Winograd, T. (1987-1988). A language/action perspective on the design of cooperative work. *Human-Computer Interaction, 3*(1), 3-30.

Wooldridge, M. (1998). Agent-based computing. *Interoperable Communication Networks, 1*(1), 71-97.

Wooldridge, M. (1999). Intelligent agents. In G. Weiss (Ed.), *Multi-agent systems*. MIT Press.

Wooldridge, M. J., & Jennings, N. R. (1995). Intelligent agents: Theory and practice. *Knowledge Engineering Review, 10*(2), 115-152.

Wooldridge, M., & Ciancarini, P. (2000). Agent-oriented software engineering: The state of the art. In P. Ciancarini & M. Wooldridge (Eds.), In *Proceedings of the First International Workshop on Agent-Oriented Software Engineering* (pp. 1-28).

Wooldridge, M., & Jennings, N. R. (1995). Intelligent agents: Theory and practice. *The Knowledge Engineering Review, 10*(2), 115-152.

Wooldridge, M.,& Jennings N.R. (1995). Agent theories, architectures, and languages: A survey. In M. Wooldridge & N.R. Jennings (Eds.), *Intelligent agents*. Berlin: Springer-Verlag.

WSArch (2004). Web Services Architecture. *W3C Working Group Note.*

WS-BPEL (2004). Web Services Business Process Execution Language. OASIS.

WS-CDL (2005). Web Services Choreography Description Language Version 1.0. W3C Candidate Recommendation.

WS-CHOR (2004). Web Services Choreography Requirements. *W3C Working Draft.*

WSDL (2006). Web Services Description Language (WSDL) Version 2.0

Wu, J., Ulieru, M., Cobzaru, M., & Norrie, D. (2000). Supply chain management systems: State of the art and vision. In *9th International Conference on Management of Innovation and Technology* (pp. 759-764). IEEE Press.

XML Encryption Syntax and Processing (2002, December). W3C recommendation. Retrieved February 12, 2007, from http://www.w3.org/TR/xmlenc-core/

XML Information Set (Second Edition) (2004, February). W3C recommendation. Retrieved February 12, 2007, from http://www.w3.org/TR/2004/REC-xml-infoset-20040204/

XML Query Working Group Public Page. Retrieved February 12, 2007, from http://www.w3.org/XML/Query/

XML Schema Part 0: Primer Second Edition (2004, October). W3C recommendation. Retrieved February 12, 2007, from http://www.w3.org/TR/xmlschema-0/

XML-Signature Syntax and Processing. (2002, February). W3C recommendation. Retrieved February 12, 2007, from http://www.w3.org/TR/xmldsig-core/

XProlog (2002). XProlog. Retrieved February 12, 2007, from http://www.iro.umontreal.ca/~vaucher/XProlog/

XSL Transformations (XSLT) Version 2.0 (2006, June). W3C candidate recommendation. Retrieved February 12, 2007, from http://www.w3.org/TR/xslt20/

XSL Working Group Public Page. Retrieved February 12, 2007, from http://www.w3.org/Style/XSL/

Xue, X., Li, X., Shen, Q., & Wang, Y. (2005). An agent-based framework for supply chain coordination in construction. *Automation in Construction 14*(3), 413-430.

Yan, Y., Kuphal, T., & Bode, J. (2000). Application of multi-agent systems in project management. *International Journal of Production Economics, 68*, 185-197.

Yan, Z., Meilin, S., & Shaohua, Z. (2004). An agent-based framework for cross-domain cooperation of virtual enterprise. In *Proceedings of the 8th International Conference on Computer Supported Cooperative Work in Design* (pp. 291-296).

Yen, B. P.-C. (2002). Communication infrastructure in distributed scheduling. *Computers & Industrial Engineering, 42*, 149-161.

Yi, D.W., Kim, S.H., & Kim, N.Y. (2002). Combined Modeling with Multi-Agent Systems and Simulation: Its Application to Harbor Supply Chain Management. In *35th Annual Hawaii International Conference on System Sciences* (HICSS'02) (ppp. 70-79). IEEE Computer Society.

Yonghe, L., & Biqing, H. (1999). Virtual enterprise: An agent-based approach for decision and control. In *Proceedings of the IEEE SMC '99 International Conference on Systems, Man, and Cybernetics* (pp. 451-456).

Yung, S.K., & Yang, C.C. (1999). A new approach to solve supply chain management problem by integrating multi-agent technology and constraint network. In 32nd *Hawaii International Conference on System Sciences* (pp. 1-10). IEEE Computer Society.

Zambonelli, F., Jennings, N., & Wooldridge, M. (2003). Developing multiagent systems: The Gaia methology. *ACM Transactions on Software Engineering and Methodology, 12*(3).

Zhang, B., & Niu, X. (2006). *Implementation of agora system.* Unpublished master's thesis, Royal Institute of Technology, Department of Microelectronics and Information Technology, Stockholm.

Zhang, D., & Zhao, K. (2004). Economic model of TAC SCM game. In *IEEE/WIC/ACM International Conference on Intelligent Agent Technology* (pp. 273-280). IEEE Computer Society.

Zhang, Z.Q., & Xi, B. (2005). Research on framework of decision support system for partner choice and measurement in supply chain. In *Proceedings of 2005 International Conference on Machine Learning and Cybernetics* (pp. 378-382). IEEE Press.

About the Contributors

Nicolaos Protogeros is an assistant professor of information systems and e-commerce at the Macedonia University of Thessaloniki (Greece). He received a PhD in information systems from the National Polytechnic Institute (France), an MSc in remote sensing from the University Paul Sabatier (France), and a bachelor degree in mathematics from Aristotle University of Thessaloniki (Greece). Dr. Protogeros has 15 years of working experience in the private sector specializing in information technology and electronic commerce applications and over 10 years of teaching experience. He has been the project leader for many research and development projects in the area of Web-based technologies, software agents, and virtual organizations. Dr. Protogeros has published papers in academic journals and he has participated in many international conferences. His current research and teaching activities are concerned with the implementation and application of e-commerce systems to support inter-organizational collaboration and virtual enterprises.

* * *

Ioannis Athanasiadis is a researcher with the Dalle Molle Institute for Artificial Intelligence (IDSIA), in Lugano, Switzerland. His areas of expertise include: environmental informatics, agent-oriented software engineering, decision support systems and machine learning. During 2000-2005 he was a scientific collaborator of the Informatics and Telematics Institute, in Thessaloniki, Greece. He holds a bachelor's and a PhD in electrical and computer engineering, both from the Aristotle University. He is a member of the iEMSs, ISEIS, IEEE-CS and ACM. He is a fully licensed professional engineer, member of the Technical Chamber of Greece. In June 2004, he has been awarded the iEMSs student prize in integrated systems. For more information go to www.athanasiadis.info.

Ali Bahrami is associate technical fellow at the Boeing Phantom Works. He is author of a software engineering textbook entitled *Object-Oriented systems Development: Using Unified Modeling Language*, published by McGraw-Hill. He has authored two other books in AI and computer graphics, many book chapters and over 20 journal papers and refereed proceedings. Dr. Bahrami holds several patents, and is the system architect and creator of the modeling and simulation management system (MS)2.

Albert Bokma is a senior research fellow in the School of Computing and Technology at the University of Sunderland. He teaches electronic commerce and information management on postgraduate programs and his current research activities concentrate on virtual enterprises, application integration and ad hoc business transaction support as well as the Smantic Web and semantic information management approaches. He graduated from University College London (1986) with a BA, and from the University of Durham (1991) with a PhD in computer science. He has been principal investigator on several European framework projects, including Nopik, Burma-x and Smartisan where information management and business process and systems integration issues were explored.

Ramón Brena is a professor at the Center of Intelligent Systems, Tech of Monterrey, Mexico, since 1990, where he is head of a research group in distributed knowledge and multiagent systems. Dr. Brena holds a PhD from the INPG, Grenoble, France, where he presented a doctoral thesis related to knowledge in program synthesis. His current research and publication areas include: intelligent agents and multiagent systems, knowledge management, representation and distribution, Semantic Web, and artificial intelligence in general. Past research includes: program synthesis and software reuse, as well as automated reasoning. Dr. Brena is member of the SMIA (AI Mexican Society), the AAAI and the ACM, and is recognized as an established researcher by the official Mexican research agency, CONACyT.

Yee Ming Chen is an associate professor in the Department of Industrial Engineering and Management at Yuan Ze University, where he carries out basic and applied research in agent-based computing. His current research interests include: soft computing, supply chain management and system diagnosis/prognosis.

Maria Manuela Cunha is currently associate professor in the Higher School of Technology, Polytechnic Institute of Cávado and Ave, Portugal. She holds a DiplEng in informatics and systems engineering, an MSci. in the field of information society and a DrSci in the field of virtual enterprises, all from the University of Minho. She coordinates the scientific domain of organizations and information systems in the Department of Information Systems and Technologies. She supervises several PhD projects in the domain of virtual enterprises. Her scientific and engineering interests are electronic business, agile and virtual enterprises and information systems. She serves as a member of editorial boards for several international journals and has served in several scientific committees of international conferences.

Yuri Demchenko is a senior researcher with the System and Network Engineering Research Group (SNE) at the University of Amsterdam. He is contributing to the development of the generic AAA architecture in application to open collaborative environment and computer grids. He participates in major EU project EGEE (Enabling Grid for E-SciencE) and Phosphorus, where he contributes to the development of the distributed multidomain access control infrastructure. His active topics of interest and contributions include: distributed multidomain policy-based access control infrastructure, dynamic trust and policy management in SOA, virtual organisation security architecture, and using SAML and XACML distributed authorization. He is contributing to the research on operational security for XML

Web services and grids and active in the open grid forum OGSA-AUTHZ working group. His additional topic of interest is Web services and grid security vulnerabilities and threats analysis and modelling. He is also a codeveloper of the incident object description and exchange format (IODEF) being standardized by IETF. Demchenko graduated from the National Technical University of Ukraine "Kiev Polytechnic Institute" (KPI) in 1981 receiving a bachelor's degree in instrumentation and measurement. In 1989 he received Cand. of Sc. (Techn.) degree. Demchenko has been active in Internet and computer networking since 1992.

Jürgen Dorn studied computer science and economics at Technische Universität Berlin. He received his PhD from Technische Universität Berlin in 1989 for a thesis on knowledge-based reactive robot planning. From 1989 to 1996, he was head of a group at Christian Doppler Laboratory for Expert Systems in Vienna that has developed several scheduling expert systems for the Austrian steel industry. He is now professor of business information systems at Vienna University of Technology and leads the Move project group at ec3.

Anastasios Economides received a bachelor's degree in electrical engineering from Aristotle University of Thessaloniki in 1984. Holding a Fulbright and a Greek State Fellowship, he received a MSc and a PhD in computer engineering from the University of Southern California, Los Angeles (1987 and 1990, respectively). He is the director of CONTA (computer networks and telematics applications) laboratory. He has published over 100 peer-reviewed papers.

Dimitris Folinas holds an MIS from the Interdepartmental Program of Postgraduate Studies, University of Macedonia and a PhD from the Department of Applied Informatics, of the same university. He works as a scientific associate in the Department of Applied Informatics, University of Macedonia, and in the Department of Logistics, Technological Educational Institute of Thessaloniki. His research and teaching interests include: e-logistics, logistics information systems, business-to-business integration, supply chain integration, virtual organization/enterprise and e-commerce models and technologies.

Chrysanthi E. Georgakarakou received her bachelor's degree in computer science from the University of Ioannina, Greece (2000), and her MSc in information systems from the University of Macedonia, Thessaloniki, Greece (2005). Her research interests are in the following areas: intelligent buildings, agents and multi-agent systems, strategic management and marketing.

Renata S. S. Guizzardi received a MSc in computer science in 2001 from the Federal University of Espírito Santo, Brazil. She completed her PhD in computer science in February 2006, as part of the architecture and services of network applications group at the University of Twente, The Netherlands. She is currently a post-doc at the Automated Reasoning Systems division of the Institute for Scientific and Technological Research (ITC-irst), in Italy. Her PhD work focuses on the application of intelligent agents to knowledge management, taking a constructivist perspective. Other research interests include agent-oriented software engineering, CSCL/CSCW, information retrieval and machine learning.

Peter Hrastnik studied business computer science and economics at University of Vienna. After receiving the degree, he was employed by an Austrian mobile telecommunications provider. Since 2001, he's been at ec3. His PhD focuses on integration of transaction models in Web processes based on Web services. Hrastnik was member of the second Web service composition contest in Bejing.

Ioannis Ignatiadis holds a master's degree in technology management from UMIST, UK, and a second master's degree in information technology from Imperial College, UK, as well as a bachelor's degree in computer science from the same university. He has worked as a software consultant in information technology projects for big multinational companies in Europe. He also worked as a researcher in the implementation of European Union-sponsored Information Society Technologies (IST) projects. His research interests evolve around e-business and the use of enterprise systems within an organization.

Bill Karakostas holds a PhD and a MSc by research from the University of Manchester and a BA from the University of Patras, Greece. He works as a senior lecturer in the Centre for HCI Design School of Informatics in the City University, London. His research interests include: distributed object computing, Web languages, standards and architectures, software component technology, workflow and collaboration technologies. Over 70 scientific publications and 1 textbook in computer science areas. He is scientific advisor to several UK and Greek software houses. Journal referee and Conference Committee member. ESSI programme technical editor (1996), proposal evaluator and project reviewer in EU FPV KA1 and KA4 (since 2000). Involved as technical coordinator and advisor in 10+ EU framework 3, 4, and 5 projects (IST) since 1988. Affiliated member of IEEE Computer Society.

Adamantios Koumpis heads the Research Programmes Division of ALTEC S.A., which he founded in 1996 (then as independent division of Unisoft S.A.). His research interests include: quantitative decision-making techniques and info society economics. He successfully lead many commercial and research projects in Greece in the areas of e-commerce, public sector and business enterprise re-organization and information logistics, concerning linking of data/information repositories with knowledge management and business engineering models.

Lea Kutvonen is a professor in the Department of Computer Science at the University of Helsinki, Finland. She leads the Collaborative and Interoperable Computing Group (CINCO) with interest to federated management of B2B collaboration lifecycle and interoperability. The themes emerging from that area include architecture issues, e-contracting, non-functional aspects such as trust management, and coordination and composition of Web services. The CINCO group is part of the distributed systems and data communication research area.

James Laffey is a professor at the University of Missouri, Columbia, and co-founder of the Center for Technology Innovations in Education. He has been the principal investigator for several NSF awards to study and advance understanding and practice for bringing technology to bear in education. His teaching and research interests are in developing technology innovations to facilitate learning and support performance. His current research includes developing new systems and new knowledge about social computing and social ability in educational computing. Before coming to MU he worked for six years at Apple Computer, Inc. conducting research and development for learning and support systems. While working at Apple he was responsible for developing award winning interactive learning systems, and designing innovative systems that enabled Apple to better meet customer requirements. Dr. Laffey earned his BA from the University of Notre Dame and his PhD from the University of Chicago, and has worked at the University of Washington and San Francisco State University.

Pablo Gomes Ludermir received a MSc in telematics (2005) from the University of Twente, The Netherlands. He is currently a PhD student in the Computer Science Department in the same university. His research interests include: information retrieval, ubiquitous computing, software architectures and aspect-oriented architecture design.

Vassiliki Manthou is an associate professor in the Department of Applied Informatics, University of Macedonia, Economic and Social Sciences. She holds a BSC in management and administration, from Louisiana State University, U.S. and a PhD in management information systems from the University of Macedonia, Department of Applied Informatics. She was also a visiting research professor at Loyola University, New Orleans, Louisiana, U.S. She is a member of the International Society for Inventory Research (ISIR), the Hellenic Management Association, Hellenic Institute of Informatics, Institute of Education and Human Resource Development, Hellenic Economic Chamber, the Hellenic Operation Research Society. Her professional expertise, research and teaching interests include: analysis and design of management information systems, office automation, use of new technologies and informatics in organizational processes, (inventory management, marketing information systems, CAD systems, material requirements planning (MRP)), supply chain management systems (SCM), logistic systems, enterprise resource planning (ERP) systems, bar coding systems, electronic commerce (EC), office automation and E-business. She is a member of the editorial board of international journals and also acts as a reviewer in journals and in many international and national conferences. She has participated and participating in European projects in the above fields, and is a reviewer in IST projects.

Mihhail Matskin is a professor of software engineering (since 2002) at the Department of Electronics, Computer and Software Systems at the Royal Institute of Technology (KTH), Stockholm and adjunct professor (since 2004) at the Norwegian University of Science and Technology (NTNU), Trondheim. His current research activities include: work on service-oriented architecture, Semantic Web services and services composition, agent technology, multi-agent systems and software engineering of distributed systems. He is a member of a large number of program committees of international scientific forums. He has published more than 100 scientific works.

Janne Metso holds an MS from the University of Helsinki and is a PhD student in the CINCO group. He works on e-contract negotiation facilities and contract management agents in the B2B middleware.

Pericles A. Mitkas is a professor of electrical and computer engineering at the Aristotle University of Thessaloniki, Greece. He is also the associate director of the Informatics and Telematics Institute of the Center for Research and Technology – Hellas (CERTH). His research interests include: databases and knowledge bases, data mining, software agents and bioinformatics. Dr. Mitkas received his diploma of electrical engineering from Aristotle University of Thessaloniki (1985) and an MSc and PhD in computer engineering from Syracuse University (1987 and 1990, respectively). Between 1990 and 2000 he was a faculty member with the Department of Electrical and Computer Engineering at Colorado State University in the U.S.

Paraskevi Nikolaidou is a PhD student at the Electrical and Computer Engineering Department of the Aristotle University of Thessaloniki, Greece. Her PhD thesis subject is "Self-evaluation and autonomous improvement of agent behaviour in multi-agent systems through data mining." She graduated in electrical and computer engineering at the same university in 2004. Her research interests include: intelligent software agents and multi-agent systems, data mining, databases and software engineering.

Tania Pavlou is currently completing her PhD thesis on the topic of supply chain management at the Centre of Human Computer Interaction Design in City University in London. Tania holds an MSc from the School of Informatics in City University in business systems analysis and design and her first degree was in applied informatics in the University of Macedonia in Thessaloniki. Her research has focused on unexpected events that cause patterns of turbulences during supply chain operations and on IT paradigms that support virtuality in supply chain networks. Her research and teaching interests include: supply chain management, business reengineering with ERP systems, e-commerce, e-business enablers and implementations of SC networks.

Joaquim Pereira da Silva is currently an assistant professor in the School of Management at the Polytechnic Institute of Cávado and Ave, Portugal. He holds a Dipl. Eng. in the field of systems and informatics engineering and an MSc in the field of virtual enterprises, both from the University of Minho. He teaches in the domain of software engineering and enterprise information systems, and his scientific interests are information and communication technologies, virtual enterprises, and systems interoperability.

Sobah Abbas Petersen is a research scientist in the Department of Computer and Information Sciences, at Norwegian University of Science and Technology (NTNU), Norway. She received her PhD at NTNU (2003). She has broad experience in enterprise modelling from industry and research. Her research has focused on applying ideas of modelling to industrial problems and finding technological solutions for them. Her current research activities include: collaborative and mobile learning and using ideas of modelling and distributed AI for designing intelligent learning environments for mobile learners.

Goran D. Putnik received his DiplEng, MSci and DrSci from Belgrade University, both MSci and DrSci in the area of intelligent manufacturing systems (IMS). His current position is aggregated professor in the Department of Production and Systems Engineering at the University of Minho, Portugal. He served as director of the Centre for Production Systems Engineering (CESP) and as director of the Master and Postgraduate Course on CIM. His scientific and engineering interests include: production systems and enterprises design and control theory and implementations, design theory, design engineering, information systems management, formal theory of production systems and enterprises, and distributed, agile and virtual enterprises, and supervises a number of PhD projects as well. Putnik serves as a reviewer and a member of editorial boards for several international journals.

Albert Rainer studied business computer science at Vienna University of Technology. He is a member of the scientific staff at ec3 since 2001 and has finished his PhD (2006) on process verification and Web service composition.

Jinghai Rao is a project scientist in the Mobile Commerce Lab, School of Computer Science at Carnegie Mellon University. He joined CMU right after he received his PhD in computer science in 2004 from the Norwegian University of Science and Technology. His research interests include Semantic Web, Web services, pervasive computing and distributed trust management. He has published more than 20 scientific papers and has consulting experience with industry projects. He is a member of program committees of international scientific conferences.

Eduardo Ramírez holds an MSc degree in information technology from the Tech of Monterrey, México, where he collaborated as a research assistant and staff engineer at the Center of Intelligent Systems. He is involved in the development and enterprise implementation of the JITIK project. He is cofounder and CTO of Ensitech, S.C. a high-tech startup with consultancy and research activities on distributed computing and Web technologies. His current research work and interests involve agent-oriented software engineering, Web services and service oriented architectures, Semantic Web, rich Internet applications and collaborative knowledge management.

Herbert Remidez is an assistant professor of management information systems at the University of Arkansas at Little Rock's College of Business. His work experience prior to joining the University of Arkansas in the fall of 2003 includes serving as an IT project and training manager at a software research and development center. He completed his PhD in information science and learning technologies at the University of Missouri, Columbia. Dr. Remidez has published articles in the *Communications of the ACM*, *International Journal of Knowledge and Learning*, and *Computers in the Schools*. His current research project focuses on template-driven messaging systems, IT project management and e-learning.

Bob Roberts is the leader of the e-business group in the Centre for Applied Research in Information Systems (CARIS) and also course director for the MSc course in e-commerce in the faculty of computing, information systems and mathematics at Kingston University. His research and teaching activities are concerned with the implementation of e-eommerce systems to support business to business (B2B) collaborative relationships as well as the sociopolitical and relational aspects of interorganisational systems and virtual organisations. Recent funded research and consultancy activities cover a range of e-business projects in the telecoms, health, construction and electronic sectors.

Toni Ruokolainen holds an MS from the University of Helsinki and is a PhD student in the CINCO group. His interests include service type safety and type management facilities in the context of interoperability middleware.

José Paulo Oliveira Santos received his DiplEng of electronics and telecommunications from the University of Aveiro. He received an MSci from the University of Coimbra in information systems, branch of Computer Data Networks, and the PhD from the University of Aveiro in automation /industrial informatics. He is currently a professor at Mechanical Department of University of Aveiro. He is responsible for the CIM laboratory, teaches several classes related with automation, industrial informatics and integrated production systems.

Diego Sona received the Laurea (MSc) and a PhD degree in computer science from the University of Pisa (Italy) (1996 and 2002, respectively). He is currently a research scientist at the Automated Reasoning Systems division of the Institute for Scientific and Technological Research (ITC-irst), Trento, Italy. His research interests include: neural networks, pattern recognition, supervised and unsupervised learning methods, bayesian learning, information retrieval, Web mining, relational machine learning, sequence learning and methods in functional brain images (fMRI).

Antonie Stam is the Leggett & Platt distinguished professor of management information systems in the management department at the University of Missouri. Prior to joining the University of Missouri in the fall of 2000, he was a professor in the Department of Management Information Systems at the University of Georgia. He holds a PhD in management science from the University of Kansas. Professor Stam has served in visiting professor and research scientist roles in Belgium, Austria, Finland, and France, and has consulted with companies and organizations in the U.S., China, and Finland. He is a member of the Association for Information Systems, the American Statistical Association, INFORMS, and the Decision Sciences Institute. His primary research interests include information systems, decision support systems, applied artificial intelligence, multi-criteria decision making, and applied statistics. He has published in journals such as *Management Science, Decision Sciences, Journal of the American Statistical Association, Operations Research, Public Opinion Quarterly, Multivariate Behavioral Research, International Journal of Production Research*, and others.

As a researcher at Institut Eurécom, France, **Adomas Svirskas** is responsible for tying together business and technical aspects of collaborative service-oriented systems and architecting innovative solutions. The projects he is involved in (e.g., R4eGov) deal with challenging problems such as trust, security and collaboration management in E-government sector. Before joining Institut Eurécom, Adomas was a researcher at CCLRC Rutherford Appleton Laboratory, UK and a senior researcher at the e-commerce research group at Kingston University, London. Adomas' more than 15 years IT experience in both academia (Lithuania, USA, UK, France) and the leading software companies in Europe and the USA (Trilogy, SAP, Kiala) cover a range of projects in the automotive, banking, telecom, logistics and the Internet business sectors.

Dimitrios Tektonidis heads the R&D Research Programmes Development Unit of ALTEC S.A. He received his bachelor's degree from the Technological Educational Institution (TEI) of Thessaloniki and a PhD candidate at the University of Sunderland. He is author of research papers, technical reports and project deliverables in the domains of enterprise application integration, enterprise resource planning and customer relationship management. He led the development teams in several EU projects. He is also a lecturer in the Technological Educational Institution (TEI). His main research fields are IS interoperability and enterprise application integration, knowledge management and Semantic Web. He is member of the ALTEC task force for the next generation of the company's ERP systems.

Fani A.Tzima received her diploma from the Electrical and Computer Engineering Department at Aristotle University in Thessaloniki, Greece (2005). She is currently a PhD candidate with the same Department. She was also a member of the team representing the Department in the worldwide software design competition "Microsoft Imagine Cup 2005", where they finished second. Her research interests include: software agents, multi-agent systems, environmental informatics and software engineering. She is a member of the Technical Chamber of Greece.

Shih-Chang Wang is currently an assistant professor of Department of Business Administration at Lung-Hwa University of Science and Technology in Taiwan. He received a master's degree in industrial management at National Cheng-Kung University, Taiwan (1994), and a PhD in industrial engineering and management at Yuan-Ze University, Taiwan (2006). He has been engaged in research on multiagent systems, computational intelligence and e-business.

Index

A

agent
  -based intelligent system 141
  management system (AMS) 145
  oriented software engineering (AOSE) 2
agile
  /virtual enterprise (A/VE) 76–96
  supply chain (ACM) 227
agile/virtual enterprise (A/VE) 7–12
AGORA multi-agent architecture 52
answer set programming (ASP) 9–12, 190–207
ant colony optimization (ACO) 229
application program interface (API) 88, 100
application service providers (ASP) 329
ARTEMIS project 328–340
  platform 336
  selling proposition 337
  target market 338
attribute
  authority (AA) 275
  certificate (AC) 273

B

B2B middleware 11–12, 288–309
  architecture 293
  functionalities 291
Bremen University semantic translator for enhanced retrieval (BUSTER) 264
Bullwhip effect 225
business
  drivers 335

network model (BNM) 289
network model repository 299
process execution language (BPEL) 218
process execution language for Web services (BPEL4WS) 39, 84
process management systems (BPMS) 175
process modeling 244–255
  framework 247
    step 1 247
    step 2 248
    step 3 250
    step 4 250
  protocol 69
  service interface (BSI) 73
business processes modeling 10–12

C

case
  -based reasoning (CBR) 234
  studies 58
choreography 38–39
  requirements 70–71
cognitive-affective model of organizational communication (CAMOC) 311
collaborative working environment (CWE) 172
commercial off-the-shelf software tools (COTS) 212
complex resource provisioning (CRP) 268
content management systems (CMS) 175

D

data acquisition language for scheduling (DALS) 137

database management systems (DBMS) 87
Datalog with disjunction (DLV) 195–207
description logics (DL) 205
desktop system 129
directory facilitator (DF) 145
distributed
  architecture for monitoring and diagnosis (DIA-
     MOND) 264
  artificial intelligence (DAI) 5
  constraints satisfaction problem (DSCP) 229
  decision-making (DDM) 229
  problem solving (DPS) 2
  service network architecture (DSN) 168
doctor 2 doctor (D2D) 337
dynamic
  enterprise model (DEM) 18
  security associations 279
    interorganizational association or federation 279
    job/workflow 279
    project or mission oriented cooperation 279
    session 279

E

ebXML business process (ebBP) 68
eCommunities 290–291
EGEE
  generic applications advisory panel (EGAAP) 277
  project 276
electronic business XML (ebXML) 339
embedded Web services architecture (EWSA)
    175–189
enterprise
  application integration (EAI) 97–114, 336
  information systems (EIS) 26
  repository 209
  resource planning (ERP) 97, 175
enterprise application integration (EAI) 8–12
environmental
  data 257
  data exchange network for inland water (EDEN-
    IW) 263
  management information systems (EMIS) 258
event process chain (EPC) 250
evolutionary computation approach 155–156
experimental studies 319
extended supply chain 237
eXtensible markup canguage (XML) 30

eXtensible markup language (XML) 48, 218
  schema for scheduling (XSS) 137

F

FIPA agent communication language (FIPA-
    ACL) 147
Food and Agriculture Organization (FAO) 257
forecast streamlining and enhancement project
    (FSEP) 264
fully qualified attribute name (FQAN) 272

G

general contractor (GC) 149
geographical information systems (GIS) 258
global middleware 297
GridShib 274–277
  GT/grid security 274
  Shibboleth 274–275
guess/check/optimize (GCO) methodology 196

H

hierarchy searching algorithm (HAS) 137
holistic approach 338
hybrid peer-to-peer (P2P) architecture 78–96

I

identity provider (IdP) 275
information
  architecture plan (IAP) 162
  management model (IMM) 161
  technology architecture 85
    logical architecture 87
    physical architecture 85
initiating activity agent (IAA) 154
integrated
  process management 208–222
    benefits 216
  situation dictionary 163
integrated process management 10–12
integration task force (ITF) 162
intelligent agents 48, 117
interoperability problems 332
inverse document frequency (IDF) 121

J

Java agent development framework (JADE) 147

just-in-time information and knowledge (JI-TIK) 184

K

knowledgeable agent for recommendations (KARe) 116–134
  prototypes 129
knowledge management (KM) 8–12, 115–134
knowledge sharing 258

M

manufacturing execution systems (MES) 175
market of resources 80–96
  structure 80–82
message transfer chain (MTC) 137
metadata management 34
multi-agents-based diagnostic data acquisition and management in complex systems (MAGIC) 264
multi-agent system (MAS) 8–12, 2, 48, 135–159, 223–243, 267
multi-agent systems (MAS) 10–12

N

negotiation strategy 155
network management agents (NMAs) 294
New Zealand distributed information system (NZDIS) 263
NSF middleware initiative (NMI) 274

O

object-to-agent (O2A) 178
ontologies 118
  -based enterprise application integration (ONAR) 97–114
    ONAR integration process 106
    ONAR methodology 101–103
ontologies-based enterprise application integration (ONAR) 8–12
open
  Applications Group 67
  collaborative environment (OCE) 268

grid services architecture (OGSA) 269
orchestration 38–39
Organization for the Advancement of Structured Information Standards (OASIS) 260

P

parallel artificial intelligence (PAI) 2
participating activity agent (PAA) 154
peer
  -to-peer communities 117
  discovery 131
populator 295
process modeling 211
project management 214

Q

quality of business (QoBiz) 69
quality of service (QoS) 69

R

recommender systems 118
regional centers (RC) 277
reinforcement learning (RL) 234
request-for-quote (RFQ) 238
Rilevamento dati Ambientali con Interfaccia DECT (RAID) 264

S

seamless semantic interoperability toolkit (SSIT) 169
security 35–36
  assertion markup language (SAML) 85
  associations 267–287
  token service (STS) 286
security associations 11–12
semantic
  language (SL) 140
  Web 97–114
semantic Web 8–12
service
  -oriented architecture (SOA) 25–45, 61
    benefits 27–28
    overview 26
  level agreements (SLA) 69

offer repository 299
oriented application integration (SOAI) 97–
    114, 169
service-oriented architecture (SOA) 6–12
service oriented application integration (SOAI)
    8–12
service oriented architecture (SOA) 7–12
shadow networkspace (SNS) 315
simple object access protocol (SOAP)
    30, 49, 83
situation
  analysis model (SAM) 161
  room (SR) 160–173
  room analysis (SRA) 160–173
    run-time environment 168
  room model (SRM) 161–173
situation room (SR) 9–12
situation room analysis (SRA) 9–12
software 109
  agent 4–24, 174–189
    architectures 9
    communication languages 10–11
    properties 6–7
    systems 5
    transportation mechanisms 11
    typology 8–9
supply chain management (SCM) 10–12, 223–
    243
  current trends 224
  problems 225
  simulation 231

T

taxonomies 118
Technical Committee (TC) 68
term frequency (TF) 121
trading agent competition 237
trust 311–326
  templates 313
    communication issues 314
    feedback 315
    introduction 314
    issue/conflict 315
    task completion/questions 315
    time management/milestones 314
type repository 297

U

unified modeling language (UML) 212, 249
universal description, discovery, and integration
    (UDDI) 30–33, 48, 83, 106, 246, 339
user-controlled service provisioning (UCSP)
    280

V

virtual
  enterprise (VE) 16–19, 25, 46–65, 160–
      173, 191–207, 267–287
    formation 51–52
      partner selection 52
    framework architecture 261
      agent roles 261
    integration 80
    main users 259
    model 49–50, 76–96
  enterprise business description 335
  laboratories (VL) 268
  organization (VO) 244–255, 267–287
    management framework 281
    operational models
      agent centric VO (VO-A) 280
      project centric VO (VO-G) 280
      resource/provider centric VO (VO-R) 280
      user-centric VO (VO-U) 280
    security services and operation 282
  organization membership service (VOMS)
      272–287
    administration client 273
    administration server 273
    user client 273
    user server 273
  resource 260
  teams 312–326
virtual enterprise (VE) 9–12
virtual enterprise (VE) model 7–12
virtual organisation (VO) 11–12

W

Web
  -Pilarcos 290–309
  service composition 194
  service description (WSD) 28
  service description language (WSDL) 31–32, 193
  services 28–45, 48, 66–75, 78–96, 106, 174–
      189, 244–255

choreography description language (WS-CDL)
     39, 68
description language (WSDL) 48, 83
flow language (WSFL) 83
infrastructure 29
JITIK 185
Web services 7–12, 10–12
workflow
  management coalition (WfMC) 209
  management system (WfMSs) 215

X

XML
  key management specification (XKMS) 85
  process definition language (XPDL) 208–222
XML process definition language (XPDL)
     10–12